Nietzsche and Law

Philosophers and Law
Series Editor: Tom Campbell

Titles in the Series:

Cicero and Modern Law
Richard Brooks

Aristotle and Modern Law
Richard O. Brooks and James Bernard Murphy

Plato and Modern Law
Richard O. Brooks

Locke and Law
Thom Brooks

Rousseau and Law
Thom Brooks

Kant and Law
B. Sharon Byrd and Joachim Hruschka

Marx and Law
Susan Easton

Hobbes on Law
Claire Finkelstein

Derrida and Law
Pierre Legrand

Hume and Law
Ken Mackinnon

Gadamer and Law
Francis J. Mootz III

Nietzsche and Law
Francis J. Mootz III and Peter Goodrich

Wittgenstein and Law
Dennis Patterson

Hegel and Law
Michael Salter

Nietzsche and Law

Edited by

Francis J. Mootz III

Pennsylvania State University's Dickinson School of Law, USA

and

Peter Goodrich

Cardozo School of Law, New York, USA

ASHGATE

Published by
Ashgate Publishing Limited
Gower House
Croft Road
Aldershot
Hampshire GU11 3HR
England

Ashgate Publishing Company
Suite 420
101 Cherry Street
Burlington, VT 05401-4405
USA

Ashgate website: http://www.ashgate.com

British Library Cataloguing in Publication Data
Nietzsche and law
1. Nietzsche, Friedrich Wilhelm, 1844–1900 - knowledge - law 2. Law - Philosophy
I. Mootz, Francis J. II. Goodrich, Peter, 1954–
340.1'092

Library of Congress Control Number: 2007930996

ISBN 978–0–7546–2620–6

Printed in Great Britain by TJ International Ltd, Padstow, Cornwall

Contents

PART III LEGAL CRITIQUE

PART IV TIMELY REFLECTIONS ON THE SCHOLARLY ENTERPRISE

Acknowledgements

The editors and publishers wish to thank the following for permission to use copyright material.

Ashgate Publishing for the essay: P. Christopher Smith (2007), 'From Strife to Understanding: Pathological Argument in Nietzsche and Gadamer', in Francis J. Mootz III (ed), *Gadamer and Law*, Aldershot: Ashgate Publishing, pp. 339–59.

Blackwell Publishing for the essays: Marianne Constable (1994), 'Genealogy and Jurisprudence: Nietzsche, Nihilism, and the Social Scientification of Law', *Law and Social Inquiry*, **19**, pp. 551– 90. Copyright © 1994 Blackwell Publishing; Peter Goodrich (1986), 'Law and Modernity', *Modern Law Review*, **49**, pp. 545–59. Copyright © 1986 Blackwell Publishing Limited.

Cardozo Law Review for the essays: Charles M. Yablon (2003), 'Nietzsche and the Nazis: The Impact of National Socialism on the Philosophy of Nietzsche', *Cardozo Law Review*, **24**, pp. 739–55; Frederick M. Dolan (2003), 'Nietzsche's Gnosis of Law', *Cardozo Law Review*, **24**, pp. 757–67; Roger Berkowitz (2003), 'Friedrich Nietzsche, the Code of Manu, and the Art of Legislation', *Cardozo Law Review*, **24**, pp. 1131–49; Adam Gearey (2003), 'African Nietzsche: Poetry, Philosophy and African Legal Thinking,' *Cardozo Law Review*, **24**, pp. 903–23; Richard H. Weisberg (1997), 'It's a Positivist, It's a Pragmatist, It's a *Codifier*! Reflections on Nietzsche and Stendhal', *Cardozo Law Review*, **18**, pp. 85–96; Adam Thurschwell (2003), 'Specters of Nietzsche: Potential Futures for the Concept of the Political in Agamben and Derrida', *Cardozo Law Review*, **24**, pp. 1193–259.

Copyright Clearance Center for the essay: Joseph Pugliese (1996), 'Rationalized Violence and Legal Colonialism: Nietzsche *contra* Nietzsche', *Cardozo Studies in Law and Literature*, **8**, pp. 277–93.

Palgrave Macmillan for the essay: Nathan Widder (2004), 'The Relevance of Nietzsche to Democratic Theory: Micropolitics and the Affirmation of Difference', *Contemporary Political Theory*, **3**, pp. 188–211. Copyright © 2004 Palgrave Macmillan.

Penn State Press for the essay: H.W. Siemens (2002), 'Agonal Communities of Taste: Law and Community in Nietzsche's Philosophy of Transvaluation', *Journal of Nietzsche Studies*, **24**, pp. 83–112. Copyright © 2002 Pennsylvania State University.

Sage Publications Limited for the essay: Francis J. Mootz III (2007), 'Responding to Nietzsche: The Constructive Power of *Destruktion*', *Law, Culture and the Humanities*, **3**, pp. 127–54. Copyright © 2007 Association for the Study of Law, Culture and Humanities.

Springer Science and Business Media for the essay: Adam Gearey (2000), 'We Fearless Ones: Nietzsche and Critical Legal Studies', *Law and Critique*, **11**, pp. 167–84.

Every effort has been made to trace all the copyright holders, but if any have been inadvertently overlooked the publishers will be pleased to make the necessary arrangement at the first opportunity.

Series Preface

The series *Philosophers and Law* selects and makes accessible the most important essays in English that deal with the application to law of the work of major philosophers for whom law was not a main concern. The series encompasses not only what these philosophers had to say about law but also brings together essays which consider those aspects of the work of major philosophers which bear on our interpretation and assessment of current law and legal theory. The essays are based on scholarly study of particular philosophers and deal with both the nature and role of law and the application of philosophy to specific areas of law.

Some philosophers, such as Hans Kelsen, Roscoe Pound and Herbert Hart are known principally as philosophers of law. Others, whose names are not primarily or immediately associated with law, such as Aristotle, Kant and Hegel, have, nevertheless, had a profound influence on legal thought. It is with the significance for law of this second group of philosophers that this series is concerned.

Each volume in the series deals with a major philosopher whose work has been taken up and applied to the study and critique of law and legal systems. The essays, which have all been previously published in law, philosophy and politics journals and books, are selected and introduced by an editor with a special interest in the philosopher in question and an engagement in contemporary legal studies. The essays chosen represent the most important and influential contributions to the interpretation of the philosophers concerned and the continuing relevance of their work to current legal issues.

TOM CAMPBELL
Series Editor
Centre for Applied Philosophy and Public Ethics
Charles Sturt University

Introduction

Ambulo, ergo sum. (Friedrich Nietzsche)[1]

According to Cato the Elder, the practice of kissing relatives had its roots in the desire to control women. The question posed and answered by the kiss was: 'Does her breath smell of wine?' Women were forbidden from drinking by Roman law because alcohol could lead them to 'unlearn altogether the art of saying No'.[2] Nietzsche uses this intriguing pneumatic example as an instance of the hidden qualities or cultural embeddedness of positive law. The norm betrays a fear and, in this instance, that fear is of the Greek, and specifically of the Dionysian. What threatens is not just the foreign and unknown, but also the satyrical tradition of the carnival, the inebriate, the joyful, the erotic and playful. The ludic or simply gay rites that drinking evoked were potentially significant as a dissipation of identity, of the immersion of the one into the many, and also of the collapse of order into ecstasy, of the unity of law into the plurality of dance.

The law, here the prohibition on women drinking, does not directly define an interior of a city-state or people, but rather betrays what the culture is not. It is a telling and touching example of the obscure, but essential, relation of law to culture and of norm to life. Consider the paradox of creating a disciplinary measure out of an erotic embrace, a juridical interrogation in the form of oral insufflation – sniffing as legal interpretation. It gives a new meaning to the hermeneutic of suspicion. Yet however one frames the instance of legal kissing for Nietzsche it has a twofold significance and can also point in the direction of the dual sources of Nietzschean jurisprudence that will be traced in the contributions to this volume. First, at a philosophical level, this rite – one that in essence juxtaposes contract and contact, law and touch – collapses legality into an interior source or before of law, tactile and internal to it. Second, in hermeneutic form, the paradox of this Judas kiss, this ulterior and opaque semiotic, is suggestive of the multi-layered quality of all juridical acts and pronouncements, of the need for interpretations and the variable moods of their illocution. Nietzsche formulates these two facets of law in terms of the opposition of the Greek to the Roman, but they can be explored just as productively by considering two encounters, those between the pre-legal and the legal, and between science and anti-science. The two traditions that Nietzsche seeks to evoke and expand are similarly the Greek – always the Greeks – and that of the Troubadours and the gay science of *rectorica*, of eloquence as law.

---

1 'I walk, therefore I am'. Friedrich Nietzsche, *Early Greek Philosophy and Other Essays*, trans. Maximilian Mügge (1911) at p. 129. The epigram is in honour of Dean Fredrick Dolan's, 'Nietzsche's Gnosis of Law', Chapter 7 in this volume.

2 Friedrich Nietzsche, *Joyful Wisdom ('La Gaya Scienza')*, trans. Thomas Common (1910), hereafter *Gay Science*, at p. 81. The history and art of kissing should never be broached without reference to magnificent and comprehensive work by Nicolas Perella, *The Kiss Sacred and Profane* (1969). Peter Goodrich, in *The Laws of Love: A Brief Historical and Practical Manual* (2006), ch. 7 outlines a positive casuistry of kissing.

The Tragedy of Legality

The return to the Greeks, the re-enactment of the antinomy of Apollo and Dionysus, and through that the re-encounter with cultural forms, dialogues and poetic disquisitions that institute a before of law, a beyond of contemporary institutions, is a fecund theme throughout. At the root of this return is another and more philosophical opposition, that between Heraclitus, the weeping philosopher, and Democritus, the laughing sage. So start with the disconsolate philosopher from Ephesus who conceived only of the one Justice, eternally swaying, and exclaims, 'The contest of the Many is itself pure justice. And after all: The One is the Many', going on to conclude:

> And if the world which we see knows only Becoming and Passing but no permanence, should perhaps those qualities constitute a differently fashioned metaphysical world … not a world of unity as Anaximander sought behind the fluttering veil of plurality, but a world of eternal and essential pluralities?[3]

The return to the Greeks, to the early Greek philosophers, is not only an attempt to go before the law – and so, beyond the law – to a pagan and plural pre-Christian *nomos*, but also a way of opening up to, and reconstructing, a painful history – that of an error. The Berkeleyan triad of Nonet, Constable and Berkowitz, the latter two having trained with the former, provide a fascinating conspectus of the dimensions of this jurisprudential error as devised through, and elicited from, Nietzsche's critique of metaphysics. The significance of the One in the Many and of the Many in the One resides in the recognition of the limitation – indeed, the inadequacy, the necessary failure – of law. This tragic story is taken up on many sides by posing the simple question 'What is positive law?'. The answer: a plurality, a tragedy, an illusion, a necessary illusion. Such is the wager of the nihilist on the certainty of law. It is formulated by Philippe Nonet (Chapter 1) in a variation on a juridical maxim: '*ubi jus incertum, ibi jus nullum*' – where law is uncertain, there it is nothing (p. 8). The more usual citation is '*misera est servitus ubi ius est vagum aut incertum*' – it is miserable to follow the law where it is vague or uncertain (Coke, p. 246). Hence pessimism as the interior of nihilism and as the unflinchingly candid path to becoming, to the *incipit* of the new.

To the extent that law is embedded in the religious instinct, in the belief in a higher and other world, it requires positivity, meaning limitation to specific procedures of norm creation and application. The key is its limitation – what Nonet terms its 'rage against time' (pp. 29–30), its slow unpacking of what the supreme jurisprudential purist, Hans Kelsen (1957), borrowing from Nietzsche, terms the history of a 'gargantuan error'. For Marianne Constable, too, Nietzschean jurisprudence is, in its most exemplary form, the *longue durée* of an error that moves from the Greeks to the moderns – Heraclitus to Hart. In Chapter 2 she correctly formulates the *Twilight of the Idols*, the demise of law, as the passage from truth to myth and thence to the abolition of both – the moment of creativity, of the humanity to come. For such a trajectory to be possible requires the progressive refusal to reduce law to another virtue or discipline. It requires constraint, honesty, mere positivity, and thus the uncomfortable recognition that law is no more than what doctrine makes on specific occasions, a merely

3 Nietzsche, *Early Greek Philosophy*, at p. 103.

human endeavour, something of a side issue in the order of disciplines and in the drama of political life.

The ending of the error – when the two laws, divine and human, are abolished; when we are done with the judgement of Jupiter, of priests and tyrants; when law is simply law – means that law too, ironically, is done. The first of the disciplines, the order of institutions, the definer of words, deprived of its sanctity, shored of its mythic unity, realizes its hybrid character, its necessary uncertainty, the power of becoming merely law, simply statement, anathema or adulation. In jurisprudential terms the interesting issue, elaborated upon lengthily by Christopher Smith in Chapter 5 and in contrary vein by Francis Mootz in Chapter 6, is that of the transition to a hybrid discipline, the opening of dialogue, the resumption of conversations that have long been abandoned. In this guise, as Nathan Widder argues in Chapter 3, difference substitutes for juridical similarity, metonymy for metaphor, and lines of flight for erroneously stable identities.

The encounter with the Greeks, the return to the roots of the philosophical tradition, is not simply an unpacking of errors, a removal of veils, but also a positive inclination towards a culture that knew, in Nietzsche's own emphasis:

> ... how *to live*: for that purpose it is necessary to keep bravely to the surface, the fold and the skin; to worship appearance, to believe in forms, tones, and words, in the whole Olympus of appearances! Those Greeks were superficial – *from profundity*![4]

There was also, of course, their commitment to conversation, 'fine talk', the avenues of dialogue that Frederick Dolan (Chapter 7) traces in the gnosis of walking, and the pursuit of ambulant and animated ideas. Putting it differently, we can say that Heraclitus has to learn to laugh, for, after all of what use is a book that does not take us beyond all books, into life, into dialogue, and in the present case, as Mootz shows, into court.

Long Live the Troubadour

The second source of Nietzschean jurisprudence, traced in the later sections of this volume moves from the Greeks to the Romans and most specifically to the Ovid of the *lex amatoria*.[5] Here the relevant transition is that of a secondary reception: the erotic norms of Roman verse, the code of contact or map of the heart, gets taken up in the laws of love, in the medieval tradition of rhetoric and, specifically, in the gay science – the poetics associated with courtly love. This less travelled road in Nietzsche's work – his return to the gay science and, specifically, to the roots of the rhetorical tradition – enjoins a second set of themes. The question posed is directly that of how to live, the aesthetic of relationship, the creation of new laws.

We find this question posed in specifically historical terms, as a question of return and of fate, as something for the laborious, in the first book of the *Gay Science*. The question is that of how to live, posed here in terms of the art of law conceived as a facet of the art of life:

---

4 Nietzsche, *Gay Science*, at p. 10.

5 On the reception of Ovid and the *lex amatoria*, and specifically its strongly legal character, see Becker (1997) and, more broadly, Bloch, (1977). See also Goodrich (2001), and Yovel (2005). For a sampling of texts, see *The Comedy of Eros* (2nd edn, 1997), trans. Norman R. Shapiro.

> Hitherto all that has given colour to existence has lacked a history: where would one find a history of love, of avarice, of envy, of conscience, of piety, of cruelty? Even a comparative history of law, as also of punishment, has hitherto been completely lacking.[6]

If law, in this formulation, is a 'condition of existence', an institution and teaching at the root of amity and community, then it has yet to find its scholars, its poets, or – to borrow from Constable's contribution – its genuinely deviationist doctrinalists, its free thinkers.

What Constable assesses in epistemological terms gets worked out in the critical terminology of 'post-legal studies', always assuming that the 'post' coined in the neologism refers primarily to a sending on, a novelty, a new ground, rather than simply a beyond, an open space, a plurality. In that more technical sense the second thematic of this volume is precisely concerned with the viscera and embodiments of legal institutions, the inhabiting of juridical texts. The guiding theme is that of desire, Nietzsche's erudition *in eroticis* as worked through law. The issue, one which was well captured by Gillian Rose in her *Dialectic of Nihilism* (1984), is that of coming to know more and not less about the law tables. In one sense Nietzsche was at least fascinated by law, by the tablets and tables, the pronouncements and legislations, and the poetic acts of creation and determination. He was not afraid of such acts of power, such will and its positive outcomes, but rather wanted to make them his own. How that is done – in other words, legal philosophy as a way of life – becomes the conjoining theme of Parts III and IV of this book.

The initial question, posed by Peter Goodrich (Chapter 12), is that of how to live with uncertainty, how to inhabit the polysemy, the simple plurality of juridical texts. The task for the Nietzschean-inspired legal scholar is that of tirelessly addressing the enfolding of meaning in text. All of life rages here, one might say, but only the most attentive – indeed, amorous – ear can hear it. We draw this time from Nietzsche's widely cited and little understood essay on truth which reaches its now familiar crescendo in the rhetorical question:

> What therefore is truth? A mobile army of metaphors, metonymies, anthropomorphisms: in short a sum of human relations which became poetically and rhetorically intensified, metamorphosed, adorned, and after long usage seem to a nation fixed, canonic, binding; truths are illusions of which one has forgotten that they are illusion … coins which have their obverse effaced and now are no longer of account as coins but merely as metal.[7]

The notion that meaning is coinage, interpretation an attribution or aspersion of price – etymologically *inter-pretium*, a bargaining as to value – should not surprise lawyers, but receives little expression in doctrine. The Nietzschean insight is into an economy of meaning, a market of signification that precisely responds to the relations that our canons and laws enshrine in a forgotten, and thus increasingly opaque, form. To reconstruct the history of such meaning, to understand the lives impacted in the history of texts, is the endless task of interpretation. Thus, in differing guises, the later contributors to this volume look to the transvaluation of values, the plurality of meanings and the failures of reason, as well as the

---

6 Nietzsche, *Gay Science*, at p. 43.

7 Nietzsche, 'On Truth and Falsity in their Ultramoral Sense' (1873), in *Early Greek Philosophy* (1911) at p. 180.

spectres of significance, of inheritance and decay, of North and South, encountered endlessly in different jurisdictions and multiple precedents.

The reference to truth as metaphor can also remind us of the source of Nietzsche's views in his early lectures on rhetoric. We should not forget that the *Gay Science* was a rebirth of an earlier institutional rhetoric and that its laws of love were rules of grammar – formulae for poetic and juristic composition. The early lectures on rhetoric are motivated by two key concerns. First is the priority of speech over writing: 'the true prose of antiquity is an echo of public *speech* and is built on its laws, whereas our prose is always to be explained more from *writing*'.[8] The second and correlative point – a necessary corollary of the public quality of language use, its intrinsic sociality, its pervasively symbolic character, in sum its legality – is the acknowledgement that language is rhetoric and that meaning is a sign: 'The *tropes*, the nonliteral significations, are considered to be the most artistic means of rhetoric. But, with respect to their meanings, all words are tropes in themselves, and from the very beginning.'[9] There is no escape from rhetoric, no end to the task of tracing the erased face of the coin, the allegory of the word. As Nietzsche himself put it, 'There is just as little distinction between actual words and tropes as there is between straightforward *speech* and *rhetorical figures*. What is usually called language is actually figuration.'[10]

Rhetoric joins the market in the figure of a coin, a mercantile metaphor of repetition and erasure, of use and forgetting. The figures that survive, that become linguistic coinage, common use, are those that appeal, persuade and have value for their auditors. It is here that the earlier reference to the priority of public speech inserts politics into language, and law into rhetoric. What matters for public speech, of which law is in modernity the most serious of forms, is precisely its proper institution, its politics in the very precise legal sense of institution: namely, *aetas*, *scientia*, *mores* and *ordo*, meaning time, knowledge, custom and order.[11] An institution is a teaching, an inculcation in formal manner of a mode of life. Truth, to pursue Nietzsche's metaphor, is the outcome of agon, an expanded trial, of successful persuasion; it is only now incorporated into institutions, into the dictation of time and place and purpose. As the essays by H.W. Siemens (Chapter 14), Joseph Pugliese (Chapter 15) and Adam Thurschwell (Chapter 16) variously indicate, it is through the genealogical reconstruction of the imperialism of truth, the mapping of its geographical projection, as well as its political repetition, that critique comes to understand and challenge the cost of belief. What price do we pay for abstraction, Adam Gearey asks in Chapter 13, and what is the cost in lives, in the quality of life, the aesthetics of knowing, if we cannot recognize difference or enjoy the hedonic particularity of different cultures and difference in law?

Taken together, this collection marks the necessarily marginal trajectory of Nietzschean inquiries into law. They mark a margin not simply in the political sense of being lateral to the concerns of 'serious' – which is to say profound, heavy, sedimented – jurisprudence, but also in the more playful sense of being before what is written, beyond the script or sentence, exergue or space of glosses and thresholds. Here it is the hybrid, the plural, the swaying – to borrow again from Heraclitus – that holds sway. The issues raised and the concerns aired are

8 Nietzsche, 'Description of Ancient Rhetoric' (1989) at p. 21.

9 Ibid., at p. 23.

10 Ibid., at p. 25.

11 This is by the 1603 Canons of the Church of England. See Gibson, *Codex juris ecclesiastici Anglicani* (1703), Vol. 2, at p. 850.

more concrete, more real and closer to speech than to writing. Recollect again Nietzsche's initial figure of law in the *Gay Science*, the regime of kissing kin that Cato viewed as a regulatory device. It overturns and undermines our accustomed interpretation of kissing as the mark of amity, of brotherhood and community. It suggests or betrays another scene of law, a complex of fears and desires whose expression is encoded in a practice of kissing whose origins have long been erased. It is a perfect example of Nietzsche's jurisprudence, that of a wisdom *in eroticis* that belongs in law, amongst in laws, a coming to know, a becoming of visceral knowledges that jurists have unhappily abandoned. This, then, could be taken as the emblem of Nietzschean jurisprudence. It is the study of juridical practices as a way of life and, here, the analysis of what the kiss betrays. More than that, it is intrinsic to philosophy which, in one etymology, is the *sophia* (wisdom) of *philein* (kissing).

But that is not all. As excoriated, deconstructed, revived and politicized Nietzsche is a gay scientist of law, an osculating jurist, an amorous rhetorician. He is an intransigent, rigorous, at times derisive and at times uncharitable hermeneut. He is great and terrible because, to paraphrase his own sentiments towards Wagner, 'love is of all the sentiments the most egotistic, and consequently, when it is wounded, the least generous'.[12] With that hermeneutic suspicion in mind, it is to Nietzsche that the last word must be given – his philosophy demands it, his philology seizes it. There is nothing we can do about Nietzsche having the last word but to attend to his word, or, to borrow again from the Latins, *nos disputatio in una, ergo sum*.[13] And so we conclude the volume with an excerpt in which Nietzsche champions the philosopher of tomorrow and the day after tomorrow, as a legislator who rises above the pablum of democratic sentiments and creates knowledge because he knows that truths cannot be discovered. His is a levelheaded cruelty, a severe spirit that is cultivated through the negativity of experience.

Opposed to the Nietzschean philosopher is the mendacious figure of the scholar. The latter is a 'specialist and nook dweller', an 'industrious worker', a 'utility man' (pp. 427–8), a parsimonious proponent of a 'theory of knowledge', one of the 'nimble smarties or clumsy solid mechanics and empiricists'(p. 433). Filling the blanks left by the great minds of yesterday, scholars toil in service to systems of thought that have outlived their usefulness and betrayed their inspiration. These are not thinkers; they are coroners.

Faced with the challenge of being a philosopher rather than a scholar, can we really talk of a Nietzschean philosophy of law? Can a Nietzschean write about law without betraying himself and descending to mere scholarship, to base legalisms, to a cellar filled with nothing more interesting than dust-besmeared files? Is it not the bad conscience of a scholar that seeks to apply philosophy to law? Nietzsche explicitly claimed not to want followers, but he did want readers – experienced, engaged, attentive, patient readers. It is our hope to have provided a space for such readers and readings here.

References

Becker, Karin (1997), 'La mentalité juridique dans la littérature française (XIIIe–Xve siècles)', *Moyen Age: Revue d'histoire et de philologie*, **103**(2), pp. 309–77.

Bloch, Howard (1977), *Medieval French Literature and Law*, Berkeley: University of California Press.

12 Nietzsche, *The Case of Wagner* (1911) at p. 5.

13 'We debate, therefore I exist.'

Coke, Sir Edward (1964), *The Institutes of the Laws of England*, Vol. 4, London: Lee and Pakeman.
Gibson, Edmund (1703), *Codex juris ecclesiastici Anglicani*, London: Baskett.
Goodrich, Peter (2001), 'Gay Science and Law', in V. Kahn and L. Hutson (eds), *Rhetoric and Law in Early Modern Europe*, New Haven, CT and London: Yale University Press.
Goodrich, Peter (2006), *The Laws of Love: A Brief Historical and Practical Manual*, Basingstoke: Palgrave Macmillan.
Kelsen, Hans (1957), *What is Justice?*, Berkeley: University of California Press.
Nietzsche, Friedrich (1910), *Joyful Wisdom ('La Gaya Scienza')*, trans. Thomas Common, in *The Works of Friedrich Nietzsche*, Edinburgh: T.N. Foulis.
Nietzsche, Friedrich (1911), *Early Greek Philosophy and Other Essays*, trans. Maximilian Mügge, London and Edinburgh: T.N. Foulis.
Nietzsche, Friedrich (1911), 'On Truth and Falsity in their Ultramoral Sense' (1873), in *Early Greek Philosophy and Other Essays*, Edinburgh and London: T.N. Foulis.
Nietzsche, Friedrich (1911), *The Case of Wagner, A Musician's Problem*, trans. Anthony M. Ludovici, Edinburgh and London: T.N. Foulis.
Nietzsche, Friedrich (1989), 'Description of Ancient Rhetoric' (1873–73), in Sander Gilman with Carole Blair and David Parent, *Friedrich Nietzsche on Rhetoric and Language. With the Full Text of his Lectures on Rhetoric Published for the First Time*, New York: Oxford University Press.
Perella, Nicolas J. (1969), *The Kiss Sacred and Profane: An Interpretative History of Kiss Symbolism and Related Religio-Erotic Themes*, Berkeley and Los Angeles: University of California Press.
Rose, Gillian (1984), *Dialectic of Nihilism. Post-structuralism and Law*, Oxford and New York: Basil Blackwell.
The Comedy of Eros: Medieval French Guides to the Art of Love (2nd edn, 1997), trans. Norman R. Shapiro, with notes and commentaries by James B. Wadsworth and Betsy Bowden, Champaign-Urbana: University of Illinois Press.
Yovel, Jonathan (2005), 'Gay Science as Law: An Outline for a Nietzschean Jurisprudence', in Peter Goodrich and Mariana Valverde (eds), *Nietzsche and Legal Theory: Half-Written Laws*, New York: Routledge.

Part I
Political Philosophy, Genealogy, Law

[1]

What Is Positive Law?

Philippe Nonet†

The following notes attempt a brief introduction to the mature works of Nietzsche that speak most pointedly and most explicitly to the fundamental questions of jurisprudence. The main texts upon which it relies are contained in *Jenseits von Gut und Böse*, first published in 1886, immediately after *Also Sprach Zarathustra*; and *Zur Genealogie der Moral*, first published in 1887.[1] By Nietzsche's own instructions, these last two books are to be read as a single work, since the latter was written as an "addition intended to complete and clarify" the former.

Oddly perhaps the title of this Essay does not even allude to the work of Nietzsche. It only asks the question: what is positive law? Wrongheaded as it may seem, the omission is deliberate. The task before us indeed calls upon us to think through the question of the essence of positive law. To study Nietzsche is not to ascertain the historical record of "what Nietzsche said," nor to seek mastery of that mass of materials in the construction of tidy "nietzschean" doctrines. Great thinkers demand that we let their words draw our attention to the matter at issue in their thought. At issue in Nietzsche's thought is the question of the essence of positive law.

I. Positive Law as Will to Power

What is positive law? We may begin with the familiar account that the word "positive" suggests immediately: positive law (Nietzsche calls it *Gesetz*) is law that exists by virtue of being posited (*gesetzt*), laid down and set firmly, by a will empowered so to will. Such law "exists" in the sense that it has validity

---

† Professor of Law, University of California, Berkeley, School of Law (Boalt Hall). Docteur en droit 1961, University de Liege, Belgium; Ph.D. 1966, University of California, Berkeley. This Essay is dedicated to Linda Helyar.

1. Several translations of these works are available. The most commonly used are F. NIETZSCHE, JENSEITS VON GUT UND BÖSE, BEYOND GOOD AND EVIL (W. Kaufmann trans. 1966) [hereinafter JGB]; F. NIETZSCHE, ALSO SPRACH ZARATHUSTRA, THUS SPOKE ZARATHUSTRA (R.J. Hollingdale ed. 1961) [hereinafter ASZ]; and F. NIETZSCHE, ZUR GENEALOGIE DER MORAL, ON THE GENEALOGY OF MORALS (W. Kaufmann & R.J. Hollingdale trans. 1967) [hereinafter GM]. No study of Nietzsche, or indeed of any great thinker, German or Greek, can rely upon translations, except as a first and dubious introduction to the original text. All quotations in this essay have been translated by the author. All references are to standard editions of the original texts. Translations of Nietzsche are based mostly on the German text in F. NIETZSCHE, SÄMTLICHE WERKE, KRITISCHE STUDIENAUSGABE, (G. Colli & M. Montinari eds. 1988) [hereinafter KSA]. Unless indicated otherwise, all references to these works are to section numbers which are the same in English translations as in the originals.

(*Geltung*). It has validity if the will (*Wille*) from which it issues has the power (*Macht*) to impose it, to demand and secure obedience to its command. Issuing from such power, the law *valet*: it is itself powerful, strong, effective. It has causal efficacy. Now the question arises: of what kind is this power of positive law? Does it prevail in the way reason demands obedience to a justified claim, or rather in the way force exacts compliance as an empirical effect? In kantian terms, does its causal efficacy belong to the causality of freedom or the causality of nature? Is positive law an intellectual or physical entity? These questions will require preparation before they can be answered, if indeed they can. Perhaps the distinctions upon which they rely—between reason and force, freedom and nature, and so on—are not applicable to the matter at hand.

Nevertheless, a hint has already been given, and should not be let pass unnoticed. For positive law, to exist is to be valid, i.e. powerful and effective. In this identity of existence and validity, there sounds a not so distant echo of a general thesis of medieval ontology, according to which the existence, *existentia*, of a being is understood as the actuality, *actualitas*, in that being of the creative power of God the Creator, *actus purus*. If this intimation is not altogether misleading, positive law stands in the same relation to the will from which it issues as do beings to the ground of being, *prima causa*, in Christian theology. As the command of a will, positive law is the actuality (*Wirklichkeit*) and effectiveness (*Wirksamkeit*) of the commanding power of the will. The will indeed rules, *is*, as effective command, i.e. as the unity of command and obedience.[2] Such a creative power cannot be reduced either to the authority of a thought or to the efficacy of a natural cause. The unity of command and obedience cancels the difference between idea and reality. Like the hegelian *Geist*, the commanding will actualizes thought in nature.

Judged by the lights of current jurisprudence, these suggestions may seem preposterous. Even the most "positivist" accounts of positive law fall far short of allowing it the unconditional power of command that the theological analogy above would require. The power to posit law is always conceived as derivative, grounded in and made possible by a prior and higher Law (*Recht*), which does not itself issue from command but grants or constitutes the power to command, and determines the conditions under which that power is legally exercised. This condition of legality defines the "validity" of positive law, which is then conceived as the formal authority of command, and sharply distinguished from empirical efficacy. The roots of positive law may thus be traced to a hypothetical *Grundnorm*, or to an already given and "accepted" rule of "recognition," or to a "natural law" the uncertainties of which it is designed to settle. However mysterious the source of the grounding Law may remain, some such foundation is thought necessary to secure the possibility of positive law. If the higher law that fixes the conditions of validity of positive law were itself to issue from

2. JGB, *supra* note 1, § 19.

command, it would depend upon yet a higher law to fix the conditions of its authority; and if this next higher law also were a command, its own validation would require the support of a still higher law, and so on *ad infinitum*. On such terms, positive law would never get grounded, or so the argument runs.

In holding positive law to a subordinate place, jurisprudence has been faithful to received legal and institutional experience. It is heir to a long tradition of lawyerly contempt for legislation. Through most human history so far, the power of command has indeed been confined to narrow domains, bounded by custom, held in delegation, premised upon and therefore conditioned by limited trust, kept within the scope of presumed expertise. But this past affords no clue to the significance of positive law in the strong sense of a law that asserts itself as binding on the sole ground that it has been so willed, subject to no other condition. If such a phenomenon has indeed made its appearance in the modern world, it requires to be thought afresh.

In its primary sense, the name "legal positivism" designates not a philosophical or legal doctrine, but the historic movement by which the power of command rises to the rank of supreme source of law, thus inaugurating the reign of positive law. Nietzsche is the thinker and prophet of legal positivism.

With Nietzsche, the relation between positive law (*Gesetz*) and higher law (*Recht*) is turned upside down. *Recht* is brought down from its eminent place as higher Law of the land, and reduced to the standing of a mere creature of *Gesetz*.

> The most decisive act that the supreme power performs . . . is the institution of *Gesetz*, the imperative declaration of what in general counts as *Recht* in its eyes, and what counts as *Unrecht*. . . . "*Recht*" and "*Unrecht*" exist, accordingly, only after the institution of *Gesetz* . . . . To speak of *Recht* or *Unrecht in itself* is quite senseless.[3]

It follows that *Gesetz*, as the self-assertion of the commanding will, is the spring of justice (*Gerechtigkeit*): the "egoism" of the will "is justice itself."[4] Thus justification (*Rechtfertigung*) is originally granted by positive law, not by *Recht*. The positing of law in *Gesetz* is the creative act from which derive all measures, standards or aims of thought and action, regarding art and truth as well as the good. Hence the philosopher, who for Nietzsche embodies the most powerfully creative spirit, is first and foremost one who posits law:

> *Genuine philosophers are commanders and legislators* [Gesetzgeber]: they say, "*thus* it *shall* be!" They first determine the Whither and For What of man . . . . With a creative hand they reach for the future, and all that is and has been becomes a means for them, an instrument, a

3. GM, *supra* note 1, pt. II, § 11.
4. JGB, *supra* note 1, § 265.

hammer. Their "knowing" is *creating*, their creating is a legislation [*Gesetzgebung*], their will to truth is—*will to power.*[5]

Positive law reaches the height of its power in the creative work of philosophy. That this creative power occupies a position analogous to that of the Creator-God of Christian metaphysics, that the supremacy of positive law therefore signifies the rising of man to claim that position for man himself, that positivism thought in its most radical implications entails a kind of deification of human power, all this is quite apparent to Nietzsche. Philosophy "always creates the world in its own image; it cannot do otherwise. [It] is this tyrannical drive itself, the most spiritual will to power, to the 'creation of the world,' to the *causa prima*."[6] The rise of positive law signals the beginning of man's "fight for the dominion of the earth."[7]

With positive law, the power of command assumes the place of ground and source of all law. What is the foundation of that power? From what and where does the will derive such an extraordinary title to rule? Now of course if positive law is truly to be fundamental, it cannot itself rest upon yet another ground outside itself. Somehow it must be capable of grounding itself. Again following the theological analogy, the *causa prima* must be *causa sui*. What indeed empowers the will to command is the will itself. In every commanding, the will wills, above and before the object of its command, its own power to command what it wills. This is why the will is essentially will to power (*Wille zur Macht*).

> Anyone who considers the basic drives of man . . . will find that each of them would like only too well to represent just *itself* as the ultimate purpose of existence and the legitimate *master* of all other drives. For every drive seeks to dominate—and it attempts to philosophize in that spirit.[8]

Even self-preservation yields priority to power in the economy of "life," i.e. the will in Nietzsche's language: "A living thing seeks above all to discharge its strength—life itself is *will to power*; self-preservation is only one of the indirect and most frequent *results*."[9] In that it wills first and foremost to empower itself to command, the will attains absolute freedom from all laws other than those it posits for itself: it may then lay claim to an unconditioned power to legislate—and thus give a radically new sense to the kantian principle of autonomy.[10]

5. *Id.* § 211.
6. *Id.* § 9.
7. *Id.* § 208.
8. *Id.* § 6.
9. *Id.* § 13.
10. *See id.* § 22.

This idea of an unconditioned power to posit law may well seem so far-fetched, so utterly removed from the ordinary understanding of legislation and positive law, that it need not concern any serious student of these matters. Who would allow any legislature such unlimited authority? Do we not hold the positive law liable to criticism, indeed open to disobedience, on "moral" or other grounds extraneous to the law? Perhaps. But Nietzsche's concept of *Gesetz* does not refer to anything like positive laws or legislatures. Positive law here means neither posited laws, i.e. instances of positive legal enactment, nor the totality of posited laws that constitutes a positive legal system, nor positive legal systems in general, nor even the process by which such laws are posited. *Gesetz*, in Nietzsche's sense, is rather that fundamental understanding of law which first opens the possibility of positing laws and instituting arrangements for such positing. Positive law so conceived is prior to any instance of posited law, or of means of positing law. In the language of *Sein und Zeit*,[11] the concept must be thought not ontic—pertaining to beings (*das Seiende*)—but ontological—pertaining to *das Sein*, an element of the prior understanding of being within which beings come to be known. Elsewhere, and more commonly, Nietzsche speaks of the positing of values (*Wert setzen*) instead of *Gesetz*. Positive law springs from the self-affirmation in and by which man assumes "the right [*Recht*] of masters [*Herren*] to set values,"[12] that is, from the moment when man understands himself in accordance with the essence of "life" as power to will, and this will as will to power. "There would be no life at all"—and to Nietzsche all being is life, and will to power—"if not on the basis of perspective estimation [*Schätzung*] and fiction [*Scheinbarkeit*]."[13]

> Setting prices, determining values, contriving equivalences, exchanging—these preoccupied the earliest thinking of man to so great an extent that in a certain sense they constitute thinking *as such*; . . . here likewise, we may suppose, did human pride . . . have its first beginnings. Perhaps our word "man" [Mensch] (*manas*) still expresses something of precisely *this* feeling of himself: man designated himself as the essence [*Wesen*] that measures values, evaluates and measures as the "estimating [*abschätzende*] animal as such."[14]

"Early" and "beginning" are meant here not in the historical, but in the philosophical sense of ἀρχή, principle, the primordial. When we criticize our laws, our legal system, or our lawmakers, we do so by way of evaluating them, by

11. M. HEIDEGGER, SEIN UND ZEIT §§ 2, 3, 4 (1927) [hereinafter SEIN UND ZEIT]. There is an English translation of this work: M. HEIDEGGER, BEING AND TIME (J. Macquarrie & E. Robinson trans. 1962). All references to this work are to paragraph numbers which are the same in the English translation as in the original. Several translations of Heidegger's works capitalize the *b* of "being" when the word translates the German *das Sein*. This practice misleads some readers to think that Heidegger somehow deifies being. It should be avoided.

12. JGB, *supra* note 1, § 261.

13. *Id.* § 34.

14. GM, *supra* note 1, pt. II, § 8.

measuring them up to the values we have set for ourselves, and thus in the light of an assumed power to legislate. Such "moral criticism" of posited laws lies entirely within the perspective of positive law, if indeed the essence of positive law rests in a certain understanding by man of his own essence and relation to the world: man as maker of his world, the man who knows "the future of man as his will."[15]

II. Positive Law as Nihilism

Positive law in that sense is nihilism. Nietzsche conceives its rise to supremacy as the fulfillment or completion (*Vollendung*) of nihilism. In this fulfillment, Nietzsche seems to think, nihilism succeeds in overcoming (*Überwindung*) itself. What is nihilism? In what sense and how is it fulfilled and overcome? These questions define the overarching concerns from which *Jenseits von Gut und Böse* draws its unity and principle of organization.

The nihilist is "a fanatic of conscience who would rather rest and die on a certain nothing than on an uncertain something, . . . a soul in despair, mortally tired."[16] In law, his principle says: *ubi jus incertum, ibi jus nullum.* The rise of such "a will to the nothing"[17] is the driving force that has determined the movement of Western history since the founding of Christendom (*Christentum*, as distinguished from Christianity, *Christlichkeit*). As Nietzsche understands it, "Christendom is platonism for 'the people.'"[18] It erects another world above and beyond the natural or sensible world, and counterposes the illusoriness of what appears to the senses in this "valley of tears" (τὰ ὁρατά), to the promise of an absolute truth attainable by the soul of the just in the beyond (τὰ νοητά). Thus Christendom, as platonism, is also called metaphysics. With it, the highest "values"—truth, and hence also the truly good and the truly beautiful, i.e. the possible forms of greatness for man that give human life an aim and make it worth living—are placed out of the reach of man in this life. This is the meaning of the ascetic ideal of Christian morality:

> [T]his hatred of the human, even more of the animal, and more still of the material, this horror of the senses, of reason [*Vernunft*] itself, this fear of happiness and beauty, this longing to get away from all appearance, change, becoming, death, wishing, from longing itself—all this means if we dare to grasp it, a *will to the nothing*, a will to counter [*Widerwillen*] life, a rebellion against the most fundamental presuppositions of life; but it is and remains a will! . . . Man would rather will *the nothing* than *not* will.[19]

15. JGB, *supra* note 1, § 203.
16. *Id.* § 10.
17. GM, *supra* note 1, pt. III, § 28.
18. JGB, *supra* note 1, *Vorrede* (Preface).
19. GM, *supra* note 1, pt. III, § 28.

In this transposing and postponing of the ends of life to the afterlife begins the movement by which "the highest values devalue themselves,"[20] namely the destructive phase of nihilism. The transposing itself already betrays a destructive impulse, which Nietzsche conceives as the slave's instinct of revenge against the master: metaphysics denies the power of mankind, of both the strong and the weak, to attain worthy ends in this world. With its scorn for the worldly feats and glories of the noble man, Christendom marks the advent of the "slave rebellion in morals."[21] As the revolt proceeds, the Christian promise of truth itself is questioned, in the very name of truth. Can the "existence" of God, i.e. the supernatural world, be proved? Although unprovable, belief may still be required as a duty of faith, provided philosophy can show the priority of duty over truth and thus "make room for faith."[22] In the end, the unprovability of the existence of God proves fatal to belief, and there occurs the great event of modern times: the death of God. The loss of faith "does not stand in antithesis to" the metaphysical ideal, but "is rather one of its concluding forms and inner consequences; it is the awe inspiring *catastrophe* of two thousand years of breeding to truth, which in the end forbids itself the *lie of belief in God*."[23] Instead of denying the metaphysical world, modern atheism succeeds only in debasing, desecrating it. In place of the promise of salvation and the beatific vision, there moves now the promise of "progress" toward "happiness" on this earth through the advance of science and democracy.

> Free-thinkers belong among the *levelers* . . . . What they would strive for with all their powers is the common green pasture happiness of the herd, with security, lack of danger, comfort, and an easier life for everyone; the two tunes and doctrines they sing most profusely are "equality of rights" and "sympathy for all suffering"—and suffering itself they take for something that one must abolish.[24]

Thus there arises the great danger of modern times, "the danger of dangers":[25] the danger of "a common war against all that is rare, strange, privileged, against the higher man, the higher soul, the higher duty, the higher responsibility,"[26] a war that would result in "the *complete degeneration of man* . . . into the

---

20. F. NIETZSCHE, WILLE ZUR MACHT § 2 [hereinafter WM]. This "work" first appeared in 1901 in the *Grossoktavausgabe* of Nietzsche's WERKE, vol. XV. It is not a work of Nietzsche, but a collection of selections from his unpublished notes, gathered under the direction of his sister. There is an English translation: F. NIETZSCHE, WILL TO POWER (W. Kaufmann & R. J. Hollingdale trans. 1968). All references to this work are to section numbers, which are the same in the English translation as in the original.

21. JGB, *supra* note 1, §§ 195, 260; GM, *supra* note 1, pt. I, *passim*.

22. I. KANT, KRITIK DER REINEN VERNUNFT *B xxx. The most commonly used translation of this work is I. KANT, CRITIQUE OF PURE REASON (N. Smith trans. 1965).

23. GM, *supra* note 1, pt. III, § 27.

24. JGB, *supra* note 1, § 44.

25. GM, *supra* note 1, Preface, § 6.

26. JGB, *supra* note 1, § 212.

perfect herd animal, . . . the animalization of man into the dwarf animal of equal rights."[27]

However, insofar as this destructive nihilism proceeds from a quest for truth, a "will to truth";[28] insofar as its devaluation of values therefore leaves unquestioned the very highest of the higher values, namely truth itself; insofar as it thus stays within the horizon of metaphysics, it remains radically incomplete (*unvollendet*), in the sense that it falls way short of the possibilities of a full devaluation of values. Nihilism, or the devaluation of values, is not completed or fulfilled until truth "in the end draws its *most severe conclusion*, its conclusion *against* itself; this occurs (*geschieht*) when it poses the question 'what does the will to truth signify (*bedeutet*)?' "[29] This questioning and denial of the value of truth Nietzsche regarded as his own task:

> [W]hat sense would our whole being have, if it were not this, that in us the will to truth had come to consciousness of itself as a *problem*? As the will to truth becomes conscious of itself, from now on—of this there is no doubt—morality collapses: this is the great spectacle in a hundred acts reserved for the next two centuries in Europe, the most frightful, most questionable, and perhaps also most hopeful of all spectacles . . . .[30]

The *Genealogie der Moral* concludes with the question of the value of truth. *Jenseits von Gut und Böse* opens with it, as though this work turned to the future—its subtitle is *Vorspiel einer Philosophie der Zukunft*[31]—out of a past the history of which is later laid out in *Genealogie*.

The first chapter of the prelude, "On the Prejudices of Philosophers," accomplishes the completion of nihilism: it denies the supremacy of the value of truth.

> The falseness of a judgment is for us no objection to a judgment; . . . The question is how far it is life-promoting, life-preserving, . . . and we are fundamentally inclined to maintain that the falsest judgments . . . are the most indispensable for us . . . that renouncing false judgments would mean renouncing life, a denial of life. To recognize untruth as a condition of life: that certainly means standing against habitual value feelings in a dangerous way; and a philosophy that dares this places itself by this alone beyond good and evil.[32]

The distinction between good and evil (*Gut und Böse*) stands here as in the title for the moral order as a whole, and more generally for metaphysics, i.e. the

27. *Id.* § 203.
28. GM, *supra* note 1, pt. III, § 27.
29. *Id.*
30. *Id.*
31. The English translation of the subtitle is *Prelude to a Philosophy of the Future.*
32. JGB, *supra* note 1, § 4.

opposition of the supernatural to the natural world. With the negation of the value of truth, "we move right over and away from morals [*die Moral*], we smother, we crush perhaps the remnants of our own morality [*Moralität*]."[33] Freed from the domination of faith, philosophy, which as "the morphology and doctrine of the development of the will to power" is now called "psychology," becomes again "the queen of the sciences."[34]

Complete nihilism would seem under its first aspect to reach the utmost level of destructiveness. Having denied truth, the spirit (the will) is liberated from every bond of subordination or dependence, even from the constraint of "reality."[35] The freedom of this "free spirit" which, as announced in the title, is the object of the second chapter of *Jenseits von Gut und Böse*, reminds of Hegel's account of the nihilism of "negative freedom."[36] It rejects every dogma, every shared understanding, every attachment—"every person is a prison"[37]—every common good, indeed everything common and even communication itself.[38] It destroys everything that might stand as a possible limitation of its independence: free spirits are "born, sworn, jealous friends of solitude."[39]

But

> whoever has endeavored . . . to think pessimism through to its depths . . . ; whoever has actually looked down into the most world-denying of all possible ways of thinking . . . may just thereby, without having properly willed it, have opened his eyes to the opposite ideal: the ideal of the most high-spirited, most alive, and most world-affirming man . . . .[40]

As a few texts of the first and second chapters have already intimated, and the third chapter, on "The Essence of Religion," proceeds to show, it appears that complete nihilism entails the overcoming of nihilism.[41] Since the devaluation of the higher values relied upon truth as a ground, and the value of truth has now been denied, the negation of values has itself been negated. Falseness is no longer an objection, and man is free to affirm himself in the creation of values. Thus the free spirit differs from the free-thinker: his independence or negative freedom is only the other side of a will that has "risen to uncondi-

33. *Id.* § 23.
34. *Id.*
35. *Id.* § 36.
36. G.W.F. HEGEL, GRUNDLINIEN DER PHILOSOPHIE DES RECHTS § 5 (1st ed. 1821) [hereinafter GPR]. The English translation of this work is G.W.F. HEGEL, PHILOSOPHY OF RIGHT (T. Knox trans. 1952). All references to this work are to paragraph numbers which are the same in the English translation as in the original.
37. JGB, *supra* note 1, § 41.
38. *See id.* §§ 27, 40, 43.
39. *Id.* § 44.
40. *Id.* § 56.
41. *Id.* § 32.

tioned power-will."[42] The skepticism of the free-thinker proceeds from weakness, tiredness, despair, from the destructive rage of the slave, whereas the radical skepticism of the free spirit exudes the strength of a will "eager for life": these "stronger and livelier thinkers . . . will at bottom to win back something of the ancient domain of the faith of earlier times, perhaps 'the immortal soul,' perhaps 'the ancient God,' ideas in short that allow to live better, namely more strongly and more cheerfully, than 'modern ideas.'"[43] The God that died in modern times was the God of Christendom, God "'the Father,' 'the Judge,' 'the Remunerator,'" but religion itself has not died: on the contrary, "the religious instinct is growing powerfully."[44] In complete nihilism, God is "sacrificed for the nothing,"[45] but in that very sacrifice a new god is created, Dionysus, the god of the love of life and of eternal return, "*circulus vitiosus deus*,"[46] who will however remain unnamed until the very end of the work.[47]

However poorly it will do, a brief explanation of the doctrine of eternal return is perhaps necessary. For present purposes, the matter may be put as follows. As long as the death of God is experienced as a loss, an absence, a lack, nihilism remains at once incomplete and destructive: incomplete, insofar as in the thought of a lack persists a belief in the necessity of a supernatural world to cure the defects of this world; destructive, because the lack makes life in this world seem senseless and worthless. What is, the present, loses significance; nothing matters in any decision; the will despairs and weakens to the point of extinction. "The aim is lacking: 'why?' finds no answer."[48] Under the spell of this nihilism,

> the *will* for man and earth was lacking; behind every great human destiny there sounded as a refrain a yet greater "in vain!" . . . [M]an was surrounded by an enormous void—he did not know how to justify, explain, affirm himself, he *suffered* from the problem of his sense. He also suffered otherwise, . . . but his problem was *not* suffering itself, but that there lacked an answer to the crying question "*to what end* do I suffer?"[49]

Nihilism fulfills itself by denying the lack, i.e. by denying that this world needs a ground outside it to give it support, that this life needs an end outside and above it to give it sense and value. As unconditioned will, life itself is the valueless positing of values, the endless giving of sense, the groundless creating of all that is. It is the lawless law-giver of positive law. Having reached this

42. *Id.* § 44.
43. *Id.* § 10.
44. *Id.* § 53.
45. *Id.* § 55.
46. *Id.* § 56.
47. *Id.* § 295.
48. WM, *supra* note 20, § 2.
49. GM, *supra* note 1, pt. III, § 28.

power of self-affirmation, the will emerges as the "religious instinct" itself: it deifies, sanctifies, justifies (in the theological as well as the legal sense of the word) what it wills, i.e. the will or life itself. The self-affirming will affirms the infinite value of what it wills, what is, the present. Projected over time, this infinite value requires the eternal return of the like.

> The world-affirming man has not only settled for and learned to endure what was and is, but wills to have it, *just as it was and is*, repeated in all eternity, calling insatiably *da capo*, not only to himself, but to the whole play and spectacle, and not only to a spectacle, but at bottom to him who has need of this spectacle—and makes it necessary: because again and again he has need of himself—and makes himself necessary . . . .[50]

Thus the triumph of positive law signifies at once the fulfillment of nihilism—the end of the longing for God—and the overcoming of nihilism—the deifying affirmation of life on earth. The rest of *Jenseits von Gut und Böse*, read in this light, appears to follow a straightforward plan, which may now be quite briefly explained. Part Four is an "interlude," consisting of some 120 epigrams,[51] many models of Nietzsche's art and thought; it separates the first three chapters, the coherence of which has just been discussed, from the last five, which form the second and last main division of the work. Here Nietzsche spells out the main features of the self-affirming will that rises in the overcoming of nihilism; he does so mainly by way of a "critique of modernity,"[52] of the incomplete and destructive nihilism of our times. Chapters Five, "Toward a Natural History of Morals," Six, "We Scholars," and Seven, "Our Virtues," form a triad on the theme of the will as a unity of command and obedience.[53] Nietzsche begins with obedience (Chapter Five), which he calls "the imperative of nature," i.e. of "instinct" or will to power: "that there be obedience for a long time in *one* direction: thus comes and has always come in the long run something for the sake of which it is worth living on earth; . . . something illuminating, refined, mad, divine."[54] The "history of morals" is the history of a slave rebellion against this imperative of life, the outcome of which is the degeneration of obedience into the "herd instinct,"[55] with the risk of a degeneration of man into a herd animal.[56] The other side of obedience is command

50. JGB, *supra* note 1, § 56.

51. *See id.* §§ 63-185.

52. F. NIETZSCHE, ECCE HOMO, *Jenseits von Gut und Böse* (Beyond Good and Evil) § 2 (1st ed. 1886) (G. Colli & M. Montinari ed. 1988) [hereinafter EH]. There is an English translation of this work: F. NIETZSCHE, ECCE HOMO (W. Kaufmann & R.J. Hollingdale trans. 1967). All references to this work are to chapter and section number which are the same in the English translation as in the original.

53. JGB, *supra* note 1, § 19.

54. *Id.* § 188.

55. *Id.* § 199.

56. *See id.* §§ 202, 203.

(Chapter Six), the creative law-giving of the philosopher-legislator,[57] whose rise and rule may well become impossible as the triumph of the slave brings philosophy under the dominion of science and scholarship. Finally virtue (Chapter Seven) achieves the unity of command and obedience. The identity of inclination and duty is attained here by the subordination of duty (morality, obedience) to instinct (nature, will): the task is to "translate man back into nature"[58] so that morality and its hostility to life may be overcome. "In man creature and creator are united: in man there is matter, debris, clay dirt, nonsense, chaos; but in man there is also creator, form-giver, hammer hardness, spectator-divinity, and seventh day."[59] The same unity manifests itself in the relation of doing to suffering, in the tragic fusion of joy with pain, indeed in the natural pleasure man takes in pain, i.e. the pleasure of cruelty: "Almost everything we call 'higher culture' rests upon the spiritualization and deepening of cruelty—this is my thesis; the 'savage animal' has not been mortified, it lives, it flourishes, it has only—deified itself."[60]

Finally, Chapters Eight, "People and Fatherlands," and Nine, "What is Noble?" announce the essential ways in which the values affirmed by a self-affirming will differ from the values of a morality that denies life. First, the platonic relation between art and truth is inverted: art takes the place of truth as the highest value (Chapter Eight). Art is here understood in the most general sense of a creative power: the power to give form to chaotic matter, to impose being upon becoming,[61] to make things appear in shining light, and thus to illuminate (*verklären*) and glorify them, to confer beauty, to deify.[62] Second, more generally and fundamentally (Chapter Nine), the slave understanding of the relation between good and evil is inverted: the ethos of the noble man is restored to rule; honor, tradition, pride, power, distance, discipline, all that the slave resents and judges evil, take the place of utility, progress, humility, selflessness, equality, freedom, the basic slave standards of the good.[63] Only such an aristocratic ethos can sustain "the elevation (*Erhöhung*) of the species 'man,' the continued 'self-overcoming of man,' to use a moral formula in a supra-moral sense."[64]

57. *See id.* § 211.
58. *Id.* § 230.
59. *Id.* § 225.
60. *Id.* § 229.
61. *See id.* §§ 244, 245.
62. *See id.* §§ 254, 255.
63. *See id.* § 260.
64. *Id.* § 257.

III. Positive Law as Absence of Law

If this were all there were to *Jenseits von Gut und Böse*, and generally to Nietzsche's account of the overcoming of nihilism in positive law, then Heidegger should never have qualified this indictment:

> Nietzsche's metaphysics is nihilism proper. This entails not only that Nietzsche's nihilism does not overcome nihilism, but also that it can never overcome it. Precisely in that in which and through which Nietzsche means to overcome nihilism, in the positing of new values by the will to power, nihilism proper announces itself: That there is nothing to being [*das Sein*] itself, as it has now become a value. . . . Value thinking is now elevated to the rank of principle. Being [*das Sein*] itself, as a matter of principle, is not let in as being [*das Sein*]. . . . Accordingly Nietzsche's metaphysics is no overcoming of nihilism. It is the last entanglement in nihilism. . . . Through this entanglement of nihilism in itself, nihilism first becomes thoroughly complete in what it is. This thoroughly complete, perfect nihilism is the fulfillment of nihilism proper. . . . Fulfilled nihilism finally shuts itself off from the possibility of ever being able to think and to know the essence [*Wesen*] of nihilism. Is this not to say that the essence of nihilism remains closed to Nietzsche's thought? How dare we say so?[65]

That formally Nietzsche's understanding of nihilism is nihilistic itself, Nietzsche himself admits, and rightly he smiles at the objection: "[W]ould you like to make this objection? Well, so much the better."[66] By his own account, the overcoming of nihilism occurs in the fulfillment of nihilism, and this fulfillment in turn proceeds from within the destructive movement of nihilism: the overcoming of morality, *alias* nihilism, is a self-overcoming by morality of morality itself.[67]

> All great things bring about their own destruction through an act of self-overcoming: thus the law of life will have it, the law of the necessity of "self-overcoming" in the essence of life—the legislator himself always eventually receives the call: "*patere legem, quam ipse tulisti.*" In this way Christendom *as dogma* collapsed struck by its own morality; in this way Christendom *as morality* must now collapse too: we stand on the threshold of *this* event.[68]

---

65. 2 M. Heidegger, Nietzsche 340-41 (1961) [hereinafter Nietzsche]. The part of this work here quoted and cited has been translated in English: 4 M. Heidegger, Nietzsche 202-03 (F. Capuzzi trans. 1982). References to this work are to the original page numbers. The corresponding pages of the English translation are indicated in parenthesis immediately thereafter.

66. JGB, *supra* note 1, § 22.

67. *See id.* § 32.

68. GM, *supra* note 1, pt. III, § 27.

Does it follow that the attempt to overcome nihilism remains so "entangled in nihilism" that it cannot succeed? Perhaps, but the matter cannot be decided by a purely formal argument, which may not add up to more than a play on words.

From the beginning, Nietzsche conceives nihilism as an essentially destructive movement, the unfolding of a will to the nothing by way of a devaluation of values. In the completion or fulfillment of this destruction, however, Nietzsche envisions the possibility of a creative transformation: that the will may free itself to posit new values. Is positive law so conceived truly free of destructiveness, so that it may indeed be regarded as an overcoming of nihilism? By no means. What positive law accomplishes rather has the appearance of a complete debasement of all law, new or old. The debasement proceeds in two steps, both consequences of the negation of the supersensible world. First, law, which had been the imperative of reason, is reduced to the rank of an "imperative of nature."[69] No longer does the will (*Wille*) reign as practical reason, the source of man's transcendence, and the ground of his freedom. Deposed, it now drives as the power of instinct, "will to power," "life," "sexuality."[70] The *animal rationale* has been brought "back in nature" as *homo natura*.[71] By itself however this downgrading of spirituality, which had in most essential respects already been accomplished by Hegel,[72] remains ambiguous. There are two sides to the identity of will and instinct: the obverse of the naturalization of spirit is the spiritualization of instinct.[73] Nature loses the character of a causality alien to the will. If freedom is denied, so is determination: "In the 'in itself' there is nothing of 'causal connections,' 'necessity,' 'psychological unfreedom,' there is *no* sequence of 'cause and effect,' there governs no 'law.'"[74] And as the will wills the eternal return of its will, it brings about the return of its future from the past as a fate it has chosen. In this embrace of *amor fati*, necessity and freedom are one.

A second and decisive move assures that the debasement of law is complete and unequivocal: the relation of life to the law is inverted so that law loses its authority as the end of life, and is instead made to serve life as a means. To deny metaphysics is to assert that life has no end outside and above it, no sense, no value measurable by any standard, no ground upon which to rest. Life is endless, senseless, valueless, groundless—an abyss (*Abgrund*). Here, however, Nietzsche retains the dichotomy of the natural and the supernatural: instead of denying their difference, he turns it upside down, so that nature occupies the

69. JGB, *supra* note 1, § 188.

70. *Id.* § 75.

71. *Id.* § 230.

72. GPR, *supra* note 36, §§ 7, 19, 154, 155, 183.

73. JGB, *supra* note 1, §§ 219, 229; GM, *supra* note 1, pt. I, § 7; F. NIETZSCHE, GÖTZEN-DÄMMERUNG, *Moral als Widernatur* §§ 1-3 (1st ed. 1869) (G. Colli & M. Montinari eds. 1988) [hereinafter GD]. There is a translation of this work: F. NIETZSCHE, *Morality as Anti-Nature*, in TWILIGHT OF THE IDOLS (R.J. Hollingdale trans. 1968). All references to this work are to chapter titles and section numbers which are the same in the English translation as in the original.

74. JGB, *supra* note 1, § 21.

position of spirit, which is henceforth to be governed by the exigencies of instinct, or will to power. Life itself becomes the ground, the end that determines the sense and the value of all standards, all ideals, indeed all ideas. Hence the philosopher-legislator "will put religions in the service of his work, just as he will employ the political and economic orders."[75] Even religions are "means in the philosopher's hand," and must not be allowed "to reign as sovereign," "to be ultimate ends and not means among other means," because "sovereign religions hold the type 'man' down on a lower rung."[76] Accordingly there are no principles at law, but only values, i.e. products of the will's evaluation of the possibilities it opens for itself, instruments of calculable worth—in current jargon: policies. Laws, and even gods are created, and therefore also killed, as the will to power commands for the heightening of its power to will. But what reverence could man have for such "gods" of his making? What sanctity could there be about such laws? They have been desecrated, brought down to a world in which nothing is inviolable, and hence nothing truly binding, everything usable and disposable at will. Such gòds, such laws can demand nothing of man. They occupy the "lower rung," utterly ungodly. Positive "law" is lawless.

If positive law, the reduction of *Recht* to *Gesetz*, accomplishes the debasement, and thus the destruction or annihilation of law, then it is nihilistic indeed, but in a sense that escapes Nietzsche's understanding of nihilism as a "devaluation of values," and in such a way that its nihilism continues to prevail in the envisioned ending of this devaluation and freeing of a "creation of values." When nihilism is conceived as the devaluation of values, it has already been determined that gods and laws count as values, and that this sacrilegious deed itself will not only stay out of the reach of the overcoming of nihilism, but will constitute this overcoming. Positive law, the self-affirming power of the will to set values, already rules supreme in the understanding by which the collapse of the realm of spirit takes on the character of a devaluation of values. From within this understanding, the debasement of spirit accomplished by positive law cannot itself be recognized as nihilism. Thus positive law blinds itself to its own destructiveness, and falls under the illusion that it will overcome all nihilism.

Now the destructiveness of positive law is not confined to the realm of spirit. If gods and laws are means, so is everything else too, except for that to which it stands as means. Outside the will all that is "is" by way of value to the will. To philosophers "all that is and has been becomes a means, an instrument, a hammer. Their 'knowing' is *creating*, their creating is legislation."[77] And this entails: all knowing, that is, the relation of thinking man to whatever is, has at bottom the character of a command. It follows that things, beings (*das*

75. *Id.* § 61.
76. *Id.* § 62.
77. *Id.* § 211.

Seiende), are never allowed by thinking simply to be what they are of their own. There is no inner order of things to which understanding must yield. There is no integrity of things before which man must bow in respect. Nothing escapes degradation at the philosopher's hand.

Nietzsche's point, however, is not that with the advent of positive law man exercises an *option* to think in the manner of command, as though the alternative were open for thought to refrain from doing violence to beings. Nor does Nietzsche mean to assert like Hegel an "absolute right of appropriation over all things of nature,"[78] that would justify man in using to his ends other beings that have no end of their own. Rather Nietzsche conceives the essence of thinking as command. Genuine thought is creative, a work of art. Positive law itself is man's creative affirmation of the full creative power of human thought. If thought is creation, beings—what thinking thinks—are creatures of thought. Beings (*das Seiende*) come to be (*sein*) as the thought-will of the artist imposes form upon formless chaos, secures duration of the transient, eternalizes the passing moment, in sum "stamps upon becoming the character of being (*das Sein*)."[79] Since beings (*das Seiende*) are—stand and last—as effects of a power to will, their being (*das Sein des Seienden*) appears as the effectiveness (*Wirksamkeit*) or actuality (*Wirklichkeit*) of that creative power. Like the "existence" of posited laws, the existence of beings lies in their "validity," the actuality of the power from which they issue. Strictly speaking indeed, because thought is command, all beings are laws: effects of the positing of a will. But: "'Will,' of course, can affect only 'will'—and not 'matter.'"[80] The will cannot will anything other than itself: what the commanding will commands is the command, what thinking thinks is nothing but thought. Therefore "the world viewed from within, the world determined and designated according to its 'intelligible character'—the world is 'will to power' and nothing outside."[81] There is nothing at all to beings and their being, nothing at all to which thought might relate outside itself.

Accordingly, outside the self-positing will there is nothing at all that this will might degrade, violate, or destroy in any way. Thus positive law here again seals itself from the possibility of recognizing its destructiveness. The same denial—that there is nothing outside the will—even enables positive law to proclaim itself the savior of being: since the being of beings is nothing but the actuality of the creative will, the self-affirmation of that will suffices to secure being from the destruction that a "will to the nothing" threatened to bring. However the denial itself exhibits another aspect of the nihilism of positive law. The claim that there is nothing outside the self-positing will, hence that the being of beings is *nothing* (*nihil*), does not by itself amount to a destructive

78. GPR, *supra* note 36, §§ 39, 44.
79. WM, *supra* note 20, § 617.
80. JGB, *supra* note 1, § 36.
81. *Id.* § 36.

force of the kind manifest in the debasement of spirit, or in the degradation of all beings to the rank of mere instruments. Nevertheless the denial of being may well be the deeper source from which such a destructive historical movement emerges.

In Heidegger's words, the triumph of positive law begins "the epoch of the unconditioned and complete objectification of all that is."[82] This objectification arises out of "the complete domination of subjectivity."[83] To every object, there belongs a subject as its ground, in this case man. The essence of all subjectivity in turn lies in the subject's assumption of the power to ground the constitution of objects. Man

> erects himself out of and above other beings [*das Seiende*] as the being [*der Seiende*] who proposes and produces [*vorstellend-herstellend*], and thus takes power over all beings [*das Seiende*] as objects. Of himself man puts his essence to rest upon security [*Sicherheit*]. He seeks to effect his securing by a complete ordering of all beings in the sense of a methodical securing of their stability [*Bestand*] . . . . The objectification of all beings, which arises out of man's uprising in the exclusive self-willing of his will, is the essence of the movement in the history of being [*das Sein*] by which man invests his essence in subjectivity. All transcendence, be it ontological or theological, is represented [*vorgestellt*] relative to the subject-object relation.[84]

Even God becomes an object of man's making.

Thus positive law is the metaphysics of modern technology, of man's rise to "dominion over the earth."[85] It is metaphysics, despite Nietzsche's effort to overcome metaphysics, in that it seeks a ground of beings "beyond" them in a superior being. The subject-will "underlies" its objects-values in the same way that the Creator-God grounded his creation and ruled as the end to which all finite beings were directed. Like older metaphysics, positive law results in denying the being of finite beings. To Pascal, with whom Nietzsche acknowledged a profound affinity,[86] "the finite is annihilated in the presence of the infinite and becomes pure nothingness. So it is with our mind before God, with our justice before divine justice."[87] To Nietzsche, there is nothing outside the unconditioned will to power. In both the old and the new metaphysics, the denial of being occurs as man falls (*verfällt*) captive of beings,[88] absorbed in his worldly concerns, ruled by common everyday wisdom (ἡ σοφία τοῦ κόσμου), the end of which may be to secure eternal salvation, or happiness in

82. NIETZSCHE, *supra* note 65, at 387 (English trans. at 241).

83. *Id.*

84. NIETZSCHE, *supra* note 65, at 378-79 (English trans. at 234).

85. JGB, *supra* note 1, at § 208.

86. *See id.* § 45.

87. B. PASCAL, PENSÉES *418. There is an English translation of this work: B. PASCAL, PENSÉES (A. Krailsheimer trans. 1967).

88. NIETZSCHE, *supra* note 65, at 378 (English trans. at 233).

this life. In positive law, the fall is complete, so that there prevails a "full concealment of being in the midst of a complete securing of beings,"[89] and "the purely actual, what counts as reality to the many," becomes "the measure for deciding that only the effective [*das Wirksame*]—the traceable and impression, the experienced [*das Erlebte*] and expression, the useful and success—shall be valid [*gelten*] as beings."[90]

Thought from within positive law, however, the conclusion that "the world is will to power, and nothing outside" cannot itself issue from any involvement of thought with something "outside" thought. The denial of being is an act of will, and indeed the will's highest self-affirmation: that by which the will empowers itself as unconditioned will to power. The assertion that there is nothing outside will to power, i.e., that there is no transcendence of thought beyond itself, repeats in different form the denial of the "value" of truth, in and by which the "will to nothing" wills itself to nothing, thus at once fulfilling and overcoming its destructiveness. But this devaluation already supposes that *truth*, alias being, is a value, i.e. the willing of a self-positing will. To deny being, the will must already presume that being lies within the reach of its power to will, a power that cannot effect anything outside itself. Accordingly, there cannot be anything outside the will corresponding to the assertion that "there is nothing outside the will to power." Nor is there anything outside the will corresponding either to "the nothing," the annihilation willed in the "will to nothing," or to the overcoming of that power of destruction. Nihilism itself has no being outside will. In this sense too positive law remains nihilistic in its understanding of nihilism. The very conception of nihilism as a destructive force, and of an overpowering of that force to bring by force an end to destruction, betrays precisely that fascination with the effective, with which fallen man approaches all beings, and finds the being of beings in the actuality of power.

Is it possible that nihilism would after all, in its essence, not be destructive? That the ravage wreaked by the "will to the nothing" would manifest not the absolute power of the will, but rather the precedence of a "nothing" that must first unleash the power of man to destroy? That this "nothing" would therefore escape and defeat any "will to overcome" it? In sum, that nihilism would neither issue from man's making, nor let itself be undone by man? If such were the case, then positive law, and Nietzsche as the thinker of positive law, would have failed entirely to grasp the essence of nihilism, and their claim to have overcome it would ring hollow.

Such is indeed the possibility that Heidegger envisions and explores. To entertain this possibility is to think the "nothing" not as *nihil negativum*, the nothing of negation, but as *nihil originarium*, a nothing that, prior to any negation or affirmation by thought, would of itself give man to think. Thought

89. *Id.* at 387 (English trans. at 242).
90. *Id.* at 376 (English trans. at 231-32).

in this way, the nothing "is" the being of beings. Being and nothing are one and the same, not in the sense of some ordinary assertion that "being is nothing," nor in the sense of Hegel's "speculative proposition" asserting the dialectical identity of being and nothing,[91] but in the sense indicated by what Heidegger calls the "ontological difference," that "[t]he being of beings 'is' not itself a being (*Das Sein des Seienden 'ist' nicht selbst ein Seiendes*)."[92] Being (*das Sein*) must not here be understood as beingness (*die Seiendheit*), what all beings have in common as beings. The German text employs the infinitive rather than the participle form to signify "being" as verb (*sein*) rather than substantive (*das Seiende*). The being of beings is the advent of their being (*sein*), not the concept of "beings as such" (*das Seiende als solchen*). In other words, being is not some substrate or substance (οὐσία) all beings have in common as beings, but the event of the coming of beings in the presence of thought. As this advent, being (*das Sein*) itself is no being (*kein Seiendes*) and never exhibits the beingness of a being. This absence of being (*das Sein*) from among beings (*das Seiende*), this staying-out (*Ausbleiben*) or withdrawal (*Entzug*) that being achieves of its own, is the nothing in which lies the essence of nihilism.

> Nihilism, i.e. metaphysics, is the thinking of fallen man. Being itself stays unthought in metaphysics, because metaphysics thinks beings as such. What does this say, that beings as such are thought? It says that beings themselves come shining to the fore. They stand in the light. Beings are lighted. Beings themselves are brought out of concealment. Beings stand in this unconcealment. This unconcealment is the essence of truth, which shows itself originally only then already to wither away.[93]

Because the being of beings "is" itself no being, man comes to think as though, in common parlance, there were "nothing to it." The unveiling veils itself, so that the unveiled alone stand in the open and shine. The unconcealment of beings fulfills itself by withdrawing back in concealment and letting the unconcealed beings shine in the light by themselves. Light, the open, truth, unveiling, unconcealment (αληθεια) are different names for the being of beings, understood as the coming of beings into the presence of thought. Now if being itself withdraws into concealment, then the fall of man to beings is at bottom not of man's doing. Nihilism leaves being unthought, not because of any failure of thought man can simply will to correct, but because being stays out of the open. The essence of nihilism is not that man neglects being, but that being abandons beings, so that man ceases to wonder at the wonder of being.

---

91. G.W.F. HEGEL, ENZYKLOPÄDIE § 87 (3d ed. 1830). The part of this work here cited is translated in English: G.W.F. HEGEL, LOGIC (W. Wallace trans. 1975).

92. SEIN UND ZEIT, *supra* note 11, at § 2.

93. NIETZSCHE, *supra* note 65, at 350-51 (English trans. at 212).

If so, in its will to overcome nihilism, positive law attempts an assault against being. But since being cannot be brought under its power, the will revolts and turns away from being. In this turning away from being, the will-thought turns against itself, and reaches the peak of its destructiveness. For thinking is the relation to being that defines the essence of man, the being who thinks, to whom comes the gift of being. By its denial of being, positive law "gives up man's essential possibility."[94] The turn away from being is now complete, in that positive law can even deny it denies being, and claim instead that it exalts the "value" of being. With positive law, being falls from absence into complete oblivion. Yet even this forgottenness of being must not be thought a product of man's forgetfulness. In it the withdrawal of being attains its fulfillment. Positive law is no creation of human will, nor can it itself be overcome by the power of will. Man did not kill God, but the gods abandoned man.

> The staying-out of the unconcealment of being releases the withering away of all that is wholesome among beings. The withering away of the wholesome takes with it and closes the openness of the holy. The closure of the holy obscures every radiance of the divine. This darkening fastens and conceals the want of God. The obscure want lets all beings stand in that eerie strangeness in which beings, made objects of a boundless objectification, seem to be secure possessions in every way familiar. The strangeness of beings as beings [*des Seienden als Solchen*] brings to light the homelessness of man within the totality of beings [*des Seienden im Ganzen*].[95]

Perhaps this desolation of the earth is also the way being demands to be remembered and recalls man to his essence.

Positive law requires to be thought, not to be overcome. To think it is to remember the absence of law.

IV. Positive Law as Rage Against Time

Heidegger was moved on several other occasions to qualify his apparent indictment of Nietzsche's "value-thinking." In the essay "*Nietzsches Wort 'Gott ist tot,'*"[96] an argument that moves along the same lines as the essay quoted above, concludes with the intimation that Nietzsche portrayed himself in the figure of "the mad man who lit a lantern in the clear light of morning, ran to

94. *Id.* at 366 (English trans. at 224).

95. *Id.* at 394-95 (English trans. at 248).

96. M. Heidegger, Holzwege 193-247 (1st ed. 1950) [hereinafter Holzwege]. There is an English translation of this essay in M. Heidegger, The Question Concerning Technology and Other Essays 53-112 (W. Lovitt trans. 1977). References to this work are to page numbers of the original; the corresponding pages of the English translation are indicated in parentheses immediately thereafter.

the market, and cried incessantly: 'I seek God! I seek God!'"[97] Heidegger asks: "Has a thinker here perhaps actually cried *de profundis*?"[98] In a later essay, "*Wer ist Nietzsches Zarathustra?*"("Who is Nietzsche's Zarathustra?")[99] which echoes the main themes of the first part of the lecture course *Was heisst Denken? (What is Thinking?)* Heidegger interprets Zarathustra's two great teachings, the overman and the eternal return of the same (*das Gleiche*), as Nietzsche's effort to think "the belonging together of being and the essence of man":[100] in willing the eternal return of the present, man frees (*erlöst*) himself from the "spirit of revenge" that had until then dominated his relation to beings, and ascends as overman (*Übergang, Übermensch*) to a mode of thinking-willing that accords with the being of beings. Nietzsche's thought, particularly his understanding of time, remains trapped within metaphysics, but in such a way that it shows what is unthought in metaphysics, what still demands to be thought, i.e. being.

Nietzsche understood the desolation of positive law. He succumbed to madness unable to escape: "The waste grows: woe to him who harbors waste."[101] That, and how he understood this devastation becomes apparent towards the end of *Jenseits von Gut und Böse*. Here even more than elsewhere it is necessary to resist a temptation by which Nietzsche himself lures the reader away from the depth of his thoughts: the temptation to read the work as just a loosely assembled collection of discrete aphorisms, which is indeed what the text seems to be here even more than elsewhere. Close attention reveals a tightly woven whole. The unity of this whole must however not be thought in the formal articulation of a doctrine. The aphorism itself and its fragmentation of the text are precisely to break every striving of the reader for access to some readily disposable pack of "ideas." The wholeness of the text must emerge from the unfolding and enduring of the thinker's deepest, most painful experience, namely the sight of the ruin of soul and world, to which man is destined under the rule of positive law.

The work concludes with a thought that implicitly refers back to the famous lines with which Hegel ended the preface to his philosophy of law. Here is Hegel's text:

97. F. NIETZSCHE, DIE FRÖHLICHE WISSENSCHAFT § 125 (1st ed. 1882) (G. Colli & M. Montinari eds. 1988) [hereinafter FW]. There is an English translation of this work, F. NIETZSCHE, THE GAY SCIENCE (W. Kaufmann trans. 1974). References to this work are to section numbers which are the same in the English translation as in the original.

98. HOLZWEGE, *supra* note 96, at 246 (English trans. at 112).

99. M. HEIDEGGER, VORTRÄGE UND AUFSÄTZE (1st ed. 1954) 97-122 [hereinafter VUA]. There is an English translation of this essay in 2 HEIDEGGER, NIETZSCHE 209-33 (D. Krell trans. 1984). References to this work are to page numbers of the original; the corresponding pages of the English translation are indicated in parenthesis immediately thereafter.

100. *Id.* at 120 (English trans. at 231).

101. ASZ, *supra* note 1, pt. IV, *Unter Töchtern der Wüste* (Among Daughters of the Wasteland) § 2.

> One word more about giving instruction as to what the world ought to be. Philosophy always comes on the scene too late to give it . . . . When philosophy paints its grey in grey, then has a shape of life grown old, and with grey in grey it cannot be rejuvenated but only understood. The owl of Minerva begins its flight only with the falling of dusk.[102]

Appearing at the end of what was to prepare a "philosophy of the future," namely the philosophy of positive law, which "teaches man the future of man as his will,"[103] the reference and Nietzsche's own words strike an eerie note:

> Alas, what are you after all, you my written and painted thoughts! . . . You have already lost your novelty, and some of you are ready, I fear, to become truths: they already look so immortal, so heartbreakingly upright, so tiresome! And has it ever been different? What things do we write and paint, . . . we eternalizers of things that *let* themselves be written, what are the only things we can paint? Alas always only what is about to decay . . . ! We eternalize what cannot live and fly much longer, only tired and broken things! And it is only your *afternoon*, you my written and painted thoughts, for which alone I have colors, many colors perhaps . . . : —but no one will guess from that how you looked in your morning, you sudden sparks and wonders of my solitude, you my old beloved—*bad* thoughts.[104]

In a few words, Nietzsche has brought together all the ominous themes introduced in the latter half of the last chapter: the mask; community, solitude, and nobility; fate, and revenge against "the eternal, grievous 'too late' ";[105] now all under the overarching theme of the sun, illumination, light and darkness.

Here Nietzsche foresees that his writing has articulated thoughts that are about to become the unthought orthodoxy of generations to come: Positive law is destined to be the rule of a godless humanity. Nietzsche's own art, which celebrated the supreme value of creative art, has itself only yielded a truth, that is, a dead thought, a thought held without question, uncreatively, thoughtlessly. Truth is the way thoughts rule the world. The greatest thought and deed ever was man's killing of God,[106] but "the greatest events and thoughts—and the greatest thoughts are the greatest events—are grasped last: the generations that are contemporaneous with them do not *live* such events—they live right past them."[107] Godless man will not think the death of God. At least since Plato, the sun has signified the light of thought. Thus as Nietzsche's thoughts become truths, the sun that had illuminated his morning and noon begins to set. Darkness envelops all being.

102. GPR, *supra* note 36, *Vorrede* (Preface).
103. JGB, *supra* note 1, § 203.
104. *Id.* § 296.
105. *Id.* § 277; *see also id.* §§ 269, 274, 279, 295.
106. FW, *supra* note 97, at § 125.
107. JGB, *supra* note 1, at § 285.

Why are these thoughts fated to die as truths? Nietzsche answers: because they have been "written and painted," i.e. given the form of art. The point is not that writing and painting themselves kill their object, but rather that they are essentially unable to capture anything other than already dying thoughts. And why should their power be so limited? Because the essence of art, even the art of the philosopher, lies in illusion—transfiguration (*Verklärung*), beautification, simplification, falsification, fiction, appearances, deception—that is, the effective communication of falsehood, the possibility of which is always already determined and limited in advance by the "truths" the world holds in common. Only the common is communicable: "To understand one another, it is not enough that one use the same words; one also has to use the same words for the same kinds of life-experiences (*Erlebnis*), one must in the end have one's experience (*Erfahrung*) in common."[108]

But if only the common can be communicated, then all communication is grounded in a prior debasement of its object.

> Easy communicability—which at bottom means the living of only average and *common* life-experiences [*Erlebnis*]—must have been the most violent of all forces that have ever had man at their command. The more similar, more ordinary men have had and always have the advantage.... One must invoke monstrous counterforces in order to cross this natural, all too natural *progressus in simile*, the steady transformation of man into the similar, ordinary, average, herdlike—into the common![109]

"All community makes somehow, somewhere, sometime—'common.'"[110] The word "common" (*gemein*) here signifies also: mean, vulgar, plebeian, ignoble, shameful, base, low,[111] petty, small.[112] Conversely, whatever separates, isolates, makes distant and different, causes misunderstanding, also brings a measure of elevation, distinction, nobility of spirit.[113] Hence the greatest virtue is solitude, the virtue of hermits, sought above all by saints[114] and philosophers.[115] Solitude rests upon "a sublime bent and urge for cleanliness, which guesses how all contact between man and man—'in society'—must inevitably bring about uncleanliness."[116] Communication soils. "One no longer loves one's knowledge enough as soon as one communicates it."[117]

---

108. *Id.* § 268.
109. *Id.*
110. *Id.* § 284.
111. *Id.* § 275.
112. *Id.* § 267.
113. *See id.* §§ 270, 271, 272, 273, 283, 284, 289, 290.
114. *See id.* § 271.
115. *See id.* § 289.
116. *Id.* §§ 284, 271.
117. *Id.* § 160.

To be communicable, thoughts must be not only common, but also shallow. To communicate something is to make it appear to others. But only the showable, only what lets itself be seen, i.e., the outer surface of things, can ever be shown. Thus by its essence art can only make surfaces shine. Everything profound—profound suffering,[118] profound thought[119]—escapes communication.

Now the idea of a surface behind or under which lies an inaccessible depth opens the possibility that in communicating a thought, i.e., showing a surface, the work of art conceals, i.e. makes the depth of its thinking impenetrable to others. Communication masks. "Does one not write books precisely to conceal what one harbors? . . . Every philosophy also *conceals* a philosophy; every opinion is also a hiding place, every word also a mask."[120] Even as it makes common, communication removes from the common what its appearance to the common masks. Just as *Also Sprach Zarathustra* claimed of itself in its subtitle, every work of art is at once "for everyone and no one." Insofar as it masks, art separates, closes a domain of protected solitude where thought may live and elevate itself. This is the theme upon which the last section of *Jenseits von Gut und Böse* ends: from his written words, Nietzsche writes, nobody will guess how his thoughts looked when their lights, wonders of his solitude, rose in the morning.

The theme of the mask is fraught with paradox. If the word masks, then the word that "the word masks" is itself a mask. But the revelation that the word masks unmasks the mask that the word had been, deprives it of the power to mask, so that the word that "the word masks" falsifies itself. When the wanderer—Nietzsche himself, the one who called himself Zarathustra's shadow, and who sang: "[T]he waste grows: woe to him who harbors waste"—is unmasked and found "on his way without scorn, without love, with unfathomable eyes; wet and sad like a sounding lead that has come back to light out of every depth unsated—what did it seek under there?"; when the wanderer unmasked is asked who he is and what he wants, he becomes impatient at these nosy questions, and asks for "one more mask! a second mask!"[121]

What does Nietzsche's work mask, in such a way that its own unmasking of that mask is at once itself a mask, and a destruction of the mask's power to mask? Nietzsche answers: the work of great artists almost always hides an inner "corruption" or "collapse," "a soul that 'cannot be saved' [*gesamte innere 'Heillosigkeit'*]," "an eternal 'too late' in every sense"; these "higher men" are often

118. *See id.* § 270.
119. *See id.* §§ 289, 290.
120. *Id.* § 289.
121. *Id.* § 278.

> taking revenge with their work for some inner soiling, seeking with their high flights to escape into oblivion in the face of an all-too-faithful memory, often lost in the slime and nearly in love with it, until they become like jack-o'-lanterns around swamps and *pose* as stars, ... often fighting against a long disgust, against a recurring specter of unbelief that chills and compels them to yearn for *gloria* and to gobble their "belief in themselves" from the hands of enraptured flatterers. . . .[122]

A profound suffering also hides itself behind the mask "to protect itself against contact with obtrusive and pitying hands"; it employs cheerfulness to conceal a "broken, proud, unredeemable [*unheilbar*] heart . . . ."[123] Elsewhere the wanderer, one of the "higher men" in the fourth part of *Also Sprach Zarathustra*, had sung: "[W]oe to him who harbors waste [*weh Dem, der Wüsten birgt*]!" Now Nietzsche explains: it is the philosopher-hermit who in his writing seeks "to conceal what he harbors [*um zu verbergen, was man bei sich birgt*]," namely "an abyss [*Abgrund*]," "a wasteland [*Öde*]," "something incommunicable," of which the writing nevertheless lets hear "an echo."[124]

What then is this inner devastation of which Nietzsche will now let the reader have an intimation? The most explicit statement is this:

> [T]he need *for* nobility is from the ground up different from the needs of the noble soul itself, and downright the telling and dangerous mark of the lack of a noble soul. It is not the works, it is the *faith* that decides here, that fixes here the order of rank ... : a fundamental certainty that the noble soul has about itself, something that cannot be sought, nor found, nor perhaps lost. The noble soul has reverence for itself.[125]

This text harks back to two earlier sections: the noble soul "does not gladly look 'up'—but either ahead of itself, horizontally and slowly, or down: *it knows itself to be a height*";[126] and by way of a quotation from Goethe: "'Truly high respect one can have only for him who does not *seek* himself.' Goethe to Rat Schlosser."[127] To seek nobility is to lack it. As Nietzsche employs it, the word "noble" (*vornehm*) must be understood as translating the Greek κάλος, which signifies more generally the admirable, and thus also the beautiful. Therefore the texts quoted above mean also: to seek beauty is to lack it. Thus the background against which the end of Chapter Nine is written becomes apparent: it is the dialogue between Socrates and Diotima in the *Symposium*.[128] There Plato explains how love, Eros, seeks beauty, and hence also

122. *Id.* § 269.
123. *Id.* § 270.
124. *Id.* § 289.
125. *Id.* § 287.
126. *Id.* § 265.
127. *Id.* § 266.
128. PLATO, SYMPOSIUM 201-13 [hereinafter SYMPOSIUM]. A commonly used translation of this work is B. JOWETT, THE DIALOGUES OF PLATO (1937). All references are to pages of the authoritative manuscript

the good, and the most beautiful of all things, σοφία (*sophia*, wisdom) itself: Eros is "a philosopher through all his life."[129] But he seeks these great things precisely because he lacks them (δι' ἔνδειαν): "[H]e is first of all always a slave [πένης], one who must work, rough, dirty, barefoot, homeless, always in need."[130] Love itself is neither noble nor good. For this reason, it cannot be true that love is a god, for gods cannot be thought wanting anything good. All gods are "in good spirits" (εὐδαίμων), in full possession of beauty and goodness: "[N]o god would philosophize, or ever desire to become σοφός, for he is already."[131]

Nietzsche concurs: his own longing for nobility betrays the soul of a slave. But he goes a step further and says: there can be no fulfillment of such longing. Nobility "cannot be sought."[132] The seeking itself proceeds from lack; it is and remains always nothing other than the experience of that lack. "The law is always in force that he who has these good things is different from him who earns them. Everything good is inheritance: what is not inherited is imperfect, is beginning . . . ."[133] Because the longing grows out of lack, its understanding of the good for which it longs is affected by the same lack, and its desiring of the good is fraught with an urge to destroy, i.e. the envy that springs from the feeling of want. Thus every end, every object of desire is necessarily degraded by the very want out of which it is desired. "Alas, whoever is knowledgeable in matters of the heart understands how poor, dumb, helpless, presumptuous, uncomprehending, more apt to destroy than to save is even the best and deepest love."[134] Accordingly, the search for nobility by way of elevation, distance, separation, solitude—and this includes every striving to escape from the common, and the wearing of a mask as such an escape—aims at falsehood, and is itself a form of baseness.

But this wretched, unknowing, and destructive love, this impossible and therefore endless longing for greatness and perfection constitutes the very essence of life, the will to power, the will—Kant's power to desire, Leibniz's *appetitus*—that seeks forever to raise itself to new heights of the power to will, a will the vitality of which requires that fulfillment never come. This is the life in which Nietzsche has found a god, Dionysus, the divinity that opens for man the possibility of creating new gods, the god of creation itself, of generation, fertility, rapture, and desire. Like Jesus, and *contra* Plato, Nietzsche has found God in love, in the lack of godliness from which springs the longing for God: he "had to find a god who is all love, all capacity to love."[135] Dionysus is

---

which are indicated in the margins of the English translation.

129. *Id.* at 203d7.
130. *Id.* at 203c6.
131. *Id.* at 204.
132. JGB, *supra* note 1, § 287.
133. GD, *supra* note 73, *Streifzüge eines Unzeitgemässen* (Raids of the Untimely) § 47.
134. JGB, *supra* note 1, § 269.
135. *Id.*

"the great ambiguous one," the god who is the absence of God, godlessness, i.e., no God at all, "the god of seeking" (*der Versucher-Gott,* which means also the temptator-god), a god therefore defined by lack: "[T]his godhead lacks," it is not at all the *ens perfectissimum,* as which God has been conceived in philosophy since Plato, and the seeking of which Dionysus himself is.[136] Being love itself, this god is a philosopher: "[T]hat Dionysus is a philosopher, and thus that gods also philosophize, seems to me a novelty that is not uninteresting, and perhaps might arouse mistrust especially among philosophers,"[137] i.e., followers of Plato, who knew the poverty of spirit and the folly from which the love of wisdom is born.

"Whoever feels this way, whoever knows this about love," as did Jesus, "*seeks* death. But why dwell on such painful matters? Assuming one must not."[138] As Plato understood, that for which all love longs is to possess the great things it lacks, indeed to possess them forever, and at bottom to secure immortality, in more than one sense. The complete and unending possession of beauty and the good, by which divinity is defined, entails the complete and everlasting absence of any need, want, desire, love, that is the absence of mortal life. In longing for its own extinction, love seeks death. Thus the god of life, Dionysus, understood as the god of love, turns out to be a god of the seeking of death, the hatred of life, the will to nothing. Nietzsche knew: "The same old story! When one has finished building one's house, one notices that in building it one has unexpectedly learned something one needed to know in the worst way—before one began to build. The eternal grievous 'too late!' The melancholy of everything finished!"[139] This is how he explains what he should have known before he began: "Men of profound sadness . . . have a way of grasping happiness [*Glück*], that is as though they sought to crush and choke it, out of jealousy—alas, they know too well that it will flee."[140] Nietzsche's own embrace of life, the god Dionysus, would destroy life in a rage against its passing, that is, against its temporality, against time itself as essentially passing, against mortality. Thus Dionysus, who is also the god of the circle of eternal recurrence, the truth of which would "redeem the past" and free man from "the spirit of revenge,"[141] turns out to have been thought in and by the spirit of revenge. How so? What is the spirit of revenge? Why this hatred of time, of the temporal as such?

What makes longing impossible to fulfill? The answer is: time. Every longing conceives and seeks its object, a desired future, out of a present lack; when this future comes to be, it is flawed by that lack, and the moment of lack

136. *Id.* § 295.
137. *Id.*; *see also id.* § 294.
138. *Id.* § 269 (emphasis in original).
139. *Id.* at § 277.
140. *Id.* at § 279.
141. ASZ, supra note 1, pt. II, *Von der Erlösung* (Of Redemption).

in which it was conceived has vanished in the past, escaping the reach of the will's power to correct the flaw. Thus now is always already "too late."[142] Because of time also, whatever good may happen out of luck (*Glück*) will pass without letting itself be held.[143] "The will cannot will backwards; that it cannot break time and time's desire, that is the will's most lonely affliction. . . . This, yes this alone is *revenge* itself: the will's counter-will (*Widerwille*) against time and its 'It was.' "[144] The hatred of life which manifests itself in metaphysics has its source in the will's rage at its own impotence before the passing of time. To overcome nihilism, the will must be freed from this rage. The past must be redeemed. The past is redeemed and the will freed when the will learns to "will backwards," to grasp its past as the future lying ahead and within the reach of its creative power. It can, indeed it must do so, because past, present, and future form a circle, the circle of eternal return, in accordance with which at every moment of decision the will is to will the eternal recurrence of the like now. This "redemption" differs from the Christian promise of immortality and eternal bliss in a world beyond. It guarantees the eternal return of this mortal life of never-fulfilled longing. But is it any less "metaphysical"? Does it not also rest on the supposition that without it life would deserve to be hated, and would so deserve precisely by virtue of its temporality? Thus the will that wills its eternal return also springs from the spirit of revenge.

The redeemed will also crushes the life it embraces. It may now be possible to fathom yet a deeper level of thought in the concluding words of this work: artists "eternalize what cannot live much longer," dying thoughts behind which hide young and growing thoughts that "no-one will guess."[145] Of Nietzsche's godlessness, only what is already common, the atheism of the "educated," a truth, can be communicated. Art and philosophy—i.e., lawmaking—come always too late, "untimely" (*unzeitgemäss*, as in *Unzeitgemässe Betrachtungen*, and *Streifzüge eines Unzeitgemässen*[146]), after their καιρός.[147] Art too suffers from time. Why then would the artist ever seek to paint or write his thoughts? Because art too, the redeemed and creative will, the will that glorifies life and wills its eternal return, takes revenge.[148] It eternalizes the dying thought. This means: it eternalizes itself, the will, life, in its dying, in its defeat at the hands of time. Then with this dying thought, it hides the living thought. The "truths" art creates are only the appearance of thought, not thought itself, which remains concealed, forever masked by the words and colors of the work. Dare one presume to guess what lies so concealed? Should one not rather "respect the mask, and not indulge in psychology and curiosity in the wrong

142. JGB, *supra* note 1, at §§ 269, 274, 277, 295.
143. *See id.* § 279.
144. ASZ, *supra* note 1, pt. II, *Von der Erlösung* (Of Redemption).
145. JGB, *supra* note 1, § 296.
146. *Untimely Meditations* and *Raids of the Untimely*; *see supra* note 133.
147. *See id.* § 295.
148. *See id.* § 269.

place"?[149] May one fail to probe at all? The hidden and living thought, one guesses, is Nietzsche's inner desolation, an impossible longing, the despair of godlessness as the seeking of death, and the distress at time that determines such a longing. But these are just the kind of thoughts to which points the idea, here painted in words, of an impenetrable mask. To say of something that it masks is to assert the existence of something else, namely Truth, or the thing-in-itself, hidden behind the surface of appearances, or the thing-for-us. By this Nietzsche allows the distinction between truth and appearance he had denied as he launched the assault against metaphysics in Part One. To say furthermore that the mask is impenetrable—"no-one will guess"—is to place Truth out of the reach of human sight. Sight is condemned to illusion, the search for truth to frustration, the soul to the absence of God. The impenetrable mask stands for nothing other than platonism, the doctrine that the "true world" resides in an unattainable beyond.[150] And Dionysus himself is shown wearing the mask: he is "the great concealed one . . . whose mastery includes the knowledge of how to seem."[151] But then to point to a mask as a mask is already to have unmasked it. The unmasked mask here is the mask itself as signifying the impossible quest for a Truth beyond.

"Always beyond"[152] is the principle of the overman, the man who determines his essence in accordance with the essence of life as endless self-overcoming, and thus reaches for superhuman, godly greatness. What his god, Dionysus, lacks most is not the divine beauty and goodness for which he longs, but the humanity he finds wanting: "[W]hat this godhead lacks is not just modesty—there is in general good ground to suspect that in several respects the gods as a group could learn at the school of men. We humans are—more human . . . ."[153] Their seeking of the divine betrays a hatred of mortal life. Has Nietzsche repudiated the god of love? By no means: "'Bad! Bad! What? Isn't he going back?'—Yes! But you understand him poorly when you complain of that. He goes back like one who will try a big jump."[154] Love is not wisdom, but it knows it is not. Ignorance, not love, is the true danger, in that "the [ignorant] man who is neither noble, nor good, nor prudent, is nevertheless satisfied with himself: he who does not know he is wanting does not desire."[155] In any event, a philosopher does not choose his thoughts. "A thought comes when 'it' wishes, not when 'I' wish."[156]

149. *Id.* § 270.
150. GD, *supra* note 73, *Wie die "wahre Welt" endlich zur Fabel wurde* (How the True World Became a Fable) § 2.
151. JGB, *supra* note 1, § 295.
152. *Id.* § 284.
153. *Id.* § 295.
154. *Id.* § 280.
155. SYMPOSIUM, *supra* note 128, at 204a4.
156. JGB, *supra* note 1, § 17.

> A philosopher . . . is struck by his own thoughts as from outside, from above and below, . . . a fateful man around whom there is always anger, grumbling, rift, and eerie [*unheimlich*] happenings. A philosopher: alas a being [*Wesen*] who often runs away from himself, often has fear of himself—but is always too curious not to "come back to himself" again.[157]

Nietzsche's thoughts too belong to the divine circle of time. But the circle of time is also the recurring cycle of birth, life, and death, and the circling of the sun around the earth, by which night follows upon day and day upon night. Ahead on that circle, in the future, there always looms death, and the darkness of night. Hence, "Dionysus is also the god of darkness."[158] Darkness in turn is that in which the light of thought will in time shine again.

The terrifying prospects Nietzsche envisioned become distinctly apparent in *Zur Genealogie der Moral*, an "uncanny" and "gruesome" work,[159] the structure of which can now be briefly sketched out. As the preface indicates Nietzsche returns here to the themes at the end of *Jenseits von Gut und Böse*, particularly time, the eternal "too late," and the impossible longing for truth. The socratic γνῶθι σαυτόν[160] is unattainable:

> We are unknown to ourselves, we who know—on good ground . . . . What concerns life, the so-called "life-experiences" [*Erlebnisse*]—who among us has enough earnestness for that? or enough time? As to such matters we were never quite "with it" [*bei der Sache*]: our heart is not there—not even our ears! Rather, as one divinely distracted and immersed in himself, into whose ears the bell has just boomed with all its power the twelve beats of noon, suddenly wakes up and asks himself: "what has just struck, properly?" so we sometimes rub our ears *afterward* and ask: "what have we just experienced, properly [*eigentlich*]?" and, afterward as aforesaid, count the twelve trembling bell strokes of our experience, our life, our being—and alas! miscount . . . . We remain necessarily strangers to ourselves, we do not understand ourselves, we must confuse ourselves, for us the law says in all eternity "Each is furthest from himself."[161]

The three essays that follow are a sustained—fated to fail—attempt at self-understanding.

In the first essay, Nietzsche explains the "corruption" of his understanding and praise of nobility: they are themselves infected with slave *ressentiment*. His affirmation of noble values proceeds from a will to "invert" (*umwerten, umkehren*) Christian values, "to unite the *unnatural* inclinations, all aspirations

157. *Id.* § 292.
158. EH, *supra* note 52, *Genealogie der Moral*.
159. *See id.*
160. "Know thyself."
161. GM, *supra* note 1, *Vorrede* (Preface) § 1. *Compare* JGB, *supra* note 1, § 281.

to the beyond, to what is counter to sense, instinct, nature, animality, in short all ideals hitherto, which are all hostile to life and all slander to this world, with the bad conscience."[162] Such an "inversion of all values"—*Umwertung aller Werte*, the title of a major work Nietzsche planned—is just the way the "spirit of priestly revenge" defeats its noble enemies:

> It was the Jews, the people with the most deeply withdrawn priestly vengefulness, who with fearsome consistency dared to invert the aristocratic value-equation (good = noble = powerful = beautiful = happy = beloved of God), and held on to that inversion with the teeth of the most abysmal hatred (the hatred of impotence), saying: "the wretched alone are the good; the poor, impotent, lowly alone are the good; the suffering, deprived, sick, ugly alone are pious, alone are blessed by God, for them alone is there blessedness—and you, the noble and powerful, are on the contrary to all eternity the evil [*Bösen*], cruel, lustful, insatiable, godless."[163]

Nietzsche attempts to invert that original inversion, but his too is a revenge, the act of a slave, not an action but "from the ground up a reaction," a negation instead of an affirmation: "[W]hile every noble morality grows out of a triumphant affirmation of itself, slave morality from the outset says No to the 'outside,' the 'other,' the 'not-itself': and this No is its creative deed."[164] Elsewhere Nietzsche confesses: "I know the pleasure in annihilating to a degree that fits my power to annihilate—in both respects I obey my dionysian nature which cannot separate doing No from saying Yes. I am the first immoralist: thus I am the annihilator par excellence."[165]

The pleasure of annihilating is at bottom "the satisfaction of being permitted without qualm to unleash one's power on a powerless victim, the sensual pleasure '*de faire le mal pour le plaisir de le faire,*' the enjoyment of violation,"[166] that is, the pleasure of cruelty. This pleasure is "so much more highly prized, the lower one stands in the social order": to a slave it appears as "a delicious morsel, a foretaste of higher rank, like taking part in a right of the masters, the exalted feeling of being permitted to despise and mistreat another being as 'beneath oneself.'"[167] This is the satisfaction that the impotent find in revenge. But as the second essay proceeds to show, revenge is the primordial source out of which all evaluations, all measuring and calculation of value, spring. In revenge occurs the first fixing of a price, of an equivalence between present pain and past injury, such that the pleasure taken in inflicting the former

162. GM, *supra* note 1, pt. II, § 24.
163. *Id.* at pt. I, § 7.
164. *Id.* at pt. I, § 10.
165. EH, *supra* note 52, *Warum ich ein Schicksal bin* (Why I am a Destiny) § 2.
166. GM, *supra* note 1, pt. II, § 5.
167. *Id.*

"pays" for the pain suffered in the latter.[168] Now the fundamental principle of justice upon which rests all positing of values asserts: "everything has its price; *all* can be paid off."[169] Thus positive law which appeared at first as the self-affirming "right of masters to set values"[170] turns out to spring from the vindictiveness of an impotent will. There lies the explanation of its radical debasement of law, indeed of all beings it touches. Only objects can have prices.[171] Since positing a value consists in setting a price, all valuing objectifies, robs its concern of every possible dignity. Positive law puts economics in God's place.

The theme of cruelty unifies the three essays of the *Genealogie*, and ties them to the end of *Jenseits von Gut und Böse*. In cruelty, understood as the pleasure of unleashing power on the powerless, the will experiences the fulfillment of its most vital and urgent desire, the desire to command. Thus the feeling that delights lower orders and brings the satisfaction of revenge, is nothing other than the basic pleasure in which the will to power feels itself rising to new heights. In the last analysis, the pleasure at suffering is what makes it possible to "say Yes" in "doing No," to break into dionysian laughter at the torture of life,[172] to will the eternal return of unfulfilled longing, to substitute a "gai saber" for the "religion of pity"[173] and in that sense to overcome nihilism in its completion. The third essay traces the greatness of man, his will to overcome himself, to man's cruelty toward himself, and thus to an "alteration in the direction of *ressentiment*"[174] away from the-external causes of his pain, toward himself. In this way, "the healing instinct of life sought . . . to use the bad instincts of all sufferers for the purpose of self-discipline, self-surveillance, and self-overcoming."[175] Man became

> the great experimenter with himself, restless, unsatisfied, who wrestles with animal, nature, and gods for the ultimate dominion—he, still unconquered, eternally aimed at the future, whose own driving force finds no peace any more, so that his future inexorably wounds him like a spear in the flesh of every present—how should such a courageous and rich animal not also be the most endangered, the most chronically and profoundly sick of all sick animals?[176]

And yet "the No he says to life brings to life as if by magic an abundance of tender Yeses; yes, if he wounds himself, this master of destruction, of self-

168. *Id.* pt. II, §§ 4, 8.
169. *Id.* pt. II, § 8.
170. JGB, *supra* note 1, at § 261.
171. I. KANT, GRUNDLEGUNG ZUR METAPHYSIK DER SITTEN *434. An English translation of this text is I. KANT, GROUNDWORK OF THE METAPHYSICS OF MORALS (H. Paton trans. 1964).
172. JGB, *supra* note 1, § 294.
173. *Id.* § 293.
174. GM, *supra* note 1, pt. III, § 15.
175. *Id.* pt. III, § 16.
176. *Id.* pt. III, § 13.

destruction—afterward it is the wound itself that compels him *to live* . . . ."[177] There lies the source of the philosopher's love of the wastelands (*die Wüste*), of solitude, self-denial, independence from all things or persons outside himself. In the waste,

> he smiles at the sight of the optimum conditions for the highest and boldest spirituality—he does not thereby deny "existence," he rather affirms *his* existence and *only* his existence, and this perhaps to such a degree that he is not far from harboring the sacrilegious wish: *pereat mundus, fiat philosophia, fiat philosophus, fiam*![178]

Such a desire for unconditional freedom is of course above all a death wish.

Positive law parades as man's proud affirmation of his creative powers. But under the masquerade there rages the violence of man's revolt against time and his finitude, a sacrilegious assault against being and the humanity of man. "*Die Wüste wächst: weh Dem, der Wüsten birgt*!"[179]

---

177. *Id.*
178. *Id.* pt. III, § 7.
179. *See supra* text accompanying notes 101, 121, 124.

[2]

Genealogy and Jurisprudence: Nietzsche, Nihilism, and the Social Scientification of Law

Marianne Constable

In Twilight of the Idols, *Nietzsche presents a history of metaphysics that can also be read as a history of jurisprudence. Nietzsche shows how—via Platonism, Christendom, Kantianism, and utilitarianism—the "real" or "true" world of ideals gives way to an "apparent" phenomenal world that is itself ultimately brought into question. This article shows how 20th-century legal thought, broadly construed, also moves away from "ideals" of law toward an understanding of law as observable social phenomena. It suggests that the move to the "apparent" world in legal thought raises questions similar to those raised by Nietzsche's work: Does sociological law point to a nihilistic destruction of the legal tradition or to a joyous possibility of overcoming that tradition?*

Marianne Constable is assistant professor in the Department of Rhetoric at the University of California at Berkeley. The author thanks Philippe Nonet for the seminar in which he first suggested how Nietzsche's history of metaphysics is a history of jurisprudence. She thanks Linda Helyar for graciously providing the (unpublished) field statement in jurisprudence discussing that history further. She also thanks Frederick Dolan, Jill Frank, Bonnie Honig, Elizabeth Mertz, and the reviewers of an earlier version for their comments.

How the 'Real World' at Last Became a Myth

HISTORY OF AN ERROR

1. The real world, attainable to the wise, the pious, the virtuous man—he dwells in it, *he is it*.

   (Oldest form of the idea, relatively sensible, simple, convincing. Transcription of the proposition 'I, Plato *am* the truth.')

2. The real world, unattainable for the moment, but promised to the wise, the pious, the virtuous man ('to the sinner who repents').

   (Progress of the idea: it grows more refined, more enticing, more incomprehensible—*it becomes a woman*, it becomes Christian . . .)

3. The real world, unattainable, undemonstrable, cannot be promised, but even when merely thought of a consolation, a duty, an imperative.

   (Fundamentally the same old sun, but shining through mist and scepticism; the idea grown sublime, pale, northerly, Konigsbergian.)

4. The real world—unattainable? Unattained, at any rate. And if unattained also *unknown*. Consequently also no consolation, no redemption, no duty: how could we have a duty towards something unknown?

   (The grey of dawn. First yawnings of reason. Cockcrow of positivism.)

5. The 'real world'—an idea no longer of any use, not even a duty any longer—an idea grown useless, superfluous, *consequently* a refuted idea: let us abolish it!

   (Broad daylight; breakfast; return of cheerfulness and *bon sens*; Plato blushes for shame; all free spirits run riot.)

6. We have abolished the real world: what world is left? the apparent world perhaps. . . . But no! *with the real world we have also abolished the apparent world!*

   (Mid-day; moment of the shortest shadow; end of the longest error; zenith of mankind; INCIPIT ZARATHUSTRA.)

—Friedrich Nietzsche[1]

1. Friedrich Nietzsche, *Twilight of the Idols* 40-41, trans. R. J. Hollingdale (London: Penguin, 1968), translator's footnotes omitted. Page citations to *Twilight* are given in parentheses in the text.

"When you get the dragon out of his cave on to the plain and in the daylight, you can count his teeth and claws, and see just what is his strength. But to get him out is only the first step. The next is either to kill him, or to tame him and make him a useful animal. For the rational study of law the black-letter man may be the man of the present, but the man of the future is the man of statistics and the master of economics,"[2] said Oliver Wendell Holmes, in an address dedicating the new hall of the Boston University School of Law in January 1897.

Those of us living in an environmentally conscious age without dragons may wonder why Holmes found it necessary to do *anything* about a dragon at all. Why not let hypothetical dragons lie? we ask. But passive acceptance of tradition—the tradition of law, if not the tradition of fairy tales—is precisely what Supreme Court Justice Holmes was not to allow. The dragon that is law, for Holmes, must be killed or made useful, and the man to do it is the social scientist.

A century after Holmes's address, the proclamation of the wedding—if not always considered a "love match"[3]—between law and social science prompts one to wonder what has become of the dragon of law? While Holmes railed against what he saw as the formalism of legal rules and the insularity of received law from actual practices, our contemporaries consider it clear that

> the courts have undergone a veritable revolution; they now make not only law but social policy, and there is hardly an area of the public bureaucracy that remains immune from what is in effect administrative supervision by the courts. This judicial activity is characteristically predicated on the basis of legislative or social facts. Accordingly, during the past twenty [now thirty-five] years the relationship between social science and law has become not only familiar but routinized.[4]

It appears that the dragon has been tamed and transformed into a spouse by the forces of social science.

2. Oliver Wendell Holmes, "The Path of the Law," 10 *Harv. L. Rev.* 457, 469 (1897). "'Black letter law'" refers "in a somewhat disparaging way" to legal doctrine. "The term is derived from the long abandoned practice of employing a gothic typeface for printing common law literature, so that a black letter lawyer was one learned in the legal tradition, and one major ingredient in law and legal reasoning is of course respect for tradition." A. W. B. Simpson, "Legal Reasoning Anatomized," 13 *Law & Soc. Inquiry* 639 (1988).

3. John M. Wisdom, "Some Remarks on the Role of Social Science in the Judicial Decision-making Process in School Desegregation Cases," 39 *Law & Contemp. Prob.* 142 (1975), cited in Michael J. Saks & Charles H. Baron, eds., *The Use/Nonuse/Misuse of Applied Social Research in the Courts* 12 (Cambridge, Mass.: Abt Books, 1980) ("Saks & Baron, *Use/Nonuse/Misuse*").

4. Paul L. Rosen, "History and State of the Art of Applied Social Research in the Courts," in Saks & Baron, *Use/Nonuse/Misuse* 11.

But let us look at the relation of law and social science more closely. From one angle, there certainly appears a cohabitation: legal opinions refer to social research; social scientists testify as expert witnesses in court; lawyers rely on social science consultants in jury selection; law students take courses in quantitative methods; law journals publish articles on econometrics in the courtroom; and social scientists and lawyers, deploring the misuse and abuse of social science research in the courtroom, explain how to improve legal use of social science.

From another angle, however, one may ask whether this domestic scene is as it appears. Articles in law and social science journals continue to note that judicial decision makers are singularly unaffected by social research.[5] Further, the distinction between *is* and *ought* adopted by many social researchers and legal historians, as well as by some lawyers and philosophers of law, seems to separate scientific or theoretical concern with identifying and describing facts and values, from legal and practical concern with what ought to be done. That is, the set of "*is* questions"—"What is law?" and "Why do individuals and groups obey the law?"—with which theorists and researchers since Montesquieu have been engaged differ from "What should the law be?" and "Why should one obey the law?"—"*ought* questions" with which some legal practitioners and philosophers remain concerned.

Moreover, recent challenges to the is/ought distinction—a distinction thought by some to parallel the separation between social science and law—add to the sense that neither routine cohabitation nor strict separation adequately captures the complicated character of current relations between law and social science. Turning to the work of Friedrich Nietzsche enables one to begin to grasp those complications and to consider some of the difficulties inhering in relations between law and social science in 20th-century American legal thought. "American legal thought" is here broadly construed to include legal theory and philosophy, legal doctrine, and social theory and research about law that takes place under the auspices of sociology, social psychology, political science, economics, history, and anthropology. The argument presented is that in all of these, admittedly in some sense disparate, areas, there nevertheless emerges a peculiarly modern understanding of law, which understanding will be termed "sociological" and which understanding will be shown to correspond to the "positive law" of an age into which Nietzsche's work provides insight.

The thrust of this essay is not itself sociological. Rather, it considers the question of law in the modern age as a question of the historical possibilities out of which modern understandings of law emerge. Yet neither is the essay intellectual history, not simply because it does not seek to review

5. See, e.g., J. Alexander Tanford, "Law Reform by Courts, Legislatures, and Commissions Following Empirical Research on Jury Instructions," 25 *Law & Soc'y Rev.* 155 (1991).

all that has been said or may be said of the variety of views about law held in law and in scholarship about law, but also because the structure of "stages" it imposes on 20th-century legal thought is not to be understood as a strict claim about chronology but rather as an aid for focusing philosophically on the possibilities of the present.

The most familiar way for jurists and jurisprudes to address the question of law "philosophically" today is to distinguish between positive law as "the law that is, in contrast to the law that ought to be," as Peter Berkowitz puts it. "This simple, preliminary formulation," he continues, "leaves open the question of the consequence of a conflict between the positive law that is and the law that ought to be, between the law of the city and the divine law, between human justice and what is right by nature or dictated by reason." The matter thus devolves into an argument between positivists and natural lawyers: "the distinction between the law that is or prevails and the law that ought to be or govern underlies a vast and fascinating array of opinions about the origins or foundations of justice, goodness, and wisdom," Berkowitz writes.[6] Because the concern of this essay is not, as such, to found or ground law or justice, but rather to understand law in the modern age and consider some of its implications, it does not engage in this familiar natural law/positive law argument. Instead it shows how the ostensible variety of modern "opinions" about law today all take the essence of law to be, in one sense or another, social construction—the creation of man in society, the product of will.

Drawing on Nietzsche's brief and famous six-stage history of metaphysics, literally "How the 'True World' Finally Became a Fable" ("Wie die 'wahre Welt' endlich zur Fabel wurde") or "The History of an Error," in *Twilight of the Idols*, the essay aims both to reveal aspects of the relation between law and social science that may be unfamiliar to those in these fields and to contribute to an understanding of the relevance of Nietzsche's thought to law. More specifically, the essay shows how 20th-century legal thought—a legal thought that, fragmented though it may be, often traces its impetus, if not its origins, to the insights of Oliver Wendell Holmes—corresponds to the final stages of Nietzsche's history of metaphysics. The first five stages of Nietzsche's history can be taken to sketch the way in which jurisprudence, like metaphysics, has, through reason, long sought its foundations in the truths residing in a "real world" (*wahre Welt*) outside of, beyond (*meta*), and even in opposition to, "life" in *this* world. Justice lies, respectively, in the virtue of the wise citizen of the *polis*, in the natural law of the divinity of the unattainable world beyond, in the moral law of Kant's categorical imperative, in the positive law of the empiricists and utilitarians, and in the social policy and distributive justice of economists and philosophers.

6. Peter Berkowitz, "On the Laws Governing Free Spirits and Philosophers of the Future: A Response to Nonet's 'What Is Positive Law?'" 100 *Yale L.J.* 701, 703, 704 (1990).

Striving for such justice signifies to Nietzsche a need and desire to escape one's condition, as one turns to an illusory better world that is believed to be "real." But the attempt of reason in its "will to truth" to destroy the nihilistic life-denying illusions at each stage of metaphysics only leads erroneously, for Nietzsche, to the unfolding of a further stage of illusions.

The end of the history of the error of reason, that is, the end of the history of metaphysics, lies, for Nietzsche, in nihilism—in the complete abolition not only of the "real" worlds erroneously constructed through reason but also of their complementary "apparent" world. Such nihilism, for Nietzsche, brings with it the joyful possibility of overcoming nihilism. It resembles both the transformative visions of critical legal studies and the denial, by pragmatic and interpretive legal thought, of the distinctions between is and ought, between the theoretical and the practical, between the observed or apparent and the "true" or the "real."[7] But the question remains whether the joyous possibility of overcoming nihilism is to be found in current legal thought as, in Nietzsche's words, it abolishes the "true" or the "real world" in the very name of truth and reality.[8]

For, as shall be seen, sociology of law in the fourth and fifth stages takes up the task of grasping the so-called reality of phenomena or appearances. As it does so, its knowledge comes to constitute the "truth" about perceptions and beliefs. And as sociology looks to appearances, justice disappears. Whether positing foundations or declaring the impossibility of doing so, sociology provides access to a law disengaged from justice and attached to "social realities," which law sociology simultaneously renders problematic. Note that for Nietzsche, the "real" corresponds to what one might commonly call the "ideal"; the "apparent" corresponds to the "phenomenal" world of what many now call "reality." Modern thought about law thus finds itself confronting the difficulties of the final stage of Nietzsche's history of metaphysics: "But no! *with the real world we have also abolished the apparent world.*"

In what follows, Part I provides, through close reading of the beginning of *Twilight of the Idols*, a very preliminary introduction to Nietzsche's history

7. Hollingdale notes the connection in German of "wahre Welt" (in quotations in the title) translated as "real world" and "Wahrheit," translated as "truth." Nietzsche, *Twilight* 40, translator's first footnote.

8. Joseph William Singer writes: "Recently, there has been a lot of talk among legal scholars about nihilism. This has been more evident in conversations among law professors than in the scholarly literature. When references to nihilism do appear in the law journals, they are vague and generally made only in passing." He notes: "I am not trying to use the word nihilism in the way philosophers have used it. Those philosophical discussions are irrelevant to the current debates among legal theorists about 'nihilism' . . . none of those theorists (myself included) has paid much attention to that literature, at least not in print." Singer, "The Player and the Cards: Nihilism and Legal Theory," 94 *Yale L.J.* 1, 4 text at n.7 (1984). This article, by contrast, uses "nihilism" in the way that philosophical discussion about Nietzsche uses it, showing the relevance of debates about nihilism to modern law and sociological study of law.

of metaphysics as a history of jurisprudence. Part II illustrates the unfolding of the fourth and fifth stages of that history through references that link the concerns of early 20th-century legal theory to Nietzsche's understanding of the "real" (suprasensible and now considered ideal) world beyond and the apparent (now often considered "real") phenomenal world. Part III turns to several modern examples to depict current relations between law and social science, *ought* and *is*, the real and the apparent worlds. These examples reveal aspects of sociological law and legal thought which, like the metaphysics of the fifth and sixth stages of Nietzsche's history, suggest a particular sort of nihilism. Part IV rests with the question of the possibilities of modern law.

I. THE PROBLEM OF NIETZSCHE

Nietzsche's "History of an Error" appears in *Twilight of the Idols* preceded by "The Problem of Socrates" and "Reason in Philosophy." The first four stages of this history correspond to Nietzsche's understanding of Platonism, Christendom, Kantianism, and positivism or empiricism. To each of these dogmas or "isms," there belongs a particular truth, justice, and reality, which serve as the grounds on which "*this*" world, the world of "life" and of the senses, of becoming, of death, change, age, procreation and growth, has been designated as worthless, secondary, *mere* appearance. According to Nietzsche, the "real worlds" on the basis of which philosophers and priests adhering to their dogmas judge *this* world are "*moral-optical* illusion[s]," constructed out of contradiction to the apparent or actual world, even as they provide the ostensible standards by which to guide this life. Appealing to these truths or real worlds, according to Nietzsche, allows us to "*revenge* ourselves on life by means of the phantasmagoria of 'another,' a 'better' life" (at 39). The division between a real and an apparent world itself is, for Nietzsche, a "symptom of *declining* life," of a life that is no longer capable of flourishing on its own and in which happiness and instinct are no longer one (at 39, 34).

Socrates, according to Nietzsche, was the first to diagnose this condition, to divine what "had begun to be the universal exigency: that no one was any longer master of himself, that the instincts were becoming mutually *antagonistic*." The ostensible cure Socrates devised for the tyranny of instincts gone awry, the countertyranny of reason, that is, was the last expedient for the Greeks, Nietzsche claims, who at the time "had only *one* choice: to perish or—be *absurdly rational*" (at 33).

Plato's formulaic imitation of Socrates—"Reason = virtue = happiness"—thus points to a pathologically conditioned moralism, according to Nietzsche, a moralism both made and believed necessary by the decadence in which Plato too found himself. Plato and the other philosophers and moralists coming after Socrates "imagine that by making war on *decadence* they therewith elude *decadence* themselves." But, Nietzsche continues, "this is beyond their powers: what they select as an expedient, as a deliverance is itself only another expression of *decadence*—they *alter* its expression, they do not abolish the thing itself" (at 33–34). Socrates—understood as the teaching of the saving power of reason—is thus, for Nietzsche, "a misunderstanding." Indeed,

> *the entire morality of improvement, the Christian included, has been a misunderstanding*. . . . The harshest daylight, rationality at any cost, life bright, cold, circumspect, conscious, without instinct, in opposition to the instincts, has itself been no more than a form of sickness, another form of sickness—and by no means a way back to 'virtue,' to 'health,' to happiness. . . . To *have* to combat one's instincts—that is the formula for *decadence*: as long as life is *ascending*, happiness and instinct are one. (At 34)

"The problem of Socrates" then, for Nietzsche, corresponds not only to Socrates *as* problem but also to both the problem *introduced* by Socrates, who accompanied the emergence of the possibility of misunderstanding reason as savior,[9] and to the problem *diagnosed* by Socrates, the weakness and degeneration characterizing the end of the older noble Athens in which authority had been "part of accepted usage" and one did not give reasons but commanded. "Wherever authority is still part of accepted usage and one does not 'give reasons' but commands," Nietzsche writes, "the dialectician is a kind of buffoon: he is laughed at, he is not taken seriously. Socrates was the buffoon who *got himself taken seriously:* what was really happening when that happened?" (At 31.)

Contrast the homage now paid to Socrates to the treatment received by Thersites, the "scurrilous babbler" depicted in Book II of the *Iliad.* Like Socrates, Thersites is impudent and malformed. At a moment in the war against the Trojans when the Aegean heroes, Agamemnon and Achilles, are fighting amongst themselves, Thersites, who in the past has criticized both Odysseus and Achilles, jeers at Agamemnon for his greed in women and gold and calls on the Aegean troops to abandon the war and return home. Odysseus tells Thersites off, threatening him and striking him—and the soldiers laugh.[10] The seriousness with which modern Thersiteses get taken

9. Socrates himself may well have *understood* that reason was no savior, according to Nietzsche, who writes of the "*wisdom*" of the "courage for death" of "this shrewdest of all self-deceivers": "Socrates *wanted* to die—it was not Athens, it was *he* who handed himself the poison cup. . . .'Socrates is no physician,' he said softly to himself: 'death alone is a physician here. . . . Socrates himself has only been a long time sick . . .'" Nietzsche, *Twilight* 34, ellipses in original). See also Plato's *Crito* and *Phaedo.*

10. Homer, *The Iliad,* Loeb ed., Book II, lines 211–277.

today—an age some characterize precisely by its so-called crisis of authority—on the other hand, is indicated by Kenneth Burke:

> And what of Thersites,
> Despised of all his tribe
> (Whipped by power, wisdom, and heroic love, all three:
> By Agamemnon, Ulysses, and Achilles),
>
> Loathed by the bard that made him,
> Ultimate filth, speaking against epic war?
> What of Thersites?
>
> Salute—
> To Saint Thersites.[11]

Already Plato's *Euthyphro*—without doubt more familiar to the 19th-century Nietzsche than the works of the 20th-century Burke!—manifests the disintegration of Greek nobility as Nietzsche understands it and the conditions that make Socrates "necessary." In this early dialogue, Socrates and Euthyphro encounter one another on the steps of the courthouse. Socrates has been accused of impiety—of corrupting the youth of Athens and of inventing new gods. Euthyphro is bringing suit against his own father for having allowed a slave who killed another slave to die while awaiting his punishment. Euthyphro claims to be doing the pious thing, so Socrates asks Euthyphro to instruct him as to piety that he may be able to defend himself against his accusers. Socrates' questioning clearly reveals that Euthyphro is unable to present a logically defensible definition of piety. While some latter-day scholars point here to the ultimate absence of a satisfactory definition of piety on Socrates' own part and to Socrates' manner of questioning to claim that the Socratic dialogue *produces* skepticism on the part of the listener/reader—if not of Euthyphro, who indeed comes across as a bit dense—Nietzsche's text would suggest that Socrates enters the scene once the deterioration of the values of the old Athens and the skepticism that accompanies it have *already* begun. That is, for Nietzsche, the very situation of a suit by the "aristocratic" Euthyphro against his own father signifies the prior breakdown of an older authority and tradition that Nietzsche associates with the ancient Hellenes.

Nietzsche does admit that, as dialectician, Socrates indeed possesses "a pitiless instrument," one with which "one can play the tyrant" and leave it to one's opponent "to demonstrate he is not an idiot: [the dialectician] enrages, he at the same time makes helpless. The dialectician *devitalizes* his opponent's intellect" (at 32). But for Nietzsche, the choice of such a

11. Kenneth Burke, *Language as Symbolic Action* 110–11 (Berkeley: University of California Press, 1966), citing his own *Book of Moments* 25. I am grateful to Fred Antczak for bringing this passage to my attention in another context.

weapon as dialectic and the compulsion to give reasons occurs only when one has "no other weapon left: one must have to *enforce* one's rights: otherwise one makes no use of it" (at 32). For the Greeks to embrace the apparent Socratic "cure" and to seek to master the instincts by reason means, for Nietzsche, that Greek "instincts" were already in such disarray that "no one was any longer master of himself" (at 33), that command and obedience were no longer one. The separation of command from obedience coincides with the disharmony and degeneration of the instincts that makes reason necessary, for without reason, the antagonistic instincts will destroy themselves. Reason thus accompanies the emergence of the problem of will as commander and introduces the divisions between is and ought, between the apparent and the real worlds, between positive law and higher law.

Following "The Problem of Socrates" then, come the distinctions—among them those between the apparent and the real worlds, sensation and concept, becoming and being—of "'Reason' in Philosophy." In each of these pairs, Nietzsche claims, reason privileges the latter half in two senses: as causally prior and as good, hence "moral." "Our prejudice in favour of reason compels us to posit unity, identity, duration, substance, cause, materiality," he writes. This "error" is advocated by *logos*, by the language of "deed and doer" or the grammar of subject and predicate which everywhere sees the separation of command and obedience in its understanding of "will as cause in general" and which projects its belief in will onto all things. That is, foisting a belief in will onto the world, the metaphysics of language or of reason posits "ego-substance" and creates the concept "being," to both of which, like will, it attributes causal power and worth. It likewise creates what for Nietzsche is the most stupendous concept, "God," who as Supreme Willing Being is both *causa sui* (its own cause) and *ens realissimum* (the most real being). "At the beginning," claims Nietzsche, "stands the great fateful error that the will is something which *produces an effect*" (at 37–38).

Nietzsche discusses the error of taking will as cause—broken down further into "four great errors"—in a later section of *Twilight*, which need not be taken up here. One notes only that Nietzsche, pointing to the beginning of this error, presents Socrates and his thought together not as cause but as "symptom" of decadence. (Thus is introduced the so-called historical method of "genealogy" adopted by such later writers as Michel Foucault.) The "first" stage of "How the 'Real World' at Last Became a Myth" seems to follow, but is not caused by, the error "at the beginning" in which will is taken to produce effects.[12] (Even the language of "following" is problematic, for any given stage in Nietzsche's history, as shall be seen especially in part III, always already collapses into the next stage or the last one.)

12. Uncited quotations that follow are from the Nietzsche excerpt quoted at the beginning of this essay.

In the first stage, writes Nietzsche, reason provides access to a "relatively sensible" reality or truth, one in which the Platonic "idea" (*eidos*, often translated as "form") while an intelligible object of knowledge, does not yet take propositional form. Truth and justice lie within reach of the wise and virtuous man living in the *polis*. But already for Plato, virtue is necessarily accompanied by a particular kind of knowledge or reason and consists in more than simple right action. Plato "already has the concept 'good' as the supreme concept," writes Nietzsche; he is "a coward in the face of reality—consequently, he flees into the ideal." In doing so, Plato is "antecedent Christian," writes Nietzsche, and "in the great fatality of Christianity, Plato is that ambiguity and fascination called the 'ideal' which made it possible for the nobler natures of antiquity to misunderstand themselves and to step on to the *bridge* which led to the 'Cross.' . . . And how much there still is of Plato in the concept 'Church,' in the structure, system, practice of the Church" (at 106–7).

The justice sought by the Christian Church, Nietzsche continues, is not attainable in this world; the Christian promise of redemption in the second stage relegates justice and right to the world beyond. Justice no longer lies in the virtue of the citizen but in a divine or natural law. Yet as Kant, in the third stage of Nietzsche's history, points out, the divine and the world beyond can neither be proven nor promised. In thinking through the conditions of the possibility of morality, Kant nevertheless posits moral law. He understands morality as duty or obligation, as the categorical imperative of persons who, partaking in the admittedly unknowable noumenal world of things-in-themselves, are subjects who will, worthy of respect as "ends-in-themselves," and not simply empirical beings governed by the causal laws of the phenomenal world of appearance. Like the God-given freedom of will that underlies the possibility of any judgment as to the guilt of the Christian sinner, an "intelligible freedom" underlies the Kantian "good" will. (In Kant's "divine will," on the other hand, one finds a unity of command and obedience that renders both moral freedom and necessity or obligation irrelevant and that resembles Nietzsche's characterization of the authority of the old Athenians.[13]) The goodness of human will for Kant shines palely "through mist and scepticism," Nietzsche writes, for no God any longer

13. Imperatives, for Kant, are "formulae for expressing the relation of objective laws of willing to the subjective imperfection of the will of this or that rational being—for example, of the human will" (at 81). In man, "reason solely by itself is not sufficient to determine the will" as "the will is exposed also to subjective conditions (certain impulsions) which do not always harmonize with the objective ones." Hence in man, actions "recognized to be objectively necessary are subjectively contingent, and the determining of such a will in accordance with objective laws is *necessitation*" (at 80). In a being such as God, on the other hand, reason "infallibly determines the will," and actions "recognized to be objectively necessary are also subjectively necessary—that is to say, the will is then a power to choose *only that* which reason independently of inclination recognizes to be practically necessary, that is, to be good" (at 80). For "the *divine* will, and in general for a *holy* will, there are no imperatives: 'I *ought*' is here out of place, because 'I *will*' is already of itself necessarily in harmony with the law" (at

"gives a human being his qualities"; instead "*he himself*" does (at 54). That is, in Nietzsche's reading of Kant, man wills the "good" freely himself or, in Kant's words, the reasoning will gives itself its own law.

It remains for the "positivists" of Nietzsche's fourth stage to point out that Kant's moral law—like divine law, which Kant himself acknowledged was unattainable to human reason—cannot serve as a guiding principle for individuals in this material world; Kantian duty remains empirically unknown.[14] Utilitarianism, by contrast, offers an approach to law ostensibly grounded in experience. Reality comes down to earth, so to speak, and the senses rise in estimation, as utilitarianism, like scientific knowledge that accepts "the evidence of the senses" (at 36), appeals to the desirability of sensations of pleasure and the undesirability of sensations of pain to determine the means to earthly happiness. The consequences of deploying this "science" whose principle is that of utility or of the maximization of happiness so defined will be felt not in the world beyond but in the future of *this* phenomenal world.

Insofar as utilitarians seek a better future world and attempt the rational calculation of pleasures and pains to determine (that is, both to ground and to judge) policies by which to govern, utilitarianism continues the tradition of the metaphysics of will that Nietzsche describes. Utility in this fourth stage serves as the standard of judgment by which to bring about utilitarian and positivist visions for the reform of the positive laws of this world.

While utilitarians, such as John Stuart Mill, still allow invokation of the language of morality or "virtue" or of what *ought* to be when it serves their purpose,[15] the free spirits of Nietzsche's fifth stage and those whom Nietzsche elsewhere calls "free thinkers" recognize the uselessness of such ideals and move to abolish references to them. The "real world" of the earlier stages appears in quotation marks in the fifth stage in Nietzsche's text, as *mere* idea, a turn of phrase whose effectiveness or value in *this* world is nil. Here, for Nietzsche, is the broad daylight of ultimate Socratic rationality; here, the return to "good" or "common" "sense" ("*bon sens*") in which Plato "blushes for shame" that, in coming down to earth, his "good" "idea" has come so far and become so exposed.

81). Immanuel Kant, *Groundwork of the Metaphysic of Morals* 80-81, trans. H. J. Paton (New York: Harper & Row, 1964).

14. See John Stuart Mill, "General Remarks," *in Utilitarianism* ch. 1 (orig. pub. 1863) (New York: William Collins Sons & Co., 1962) ("Mill, *Utilitarianism*").

15. Indeed, Mill tolerates a number of acquired desires, among them virtue, claiming that "the utilitarian standard, while it tolerates and approves those other acquired desires, up to the point beyond which they would be more injurious to the general happiness than promotive of it, enjoins and requires the cultivation of the love of virtue up to the greatest strength possible, as being above all things important to the general happiness." Mill, *Utilitarianism* 291–92.

Nietzsche's own free spirits now "run riot" at the inversion of Platonism. They hail the nihilism to come for what they anticipate as the overcoming of the nihilism of the previous stages. In this overcoming of nihilism—both nihilism's overcoming and an overcoming that is itself nihilistic—they foresee the affirmation and enhancement of a flourishing healthy life that need not appeal to the standard of an illusory "other" world simply to maintain itself. The sickness and decadence that, from Socrates on, has been symptomatic of a "declining, debilitated, weary, condemned life," which has devalued itself by its continual appeals to a truer "real" world and to a morality that seeks to "'improve' men," is about to end.

This moment of the overcoming of metaphysics is the "end of the longest error" and the "zenith of mankind," for Nietzsche. Its time is "now," a moment that, in Zarathustra's teaching of the eternal return of the same, is no longer the eternal "too late" of philosophers who are ruled by the static categories of reason. Instead comes a time in which the will to life again affirms the joy of becoming, creation, and change; in which command and obedience once more are one; in which will to power triumphs—and in which will is no longer "something which *produces an effect*" on the basis of which human beings can be held accountable, but instead and again becomes the powerful "rush" of "sublimating" energy that belongs to an intoxicated, pulsing life.

The triumph of will to power comes with the demise of the distinctions between the real and the apparent worlds and of the other distinctions made *necessary* by the conditions in which reason was called on as a means of strengthening weak and declining life and as an instrument of command over clashing instincts.[16] With the end of the error, reason and instinct *together* will be one with happiness, for Nietzsche; no means or instruments will be required to produce happiness and—in an inversion of morality which proclaims that if you do this, then you will be happy—virtue will be the "consequence" of happiness (at 48).

Martin Heidegger, writing on Nietzsche, emphasizes another aspect of the changing of the essence of truth in the modern or final stages of Nietzsche's history, however. Nietzsche's inversion of Platonism for Heidegger, although not gloomy, is not joyful.[17] With its rejection of virtue, natural law, and moral law as unattainable, unknowable, and ultimately useless,

16. As Heidegger puts it, Nietzsche's wording sometimes does "revert to the most ordinary of opinions, to wit, that something is true because and to the extent that it is useful to that much-touted thing called 'life.' Yet Nietzsche's wording means something altogether different. The securing of permanence is necessary, but not because it yields an advantage; knowledge is necessary for life because it enables a necessity to arise in and from itself, and carries out that necessity, inasmuch as knowledge is itself *commanding*. And it is commanding because it stems from a command." Martin Heidegger, *Nietzsche*, vol. 3: *The Will to Power as Knowledge and as Metaphysics* 118, trans. Joan Stambaugh *et al.* (New York: Harper & Row, 1987) ("Heidegger, *Nietzsche*").

17. *Id.* at 157.

such inversion indeed manifests itself, as Nietzsche suggests, in modernity's embrace of a world that is attainable, knowable, useful. This "social" world, as Foucault points out, presents itself in terms of the regularities or laws that comprise the domain of knowledge of the social sciences, which knowledge in turn informs the social policies of government.[18] But rather than portending the simultaneous destruction and completion of nihilism that Nietzsche associates with the joyous overcoming of metaphysics, this new world, Heidegger warns, is a "fulfillment" of nihilism in which all-consuming "will to power," obscuring and forgetting its own nihilism, completes metaphysics. Roughly speaking, for Heidegger, Nietzsche's will to power loses sight of the being of the world as, in its permanent transfiguring of all into becoming, commanding itself becomes absolute.

[Heidegger's claim is more complicated than it at first may seem. The simple version—that because Nietzsche associates the other or real (suprasensible) world with being and *this* apparent world with becoming, then what remains after the abolition of the real and the apparent worlds is still *this* world of becoming and hence not being—will not do. It will not do because becoming cannot be identified with any previous world, because these have been abolished. What remains after the abolition of the real and the apparent worlds is becoming and not world of any sort or, rather, what remains is only world insofar as it is already becoming. That is, becoming—or will to power or what Nietzsche sometimes calls "life"—has total (non-causal ontologically prior) control, if one will allow the phrase. To ask "Control over what?" makes no sense, however, for this takes the "what" as some thing independent of becoming or will to power. A thing cannot be independent this way since the being of any thing depends on becoming. But when becoming becomes the whole of being this way, being is not distinguished from beings/things that are—and here lies what Heidegger calls metaphysics, the forgetting of the ontological difference between being and beings. Note that this difference is not the same as the difference between the real and the apparent in Nietzsche's history of metaphysics; the "real" from Plato on, both Heidegger and Nietzsche recognize, predominantly has been thought precisely as *a* being, if not "*the* most real being." Western philosophy since Plato then, Heidegger claims, has been metaphysical and "in the thought of the will to power, Nietzsche anticipates the metaphysical ground of the consummation of the modern age. In the thought of the will to power, metaphysical thinking itself completes itself in advance. Nietzsche, the thinker of the thought of will to power[,] is the *last metaphysician* of the West."[19]]

18. See Michel Foucault, "Governmentality," 6 *Ideology and Consciousness* 5–21 (1979); and Michel Foucault, "Politics and Reason," *in* Lawrence D. Kritzman, ed., *Politics, Philosophy, Culture: Interviews and Other Writings, 1977-1984*, at 57–85 (New York: Routledge, 1988).

19. Heidegger, 3 *Nietzsche* 8.

This is not the place to consider Heidegger's reading of Nietzsche as such. The stage has been set for two issues. The first concerns the relevance of Nietzsche's thought to modern law. One can understand this issue philosophically, without requiring strict chronological correlation of particular works with Nietzsche's stages. One can inquire, for instance, into the extent to which thought about law in the modern age is heir to what Nietzsche characterizes as the Socratic belief in "rationality at any cost" as cure to decadence and into the way that this belief reveals aspects of a Western "morality of improvement." To what extent is modern law heir to what Nietzsche calls the "sickness" that accompanies degeneration of will or of the instinct to command and to obey—of the instinct to know law? To what extent is it symptomatic of a nihilistic "misunderstanding" and "error" that culminates in the abolition of both the true and the apparent worlds? And second, to the extent that law and social science, taken together, indeed epitomizes the final stages of Nietzsche's history of metaphysics, one can ask whether law and social science points to the possibility of a Nietzschean overcoming of nihilism—or whether it points to what Heidegger describes as the fulfillment of nihilism, a completion of metaphysics that remains blind to its own essential character as metaphysical? Addressing the first issue in parts II and III enables more careful elucidation of the second in part IV.

II. 20TH-CENTURY LEGAL THEORY

Historians of American legal theory have characterized the first third of the 20th century as involving a shift from "legal formalism" and "mechanical jurisprudence" to "sociological jurisprudence" and "legal realism."[20] Arguing against what they considered to be sterile adherence to immutable, universal principles and to a deductive logic unresponsive to social needs, early 20th-century writers and judges called for what Roscoe Pound, later dean of Harvard Law School, called "the adjustment of [legal] principles and doctrines to the human conditions they are to govern rather than to assumed first principles."[21]

In 1908, Pound hailed Oliver Wendell Holmes's dissent in the 1905 case of *Lochner v. New York* as "'the best exposition of . . . sociological

20. See Edward A. Purcell, Jr., *The Crisis of Democracy* chs. 5 ("The Rise of Legal Realism") & 9 ("Crisis in Jurisprudence") (Lexington: University of Kentucky Press, 1973) ("Purcell, *Crisis of Democracy*"); John Henry Schlegel, "American Legal Realism and Empirical Social Science: From the Yale Experience," 28 *Buffalo L. Rev.* 459 (1979); G. Edward White, "From Sociological Jurisprudence to Realism: Jurisprudence and Social Change in Early Twentieth-Century America," 58 *Va. L. Rev.* 999 (1972).

21. Roscoe Pound, "Liberty of Contract," 18 *Yale L.J.* 454, 464 (1909), cited in White, 58 *Va. L. Rev.* at 1004.

jurisprudence' extant in America."[22] In *Lochner*, the majority had invalidated a state law regulating bakers' hours, on the grounds of "liberty of contract."[23] Holmes, in his dissent, maintained that "a Constitution is not intended to embody a particular economic theory, whether of paternalism and the organic relation of the citizen to the state or of *laissez faire*." He argued that at issue was "the right of a majority to embody their opinions in law," and he suggested that the Court's reliance on "general propositions" to decide "concrete cases" served to disable rational legislation that represented "the natural outcome of a dominant opinion."[24]

As Thomas Grey points out, a variety of views about Holmes exists. Holmes has been read admiringly as the critic of Langdellian legal formalism, perceived more ambivalently as a Social Darwinist, and criticized as an amoral positivist. While some recognize him as a complex legal thinker, others suggest that behind Holmes as stylist of "eclectic aphorism" lies "a muddle of mutually inconsistent ideas." Grey himself argues for the usefulness of understanding Holmes as a legal pragmatist, in part, he acknowledges, "in furtherance of a neo-pragmatist approach to legal theory."[25] For the purpose of this essay, it is less important to understand the biographical "truth" about the man Holmes than to grasp the extent to which those who have come after him have taken themselves to be following him. For our purpose, Holmes, in some ways like the misunderstanding that is Socrates in Nietzsche's *Twilight*, may well be a "misunderstanding" of his own thought, but in this essay, Holmes is what his work has been taken to be. In this context, that Holmes is perhaps most often invoked as the author of "a few memorable anti-formalistic jurisprudential slogans"[26] is itself telling.

Both sociological jurisprudence and legal realism took up Holmes' challenge to the "judicial tendency to announce general social propositions as truths and to reason downward from them in the decision of specific cases."[27] Those in these movements drew on and made famous such Holmesian wisdom as "The life of the law has not been logic: it has been experience."[28] For Holmes, the "experience" that is to animate law in the future is to be sought in knowledge of the actual world. Distinguishing between a tradition of "dead law" and science, Holmes articulates faith in a law that will look to science that can then become tradition:

> The law, so far as it depends on learning, is indeed, as it has been called, the government of the living by the dead. To a very considera-

22. *Id.*
23. Lochner v. New York, 198 U.S. 45 (1905).
24. *Id.*
25. Thomas C. Grey, "Holmes and Legal Pragmatism," 41 *Stan. L. Rev.* 787, 787 (1989).
26. *Id.*
27. White, 58 *Va. L. Rev.* at 1003.
28. Oliver W. Holmes, *The Common Law* 1, ed. Mark DeWolfe Howe (Boston: Little, Brown & Co., 1963).

> ble extent no doubt it is inevitable that the living should be so governed. The past gives us our vocabulary and fixes the limits of our imagination; we cannot get away from it. There is, too, a peculiar logical pleasure in making manifest the continuity between what we are doing and what has been done before. But the present has a right to govern itself so far as it can; and it ought always to be remembered that historic continuity with the past is not a duty, it is only a necessity. I hope that the time is coming when this thought will bear fruit. An ideal system of law should draw its postulates and its legislative justification from science. As it is now, we rely upon tradition, or vague sentiment, or the fact that we never thought of any other way of doing things, as our only warrant for rules which we enforce with as much confidence as if they embodied revealed wisdom.[29]

The Holmesian claim that continuity with the past is "only a necessity and not a duty" is, as Grey argues, "to repeat that law is always situated" and to indicate that "continuity with the past is no categorical imperative—law is a functional instrument meant to meet present and future human needs."[30] Law will ideally "draw its postulates and its legislative justification from science," declares Holmes (above), compatible with his efforts on the bench to make legal doctrine, concerning contracts for instance, more "objective.[31]

For followers of Holmes, it seemed clear that the experience that was to inform law would have to be sought in the knowable world, in a knowledge that, for many, social science would provide. Pointing to the distinction between "so called legal justice" and "social justice," Pound declared that "the time is now ripe for a new tendency, . . . which I have ventured heretofore to style the sociological tendency" in the teaching and expounding of law. "The modern teacher of law," Pound claimed, "should be a student of sociology, economics, and politics as well. He should know not only what the courts decide and the principles by which they decide, but quite as much the circumstances and conditions, social and economic, to which these principles are to be applied; he should know the state of popular thought and feeling which makes the environment in which the principles must operate in practice."[32] Like the positivists in Nietzsche's history of metaphysics, who asked of Kant's "real world—unattainable?" sociological jurisprudence asked of the abstract legal principles conceived of by Holmes's predecessors "unattainable?" and answered, again in Nietzsche's words, "Unattained, at any rate. And if unattained also *unknown*. Consequently

29. Oliver W. Holmes, "Learning and Science," Speech 1895, in *Collected Legal Papers* 138-39 (New York: Harcourt, Brace & Co., 1920) ("Holmes, *Collected Papers*").

30. Grey, 41 *Stan. L. Rev.* at 807.

31. Morton Horwitz, *The Transformation of American Law 1870-1960* (New York: Oxford University Press, 1992) ("Horwitz, *Transformation*").

32. Roscoe Pound, "The Need of a Sociological Jurisprudence," 19 *Green Bag* 607, at 614, 609, 611–12 (1907).

also no consolation, no redemption, no duty: how could we have a duty towards something unknown?" Rejecting the principles and deductive logic of legal formalism or "slot-machine justice" then, while retaining like early positivists a commitment to the reform of positive law, sociological jurisprudence sought to shift analysis from doctrine to the social effects of law.

The legal realists of the 1920s and 1930s took up the stance of sociological jurisprudence, only more so. The variety of views held by legal realists as well as the history of their "movement" makes it almost *de rigeur* today to begin discussion about legal realism with a caveat as to the difficulty of defining it. The multiplicity of ways in which the realists are now appropriated also renders clear definition problematic. Karl N. Llewellyn, among the most effective in disseminating a meaning for the term "legal realism," traced the roots of legal realism in part back to what he saw as Pound's unfulfilled calls for sociological jurisprudence. He insisted in 1931 in response to Pound's critique of legal realism, that legal realism was not a "school" nor likely to be, although he acknowledged a "movement" afoot in thought and work about law. Identifying nine common points of departure among the realists, he claimed five were peculiar to the movement: the "*temporary* divorce of Is and Ought for purposes of study"; the "distrust"—although not necessarily "negation in any given instance"—of traditional rules; the grouping of cases and legal situations into narrower categories than in the past; "an insistence on evaluation of any part of law in terms of its effects, and an insistence on the worthwhileness of trying to find these effects"; and, finally, an "insistence on *sustained and programmatic attack* on problems of law along any of these lines."[33]

Historian Morton Horwitz, for one, argues that historians have relied too heavily on Llewellyn's admittedly limited survey and statement concerning realism. Llewellyn, claims Horwitz, was in no position in 1931 to present what would become the touchstone for all future discussion as to the meaning and significance of legal realism. The result of looking to Llewellyn in this way has been, Horwitz claims, in part to draw too sharp a line between sociological jurisprudence and legal realism. "[B]oth intellectual movements," he writes, "should be understood as subcategories of pre- and post-World War I Progressive legal thought, and Legal Realism needs to be seen primarily as a continuation of the reformist attack on orthodox legal thought."[34] Although what Pound perceived as the realists' extreme rejection of the practical impact of legal rules lost them his support,[35] and although realism shifted focus from court-centered reform to statutory and administrative change, especially after the New Deal, Horwitz claims that

33. Karl N. Llewellyn, "Some Realism about Realism: Responding to Dean Pound," 44 *Harv. L. Rev.* 1222, 1233–34, 1226–28 (1931).

34. Horwitz, *Transformation* 170–72.

35. See Roscoe Pound, "The Call for a Realist Jurisprudence," 44 *Harv. L. Rev.* 697 (1931).

realism essentially continued the Progressive attack on classical legal thought that characterized sociological jurisprudence.[36]

That said, Horwitz identifies a "skepticism about reason and morality" as the "most significant difference" between legal realism and "its pre-war reformist predecessors[:] . . . The Realist generation . . . had lost much of the pre-war faith in reason, both as a reliable source of moral understanding and as a powerful internal guide to law," he writes.[37] Despite their skepticism as to completely objective and moral knowledge though, many realists nevertheless looked to the social sciences, especially economics, statistics, and psychology, to explain and predict the behavior of law and legal process. Like Holmes, for whom the man of the future was the man of statistics and master of economics, and like Pound,[38] Llewellyn suggested that economic theory offered "amazing light" in discovering how much law does or can effect. Hessel E. Yntema and Jerome Frank believed that statistical studies of judicial decisions could prove judges' subjectivity and confirm the realists' claims.[39]

Llewellyn argued further that the *language* of law bears little relation to the real (actual) world. As he wrote:

> [T]he trend of the most fruitful thinking about law has run steadily toward regarding law as an engine (a heterogenous multitude of engines) having purposes, not values in itself; . . . the clearer visualization of the problems involved moves toward ever-decreasing emphasis on words, and ever-increasing emphasis on observable behavior (in which any demonstrably probable attitudes and thought-patterns should be included).[40]

For Llewellyn then, as in one version of Holmes's lore, "What officials do about disputes is law itself."[41] For Frank too: "Until a court has passed on these facts, no law on that subject is yet in existence."[42] Or, as Yntema claimed: "The ideal of a government of laws and not of men is a dream."[43]

36. Horwitz, *Transformation* 170–72.

37. *Id.* at 170.

38. Rumble notes: "Both Pound and Brandeis were prone to cite the statement of Arthur Henderson that 'a lawyer who has not studied economics and sociology is very apt to become a public enemy.'" W. E. Rumble, Jr., *American Legal Realism: Skepticism, Reform and the Judicial Process* 11 (Ithaca, N.Y.: Cornell University Press, 1968) ("Rumble, *American Legal Realism*").

39. Purcell, *Crisis of Democracy* 86–87 (cited in note 20).

40. Llewellyn, "A Realistic Jurisprudence—The Next Step," in *Jurisprudence: Realism in Theory and Practice* 3, 39–40 (Chicago: University of Chicago Press, 1962); reprinted from 30 *Colum. L. Rev.* 431 (1930).

41. Karl N. Llewellyn, *The Bramble Bush: On Our Law and Its Study* 3 (2d ed. Dobbs Ferry, N.Y.: Oceana, 1951), cited in Purcell, *Crisis of Democracy* 83. Compare to Holmes: "The prophecies of what the courts will do in fact, and nothing more pretentious, are what I mean by the law." Holmes, *Collected Papers* 173 (cited in note 29).

42. Purcell, *Crisis of Democracy* 83.

43. *Id.* at 89.

Yet again, despite their skepticism as to legal principles and ideals, the legal realists retained a faith, compatible with the aura of a New Deal that looked to social ends and means, in planning, technocracy, and expertise. They in effect contended and strove to show—although perhaps more in the manner of Nietzsche's "free thinkers" and "last man" than his "free spirits"—that law understood as the mouthing of higher principles, like truth, like the metaphysical "real world" of the fifth stage of Nietzsche's history, was "an idea no longer of any use, not even a duty any longer—an idea grown useless, superfluous, *consequently* a refuted idea: let us abolish it." Like Nietzsche, who here laughs at science for loving error, they laughed at law that, in affirming the so-called rules and principles of justice, loved error and not truth or justice.

The late 1930s and 1940s brought a reaction against legal realism, in which the realists were variously accused of relativism, totalitarianism, and antidemocratic views. Law for the realists had become what sociologist Lon Fuller would call the "Pure Fact of Law,"[44] in which justice and *ought* dropped out. Although the realists themselves denied that they rejected all ethical goals for law or the possibility of justice, legal realism had apparently "run itself into the sand."[45] Early sympathizers turned against what was dubbed by Fuller "legal positivism," which positivism Fuller blamed in part on Holmes's "enormous influence."[46] Fuller characterized legal positivists as ethical skeptics who limited the study of law to what they could know empirically.

For Fuller, as Edward Purcell argues, legal scholars confronted a choice between the legal positivism of the realists and a natural law that *denied* the distinction between *is* and *ought*. The choice "was not between concrete existing law or speculating about an unattainable ideal. Rather it was between two different theoretical modes—one that tried to isolate a nonexistent 'law that is' [from what it claimed was a metaphysical 'law that ought'] and another that tried to understand the full scope and nature of law in process, a nature that necessarily included both an is and an ought."[47] Fuller thus provides an early and explicit articulation in sociology of law of the (re)unification—or collapse—of *is* and *ought*, a proclaimed end to the distinction between Nietzsche's "apparent" (understood as actual) and "real" (understood as ideal) worlds.

Such unification/collapse is of course also found in the legal pragmatism that some trace back already to Holmes or to Pound's sociological jurisprudence and that others take to be an aspect, via Holmes and Pound, of

44. *Id.* at 162.

45. Schlegel, 28 *Buffalo L. Rev.* at 459.

46. See Purcell, *Crisis of Democracy* 162 ff.; Jan Vetter, "The Evolution of Holmes, Holmes and Evolution," 72 *Cal. L. Rev.* 343 (1984); and Lon Fuller, *The Law in Quest of Itself* (Chicago: Foundation Press, 1940) ("Fuller, *Law in Quest*").

47. Purcell, *Crisis of Democracy* 162-63, citing Fuller, *Law in Quest* 4-6.

legal realism.[48] American pragmatism, as Grey argues, can be distinguished "from the scientific empiricism out of which it grew," by its "doubly practical account of inquiry as at once situated in existing practice and instrumental to practical ends." "The pragmatist breakthrough," according to Grey, "was to reject all mind-body dualisms," thereby escaping "from the philosophical paradoxes inherent in the confused conception of the Platonic-Christian-Cartesian-Lockean mind-soul, that hybrid entity with its many and conflicting roles . . . [which include that of] active organ of decision."[49]

In critiques of legal realism, legal scholars of the 1950's and philosophers of law of the 1960's, however, were far from hailing legal realism for its pragmatic insights. On the contrary, the "legal process" school took issue with what it perceived to be the "result-oriented jurisprudence" of legal realism and, by contrast, emphasized the use of procedural institutional arrangements to safeguard against decision makers' discretion.[50] When in 1961 legal philosopher H. L. A. Hart, in *The Concept of Law*,[51] also challenged the "rule skepticism" of the legal realists, he did so, *contra* Fuller, in the name of a legal positivism inherited from John Austin through which Hart *affirmed* the distinction between *is* and *ought*. As adherents of both so-called natural law and positive law, such as Fuller and Hart, declared themselves for different reasons against legal realism, the debate about the meaning of law seemed to return to its conventional philosophical framework: still often characterized as a disagreement between natural lawyers, who maintain that a higher moral law is the measure of the lawfulness of manmade laws, and positivists, who provide factual, nonmoral criteria, such as procedural regularity or the command of the sovereign, as the test of a law's validity and hence existence. In answering the question, What is the law? natural lawyers—harking back to the second and third stages of Nietzsche's history—look to a higher law and hold that a manmade "law" that is not just cannot be law. The positivist confines the concept of law to the manmade law that exists, distinguishing the question of the existence of law from questions about justice and morality.

But the terms of the debate had actually shifted. For one thing, from whichever natural law or positive law perspective philosophers, legal scholars, and sociologists explicitly repudiated legal realism, they too shared the

48. See, e.g., Grey, 41 *Stan. L. Rev.* (cited in note 25); see also Rumble, *American Legal Realism* 4 (cited in note 38), tracing the impact of pragmatism on the legal realists by way of James's and Dewey's "marked effect upon Pound and, to a lesser degree, upon Holmes."

49. Grey, 41 *Stan. L. Rev.* at 793, 797, 798.

50. See Henry Hart, "Supreme Court 1958 Term Foreword," 73 *Harv. L. Rev.* 84 (1959); Henry M. Hart & Albert M. Sacks, "The Legal Process" (unpublished, 1958); G. Edward White, "The Evolution of Reasoned Elaboration: Jurisprudential Criticism and Social Change," 59 *Va. L. Rev.* 279 (1973).

51. H. L. A. Hart, *The Concept of Law* (Oxford: Clarendon Press, 1961) ("Hart, *Concept of Law*").

realist faith in a sociological knowledge of law as institutions or practices of *this* world—of the phenomenal world of observable appearances. Even the "justice" of concern to ostensibly nonpositivist philosophers such as John Rawls would be "economic," treating of the distribution of the goods of this world. Furthermore, legal realism had not been forgotten. In studies of the "gap" between "law on the books" and "law in action" (one of Pound's formulations),[52] in the shift in interest to law in everyday life, and in critical legal studies of doctrine, sociologists and lawyers in the 1970s and 1980s explicitly drew on the insights of legal realism. The following section shows the entrenchment of modern American law and thought about law in the legal realist orientation toward a science or knowledge of society—an entrenchment in, literally speaking, "socio-logy."

III. LAW AND THE TRUTHS OF SOCIOLOGY

Today, despite differences between and among legal scholars, legal sociologists, and legal philosophers as to the separability and the desirability of the separation of *is* from *ought*, or of the apparent from the real, the differences fade in the enormity of a common worldview. That view consists in a commitment to the questions and the truth of the answers of sociology, a knowledge born of the observation of law as social phenomena. It manifests itself in the current understanding of law as the regulatory policy, grounded in facts and values or in the observable regularities of a population, of a governmental state. It manifests itself too in a vision of the future which, although not always articulated this way, approaches what one sociologist calls a "sociological society," in which justice disappears.

The discussion below is far from exhaustive. It simply brings together some examples from philosophy of law, social research, legal opinions, critical legal theory, and interpretive sociology, which would commonly be thought to represent a range of approaches, to suggest how, in the context of Nietzsche's thought, the "sociology" characterizing these and other modern works about law might be understood as the modern unfolding—again in a non-strictly chronological sense—of nihilism.

The preface to Hart's now-famous *The Concept of Law* points immediately to the situatedness of law in society and of philosophy in sociology. Although Hart's book is "primarily designed for the student of jurisprudence,"[53] Hart's project in *The Concept of Law* is to provide an "analysis of the distinctive structure of a municipal legal system and a better understanding of the resemblances and differences between law, coercion, and

52. See Roscoe Pound, "Law in Books and Law in Action," 44 *Am. L. Rev.* 12 (1910). For examples of such studies, see Richard Abel, "Law Books and Books about Law," 26 *Stan. L. Rev.* 175, 185–89 (1973).

53. Hart, *Concept of Law* v.

morality, *as types of social phenomena*."[54] Thus, as Hart writes, the book "may also be regarded as an essay in descriptive sociology."[55] (The core of the book consists in Hart's identification of the "two minimum conditions of a legal system"—that members obey rules of behavior that are valid according to secondary rules; and that the secondary rules themselves be accepted by the officials who use them.)

While philosopher Ronald Dworkin's aim, in contrast to Hart, is not strictly descriptive, he presents his "interpretation" of "law as integrity," too,[56] within the confines of an ahistorical and sociological view of law as the law of the state or as what justifies governmental force.[57] "Governments have goals," he writes,

> They use the collective force they monopolize to these and other ends. Our discussions about law by and large assume, I suggest, that the most abstract and fundamental point of legal practice is to guide and constrain the power of government in the following way. Law insists that force not be used or withheld, no matter how useful that would be to ends in view, no matter how beneficial or noble these ends, except as licensed or required by individual rights and responsibilities flowing from past political decisions about when collective force is justified.[58]

Both positivist social scientists and interpretivists in the "human sciences" fault Hart and Dworkin, despite their differences, for an "unrealistic"—and, according to positivists, "unscientific"—jurisprudence of rules that conflates law and justice. The very "realism" shared by these positivist and interpretivist critics however, reveals a similar, although not identical, conflation of law and justice, as shall be seen. The realism of both positivist and interpretivist critics of Hart and Dworkin transforms both law and justice into sociological phenomena, into "mere" appearances, in which justice, paradoxically, *dis*appears.

Donald Black's *Sociological Justice*,[59] to take an extreme instance of positivist social science, shows one version of this unfolding. Appealing to sociology as strict "science," Black views law as a "quantitative variable" alternately defined as "governmental authority brought to bear on a person or group" and as "governmental social control."[60] Just as "pure sociology of

54. *Id.* at 17; emphasis added.

55. *Id.* at v.

56. Ronald Dworkin, *Law's Empire* (Cambridge, Mass: Harvard University Press, 1986) ("Dworkin, *Law's Empire*").

57. Although this view is sometimes attributed to Max Weber, it is misleading to do so. Weber acknowledged the historical aspects of his analyses, claiming: "*Today* legal coercion by violence is the monopoly of the state" (emphasis added). Weber, 1 *Economy and Society* 314, ed. Guenther Roth & Claus Wittich (Berkeley: University of California Press, 1978).

58. Dworkin, *Law's Empire* 93.

59. Donald Black, *Sociological Justice* (New York: Oxford University Press, 1989).

60. *Id.* at 8; ch. 5 n.5.

law" concerns itself with "legal reality alone—the facts—and pass[es] over in silence all matters of a critical nature,"[61] Black himself maintains the distinctions he elsewhere accuses others of confusing—between facts and values, between what is and what ought to be, between science and policy. Black faults the jurisprudence of rules that he attributes to Fuller and Hart as unrealistic and also criticizes those who seek to get rid of discrimination in law. Doing so would be sociologically impossible, Black claims, since law inevitably varies with social differentials and discrimination is "an aspect of the natural behavior of law, as natural as the flying of birds or the swimming of fish."[62]

While never explicitly endorsing particular reforms, Black suggests to those interested in legal reform that they seek not to make law more equal but to equalize social differentials or to "desocialize" law, or at least courts. Such desocialization, according to Black, ultimately requires "the exclusion of people" (their names, their presence, their representation on videotapes, their voices), because people represent the "contamination" of trials with "social information" (or information about social differentials). The "final step in the desocialization of courts" for Black involves eliminating judges and juries and "closing the courtrooms themselves," in favor of electronic justice or computers "programmed to process complaints and testimony and to select disposition."[63]

The jurisprudential nihilism—no people, no courts, no law—in which Black's reforms all culminate reflect the extremes to which Black takes the is/ought distinction. *Sociological Justice* concludes in language that is uncannily resonant of that in Heidegger's "The Question concerning Technology."[64] Black writes:

> Social space is still being discovered and explored. . . . Sociological knowledge will surely grow, creeping throughout the world with a fatefulness unknowable. We only know that the science of society changes society. Social action increasingly becomes a self-conscious application of sociology. Sociological power is harnessed, a new form of energy generated, its uses impossible to imagine. A sociological society.
>
> This must be a new stage of human evolution.[65]

But unlike Heidegger, who questions technology, Black seems to *celebrate* the entrance of law into "an age of sociology" where "life will inevitably change."[66] The "sociological society" that results from the separation of *is*

61. *Id.* at 3.
62. *Id.* at 21–22.
63. *Id.* at 69–71.
64. Martin Heidegger, *The Question Concerning Technology and Other Essays* 3-35, trans. William Lovitt (New York: Harper Torchbooks, 1977).
65. Black, *Sociological Justice* 103.
66. *Id.* at 4.

from *ought* is nevertheless one in which the social scientific observer treats the presence of justice (or of any *ought*) as "value" or as no more than *the fact of its perception*, a perception whose "reality" Black, for one, is then unwilling to grant.

Few others explicitly share Black's radical separation of *ought* and *is* or the abolition of both justice and law to which Black's views lead.[67] But at least some social research about law implicitly suggests an understanding of law and of the desirability of a "sociological society" that is similar to Black's. Insofar as courts adopt such research, adoption reveals an attempt at law to substitute the truths of the "apparent" observable sociological world for those of the "real" world of *ought*, right, and justice abolished by social science.

A look at empirical jury research, for example,[68] shows this substitution. Jury studies presume that "law" makes certain assumptions about human behavior and aim to correct those assumptions. Despite their appeals to neutrality and to the distinction between fact and value, however, these studies affirm a particular view of law: that of a legal positivism in which law is the law of officials and in which validity, rather than morality, is at issue. Presenting themselves as strictly empirical,[69] such studies nevertheless ask not simply, What do juries do? but rather, Do juries obey the law? (where the jury's performance is measured, for instance, against that of "the judge as a baseline"[70]) and even, How can we get juries to obey the law? They propose "improvements" to jury trial designed to make the jury more effective, more acceptable to the public, or more in keeping with "the law." While not all researchers go so far as to take courts, judges, and officials as the standard against which to measure jury performance, they take for granted that "law" refers to the rules of the court or to judges' instructions.[71]

67. For more about Black's nihilism, see Marianne Constable, "Sociological Justice and Jurisprudential Nihilism," 11 *Oxford J. Legal Stud.* 114 (1991).

68. For details, see Marianne Constable, "What Books about Juries Reveal about Social Science and Law," 16 *Law & Soc. Inquiry* 353 (1991), concerning Harry Kalven, Jr., & Hans Zeisel, *The American Jury* (Chicago: University of Chicago Press, 1966; rev. ed. (Phoenix Ed., 1970), printed 1971; Midway Reprint Ed., 1986) ("Kalven & Zeisel, *American Jury*"); Rita J. Simon, *The Jury: Its Role in American Society* (Lexington, Mass.: D. C. Heath & Co., 1980) ("Simon, *Jury*"); Reid Hastie, Steven D. Penrod, & Nancy Pennington, *Inside the Jury* (Cambridge, Mass: Harvard University Press, 1983) ("Hastie *et al.*, *Inside the Jury*"); Valerie Hans & Neil Vidmar, *Judging the Jury* (New York: Plenum Press, 1986); Saul M. Kassin & Lawrence S. Wrightsman, *The American Jury on Trial* (New York: Hemisphere, 1988) ("Kassin & Wrightsman, *American Jury on Trial*"); and John Guinther, *The Jury in America* and *The Civil Juror: A Research Project Sponsored by the Roscoe Pound Foundation* (New York: Facts on File Publications, 1988).

69. The studies variously attempt to get away from "images," "intuitions and personal experience," "rhetoric," "anecdotes," "a priori guess[es]" and "sentimentality," and distinguish factual questions from value questions, empirical from political or ethical ones, the actual from the ideal, the empirical from the theoretical.

70. Kalven & Zeisel, *American Jury* 10.

71. Simon, *Jury* 147, for instance, mentions that "experts in law" respect the jury's opinion. Hastie *et al.* look to the record of decided cases to establish a systematic set of principles

At the same time as they associate law with the apparent standards of officialdom then, jury studies also treat justice as perception or appearance. In jury studies, as in social-psychological studies of "perceptions" of justice,[72] justice appears as public belief or as the public confidence in a system that is necessary to legitimate it or to make it—again—*appear* just. The studies present seemingly innocuous suggestions for enhancing the appearance of justice: they propose strengthening jurors' memories, for example, by substituting written for oral instructions, by allowing jurors to take notes, by providing videotapes and charts, and by instructing the jury at the beginning as well as the end of trial. Like proposals to introduce social scientific findings about the reliability of eyewitness testimony to guide the jury in its decision making, however, these proposals presuppose that a jury informed by the truths of social science is *preferable* to a jury informed by "common sense."[73]

Analyzing juror decision making by, for instance, "describing trial as a psychological stimulus, identifying the processing demands of the juror's decision task, and outlining the sequence of cognitive processes performed by the juror,"[74] these studies take as ideal type—in both the Weberian and the "normative" sense—a jury whose verdict is the product of "information-processing" very like the sort of processing believed to occur in the social sciences. One study describes the jury as a "human lie detector" and as "a fact-finding machine."[75] Another claims that "legal discussion of the right to trial by jury" focuses on the "products of deliberation," in other words on "jury verdicts and individual jurors' intellectual and evaluative reactions to the stimulus trial and the experience of deliberation."[76] The trial itself becomes "a search for probabilities" such that the jury, "confronted with a vast array of input from the bench, the bar and the witness stand, . . . must acquire, comprehend, store and retrieve all verdict-relevant information before it can dispense justice. It is no small feat to live the life of a

by which to measure jury performance. Kassin and Wrightsman construct their ideal of how the jury should conduct itself by looking at the opinions of the legal community. They introduce a problem this way: "The courts want juries to comply with their judges' instructions. With that reasonable assumption as a point of departure, we ask: so why do they cling to psychologically unsound methods of communication?" (*Inside the Jury* 144).

72. See, e.g., E. Allan Lind & Tom R. Tyler, *The Social Psychology of Procedural Justice* 91–92 (New York: Plenum Press, 1988); E. Allan Lind *et al.*, "In the Eye of the Beholder: Tort Litigants' Evaluations of Their Experiences in the Civil Justice System," 24 *Law & Soc'y Rev.* 953 (1990); Tom R. Tyler, *Why People Obey the Law* (New Haven, Conn.: Yale University Press, 1990).

73. For more direct proposals to replace common sense with social science, see, e.g., John Monahan & Laurens Walker, "Social Authority: Obtaining, Evaluating, and Establishing Social Science in Law," 134 *U. Pa. L. Rev.* 477 (1986); and Laurens Walker & John Monahan, "Social Frameworks: A New Use of Social Science in Law," 73 *Va. L. Rev.* 5559 (1987).

74. Hastie *et al.*, *Inside the Jury* 15.

75. Kassin & Wrightsman, *American Jury on Trial* 66, 120.

76. Hastie *et al.*, *Inside the Jury* 59.

flowchart."[77] The ultimate goal in such studies becomes a jury whose "perception, memory, information and decision processes" best approximate the processes of social science, a science that serves to correct the mistaken assumptions of official law.

The "disappearance" of justice thus not only accompanies Black's strict distinction between *is* and *ought* but also accompanies the substitution for law of the findings of social research that, paradoxically, looks precisely to appearances or perceptions of justice. And the privileging of the sort of social knowledge implicit in these empirical social scientific texts extends also to classically conceived law. Judicial reasoning, for instance, draws increasingly on social science. Further, even when judges and courts ignore the particulars of social research—quite often, judging from complaints in law and social science literature—courts may adopt social scientific *approaches* to law without saying so.

To take another jury-related example, the law of jury selection requires that the jury be a "fair cross-section of the community."[78] This requirement does not refer to peers or neighbors, or to any particular substantive composition of a jury.[79] It refers instead to a *method* of selecting jurors, a method that finds its grounding in statistics understood, in Foucault's terms, as the science of the state. The statistical model of the jury views the community as a population of individuals having different values, from which the jury is to be drawn, and it views the jury as a representative sample of that population. That courts do not require the composition of any particular jury to reflect the composition of the population is in keeping with a statistical approach for, as every statistician knows, a normal distribution, or a perfectly representative sample, is the ideal average of many random samples of a population and is not to be expected in any particular randomly drawn sample—or on any particular jury. Accordingly, the cross-sectional requirement does not mandate a perfectly representative jury in any given case; it only requires a jury selection *procedure* that provides for *reliable* and *random* sampling of the relevant population.[80]

77. Kassin & Wrightsman, *American Jury on Trial* 66, 119.

78. Taylor v. Louisiana, 419 U.S. 522 (1975).

79. See Batson v. Kentucky, 106 S.Ct. 1712, 1717 n.6 (1986): "We have never held that the Sixth Amendment requires that 'petit juries actually chosen must mirror the community and reflect the various distinctive groups in the population.' Indeed, it would be impossible to apply a concept of proportional representation to the petit jury in view of the heterogeneous nature of our society" (citations omitted).

80. I discuss reliability for statistical purposes and its analogy in jury selection more extensively elsewhere. Briefly: first, the pool from which to sample must approximate the population. In recent years, legislatures and state courts have required the expansion of the pool of potential jurors beyond the traditional voter registration lists to driver registration lists, tax rolls, and so forth. Second, every item in the population must have an equal probability of being selected, and each item selected must be selected independently of the selection of any other particular item. In the 1960s and 1970s, specially appointed blue-ribbon juries were abolished. In the 1970s, too, restrictions were placed on judges' discretion to excuse potential jurors before voir dire and to limit possible excuses. In the 1980s, the constitutionality of

Courts have adopted "statistical" approaches not only in jury law but in all sorts of discrimination cases. They have acknowledged social research not only concerning jury size but also on other more "value-laden" issues. In *Plyler v. Doe*, for instance, the Supreme Court held that a Texas statute withholding state funds from local school districts for the education of illegal alien children was unconstitutional under the equal protection clause of the Fourteenth Amendment.[81] As part of its argument, the Court referred to social science to validate its claims about the link between democratic values and education: the "historic perceptions of the public schools as inculcating fundamental values necessary to the maintenance of a democratic political system have been confirmed by the observations of social scientists," wrote the Court.[82]

In such decisions as elsewhere, the Court displays the type of rationality that Foucault, for one, associates with the "governmentality" of the modern age. Rational government, Foucault claims, rather than seeking conformity with external laws, whether those of God, nature, or man, aligns reason of state with an interest in maintaining the *social* order. Modern law, understood as the power of the modern state, articulates the need to sustain if not enhance the economic, demographic, and biological regularities particular to that unit known as the population. As knowledge of the regularities of the population, the subject matter of social science and statistics, comes to inform and justify law, law and social science become social policy concerned with the management of the interests of a population, of its health, safety, and welfare.[83]

Legislatures and administrative agencies have long been known as fora in which technical expertise is deployed to manage competing interests. Less noted is the increasing reliance of courts on techniques that resemble social scientific approaches to "facts" and "values" and to social regularities

peremptory challenges—or challenges without cause which, in statistical terms, could "skew" the sample—came under attack. Finally, a sample must be large enough. In the 1970s, the Supreme Court considered the question of jury size. Turning to social science research, it found "no evidence that the reliability of jury verdicts diminished with six-member panels," and held six-member juries to be constitutional. Williams v. Florida, 399 U.S. 78 (1970). A few years later, it again turned to "recent empirical data" to declare five-member juries unconstitutional: "the data now raise doubts about the accuracy of the results achieved by smaller and smaller panels. Statistical studies suggest that the risk of convicting an innocent person (Type I error) rises as the size of the jury diminishes. Because the risk of not convicting a guilty person (Type II error) increases with the size of the panel, an optimal jury size can be selected as a function of the interaction between the two risks." Ballew v. Georgia, 435 U.S. 223 (1977). See Marianne Constable, *The Law of the Other: The Mixed Jury and Changing Conceptions of Citizenship, Law and Knowledge* (Chicago: University of Chicago Press, 1994).

81. Plyler v. Doe, 457 U.S. 202 (1982).

82. *Id.*

83. For examples of the kind of rationality Foucault discusses in "Governmentality" and "Politics and Reason," see the essays collected in Graham Burchell, Colin Gordon, & Peter Miller, eds., *The Foucault Effect: Studies in Governmentality* (Chicago: University of Chicago Press, 1991), and Marianne Constable, "Sovereignty and Governmentality in Modern American Immigration Law," 13 *Stud. L., Politics & Soc'y* 249 (1993).

or "norms."[84] The growing use of expert witnesses at trial,[85] the proliferation of law and economics in legal literature,[86] and the judicial reliance on balancing tests[87] all suggest ways in which social scientific approaches captivate, if social research does not capture, even the "least dangerous branch."[88] Similarly, the management of risk implied by the adoption of no-fault auto insurance, the encroachment of strict liability doctrines over traditional negligence in tort law, and the development of "dangerousness" as a concern in sentencing point to the emergence of an "actuarial justice" in which law—or rather legal process and administrative policy—would not be possible without social studies.[89]

The positivist versions of sociology described so far present their claims as scientific observations of the phenomenal world, as factual knowledge of the things that appear in *this* world and of reported perceptions thereof. Judgments by courts and by administrative officials based on similar knowledge of facts and values incorporate, no matter how unintentionally, social scientific approaches to law. Insofar as legal officials adopt social scientific approaches, the world of appearance that is the subject matter of social science steps into the place vacated by the "real" world, the metaphysical world beyond, the world of justice that has been discredited or at least declared unusable by social science. This realist displacement of the "real"

84. "Norm" is a peculiar word, whose very different meanings, significantly enough, often seem indistinguishable in the sociology of law. A societal "norm" can indicate an observed convergence of behavior, an average (the "normal"), or acceptance of a rule or a practice as what *ought* to be done (what is *taken as* "normative"). See Georges Canguilhem, *The Normal and the Pathological* 125 (orig. pub. 1966; New York: Zone Books, 1989), discussing Lalande's medical dictionary.

85. Technically speaking, witnesses are to testify about facts (not opinion or law). The most common expert witnesses testify about medical, psychological, economic, and engineering subjects. (Several instances in which testimony by law professors on questions of "fact" concerning (nonforeign) law have also been mentioned to me, although I have not yet verified them.)

86. The best-known defender of law and economics is Justice Richard Posner, author of *The Economics of Justice* (Cambridge, Mass.: Harvard University Press, 1982) and numerous other works. The seminal works of Coase and Calabresi first appeared a good 30 years ago. Since then, articles in law and economics have become common not only in the *Journal of Law and Economics* and the *Journal of Legal Studies* but in all of the mainstream law reviews.

87. Balancing tests as such are discussed relatively little in legal journals although they are common in certain areas of law. But see Louis Henkin, "Infallibility under Law: Constitutional Balancing," 78 *Colum. L. Rev.* 1022 (1978); Donald H. Regan, "The Supreme Court and State Protectionism: Making Sense of the Dormant Commerce Clause," 84 *Mich. L. Rev.* 1091 (1986); T. Alexander Aleinikoff, "Constitutional Law in the Age of Balancing," 96 *Yale L.J.* 943 (1987); and Barbara Ann White, "Risk-Utility Analysis and Learned Hand Formula: A Hand that Helps or a Hand that Hides?" 32 *Ariz L. Rev.* 77 (1990). Recall the Learned Hand "formula" for tort liability and the balancing of interests in antitrust and areas of constitutional law. A balancing tests implies an "evaluation of interests" such that judgment seems to be the outcome of elaborate cost-benefit analyses of "values."

88. Alexander Bickel, *The Least Dangerous Branch* (Indianapolis: Bobbs-Merrill, 1962).

89. Jonathan Simon, "The Emergence of a Risk Society: Insurance, Law, and the State," 17 *Socialist Rev.* 61 (1987). See also François Ewald, "Norms, Discipline, and the Law," 30 *Representations* 138 (Spring 1990), and for a striking analysis of the emergence of an insurantial legal order in France, François Ewald, *L'Etat providence* (Paris: Bernard Grasset, 1986).

from the world beyond to this phenomenal world, reinforces an understanding of law as the implementation of values or norms, as policies that are the sum of facts plus values, empirically determinable, and designed to bring about social improvement in the future.

"Justice" at this stage now becomes the distribution of the "goods" of human society in accordance with societal values.[90] To political philosophers and theorists of public affairs concerned with such distribution, like the social researchers mentioned above, justice is a matter of "perception." The problem of distributive justice is to develop allocative mechanisms to which a public agrees; consensus or agreement points to legitimate or, again, *seemingly* fair arrangements. John Rawls's *A Theory of Justice* is an especially apt example of such work. Criticizing utilitarianism, Rawls claims to follow a Kantian line of thought, but it is clear from the situation of limited resources with which he begins, that his interest lies in improving conditions in the phenomenal world. Justice, for Rawls, is the first virtue of social institutions and it raises the very un-Kantian problems of coordination, efficiency, and stability. Rawls' project is to find a way of choosing and prioritizing among competing claims for shares of socially valued resources. He argues that his two principles are those that free and rational persons would choose in an initial position of equality, and he urges us, the readers, to think about how that initial position and the principles to which it leads match our considered convictions.[91]

While Rawls' philosophy is clearly more grounded in the social world than Kant's, it remains for Roberto Unger, in little more than three remarkable pages,[92] to offer a critique of Rawls' "social contract theory" that escapes the limitations of a return either to utilitarianism or to so-called Kantian moral theory and that ushers jurisprudence into the final stages of Nietzsche's history. At one level, Unger's comments are familiar; they relate to the abstraction from reality of the situation of persons in the Rawlsian original position (POPs, as they are sometimes called), who choose the principles of justice from behind a "veil" of ignorance as to their own conceptions of the good and their actual place in society. They relate, too, to the "economic" rationality with which the risk-averse POP is endowed.

90. See Michael Walzer, *Spheres of Justice* (New York: Basic Books, 1983), regarding the multiplicity of what count as "goods" (or the things of this world that we value) subject to distribution by political arrangements: "membership, power, honor, ritual eminence, divine grace, kinship and love, knowledge, wealth, physical security, work and leisure, rewards and punishments, and a host of goods more narrowly and materially conceived—food, shelter, clothing, transportation, medical care, commodities of every sort, and all the odd things (paintings, rare books, postage stamps) that human beings collect."

91. John Rawls, *A Theory of Justice* (Cambridge, Mass.: Harvard University Press, 1971) ("Rawls, *Theory of Justice*").

92. Roberto Mangabeira Unger, *The Critical Legal Studies Movement* 99-102 (Cambridge, Mass.: Harvard University Press, 1983) ("Unger, *Critical Legal Studies Movement*"). In the following pages, most citations to this work are given in parentheses in the text.

In the context of Nietzsche's history and of Unger's call for "destabilization rights," however, Unger's critique takes on more significance. Unger writes that despite their claimed interest in the problems of *this* world, both utilitarianism and social contract theory "share a notion of a choosing self whose concerns can be defined in abstraction from the concrete social worlds to which it belongs." In their haste to avoid the indeterminacy to which choice might lead, both utilitarians and social contract theorists "define the wants or intuitions that constitute the primary data of the method restrictively, in fact so restrictively that all of the important conclusions are already included in the characterization of the starting points." Utilitarianism, in its need for a single sympathetic spectator or authority to compute the pleasure of the whole, keeps multiplicity and complexity, especially in the sense of ambivalent and conflicting desires, at bay (at 99–100). As Rawls puts it, utilitarianism does not take the differences between persons seriously.[93] The "ideal choice" situations that contractarians construct are also limited however, Unger writes: they "avoid the partiality of people to their own interests or even to their own visions of the good." Even the "subtle contractarian" like Rawls who "defends the features imposed upon the ideal choice situation as the justified result of an earlier interplay between our existing moral intuitions and critical reflection about them" does at a "prior stage of analysis what he would otherwise have to do at the subsequent one: anticipate his conclusions in his starting points while claiming for the latter an authority that this anticipation undermines." In other words, Unger argues, as do some feminist legal scholars, that neither does Rawls's "justice as fairness" take difference seriously. Instead, insulated from the risks and conflicts that differences imply, its principles of justice reimpose the uniform "ideals" that already more or less exist, if not in institutional arrangements, at least in the chooser's desires and beliefs that are in part shaped by those arrangements.[94]

Unger, again like some feminist legal scholars, objects to the schemes of such mildly reformist theory because in abstracting from the concrete world to particular ideals, these schemes turn to ideals that restrict visions of transformation. Unger finds that in these schemes, the "real" has become too realistic. What exists, in other words, has colonized the metaphysical "real" or "ideal" of Nietzsche's history to such an extent that ideals now barely call for improvement in and change of *this* world. Modern jurists and their philosophers, Unger writes, have sought to avoid transforming legal doctrine into an "arena for continuing the fight over the right and possible forms of social life. . . . They have avoided it at the cost of a series of violent and arbitrary intellectual restrictions whose ultimate effect is to turn legal doctrine into an endless array of argumentative tricks" (at 18). Jurispru-

93. Rawls, *Theory of Justice* 27.

94. Unger, *Critical Legal Studies Movement* 99-102 (without referring to Rawls by name).

dence still turns to reason (now known as "rationality") to enmesh itself in metaphysical ideals, but those ideals are now associated with existing conditions—with the stability and certainty of the market and of public order, claims Unger (and with the authority and/or domination of the white race and/or the male sex, claim others).

The critical legal studies movement that Unger describes, in contrast to the social policy of the fifth stage, thus seeks a "loosening of the fixed order of society" such that "no part of the social world can lie secluded from destabilizing struggle" (at 23). Proposing a counterprogram to liberal legalism, critical legal studies, as Unger describes it, claims that older ideas of rights and justice are obsolete and calls for the abolition of the "real": "Let us abolish it!" it cries, along with those of Nietzsche's fifth stage, of the older "reality." Yet unlike the social researchers who point to the actual limits of formal equality and the political theorists who refute empty morality in the name of minor reform (Nietzsche's "free thinkers"), these scholars of the critical legal studies movement along with Nietzsche's "free spirits" recognize that abolishing the real world opens up radical change.

They thereby move into the final stage of Nietzsche's history where, locating themselves in history, they acknowledge the former usefulness of the old theory of rights and justice. "There was a time in modern Western history, in the prerevolutionary Europe of aristocratic and corporatist polities," Unger writes,

> when the most influential doctrines held that law in general and the constitution in particular should be an expression and a defense of the underlying order of social division and hierarchy. . . . [T]he most important shift in the history of modern legal thought may have been the turn from this conception to the idea that the constitution and the law should describe the basic possible dealings among people, as property owners and as citizens, without regard to the place individuals occupy within existing society. According to this modern view, the system of rights would rise above the real social order. Rights would work either as if this order did not exist or as if it could be adequately tamed and justified by the mere expedient of treating it as nonexistent for purposes of rights definition. (At 24)

Now, however, modern legal thought threatens to reimpose a stagnant and rigid social structure, to which threat the critical legal studies movement addresses itself:

> The critical legal studies movement has committed itself to another change in the conception of the relation of law to society, potentially equal in scope and importance to the shift to rights indifferent to social rank and place. Law and constitution are now to be seen as just the reverse of what prerevolutionary theory demanded. They become the

> denial rather than the reaffirmation of the plan of social division and hierarchy. The ideal aim of the [critical legal studies movement's] system of rights taken as a whole and in each of its branches, is to serve as a counterprogram to the maintenance or reemergence of any scheme of social roles and ranks that can become effectively insulated against the ordinarily available forms of challenge. (At 24)

Seeking alternative forms of democracy and economy, Unger turns toward "deviationist doctrine," which includes an institutional program that looks to four types of rights. Among them are "destabilization rights," which "represent claims to disrupt established institutions and forms of social practice that have achieved the insulation and have encouraged the entrenchment of social hierarchy and division that the entire constitution wants to avoid" (at 39). The program as a whole, Unger claims, is neither antiliberal nor adulterated liberalism, but what he calls "a superliberalism," which "pushes the liberal premises about state and society, about freedom from dependence and governance of social relations by the will, to the point at which they merge into a large ambition: the building of a social world less alien to a self that can always violate the generative rules of its own mental or social constructs and put other rules and other constructs in their place" (at 41).

While other critical scholars of law may not share Unger's program of superliberalism as such, they share Unger's understanding of society as "made and imagined rather than merely given" (at 18) and, further, as the making and imagining of an infinitely generative and transfigurative self that no longer need rely on reason as such. Calling his own position "irrationalism," for instance, Joseph Singer links it with pragmatism and argues:

> When we give up the idea that the legal system has a foundation, a "rational basis," we are not left with nothing. We are left with ourselves. . . . We imagine a better life in the context of living with others and we work to bring it about. Whether some imagined practice will be better or worse than current practice is a question of moral judgment. It is not a matter of finding a foundation on which to stand, or of finding the truth. It is a matter of conviction. . . . We will have to take responsibility for making up our minds."[95]

Turning to "arational, sympathetic knowledge of the other" to criticize law, Robin West looks to "the ideal community central to civic republicanism and the ideal individual central to liberal utilitarianism and the commitments to freedom, welfare, tolerance, nurturance, egalitarianism, individualism, and communitarianism that compete within and between them," but

95. Singer, 94 *Yale L.J.* at 66 (cited in note 8).

finds these moral convictions to be "grounded not in reason but in love, nurtured not in the head but in the heart."[96]

Like the critical scholars above, those who call for a new way to think about law by offering personal and/or allegorical narratives also suggest the interpretability and constructedness of the world and of law. As Pound notes of the "psychological stage" of sociological jurisprudence, law, for latter-day critics and interpretivists alike, "like all psychical creations, . . . has been and will forever continue to be in a process of becoming."[97] For these scholars, law is no longer a matter of reason (and some claim it never was), yet it is nevertheless a product of psyche, the outcome of social imagination, desire, and will.

On this point, critical legal scholarship and interpretivism join with some recent feminist jurisprudence. Generalizations again are difficult because the latter work, like the legal realism from which interpretivism often claims its origins, displays the heterogeneity that has become "a familiar feature of contemporary critical debate about law."[98] To consider feminist scholarship properly would entail another essay. If pressed to connect such work to Nietzsche, one could use the parallels between recognized strands of feminist legal thought and the approaches to law of Rawls, Unger, and the interpretivists, to suggest possible links between feminist jurisprudence and the stages of Nietzsche's history—but it is doubtful that this is the fairest feminist reading. Nevertheless, if pressed, one could begin for instance with Judith G. Greenberg's identification of three main models of feminism: the "sameness/difference" model, the "dominance" model, and the "postmodern" approach.[99] One could argue, first, that feminist appeals to the similarities and/or differences between women and men to achieve equality raise issues similar to those raised by Rawls's appeal to abstracted or disencumbered POPs to justify the principles of justice as fairness that are to govern society. The issue for sameness/difference feminists, as for Rawls and his critics, could be said to concern the status and recognition of actual difference. For these thinkers, the "ideal" of formal equality is unattainable in *this* world and must be revised to deal with actuality. At issue is what counts as actual, as relevant knowable characteristic or difference. Second,

96. Robin West, "Disciplines, Subjectivity, and Law," *in* Austin Sarat & Thomas R. Kearns, eds., *The Fate of Law* 119, 155, 157 (Ann Arbor: University of Michigan Press, 1991) ("Sarat & Kearns, *Fate*").

97. Roscoe Pound, "The Scope and Purpose of Sociological Jurisprudence," 25 *Harv. L. Rev.* 489, 505 (1912).

98. Austin Sarat & Thomas R. Kearns, "Editorial Introduction," *in* Sarat & Kearnes, *Fate* 5 ("Sarat & Kearns, 'Editorial Introduction'").

99. Greenberg also notes the existence of "feminists of color" who work within these and other approaches. See Judith G. Greenberg, "Introduction to Postmodern Legal Feminism," *in* Mary Joe Frug, *Postmodern Legal Feminism* (New York: Routledge, 1992). Frug herself describes four approaches to feminist legal scholarship, distinguishing "sameness" from "difference" scholarship by classifying them as concerned respectively with "equality doctrine" and "equality theory."

the "dominance" model of feminism, in some ways like Unger, challenges sameness/difference feminists to recognize that even the emended ideals of nonidentical equality no longer represent meaningful change: those ideals themselves, as the artifacts of existing—and oppressive—conditions that they cannot reverse, are useless.[100] Finally, "postmodern" legal feminism, as Greenberg notes, "is about interpretation." As such, it displays the attachment to the constitutive character of discourse and the commitment to a multiplicity of perspectives that characterize, despite its variety, much interpretive work.

This is not the place to deal exhaustively with that variety. Some suggest, for instance, that humanistically inspired interpretivist work infers from the socially constructed character of law a "shared community" of sorts, while more social-scientifically oriented work downplays or denies the extensiveness of such community. Suffice it to say that whatever the constitutive character of society expressed in interpretivist sociolegal work, much of this work reveals the problematic unification of realism and of self-transforming will that marks the "sociological" legal thought of the modern age.

"Interpretive sociolegal research,"[101] in other words, claims—in what is sometimes misleadingly considered to be in explicit contrast to a jurisprudence of rules—to construe law realistically: first, as what society believes—"ideology," whether particular persons or groups realize it as such—and/or, second, as an effective power—as social control. Yet more important than realism in understanding how interpretivism epitomizes the "final" stage in a Nietzschean history of jurisprudence is the notion of self-transformative will—of a will or a law that is of course social but that is also self-produced and producing, in constant flux and, most important, in some sense beyond reason.

The interpretivist work of Austin Sarat and Thomas Kearns radically illustrates this understanding of law. Although Sarat affirmed "science as a tool of persuasion" in a discussion of "postempiricist" scholarship in 1990,[102] Sarat turns a year later with Kearns to interpretive critics who reject social science.[103] These critics, the two write, are "hopeful, if not confident, that law can and should be reimagined, reconfigured, and rescued." While Sarat and Kearns imply that the work they present "refute[s] any claim that today's critics are inescapably unconstructive or nihilistic," their refutation relies on the "vague" and nonphilosophical understanding of nihilism of

100. See, e.g., Catharine A. MacKinnon, *Toward a Feminist Theory of the State* (Cambridge, Mass.: Harvard University Press, 1989).

101. See 15 *Law & Soc. Inquiry* 135–80 (1990), containing a "Review Section Debate" on "Interpretation in Sociological Research." See also on "post-realism," John Brigham & Christine B. Harrington, "Realism and Its Consequences: An Inquiry into Contemporary Sociological Research," 17 *Int'l J. Soc. L.* 41, 55–57 (1989).

102. See Austin Sarat, "Off to Meet the Wizard: Beyond Validity and Reliability in the Search for a Post-empiricist Sociology of Law," 15 *Law & Soc. Inquiry* 155 (1990).

103. Sarat & Kearns, "Editorial Introduction" (cited in note 98).

some recent legal scholarship.[104] If one relies instead on Nietzsche's understanding of nihilism, Sarat and Kearns's own interpretive work "toward a jurisprudence of violence" reveals the nihilism of a self-transforming force that, in Stanley Fish's terms, is a law responsive only to its own needs or that, in Niklas Luhmann's and Gunther Teubner's, is an autopoetic law.

Sarat and Kearns begin by adopting and adapting Robert Cover's claim that law is interpretation understood "in the context of the organized social practice of violence."[105] Cover shows how law is not simply a matter of policy nor of the implementation of values, but necessarily implies en-*force*-ment of norms. Taking up the problem of what they then call "law's violence" (their distinction between "violence" and "force" is unclear), Sarat and Kearns argue:

> [R]eason and force have no way to share control of human agency. Where the two meet in battle only one can win, and given the levels of force, pain, and violence at law's disposal, law, wherever it wants, is assured of victory. It appears, then, that law's violence does not sit well—indeed, it wars with—the conception of human agency that is built into, and held out to us by, a jurisprudence of rules.[106]

Ostensibly seeking to argue "from law's monopoly of legitimate violence to the wholesale erosion of human agency in the face of that monopoly," Sarat and Kearns claim that there is more at stake in law's violence than "an instrumental conception of law." They invoke law's violence "to speak about its pervasive cultural residue [and] the way it insinuates itself into consciousness and conditions responses." Each instance of legal force, they write, "coldly reminds us of the way social life is forged and maintained."[107]

Yet even as Sarat and Kearns point to the erosion of human agency, the law that is at stake in their work—which is indeed more than a "conception"—is nonetheless thoroughly instrumental. Through "law" is created the "elaborate social organization" required by a violence that is felt in the "actual experience of ordinary legal subjects" as well as in "the consciousness and practices of legal officialdom."[108] And conversely, through violence is law effective. "Once established, law is maintained through force . . . as an apparatus of violence that disorders, disrupts, and repositions preexisting relations and practices all in the name of an allegedly superior order. That order demonstrates its 'superiority' in ferocious displays of force,

104. *Id.* at 4–5. Regarding the vagueness of the meaning of nihilism in current legal scholarship, see note 8 above.

105. Robert Cover, "Violence and the Word," 95 *Yale L.J.* 1601, 1602 n.2 (1986).

106. Austin Sarat & Thomas R. Kearns, "A Journey through Forgetting: Toward a Jurisprudence of Violence," *in* Sarat & Kearns, *Fate* 268.

107. *Id.* at 270, 269–70.

108. *Id.* at 272–73.

and in subjugating, colonizing, 'civilizing' acts of violence."[109] Law is both cause and effect of a violence that is itself both effect and cause of law.

Sarat and Kearns look to Nietzsche to say that violence is "a perverse utopia of action without form and instinct without deliberation from which all law—natural or positive—is the fall."[110] For Nietzsche, though, instinct without deliberation points to the nobility of an ancient tradition of law as command in which reason and the separation of doer from deed were neither needed nor known. If natural law and positive law represent a "fall" for Nietzsche, the fall occurs with the introduction of reason. The violence of law discussed by the latter-day Sarat and Kearnes is not "prior" to reason, however, as Sarat and Kearns in effect acknowledge when they argue for resisting the "congenial notion" in official stories "that law's violence can be tamed by reason."[111] Attending to "the ways law is conquered by violence" instead of by reason, they show law to be a "doer of literal violence" and a "regulator of force and coercion."[112] Their image is precisely of the causal power of a violent law that escapes reason and, unlike the instinct without deliberation of Nietzsche's nobles, is in need of some savior or cure. The hopelessness with which Sarat and Kearns approach this need becomes explicit in their essay on Cover's work. "Cover was hopeful about law even in the shadow of violence," they write, but

> [w]e are much less hopeful. He sought to acknowledge law's violence and temper or domesticate it in a reconstruction of the premises of law's relationship to society. We, however, fear that the violence of law stands in the way of such a reconstruction. To use his own language, he believed that law could be homicidal without being "jurispathic." We do not share his belief.[113]

Nihilism, of course, is not hopelessness (just as hopefulness does not indicate the absence of nihilism). But the hopelessness Sarat and Kearns express (like the hopefulness of the critics they turn to) indeed accompanies a nihilistic sociological jurisprudence that denies the distinction between the real and the apparent worlds, the *ought* and the *is*, while affirming a law/force that threatens to become absolute. In their reimagining (to borrow their term) of law as the particular social phenomena of violence, Sarat and Kearns find themselves unable to affirm the better nonjurispathic law for

109. Austin Sarat & Thomas R. Kearns, "Introduction," in Austin Sarat & Thomas R. Kearns, eds., *Law's Violence* 3 (Ann Arbor: University of Michigan Press, 1992) ("Sarat & Kearns, 'Introduction'").

110. Austin Sarat & Thomas R. Kearns, "Making Peace with Violence: Robert Cover on Law and Legal Theory," in Sarat & Kearns, *Law's Violence* 211 ("Sarat & Kearns, 'Making Peace'").

111. Sarat & Kearns, "Editorial Introduction," at 12.

112. Sarat & Kearns, "Making Peace," at 214; *id.*, "Introduction," at 3, 4.

113. Sarat & Kearns, "Making Peace," at 214–15.

which they feel the need. In their need to escape what they treat as the law of *this* world, Sarat and Kearns's nihilism is revealed. As causal force or effectivity that escapes reason and human agency (and that even conquers and dictates to them), law's violence becomes a circular and eternal imperative, a command of which the commander is lacking. Law's violence threatens to become its own commander or limit, which is to say that it threatens to become limitless or absolute.

To sum up, the "law" about which one speaks in a variety of fields today is a social phenomenon belonging to an observable world that is the proper subject matter of sociology. Virtue, divine or natural law, moral law, and positive law characterize the jurisprudence of the first four stages of Nietzsche's history of metaphysics. Social policy and distributive justice correspond to the fifth stage, in which the justice of the "real world" is abolished ostensibly in favor of that of the apparent world. For philosophers and researchers, for those who accept sociological knowledge as the truth about law and for those who live in a society that accepts such truths, law becomes what sociology knows it to be: the norms (in their double sense) of a population; the management of risks and interests; the policies enforced by officials in the context of belief in the justice of state violence or, in other words, positive law. Sociology—whether as science or as interpretation, as law or as philosophy—speaks the truths of positive law in the language of belief and appearance, the language of "legitimacy," "values," "norms," "distribution," and "policy"—from which "justice" and the "true" world disappear.

Critical scholars moving into the sixth stage acknowledge the collapse of the earlier is/ought and appearance/reality distinctions. Conjoined with the prior abolition of the real world, the collapse of these distinctions, like their pragmatist unification, leads to the question What remains? This question, as yet unanswerable despite the claims of sociology to do so, raises a matter of far greater import than the admittedly somewhat schematic classifications presented so far. That matter concerns a world whose law is sociologically determined and socially constructed—whether through imagination or violence or other ultimately inaccessible self-transformative force.

IV. WHAT WORLD IS LEFT?

For Nietzsche, the end of the history of metaphysics is the end of the longest error, the error that will is taken to produce effects. Has jurisprudence—here understood as thought about law—now reached its end?

Sociology has indeed abolished the real world. What remains? The apparent one? Certainly, there remains a sociological collaboration and production of what some have called the actuarial justice of administrative government. A diffuse network of power relations that have supplanted the centralized sovereign or will that was variously identified as the source of law in earlier times. The transformative superliberalism of recent critical movements and the socially constitutive and socially controlling "beliefs" of the interpretivists. All are factors bearing some resemblance to strong "will to power" as a creative plurality of forces that, at the end of Nietzsche's history, points to the transformation of the error of will that characterizes what has come before.

Yet at the end of this error, for Nietzsche, Zarathustra enters. For Zarathustra, "state is the name of the coldest of all cold monsters. . . . [T]he state tells lies in all the tongues of good and evil; and whatever it says it lies—and whatever it has it has stolen. . . . Even its entrails are false. Confusion of tongues of good and evil: this sign I give you as the sign of the state." Zarathustra counsels, "where the state *ends*—look there, my brothers! Do you not see it, the rainbow and the bridges of the overman?"[114] The end of the state reveals to Zarathustra the "overman," a species or race that is not human, a self-overcoming being of strong will to power whose condition neither necessitates nor has necessitated it to reason and error.

For human beings of the modern age, however, for those whose knowledge and reality are precisely of statistics and the law of the state and of the regularities and regulations of sociological society, the social scientification or sociologization of law again reveals, one suspects, the conditions of human weakness and of reaffirmation of will. The constructive and transformative force of modern law, its urge to create and recreate itself in its own sociological image—whether in actuarial justice or through new constitutions, whether through public policies or destabilization rights—betrays a desire to escape modern conditions. The power of modern law lies in a mastery of social organization that is indeed neither the outcome of a divine sovereign nor exactly the product of human will. But neither is it the strong will to power of an overman. Such mastery is that of sociology, of knowledge of the "social," a knowledge and power which takes itself as and makes itself sovereign.

Sociology takes social creation to be the whole of what is and will be. It makes all that presents itself otherwise—science, religion, history, for instance—into socially constructed phenomena. It takes law as social construction—as both socially created or imagined and as social creator or maker. In the union of this sociological recognition only of the social and the privileging of sociology as knowledge, sociology simultaneously provides and becomes the law of society.

In its transfiguration into law, sociology does not thereby become divine or moral, although it does reveal its continuity with the metaphysical

114. Friedrich Nietzsche, "On the New Idol," *Thus Spoke Zarathustra*, trans. Kaufmann (New York: Viking Press, 1954).

tradition of which divine law and Kantian moral law are part. Sociology becomes the culmination of the positive law that corresponds to the realism and empiricism of Nietzsche's fourth stage and that descends, like divine and moral law, from the fateful error at the beginning of metaphysics, the necessitated error that will produces an effect. In the sociological mastery that governs the modern age lies a particular sort of positive law or command though. For sociology denies the status of law to all that does not pertain to the domain of the social and remains oblivious to all that it does not itself command. The law of sociology threatens to become absolute command—commandment as its own commander. Sociological law threatens to become, for the history of jurisprudence, what Heidegger considered to be the consummation Nietzsche's history of metaphysics: the permanent transfiguring or becoming of absolute subjectivity.[115]

* * * * *

Although Holmes began his lecture by saying that "when we study law we are not studying a mystery but a well-known profession," he concluded with a claim about

> the remoter and more general aspects of the law . . . which give it universal interest. It is through the[se aspects of the law] that you not only become a great master in your calling, but connect your subject with the universe and catch an echo of the infinite, a glimpse of its unfathomable process, a hint of the universal law.[116]

Holmes's ideas may hint at universal law, but the "echo of the infinite" that accompanies the social scientificated law toward which Holmes moved is a variation on the nihilistic metaphysics Nietzsche describes. The notes that sound are those of our eternally optimistic desire to escape the past that is our present for an illusory future. That this is so is, of course, no reason not to listen; on the contrary, the failure to hear these notes is precisely what threatens to make sociology absolute law. To those who hear, as to those who would heed Zarathustra's call to look where the state ends, something other than the law of sociology shows itself.

115. This is not to say that sociological law is *Nietzschean* will to power; "life" as Nietzsche understands it when he speaks of will to life as strong will to power is not the same as the sociologist's "social." The claim is simply that sociological law falls prey to the criticism Heidegger makes of what *he* takes to be Nietzschean will to power. Heidegger's reading of Nietzsche as such has not been addressed. By contrast with the above, Philippe Nonet in "What Is Positive Law?" 100 *Yale L.J.* 667, 669 (1990), also identifies legal positivism with the law of the modern age or rather with "the historic movement by which the power of command rises to the rank of supreme source of law," but shows precisely how Nietzsche is "the thinker and prophet of legal positivism."

116. Holmes, 10 *Harv. L. Rev.* at 457, 478 (cited in note 2).

[3]

The Relevance of Nietzsche to Democratic Theory: Micropolitics and the Affirmation of Difference

Nathan Widder
Department of Politics, University of Exeter, Exeter EX4 4RJ, UK
E-mail: n.e.widder@exeter.ac.uk

This paper argues that Nietzsche presents an ontology of excess that, by problematizing the logic of identity, can positively contribute to democratic theory and practice. This ontology is missed by a wide range of interpreters who try to depoliticize Nietzsche's thought, align it with the agonisms of contemporary mass democracy, or re-align it with an aristocratic politics of fixed hierarchy. While Nietzsche himself may not extend this ontology onto the political domain, the writings of Foucault, and Deleuze and Guattari demonstrate how it can provide greater appreciation of the subtleties and complexities of power relations that operate at a micropolitical level.
Contemporary Political Theory (2004) **3,** 188–211. doi:10.1057/palgrave.cpt.9300113

Keywords: Nietzsche; Foucault; Deleuze; democratic theory; political ontology; micropolitics

> We want *equality* without its compelling us to accept identity; but also *difference* without its degenerating into superiority/inferiority. (Tvetan Todorov, 1984, *The Conquest of America*, p. 249)

> The familiar argument of tolerance, that all people and all races are equal, is a boomerang. (Theodor Adorno, 1974, *Minima Moralia*, n. 66)

Ideas need not be 'democratic' to be relevant to democratic concerns, especially where there is a desire to rethink the nature of democratic theory and politics.[1] Given this desire, it is important to be wary of reducing a seemingly anti-democratic thinker to being an enemy to democracy, useful only for highlighting what democracy must avoid or prompting democratic theorists to defend themselves against the strongest possible opponent. This is certainly the case with Nietzsche, who has lost his reputation, at least within academic circles, as a forebear of fascism, but whose thought is still not generally held to be of positive value for democratic theory. Nietzsche's political pronouncements are clearly hostile to modern mass democracy. Nonetheless, his virulent attacks embody a suspicion that should be at the forefront of any democratic thinking: the suspicion that the democratic call for equality conceals an intolerance of difference, hiding an immorality built into a purportedly democratic ethos. The object of Nietzsche's most specific attacks is perhaps more recognizable now than it was in the late 19th century: the close link between the liberal demand for equality and the nationalist demand for purity, sameness, and identity. This link, for Nietzsche, rests upon an insistence that two individuals must be the same to be treated equally and, as a corollary, that what is different must fit into a hierarchy of superiority and inferiority. In this respect, democratic equality is no different from the aristocratic hierarchies it opposes, insofar as both are premised on a logic of identity, and hence Nietzsche holds that democratic politics rests upon the same metaphysical assumptions that modern, Western society, celebrating the death of God, purports to move beyond.

Nietzsche identifies a 'democratic idiosyncrasy' that betrays 'a prejudice in the modern world toward all questions of origin' (Nietzsche, 1967a, 28); that, in the realm of science, 'opposes everything that dominates and wants to dominate' by positing a mechanistic world order that replaces all action with reaction and adaptation (*ibid.*, 78–79); that infects scholars who 'consider a problem almost as solved when they have merely schematized it' (Nietzsche, 1974, 290); and that, in the realm of morality, reflects a herd mentality that proclaims 'I am morality itself, and nothing besides is morality' (Nietzsche, 1966, 116). All of this makes the modern democratic movement a sign of declining life (1967a, 154). Yet Nietzsche also criticizes traditional social hierarchies, just as he attacks the metaphysical hierarchies of Platonism and Christianity. He speaks of 'ages when men…simply refused to acknowledge the element of accident, role, and caprice…[and] managed to erect those monsters of social pyramids that distinguish the Middle Ages' (1974, 302). Against such rigid orders, which did have the virtue of 'durability' (*ibid.*), Nietzsche distinguishes

> opposite ages, really democratic, where people give up this faith, and a certain cocky faith and opposite point of view advance more and more into the foreground — the Athenian faith that first becomes noticeable in the Periclean age, the faith of the Americans today that is more and more becoming the European faith as well: The individual becomes convinced that he can do just about everything and can *manage almost any role*, and everybody experiments with himself, improves, makes new experiments, enjoys his experiments; and all nature ceases to become art. (*ibid.*, 302–303)

The danger of the democratic herd complex lies in its incompatibility with this brave individualism. As a result of the modern incarnation of the latter, 'What will not be built any more henceforth, and *cannot* be built any more, is — a society in the old sense of that word; to build that, everything is lacking, above all the material. *All of us are no longer material for society*' (*ibid.*, 304). The democratic idiosyncrasy, however, presses for such a society, and, not surprisingly, its calls for equality reflect intolerance towards anything brave enough to be democratic in the sense of being aggressively individual. In the democratic herd, as in the theatre, 'one is honest only in the mass; as an individual one lies, one lies to oneself' (*ibid.*, 325).

The relation of Nietzsche's thought to politics in general and to liberal and democratic politics in particular is subject to diverse interpretations. Walter Kaufmann (1974) argues that Nietzsche's philosophy is not concerned with politics but rather with purely private self-creation. Richard Rorty (1989) maintains that Nietzsche *must* be treated as an apolitical thinker because his philosophy is disastrous when introduced into the public sphere. Moreover, Rorty contends, depoliticizing Nietzsche makes him compatible with liberalism, which provides the freedom in the private sphere necessary for Nietzschean experimentation and self-creation. Others seek to politicize Nietzsche and show that his politics is actually compatible with democracy, even if Nietzsche never realized this. Thus Lawrence Hatab (1995) argues that the contestations of democratic elections, legislative and judicial battles, and social movements embody the agonism that Nietzsche prizes. David Owen (1995) argues that a political agonism drawn from Nietzsche's perspectivism and his doctrines of will to power and eternal return is superior to both classical liberalism, which rests upon shaky metaphysical foundations, and contemporary political liberalism, which is concerned more with conciliation than contestation. But those such as Bruce Detwiler (1990) and Frederick Appel (1999) oppose this adoption of Nietzsche by theorists of the democratic left, holding that Nietzsche's aristocratic political statements cannot be divorced from his overall philosophy. Nietzsche's agonism, they point out, is a contest among equals, but these equals are superiors who stand well above the ordinary democratic man. Today's democratic Nietzscheans, they argue, domesticate Nietzsche's thought through a selective reading meant to make him more egalitarian and therefore appealing to contemporary ears.[2]

This paper, however, will take a different route, drawing upon the Nietzsche-inspired work of Michel Foucault and Gilles Deleuze to show how Nietzsche's thought, despite its many aristocratic formulations, may be brought into democratic thought and practice. Specifically, it will explore how Foucault and Deleuze apply Nietzsche's ontology of power relations to the micropolitical domain. 'Micro' here refers to a constitutive level where subjects and meanings are formed and dissolved, while 'macro' refers to the level where precariously constituted subjects relate to one another, taking up places perhaps in an egalitarian contest of interests or perhaps in hierarchies of status. The micro-level must not be confused with the liberal private sphere, which might be bracketed off from 'real politics', nor with the purely personal realm invoked to portray Nietzsche as radically individualist and apolitical. It also does not refer to the psychological domain of unequal types often used by interpreters to ground Nietzsche's aristocratic politics (see Appel, 1999, esp. Chapter 2). Both micro- and macro-levels are domains of power relations, but these too must not be confused. Crucially, while micro-power relations are relations of inequality, this inequality is itself *unequal or in flux*. From this flux emerge the various characters that comprise Nietzsche's hierarchy of types: on the one hand, those whose moral valuations affirm strife, conflict, and overcoming, and, on the other hand, those who will a logic of identity that may be either hierarchical or egalitarian. The second, slavish type might even affirm a democratic contestation of wills, but it is nevertheless a slavish contest that has already effaced the constitutive level of strife.

By focusing on this micro-political domain, Foucault and Deleuze bring Nietzsche into conversation with democratic thought and practice in a way that moves beyond conceptions of politics often shared by those who would depoliticize Nietzsche, integrate him into a standard conception of democratic politics, or insist that he remain an advocate of a standard conception of aristocracy. When Foucault maintains that Nietzsche managed to theorize power outside the restraints of political theory, it is because Nietzsche's ontology of constitutive disequilibrium has been ignored by liberalism, Marxism, and other mainstream positions that focus exclusively on macro-relations among subjects (see Foucault, 1977a; Ansell-Pearson, 1995). By stressing how both a fixed aristocratic hierarchy and a democratic contest among equals reflect a slavish will to truth or a desire that desires its own repression, Foucault and Deleuze put Nietzsche in the service of a democratic micro-politics that works to overcome the binary divisions that construct and maintain the democratic herd. It is not surprising that, against some self-proclaimed Nietzschean democrats, Foucault and Deleuze show little interest in the agonism of contemporary democracy. As William Connolly would argue, what matters to Nietzsche, Foucault, and Deleuze is how these democratic contestations rest upon codings and overcodings that have already occurred at the micro-political level and that are problematic for any politics purporting to be democratic in a 'postmodern' age.[3]

Foucault and Deleuze are often admonished for abusing Nietzsche in order to promote an emancipatory politics for the marginalized and excluded (see Appel, 1999, 2, 9–11; Donaldson, 2002). Yet although their work does touch upon these forms of exclusion, they are hardly their real concern.[4] Rather, at least with respect to democratic theory and practice, they are concerned with the micro-level closures inherent in the democratic herd mentality and with the development, against these closures, of micro-level practices that do not assert the identity of the individual against the collective so much as debunk the logic of identity itself. In this way, Foucault and Deleuze use Nietzsche to press democratic theory and practice beyond good and evil. Foucault's examinations of modern disciplinary society and Deleuze's studies (with and without Félix Guattari) of patterns of reterritorialization within late capitalism not only explore the pervasive mechanisms of normalization woven into purportedly liberal societies, but also introduce distinctive conceptions of selfhood and of individual and collective practices, which can help reshape the democratic imaginary. It should not be surprising that Foucault and Deleuze's use of Nietzsche has become salient precisely where the dangers of identity-based political thought and action have become most apparent: feminism, gay and lesbian politics, post-Marxism, and the New Left generally. The importance of such thinking for democratic politics therefore ought to be obvious.

Dynamics of Agonism and its Oblivion

We can begin to grasp Nietzsche's understanding of micro-relations of strife and their connection to identity by considering his admonishment of English utilitarians in the first essay of the *Genealogy of Morals*. Their moral history takes as given the contemporary meaning of 'goodness' as unegoistic action and seeks its origin through a timeless principle of utility. Thus, they argue that unegoistic actions were originally called good by the recipients of action, but this specificity was progressively forgotten until the actions were called good *per se*. Aside from its 'inherent psychological absurdity' (Nietzsche, 1967a, 27) — since unegoistic action is by definition beneficial only to the receivers, how could the specificity of its utility be forgotten? — this view is condemned for repeating the great error of all rationalist thought: understanding history through unhistorical laws, it posits the eternal, identical, or final, as governing the world of becoming. This manoeuvre, designed to comprehend change, illustrates the first idiosyncrasy of philosophers: 'their lack of historical sense, their hatred of even the idea of becoming, their Egyptianism. They think they are doing a thing *honour* when they dehistoricize it, *sub specie aeterni* — when they make a mummy of it' (Nietzsche, 1990, 45). The lack of historical sense effects an error of domestication, rendering becoming compatible with the will to truth by positing fixed markers that measure and order change. What normally passes for history — a sense of passage from past to present and into the future — amounts to a lack of historical sense.

Historical sense, for Nietzsche, is more than an awareness of past events, even in their contingency. It involves the strength to bear the heterogeneous within oneself — 'the *plastic power*... to transform and incorporate into oneself what is past and foreign' (Nietzsche, 1983, 62). One cannot live completely historically, Nietzsche says, as the man unable to forgot cannot establish the markers of identity necessary to give his world solidity. Immersed in the flux of becoming, such a man, like Borges's Funes (1993), would be unable to overcome the singularity of each experience in order to grasp himself or the objects around him as unities (Nietzsche, 1983, 60–62). Without a certain kind of amnesia, therefore, identity is impossible. Subjects and objects cannot be identified and placed within a chronological passage, understood as having once existed but no more or being in a process of development towards a future finished form: 'The principle of identity has behind it the 'apparent fact' of things that are the same. A world in a state of becoming could not, in a strict sense, be 'comprehended' or 'known'' (Nietzsche, 1967b, 281). Forgetting constitutes identity and becoming compatible with it by ironing out a heterogeneity that cannot be located on either a spatial or a temporal continuum. This forgetting distinguishes man from the animal that lives completely unhistorically but contently, unable to forget because it cannot even remember; yet it also makes man a fragile being whose identity rests upon a memory that he is incapable of forgetting at a different level (Nietzsche, 1983, 60–62).[5]

Insofar as a being exists historically, then, it does not simply exist within a chronological continuum but is permeated by an unlocalizable excess. To think historically — or, using Nietzsche's later terminology, genealogically — thus requires an engagement with this unrepresentable difference through a displacement of identity and its correlate, opposition. Opposition, like identity, involves a forgetting of heterogeneity. In its dominant metaphysical (i.e., Platonist and later Christian) form, one opposite exists positively and independently and the other is defined as the first's lack or absence. The difference between opposing terms is therefore one of simple hierarchy and inequality, resulting in a crude idealism. In its dialectical form, opposites are mutually constitutive, each one passing into and defining the other, resulting in an equality and synthetic unity of opposites. Against both strategies, Nietzsche declares oppositional values to be 'merely foreground estimates, only provisional perspectives, perhaps even from some nook, perhaps from below, frog perspectives, as it were, to borrow an expression painters use' (Nietzsche, 1966, 10). Against metaphysical transcendence, Nietzsche maintains that no being exists as a thing-in-itself but instead is constituted through its relations to others:[6] a being exists historically because it cannot have a positive essence. The relations constituting this being, however, cannot be reduced to equality, for this manoeuvre reinvokes a sameness, identity, or ground. Constitutive relations are therefore necessarily unequal relations of domination and submission. But they are also relations of power and resistance. This resistance is not a simple counteraction to power, but a consequence of the discontinuity in power relations themselves — the very heterogeneity that the logic of identity forgets. Resistance is thereby implicated even in relations that can be characterized as 'cooperative', as Nietzsche indicates when speaking of 'the noise and struggle of our underworld of utility organs working with and against one another' (Nietzsche, 1967a, 57). Constitutive relations are *never* oppositional, for they can be neither strictly separated nor resolved through a dialectical synthesis. Power, strife, heterogeneity, and reversal are thus implicated in all relations as basic components.

Nietzsche's *Genealogy* examines the kinds of beings constituted by these relations of strife. In unequal relations within and between beings, there must be a dominator and dominated, even if resistance allows this inequality to be inverted. The character types that emerge are the noble, who, affirming himself in his agonistic relations with other nobles, engages in contests of strength in order to test his limits and overcome himself, and the slave, who, unable to affirm himself in his weakness, defines the noble as evil in order to secure his own identity as good. Without recounting the details of Nietzsche's analysis,[7] two points must be noted. First, only from the viewpoint of the slaves, who create the schema of identity and opposition from the *ressentiment* that forms when their will to power is unable to express itself outwardly, are strife and heterogeneity papered over by a strict divergence of good and evil. In other words, while the dynamic of strife is constitutive, a certain perspective on the world consigns it to oblivion. The slaves secure their own identity through a distortion of noble affirmation, one that pins the latter within boundaries paralleling those that the slaves seek for themselves. Slave morality thereby functions by a *reduction* of noble affirmation and agonism: the self-overcoming of the latter so exceeds the slaves' capacities that it is ultimately distorted onto the oppositional schema of good and evil. It is compressed onto a moral logic of identity just as becoming is domesticated in order to constitute the identity needed for the chronological conceptualization of time. Ironically, the slavish will to truth emerges from a falsification that links together purity, goodness, and truth. This valuation overcodes constitutive heterogeneity by translating it into a schema of identity and opposition ill-suited to it. Regardless of whether this schema is one of a transcendent purity measuring the physical world or one of immanence that translates the ideals of identity and purity into modern science and dialectical philosophy, an intolerance for excessive difference is already in place. The immorality of slave morality appears not in the particular actions it sanctions or condemns, but in the spirit of revenge and intolerance from which its judgements issue.[8]

Second, despite some portrayals of the nobles as brutish and stupid, Nietzsche draws from them a pluralist ethics that is neither nihilist nor relativist. The pluralism of noble morality comes from its will to overcome any semblance of identity by affirming the conflict within oneself, 'born as one is to a subterranean life of struggle' (Nietzsche, 1967a, 44), through conflict with others. These others must be worthy opponents capable of compelling one to overcome oneself — they must be other nobles, who need not be recognized by the first noble as being of the same kind, but must simply be strong enough to offer a challenge.[9] This agonistic struggle sanctions conflict and violence, yet the very strength through which the noble affirms himself, his opponent, and the strife between them also outlines a set of noble alternatives to slavish conceptions of conscience, justice, law, and self-restraint.

For the 'active, aggressive, arrogant man' who 'is still a hundred steps closer to justice than the reactive man' (Nietzsche, 1967a, 75), who has not yet become 'ashamed of all his instincts' (*ibid.*, 67), and whose conception of punishment 'evolved quite independently of any presupposition concerning freedom or non-freedom of the will' (*ibid.*, 63), justice involves equivalent punishment inflicted for unpaid debt, without any further compulsion to identify the offender as a type.[10] This, however, allows mercy to emerge and to overcome justice through a '*consciousness of power* that…could allow itself the noblest luxury possible to it — letting those who harm it go *unpunished*' (*ibid.*, 72). Related to this is a different function of law. Rather than a tool for revenge, law operates in 'the struggle *against* the reactive feelings…Wherever justice is practiced and maintained one sees a stronger power seeking a means of putting an end to the senseless raging of *ressentiment* among the weaker powers that stand under it' (*ibid.*, 75). Law as a partial restriction on aggression, Nietzsche says, serves strength — this is the creed of the strong. Conversely, law that seeks to eliminate all struggle and strife is 'a principle *hostile to life*' (*ibid.*, 76). Life, for Nietzsche, is necessarily implicated in struggle and conquest, but it is not for that reason lacking control. Unlike the constraint counselled by slave morality, however, which is driven by *ressentiment*, noble self-control follows from a healthy life.

> The three great slogans of the ascetic ideal are familiar: poverty, humility, chastity. Now take a close look at the lives of all the great, fruitful, inventive spirits: you will always encounter all three to a certain degree…It is quite possible that their dominating spirituality had first to put a check on an unrestrained and irritable pride or a wanton sensuality, or that it perhaps had a hard job to maintain its will to the 'desert' against a love of luxury and refinement or an excessive liberality of heart and hand. But it did it, precisely because it was the dominating instincts whose demands prevailed against those of all the other instincts — it continues to do it; if it did not do it, it would not dominate. (*ibid.*, 108–109)

Here, the central aspects of an ethics 'beyond good and evil' can be glimpsed. It is an ethics that, rather than seeking to secure the identity of oneself and another through mutual recognition and respect — a view containing the hidden proviso that the other may be different only insofar as he/she is also the same — presses beyond such traditional oppositions of self and other.

This portrayal of a noble ethics must certainly appear surprising to those who doubt Nietzsche has any, and who portray him as either deconstructing moral foundations and sanctioning an 'anything goes' nihilism or — what amounts to the same thing — desiring a return to an aristocratic politics in which the dominating few impose themselves on the masses. Although Nietzsche himself may not turn his critique of the democratic idiosyncrasy into a positive rethinking of democratic politics, his conceptions of law, justice, and agonism can be put to such use. Although these ideas do not amount to a political theory in the traditional sense of a worked-out social order, their import comes in exposing the microscopic conditions that underpin the demands found in traditional political theory and indicating a way to move beyond these demands. Nietzsche's political contribution thus comes in his presentation of an ontological dynamic in which identity and opposition appear only as reductive misinterpretations. A political or social theory that puts primacy on identity is therefore necessarily missing something.

Micro-powers and Dispersion

A dynamic in which power constructs identities against resistance is often ascribed to Foucault.[11] Yet in his genealogical studies of criminality and sexuality, disciplinary and normalizing powers produce neither normalized, disciplined selves nor identifiable, knowable deviants whose distance from the norm can be measured and corrected. Certainly, the norm and the various deviant categories mapped out in opposition to it are developed and used to coordinate the deployment of disciplinary power. But the products of this power remain enigmatic, as Foucault's case studies of Herculine Barbin and Pierre Rivière demonstrate (see Foucault, 1975, 1980). Foucault thus maintains that the prison system aims not to eliminate delinquency or even to genuinely comprehend it, but rather to manage deviance, and the consistent failure of the prison to reform inmates must be understood in this light (see Foucault, 1979, esp. Part 4). Disciplinary society seeks an efficient use of resources for the management of life, but while a will to identity is wrapped up in this project, the mechanisms of power do not produce identity as a result.

> What is to be understood by the disciplining of societies in Europe since the eighteenth century is not, of course, that the individuals who are part of them become more and more obedient, nor that they are set about assembling in barracks, schools, or prisons; rather that an increasingly better invigilated process of adjustment has been sought after — more and more rational and economic — between productive activities, resources of communication, and the play of power relations. (Foucault, 1982, 219)

Crucially, this drive for efficiency is replete with inefficiencies, which only reinforces the project's strength. While modern society, compelled by a will to truth to name, locate, observe, measure, and know, is driven to identify deviations from a norm that no one even fits in the first place and to police and correct these deviations in the name of promoting conformity with this fictitious standard, the effect is very much the reverse: differences are multiplied rather than gathered under an umbrella of normality. Yet through the persistent failure of the powers of individution, classification, and correction to manifest an efficient social system, these same disciplinary mechanisms are extended into more areas of modern life. Declarations of prison failure are always followed by moves to maintain them (Foucault, 1979, 272) and the entire system of disciplinary power ends up trapped in its own logic, unable to do anything more than increase its policing. Ultimately prisons look like factories, which look like hospitals, which look like schools. And when one examines the personal histories of the various 'deviants' that modernity seeks to police, they all have already passed through a myriad of institutions purportedly designed to normalize them (*ibid.*, 301).

If Foucault's overall project can be seen as a challenge to this pervasive will to identity or truth, then as with Nietzsche the will to truth must be distinguished from the dynamic of power that constitutes it. Just as Nietzsche's genealogy traces oppositional logics to a slavish perspective that denies constitutive strife, Foucault's genealogy shows how these same logics justify the use of power in modern society while falsifying or masking a substantial part of power's operations.[12] The difference between norm and deviancy is delineated through binary categories, the inadequacy of which is demonstrated by the need to reinforce these judgements by constantly invoking other, heterogeneous oppositions: 'When a judgment cannot be framed in terms of good and evil, it is stated in terms of normal and abnormal. And when it is necessary to justify this last distinction, it is done in terms of what is good or bad for the individual' (Foucault, 1977b, 230). Foucault contends that the will to truth seeks to tame the excessive power of discourse[13] and today it has eclipsed and absorbed other controls, such as prohibition or the dismissal of certain discourses as irrational (Foucault, 1984, 113–114). This shift corresponds to an apparent democratization that allows different discourses to contest one another, yet at a different level the terms of contestation have already been enframed. Discourse appears increasingly liberated, but this must be understood against a background demand that discourses demonstrate their truthfulness, with truth linked to purity, goodness, utility, and universality. Our apparently liberated post-Victorian sexuality, for example, rests upon a prior explosion of discourse that links sex and desire to the truth of the individual (Foucault, 1990, Parts 1–2). The ideas that power and liberation are opposed and that discourse can be power-free or can free oneself from power hide more subtle forms of power and discourse that condition this liberation by constituting sexuality as repressed truth. The will to truth operates still more subtlety by reducing events to chronological history. This history, Foucault says, need not judge the present in terms of progress or decline and can accept the contingency of events. Nonetheless, it is a form of history that lacks Nietzschean historical sense.

> History as practiced today does not turn away from events…But the important thing is that history does not consider an event without defining the series of which it is part, without specifying the mode of analysis from which that series derives, without seeking to find out the regularity of phenomena and the limits of probability of their emergence, without inquiring into the variations, blends and angles of the graph, without wanting to determine the conditions on which they depend. Of course, history has for a long time no longer sought to understand events by the action of causes and effects in the formless unity of a great becoming, vaguely homogeneous or ruthlessly hierarchized; but this change was not made in order to discover prior structures, alien and hostile to the event. It was made in order to establish diverse series, intertwined and often divergent but not autonomous, which enable us to circumscribe the 'place' of the event, the margins of its chance variability, and the conditions of its appearance. (Foucault, 1984, 128)

For this reason, Foucault notes that although he has operated within the sphere of historical events, his work is not one of history.[14] Rather, it is a genealogical investigation into agonistic power relations operating at a microscopic level and exceeding any movement of identity and opposition. Although this genealogy makes historical claims regarding changing configurations of power, its underlying principle is that the connections between power relations and meaning cannot be grasped according to any logic of spatial or temporal continuity.

Juridico-discursive and psychoanalytic models of power continue the will to truth's forgetting of microscopic discontinuities. The first focuses exclusively on the macroscopic level where already constituted subjects wield power in a negative fashion and where power and freedom can be opposed. The second treats power as constitutive, but conceives it in oppositional terms, with repressive power constructing the desire to transgress power's boundaries. Psychoanalysis thereby takes the binary system of licit and illicit that is part of the juridico-discursive model and extends it to all levels of power relations (see Foucault, 1990, 81–85). Social agents such as a judge, parent, police officer, or psychiatric expert certainly possess powers that they may choose to exercise or not exercise, but these agents and their possessed powers refer back to a context of meanings and truths. These meanings and truths are not pregiven, but the power that produces them is not one possessed by agents. Instead, it constructs the social positions they occupy. This network of constitutive power relations, like Nietzsche's, consists of relations of strife. Foucault thus presents his micropowers as a 'moving substrate of force relations which, by virtue of their inequality, constantly engender states of power, but the latter are always local and unstable' (*ibid.*, 93). This inequality in flux constitutes the repetitive mechanisms of repressive power as 'the over-all effect that emerges from all these mobilities, the concatenation that rests on each of them and seeks in turn to arrest their movement' (*ibid.*). Through a composition of micro-forces that is in no way a mere aggregation or totalization,[15] 'far-reaching, but never completely stable, effects of domination are produced' (*ibid.*, 102).

Micro-power relations are immanent in all things — power is everywhere though, importantly, it is *not* everything — but inscribed within them is a plurality of sites of resistance. Power at this level is never simply opposed to freedom,[16] and resistance, in turn, is never reducible to some thermodynamic, 'equal and opposing' force to power. Instead, resistances appear in the discontinuity of power relations themselves. They are 'the odd term in relations of power…Hence they too are distributed in irregular fashion' (Foucault, 1990, 96). While the dynamics of constitutive relations occasionally produce binary oppositions of power and resistance — as when the treatment of prisoners produces resentment towards the system, leading not to reform but recidivism (Foucault, 1979, 264–268) — resistance more often takes the form of indeterminate dispersions of subject positions and internal incompatibilities arising within and among disciplinary institutions and practices. For example, the exercise of power to observe and investigate sexual deviance, by virtue of the voyeurism and erotic 'hide and seek' games it encourages, proliferates rather than controls sexual desire (Foucault, 1990, 44–45). On an institutional level, the family and psychiatric bodies cooperate to monitor sexuality in the home, but also come into conflict when psychiatrists seek to institutionalize family members (*ibid.*, 111–112). Further discontinuities and cross-purposes follow from the lack of correspondence between objects and discourses of knowledge and the sites of their production, whereby the hospital as an institution to deal with insanity has its origins not in medicine but law enforcement, while the discourse on madness is located not in the hospital but the courts; and the delinquent, as an object of penal law, is produced in prisons, while prisoners are created by the judiciary (see Deleuze, 1988, esp. Part 2).

What therefore emerges in Foucault's work, just as in Nietzsche's, is a difference exceeding the orders of identity. A lack of homogeneity within the self corresponds to an inability to securely place different selves in schemas of identity and opposition. Foucault's later turn to the care for the self must be understood in light of this. It is in no way a theorization of resistance, if resistance means a liberation from power relations — although it can involve liberation from certain formations of power (Foucault, 1988b). The care for the self, or the relation of the self to itself, is a terrain presupposed by the very power relations that produce disciplinary practices and institutions. Social meanings and 'games of truth', constituted by relations of strife, include social types that are classified and disciplined and moral rules that establish prohibitions. But moral rules also presuppose a subject who relates to them and, consequently, a set of self-to-self practices through which the subject is ethically positioned. The shifts in these practices — in terms of the ethical substance modified, the mode or command motivating subjection to the moral law, the practices employed in adjustment, and the telos of ethical formation[17] — demonstrate their political and ethical import not by articulating a more ideal past,[18] but by problematizing contemporary meanings and binaries that otherwise remain unquestioned. Specifically, they problematize the link between desire, sex, and the truth of the individual, which is made at the expense of pleasure,[19] and the consequent anxiety to locate and normalize delinquency.

Alternative ways of thinking and acting follow the articulation of the contingency of contemporary truths and identities, supporting an experimentalism with living, which, by calling into question the need to see oneself as an identity, promotes a political and ethical affirmation of difference.[20] Foucault calls this a matter not of escaping games of truth but of playing them differently (Foucault, 1988b, 15). Playing them differently means approaching them with curiosity and care for what remains opaque and different, and with a willingness to press thinking beyond its traditional limits.[21] This is Foucault's means to endeavour beyond good and evil, or to struggle, as he puts it, against the fascism not only around us but inside us (see Foucault in Deleuze and Guattari, 1983, xi–xiv). Like Nietzschean noble morality, this Foucauldian ethics renounces those oppositional politics that construct the opponent as an 'evil enemy' in order to secure the sanctity of one's own identity.

> Furthermore: might not this 'struggle' that one tries to wage against the 'enemy' only be a way of making a petty dispute without much importance seem more serious than it really is? I mean, don't certain intellectuals hope to lend themselves greater political weight with their 'ideological struggle' than they really have?... And then I'll tell you: I find this 'model of war' not only a bit ridiculous but also rather dangerous. Because by virtue of saying or thinking 'I'm fighting against the enemy', if one day you found yourself in a position of strength, and in a situation of real war, in front of this blasted 'enemy', wouldn't you actually treat him as one? Taking that route leads directly to oppression, no matter who takes it: that's the real danger. (Foucault, 1991, 180–181)

Foucault, therefore, refuses to engage in ideological forms of politics that, by virtue of being totalizing, 'are always, in fact, very limited' (Foucault, 1988d,

375). Instead, he raises problems ignored by established political outlooks committed to party politics or identity-based politics. This task of thought, governed by an ethical sense, flows into politics: 'Thinking and acting are connected in an ethical sense, but one which has results that have to be called political' (*ibid.*, 377).[22]

> Let's take an example that touches us all, that of Poland. If we raise the question of Poland in strictly political terms, it's clear that we quickly reach the point of saying there's nothing we can do. We can't dispatch a team of paratroopers, and we can't send armored cars to liberate Warsaw. I think that, politically, we have to recognize this, but I think we also agree that, for ethical reasons, we have to raise the problem of Poland in the form of a nonacceptance of what is happening there, and a nonacceptance of the passivity of our own governments. I think this attitude is an ethical one, but it is also political; it does not consist in saying merely, 'I protest', but in making of that attitude a political phenomenon that is as substantial as possible, and one which those who govern, here or there, will sooner or later be obliged to take into account. (*ibid.*)

The problems ignored by the normal mechanisms and institutions of politics include those of asylums, prisons, and clinics. These are specific fields, but they highlight the most general issues of modern Western society: power relations and the disciplinary strategies that organize them.[23]

In these ways, Foucault takes Nietzsche's critique of identity and his dynamic of agnostic relations onto terrains in need of politicization. As these areas are occluded by the demand for identity that traverses modern democratic life, they require alternative modes of theorization and engagement. Theory and practice become more subtle and layered than traditional conceptualizations allow. The first can no longer be an abstract doctrine providing a priori rules and justifications for the second. Political theory in particular cannot remain the explication of procedures to conduct and police disputes, the elaboration of the conditions for a more inclusive social milieu to resolve them, or the development of a utopian model to inspire political action. All of these options paper over excess by giving primacy to the reconciliation — through either simple inclusion or simple exclusion — of divergent elements. Submerged within any binarism is a multiplicity to be exposed. Politics is the strategic attempt to do this.

A Many-Layered Politics

Our social and political worlds consist of many levels that cannot be fully separated from one another but must not be conflated. These levels create possibilities and necessities for understanding power, knowledge, and change, and thus for politics. Like Nietzsche and Foucault, Deleuze and Guattari aim to trace these multiple layers in their heterogeneity and mutual imbrication.

There is, first, a molar level of segmentarity: domains and classifications such as school, profession, holiday, prison, working class, childhood, adolescence, and homosexuality. In this realm of sharp divisions, one's place or identity is located. No doubt one assumes several roles within and across these segments, but only one at a time or only within specific relations: one passes from childhood to adulthood and from school to work; one can be a father, son, and husband simultaneously, but to different people; one is a worker from 9 to 5 and a pensioner after 65. The segments amount to organized binaries, even where more than two choices are available.[24] Regardless of the choices or assignments made, however, these quite different segments seem ominously the same — undoubtedly because they all function on a disciplinary model.

There is also another level of micro- or molecular fluxes, where molar identities and differences are composed and dissolved. At this level of constitutive relations of power and resistance, the same power creates both 'normal' identities and opposing forms of madness, delinquency, and perversion. The latter are found in the marginals society tries to constrain, but something of them is in all of us.[25] They are a pervasive and potentially revolutionary element within the segments that threatens to overturn them.

And there is a third level, also relational, but where relations are not oppositional. They are affirmative and creative in the same way as Nietzsche's noble overcoming. There is a politics we direct against molar segments in order to modify or reform them, perhaps radically; and there is a political struggle waged at the level of meaning in the name of the marginal and the excluded. But this third level provides yet another politics, not of reform or even revolutionary opposition, but of doing something different: an a-systematic rather than anti-systematic politics (see Kazarian, 1998).

Deleuze and Guattari give many names, each stressing different characteristics, to this relational terrain that does not conform to identity and opposition. They include:

- A *war machine*, which expresses the agonism of this relationality while differentiating it from the 'institution of war' that appropriates it into an oppositional schema: '*The State has no war machine of its own;* it can only appropriate one in the form of a military institution, one that will continually cause it problems' (Deleuze and Guattari, 1987, 355).
- A *rhizome*, which expresses how this network of relations does not conform to any arboreal model of pluralism where diverging branches and roots are

unified by a common trunk. The rhizome is a plurality with no central point and therefore no defined limit (see Deleuze and Guattari, 1987, 3–25).

- A *multiplicity* that differs from the One and the Many, from any plurality that refers back to unity.
- A *smooth space* or *plane of consistency*, which is not an indifferent terrain where all parts are the same, but rather one where differences are not hierarchized or striated by a central point or identity standing above and organizing them. This space is consistent by virtue of having no transcendent dimension, making it smooth but also differentiated.[26]
- *Desire*, understood as an a-teleological movement not related to any particular object: 'desire implies no lack; neither is it a natural given. It is an *agencement* of heterogeneous elements that function' (Deleuze, 1997, 189). Desire must not be confused with pleasure or feeling, which might judge it.[27]
- *Nomadism*, as contrasted with migration, the latter perhaps ignorant of its final destination but nonetheless seeking one. The nomad has no such concern with locale.[28]
- A *line of flight* or *deterritorialization*, which 'flattens' or decomposes structures of identity that organize differences from on-high. This is achieved not by opposing striated organizations but simply by exceeding them.

This final level is in some sense outside the others, but all three are also immanent to each other, forming a single assemblage. Micro-levels of desire and molecular fluxes constitute the macroscopic segments that fix and incorporate them, (re)territorialing desiring lines of flight; and lines of flight continue within molar organizations and deterritorialize them.

The molar segments work by coding differences. Each domain has markers of normality and deviance appropriate to it. The domains are independent, but they also communicate with one another. Prisons and courts, for example, have different norms and practices, but they resonate together, the courts producing convicts through a judgement of guilt passed upon actions and the prisons receiving convicts and turning them into delinquents through disciplinary tactics, so that each passes its subjected products to the other. Every domain similarly refers outside itself and the State is the mechanism by which these diverse domains communicate. It overcodes the domains, not by reducing them to a homogeneous blob, but by enabling and regulating transferences. This makes the State an important but limited site of political struggle: the problem of crime cannot be adequately dealt with at the level of the State only, since it is a relay rather than an all-or-nothing power holder.

If the level of desire is in some sense primary, it is because its strife constitutes the very segments that seem to arrest it. As with Nietzsche's analysis of master and slave moralities, certain formations of desire posit a transcendence organizing all relations and becomings — desire comes to desire its own repression. But this organization, structured by identity and opposition, necessarily distorts, reduces, and only partially captures the dynamic it seeks to grasp. The State and its molar organizations are thus always pitted against the chaotic excess of the war machine, which they cannot fully incorporate. It is a mistake to see this excess from the point of view of the State, which sees chaos as mere anarchy, a Hobbesian state of nature. Chaos is not the polar opposite of order and it presupposes rules or laws — a nomos. This makes possible a 'nomad science' and a thinking extricated from the State model. Like the becoming that both Nietzsche and Foucault argue is domesticated by the logic of identity, this nomadism is untimely and therefore not captured by history.

There are many aspects of nomad or minor science,[29] but they are all linked through an idea of unlocalizable discontinuity incompatible with identity and opposition and their accompanying notions of boundaries. Against a Euclidian space that is consistent with this logic of boundaries, Deleuze suggests 'another, 'topological', space which establishes contact between the Outside and the Inside, the most distant, the most deep' (Deleuze, 1988, 110). This new space subverts the possibility of treating differences in terms of opposition. The latter is an abstraction, 'roughly cut from a delicate milieu of overlapping perspectives, of communicating distances, divergences and disparities, of heterogeneous potentials and intensities…'

> As for opposition…it is as though things were spread out upon a flat surface, polarised in a single plane, and the synthesis itself took place only in a false depth — that is, in a fictitious third dimension added to the others which does no more than double the plane. In any case, what is missing is the original, intensive depth which is the matrix of the entire space and the first affirmation of difference: here, that which only afterwards appears as linear limitation and flat opposition lives and simmers in the form of free differences. Everywhere, couples and polarities presuppose bundles and networks, organized oppositions presuppose radiations in all directions. (Deleuze, 1994, 50–51)

This is a realm of elusive and 'intensive' becomings, which appear to move nowhere from the perspective of identity and yet pass with 'infinite speed' by virtue of being 'beyond' the limits of spatio-temporal continuity. Deleuze and Guattari relate this movement to the Epicurean idea of the swerve of atoms — the *clinamen* — occurring in a time and space smaller than the minimum thinkable continuity.[30] The nomadic movement of this line of flight is experienced as 'a curious stationary journey' (Deleuze and Parnet, 1987, 127).

From this multi-layered complex of movements and sedimentations comes the need for a multiform politics and an appreciation of the way all things, at whatever level, are political. The personal is political, though in a peculiar sense. It is not simply because the barrier between private and public is drawn in the public or political realm; nor because both public and private refer to large-scale powers such as capitalism, patriarchy, and racism, which organize them. More than these, it is because of the way that any thing, in the molecular fluxes that constitute it and in which it participates, and in the creative deterritorializations it can enact, ultimately effects the reification or overcoming of formations of power, identity, and opposition. And it is because a thing, existing historically, is always tied to an excess that eludes full capture by the terms of identity.

Politics must therefore involve more than reform of existing institutions or revolutionary opposition to them. A creative experimentalism and a corresponding affirmation of hybridity are also requisite for a politics that aspires beyond good and evil. Hybridity means, first, that there is no pure identity because in referring outside itself any identity is always already mixed. More profoundly, however, hybridity means that this mixture is never homogeneous: the hybrid does not mix black and white into a continuous shade of grey. The hybrid instead forms a nexus of heterogeneous differences that are incommensurable but nonetheless indispensable to one another, tied together in a kind of Gordeon knot beyond any possible untying. This is the heterogeneity articulated by Nietzsche's ontology and brought to bear on democratic politics by Foucault and Deleuze. But this democratic politics is a micro-politics where what matters is not the affirmation of some egalitarian sameness among differences nor the celebration of different and heterogeneous identities that establish themselves by opposing themselves to what they are not. Rather, what matters here is the ability to dissolve both identity and its abstract corollary, opposition. To be a Nietzschean democrat is to pluralize through an overcoming of identity and the introduction of an excessive discontinininuity.

It seems clear that the link regularly made between identity and politics, whereby the construction of an efficacious identity is seen as a necessity for political action, has become problematic in a 'postmodern' world of blurred boundaries. This is reason enough to think that recognition of the micro-political domain of power relations is indispensable for any politics that claims to speak to contemporary concerns. Indeed, when the micro-political domain is taken into account, the issue of Nietzsche and democracy shifts. It is no longer a question of whether Nietzsche is really a democrat or not, or whether his thought can be squared with democracy, but whether those who would depoliticize Nietzsche or interpret his thought in support of either a macropolitical egalitarianism or a macropolitical aristocratism are as pro-democratic as they might like to think. By holding on to an anachronistic conception of politics, these interpreters have remained in the orbit of the very thinking Nietzsche criticizes as a slavish simplification. If the will to identity indeed embodies the desire of desire to repress itself, and if our politics still tends towards identity striations, then the political lesson of Nietzsche, Foucault, and Deleuze is that we are not yet democratic enough.

Date submitted: 20 November 2002
Date accepted: 26 February 2003

Notes

1 This article is a revised version of a paper originally titled 'The Relevance of Nietzsche to Democratic Theory: Agonism as an Affirmation of Difference,' which was presented at the 2000 Political Studies Association Conference at the London School of Economics on a panel on 'Nietzsche and Democratic Theory' with Ian Donaldson as the second paper presenter, Iain MacKenzie as discussant, and Diana Coole as Chair. I would like to thank the two anonymous reviewers for *Contemporary Political Theory* for their helpful and encouraging comments.

2 Hatab (1995, 96–108) tries to sidestep this problem by maintaining that that substantive equality is not necessary for Nietzschean democracy. All that is required, he says, is a fair and open opportunity to compete that is consistent with differential outcomes for the winners and losers of the contest. Whether this simply domesticates Nietzsche by turning him into a free market political liberal is a point worth considering.

3 Those who are critical of the employment of Nietzsche's thought for democratic ends have attacked Connolly's use of Nietzsche's theme of *ressentiment* to argue for economic equality. It is true that Connolly has made this argument (see, in particular, Connolly, 1988, 171–173) and that Nietzsche himself would not care much about economic equality. Nevertheless, it is also clear that in the main Connolly's deployment of Nietzsche — and of Foucault and Deleuze — has not been to make arguments for economic equality but to explore forms of power that reside below the domain of standard democratic contestation or reflection. See, for example, his analysis of Tocqueville in Connolly, 1995, Chapter 6. See also the exchange between Connolly and Mark Redhead (Redhead, 1997; Connolly, 1997).

4 Deleuze perhaps makes this point more explicitly than Foucault: 'Marginals have always inspired fear in us, and a slight horror. They are not clandestine enough' (Deleuze and Parnet, 1987, 139).

5 Against the man who can bear the historical within himself, Nietzsche contrasts the fragility of those 'who possess so little of this power that they can perish from a single experience, from a single painful event, often and especially from a single subtle piece of injustice, like a man bleeding to death from a scratch' (Nietzsche, 1983, 62).

6 'The properties of a thing are effects on other 'things': if one removes other 'things', then a thing has no properties, i.e., there is no thing without other things, i.e., there is no 'thing in itself'' (Nietzsche, 1967b, 302).

7 For a more detailed account, see Widder (2003a).

8 As Nietzsche maintains, the revaluation of values does not mean a wholesale rejection of the judgements made by the slaves, but rather of the soil from which they grow: 'It goes without saying that I do not deny — unless I am a fool — that many actions called immoral ought to be avoided and resisted, or that many called moral ought to be done and encouraged — but I think the one should be encouraged and the other avoided *for other reasons than hitherto*. We have to *learn to think differently* — in order at last, perhaps very late on, to attain even more: *to feel differently*' (Nietzsche, 1982, 60).

9 As already mentioned, defenders of the aristocratic reading of Nietzsche like to point out to democratic Nietzscheans that this affirmation of one's adversaries applies only between noble beings of the same high rank and so cannot be turned into a democratic ethos that applies to the whole of society (see, for example, Redhead, 1997, 189). Nevertheless, to rest on this point is to overlook Nietzsche's implicit critique of noble morality in the *Genealogy*. Nietzsche makes clear that the nobles misunderstand the slaves, just as the slaves misunderstand the nobles (1967a, 37) and it is this misunderstanding that leads to their downfall. In treating the slaves as weak in simple opposition to their strength, the nobles fail to see the slaves as a threat. Ironically, the nobles' errors are a failure to extend affirmation to the slaves and a reduction of this difference to opposition.

10 In this regard, Nietzsche contends that 'during the greater part of the past the judges and punishers themselves were *not at all* conscious of dealing with a 'guilty person'' (1967a, 82). The result is a justice that avoids the mania that Foucault finds throughout modern disciplinary society to name character types to be observed, analysed, and disciplined.

11 See, for example, McNay, 1992 and 1994, which argue that Foucault's work maintains an unresolved ambivalence concerning the subject and power, holding to a concept of power as a positive force that includes resistances, yet never developing this idea and by default articulating an understanding of power as repression of the individual. Concomitant with this, the body is treated as a site of both inscription and resistance, but the lack of an essence makes such resistance impossible. Throughout McNay's analysis, it is taken as given that the dynamics of power relations are embodied in identity constitution and its failure. The depth of her misunderstanding can be seen in her turn to Habermasian communicative rationality as a supplement to Foucault's thought that resolves these difficulties. I have recently taken issue with readings of Foucault that ascribe to him an opposition between power and resistance in Widder (2003b).

12 As Foucault says, 'power is tolerable only on condition that it mask a substantial part of itself. Its success is proportional to its ability to hide its own mechanisms' (1990, 86).

13 '[I]n every society the production of discourse is at once controlled, selected, organized and redistributed by a certain number of procedures whose role is to ward off its powers and dangers, to gain mastery over its chance events, to evade its ponderous, formidable materiality' (Foucault, 1984, 109).

14 'The studies that follow, like the others I have done previously, are studies of 'history' by reason of the domain they deal with and the references they appeal to; but they are not the work of a 'historian.' Which does not mean that they summarize or synthesize work done by others. Considered from the standpoint of their 'pragmatics,' they are the record of a long and tentative exercise that needed to be revised and corrected again and again. The object was to learn to what extent the effort to think one's own history can free thought from what it silently thinks, and so enable it to think differently' (Foucault, 1985, 9).

15 'There is no discontinuity between them, as if one were dealing with two different levels (one microscopic and the other macroscopic); but neither is there homogeneity (as if the one were only the enlarged projection or miniaturization of the other); rather, one must conceive of the double conditioning of a strategy by the specificity of possible tactics, and of tactics by the strategic envelope that makes them work' (Foucault, 1990, 99–100).

16 'This means that in the relations of power, there is necessarily the possibility of resistance, for if there were no possibility of resistance — of violent resistance, of escape, of ruse, of strategies that reverse the situation — there would be no relations of power. This being the general form, I refuse to answer the question that I am often asked: 'But if power is everywhere, then there is no liberty'' (Foucault, 1988b, 12).

17 Without recounting the details here, see Foucault (1985, 1986, 1988a).

18 'I am not looking for an alternative; you can't find the solution of a problem in the solution of another problem raised at another moment by other people' (Foucault, 1988a, 343).
19 'And I could say that the modern 'formula' is desire, which is theoretically underlined and practically accepted, since you have to liberate your own desire. Acts are not very important, and pleasure — nobody knows what it is' (Foucault, 1988a, 359).
20 Thus, Foucault distances himself from the 'Californian cult of the self' and from the Sartrean theme of authenticity in self-creation (1988a, 349–351, 362).
21 'I like the word [curiosity]. It evokes 'care'; it evokes the care one takes of what exists and what might exist; a sharpened sense of reality, but one that is never immobilized before it; a readiness to find what surrounds us strange and odd; a certain determination to throw off familiar ways of thought and to look at the same things in a different way…; a lack of respect for the traditional hierarchies of what is important and fundamental' (Foucault, 1988c, 328).
22 These words are those of a questioner, but Foucault states his agreement with them.
23 'Another old accusation: that I take up particular problems in order to distract attention from others that are general and essential. I repeat: what I take up *is* general, perhaps more so than anything else. We live in a social universe in which the formation, circulation, and utilization of knowledge present a fundamental question. If the accumulation of capital has been an essential feature of our society, the accumulation of knowledge has not been any less so. Now, the exercise, production, and accumulation of this knowledge cannot be dissociated from the mechanisms of power; complex relations exist which must be analyzed' (Foucault, 1991, 164–165).
24 'Segments depend on binary machines which can be very varied if need be…And they are not roughly dualistic, they are rather dichotomic: they can operate diachronically (if you are neither *a* nor *b*, then you are *c*: dualism has shifted, and no longer relates to simultaneous elements to choose between, but successive choices; if you are neither black nor white, you are a half-breed; if you are neither man nor woman, you are a transvestite: each time the machine with binary elements will produce binary choices between elements which are not present at the first cutting-up)' (Deleuze and Parnet, 1987, 128).
25 Deleuze and Guattari hold that this molecular level corresponds to Foucaultian micro-powers, and yet they seem systematically to misread Foucault on this point, treating power and resistance in Foucault as oppositional forces, although as should be clear from this paper's earlier analysis of Foucault this is a mistaken portrayal: resistance for him results not simply from opposition but from discontinuities inherent in power relations themselves. Deleuze and Guattari use their reading to posit a dynamic of desire which they say undercuts Foucault's analysis of power: 'Our only points of disagreement with Foucault are the following: (1) to us the assemblages seem fundamentally to be assemblages not of power but of desire (desire is always assembled), and power seems to be a stratified dimension of the assemblage; (2) the diagram and abstract machine have lines of flight that are primary, which are not phenomena of resistance or counterattack in an assemblage, but cutting edges of creation and deteritorialization' (Deleuze and Guattari, 1987, 531). Deleuze elsewhere provides a more sustained and subtle account of his differences with Foucault (see Deleuze, 1997), but his analysis is still based on the contention that for Foucault power and resistance are in opposition. That contention and the resulting critique, however, are absent from Deleuze's monograph on Foucault (Deleuze, 1988).
26 'A field, a heterogeneous smooth space, is wedded to a very particular type of multiplicity: nonmetric, acentrered, rhizomatic multiplicities that occupy space without 'counting' it and can 'be explored only by legwork.' They do not meet the visual condition of being observable from a point in space external to them; an example of this is the system of sounds, or even of colors, as opposed to Euclidean space' (Deleuze and Guattari, 1987, 371).
27 See Deleuze (1997, 189–190). Nietzsche perhaps best expresses the Deleuzo–Guattarian concept of desire and its affirmative character when he writes: 'Physiologists should think before putting

down the instinct of self-preservation as the cardinal instinct of an organic being. A living thing seeks above all to *discharge* its strength — life itself is *will to power*; self-preservation is only one of the indirect and most frequent *results*' (Nietzsche, 1966, 21; see also 1967b, 344).

28 'The nomad is not at all the same as the migrant; for the migrant goes principally from one point to another, even if the second point is uncertain, unforeseen, or not well localized. But the nomad goes from point to point only as a consequence and as a factual necessity; in principle, points for him are relays along a trajectory' (Deleuze, and Guattari, 1987, 380).

29 Some of these are detailed in Deleuze and Guattari (361–423), but it can be said the Deleuze's entire corpus is itself a sustained exposition of this form of thought.

30 'The *clinamen*, as the minimum angle, has meaning only between a straight line and a curve, the curve and its tangent, and constitutes the original curvature of the movement of the atom. The clinamen is the smallest angle by which the atom deviates from a straight path. It is a passage to the limit, an exhaustion, a paradoxical 'exhaustive' model' (Deleuze and Guattari, 1987, 361). For further analysis of the Epicurean *clinamen,* see also Deleuze (1990) and Widder (2002, 76–82).

References

Adorno, T. (1974) *Minima Moralia: Reflections on Damaged Life*, E.F.N. Jephcott (trans.), London and New York: Verso.

Ansell-Pearson, K. (1995) 'The Significance of Michel Foucault's Reading of Nietzsche: Power, the Subject, and Political Theory', in P.R. Sedgwick (ed.) *Nietzsche: A Critical Reader*, Oxford: Blackwell, pp. 13–30.

Appel, F. (1999) *Nietzsche Contra Democracy*, Ithaca and London: Cornell University Press.

Borges, J.L. (1993) 'Funes, the Memorious', in *Ficciones*, Intro. John Sturrock, London: Everyman's Library.

Connolly, W. (1988) *Political Theory and Modernity*, New York and Oxford: Basil Blackwell.

Connolly, W. (1995) *The Ethos of Pluralization*, Minneapolis and London: University of Minnesota Press.

Connolly, W. (1997) 'Reworking the democratic imagination', *The Journal of Political Philosophy* 5.2: 194–202.

Deleuze, G. (1988) *Foucault*, Séan Hand (trans.), London: The Athlone Press.

Deleuze, G. (1990) 'Lucretius and the Simulacrum', in Constantin V. Boundas, Mark Lester and Charles Stivale (ed.) (translator) *The Logic of Sense*, New York: Columbia University Press, pp. 266–279.

Deleuze, G. (1994) *Difference and Repetition*, Paul Patton. (trans.), London: The Athlone Press.

Deleuze, G. (1997) 'Desire and Pleasure', in A. I. Davidson (ed.) *Foucault and his Interlocutors*, Chicago and London: University of Chicago Press, pp. 183–192.

Deleuze, G. and Guattari, F. (1983) *Anti-Oedipus: Capitalism and Schizophrenia*, Robert Hurley, Mark Seem and Helen R. Lane (trans.), Minneapolis: University of Minnesota Press.

Deleuze, G. and Guattari, F. (1987) *A Thousand Plateaus: Capitalism and Schizophrenia*, Brian Massumi (trans.), Minneapolis: University of Minnesota Press.

Deleuze, G. and Parnet, C. (1987) *Dialogues*, Hugh Tomlinson and Barbara Habberjam (trans.), New York: Columbia University Press.

Detwiler, B. (1990) *Nietzsche and the Politics of Aristocratic Radicalism*, Chicago: University of Chicago Press.

Donaldson, I. (2002) 'Hierarchy and Ontological Dualism: Rethinking Gilles Deleuze's Nietzsche for Political Philosophy', *History of Political Thought* 23.4: 654–669.

Foucault, M. (ed.) (1975) *I Pierre Rivière, Having Slaughtered my Mother, my Sister, and my Brother: A Case of Parricide in the 19th Century*, Frank Jellinek (trans.), Lincoln, NE and London: University of Nebraska Press.

Foucault, M. (1977a) 'Nietzsche, Genealogy, History', in D.F. Bouchard (ed.) (trans.) *Language, Counter-Memory, Practice: Selected Essays and Interviews*, Ithaca: Cornell University Press, pp. 139–164.

Foucault, M. (1977b) 'Revolutionary Action: 'Until Now'', in D.F. Bouchard (ed.) *Language, Counter-Memory, Practice: Selected Essays and Interviews*, Ithaca: Cornell University Press, pp. 218–233.

Foucault, M. (1979) *Discipline and Punish: The Birth of the Prison*, Alan Sheridan (trans.), New York: Vintage Books.

Foucault, M. (1980) *Herculine Barbin: Being the Recently Discovered Memoirs of a Nineteenth-Century French Hermaphrodite*, Richard McDougall (trans.), New York: Pantheon Books.

Foucault, M. (1982) 'Afterword: The Subject and Power', in H. Dreyfus and P. Rabinow (eds.) *Michel Foucault: Beyond Structuralism and Hermeneutics*, Chicago: University of Chicago Press, pp. 208–226.

Foucault, M. (1984) 'The Order of Discourse', in M. Shapiro (ed.) *Language and Politics*, New York: NYU Press.

Foucault, M. (1985) *The History of Sexuality, Volume 2: The Uses of Pleasure*, Robert Hurley (trans.), London and New York: Penguin Books.

Foucault, M. (1986) *The History of Sexuality, Volume 3: The Care of the Self*, Robert Hurley (trans.), London and New York: Penguin Books.

Foucault, M. (1988a) 'On the Genealogy of Ethics: Overview of a Work in Progress', in P. Rabinow (ed.) *The Foucault Reader*, New York: Pantheon Books, pp. 340–372.

Foucault, M. (1988b) 'The Ethic of Care for the Self as a Practice of Freedom', in J. Bernauer and D. Rasumusson (eds.) *The Final Foucault*, Cambridge, MA and London: The MIT Press.

Foucault, M. (1988c) 'The Masked Philosopher', in DK Lawrence (ed), Alan Sheridan *et al.*, (trans.) *Philosophy, Politics, Culture*, London: Routledge, pp. 323–330.

Foucault, M. (1988d) 'Politics and Ethics: An Interview', in P. Rabinow (ed.) *The Foucault Reader*, New York: Pantheon Books, pp. 373–380.

Foucault, M. (1990) *The History of Sexuality, Volume 1: An Introduction*, Robert Hurley (trans.), New York: Vintage Books.

Foucault, M. (1991) *Remarks on Marx: Conversations with Duccio Trombadori*, R. James Goldstein and James Cascaito (trans.), New York: Semiotext(e).

Hatab, L. (1995) *A Nietzschean Defense of Democracy: an Experimentation in Postmodern Politics*, Chicago and La Salle: Open Court Publishing Company.

Kazarian, Ed. (1998) 'Deleuze, Perversion and Politics', *International Studies in Philosophy* 30(1): 91–106.

Kaufmann, W. (1974) *Nietzsche: Philosopher, Psychologist, Antichrist*, 4th ed, Princeton: Princeton University Press.

McNay, L. (1992) *Foucault and Feminism: Power, Gender and the Self*, Oxford: Polity Press.

McNay, L. (1994) *Foucault: A Critical Introduction*, Oxford: Polity Press.

Nietzsche, F. (1966) *Beyond Good and Evil: Prelude to a Philosophy of the Future*, Walter Kaufmann (trans.), New York: Vintage Books.

Nietzsche, F. (1967a) *On the Genealogy of Morals*, Walter Kaufmann and R.J. Hollingdale (trans.), New York: Vintage Books.

Nietzsche, F. (1967b) *The Will to Power*, Walter Kaufmann and R.J. Hollingdale (trans.), New York: Vintage Books.

Nietzsche, F. (1974) *The Gay Science*, Walter Kaufmann (trans.), New York: Vintage Books.

Nietzsche, F. (1982) *Daybreak*, R.J. Hollingdale (trans.), Cambridge: Cambridge University Press.

Nietzsche, F. (1983) 'On the Uses and Disadvantages of History for Life', in R.J. Hollingdale (trans.) *Untimely Meditations*, Cambridge: Cambridge University Press, pp. 57–123.

Nietzsche, F. (1990) *Twilight of the Idols*, R.J. Hollingdale (trans.), Harmondsworth: Penguin Books.

Owen, D. (1995) *Nietzsche, Politics and Modernity: A Critique of Liberal Reason*, London, Thousand Oaks, and New Delhi: Sage Publications.

Redhead, M. (1997) 'Nietzsche and Liberal Democracy: A relationship of Antagonistic Indebtedness?' *The Journal of Political Philosophy* 5.2: 183–193.

Rorty, R. (1989) *Contingency, Irony, and Solidarity*, Cambridge: Cambridge University Press.

Todorov, T. (1984) *The Conquest of America: The Question of the Other*, Richard Howard (trans.), New York: Harper & Row, Publishers.

Widder, N. (2002) *Genealogies of Difference*, Urbana and Chicago: University of Illinois Press.

Widder, N. (2003a) 'Nietzsche', in D. Boucher and P. Kelly (eds) *Political Thinkers: From Socrates to the Present*, Oxford: Oxford University Press.

Widder, N. (2003b) 'Foucault and Power Revisited', Paper Presented at the 2003 Political Studies Association Conference in Leicester, UK.

[4]

NIETZSCHE AND THE NAZIS: THE IMPACT OF NATIONAL SOCIALISM ON THE PHILOSOPHY OF NIETZSCHE

*Charles M. Yablon**

INTRODUCTION

Time moves in only one direction, but causation moves in two. That prior events affect those that follow is fundamental to our understanding of the world, Humean skepticism notwithstanding. But almost equally fundamental to our modern understanding of the world is the realization that absolute knowledge of the past is not possible, that our perception of historical events must always and inevitably be shaped by current concerns and perspectives, including our knowledge and judgment about events subsequent to those being studied. In short, the past affects the future, but the future also affects the past.

This is perhaps particularly true when the historical subjects involved are not discrete and isolated events, like the Second Punic War or the reign of Henry the Eighth, but philosophical ideas associated with a particular historical figure. Two forms of philosophical history uneasily co-exist within the modern academy. One seeks, within the limitations of all historical inquiry, to understand the works of Plato, or Aristotle, or Hegel, as products of their age, to recapture, if you will, the original intentions of their authors. Such works are philologically informed and very sensitive to historical context. The other form of scholarship is more concerned with taking philosophical ideas associated with the works of Plato, Aristotle, Hegel or others, and analyzing, refining, modifying and extending them in light of modern day issues and concerns. These scholars are less concerned with historical accuracy than with the cogency, power and philosophical coherence of their positions. Of course, these are tendencies and predilections rather than exclusive categories. Even the most

* Professor of Law, Benjamin N. Cardozo School of Law. I wish to thank all the participants in the Nietzsche conference and particularly Peter Goodrich, the conference organizer, for support and helpful comments.

freewheeling post-modern Aristotelians or Hegelians feel a certain obligation to find a source for their idea in the writings of the Master. Even the most scrupulous historicists will explain that they study Plato in the original Attic Greek because his ideas are still relevant and important to us today.

Accordingly, when we speak of the philosophy of Aristotle, or Hegel, or Nietzsche, we are speaking of both more and less than the philosophical ideas in the mind of a single individual who wrote books many years ago. We are speaking about a set of ideas, and perceptions of those ideas, which had their historical origins in the writings of a specific individual, but which can and do change in response to subsequent events.

This paper is titled *Nietzsche and the Nazis: The Impact of National Socialism on the Philosophy of Nietzsche.* I hope that my prior discussion of causation and philosophical history makes it clear that this title is neither a misprint, nor an impossibility, nor a category mistake. Rather, it is an attempt to examine how the extensive adoption, interpretation and use of Nietzschean philosophical concepts by the Nazi regime, including, most importantly, the philosophers and interpreters of Nazi ideology, have affected and influenced the perception and interpretations of Nietzschean philosophy in the periods that followed. The existence of such an impact seems both undeniable and inevitable. Nietzsche was by far the most prominent and respected philosopher utilized by the Nazis as a source and justification for their ideology. Nietszchean concepts pervade Nazi propaganda, as well as the more academic work of Nazi philosophers. Indeed, it is not an exaggeration to say that Nietzsche's work occupied a position of influence and authority in Nazi Germany not unlike that of Marx' work in the Soviet Union.

For post-Nazi era interpreters of Nietzsche, the central role that Nietzschean philosophy played in the Third Reich is an unavoidable fact, yet one that poses enormous difficulty for subsequent scholarship. For the many who find Nietzschean philosophy brilliant, deeply rewarding of intense study, and the source of powerful insights about humanity and the world, must somehow explain how the most brutal and murderous regime in the history of the world, and a nation with considerable philosophical sophistication, could find justification and support in those same works.

It is tempting perhaps, to say that the use of Nietzschean philosophy by the Nazis was largely pretextual, that Nietzsche was not so much the source of Nazi ideology as a convenient prop, a famous name to lend some intellectual respectability to the brutal, racist and stupid ideas that made up the true Nazi ideology. There is undoubtedly much truth to this. Yet the fact remains that when the Nazi apologists sought an intellectual forebear to justify their horrific regime, they had the whole rich German philosophical tradition to choose from. It was no accident that they chose Nietzsche rather than Kant, or Hegel, or Liebniz. They saw something in Nietzschean philosophy that they could use. Indeed, they saw many things.

It is also tempting to say that the Nazis perverted the philosophy of Nietzsche, distorted many concepts, like the *ubermensch*, so that they were vastly different from their original meaning, and simply ignored other Nietzschean concepts that were incompatible with Nazi ideology. Again, there is undoubtedly much truth to this. But in order for this to be a fully satisfactory answer to the problem of Nietzsche and the Nazis, one must explain why certain accounts of Nietzschean philosophy which modify some concepts and de-emphasize others constitute "perversions" of the philosophy, while others are merely "interpretations." In short, one needs not just a theory of interpretation, but also a theory that will enable one to recognize incorrect, invalid or perverted interpretations of complex and ambiguous texts. In our post-modern world, informed, in no small part, by the philosophy of Nietzsche itself, it is hard to find such theories and harder still to believe in them. These statements are not meant as an indictment either of Nietzsche or of Nietzschean philosophy. Rather, they are intended to elucidate the way in which the Nazis' use of Nietzschean philosophy created deep and serious issues for the subsequent understanding of Nietzschean philosophy.

Let me be perfectly clear. I am not arguing, as some have previously done, that Nietzschean philosophy was, in fact, a forerunner of Nazi ideology, or at least contained the seeds of Nazism in some of its aspects. Even less plausible and more repugnant is the claim that Nietzsche himself was a proto-Nazi or had any sympathy for Nazi ideas and doctrines. I will stipulate that Nietzsche himself, unlike his egregious sister, was not an anti-Semite, but tended rather to philo-Semitism. He was not a German nationalist, but generally espoused a pan-European perspective. Indeed, to the extent that any ahistorical statements can be made with certainty, it seems certain to me that the historical Nietzsche would have been disgusted and repelled by Nazi ideas and Nazi ideology. However, except for those who are willing to limit the proper interpretative scope of a text to the ascertainment of the actual intentions of its author, I do not see how this fact makes much of a difference to the problem I am posing.

Because it is an equally undeniable fact that the Nazis interpreted Nietzsche. They studied him assiduously, quoted him extensively, analyzed and expanded on key concepts, de-emphasized others and even "corrected" his "mistakes." In short, the Nazis engaged in pretty much the same enterprise we recognize as the study of philosophy, and concluded that the philosophy of Nietzsche anticipated and justified their goals of world domination and racial hegemony. These were not people lacking in philosophical sophistication. Indeed, it is probably the case that during the 1930s and early 1940s, the philosophers of the Third Reich constituted the most active and well-trained "interpretive community" of Nietzschean scholars in the world.

This paper is divided into two parts. The first part, which draws mainly from the excellent book by Steven Aschheim, *The Nietzsche Legacy in Germany 1890-1990*,[1] provides a brief overview of the facts concerning the relationship of Nietzschean philosophy to national socialism, and seeks to describe the ways in which certain key Nietzschean concepts were understood and interpreted by philosophers during the Nazi period. The second part of this paper examines the ways in which writings about Nietzsche in the post-Nazi period have responded to the Nazis' interpretation and use of Nietzschean philosophy. I will seek to set out a brief taxonomy of responses to the Nazi interpretations of Nietszchean philosophy, both as a means of understanding some post-Nazi writing about Nietzsche and the impact that national socialism has had on the philosophy of Nietzsche.

I. Nietzschean Philosophy During the Nazi Period

During the 1930s and 1940s, the association of Nietzschean philosophy with national socialism was considered by many philosophically trained individuals to be quite evident and obvious. This view was held by many (but not all) Nazi proponents and sympathizers, and also by many strongly opposed to the Nazi regime, as well as philosophically trained individuals who were ambivalent about the rise of national socialism. Even before the Nazis obtained power, Nietzsche had become the favorite philosopher of the radical right in post-World War I Germany. A key figure in this development was Alfred Baumler, a professor of

[1] Steven E. Aschheim, The Nietzsche Legacy In Germany 1890-1990 (1992).

philosophy at the University of Berlin who was to become the Third Reich's authorized Nietzsche scholar. As early as 1931, Baumler portrayed Nietzsche as a prophet of Nazism, a primarily political thinker whose writings predicted the revolutionary conflicts in European society which the Nazis sought to bring about. Other well established Nietzscheans of the pre-Nazi period saw the rise of national socialism as a Nietzschean revolution which both fulfilled and elucidated the meaning of Nietzsche's work. For example, Ernst Horneffer, an editor of the *Nietzsche Archive* who in the pre-Nazi period is described by Ascheim as one of the foremost champions of a neo-pagan "Germanic Nietzscheanism"[2] had by 1934 become a committed Nazi who declared that Nietzsche did not belong to the nineteenth century but to "our time. It is as if he lingered on living among us."[3] Similarly, Gottfried Benn, a talented German expressionist whose work in the pre-Nazi period focused on Nietzschean nihilism and the death of God, saw, in national socialism, at least for a time, the possibility of a transcendent Nietzschean community that was both "primal and future oriented,"[4] since it portended the creation of a "new biological type—the Aryan, whose great task it was to do battle against decadence in all its guises."[5]

Whatever other sins these Nietzschean Nazis were guilty of, it seems clear from Ascheim's account that they were not insincere. They recognized that there were important differences and inconsistencies between the writings of Nietzsche and the doctrines of national socialism (although they obviously believed that the affinities and similarities were even greater). Accordingly, they developed a hermeneutics of Nietzschean thought which not only permitted reinterpretations and new understandings of Nietzsche's work, but actually justified such reinterpretations as superior to contemporaneous nineteenth century understandings of Nietzsche, including perhaps, even those of Nietzsche himself. On this view, it was the triumph of the Nazi regime itself which for the first time made a full understanding of Nietzsche possible. This was the meaning of Ernst Horneffer's statement that Nietzsche belongs "to our own time." It was echoed by Alfred Rosenberg's statement in 1944 that only "in our time" was a true appreciation of Nietzsche possible.[6]

At the level of popular culture in the Third Reich, these

[2] *Id.* at 222.
[3] *Id.* at 236.
[4] *Id.* at 68.
[5] *Id.* at 69.
[6] *Id.* at 237.

hermeneutic issues were cast aside, and Nietzsche was simply portrayed as the great prophet of the Nazi revolution. In the words of Franz Neumann, Nietzsche "provided National Socialism with an intellectual father who had greatness and wit, whose style was beautiful and not abominable, who was able to articulate the resentment against both monopoly capitalism and the rising proletariat."[7] At a ceremony commemorating Germany's victory over Russia in the First World War, three books were placed in the Tannenberg Memorial: *Mein Kampf*, Alfred Rosenberg's *Myth of the Twentieth Century*, and *Thus Spake Zarathustra*.[8] Nietzschean concepts provided a critical source and justification for many of the policies and reforms advocated in the Third Reich. Assaults on scientific objectivity were made in the name of Nietzsche, "the intellectual Fuhrer to a new culture." Concepts of universal law and equal rights based on immanent reason were rejected in favor of a Nietzschean conception of law as embodying "the strong unbreakable tie of the law to the power-political necessity of every Volk." Eugenic measures were justified by Nietzschean concepts of biologism and the doctrine of "holy cruelty." Yet, as Aschheim reminds us, although Nietzsche's works were published and distributed throughout the Third Reich "at a dizzy pace," those published works first went through a process of "appropriate editing."[9]

Although Nietzsche was in some respects the official philosopher of the Third Reich, unlike Hitler and the Nazi regime itself, he was not immune from criticism. It was possible in the Nazi era to espouse philosophies and doctrines totally antithetical to Nietzscheanism, to criticize Nietzschean concepts as wrong or incoherent, just so long as one remained a committed Nazi. For example, the Nietzschean rejection of objective value was criticized by neo-Kantian German philosophers, who argued that such a concept of objective value was necessary to ground the doctrines of national socialism. They sought to reinterpret Nietzsche not as a proponent of extreme relativism but as someone whose insights could be limited to an *a posteriori* account of human will and action.[10]

More severe critics of Nietzsche than the neo-Kantians were representatives of the Christian churches, who recognized in Nietzsche a powerful antagonist. Despite the expurgated nature of the Nietzschean texts being published in Germany, these critics

[7] *Id.* at 235.

[8] *Id.* at 239.

[9] *Id.* at 245.

[10] *See id.* at 256.

had no difficulty citing Nietzsche's "antinationalist, antiracist and pro-Jewish positions" as grounds for his rejection as philosopher of national socialism.[11] The fact that these groups and many other anti-Nietzscheans were free to criticize Nietzsche as insufficiently reflective of true national socialism indicates that the many other German intellectuals, including most German Nietzscheans, who saw Nietzsche as the great prophet and forerunner of national socialism were likely to have held such views sincerely, a reflection of serious study of Nietzsche's work, and not merely to ingratiate themselves with the current regime.

Even more indicative of the widespread belief among intellectuals in Nazi Germany that Nietzsche was the great philosopher of national socialism was the acceptance of this idea among intellectuals trained in other traditions. After all, for Nietzscheans like Baumler and Horneffer, the association of Nietzsche with national socialism, however sincerely held, was also a good career move given their chosen specialty. It is even more significant, therefore, that many non-Nietzscheans, both in and outside the Third Reich, saw essentially the same connection. We have already noted how German neo-Kantians, in an attempt to provide the proper philosophical grounding for national socialism, sought to merge Kant and Nietzsche. Outside the Third Reich, in 1934, Carl Jung began a five-year marathon seminar analyzing Nietzsche's *Zarathustra.* The analysis, of course, was a Jungian one, with Jung detecting a powerful resonance between Nietzsche's unconscious and the collective unconscious of modern man, particularly in the form it was taking in Nazi Germany. Jung's statements in that seminar indicate a deep ambivalence about the Nazi regime, praising it faintly at times and referring to "this modern political evil" at others. He did not waver, however, in his identification of Nietzsche with events in Nazi Germany, describing Nietzsche as "in a way the great prophet of what is happening in Germany" yet also viewing the actually Nazi understanding of Nietzsche's work as somewhat crude and pathological.[12]

Finally, there is Heidegger. The extent to which Heidegger supported national socialism in the early years of the Nazi regime, and had, by his own account, rejected it by the late 1930s, is a complex and much debated issue. What appears beyond dispute, however, is that for Heidegger, his position on national socialism was inextricably tied to his acceptance or rejection of Nietzscheanism. While Heidegger's works, particularly in the

[11] *Id.* at 254.
[12] *See id.* at 260-62.

early 1930s, contain positive references to Nietzsche and Nietzschean concepts, Heidegger claimed to have broken with Nazism by the late 1930s, and cited as evidence of that his lectures on Nietzsche in 1936-1937 and in 1939-40 which have been published and translated as a four-volume treatise titled "*Nietzsche.*" The extent to which these lectures constitute a repudiation of Nazism is certainly open to debate, although they clearly reject the sort of simplified political Nietzsche of Baumler and other Nietzschean Nazis. For our purposes, it is sufficient to note that Heidegger too viewed his positions on Nietzsche to be intimately linked to his position on national socialism.

In short, there can be no serious dispute that during the Nazi period, Nietzschean philosophy was strongly identified with national socialism, was seen as providing Nazism with intellectual depth and potential philosophical justification. This view was held not only by Nietzschean scholars in the Third Reich, but by German intellectuals trained in other philosophical traditions, as well as by many non-German, non-Nazi intellectuals.

Yet Nietzschean pronouncements were never accepted blindly. Despite the expurgated versions used as school texts, Nietzschean scholars were well aware that while many Nietzschean concepts seemed compatible with or even to instantiate basic principles of national socialism, others Nietzschean concepts seemed incompatible or downright subversive to Nazi ideas. Intellectual work was required by Nietzchean Nazis so that these latter concepts could be reinterpreted, clarified and understood in new ways.

Among the Nietzschean concepts favored by the Nazis was undoubtedly the "will to power." The notion that one could escape nihilistic despair by an act of will whereby good and evil were transcended to create a more primitive, vital and natural society seemed like a thorough endorsement of the basic goals and methods of the Nazi regime. Similarly, the concepts of *ubermensch* and the much less used Nietzschean term, *untermensch*, were also of immense value to the Nazis in providing intellectually respectable pedigrees to brutal racist categories.[13] The Nazis also found much value and support in Nietzsche's biologism, his emphasis on bodily health and vigor. Unlike their racial and nationalist agendas, the Nazi policies of eugenics and euthanasia, as well as repression of homosexuals, could be clearly and easily justified by quotations from Nietzschean texts. Hadn't Nietzsche written in *The Will to Power* that "[s]ympathy for

[13] *See id.* at 237.

decadents, equal rights for the ill-constituted—that would be the profoundest immorality, that would be antinature itself as morality!"?[14]

What about those Nietzschean concepts which appeared inconsistent with Nazi doctrine? Different concepts created different levels of difficulty. Nietzsche's rejection of collective values in favor of a heroic individualism, for example, could be modified by emphasizing those statements where Nietzsche saw the individual as part of a larger historical destiny, and by Nietzsche's biologism, which often manifested itself in discussions of the vitality of various "races" and species. Nietzsche's rejection of nineteenth century German nationalism and his vision of the "good European" was converted by the Nazis into a useful recruiting tool among non-German Europeans sympathetic to the Nazi cause. Non-German volunteers for the Waffen SS, (and there were a significant number) were often inspired by a Nietzschean vision of good Europeans forging a new, war-like aristocracy of the future.[15]

With respect to Nietzsche's many condemnations of anti-Semitism and "the race swindle" however, the Nazis needed and discovered a more radical reinterpretation of Nietzsche. Aside from Baumler's assertion that, in his personal life, Nietzsche really didn't care much for Jews at all, [16] they pointed to Nietzsche's many attacks on Christianity and priestly religion generally as indications of his true and much more thoroughgoing anti-Semitism. Nietzsche's statements in, for example, *Genealogy of Morals*, where Christianity itself is presented as a secret Jewish plot, through which "Israel, with its vengefulness and revaluation of all values, has hitherto triumphed again and again over all other ideals, over all nobler ideals"[17] was be viewed as a form of anti-Christian anti-Semitism, and the "nobler values" presumed to be the Volkish ideology of the Third Reich. As for Nietzsche's claim that there were no pure races and his suspicion of the "race swindle," these were viewed as merely an empirical mistake on his part, ameliorated by Nietzsche's obvious concern for eugenics and racial improvement.[18]

In short, it is beyond dispute that during the Nazi period,

---

[14] FRIEDRICH NIETZSCHE, THE WILL TO POWER para 734, at 389 (Walter Kaufman ed., Walter Kaufman & R. J. Hollingdale trans., 1967). *See generally* ASCHHEIM, *supra* note 1, at 243.

[15] *See* ASCHHEIM, *supra* note 1, at 247-48.

[16] *See id.* at 250.

[17] FRIEDRICH NIETZSCHE, *On the Genealogy of Morals*, *in* BASIC WRITINGS OF NIETZSCHE 439, 471 (Walter Kaufmann ed. & trans., 1968).

[18] *See* ASCHHEIM, *supra* note 1, at 244.

many and probably most scholars and intellectuals, Nietzscheans and non-Nietzscheans, Nazis and non-Nazis, geniuses and intellectual hacks, all viewed Nietzsche as a forerunner, a source and a potential justification for national socialist ideas and practices.

II. THE EFFECT OF NATIONAL SOCIALISM ON THE PHILOSOPHY OF NIETZSCHE

What are we to make of the strong identification of Nietzsche with Nazi ideology during the period of the Third Reich? For many, particularly in the immediate post-war period, it led to the condemnation of Nietzsche and Nietzschean philosophy. After all, if most of the trained Nietzschean experts, or if you prefer, most of the Nietzschean interpretive community, identified Nietzsche with Nazi ideas, wasn't the characterization of Nietzsche as a proto-Nazi likely to be correct? This argument has, of course, raged for years, and I am not going to add anything to it here, except to point out that the argument itself only makes sense if one takes a fairly determinate view regarding the meaning and interpretation of texts. That is, if you believe the writings of Nietzsche have a fixed and determinate meaning which can be ascertained through the correct hermeneutic process, then the question of whether the ideas set forth in the Nietzschean texts corresponds to those of the Nazis is at least intelligible and coherent, if not necessarily answerable.

If, however, one is inclined to view the meaning of texts, particularly complex aphoristic ones, as relatively indeterminate, malleable and contingent over time, then the fact that a text has been interpreted a certain way at a particular time sheds little light on its actual meaning. Indeed the very project of ascertaining true or actual meaning begins to seem misguided.

However, recognition of the indeterminacy of textual interpretation raises a different question, a question not about the meaning of Nietzsche prior to the Nazis, but about the meaning of Nietzsche *after* the Nazis. If the interpretation and understanding of Nietzsche is indeed relatively indeterminate, malleable, and contingent over time, then how have the meaning of those texts been affected by the indisputable fact that they can be and have been interpreted and understood to justify the most evil and destructive regime in world history? The facts concerning the Nazi interpretation of Nietzsche, the knowledge that such vicious, evil readings of the texts are available, that they were made, debated and believed by serious scholars, must necessarily inform the work and the interpretations of every student of Nietzsche who has written about him since that time. In the pages that follow, I will attempt to give a preliminary taxonomy of the kinds of responses that this knowledge has generated in post-Nazi writings about Nietzsche.

The first response, perhaps unsurprisingly, is denial, both implicit and explicit, a refusal to recognize that the Nazi interpretations of Nietzsche could possibly constitute sincere, genuine and sophisticated understandings of the texts. Consider, for example, the essay by Walter Kaufmann which introduces his translations of the *Basic Writings of Nietzsche*.[19] In that essay, Kaufmann talks about the widespread influence of Nietzsche's works, not only on philosophers, but on literature, psychology and other humanistic endeavors. Among the many he names as influenced by Nietzschean ideas are Freud, Sartre, Buber, Camus, Malraux, Bernard Shaw, James Joyce, and virtually every "German philosopher of note" since Nietzsche's time, with the single exception of Husserl.[20] Of course, most of these people cannot by the broadest stretch of the imagination be considered faithful interpreters of Nietzsche, and Kaufmann makes no such claim. Rather he says that they were people on whose work Nietzsche's ideas had an impact. For example, Kaufmann approvingly quotes Freud's statement that Nietzsche's "premonitions and insights often agree in the most amazing manner with the laborious results of psychoanalysis," and states that some of Sartre's best known literary works contain "dozens of echoes of Nietzsche's writings." But Kaufmann's listing of the various intellectual influences of Nietzsche in the twentieth century, extensive though it is, contains a curious omission. Clearly there was another group of influential thinkers in the early twentieth century who also believed that Nietzsche's work contained "premonitions and insights" that often agreed with their own, and whose work also often contains "echoes of Nietzsche's writings." Yet Kaufmann chooses simply to exclude Nazis and Nazi thought from his otherwise expansive list of those influenced by Nietzsche's works.

Later in the same essay, Kaufmann explicitly rejects the claim that Nietzsche was a "Nazi philosopher" as an "absurdity" that can only be held by those showing either "rank ignorance" or "an

---

[19] *See generally Introduction to* FRIEDRICH NIETZSCHE, BASIC WRITINGS OF NIETZSCHE (Walter Kaufmann ed. & trans., 1968).

[20] *Id* at ix-x.

incredible lack of intellectual integrity."[21] As a lawyer, I perceive in these words a familiar litigation strategy—restate your opponent's position in the weakest formulation possible, and then attack it vigorously. Kaufmann can easily deny that Nietzsche was a Nazi. He can much less easily deny that Nietzschean ideas had an impact on Nazi thought, or that all those who saw parallels between Nietzschean ideas and Nazi thought were either ignorant or guilty of a lack of intellectual integrity. Yet Kaufmann dedicated his life to a noble attempt to deny precisely that. His translations and commentaries on Nietzsche, written after the Nazi period, are designed to set forth an authoritative, positive, non-Nazi interpretation of Nietzsche as the only intellectually honest possible reading. Like many forceful advocates, however, Kaufmann is always in danger of overstating his case. In attempting to deny that anything in Nietzsche's writings can plausibly be interpreted to support Nazi ideas, he offers, as authoritative, positive readings of Nietzsche, concepts that are no more inherently plausible than the Nazi concepts they are intended to replace. For example, in footnotes to his translation of the term "blond beast" in *Genealogy of Morals*, Kaufmann takes pains to provide a non-racial interpretation, associating blondness with "the beast, the lion" rather than with Aryans. While this reading is not clearly wrong, it is certainly hard to reconcile with the phrase "blond Germanic beast" which appears in the very next paragraph of the *Genealogy*.[22]

The project of denying the validity of the Nazi interpretation of Nietzsche by positing a correct authoritative non-Nazi reading of Nietzsche runs afoul of many of the same problems that the Nazi interpreters of Nietzsche encountered. Indeed, it threatens to become a mirror image of the Nazi project. Some concepts fit easily into a positive non-Nazi reading of Nietzsche, but others, the will to power, the *ubermensch*, the Blond Beast, the very concepts the Nazis found so congenial, must be de-emphasized or reinterpreted or suppressed.

A second, rather different response to the Nazi interpretation of Nietzsche is what we might call "radical indeterminacy." This view denies the validity of the Nazi interpretation of Nietzsche by denying the possibility of making any single positive interpretation of Nietzschean works. Nietzsche's writings readily lend themselves to such a reading containing, as they do, contradictory statements on some matters, vague and aphoristic statements on many others, and a plethora of different styles and statements on many matters,

---

[21] *Id.* at xii.

[22] NIETZSCHE, *supra* note 17, at 477-78.

including the nature of truth itself. The problem is how to give an account of such radical indeterminacy without making Nietzsche's work appear hopelessly confused and incoherent.

One of the earliest thinkers to adopt this approach was Karl Jaspers. His book on Nietzsche, written in 1936, was a clear challenge to those Nazi thinkers, like Baumler, who sought to find in Nietzsche a coherent political philosophy. Instead, Jaspers emphasized the contradictions in Nietzsche's thought. He stated that one could ground a Nazi position "down to every detail" in Nietzsche's work, but that "one can see the exactly opposite position represented by Nietzsche with equal vehemence."[23] For Jaspers, Nietzsche's method was to embrace contradiction in order to free the mind from all ideological and other conceptual constraints, in order to achieve "systematically conscious domination of one's own thinking."

Another philosopher I would place in this same radical indeterminist tradition is Jacques Derrida. Although Derrida does not write expressly about Nazi interpretations of Nietzsche, in his famous essay, *Spurs*, Derrida confronts a more commonly accepted charge against Nietzsche, his hatred of women. Where others have found in Nietzsche's work only "incurable misogyny," Derrida finds three contradictory positions. First, "[w]oman is condemned, debased and despised as a figure or power of falsehood." Second, "Woman is condemned and despised as a figure or power of truth." Finally, "Beyond this double negation, woman is recognized, affirmed as a power of affirmation, dissimulation, as an artist, a dionysiac."[24] Accordingly, there is no single true Nietzschean position on women or any way of arriving at one, and if there is no Nietzschean truth about woman, neither is there a Nietzschean truth about anything else. As Derrida tells us:

> [T]here is no one truth of Nietzsche or of his text. The phrase one reads in *Beyond Good and Evil*, "these are only—my truths" .... *My* truths implies no doubt that these are not truths because they are multiple, variegated, contradictory. There is no one truth in itself, but what is more, even for me, even about me, the truth is plural."[25]

Of course, this Derridean position makes statements about Nietzsche which are themselves subject to a radical indeterminist

[23] KARL JASPERS, *Reply to My Critics*, *in* THE PHILOSOPHY OF KARL JASPERS 857-63 (Paul Arthur Schilpp ed., 1957).

[24] JACQUES DERRIDA, *Spurs: Nietzsche's Syles*, *in* A DERRIDA READER: BETWEEN THE BLINDS 370-71 (Peggy Kamuf ed., 1991).

[25] *Id.* at 373.

critique, but that is a subject for a different day, (or at least a different panel).

A third category of reaction is what we might call the dialectical response to the Nazi interpretation of Nietzsche. These thinkers considered the Nazi interpretation of Nietzsche a misreading, but not an ignorant or pretextual misreading. Rather, applying a dialectical approach to Nietzschean interpretation, they viewed the Nazi embrace of Nietzsche as an understandable, even predictable view of Nietzsche which was the product of the social, economic and psychological conditions under which it was made. These dialectical thinkers see Nietzsche as a prophetic voice who was doomed to be misunderstood, perhaps did not even fully understand his own message, but whose works helped propel a process whereby a fuller understanding of his own significance could later be achieved.

The paradigmatic work in this category is Adorno and Horkheimer's *Dialectic of Enlightenment.* Although utilizing concepts of dialectical reasoning derived from Hegel and Marx, Adorno and Horkheimer apply these insights to the Enlightenment itself, which is seen as simultaneously a tool for both popular liberation and oppression. Nietzsche, on this view, was one of the few nineteenth century thinkers to recognize the potential for oppression, the "nihilistic anti-life force" inherent in the progressivism of the Enlightenment. Adorno and Horkheimer compare Nietzsche to that other great flouter of nineteenth century enlightenment values, the Marquis de Sade, and see Nietzsche and Sade's *Juliette* as engaged in similar projects of critiquing the oppressiveness of Enlightenment thought and asserting a vital primitive resistance against concepts of rationality and conventional morality.

For Adorno and Horkheimer, the context in which Nietzschean ideas are set forth is critical. The Nazi exaltation of power, strength and barbarism over civilization and morality were indeed Nietzschean themes, but when coming from a little-read nineteenth century philosopher such statements were liberating attacks on a dominant world-view. Their adoption by a State power inevitably distorted and converted them to an instrument of oppression. As Adorno and Horkheimer state:

> By raising the cult of strength to a world-historical doctrine, German Fascism also took it to an absurd extreme. As a protest against civilization, the master's morality conversely represents the oppressed. Hatred of atrophied instincts actually denounces the true nature of the task-masters—which comes to light only in their victims. But as a Great Power, or state religion, the master's morality wholly subscribes to the civilizing

> powers that be, the compact majority, the resentment, and everything that it formerly opposed. The realization of Nietzsche's assertions both refutes them and at the same time reveals their truth, which—despite all his affirmation of life—was inimical to the spirit of reality.[26]

Georges Bataille, another prominent post-war thinker strongly influenced by Nietzsche, also views Nietzsche from a dialectical perspective, not a dialectic of world-historical events, but a dialectic of personal liberation struggle. Like Adorno and Horkheimer, he sees de Sade, along with Nietzsche, as the two great nineteenth century apostles of total liberation, of freedom from conscience and rationality. Yet Bataille's deep ambivalence about the Nietzschean project of liberation comes from his own attempts to live it. He tells us that "Nietzsche's work, seen from the perspective of action, is an abortion—a strongly defensible one; his life is a failed life, like that which attempts to put his writing into action."

For Bataille, Nietzsche cannot be understood by simply reading him, but only by living the same struggle he lived. All mere readings of Nietzsche, therefore, including the Nazis', are inevitably misreadings:

> One has truly not heard a single word of Nietzsche's unless one has lived this signal dissolution in totality; without it, this philosophy is a mere labyrinth of contradictions, and worse, the pretext for lying by omission (if, like the fascists, one isolates passages for purposes which negate the rest of the work).[27]

Missing from all the previously discussed responses to Nazi Nietzscheanism is any feeling of complicity or responsibility. All these various commentators seem quite sure that what the Nazis saw and valued in Nietzsche is quite different from what they find valuable and powerful in his work, whether it be Kaufman's positive non-Nazi Nietzcheism, Jaspers and Derrida's radical indeterminacy, or the dialectic perspectives of Adorno, Horkheimer and Bataille.

Another position is of course possible, a position which states that the concepts that the Nazis saw and valued in Nietzsche are indeed an essential and valuable part of Nietzsche. This does not imply that Nietzsche was in any sense a Nazi philosopher, far less that Nazism was a correct or necessary result of Nietszchean thought. But it does lead to what we might call a tragic view of

---

[26] MAX HORKHEIMER & THEODOR W. ADORNO, DIALECTIC OF ENLIGHTENMENT 100-01 (John Cumming trans., 1972).

[27] GEORGES BATAILLE, *On Nietzsche: The Will to Chance*, *in* THE BATAILLE READER 340 (Fred Botting & Scott Wilson eds., 1997).

Nietszchean philosophy, of a set of ideas whose power does indeed transcend good and evil, whose conscious ambiguity both reveals and obscures, and whose potential for unleashing barbarity upon the world must be recognized and regretted. Although there does not appear to be any post-war philosopher who has adopted this view, it is the pervasive theme of Thomas Mann's great post-war novel, *Doctor Faustus*.

Mann himself seems to have had reservations about *Doctor Faustus* as a literary work. He called it "joylessly earnest, not artistically happy." The impact of the book lies as much in its allegorical power as in its novelistic technique. It tells the story of Adrian Leverkuhn, a brilliant, driven and solitary composer, who seeks in his work to shatter all artistic norms, who contracts syphilis, and who goes mad. Leverkuhn obviously represents Nietzsche, whose life and illness are paralleled in many respects, but he also represents the German nation, itself descending into madness and destruction, as well as the legendary Faust. Leverkuhn, however, is not seduced or deceived by the Devil, but has actively sought him, has made his pact willingly, even before the Devil himself arrives to seal it.

The story of Leverkuhn is narrated in the novel by his friend, Serenus Zeitblom, an earnest, pedantic, and thoroughly conventional man, whose own reactions and responses to Leverkuhn and to the Nazi tragedy are the central theme of the book. Zeitblom himself describes the book as "a monumental work of lamentation" and so it is. Mann clearly saw a link between the works of Nietzsche and the Nazi catastrophe, and whether that is an accurate portrayal of the relationship is less important than the fact that it was so viewed. *Doctor Faustus*, therefore, is not so much about Nietzsche as about the perception of Nietzsche, while recognizing that reality and perception are not only linked, but indistinguishable. The dominant mode of the book is indeed one of lamentation, not condemnation. Leverkuhn's work is brilliant, exhilarating, frightening and dangerous. Yet viewed, as Mann and Zeitblom view it, with knowledge of the madness and destruction that were to follow, it is also, and perhaps predominantly, tragic.

Let me conclude then with a quotation from *Doctor Faustus*, a description of Leverkuhn's music, which may also be taken as a description of Nietzsche's writing, and must therefore also be taken as a description of the perception of Nietzsche's writing in the aftermath of the Nazi destruction:

> Yes, in the contemplation of this music, admiration and sadness mingled in the most peculiar way. "How beautiful!"

one's heart said—or at least mine said to itself—"and how sad!" For what one admired was a wittily melancholy work of art, an intellectual feat worthy of the name heroic, laconic anguish behaving like playful travesty—which I do not know how to characterize other than to call it an unrelenting, tense, breakneck game played by art at the very edge of impossibility. And that was what made one sad.[28]

[28] THOMAS MANN, DOCTOR FAUSTUS 233 (John E. Woods trans., 1997).

Part II
Legal Hermeneutics

[5]

From Strife to Understanding: Pathological Argument in Nietzsche and Gadamer

P. Christopher Smith*

To be sure, Gadamer's idea of *Gespräch*, of dialog or conversation, goes a long way toward undercutting the Platonic/Aristotelian paradigm for argument, namely *apodeixis* or logical "demonstration" by the inclusion of classes of things in, or exclusion from, other classes – as in "All p are q; r is p; therefore r is q," or "No p are q; r is p; therefore no r is q." In this regard Gadamer, like Steven Toulmin, has done much to reestablish an earlier paradigm for legal argument, *dikanikê rhetorikê*, or judicial rhetoric.[1] In this paper I maintain first, however, that Nietzsche's destruction of rational argument altogether, is an even more profound step insofar as Nietzsche penetrates to the affective *Untergrund* and *Abgrund*, the underground and non-ground abyss of *pathos*, on the surface of which any so-called "reasoning" or *logos* floats unsteadily.[2] Gadamer, for all his challenges to the apodictic form of argument, still seems to perpetuate Plato's abstraction of some sort of impartial, dispassionate, disembodied

---

* Philosophy Department, The University of Massachusetts Lowell, One University Avenue, Lowell, MA 01854.

[Ed. Note: Smith's paper is published in this form for the first time in this volume. Smith's paper was presented at the 2003 Annual Meeting of the Association for the Study of Law, Culture and the Humanities in New York City. An earlier version was publised as P. Christopher Smith, 'Nietzsche and Gadamer: From Strife to Understanding, Achilles/Agamemnon to Achilles/Priam,' CONTINENTAL PHILOSOPHICAL REVIEW 35 (2002), p.379, but the published version does not contain Smith's application of his thesis to legal hermeneutics. This previously unpublished paper is published with Smith's permission.]

1. See my "Towards a Discursive Logic: Gadamer and Toulmin on Inquiry and Argument" in *The Specter of Relativism*, ed. Lawrence Schmidt, (Evanston, Northwestern University Press, 1995), 183-191.

2. There is not space in this study for an extended account of Nietzsche's *Die Geburt der Tragödie aus dem Geiste der Musik* (The Birth of Tragedy out of the Spirit of Music), *Kritische Studienausgabe I* (Munich, de Gruyter, l998), from which these anti-foundationalist expressions derive. See §§ 4,5. Nevertheless, this book's subversion of Platonic rationality is crucial for the exposition here. For a more detailed account see my *Hermeneutics of Original Argument* (Evanston, Northwestern U.P., l998) (henceforth "HOA"), 291-310.

psukhê or self that looks on and reasons from a distance about some *Sache* or subject matter. Nietzsche, on the other hand, embeds "reason" in the physical experiences that the body undergoes, which is to say, in what Homer calls the *thumos* or "gut." One thought does not cause another thought in some sort of logical sequence, Nietzsche tells us, rather each thought is the completely atomic last manifestation in consciousness of a basic underground drive: the will to power. Nietzsche's destruction of reasoned argument will be supported here with a concise exposition of Achilles' altercation with Agamemnon in the *Iliad,* Book I. For the argument there, is clearly "not about what it's about," not about how to appease Apollo so that he would cease visiting a plague upon the Greeks forces. Rather, at its pre-rational non-ground it is a contest of will about who, Achilles or Agamemnon, will be acknowledged as "the best of the Achaeans," which is to say, who will have to submit to whose power.

Still, along the way Gadamer alerts us to something to which Nietzsche is deaf. There really is *Verstehen* that comes from *Sichverständigen* in a *Gespräch*, which is to say, understanding that comes from reaching an understanding in conversation, but *Verstehen* here becomes *Verständnis*; understanding becomes the understanding partners in conversation show for each other. And for this to happen the underground affect of these partners must become something other than the will to power. For Gadamer, it turns out, reaching an understanding is based in an affect or *pathos* after all. *Logos* is patho/logical in Nietzsche's sense, save that instead of the will to power the underlying *pathos* which alone sustains genuine conversation is a feeling of kinship and *Zugehörigkeit*, a shared feeling that the speakers are bound to each other in belonging the same community. Thus, rather than speaking, as Gadamer does, of a "fusion of horizons," one might better speak of a "fusion of affects" by virtue of which conflict yields to shared compassion, antipathy to sympathy. In the closing Book XXIV of the *Iliad,* Achilles reaches an understanding with the aged and helpless Priam, regarding the return of his son Hector's body for appropriate funeral rites. This scene will display for us just how such an affective concord makes Gadamer's reaching and understanding in conversation possible in the first place.

In conclusion we will consider the relevance of our findings for legal reasoning.We will see that rather than serving as a paradigm for legal reasoning, Gadamer's account of *Sichverständigen* or reaching an understanding serves as a critical standard against which its deficiencies are to be measured. For in the end, legal reasoning has as its affective underground and non-ground the Nietzschean contest of wills to power. It cannot, therefore, get beyond the strife of Achilles and Agamemnon to any sense of kinship and community. As a consequence, reaching an understanding in Gadamer's sense is impossible for it.

1. Nietzsche's advance over Gadamer.

Ever since the Pythagorean/Platonic catharsis of the *psukhê*, the conscious thinking self, from the influences of the body and its affects, the prevailing prejudice in the philosophy of language has been that the communication of intelligible content should the single concern. Consequently, of the three forms of *peithein* or convincing acknowledged by Aristotle in his retrospective review of rhetorical persuasion, *logos*, *êthos* and *pathos* (*Rhetoric* I,2,1356a1-20), communication of the *logos*, the logical content, has received nearly exclusive attention. At the same time, communication of the other two, the good character of the speaker and the appropriate affect, have been treated as matters of extrinsic ornamentation at best and, at worst, of sophistical manipulation. Gadamer, as we will see here, modifies the Aristotelian idea of *logos* but without penetrating, as Nietzsche does, to its underlying groundless abyss of Dionysian *pathos*. Thus Gadamer, it would seem, remains very much within the intellectualist tradition insofar as "what it's about," *die Sache* or subject matter, as this is clarified in the *Mitte der Sprache*, the medium of discourse, is his primary concern.[3] If, therefore, we are to push Gadamer in the direction Nietzsche might move him, we will have to let go entirely of philosophy's naïve fixation on the supposedly "rational content" of what is said and delve beneath it to the undercurrents of feeling on which this supposed "rational content" rides ever so precariously.

In Gadamer, to be sure, *Verstehen* unfolds in *Gespräch*, in conversation with others: we undergo together — physically, one

3. See H.-G. Gadamer *Wahrheit und Methode* (Truth and Method) in Gesammelte Werke 1 (Tübingen, Mohr (Siebeck), l986) (henceforth "GW1"), 460-68. Page numbers in brackets, here [432-49], refer to *Wahrheit und Methode* (Tübingen, Mohr (Siebeck), 1965). Translations from German and Greek will be my own except where noted.

might assume — the experience of what we say to each other, the *pathos tôn logôn.*[4] Thus in the end, understanding in Gadamer becomes not just *Verstehen* as the understanding of some subject matter or *Sache*, but understanding shown for someone else, *Verständnis,* and an understanding reached with someone else, *Sichverständigen*. As Gadamer puts it,

> In the first place, understanding *(Verstehen)* means coming to an understanding with one another *(sich miteinander verstehen)*; in the first place, an understanding *(Verständnis)* is always an understanding reached with someone else *(Einverständnis).* Thus human beings for the most part understand each other right away, or if not, they make themselves clear *(sie verständigen sich)* until they have reached their goal of agreement *(Einverständnis).* (GW1 183 [168])

We note, however, Gadamer's conclusion here: he goes on to say that "An understanding *(Verständigung)* is thus always an understanding *about something (über etwas).* To understand one another *(Sich verstehen)* means understanding one another *(Sichverstehen)* in regard to something *(in etwas)"* (GW1 183-84 [168] emphasis added). For our Nietzschean radicalization of Gadamer the point is that *Sichverständigen*, reaching an understanding, is only secondarily *Sichverständigen in einer Sache*, reaching an understanding about some subject matter.

One could say that Gadamer's idea of "dialectical" reasoning as *Gespräch* or conversation returns to Plato's original, pre-mathematical sense of *dialegesthai*, namely "talking through" things inconclusively, where any understanding reached is always a blend of *euporia* and *aporia*, of "getting through well" to a partial insight while at the same time coming to an "impasse," losing our way, in what remains ultimately opaque and impenetrable.[5] We see, accordingly, that reasoning here, contrary to the Platonic/Aristotelian paradigm of logical demonstration *(apodeixis),* stays with questionable things that, in perpetual

4. The full phrase *tôn logôn autôn athanaton te kai agêrôn pathos en hêmin* is from Plato's *Philebus* 15d. Gadamer renders this freely but accurately as "Jenes nie alternde Widerfahrnis der *Logoi*" (The never aging experiential encounter with the *logoi*) (H.-G. Gadamer, Gesammelte Werke 6 (Tübingen, Mohr (Siebeck) l985) (henceforth "GW6"), 106. I will have more to say about this matter subsequently.

5. See *Philebus* 15c; compare Gadamer on this passage in GW6, 106, and GW1, 383-84, 387-93 [360,361-67]).

violation of logic's laws of self-identity and non-contradiction, oscillate unsteadily between being and not being what they are in our ever equivocal speaking of them. Thus Gadamer, in returning to the original idea of conversational *dialegesthai*, reintroduces Heraclitian ontological fluidity into a world made static by the derivative Platonic dialectic of the *eidê* and *genê*,[6] and thereby returns cognition to its origins in understanding. Nevertheless, insofar as his hermeneutical theory concentrates on the *Sache* or intelligible subject matter *about* which the parties in conversation are speaking, he seems, at the same time, to perpetuate the intellectualist ideal of pure reason that transcends anything emotional, sensual, or bodily.[7] Let us, therefore, turn to Nietzsche to see how his *"Destruktion"* of discourse is in important ways deeper and more radical than Gadamer's hermeneutics.

We take as our point of departure a seminal quotation from Nietzsche's *Will to Power* that articulates concisely the thesis proposed here: that for Nietzsche "reasoning" is a mere façade, which only thinly conceals what is really going on behind it.[8] In § 477 he writes,

> [T]he assumption, made by logic, that there is an immediate causal connection between thoughts—this is the result of the most crude and heavy-handed kind of observation imaginable. *To be sure, every affect possible plays its game between two thoughts,* but their movements are too sudden, so we mistake them for something else, deny them. . . . 'Thinking' as the theorists of cognition *(Erkenntnistheoretiker)* assume it to be, is nowhere to be found. (Emphasis added.)

It is logic's assumption that one thought "follows from" another and is "caused," which is to say, logically entailed, by that other thought; thought x "implies" thought y. "We believe," says Nietzsche,

> that one thought and the next, as these follow one another in us, stand in some sort of causal chain. The logician, for one, who talks about nothing but cases that in reality never occur,

6. Though *eidê* and *genê* might be translated as species and genera, Plato does not distinguish them in this way. Still, the reasoning based on them is by static universal" classes" of things. See n.14 below.

7. See the *Phaedo*, in particular, the account of the soul "itself by itself" at 79d.

8. F. Nietzsche, *Der Wille zur Macht* (The Will to Power) (Stuttgart, Kröner l964) (Henceforth "WzM").

> has gotten used to the prejudice that thoughts cause thoughts. . . . But everything that reaches consciousness is an appearance at the end of a process, a conclusion, and causes nothing. In consciousness every sequence of one thing after another is completely atomic" (§ 478).

Reason's "line of thought," any apparently logical inference of one thought from another, is in fact an artificial construction superimposed on disconnected non-sequiturs.

The fictions of reason and the logical entailment of one thought by another, it turns out, are but manifestations of a single underlying *pathos*, the will to power. "[T]here are no facts, only interpretations," Nietzsche tells us, and

> Our needs are what interpret the world, our drives and their pro and contra. Every drive is a kind of compulsion to dominate and has its perspective that it wants to force upon the others as the norm (§ 481).

All "thinking" is perspectival interpretation to sustain and increase life, and, Nietzsche adds, extending his destruction of the unified self, "One may not ask, 'Who, then, is interpreting?' Rather, interpretation itself, as a form of the will to power, exists," Nietzsche tells us, "as an affect—'exists,' not 'is,' as a process, a becoming" (§ 556).

Indeed, logic's ideas of valid reasoning and truth *per se* are nothing but fabrications useful for life in its will to simplify complexities and reduce infinite differences to falsified similarities. "This assimilation," he says, "is the same as the amoebae's incorporation of appropriated matter." ('500), and, applying this physiological, assimilative model to human cognition, he concludes, that "the whole apparatus of cognition (*Erkenntnis*) is an apparatus of abstraction and simplification aimed not at cognition, but at getting things in our power" (§ 503):

> Cognition (*Erkenntnis*) works as the tool of power. Thus it is obvious that it expands with every "more" in power. . . . In order that a particular species maintain itself and grow in its power, it must grasp in its conception of reality enough that is calculable and that stays the same so that from then on, a schema for that species' behavior can be constructed. . . . The measure of the will to know depends on the measure of growth in the species' will to power. A species grasps so and so much reality in order to become master of it, to put it in its service" (§

480).

All discourse, it turns out, is a mere front for the basic life drive to extend control, and Gadamer's dream of impartial, mutual clarification of some *Sache* or subject matter in the medium of speech shared between us begins to look like a sheer illusion. If Nietzsche is right, all that any speaker is trying to do is to outmaneuver her or his opponent in an *agôn*, *Kampf*, contest, in which "winning isn't everything, it's the only thing."

2. Strife: Achilles and Agamemnon.

To test the validity of this destruction of "rational" discourse we turn now to Homer's *Iliad*. For as oral poetry, the *Iliad* shows us basic communicative phenomena prior to the disembodiment of speech introduced by writing and literacy. In particular, it displays the original basis of all speech in the *pathê* or affects undergone by the body. For Homer, not the eviscerated mind but the *phrenes*, *stêthes*, *thumos*, the chest, viscera, and spirit or heart, the "gut" in other words, is the location of thought. To exemplify this very Nietzschean idea, I have chosen Achilles' argument with Agamemnon in Book I of the *Iliad* despite the entirely objectionable subject of their dispute, namely the distribution to men warriors of two captured young women as prizes of honor.[9] It is asking a great deal to plea for a suspension of revulsion here, but I know of no better illustration than this clash of wills to power, to display that, contrary to Gadamer, the ostensible "question" for supposedly rational discussion, *die Sache* or subject matter in question, is not at all what is at stake (compare GW1 368-84 [344-60]). Rather this conversation, if we can call it that at all, is really and only a contest to decide which of the opponents will prevail, Achilles or Agamemnon, as the "best of the Achaeans" (see *Iliad*, I, 91, 412). Power, acknowledged by others with the honors they bestow, is the real concern.

The occasion for Achilles' and Agamemnon's dispute is a council called, not by Agamemnon, who as the aggrieved Menelaus' older brother is the rightful commander of the entire Argive expedition to Troy, but by the supposedly subordinate

9. For my analysis of this passage on numerous occasions I have drawn upon the fine textual scholarship of both Simon Pulleyn, *Homer Iliad I* (Oxford, Oxford U.P, 2000), and G.S Kirk, *The* Iliad: *a Commentary*, Vol. I: books 1-4 (Cambridge, Cambridge U.P, l985), 51-83.

Achilles. Insubordination, this is to say, or at least Agamemnon's perception of it, figures in what goes on here from the beginning. Taken on the surface level of Gadamer's hermeneutics, the "question" to be answered is how to get Apollo to call off the plague he has visited upon the Argives, Danaans, or Achaeans, as these same troops are variously named to preserve the dactylic hexameter. To find out, Achilles, again upstaging Agamemnon, proposes that the prophet Calchas be summoned. Calchas agrees, in the presence of all, including most notably Agamemnon himself, to speak only if Achilles swears to protect him against "a great man who has power over all the Argives and to whom the Achaeans are obedient" (I.78-79), and who is sure to be angered by what he has to say. In promising his protection Achilles says straight out what Calchas deferentially only implied: that this powerful king is none other than Agamemnon himself, who, as Achilles says provocatively to his face, "now boasts of being the best of the Achaeans by far" (91). Thus threatened, Agamemnon must already sense collusion between these two in attempting to undermine his domination. And indeed, Calchas announces that it was Agamemnon's abrupt and brutal refusal to accept a ransom from Apollo's priest Chryses and to release Chryses' daughter, that caused the wrath of Apollo, and that Apollo is only to be placated if Agamemnon gives up his "prize of honor" and returns her to her father with appropriate sacrifices to the god.

Agamemnon's response on the basic affective level is *mênis*, rage, the very same *pathos*, in fact, that, in Achilles, is the theme for the whole poem announced in the *Iliad's* first verse, "Sing goddess of the rage *(mênis)* of Achilles." And everything Agamemnon says is a manifestation of his own rage. *Manti kakôn*, "Evil prophet," he growls, *kak' ossomenos*, "glaring evilly" (104-105): "And now you prophesize and speak *in the midst of the Danaans*." (109). His rage, as we hear the beneath the surface of what he says, results from the open threat to his status in front of those on whose respect his understanding of himself as the "best" and most powerful depends. Lest he look bad, he allows that he will "give up the girl," but his yielding is purely tactical and the result not of any dispassionate reasoning but solely of his selfish wanting and willing: "I did not *want (ethelon)* to accept the splendid ransom for the girl Chryseis," he says churlishly, "since I very much *wish (boulomai)* to have her at my beck and call back home." "Indeed I *want her in preference (probeboula)* to

Clytemnestra, my lawful wife" (111-113). "But even so, I am *willing (ethelô)* to give her back, if you say that's best. I *wish (boulom')* the army to be saved rather than destroyed" (116-17). Though his willing and wanting seems for a moment to have the well-being of others at heart, his predominant self-centeredness immediately resurfaces, and it becomes clear that the gut fear for his own power status relative to others drives everything he says: "But get another prize ready for *me (emoi)* right away," he adds, "so that I alone of the Argives *(mê hoios argeiôn)* do not go without a prize" (118-19).

In listening to Agamemnon's, and in fact any Homeric direct speech, two things that confirm Nietzsche's destruction of "rational" discourse are immediately evident: first, as is typical of pre-literacy, the "arguments" are paratactic, not hypotactic-periodic. This is to say that clauses are not yet subordinated, one to another, in some logical or causal sequence — this *because* this — rather one thought follows another only temporally, not logically. The thoughts are, as Nietzsche has put it, "completely atomic." Second, and in accord with this atomism, the thoughts expressed are caused by passions, not by each other. They are each, as Nietzsche says, the end result, the manifestation in consciousness, of the unconscious processes the speaker is undergoing; we find in Agamemnon that, "every affect possible plays its game between [his] thoughts." Agamemnon is threatened; he feels fear and this manifests itself in anger. Relinquishing Chryseis, Agamemnon's prize of honor, without compensation would only sustain Achilles' threat to him. The "reasons" Agamemnon gives why he won't relinquish her, namely that she is more beautiful, talented, and intelligent than his wife, Clytemnestra (113-15), are thus a front for what is really going on with him, as is made obvious when he allows he will give Chryseis up, but not without having a replacement prize awarded to him. A loss in honor equals a loss in power, and this he will avoid at all cost.

Similarly, Achilles' response only transparently disguises the passions that drive him to say what he does: the indignation, rancor, hostility, and hatred that are ultimately manifestations of his own rage. He addresses Agamemnon with contemptuous irony that shifts directly into insult: "Most praiseworthy son of Atreus, of all men most loving of his possessions," he says (122). With that we have the affective voicing which underlies the entire speech that follows. Positioning himself over against Agamemnon and with all the others by presuming to speak for them and not himself, he too gives "reasons" — paratactically without causal connectives — why Agamemnon's demands cannot be met: "*We* do not know of goods laid up in common. What *we* plundered from cities, that has been divided up" (124-25). In severing the "cognitive" from the "emotive," we today might reconstruct this as a "rational" argument that there is no prize available *because* they have all been distributed already, *therefore*, Agamemnon can't have a replacement. Such a reconstruction, however, would completely suppress the fact that the reasons Achilles gives are but the expression of the *pathos* he is undergoing, namely hatred of the man who slights *his* honor and refuses to recognize *his* superiority. What is really going on here becomes clear in the way Achilles advances his second "reason," namely in a *command* that Achilles gives Agamemnon: "But come, *you (su)* give up this girl to the god, moreover we Achaeans will recompense you three and fourfold if ever Zeus grants us to take the strong walled city of Troy" (127-29).

Agamemnon senses immediately what is at stake, namely that in this *agôn* of wills to power, Achilles is maneuvering rhetorically to undermine his authority and rule. "Not so fast, splendid though you may be, Godlike Achilles, with your thieving intent," he fires back with caustic irony of his own, "Do you *want (etheleis)*, so long as you yourself have a prize, that I, however, should sit here like this with nothing, and so *you* order *me* to give her back? (131-34). The issue then, is who is in whose power, who commands and who obeys. Agamemnon does not bother any longer to disguise his feelings as reasons. He says next, in effect, I'll just take someone else's prize, maybe yours Achilles, and I have the power to do it! (136-39). To be sure, he then tries to obscure the underlying power struggle with a dismissive kingly "we": "But *we* will consider these things later," he says, and trying to draw the "we" back over to his side, he continues with sovereign second person plural directives of his own: "For now *let us* draw a black ship down into the shining sea, . . . a hecatomb *let us* place on board, . . . and fair cheeked Chryseis herself let us put aboard" (140-144). But this is a feint, and he quickly slips back into verbal conflict, hurling an epithet of his own in return for Achilles' previous insult "Of all men most loving of possessions": "Let a single man," says Agamemnon, still feigning sovereign composure, "be master of the ship, either Ajax or Idomeneus or shining Odysseus, or *you* son of Peleus, of all men the most terrible" (144-46). Any foreground/background distinction between what these two are saying and what drives them to say it, collapses here as the background history of strife between them erupts into the apparent foreground of "reasoned" persuasion.

This is too much for Achilles, who, like Agamemnon, has been completely attuned all along to the affective clash communicated behind the façade of "reasonable" proposals exchanged. "What it's really about" now shatters any veneer of civility: "Shameless — armored in shamelessness — always shrewd with greed!," retorts Achilles, choking with rage: "How could any Argive soldier obey *your* orders, freely and gladly do *your* sailing for you or fight *your* enemies, full force? Not I, no" (149-52); "No, you colossal, shameless — we all followed you to please you, to fight for you, to win your honor back from the Trojans — Menelaus and you, you dog-face! (157-59).[10] To which Agamemnon replies in kind: "I'll send her back in my own ships with my crew. But I, *I (egô)* will be there in person at your tents to take Briseis in all her beauty, your own prize — so you can learn just how much greater I am than you, and the next man up may shrink from matching words with me, from hoping to rival Agamemnon strength for strength!" (183-87 (Fagles 83)).

If we apply Nietzsche's destruction of "rational" discourse to this, we can see only the absolute impossibility of Gadamer's *Gespräch* and *Sichverständigen*, of dialog in which the partners reach an understanding. What has happened in the exchange of Achilles and Agamemnon is in no sense an intellectual misunderstanding, and the cause of communicative collapse is not at all, as Gadamer might claim for failed conversations, that the question asked was skewed *(schief)* and the answers given therefore misdirected (GW1 370 [346]). No, we have here two wills to power in conflict with each other, and both antagonists in this *agôn* are doomed to irreconcilable strife for so long as their fundamental hostility defines what they say. Nietzsche, of course, would tell us that this hostility is inevitable and final; from his point

10. Robert Fagles does beautiful work here rendering the epistrophe "you . . . you . . . you," and the aposiopesis "colossal, shameless" — and hence making audible the ultimately ineffable hatred of each other which these figures communicate. Hence here I have used his translation of the *Iliad* (New York, Penguin, 1990) (henceforth "Fagles"), 82.

of view Gadamer's *Sichverständigen* is fiction.

3. Gadamer's advance over Nietzsche.

Nietzsche's account seems to elucidate perfectly the real affective basis beneath the "lies" of supposedly reasonable "truths" in Achilles' exchange with Agamemnon, whom he would have stabbed to death had he not been restrained by Athena's divine intervention. The actions each proposes, it turns out, and the "reasons" given in support of these, are nothing but thrusts and parries in a contest of will for supremacy. But is this always the case? Or can we, while accepting Nietzsche's claim that *pathos* is the ground and basis of any *logos*, and acknowledging, accordingly, the indissoluble unity of the Apollonian and Dionysian, still allow for the possibility of genuine dialog and consultation that, to invert Clausewitz, is not a continuation of war with other means? Is it possible that people can reach an understanding with each other after all, but on the basis of a different complex of affects from the fear, hate, anger and hostility that surround the will to power? Could strife give way to understanding in the deeper sense of an affective concord? This, I suggest, would be well beyond Nietzsche's ken, but not Gadamer's.

A good place to start in this regard is Gadamer's appropriation of the social adjuncts to *phronêsis*, or ethical and political discernment, as Aristotle treats these in the *Nicomachean Ethics*, Book VI. In treating the first of these, *sunesis* (see EN 1142b35-1143a19), Gadamer changes the usual translation, *Verstehen* or understanding, into *Verständnis* or the understanding I show for another person. To illustrate what he intends with this change, Gadamer writes that in giving counsel, particularly in matters of conscience,

> [t]hose asking for counsel *(Rat),* just as much as those who give it, assume that the other person is obligated to them as a friend. Only friends can give counsel to each other, which is to say that only counsel intended in a friendly way is meaningful for the one receiving it. *Thus it is evident here too that the one who shows understanding* (Verständnis) *does not think of himself as standing, unaffected and dispassionate* (unbetroffen), *over against the other and judging him or her. Rather, out of a specific sense of kinship* (aus einer spezifischen Zugehörigkeit) *which binds him together with the*

> *other, he is affected and feels along with him, thinks along with him.*" (GW1 328 [306]) (Emphasis added.)

Gadamer supports this com-passionate or sym-pathetic interpretation of *sunesis* with reference to the next "modifications" of *phronêsis* that Aristotle introduces, namely *gnômê* and *sungnômê* (EN 1143a19-35). These he renders as *Einsicht* and *Nachsicht*, that is to say, considerateness and forbearance (WM 306). Crucial for Gadamer here is EN 1143b19-23:

> That which is called considerateness *(gnômê)*, and according to which we say people are well disposed to show consideration *(eugnômnes)* and have forbearance *(sungnômê)*, is right judgment concerning what is fair *(epieikes)*. A sign of this is that we say that the fair person *(ho epieikês)* is most forbearing *(malista sungnômonikos)* and that it is fair *(epieikes)* to show forbearance in regard to certain people.

We see here that the key to all of these extensions of *phronêsis* to one's relationships with other people is *epieikeia*, fairness, or what Gadamer calls *Billigkeit* (GW1 323 [301]). But Gadamer has another translation closer to the original sense of *epi-eikein* as "letting up" or "easing off," namely *nachlassen* or relenting, that will serve us well when we come to Achilles and Priam. Along with *philia*, friendship, kinship, holding dear, this possibility of relenting, so foreign to anything in Nietzsche, provides the affective basis for reaching an understanding. "To reach an understanding in conversation," Gadamer writes,

> is not at all to play one's trump card and force one's own standpoint through. Rather it is the transformation of the partners into a community in which one does not remain what one was. (GW1 384 [360])

Understanding can be reached between Achilles and Agamemnon, in Book XIX only after they have both suffered absolute disaster and must abandon their ferociously *un*relenting attack on each other, but with the distraught Priam Achilles can relent. With that, the affective basis for a genuine conversation is given and, indeed, the two of them are transformed into partners in a community in which neither remains what he was.

4. Understanding: Achilles and Priam.

Let us turn now to the concluding Book XXIV of the *Iliad*, to see how this comes about.[11] This book begins, not coincidentally, I suggest, with the words, *Luto d' agôn*, "Now the contest was over." The immediate reference, of course, is to the funeral games held for Patroclus, whose death at the hand of the Trojan hero Hector had turned Achilles' *mênis* or rage away from Agamemnon and against the Trojans, whom he slaughters mercilessly, and most of all, against Hector. So violent is his rage that, having killed Hector, he would desecrate his body by dragging it behind his chariot around his fallen comrade Patroclus's grave again and again. In Book XXIV, however, the rage driven *agôn* of Achilles against Agamemnon, against the whole Argive army, against the Trojans, and finally against Hector, is over. Or as the *luto* of this first verse might foreshadow, it is diffused, resolved, and thus the *Iliad*, whose very theme was the rage of Achilles, can now come to its conclusion.

Aided by Hermes, the old and grievously afflicted Priam surprises Achilles in his camp with a "shining ransom" and pleads for the release of his son Hector's body to him so that he might save it from "the birds and the dogs" and provide appropriate funeral rites. However, prior to his saying anything, he throws himself at Achilles' knees and even kisses his hands, those "terrible man-killing hands" (XXIV, 477-79). These are truly astonishing gestures that confirm for us the original basis of any verbal communication in communication by the body.[12] To

11. In regard to this passage Nicholas Richardson's careful textual analysis has been most instructive. See his *The* Iliad: *A Commentary*, Vol. VI: books 21-24 (Cambridge, Cambridge U.P. l993), 272-361.

12. It is remarkable that with only a few exceptions, most notably Nietzsche, philosophy has traditionally omitted corporeal communication from its considerations. Until Ramus's and Port-Royal's turn to the oxymoron "literary rhetoric," rhetoric, which is to say, oratory, with its emphasis on delivery *(hupokrisis, pronuntiatio)* as a physical act, did much better than philosophy in acknowledging the importance of the body. See HOA 318n.2. Philosophy's failure in this regard reaches its radical form in the hyperliteracy of French postmodernism when *le geste,* the gesture, becomes a function of writing. For all of his emphasis on *die Sache*, the intelligible subject matter, and the communication of it in written texts, Gadamer certainly does not go to this extreme. On the one hand, Gadamer can say that, "Speech *(die Sprache)* attains its true *intelligible* being *(ihre wahre Geistigkeit)* in writing" (GW1 394 [368]); on the other hand, he will maintain that, "Emphasis, rhythmic division, and the like, are intrinsic to even the most silent reading," and that "Any understanding of what is meaningful is plainly so closely tied to *bodily* speech

comprehend their powerful affective message we might best recall Priam's earlier prayer to Zeus. "Grant me," he says, that at Achilles' I find kinship and mercy *(philon êd' eleeinon)*" (309). Kissing Achilles' hands, even if they are the murderous hands of the archenemy, is a gesture of kinship. Here it is combined for the only time in Homer with a suppliant's gesture of submission and a plea for mercy.[13] By these bodily gestures circumstances are created that are completely different from the confrontation of Achilles and Agamemnon: There can no longer be any contest for power and domination here, any Nietzschean *Kampf*, nor any question of winning honor from others in recognition of one's power. Nor, conversely, can there be any question of losing face before others.

Homer tells us this with one of his most imaginative similes in which everything is turned on its head:

> Just as a man overcome by dreadful madness, slays a man at home and comes to a rich man in a foreign land for mercy and protection, and evokes astonishment in everyone who sees him, so Achilles was astonished when he saw Priam. (480-484).

We note how the references oscillate ambiguously here. It is Priam who comes as a suppliant to the foreigner Achilles, yet he is the rich man and Achilles is the killer overcome by rage. Just who is seeking kinship and mercy from whom shifts unstably. For evidently it is not just Priam who seeks kinship and mercy from Achilles but, on a deeper level, Achilles, too, who seeks kinship and mercy from Priam for having killed his son. Thus with these gestures the basic affects of fear on the one side, Priam's, and rage on the other, Achilles', already begin to yield to the compassion of each one for the other. Indeed, Homer will make it clear in what follows that Achilles sees his next of kin, his father Peleus, in Priam, but there are strong indications also that Priam will be able to see in Achilles his son. Hector, after all is called "man-killing" too (509). Thus the feeling of kinship (Gadamer: *Zugehörigkeit*) develops reciprocally.

If we are to follow how an understanding is reached in dialog, in *Gespräch*, here, we must, therefore, not focus primarily on the

---

(dem Sprachlich-Leibhaften), that understanding always contains an interior speaking within itself" (GW1 165-66 [153]) (emphases added).

13. See Richardson, *The* Iliad, etc. 322.

Sache or subject matter about which these partners in conversation come to an agreement. Rather, we must take care to trace the deeper affective changes communicated in the gestures of the body and in the tone and voicing of what Achilles and Priam say. For these affective changes are what make reaching any understanding possible in the first place. Significantly, Priam does not start with the "subject matter," with some question or issue to be resolved. Rather he begins with a verbal supplication based in his posture of submission, "Remember your own father, godlike Achilles" (486). In this way he communicates both corporeally and vocally his own passion of overwhelming sorrow and fear while drawing Achilles in to compassion for him. He brings about a change in Achilles from *mênis* or rage, first, to *philia* and then to *eleos*, first to kinship and then to mercy: to kinship, or even affection, because Achilles can see his own father, in this defenseless old man crouching submissively before him, and to mercy, because in identifying with his sorrows he must feel pity for him. And with that the hostility, enmity, hatred, which had made any understanding between Achilles and Agamemnon impossible, begins to fade.

Only this somatic/tonal shift in the ungrounded underground of affect can provide the basis for Priam to reason with Achilles, that is, to give grounds, *(logous didonai).*[14] To paraphrase: Like me, says Priam, your father is abandoned and defenseless with his enemies closing in on him, but he can expect the return of his son. (That Achilles and presumably Priam, too, know Achilles is fated to die in Troy only heightens the pathetical effect.) I, Priam, however, am even worse off than he is, for you killed the only son who could have protected me. The end of this "argument" is again significant, for, just as at the beginning there is no question raised, here at the end there is no conclusion drawn. There is no answer given in the order of "Therefore, you should at least return the body to me." Rather his speech issues in near desperate pleas: "Hold the gods in awe, Achilles, remembering your father, have mercy on me" (503-504).

Achilles' ambivalence, then, is not about whether to assent intellectually to a proposition; rather he is torn viscerally between

14. Not deductively, of course, but by the rhetorical loci of "similarity and difference" and "the more and the less." See my HOA, 56-71 on original reasoning by the topics as opposed to logical deduction by the inclusion of classes *(eidê, genê)* in each other or exclusion from each other.

residual anger and newly felt sympathy. At first this affective ambivalence shows up, accordingly, not in what he says, but in physical gestures of his own. He takes Priam by the hand, a gesture of reconciliation, but pushes him away, if ever so "gently" *(êka)* (508), a gesture of rejection, but softened.[15] There is at this moment in Achilles a precarious balance in affective weights that could just as easily tip one way as the other, but for the moment com-passion, shared grief, overcomes both him and Priam and they burst into tears: "The one cried painfully for man-killing Hector, cowering at the feet of Achilles, but Achilles cried now for his father and now for Patroclus" (509-10). Then Achilles, ever frighteningly impulsive, leaps from his chair and pulls the old man up by the hand. "Ah, you poor man," he says in an expression of heartfelt sympathy, "How many awful things your spirit *(thumos)* has had to endure (518), but we should not think that Achilles' countervailing anger has been wholly banished. When Priam, with a physical gesture of his own, rejects the chair Achilles offers him and then asks directly for the release of Hector's body (551-52), Achilles glares at him in the same way he had once looked at Agamemnon, *hupodra*, darkly, fiercely, from beneath his brows (I, 158, XXIV, 559). "Don't anger me old man!" he shouts (560), disrupting the tie of kinship, and on Priam's side the affective response to a stronger man's anger returns: "The old man was terrified" (571 (Fagles 607)). Still, awe before the gods, to which Priam had appealed, restrains Achilles. He is mindful, he says, that "Thetis, daughter of the old man of the sea, who bore me, came as a messenger from Zeus." "And you too, Priam" — Achilles addresses him intimately now by name — "I know, nor was it concealed from me, that one of the gods brought you to the Achaeans' ships" (562-64).

Though restrained still by piety, Achilles nonetheless bolts out the door, jumping up "like a lion" (572), to prepare Hector's body. But now his attitude in regard to Hector has come round to its opposite: what was once wrath and shameless impropriety is now reverence for the gods. Or should we say, the balance has tipped deeply toward reverence. For the wrath, if now latent, is still there. Knowing this, Achilles covers the body, for he is aware that Priam, were to see his son, might grow angry himself drawing Achilles' wrath in return. And indeed, should that happen, they would be thrown back to the affective condition of Achilles' and

15. See Richardson, *The* Iliad, etc. 327.

Agamemnon's strife in Book I. The chance of reaching an understanding would be lost. "Your son is released *(lelutai),* old man, as you commanded" is his salutation to Priam when he returns (599)[16] "Now let us set our minds to eating," he adds with the ultimate gesture of friendship to a stranger who has become a kinsman (601). With the formulaic "But once the desire for drink and food was satisfied" Homer begins to close this scene. "Priam the Dardanian," he tells us, "marveled first at Achilles, how tall and powerful he was, for he was like the gods in appearance. And Achilles marveled at the Dardanian Priam, seeing how good was his visage and listening to his words" (629-32).

At the end of Achilles' encounter with Priam antipathy becomes sympathy. His fear having abated, Priam asks for a bed, and Achilles responds, "playfully" even *(epikertomeôn)*, "Bed down outside, dear old man *(geron phile)*" lest any of Agamemnon's people find you here (649-50). Achilles then asks Priam how many days he needs for the preparation and proper execution of the funeral, and when Priam answers eleven, Achilles responds, calling him by name, "Then it will be what you demand, old man Priam" (669). Next, Homer tells us, "he grasped him by the right wrist that he might not feel fear in his heart *(eni thumôi)"* (672). With that physical gesture strife has given way to understanding.

5. Conclusion.

In this passage, then, we recognize that, contrary to Nietzsche, Gadamer's *Sichverständigen* or reaching an understanding does indeed occur. As we have verified in our exploration of the altercation between Achilles and Agamemnon, Nietzsche's destruction of discourse is strikingly sharp sighted in revealing that any human exchange is not primarily "about what it's about," not "about" some intelligible *Sache* or subject matter. Rather, beneath its conscious, "rational" surface, what we say to each other is always driven by the body and its affects. At the same time, Nietzsche is equally striking in his obliviousness to any basic affective dispositions other than the will to power. As a consequence, he is unable to conceive of any communicative experience except contention for dominance, and he is incapable of accounting for what happens in the exchange of Achilles and

16. The *lelutai* here resonates with the *luto* motif first sounded in verse 1.

Priam. In this regard Gadamer, who stresses *Zugehörigkeit*, a sense of kinship, and *Nachlassen* or relenting, as prerequisites for any genuine dialog, clearly surpasses him.

Nevertheless, our exposition of how understanding comes about between Achilles and Priam shows us that there is something to be learned about *Sichverständigen* from Nietzsche after all. For as Gadamer could have made clear, had he further developed his ideas of kinship and relenting, the ground and basis of *Sichverständigen* is surely not found at the level of a "fusion of horizons" in regard to some intelligible subject matter. "Horizon," after all, comes from the Greek *horaô*, meaning "I see," and it is far too ocular to name what really goes on in corporeal, vocal communication, where the response sought from an audience is "I will." Thus, using Nietzsche's emphasis on the bodily, affective basis of discourse to get behind Gadamer's residual intellectualism,[17] we can uncover the real [un]ground of *Sichverständigen.* As the encounter of Achilles and Priam shows us, reaching an understanding consists fundamentally, not in agreement about something, but in the reconciliation of previously conflicted *pathê* or passions, a fusion of affect.

What conclusions, then, can we draw from all this for legal reasoning? A Hegelian distinction between *sittliche Substanz* and the *Rechtszustand*, between the "ethical substance" of a genuine community and the rule of law or "legal status," might be of use here.[18] *Sittliche Substanz* refers to the basis of any community in which the participants are bound to each other, not by a system of inviolable, unalienable rights of the individual person, but by the obligations that the participants in the community owe to each other. In such a community the members are not self-sufficient islands unto themselves, rather they are defined by the roles they play in their multiple relationships, say, as a mother or father, wife or husband, daughter or son, sister or brother. What holds such a

17. See F. Nietzsche, *Also Sprach Zarathustra*, I, "Von den Verächtern des Leibe" (About those who scorn the body) (Stuttgart, Kröner, 1960), 34: "Leib bin ich ganz und gar, und nichts außerdem; und Seele is nur ein Wort für etwas am Leibe" (I am body, completely, and nothing else besides; and 'soul' is just a word for something that happens with the body).

18. For *sittliche Substanz* see G.W.F. Hegel, *Phänomenologie des Geistes* (Hamburg, Meiner, 1952) (henceforth "PhG"), 311-12, 313-16, and *Grundlinien der Philosophie des Rechts* (Hamburg, Meiner, 1955) (henceforth"GPhR"), §§ 142-69. For the *Rechtszustand* see PhG, 342-46, and GPhR § 184. I have treated Hegel's distinction here extensively in my Hermeneutics and Human Finitude (Bronx, Fordham, 1991), 14-38.

community together is the members' sense of kinship, their belonging together, or, with Gadamer, their *Zugehörigkeit.* Hegel speaks of "substance" here in order to draw a contrast with the insubstantiality of moral "principles" constructed by the autonomous individual out of pure reason. What people do in a *sittliche Gemeinschaft* or ethical community based on received traditional customs from time out of mind *(Sitten),* not intellectual reflection.

Obviously, where the will to power ruins any possibility of *Zugehörigkeit*, where all sense of kinship and belonging together in an ethical community is destroyed, the only thing standing between civility and the collapse into Hobbes's anarchic "pursuit of power after power," is the rule of law, the *Rechtszustand* or legal status. For example, when a marriage degenerates into a *Machtkampf*, an *agôn* for power and property, or when, for that matter, any partnership devolves into the irreconcilable antagonism of an Achilles and Agamemnon, only regulation by a legal instance of authority can prevent the domination and exploitation of one party by the other. (Aeschylus's invocation of the Areopagus takes this step beyond Homer.)

Nevertheless, arguments of the parties before the court in these circumstances will still be adversarial, not conversational. To invert Clausewitz, legal argument will inevitably be the continuation of war by other means. Furthermore, Nietzsche's destruction of reason makes clear that those empowered by the legal system to adjudicate such conflicts are far from impartial, rational onlookers "above" these conflicts. In reality they too are power players deeply involved in them. Legal arguments before judges as well as the arguments judges make to each other in their deliberations, are all rather thinly disguised Nietzschean tests of will. Of necessity, therefore, they exclude any Gadamerian *Zugehörikeit.*

Hence, hence far from being a useful paradigm for legal reasoning, Gadamer's idea of conversation, based in the sense of kinship that the partners feel for each other, poses a special challenge to it. The task would now be to acknowledge the inevitably contentious, derivative nature of legal reasoning and, by establishing its boundaries, prevent its usurpation of the entire ethical-political realm of conversational deliberation. Legal reasoning must not, as in Toulmin, become the new paradigm that replaces *apodeixis*. Indeed, the way must always be left open to recover the deliberative community from which legal reasoning removed itself in the first place. The antagonistic non-conversation of Achilles and Agamemnon must eventually be returned to the understanding Achilles and Priam show for each other.

For as Hegel points out, we must not be condemned for all time to be nothing but abstract "persons" in purely contractual relationships concerning property, and who accept external legal regulation lest their all-determinant will to power throw them back into Hobbes's war of all against all (see PhG 343, GPhR § 182). Nor is my "original position," as a latter day Lockean would have it, that of an individual bargainer for a fair slice of the pie who, in pure self-interest, restrains his or her competitive tendencies. On the contrary, originally *we* take counsel with each other concerning what is best for *us*. And not the will to power is basic here, but our feeling of being obligated to each other in kinship. That Rawls would enjoy such widespread acclaim shows how near the *Rechtzustand's* legal reasoning has come to suppressing this fundamental truth and displacing *sittliche Substanz* altogether.

[6]

Responding to Nietzsche: The Constructive Power of *Destruktion*

Francis J. Mootz III

Penn State University, Carlisle

As a student of Hans-Georg Gadamer, and later a translator and important commentator on Gadamer's philosophy, P. Christopher Smith is widely acknowledged to be a leading hermeneutical philosopher. In a series of works, Smith has argued that Gadamer provides an important corrective to Nietzsche's caustic critical challenges, but that Gadamer's hermeneutics has no relevance for legal theory because law is just the manifestation of will to power. In this paper I argue that Smith misunderstands the nature of legal practice. Starting with a re-reading of the debate between Gadamer and Jacques Derrida about the legacy of Nietzsche's philosophy, I argue that Gadamer responds to Nietzsche's challenge in a manner that is exemplified in the critical dimensions of legal practice. Using the example of family law that Smith offers, I contend that Smith underestimates the critical and interpretive elements inherent in legal practice and captured in Gadamer's philosophy. I conclude that Gadamer offers a persuasive answer to Nietzsche's challenge. *Law, Culture and the Humanities* 2007; **3**: 127–154

I. Recovering Shades of Gray in Nietzsche's Shadow

More than one hundred years after his death, Nietzsche's long shadow continues to cloud the self-assurance of legal reasoning to the point of casting legality itself into doubt. There is no convincing demonstration that law can survive Nietzsche's scathing insights, which are carried forward today through various critical interventions; there is no alleviation of the suspicion that the "rule of law" is yet another modernist fable that conceals the play of power. For the most part, theorists either turn away from the corrosive effects of Nietzschean critique, or they revel in the anarchy seemingly invited by Nietzsche. In this article, I respond to Nietzsche's formidable challenge more directly by way of confession and avoidance: Even if we accept Nietzsche's claims in their full radicality, I argue that it is possible to defend both a critical engagement *with* law and the critical potential *of* law. I endorse Gadamer's thesis that *Destruktion* is

Address for correspondence: Francis J. Mootz III, Professor of Law, Penn State University, Dickinson School of Law, 150 South College Street, Carlisle, PA 17013. E-mail: fjmootz@psu.edu

a constructive power that girds legal practice, even if all too often this critical power is suppressed.

Nietzsche's as-yet unanswered challenge to law has been carefully recounted by P. Christopher Smith in the course of his efforts to recover "the hermeneutics of original argument."[1] Smith locates original argument in consultation and deliberation with others. He describes how the communal understanding of reasoning that animates the pre-literate Homeric epics – in which one takes counsel with others by *hearing* them and *feeling* the force of their demands – has, since Plato, increasingly been covered over by the univocal and demonstrative model of modern argumentation in which insular contestants seek to *demonstrate* a truth that they have *seen* with their solitary mind's-eye. Smith lauds Nietzsche for forcefully undermining the pretense of logical-deductive legal reasoning and the conceit of demonstrative legal argumentation by uncovering the untamed, embodied *pathos* that resides at the heart of all reasoning and persuasion. Unfortunately, Smith charges, law turns a deaf ear to this challenge and embraces a hopelessly abstract model of reasoning. Smith concludes that "judicial reasoning . . . has effectively displaced and buried the original ways we exist and talk with each other in availing ourselves of the words said from time out of mind that we have first heard from others."[2]

Smith's creative readings of Greek philosophy and drama in the course of recovering the experience of original argument inspire me to undertake the complementary project of investigating the role of original argument in legal practice. By doing so, however, I challenge Smith's characterization of legal practice as the institutionalization of an inauthentic form of understanding. At first, Smith suggested that his work on original argument has "important, challenging consequences" for "judicial theory," and he emphasized that all reasoning, "even judicial reasoning, originates in our belonging together, our [embeddedness in tradition], in a community of reasoners . . ."[3] More recently, however, Smith retrenches his claim in important respects by suggesting that Gadamer's hermeneutics does not provide a model for legal argumentation, but rather a "challenge."[4] The task for legal theory, Smith

---

1. See P. Christopher Smith, *The Hermeneutics of Original Argument: Demonstration, Dialectic, Rhetoric* (Evanston, IL: Northwestern University Press, 1998).
2. P. Christopher Smith, "The Uses of Aristotle in Gadamer's Recovery of Consultative Reasoning: Sunesis, Sungnômê, Epieikeia, and Sumbouleuesthai," *Chicago-Kent Law Review* 76 (2000), p. 749.
3. Op. cit., pp. 749–50.
4. P. Christopher Smith, "From Strife to Understanding: Pathological Argument in Nietzsche and Gadamer," unpublished conference paper, p. 21, 2003 Annual Meeting of the Association for the Study of Law, Culture and the Humanities, New York University. An earlier version of Smith's paper was published as P. Christopher Smith, "Nietzsche and Gadamer: From Strife to Understanding, Achilles/Agamemnon to Achilles/Priam," *Continental Philosophical Review* 35 (2002), p. 379, but the published version does not contain Smith's application of his thesis to legal hermeneutics. I am grateful to Chris for permitting me to quote from his unpublished manuscript.

argues, is "to acknowledge the inevitably contentious, derivative nature of legal reasoning and, by establishing its boundaries, prevent its usurpation of the entire ethical realm of conversational deliberation ... Indeed, the way must always be left open to recover the deliberative community from which legal reasoning removed itself in the first place."[5] Smith concludes that Gadamer and Nietzsche both offer insights into understanding and interpretation, but that Gadamer's approach holds no real significance for the demonstrative contest of legal argumentation. More pointedly, Smith appears to argue that legal argumentation must be demystified by Nietzschean critique and then cabined, given that legal argumentation precludes genuine hermeneutical exchanges.

In response, I contend that contemporary legal practice need not be a paradigm of modernity's forgetfulness of original argumentation, even if it too often plays this role. My thesis is that Nietzsche announced the destruction of a certain understanding of legal argumentation but not the destruction of law, and that the hermeneutical characteristics of legal practice have not been occluded irreversibly by the ascendency of technical rationality and the clash of wills to power. Working from Smith's creative and stimulating insights, but against his conclusions, I pursue a hermeneutical defense of law and critical legal theory in response to Nietzsche's challenge.

This paper is organized in two parts. In the first part, I reclaim the constructive elements of Heidegger's *Destruktion* as an appropriate response to Nietzsche's seemingly uncompromising rejection of the potential for philosophy in the face of will to power. Gadamer extends the guiding concept of *Destruktion* by connecting it to the experience of dialogue, focusing on life as it is lived rather than abstract philosophical concepts. I return to the 1981 encounter between Gadamer and Derrida and argue that Gadamer effectively answered Derrida's Nietzschean reading of Heidegger, as evidenced in the reverberations of this debate in their subsequent writings. I conclude that Gadamer's elaboration of Heideggerian *Destruktion*, particularly in response to Derrida's Nietzschean critique, provides a viable response to Nietzsche's unremitting critical challenge.

In the second part, I bring Gadamer's philosophy to bear on legal practice and legal theory. Gadamer's argument that dialogical risk in conversation fuels *Destruktion* does not provide a methodology for correct decision making, but it does clarify how legal practice might be facilitated by acknowledging the nature of hermeneutical understanding and critical insight. I conclude by demonstrating the power of this perspective to answer Smith's Nietzschean critique of law by working through Smith's example of the agonistic contest of family law litigation.

5. Smith, "Strife," p. 21.

II. Reclaiming Heidegger's Legacy: Revisiting the Gadamer-Derrida Encounter

A hermeneutical response to Nietzsche must begin with Heidegger, who directly confronted the power of Nietzsche's thought as part of his masterful recasting of the philosophical tradition. Heidegger's initial effort in *Being and Time* to construct a fundamental ontology of the finitude of existence collapsed of its own weight,[6] leading to his "turn" away from the "language of metaphysics." In his later period, Heidegger waited upon the gods, who speak through the ineffable language of poetry. Heidegger's account of the experience of truth reflects this development in his thought: evolving from his early notion of truth as emerging from a tarrying with the disclosure of meaning, to truth as the product of a momentary grasping (*Augenblick*), and finally to truth experienced as a flash of insight that strikes like lightning loosed by the gods.[7] With his "turn," in which truth is no longer a project but only an event, Heidegger would appear to have encountered the dead-end of Nietzsche's relentless critical theory. This judgment is perhaps most clearly supported by Heidegger's intimation to family members shortly before his death that Nietzsche had "ruined" him.[8] One plausible interpretation of this self-evaluation is that, in the end, Heidegger found it impossible to philosophize while simultaneously remaining true to Nietzsche's radical dismantling of the philosophical enterprise.

Heidegger's lament need not become a cause for resignation. His original and provocative thinking has been carried forward in productive ways that grapple with Nietzsche's legacy. Gadamer and Derrida represent two major divisions of thought that follow Heidegger's lead, with the resulting debate (to paraphrase Paul Ricoeur) between hermeneutical dialogue (belonging) and deconstructive wariness (suspicion). I endorse Gadamer's claim that his "philosophical hermeneutics" pursues Heidegger's "turn" away from fundamental ontology in a productive, even if surprising, way. Gadamer brings life to Heidegger's turn by "re-turning" to Heidegger's early path-breaking interpretations of Aristotle's philosophy of factical life, interpretations that had jolted the student Gadamer like "an electric shock."[9] If

6. Gadamer succinctly explains this collapse as Heidegger's recognition that he had not made a complete breakthrough in his challenge to the idealism of consciousness. "For what he called the 'fundamental ontology of Dasein' could not – despite all the temporal analyses of how Dasein is constituted as *Sorge* ["care"] – overcome its own self-reference and hence a fundamental positing of self-consciousness. For this reason, fundamental ontology was not able fully to break away from immanent consciousness of the Husserlian type." Hans-Georg Gadamer, "*Destruktion* and Deconstruction," in Diane P. Michelfelder & Richard Palmer, eds., *Dialogue and Deconstruction*: *The Gadamer-Derrida Encounter* (Albany, NY: State University of New York Press, 1989), p. 104 (Geoff Waite and Richard Palmer, trans.).
7. Robert J. Dostal, "Gadamer's Relation to Heidegger and Phenomenology," in Robert J. Dostal, ed. *The Cambridge Companion to Gadamer* (Cambridge, UK: Cambridge University Press, 2002), p. 247.
8. Op. cit., p. 261 (quoting from an interview with Gadamer, "Heidegger und Nietzsche: Nietzsche hat mich kaputtgemacht!," *Aletheia* 5 (1994), pp. 6–8.
9. Hans-Georg Gadamer, *Philosophical Apprenticeships* (Boston, MA: The MIT Press, 1985), pp. 46–47 (Robert R. Sullivan, trans.).

Heidegger, in the end, awaited an unrequited conversation with the gods, Gadamer "re-turns" to Heidegger's origins and finds in ordinary conversation the key to responding to Nietzsche's initiatives.

2.1 Destruktion as Dialogic Encounter, not Poetic Event

Gadamer is surprisingly silent about Nietzsche,[10] but he did grapple with Nietzsche's philosophy in his infamous (non–)encounter with Derrida in 1981. After acknowledging that he and Derrida are both indebted to the later Heidegger, Gadamer used his introductory comments to recount important differences in their developments of Heidegger's insights. Against Derrida's deconstructive criticism of Heidegger for remaining in the grip of the language of metaphysics and failing to embrace the depth of Nietzsche's critique, Gadamer insists that Heidegger was "not exhausted in a mere gesture of protest, as was the case with ... Nietzsche. Rather, he attacked his task as being a matter of hard conceptual labor, which one should learn from the study of Aristotle."[11]

Heidegger's early Aristotle lectures pursued *Destruktion* of the philosophical tradition, and Gadamer insists that with his "turn" Heidegger "actually held to his fundamental project by maintaining, in a sublimated form, the *destruktive* achievement present in its beginnings."[12] Gadamer joins Hannah Arendt and others who find in the early Heidegger the key to understanding his later philosophical initiatives.[13] Gadamer argues that Heidegger's early Aristotle studies provide models of *Destruktion*, in which he abandons the philosophical pretensions problematized by Nietzsche without abandoning philosophical critique altogether.

> Anticipating Gadamer's notion of "fusion of horizons," Heidegger wrote regarding the destruction of Aristotle and the tradition based on him,

10. Elsewhere I have argued in detail that reading Gadamer and Nietzsche together as challenging supplements to each other is not only possible, but productive. Francis J. Mootz III, "Nietzschean Critique and Philosophical Hermeneutics," *Cardozo Law Review* 24 (2003), p. 967.
11. Gadamer, "*Destruktion*," p. 110.
12. Op. cit., p. 109.
13. See John van Buren, *The Young Heidegger: Rumor of the Hidden King* (Bloomington, IN: Indiana University Press, 1994). Ironically, Heidegger's autobiographical tendency to dismiss his early work as having been superceded by his "turn" served to undermine his themes of flux and plurality and contributed to the scholastic development of "Heidegger, Inc." Op. cit., pp. 21–23. Summarizing the ambivalence in Heidegger's self-assessment, van Buren writes:

    > In his autobiographies, the right hand does not appear to know what the left hand is doing. On the one hand, he indicated that his enduring topic was discovered in his youthful thoughtpaths, and that this topic is characterized by a radical openness and diversity of byways, incomplete ways, and errant ways. On the other hand, he downplayed and often even dismissed his youthful thought, placing it into a hierarchical-teleological relationship to "the way" of his subsequent writings.
    > Op. cit., p. 9.

> "Corresponding to our position, the original position is to be again worked out anew, i.e., corresponding to our altered historical situation, it is something other and yet the same." The "effective possibility" of Aristotle's thought "for its future" was to be sprung loose through "repetition," in which it kairologically and "constantly becomes a new present." The young Heidegger, Gadamer reported, was an "Aristotle redivivus."[14]

Heidegger's creative repetition of Aristotle's "hermeneutics of facticity" not only animates Heidegger's later work, it fueled Gadamer's philosophical hermeneutics.

Heidegger uses the word *Destruktion* to mean "dismantling and reviving," rather than "obliterating and moving past." The purpose of *Destruktion* "is to take concepts that have become rigid and lifeless and fill them again with meaning. Such an activity does not serve the purpose of pointing back to a mysterious origin, an *arché*, or the like. That is a fatal misunderstanding, which gets used as an objection above all against the later Heidegger."[15] Gadamer insists that Heidegger's philosophical

---

14. Op. cit., p. 226 (quoting from the author's translations of the German texts of the following books: Martin Heidegger, *Phenomenological Interpretations of Aristotle* (Bloomington, IN: Indiana University Press, 2001) (Richard Rojcewicz, trans.); Martin Heidegger, *Ontology: Hermeneutics of Facticity* (Bloomington, IN: Indiana University Press, 1999) (John van Buren, trans.); and Hans-Georg Gadamer, *Truth and Method* (New York, NY: Crossroad Publishing, 2nd rev. ed., 1989) (Joel Weinsheimer and Donald G. Marshall, rev. trans.).
15. Hans-Georg Gadamer, "Letter to Dallmayr," in Diane P. Michelfelder & Richard Palmer, eds., *Dialogue and Deconstruction: The Gadamer-Derrida Encounter* (Albany, NY: State University of New York Press, 1989), p. 99 (Richard Palmer and Diane Michelfelder, trans.). Later, Gadamer offers a similar definition, explaining that in *Destruktion* the goal "is to let [an encrusted concept] speak again in its interwovenness in living language. This is a hermeneutical task. It has nothing to do with obscure talk of origins and the original." Op. cit., p. 100. Heidegger provides a succinct account of the role of *Destruktion* in the Introduction to *Being and Time*:

    > If the question of being is to achieve clarity regarding its own history, a loosening of the sclerotic tradition and a dissolving of the concealments produced by it is necessary. We understand this task as the [*Destruktion*] of the traditional content of ancient ontology which is to be carried out along the *guidelines of the question of being*. This [*Destruktion*] is based upon the original experiences in which the first and subsequently guiding determinations of being were gained.
    >
    > This demonstration of the provenance of the fundamental ontological concepts, as the investigation which displays their "birth certificate," has nothing to do with a pernicious relativizing of ontological standpoints. The [*Destruktion*] has just as little the *negative* sense of disburdening ourselves of the ontological tradition. On the contrary, it should stake out the positive possibilities of the tradition, and that always means to fix its *boundaries* ... the [*Destruktion*] does not wish to bury the past in nullity; it has a *positive* intent. Its negative function remains tacit and indirect.

    Martin Heidegger, *Being and Time* (Albany, NY: State University of New York Press, 1996), p. 20 [§6] (Joan Stambaugh trans., 7th German ed., 1953).

    Heidegger's famous promissory note for Part II described his intent to outline the basic features "of a phenomenological [*Destruktion*] of the history of ontology on the guideline of the problem of temporality." Op. cit., p. 35 [§8]. Gadamer's philosophical hermeneutics offers payment on this promise by carrying forward the project of *Destruktion* while still avoiding the metaphysical entanglements that Heidegger came to recognize in the first part.

practice of *Destruktion* is a creative activity that creates a future through a de-structuring repetition of the situation. *Destruktion* occurs within an ongoing philosophical conversation; it is *not* achieved by "freeing" ourselves from metaphysics by casting it aside as if it were an historical artifact.[16] In other words, it is an empty gesture to *reject* the language of metaphysics rather than to *work through* this heritage by means of a *Destruktion*.

Gadamer revives early Heideggerian *Destruktion* against Heidegger's later claims to deconstruct the "language of metaphysics," arguing that Heidegger's embrace of Nietzschean excess temporarily – but never completely – derailed his initiatives.[17] Gadamer's contribution is to locate the *Destruktion* of stale concepts within the de-centering experience of dialogue rather than in the solitary efforts of the great philosopher, advancing Heidegger's early initiatives by taking "the path from dialectic back to dialogue, back to conversation."[18] Gadamer readily admits that Heidegger was disappointed by Gadamer's philosophical direction, and that he considered Gadamer's hermeneutical philosophy to be insufficiently radical. But Gadamer insists that his return to the practical engagement of dialogue uncovers the key to undermining the "subjectivity of the subject" by disrupting the assumption "that the subject takes hold of empirical reality with methodological self-certainty by means of its rational mathematical construction, and that it then expresses this reality in propositional statements."[19] Gadamer concludes that his contribution to post-Heideggerian philosophy

> is the discovery that no conceptual language, not even what Heidegger called the 'language of metaphysics,' represents an unbreakable constraint upon thought if only the thinker allows himself to trust language; that is, if he engages in dialogue with other thinkers and other ways of thinking. Thus, in full accord with Heidegger's critique of the concept of

---

16. Gadamer argues that *Destruktion* represents a feature of an unending tradition of philosophical thinking, and so even Plato's dialogues provide resources and are not just a metaphysical straight-jacket against which Nietzsche and Heidegger rightfully struggled. Gadamer, "Dallmayr," p. 101.
17. Gadamer argues that Heidegger's mistaken efforts to follow Nietzsche's most extreme paths in an attempt to break free of the language of metaphysics led to "*Holzwege*, the kind of circuitous dead-ends cut by loggers on wooded hillsides. And these paths, after the *kehre*, or turn of the way of Heidegger's thinking toward Being, led into impassable regions [and] remained an adventurous journey into error." Gadamer, "*Destruktion*," p. 104.
18. Op. cit., p. 109.
19. Hans-Georg Gadamer, "Text and Interpretation," in Diane P. Michelfelder & Richard Palmer, eds., *Dialogue and Deconstruction: The Gadamer-Derrida Encounter* (Albany, NY: State University of New York Press, 1989), p. 26, 29 (Dennis J. Schmidt and Richard Palmer, trans.).

> subject, whose hidden ground he revealed as substance, I tried to conceive the original phenomenon of language in dialogue.[20]

Too respectful of Heidegger's pathbreaking work to say it directly, Gadamer develops philosophical hermeneutics as a means of realizing Heidegger's ambition to confront Nietzsche without getting lost in the later Heidegger's elitist and poetic monologue.[21]

Gadamer places great importance on Heidegger's work for showing that *Destruktion* occurs not just as a product of genuine dialogue between two persons, but also in a dialogic confrontation with tradition. In both cases, truth is not experienced as a flash of insight, but rather emerges from a tarrying and attentiveness to a challenging disclosure that takes time and requires the relinquishment of subjective designs. This engagement is revealed in the colloquial expression, "falling into a conversation," which signals that a conversation is more than the goal-oriented strategies of its participants, and that it develops over time rather than being accomplished instantly. Gadamer's focus on dialogue leads him to conclude that there simply is no mistaken "language of metaphysics" that we can identify from afar and then abandon once and for all through deconstructive thinking that purports to be radically Nietzschean.

> There is only a metaphysically thought-out coinage of concepts that have been lifted from living speech. Such coinage of concepts can, as in the case of Aristotelian logic and ontology, establish a fixed conceptual tradition and consequently lead to an alienation from the living language. ... Thus, the task of a *Destruktion* of the conceptuality of metaphysics was posed. This is the only tenable sense of talk about the "language of metaphysics": this phrase simply refers to the conceptuality that has been built up in the history of metaphysics.
>
> Early on, Heidegger was to put forward as a rallying cry the task of a *Destruktion* of the alienated conceptuality of metaphysics: the ongoing task of contemporary thinking. With unbelievable freshness, he was able to trace in thinking the concepts of the tradition back to the Greek language, back to the [now forgotten] natural sense of words and the hidden wisdom of language they contain, and in so doing, to give new life

20. Op. cit., p. 23.
21. In an essay on Hegel's continuing relevance to contemporary philosophical dialogue, Gadamer most clearly makes the case that he is continuing Heidegger's later initiatives precisely by returning to dialogue. Hans-Georg Gadamer, "The Heritage of Hegel," in *Reason in the Age of Science* (Cambridge, MA: The MIT Press, 1981), pp. 56–58 (Frederick G. Lawrence, trans.). Suspicious of Heidegger's turn away from everyday dialogue, Gadamer finds the key to *Destruktion* in the challenge to subjectivity that comes from dialogue, and he rejects the claimed expertise of the profound thinker who is able to gain access to an event that is invisible to most persons.

> to Greek thought and its power to address us today. Such was Heidegger's genius. He had a penchant for restoring to words their hidden, no longer intended sense, and then from this so-called etymology to draw fundamental consequences for thinking.[22]

Hermeneutical retrieval of philosophical concepts is a *Destruktion* that opens the potential for breaking the grip of stale conceptualism and undermining the pervasive subjectivism that is the legacy of this calcified tradition. Gadamer's signature insight that "we understand in a *different* way, *if we understand at all*," emphasizes the dynamic effects of dialogic understanding.[23]

Gadamer's retrieval of Heideggerian *Destruktion* responds to Nietzsche's challenge by returning to dialogue and factical life. In this manner, Gadamer avoids the increasingly insular and enigmatic qualities of the later Heidegger without relapsing to the abandoned project of devising a fundamental ontology. In essence, Gadamer is arguing that Nietzsche's philosophical challenge to modernist subjectivity is realized in the de-centering experience of dialogue, a broad term that Gadamer uses to characterize hermeneutical experience. Gadamer argues that a variety of experiences – engaging a work of art, participating in a genuine conversation, and even rendering a legal judgment – exemplify the kind of de-centering experiences that Nietzsche seeks to promote with his disruptive interrogations of received wisdom. Of course, Gadamer does not suggest that a quick walk through a museum, casual chit-chat, or the bureaucratic practices of traffic court inevitably promote a Nietzschean *Destruktion* of the metaphysical tradition. His point is that these practices and experiences simultaneously reveal and conceal the de-centering of subjectivity anticipated by Nietzsche. By working through these practices and experiences and recuperating their dialogic character, Gadamer suggests, we can *live* Nietzsche's critique rather than just *study* it.

2.2 Confronting Derrida's Nietzschean Critique of Heidegger

Gadamer used the occasion of his exchange with Derrida to show that the dialogic conception of *Destruktion* that he developed by reading Heidegger's "turn" through the lens of Heidegger's early work provides an intriguing

22. Gadamer, "*Destruktion*," p. 107. Put succinctly, Heidegger's project claimed that Aristotelian conceptual analysis had been lost in translation – first into Latin and then into modern language – thereby literally rendering "Aristotle's commentary speechless." Gadamer, "Dallmayr," p. 99. Gadamer's point is that "this alienation confronts us with a task: the task of *Destruktion*." Op. cit.
23. Gadamer, *Truth and Method*, p. 297 (emphasis in original).

response to the Nietzschean challenge. In the course of describing his response to Nietzsche, Gadamer attempted to give full recognition to Derrida's Nietzschean rebuttal:

> Now Derrida will certainly object that I do not take Nietzsche seriously enough: that is to say, the end of metaphysics, that break which, since Nietzsche, makes all identity and continuity with oneself and with the other illusory. He takes these to be logocentric illusions from which even Heidegger did not escape, as [Heidegger's] Nietzsche-interpretation shows.[24]

Gadamer insists that human finitude precludes attaining a "complete" or "timeless" understanding, but he acknowledges Derrida's persistent challenge that he still has conceded too much "to reciprocal understanding and mutual agreement" in the face of irreducible difference, and that his celebration of dialogue betrays an implicit assumption that we truly can come to know another, whether the other is a person, idea, or culture.[25] Gadamer responds that Derrida's efforts to move beyond *Destruktion* and to escape the grip of metaphysics through deconstruction is a hopeless dream, one that builds on Heidegger's *failures* in his response to Nietzsche, rather than on Heidegger's earlier *innovations*.

Unfortunately, Derrida did not engage Gadamer directly on these issues during their exchange. It should not be surprising that Gadamer, the sensitive and responsive hermeneutic critic, attempted to anticipate and fairly articulate Derrida's challenges to his approach. But it was surprising to many that Derrida's response to Gadamer's detailed effort to take account of convergences and departures in philosophical hermeneutics and deconstruction came in the form of "three questions" that appeared to be wholly non-responsive.[26] For example, in response to Gadamer's emphasis on the interpreter's willingness to allow a text to speak rather than subordinating the text to the interpreter's designs, Derrida questions whether hermeneutical "good will" merely re-instantiates the Kantian metaphysics of will.[27] In Derrida's principal paper, he elliptically mused about the difficulty of ascribing positions to Nietzsche and

24. Gadamer, "Dallmayr," p. 96.
25. Gadamer, "Dallmayr," p. 97.
26. Gadamer's reply to Derrida's brief questions begins by making clear his puzzlement: "Mr. Derrida's questions prove irrefutably that my remarks on text and interpretation, to the extent they had Derrida's well-known position in mind, did not accomplish their objective. I am finding it difficult to understand these questions that have been addressed to me." Hans-Georg Gadamer, "Reply to Jacques Derrida," in Diane P. Michelfelder & Richard Palmer, trans. and eds., *Dialogue and Deconstruction: The Gadamer–Derrida Encounter* (Albany, NY: State University of New York Press, 1989), p. 55.
27. Jacques Derrida, "Three Questions for Hans-Georg Gadamer," in Diane P. Michelfelder & Richard Palmer trans. and eds., *Dialogue and Deconstruction: The Gadamer–Derrida Encounter* (Albany, NY: State University of New York Press, 1989), pp. 52–53.

Heidegger, thereby effectively refusing to engage Gadamer directly on their different interpretations of Heidegger's confrontation with Nietzsche's thought.

In the space created by Derrida's silence, some of Derrida's followers joined the debate and argued that Gadamer's exegetical optimism reflects a misunderstanding of the Nietzschean challenge with which Heidegger grappled and which gives rise to Derrida's deconstruction. John Caputo characterizes Gadamer's hermeneutical reading of Heideggerian *Destruktion* as "half-hearted, indeed reactionary, even resistant to the momentum, the direction, the tendency of Heidegger's critique of metaphysics."[28] Advancing a "radical hermeneutics," Caputo argues that Gadamer missed the radicalism of Heidegger's *Kehre* and that Derrida has surpassed Heidegger's initiatives.[29] For Caputo, Derrida's mysterious approach to the debate demonstrates that there "is a more Nietzschean side to Derrida than in Heidegger or Gadamer, a more deeply suspicious eye, a greater sense of the fragility of our thought constructions and the contingency of our institutions."[30] In a later book Caputo treats Gadamer with a gentler hand, but he continues to indict philosophical hermeneutics for failing to address Nietzsche's radicalism.[31] Caputo's Derridean critique of Gadamer exemplifies the received wisdom among self-proclaimed radical theorists: Gadamer's *Destruktive* return to dialogue remains trapped within the metaphysics of presence.

Gadamer's commentators responded in kind, criticizing Derrida for failing to risk his ideas in dialogue with Gadamer. Neal Oxenhandler alleges that Derrida chose to subject Gadamer to "the cutting edge of irony" rather than entering a dialogue with him, despite the considerable overlap in the motivation and implications of their work.[32] In more accusatory tones, G.B. Madison suggests that Derrida would risk "alienating that specialized audience which is composed of the addressees of his particular brand of ultra-ironic discourse" if he dialogically engaged Gadamer on the problem of power within hermeneutic understanding, concluding: "How else are we to make sense of what in Derrida's response to Gadamer (and in remarks of his elsewhere) is manifest nonsense, a caricaturial misreading of Gadamer

28. John D. Caputo, "Gadamer's Closet Essentialism: A Derridean Critique," in Diane P. Michelfelder & Richard Palmer, eds., *Dialogue and Deconstruction: The Gadamer–Derrida Encounter* (Albany, NY: State University of New York Press, 1989), p. 261.
29. John D. Caputo, *Radical Hermeneutics: Repetition, Deconstruction, and the Hermeneutic Project* (Bloomington, IN: Indiana University Press, 1987), pp. 95–119.
30. Op. cit., p. 97.
31. John D. Caputo, *More Radical Hermeneutics: On Not Knowing Who We Are* (Bloomington, IN: Indiana University Press, 2000), pp. 8, 41–59.
32. Neal Oxenhandler, "The Man with Shoes of Wind: The Derrida–Gadamer Encounter," in Diane P. Michelfelder & Richard Palmer, eds., *Dialogue and Deconstruction: The Gadamer–Derrida Encounter* (Albany, NY: State University of New York Press, 1989), p. 265.

and hermeneutics? Can it be anything other than a calculated and deliberate misunderstanding?"[33] Similarly, Donald Marshall suggests that to "read so feeble a 'response' from the most distinguished French philosopher since Sartre is certainly embarrassing and can be explained only on the assumption that Derrida knows little or nothing of Gadamer's work and was too preoccupied with what he intended to say in his own lecture on this occasion to give much attention to Gadamer's remarks."[34]

The perceived incommensurable interpretations of Nietzsche by Gadamer and Derrida is an enduring legacy of the commentary on the 1981 encounter, but the standoff is overly dramatized. Caputo's endorsement of Derridean deconstruction does not fall victim to simplistic readings of Derrida's radically Nietzschean perspective by abandoning reasoning to chaotic flux. Instead, he reaffirms that he is "trying to restore the difficulty in life, not to make it impossible," which is to say that he regards deconstruction as problematizing congealed forms of understanding, rather than precluding understanding altogether.[35] Having misread Gadamer for polemical reasons, Caputo fails to recognize that deconstructive interventions challenging all claims of necessity, universality, and timelessness without precluding ongoing debates about which understandings better serve social needs in present circumstances are the very hallmarks of Gadamer's philosophical hermeneutics. Gadamer's emphasis on dialogue provides a non-subjectivist means of breaking the grip of subjectivism that provides a more promising response to Nietzsche than Caputo's polemical account of Derrida's deconstruction. Caputo is not wholly to blame, inasmuch as Derrida's refusal in 1981 to engage an actual "other" in a dialogue that would risk his self-understanding and prejudices was rather remarkable in light of his longstanding attention to "the Other." Derrida's undeniable dexterity in reading texts – literary, philosophical, poetic, legal – was exhibited in a *tour de force* of exegetical originality rather than devoted to a dialogic exchange with another thinker. This is the most dramatic and telling lesson of his 1981 meeting with Gadamer: Derrida literally was unable to hear and respond to another thinker, even one with whom he shared substantial common ground and who was approaching him in an earnest attempt to identify helpful points of departure for discussion.

Gadamer's supporters have too often attempted to freeze the debate in its unproductive 1981 posture rather than pursuing its developing legacy, thereby violating a fundamental tenet of philosophical hermeneutics. Oxenhandler reports that Derrida conceded in a private conversation that "nothing really happened" at the Paris encounter because developing

---

33. G.B. Madison, "Gadamer/Derrida: The Hermeneutics of Irony and Power," in Diane P. Michelfelder & Richard Palmer, eds., *Dialogue and Deconstruction: The Gadamer–Derrida Encounter* (Albany, NY: State University of New York Press, 1989) pp. 198, 194.
34. Donald G. Marshall, "Dialogue and *Écriture*," in Diane P. Michelfelder & Richard Palmer, eds., *Dialogue and Deconstruction: The Gadamer–Derrida Encounter* (Albany, NY: State University of New York Press, 1989), p. 206.
35. Caputo, *Radical Hermeneutics*, p. 209.

a "position in response to Gadamer . . . would take a great effort and that is not what I want to do now."[36] Pejoratively characterizing Derrida as a disseminating prophet who necessarily is "exclusionary" in that he has "many acolytes but no equals," Oxenhandler concludes that "the time will come when Derrida will assume the responsibility of developing 'a position in response to Gadamer' . . . " and that it will prove to be productive.[37] Madison also concedes that if Derrida ever took this risk, "a genuine and lively dialogue would surely ensue,"[38] a project that regrettably is now left to their commentators in light of the recent deaths of both philosophers.

Rather than focusing on the personalities involved in the highly charged event, commentators should seek openings for a fresh reading of the debate. Gadamer's philosophy poses important questions that remain unanswered by those who promote a deconstructive reading of Nietzsche's critique. Can the role of deconstructive prophet (whether the later Heidegger or Derrida) facilitate *Destruktion*, or does this posture inevitably reinforce the grip of subjectivist metaphysics even as it strives to become ever more radical? Is Nietzsche's challenge a call to philosophical radicalism, or is Nietzsche best interpreted as issuing a call to live life without hiding behind philosophical walls of any kind? In the end, isn't it only putting oneself at risk in dialogue that can facilitate the *Destruktion* of metaphysics, which is the experience of being brought up short by one's engagement with an actual other, rather than the product of philosophical lessons about "the Other?" Doesn't Gadamer's dialogic risk embody the Nietzschean critical spirit – the dangerous maybe – in ways that the efforts by Heidegger and Derrida do not?

Following the Paris encounter, Derrida's work undoubtedly closed the gap that Gadamer identified between their positions. This movement is perhaps most starkly illustrated by Derrida's surprising conference address, "Deconstruction and the Possibility of Justice," which he begins by noting that it would be easy to refuse to see any connection between deconstruction and justice, but that such a posture would reveal the speaker to be not only "in a bad temper," but also "in bad faith."[39] Derrida does not explain this seeming reversal of his critique of Gadamerian hermeneutic charity, but the

36. Oxenhandler, "Shoes of Wind," p. 268 (quoting a private conversation with Jacques Derrida at Hanover, NH on 8 July 1987).
37. Op. cit., p. 268.
38. Madison, "Gadamer/Derrida," p. 198.
39. Jacques Derrida, "Force of Law: The 'Mystical Foundation of Authority'," *Cardozo Law Review* 11 (Mary Quaintance, trans., 1990), p. 921. Derrida dramatically announced that deconstruction has always been concerned with justice, and stated his intention "to show why and how what is now called Deconstruction, while seeming not to 'address' the problem of justice, has done nothing but address it, if only obliquely, unable to do so directly." Op. cit., p. 935. Derrida's reflections on law are quite congenial to Gadamer's argument that law exemplifies the hermeneutical situation. Derrida's address was substantially enlarged in 1994 and the complete version first appeared in translation to English in Jacques Derrida, *Acts of Religion* (New York, NY: Routledge, 2002) pp. 230–98 (Gil Anidjar, ed. and rev. trans.).

gesture appears to be intentional. He characterizes the conference title as requesting a violent "either/or," in the form of a polemic, to which he attempts to respond with an attitude of (what he apparently would call) good faith.[40] Similarly, Derrida, in his homage to Emmanuel Levinas, asks whether "without exonerating myself in the least, decision and responsibility are always *of the other*," and "whether the ethics of hospitality that we will try to analyze in Levinas's thought would be able to found a law and a politics, beyond the familial dwelling, within a society, nation, State, or Nation-State," even if the hope of *deducing* such a politics is without warrant.[41] In these and other developments of his thought, Derrida might very well have provided a basis for a dialogue with Gadamer that was not present in 1981.[42]

I do not wish to argue that Gadamer convincingly "won" their debate such that no additional dialogue is necessary. Rather, I argue only that following the path Gadamer blazed in response to the posture of deconstruction in 1981 remains a productive path for responding to Nietzsche's challenge that is not as starkly opposed to Derrida's important initiatives as the commentators have supposed.[43] Gadamer's insistence that

40. Op. cit., p. 923.

41. Jacques Derrida, *Adieu: To Emmanuel Levinas* (Stanford, CA: Stanford University Press, 1999), pp. 23, 20 (Pascale-Anne Brault & Michael Naas, trans.). See also Jacques Derrida, *Spectres of Marx: The State of the Debt, the Work of Mourning, and the New International* (New York, NY: Routledge, 1994) (Peggy Kamuf, trans.); Jacques Derrida, *Politics of Friendship* (New York, NY: Verso Press, 1997) (George Collins, trans.).

42. Caputo admits that "insofar as Derrida, very much under Levinas's influence, has come to regard faith as the medium in which we communicate – as soon as I open my mouth, I try to speak the truth – his work has come closer to Gadamer than to Heidegger." Caputo, *More Radical Hermeneutics*, p. 42.

43. Jean Grondin concludes his biography of Gadamer by quoting Derrida's published reaction to the news of Gadamer's death in 2002: "how right he was, then [in 1981] and still today!" Jean Grondin, *Hans-Georg Gadamer: A Biography* (New Haven, CT: Yale University Press, 2003), p. 338 (Joel Weinsheimer, trans.) (quoting Jacques Derrida, "Wie recht er hatte! Mein Cicerone Hans-Georg Gadamer," *Frankfurter Allgemeine Zeitung* (28 March, 2002)). In an interview near the end of his life, Gadamer claimed that Derrida later understood that his allegation of "logocentrism" was a "gross misunderstanding" of Gadamer's position, and that "in the meantime, Derrida and I became quite well attuned to one another . . . Since then he has been entirely on my side." *A Century of Philosophy: Hans-Georg Gadamer in Conversation with Riccardo Dottori* (New York, NY, Continuum, 2004), pp. 60–61 (Rod Coltman with Sigrid Koepke, trans.).

It is my natural lawyering instinct to quote these "party admissions" prominently in my text as conclusive proof of my thesis, but to do so would surely undermine my thesis. Gadamer and Derrida do not represent fixed interpretations of Nietzsche that collided in 1981, with one to emerge finally as a "victor." Rather, their dialogue itself became the test case for their interpretations, and Derrida's gracious comments can perhaps best be interpreted as an agreement that Gadamer's invitation to converse would have been a more productive, more provocative, more piercing experience. In this sense, Gadamer was a cicerone, or guide, for Derrida. But it is Gadamer's insights that prevent me from declaring an easy "victory" over Derrida, and lead me instead to call for a more probing engagement of Nietzsche in light of the dynamic challenge of Derrida's deconstruction. Gadamer's indication that they later both recognized the commonality between their approaches is offered in the spirit of dynamic hermeneutical understanding, as revealed by his concluding observation on the 1981 encounter: "The horizon of interpretation changes constantly, just as our visual horizon also varies with every step that we take." Op. cit.

conversational dialogue breaks the gripping prejudice of insular subjectivity, and the connection between this experience and the philosophical project of *Destruktion* in which one critically engages with tradition, provide a compelling orientation for critical legal thinking. Gadamer's elaboration of Heidegger's *Destruktion* opens a path between unthinking conventionalism and unceasing challenge, but his philosophy remains notoriously silent about how we can facilitate the work of ordinary dialogue to overcome "unproductive prejudices." Rather than asking how a challenging *Destruktion* of law becomes possible, he asks whether modernity's prejudices can completely silence the *Destruktion* of legal practice. As with Derrida, Gadamer's later work appeared to take more account of his opponent's insights,[44] but nevertheless the role of critical legal theory remained woefully underdeveloped. Having argued that Gadamer responds to Nietzsche to the extent that he avoids the problems encountered by Heidegger and Derrida, I now develop Gadamer's response to the Nietzschean challenge in its own right by returning to Smith's critique.

III. *Destruktion*, Law and Critical Legal Theory

Gadamer's philosophical hermeneutics does not translate to the setting of legal practice and theory in an obvious manner. What do legal theorists gain, even if I am correct that Gadamer has effectively responded to Nietzsche's philosophical challenge? Can Gadamer's emphasis on dialogic risk in conversation, which serves as the engine of *Destruktion*, shed light on the role and prospects for critical legal theory? The answer to these questions is not a matter of specifying what Gadamer's philosophy can teach legal practitioners and legal theorists from the supposed heights of philosophical insight. Gadamer does not provide a unique and determinant methodology for engaging in legal practice or critical legal theory, and his philosophy pointedly disclaims any such goal. Notwithstanding this limitation, theorists can illuminate Gadamer's themes by referring to legal practice, and can also suggest how legal practice might be facilitated by an explicit recognition of those themes. These seemingly modest accomplishments are more than sufficient to permit us to see beyond Nietzsche's shadow.

3.1 Philosophical Hermeneutics and Legal Practice

At a critical juncture of *Truth and Method* Gadamer turns to Aristotelian practical philosophy to characterize the activity of interpretation, and he suggests that legal practice provides an excellent model of this interpretive practical engagement.[45] Likewise, in his exchange with Derrida, Gadamer

44. I believe that Gadamer's attention to multiculturalism in his later work reflects this recognition of the significance of work by Derrida and others.
45. Gadamer, *Truth and Method*, pp. 324–41.

turned to legal interpretation at a key point of his discussion of the philosophical significance of textual interpretation.[46] At first glance, however, Gadamer's characterizations of legal practice appear to be self-contradictory, if not incoherent. After carefully reconstructing Gadamer's assessment of legal hermeneutics, I will explore how his philosophy provides a model of critical legal theory that responds to Nietzsche's legacy.

Gadamer regards "reading and understanding" as the process of leading the "announcement" of the text back to its "original authenticity," by which he means back to the communicative event from which the text now appears as a residue.[47] Due to the inevitability of textual distanciation, drafting legal texts must be "especially exacting," with the effort "always to avoid strife, to exclude misunderstandings and misuse, and to make univocal understanding possible."[48] To the extent that this characterization suggests that legal texts can be promulgated in a manner that permits a later interpreter to creatively reconstitute the original directive as intended by the text's author, Gadamer appears to endorse the romantic conception of hermeneutics that has always been one of his principal targets.[49] Needless to say, Gadamer's invocation of a "univocal meaning" resonates with conservative themes and appears to align him with metaphysical commitments to a knowing subject before whom the textual object of interpretation can be rendered fully present.

A careful assessment of Gadamer's discussion of legal hermeneutics, however, disrupts any such romantic or conservative reading. References to returning to the "original communicative event" and attempting to express a "univocal meaning" do not signal Gadamer's belief that legal texts are capable of fixing a perspicacious meaning that can be recovered intact and then applied. Gadamer begins with the longstanding recognition that laws cannot be construed as simple directives that are self-executing, but instead must always be read according to their general sense. "Accordingly, we must say that a text is not simply a given object but a phase in the execution of the communicative event [*Verständigungsgeschehen*]."[50] This means that a legal text always contains the "free space of meaningful concretization, a concretization that has to carry out the interpretation for the purpose of practical application."[51] Legal texts do not require interpretation only when they are vague, as a prelude to their application to a particular problem; instead, understanding is

46. Gadamer, "Text and Interpretation," pp. 35–36.
47. Op. cit., p. 35.
48. Op. cit., pp. 35–36.
49. In *Truth and Method*, Gadamer specifically relies on Heidegger's hermeneutic phenomenology to avoid the pitfalls of Wilhelm Dilthey's romantic hermeneutics. Gadamer, *Truth and Method*, pp. 218–64.
50. Gadamer, "Text and Interpretation," p. 35.
51. Op. cit., p. 36.

possible at all only in an interpretive application of the law to a case at hand.[52] Gadamer concludes that legal "decisions, precedents, or the prevailing administration of the law therefore always have a creative legal function" by applying the law to a set of facts.[53]

These seemingly contradictory themes, once properly understood, underscore why Gadamer emphasizes that the concrete setting of legal practice reveals the hermeneutical situation with "exemplary clarity,"[54] and why the hermeneutical situation can accommodate Nietzschean critique. Legal hermeneutics always involves the interpretation of binding texts, texts that make a claim on the interpreter and to which the interpreter must submit if she is to understand the law. This motivates the legal practitioner's claim that she can discover a univocal meaning: the rule of law requires that the law is obeyed, and that the interpreter does not freely twist the law to her subjective designs. An interpreter who objectifies and contorts a text for his own purposes risks nothing and remains within the grip of a subject-centered orientation that precludes genuine interpretive activity. The rule of law depends on the interpreter's good faith, which means that the interpreter acts in accordance with the law and does not manipulate the legal texts in a cynical, strategic, or ironic manner. Although this reality is particularly evident in legal practice where a decision must be made in accordance with law, it is true no less of ordinary conversational exchange and of the activity of reading literature.

The experience of giving oneself over to the text does not mean that legal texts are self-executing, such that the interpreter disappears and meaning emerges solely from the circumscribed and fixed world of the text. Lacking an insular, acontextual and autonomous meaning, texts acquire meaning only through their application to a particular concern. Legal hermeneutics exemplifies this lesson, inasmuch as attorneys and judges recognize that legal texts have meaning only in the context of a particular case. Legal practice reveals clearly that interpretation always involves application, which is to say that meaning is always meaning for the interpreter, in response to the questions posed by the interpreter. This "free play" through

52. In *Truth and Method*, Gadamer stresses that the fundamental problem of hermeneutics is application, and that interpretation "is not an occasional, *post facto* supplement to understanding; rather, understanding is always interpretation" that occurs in application. Gadamer, *Truth and Method*, p. 307. He elaborates:

> The work of interpretation is *to concretize* the law in each specific case – i.e. it is a work of *application*. The creative supplementing of the law that is involved is a task reserved to the judge, but he is subject to the law in the same way as is every other member of the community. It is part of the ideal of the rule of law that the judge's judgment does not proceed from an arbitrary and unpredictable decision, but from a just weighing up of the whole.

Op. cit., p. 329. Gadamer's extended discussion of legal hermeneutics serves to reveal that "all reading involves application, so that a person reading a text is himself part of the meaning he apprehends." Op. cit., p. 340.

53. Gadamer, *Text and Interpretation*, p. 36.

54. Op. cit.

application does not collapse into a celebration of the unfettered subjective manipulation of the text. As a law professor I constantly hear students propose interpretations of legal texts that don't make any sense and would never be advanced by competent lawyers, despite the linguistic plausibility of their analysis. Free play in the interpretation is never unbounded and indiscriminate, even if these boundaries always are in flux and subject to free play.

Gadamer's point, then, is that legal interpretation shows in particularly vivid ways that textual interpretation is conversational in structure no less than a spoken exchange between two persons. Understanding is not the product of a methodology that can be imposed on a text as if it were an object; rather, it emerges from the dialogic risk of conversational engagement. Legal practice reinforces the historically-effected character of interpretation, in which the interpreter's horizon of pre-understanding fuses with the text's effective-history of reception and re-circulation within a particular culture to generate a meaning within a context. Gadamer's conversational model of understanding accords with Nietzsche's perspectivism and emphasis on rhetoric, but it also accommodates his genealogical critique.[55] Nietzsche's critique emerges from within contemporary practices, and he finds in tradition sufficient resources for overcoming the historical contingencies that have solidified into dogma. Gadamer's development of Heideggerian *Destruktion* pursues similar goals. Gadamer places emphasis on the legal tradition precisely because the everyday experience of lawyers involves *Destruktion*, despite the irony that lawyers and judges attempt to suppress the nature of their dynamic activity by describing it as 'just following the rules.'

3.2 Critical Legal Theory and Destruktion *as a Practical Engagement*

Smith endorses Gadamer's characterization of the hermeneutical situation, and he acknowledges that Gadamer exposes a limitation in Nietzsche's account by revealing that genuine dialogue and consultation may lead to understanding. Nietzsche's unremitting critical posture renders him "unable to conceive of any communicative experience except contention for dominance,"[56] and thus he is blind to the communal experience of understanding that Gadamer characterizes by the notion of a "fusion of horizons." Emphasizing the kinship that makes understanding possible, Gadamer successfully avoids an overly-intellectualized account of interpretation by rejecting all manner of foundationalism and formalism.[57]

55. I have drawn the connections between Gadamer and Nietzsche in these ways in some detail in Mootz, "Nietzschean Critique."
56. Smith, "Strife," p. 19.
57. Op. cit., pp. 12–14.

But Smith cautions that Gadamer has not responded to the full depth of Nietzsche's critique, which extends beyond rejecting the primacy of foundational and logically formalistic reasoning. Smith argues that Nietzsche exposes the radically corporeal root of will to power, and that Gadamer exhibits a "residual intellectualism" by failing to acknowledge fully that understanding also is rooted in our corporeal existence.[58]

Smith concludes that Gadamer's advance over Nietzsche regarding the possibility of understanding through conversation does not extend to Gadamer's account of law. Simply put, Gadamer errs by attempting to translate the corporeal and affective experience of hermeneutical understanding that can occur between two people to the very different institutional setting of legal practice. Even if it is possible for interpersonal understanding to rise above a Nietzschean contest of wills, Smith insists that matters addressed in the legal realm are subject only to the bureaucratic management of an agonistic contest of wills. He then offers an intriguing illustration:

> Obviously, where the will to power ruins any possibility of *Zugehörigkeit*, where all sense of kinship and belonging together in an ethical community is destroyed, the only thing standing between civility and the collapse into Hobbes's anarchic "pursuit of power after power," is the rule of law, the *Rechtszustand* or legal status. For example, when a marriage degenerates into a *Machtkampf*, an *agôn* for power and property, or when, for that matter, any partnership devolves into ... irreconcilable antagonism ..., only regulation by a legal instance of authority can prevent the domination and exploitation of one party by the other.[59]

Smith agrees that kinship leading to understanding is possible, but he regards it as a rare and fragile achievement. Legal practice is just a means of dealing with *failures* of kinship and *breakdowns* in a consultative being-with-another. In response to hermeneutical impasse, legal practice vaguely acknowledges and then seeks to buffer the Nietzschean side of our embodied, affective lives by retreating behind formalistic and deductive shibboleths. When an organic relationship such as a marriage dissolves in fact, the law can only step in and provide neutral (which is to say, disembodied) procedures to divide the material residues of the relationship so as to avoid an open enactment of the ongoing conflict. The essence of legal practice is best understood as the management of Nietzsche's "contest of wills," Smith concludes, rather than Gadamer's notion of friendship, deliberation and understanding.

58. Op. cit., p. 19.
59. Op. cit., p. 20.

Smith's Nietzschean critique of Gadamer's hermeneutical account of legal practice has undeniable power, and it echoes Derrida's interrogation of hermeneutics. Surely it is idealistic, if not naive, to suggest that legal practice is a "conversation" oriented toward "understanding," rather than recognizing that legal practice is a bureaucratically-managed exercise of power.[60] Under my reading, though, Gadamer's claim that legal practice exemplifies hermeneutical understanding does not fall victim to such a simplistic view. Legal practice is conversational in structure, which means that it is structured as a playful movement of questioning and answering, but this is not to say that legal practice unfolds as if two intimates are engaged in a meaningful conversation. Law is structured conversationally even if it clearly is not just a conversation. Gadamer's response to Derrida establishes the basis for demonstrating the significance of philosophical hermeneutics in response to Smith's Nietzschean critique.

Smith is correct to insist that there is a critical difference between interpersonal conversation and textual interpretation, but this distinction has always been an important feature of Gadamer's hermeneutics. Arguing against Derrida's deconstructive reversal that the distanciation of textual interpretation reveals more about interpretative encounters than the personal character of oral exchanges, Gadamer steadfastly insists (as does Smith) that hermeneutical understanding is rooted in a (literal) "full-bodied" encounter with another.[61] Nevertheless, Gadamer gives textual interpretation its due in our modern literate culture. A principle goal of his exchange with Derrida was to explore the extent to which Derrida's focus on textuality provides important guidance to modern hermeneutical philosophy. Gadamer does not posit a fanciful account of law as a conversation among friends seeking agreement in the agora. He acknowledges that a new hermeneutical experience is called forth in

60. Sanford Levinson's assessment of the law and literature movement twenty years ago included what may be the best succinct articulation of this criticism.

> Yet there are obvious difficulties in adopting Rorty's metaphor of the conversation (rather than the argument), for the principal social reality of law is its coercive force vis-à-vis those who prefer to behave other than as the law 'requires.' As Chairman Mao pointed out, a revolution is not a tea party, and the massive disruption in lives that can be triggered by a legal case is not a conversation. The legal system presents a conversation from which there may be no exit, and there are certainly those who would define hell as the vision of their least favorite constitutional interpreter, whether the Court or a benighted law professor.

Sanford Levinson, "Law as Literature," *Texas Law Review* 60 (1982), p. 386. Septicism about conversational models of law was famously voiced several years later by Robert Cover. Speaking about the function of law in convicting and sentencing criminal defendants, Cover writes:

> . . . I do not wish us to pretend that we talk our prisoners into jail. The 'interpretations' or 'conversations' that are the preconditions for violent incarceration are themselves implements of violence. To obscure this fact is precisely analogous to ignoring the background screams or visible instruments of torture in an inquisitor's interrogation. The experience of the prisoner is, from the outset, an experience of being violently dominated, and it is colored from the beginning by the fear of being violently treated.

Robert Cover, "Violence and the Word," *Yale Law Journal* 95 (1986), p. 1608.

61. Smith, *Original Argument*, pp. 134–56.

modernity by a text-based culture that facilitates increasingly complex forms of social organization.

Smith's elegant book, *The Hermeneutics of Original Argument*, provides a case in point of this new hermeneutical situation. Drawing from multiple resources in the Western canon, with a particular emphasis on Nietzsche and Gadamer, Smith chronicles the abstraction from our affective life that has accompanied the ascent of modern technical and logical models of thinking that are removed from the aural nature of deliberating with another person. In concluding his study, though, Smith acknowledges the irony of having made the case for a hermeneutical retrieval of the aural (corporeal) dimensions of original argument by means of a complex and lengthy text that is produced and shipped off to anonymous readers.[62] Smith concedes that his account unavoidably is demonstrative rather than deliberative, and his demonstration of the "true" character of our corporeal being-with-others occurs only by virtue of his disembodied, textual being-with-readers. Gadamer's emphasis on legal hermeneutics is important for this very reason: he embraces this irony and investigates the hermeneutical character of reality not only in the modern literate world, but also in the emerging postmodern world of computerized data and text processing. I would not hesitate to cite Smith's book as an exemplary instance of inviting hermeneutical understanding in the manner described by Gadamer and as exemplified in legal practice.

Derrida took Heidegger's *Destruktion* as the starting point for his deconstruction, but Gadamer's different development of *Destruktion* proves its worth by responding to Nietzsche's challenge by articulating the potential for the creative and critical development of a textual tradition. This carries forward Heidegger's insight that *Destruktion*

> of Western metaphysics does not destroy or even destructure metaphysics; on the contrary, it decomposes or decompiles metaphysics' sedimented historical layers, reconstructing their hidden ontotheological structure and seeking to uncover the 'decisive experiences' responsible for this shared structure (experiences which Heidegger hopes will help us to envision a path beyond ontotheology).[63]

Smith's textual uncovering of the depth of Nietzsche's challenge is an example of this *Destruktion* in action. Although there can be no methodology of *Destruktion*, there is a critical engagement with textual tradition that opens pathways for more productive thinking by working through the inadequacies of that tradition.

62. Op. cit., p. 310.
63. Iain Thomson, "Ontotheology? Understanding Heidegger's *Destruktion* of Metaphysics," *International Journal of Philosophical Studies* 8 (2000), p. 323, n.2.

> Heidegger's hope is that careful philosophical study of such roads not taken might help us envision alternatives to our own metaphysical epoch of 'enframing.' This it might do not only negatively, by contesting the necessity of the Nietzschean metaphysics underlying our increasingly homogenized 'age of technologically-leveled world-civilization,' and thereby clearing the conceptual space for understandings of Being other than the metaphysics of the atomic age (now fulfilling itself in the almost uncontested spread of the cybernetic paradigm), but also positively, by recovering concrete (if fragmentary) historical examples of a non-metaphysical understanding of Being, elements of which (such as the temporal dynamism of Heraclitean *physis* and the active conception of truth as a historical clearing inherent in Parmenidean *alētheia*) we might draw on in order to elaborate heretofore unthought-of historical paths leading beyond our own late-modern Nietzschean impasse. Here we touch again upon the later Heidegger's central philosophical project, the vision behind his enigmatic call for 'an other beginning,' a beginning which he always insisted could only emerge out of a renewed and sustained hermeneutic altercation with the first beginnings of Western thought.[64]

To recover from the bad dream of modernity we need not rise above our situation through the prowess of critical insight; instead, we must invite and enact a *Destruktion*. Nietzsche's genealogical critique and rhetorical philosophy anticipate this development, but it is through Gadamer's dialogical development of Heideggerian *Destruktion* that it becomes concrete.

The best means of illustrating the practical significance of Gadamer's development of *Destruktion* is to work through Smith's contrast between the hermeneutically-defined marital relationship and the clash of power-interests that occurs in family court. At the outset, Smith errs by sharply distinguishing the public realm of law from the private realm of familial relations.[65] The kinship of the marital relationship is not purely a hermeneutical encounter between two persons. The relationship unavoidably is shaped and enabled by law inasmuch as marriage is a legal term rather than a natural term. To be married is to be recognized as such in the eyes of the law, and to see oneself accordingly. It is the legal character of the marriage relationship that motivates some gays and lesbians to seek such recognition of their life partnership, and leads other gays and lesbians to eschew any such legal status for their relationship. Marriage, for better or worse, has lived significance by virtue of our legal framework and heritage; hermeneutical intimacy is inextricably entwined with law.

---

64. Op. cit., pp. 319–20.
65. Debunking this distinction has been one of the lasting contributions of the critical legal studies movement and has been particularly emphasized by feminist scholars. Examples include Frances E. Olsen, "The Myth of State Intervention in the Family," *University of Michigan Journal of Law Reform* 18 (1985), p. 835; Ruth Gavison, "Feminism and the Public/Private Distinction," *Stanford Law Review* 45 (1992), p. 1. See generally Duncan Kennedy, "The Stages of the Decline of the Public/Private Distinction," *University of Pennsylvania Law Review* 130 (1982), p. 1349.

In addition, marriage is shaped by more than the family law statutes that define the legal significance of marriage. The general law of property, contract and torts enables the civil, social and economic world in which life partners realize their shared plans. This general structuring is now supplemented by the vast regulatory reach of the modern administrative state, which channels and facilitates the life plans of all couples in countless ways. To be married is just to take up one's life with another person in the complex matrix that is significantly, although certainly not exclusively, shaped by legal norms. Smith mistakenly regards the married couple as existing in a pre-legal state, reducing the legal system to its dispute resolution function.

By way of reply to this general critique, Smith might join with Habermas in concluding that the lifeworld of interpersonal relations has been colonized by juridical imperatives,[66] and then argue further that this colonization is nothing less than the covering over of original argument by a derivative manner of being-with-another as legal subjects. Habermas presses this point against Gadamer with a vengeance, arguing that we cannot reverse the colonization by technocratic rationality of the lifeworld by introducing "conversational" capacities from the bygone era of the *polis* at the level of system in the modern bureaucratic state.[67] But this rejoinder is likely to blunt the force of Nietzsche's critique rather than to reinvigorate it. Theorists tend to fall victim to one of two equally disabling orientations: either they follow Habermas in positing a quasi-transcendental principle to save the day, or they embrace a wistful and romantic desire to return to the dialogic encounters of the agora. Gadamer chooses instead to recognize the textuality of modernity, to identify the misunderstandings of understanding that textuality has spawned, and to characterize the hermeneutical situation by identifying legal practice as an exemplar of the activity of understanding in textual culture.

Although there is no definitive separation between law and personal life, certainly there is a valid and meaningful distinction that can be drawn between the understanding fostered by marital intimacy and the understanding achieved in legal interpretation. Smith compares the family law response to a failed marriage to the kinship of a healthy marriage in concluding that law does not recuperate the hermeneutics of original

66. See Jürgen Habermas, *Between Facts and Norms: Contributions to a Discourse Theory of Law and Democracy* (Cambridge, MA: The MIT Press, 1996), pp. 94–99 (William Rehg, trans.) (describing the breakdown of natural law paradigms and the modern necessity of justification of social organization through legal principles of human rights and sovereignty). For extended discussions of these themes, see Jürgen Habermas, *The Theory of Communicative Action: Reason and the Rationalization of Society I* (Boston, MA: Beacon Press, 1984), pp. 243–71 (Thomas McCarthy, trans.) (discussing Max Weber's analysis of the rationalizing role performed by law in the wake of the demythologization of religious and metaphysical worldviews) and Jürgen Habermas, *The Theory of Communicative Action: Lifeworld and System, A Critique of Functionalist Reason II* (Boston, MA: Beacon Press, 1989), pp. 356–73 (Thomas McCarthy, trans.) (analyzing the juridification of family relations and educational relationships as an instance of the colonization of the lifeworld by instrumental reason and the supplanting of communicative reason).

67. Habermas rejects the hermeneutic account of modern legal systems in Habermas, *Between Facts and Norms*, pp. 199–200.

argument. However, his distinction works only by confusing the level at which law operates in a conversational manner. No competent lawyer or judge would suggest that the purpose of family law is to rekindle the failed relationship, but the marital relationship is not the only community served by law.[68] The failure of a marriage reverberates throughout the social fabric, and this personal strife risks introducing violence and recrimination into this broader community. Family law is just an assertion of communal values to shape the manner in which the effects of the failed marriage are felt by the couple, their children, and the wider community in which they will continue to live.

The division of the marital property undeniably can be a contest of wills in the sense that each spouse's attorney seeks the maximum economic value for her client, but this battle is fought against the backdrop of legal norms that are articulated through the case at hand, or are legislated in response to the accumulation of experience in cases. The rules regarding alimony and

68. I do not want to discount the importance of, and perhaps the growing significance of, the "therapeutic jurisprudence" movement. This trend is represented generally in the work of scholars who argue that law should provide more than a dispute resolution procedure, and have encouraged the reconsideration of legal procedures and institutions in light of their effect on the parties. Examples include *Practicing Therapeutic Jurisprudence: Law as a Helping Profession*, ed. Dennis P. Stolle et al. (Durham, NC: Carolina Academic Press, 2000); *Law in a Therapeutic Key: Developments in Therapeutic Jurisprudence*, eds. David B. Wexler and Bruce J. Winick (Durham, NC: Carolina Academic Press, 1996); *Essays in Therapeutic Jurisprudence*, eds. David B. Wexler and Bruce J. Winick (Durham, NC: Carolina Academic Press, 1991). This movement recognizes that the legal imposition of communal values can exacerbate the personal strife of the individuals engaged in a dispute, and attempts to resolve matters in an integrated manner that attends both to the needs of the community and to the lived experience of those involved in the specific legal matter.

There are a number of related developments, such as the rise of the mediation movement. For example, Nancy Welsh has written about the potential for mediation to introduce procedural justice into the settlement of litigated civil cases, thus affirming the social value and dignity of litigants who then are more likely to perceive the courts and their settlement efforts as legitimate. Nancy A. Welsh, "Disputants' Decision Control in Court-Connected Mediation: A Hollow Promise Without Procedural Justice," *Journal of Dispute Resolution* (2002), p. 179; Nancy A. Welsh, "Making Deals in Court-Connected Mediation: What's Justice Got to Do With It?," *Washington University Law Quarterly*, 79 (2001), p. 787.

More specifically, the principles of "therapeutic jurisprudence" have had a large impact on family law scholarship and law reform. As explained recently in the context of exploring how courts deal with substance-abusing fathers,

> therapeutic jurisprudence involves the study of family law as a social force in the lives of family systems affected by paternal substance abuse with acknowledgment that legal proceedings can have both positive and negative consequences for fathers, mothers, and children. Ultimately the value of any legal process is determined by the extent to which it enhances the well-being of the people it affects, and the goal of legal reform is to restructure court systems so that they maximize the therapeutic consequences of legal intervention.

Thomas J. McMahon and Francis Gianni, "Moving from Popular Stereotypes to Therapeutic Jurisprudence," *Family Court Review*, 41 (2003), pp. 347–48. Toward this end, a number of scholars advocate for a unified family court system that would serve families therapeutically, rather than merely responding sporadically to discrete legal conflicts that involve members of the family. Examples include Barbara Babb, "Fashioning an Interdisciplinary Framework for Court Reform in Family Law: A Blueprint to Construct a Unified Family Court," *Southern California Law Review*, 71 (1998), p. 469; Barbara Babb, "An Interdisciplinary Approach to Family Law Jurisprudence: Application of an Ecological and Therapeutic Perspective," *Indiana Law Journal*, 72 (1997), p. 775.

property settlement reflect communal understandings of how we should justly recognize the couple's history together and then fairly appraise how they can best move into the future as individuals within the broader community. These rules constantly are in play as new situations arise that require clarification of these values. For example, when an unmarried cohabitating partner demands alimony-type payments after the termination of the relationship, or when a lesbian demands child support payments from her partner after their (necessarily) non-marital relationship ends, the law must simultaneously invent and reinscribe the norms of the wider community. The legal resolution of these issues is not designed to rebuild the hermeneutical ground of the couple's relationship, but rather is designed to reaffirm the broader bonds of the community in which the former life partners continue to live. The communal interest is even more apparent in the heart-wrenching battles over child custody, when the law seeks to elevate the communal value of promoting the "best interests of the child" over the bitter strife of the competing parents who may be pursuing venal and mean-spirited ends.

One should not confuse the hermeneutical function of law with a rosy-eyed view that litigation effectively instantiates justice in all cases. The law, no less than life partners, too frequently devolves into a contest of wills that betrays its important role in facilitating community. But to recognize that a "perfect" legal system is as elusive as the "perfect" marriage only highlights that it is the very idea of "perfect" in these contexts that raises difficulties. Gadamer's lesson is not that legal practice is a guarantor of hermeneutical integrity, but rather that legal practice reveals the hermeneutical *potential* of textual traditions, which have indelibly shaped the modern age. Legal practice has the potential to enact a form of Smith's "original argument," although the predominantly textual character of legal practice certainly means that the risky openness to another is experienced differently. A more genuine "conversation" emerges in legal practice when the parties break from the routinized bureaucracy and attend to the questions of justice in the case at hand. This provides the opening for Nietzschean critical insight, not as a dictate from principles on high, but as an announcement from *within* practice.[69] Nietzsche's announcement that Christianity had run its course in Western culture drew from his many contemporaries and precursors and itself was a product of Christian acculturation. Similarly, lawyers who challenge the conventional understanding of family law in new contexts simultaneously work within and against legal traditions (as well as within and against cultural, political, and economic traditions).

Gadamer's notion of interpretive *Destruktion* incorporates critical insight. Law is neither a purely mechanical and deductive exercise, nor is it just a clash of power. The decision in *In the Matter of Jacob*[70] by the New York

69. This is the enduring wisdom of Holmes's pragmatism: law is not a "brooding omnipresence in the sky" that operates "logically," but rather is a practical engagement grounded in "experience."

70. 636 N.Y.S. 2d 716 (1995).

Court of Appeals provides an example of the *Destruktive* element at work in the family law context. The Court considered a consolidated appeal regarding two petitions for adoption: in one case the biological mother wished to consent to the adoption of her child by her co-habitating partner, and in the other case the biological mother wished to consent to the adoption of her child by her co-habitating female partner. These petitions were problematic because the adoption statutes permitted only an "adult unmarried person" or "an adult husband and his adult wife" to adopt, and also provided that upon adoption the "natural parents of the adoptive child shall be relieved of all parental duties toward and of all responsibilities for and shall have no rights over such adoptive child ..."[71] Reading these statutory provisions in a crudely literal manner suggested that the biological mothers' legal rights must be terminated upon the adoption of the children by their co-habitating partners. Reading these statutory provisions against the background assumption that adoption was not designed to permit an unmarried adult to share parental rights with the biological mother suggested that the adoptions could not proceed in the first instance. By a narrow margin, the Court read the adoption statutes to permit the biological mothers to retain parental rights when their co-habitating partners adopted the children.

The dissenting judges assailed this case as an example of improper judicial lawmaking, arguing that "cobbling law together out of interpretive ambiguity that transforms fundamental, societally recognized relationships and substantive principles is neither sound statutory construction nor justifiable lawmaking."[72] Partisan political campaigns emphasize the social stakes for judicial appointments in similar terms, concluding that judicial will to power is the name of the game rather than reasoned elaboration. But a careful reading of the case makes clear that the majority does not simply recognize unmarried partners as suitable adoptive parents and then spin a gossamer of legal analysis to hide its exercise of raw power. The majority opinion provides a detailed interpretation of the statutes in the context of the case at hand, and delivers a critical assessment of that context. Space constraints preclude a detailed reconstruction of the opinion, but the court clearly is thinking through inherited concepts and language in charting a new path for the development of law rather than creating an entirely new path. If it appears other-worldly to talk of *Destruktion* as the revitalizing of lifeless concepts by working through them without purporting to overcome them, the majority opinion in *Jacob* provides a concrete example of this process at work.

The Court begins by noting the underlying purpose of the adoption statute – to secure the best possible homes for children – and then concludes that the adoption statutes do permit two unmarried adults who function as a child's parents to obtain legal status as parents. This is not

71. The court was interpreting N.Y. Domestic Relations Law § 110 and N.Y. Domestic Relations Law § 117.

72. *In the Matter of Jacob*, 636 N.Y.S. 2d at 733 (Bellacosa, dissenting).

purely a result-oriented exercise, inasmuch as the court carefully recounts legislative developments and administrative regulations that have effectuated this purpose under the statutory scheme. The court articulates what the law means in the current context and does not create law *ex nihilo*, even if the interpretation of the statutes involves a simultaneous critique of the context in which it is applied. This is *Destruktion* in action, and is precisely what Gadamer attempts to capture by characterizing legal texts as containing a "free space of meaningful concretization that has to carry out the interpretation for the purpose of practical application" through the "creative legal function" of applying the law to a set of facts. This is possible by virtue of the community of legal interpreters who reinscribe (which is to say, critically and creatively apply) communal values in the manner in which they adjudicate family law disputes. Interestingly, both formalists and radical deconstructionists would argue that *Destruktion* provides cover for the imposition of political will, with the former retreating to a mythical linguistic "plain meaning" to serve as an anchor while the latter embrace the "free play" of the text. Both perspectives ring hollow in the ears of lawyers and judges who struggle through the de-centering experience of interpretation, and experience of *Destruktion* that animates Gadamer's middle path.

Finally, Smith's family law example assumes that the role of the lawyer is just to resolve interpretive disputes within a textual tradition. In fact, the lawyer's role as counselor is paramount, even though it is often forgotten in the litigation models that dominate even Gadamer's image of legal practice. Much of legal practice involves deliberating with one's clients in order to determine the best means (often in tandem with other professionals such as accountants, therapists, doctors, and others) of realizing their clients' goals within the given situation. The first hermeneutical challenge for a lawyer is to hear her client's story and to enable the client to understand competing stories told by the client's adversary and by the society writ large. The rhetorical exchanges that comprise the lawyer–client relationship in the initial interviews preceding a divorce are key features of an original argument that eventually might be translated and filtered into legal briefs and motion arguments. The client's pain and anguish is heard and felt by the lawyer when she is representing her client effectively, and it is this corporeal experience that the lawyer brings into the legal venue for a hearing. The interactions of lawyers and judges in settlement conferences, pretrial hearings, negotiations and even within the stylized drama of litigation raise the potential for understanding through full-bodied original argument.

IV. Conclusion

Smith's argument that law is a contest of wills that might benefit from Nietzschean insight but cannot aspire to Gadamerian dialogue rests on too narrow a reading of Gadamer's revival of Heideggerian *Destruktion* and too narrow a picture of legal practice. The hermeneutical-rhetorical reality of legal practice points toward a text-based experience of "original argument" that cannot be completely covered over by the pretense of logical formalism. Gadamer is correct: legal practice is exemplary. Because the rhetoric of legal practice is to deny its rhetoricity, however, legal practice cannot be taken at its word, but only in its activity. Smith argues that legal practice covers over the original argument of belonging, but Gadamer shows that legal practice resists the leveling descriptions offered by too many of its participants and instead represents a belonging-together and community-of-interest that is mediated textually rather than corporeally. The task of critical legal theory is to facilitate *Destruktion*, a creative overcoming that is always potentially present but all too often is concealed in the overt moves of practice. Legal theorists oriented by this understanding of law can avoid the twin dangers of deductive formalism and postmodern *ennui*. Rather than attempting to set a methodological agenda that would straight-jacket practice with top-down conceptions of how practice should unfold, or standing aloof by ironically refusing to engage in the dynamism of practice, critical legal theory should work from a Nietzschean model of critique and on the basis of a Gadamerian dialogic model of interpretation. In this paper I have charted the ontological space in which this critical activity can flourish, with a few examples offered as guideposts. The project of critical legal theory is to unleash the dynamism of practice through *Destruktion*, to render original argument audible once again, even if only as a whisper amidst the cacophony of power and domination that mark the bureaucratic imperatives of modern law.

Acknowledgements

This article is based on a talk given at the 2003 Annual Meeting of the Association for the Study of Law, Culture and the Humanities in New York City. I thank Chris Smith for his incisive comments during the panel, and that audience for their important interventions. I also benefitted substantially from the detailed comments by three anonymous reviewers, and I owe Peter Fitzpatrick a special debt for his assistance in the final stages of the project.

[7]

NIETZSCHE'S GNOSIS OF LAW

Frederick M. Dolan

Laws, I suppose, are more like maxims and imperatives than like arguments. Maxims and imperatives tell us what to do or what to believe, while arguments offer reasons for doing or believing something. Friedrich Nietzsche was very much concerned with the questions of what to do and what to believe, and with the tortured relationship between doing or believing something and having a reason to do or believe it. A characteristic gesture of Nietzsche's is to bring to a close an elaborate skeptical argument, one that seems to dissolve grounds for action or knowledge, by issuing a bold, severe, pithy injunction, such as: "*Become hard*!"[1] Indeed, resolve in the face of chaos, equanimity at the brink of the abyss of nihilism, is more or less Nietzsche's ethos. It was also, regrettably, one of Nietzsche's legacies to the spiritual bearing of the twentieth century—I have in mind the grotesque, hyperbolic enactments of courageous self-sacrifice and facing-up-to that we find in Martin Heidegger, for example, and Michel Foucault, when they are at their worst. For Heidegger in his Nietzsche period, it is nothing less than the destiny of the West for which we are to accept responsibility. For Foucault, I suspect, it is something like the unintended consequences of the history that engendered us for which we are somehow to answer. Happily, both Heidegger and Foucault found in their later years more mature, generous, and edifying stances. Moreover, Nietzsche's ethos of command and severity turns out, upon inspection, to be an impression made by mere rhetoric, hiding a more nuanced and paradoxical understanding of action, reason, and rule.

The paradox is that the only rule is that there are no rules. Acknowledging the truth of this paradox—that is, acknowledging that there are no rules, but also that to say so is paradoxical, that, indeed, such a truth cannot quite be said, since it negates itself—is part of what I mean by "gnosis." If we attend to Nietzsche's gnosis

---

[1] FRIEDRICH NIETZSCHE, *Of Old and New Law—Tables* para. 29, *in* THUS SPOKE ZARATHUSTRA 231 (R. J. Hollingdale ed., 1969).

of law rather than to the rhetoric of severity with which he (or his Zarathustra) announces a new table of laws for a new *Rangordnung*, we will see that, far from telling us what to do or believe, Nietzsche offers no prescriptions or commands, and in that sense has almost nothing to say. (The "almost" is crucial, as that is what distinguishes Nietzsche from nihilism.) If law tells us what to do, Nietzsche is neither criticizing nor inventing law, but twisting free of it. Twisting free of what we have heard about what law has told us to do.

I said that (as I imagine) law is closer to maxims and imperatives than to arguments, but it is worth noting that Nietzsche is extremely skeptical about the latter. Argument, *pace* Heidegger, is the piety of thought, mobilizing all the verities of obligation, responsibility, and justification. Nietzsche the immoralist will have none of that. It is not only that insights are worth more than arguments, as Nietzsche affirms in the first sentence of his first book. It is also because when the most important insights prove upon reflection to be philosophically scandalous, the insight is at odds with philosophy as it is traditionally conceived, with its essentially public values of communicability, demonstration, and dialectic. Nietzsche's attraction to this view has very often made philosophers and political scientists reluctant to admit that Nietzsche has a truly compelling claim on our attention. If insights without arguments scandalize the philosophers and politicians, however, arguments barren of insight are equally offensive to Nietzsche. Even more to the point, offering arguments for insights can actually do harm to the insights Nietzsche wishes to articulate and shelter.

How so? Nietzsche's answer to that question is part of an ancient puzzle concerning the ineffability of particular things. Consciousness is first and last an effect of language, and language, as Nietzsche imagines it, is first and last an instrument of social cohesion. When we learn to speak, we learn no more than crudities, maxims, and rough approximations that pertain to human, all-too-human necessities. As Nietzsche writes in Book Five of *The Gay Science*:

> This is the essence of phenomenalism and perspectivism as *I* understand them: Owing to the nature of *animal consciousness*, the world of which we can become conscious is only a surface—and sign—world, a world that is made common and meaner; whatever becomes conscious *becomes* by the same token shallow, thin, relatively stupid, general, sign, herd signal; all becoming conscious involves a great and thorough corruption, falsification, reduction to superficialities, and

generalization.[2]

What is most real is only ever the singularity present before and in us—*haecceitas*—and that forever escapes our attempts to articulate it through names, categories, and concepts, however elaborate. This strange inaccessibility of language to the unique, concrete individual experience of being—what Heidegger calls *Dasein*, hyphenating the term in order to stress the irreducible "thereness," or singularity, of human being—the way in which who and how we are eludes our descriptions of ourselves—is part of what Nietzsche means by the Dionysian, or, in *Thus Spoke Zarathustra*, simply "life." We grasp at life with our ideas and systems, hoping to fix its constants once and for all, but we never succeed. Or rather, we succeed all too well, mistaking the name for the thing itself and regarding particular things and events as lower or less substantial than the invisible but universal laws we formulate. As Ralph Waldo Emerson says, reality slips through our fingers when we clutch hardest, and Nietzsche agrees: the traditional philosopher's approach to truth—the identification of universals—makes him the intellectual equivalent of a boorish bounder:

> Supposing truth to be a woman—what? is the suspicion not well founded that all philosophers, when they have been dogmatists, have had little understanding of women? that the gruesome earnestness, the clumsy importunity with which they have hitherto been in the habit of approaching truth have been inept and improper means for winning a wench?[3]

As with lovers, the proper method for winning truths is to offer them nourishment by making them a part of one's life. To share them, to show them off to others, given the perspective character of language, is to make them "common and meaner." Having done just that in *Beyond Good and Evil*, Nietzsche concludes that book by lamenting that his thoughts are now "ready to become truths—they already look so immortal, so pathetically righteous, so boring!"[4] Only those thoughts that are about to depart one's life anyway may in good conscience be given over to communication.

Hence Nietzsche's secretiveness about his highest thought, eternal recurrence. Nietzsche's key insight is that meaningful life, with its roles, rules, responsibilities, rewards, and punishments, is

---

[2] FRIEDRICH NIETZSCHE, THE GAY SCIENCE para. 354, at 299-300 (Walter Kaufmann trans., 1974).

[3] *Preface to* FRIEDRICH NIETZSCHE, BEYOND GOOD AND EVIL 13, 13 (R. J. Hollingdale trans., 1973).

[4] *Id.* para. 296, at 201.

an illusion. This is what Zarathustra (and Nietzsche himself) experiences as eternal recurrence. The latter is expressed in the story of Zarathustra's encounter with a dwarf who mocks his ambitions for mankind. Zarathustra replies by saying in effect that he is well aware that his hope for a new rank ordering is a delusion, because behind the thought of the *Übermensch* lie his *Hintergedanken*, the thoughts behind his thoughts:

> "Behold this gateway, dwarf!" I went on: "it has two aspects. Two paths come together here: no one has ever reached their end.
>
> "This long lane behind us: it goes on for an eternity. And that long lane ahead of us – that is another eternity.
>
> "They are in opposition to one another, these paths; they abut on one another: and it is here at this gateway that they come together. The name of the gateway is written above it: 'Moment.'[5]

The thought of eternal recurrence says that time only seems linear; it is really circular, utterly lacking in any external or final regulating or ordering intelligence, purpose, or point. Colloquially, it is going nowhere. On that assumption, each moment is an utterly unique emerging from nothingness (what Zarathustra calls "eternity," that is, timelessness) and returning to nothingness. Resentful of their inability to master the moment—their powerlessness to affect eternity's coming forth and slipping away—the philosophers (as well as the priests and politicians before and after them) have asserted that time is a mere bridge between origin and destination, teaching guilt and responsibility to persuade us to use our moment in time as the mere instrument of a Higher End. Instead of seeing the moment as a platform from which to will himself towards a *telos*, Zarathustra dwells in the moment itself, either plunging into its depths or scaling its heights. From his perspective there is no doer behind the deed, no self-distinct from its actions or even from its world. *Sub species aeternitatus*—that is, from the point of view of having welled up here just for a moment—one's sense of oneself as a separate entity, actively shaping the world, responsible to it or to oneself, is revealed as an illusory, social, moral interpretation—that is to say, a perspective.

Eternal recurrence is not only a fiction in the larger fiction of the philosophical drama titled *Thus Spoke Zarathustra*. It is also a concretely embodied experience, or *gnosis*, of Friedrich Nietzsche's. Nietzsche describes the event in *Ecce Homo*:

---

[5] FRIEDRICH NIETZSCHE, *Of the Vision and the Riddle* para. 2, *in* THUS SPOKE ZARATHUSTRA 178 (R. J. Hollingdale ed., 1969).

> [T]he idea of the eternal recurrence, this highest formula of affirmation that is at all attainable, belongs in August 1881: it was penned on a sheet with the notation underneath, "6,000 feet beyond man and time." That day I was walking through the woods along the lake of Silvaplana; at a powerful pyramidal rock not far from Surlei I stopped. It was then that this idea came to me (*Da kam mir dieser Gedanke*).[6]

That winter, in Rapallo, the thought of recurrence was personified:

> Mornings I would walk in a southerly direction on the splendid road to Zoagli, going up past pines with a magnificent view of the sea; in the afternoon, whenever my health permitted it, I walked around the whole bay. . . . It was on these two walks that the whole of *Zarathustra I* occurred to me, and especially Zarathustra himself as a type; rather, he *overtook me*.[7]

Against a long tradition, Nietzsche does not show that the validity of his insight can be established independently of the way he personally acquired it. On the contrary, that the insight could have come to him alone is, if anything, a central dimension of its authority: "One hears, one does not seek; one accepts, one does not ask who gives; like lightning, a thought flashes up, with necessity, without hesitation regarding its form—I never had any choice."[8]

Nietzsche, the connoisseur of music, receives the thought of recurrence as something that is heard—indeed, *over*heard, as if by accident—while treading a path. His Zarathustra is fellow-hiker who *overtakes*—catches up with, and then passes—his creator, who is swept up by his idea. Zarathustra's account of eternal recurrence, appropriately enough, includes visions of lanes that stretch into eternity and of creatures that have traversed and will traverse them an infinite number of times. Paradoxically, the most concrete and embodied experience of knowledge yields the revelation that *this moment* is in effect *everything*.

Nietzsche's gnosis of the moment frees him—momentarily—from the illusion of the ego and the compulsion to control, enabling him to twist free of guilt, responsibility, and resentment and to live joyously and affirmatively. It also yields an anti-Cartesian philosophical position: the ego is conferred upon us by "the metaphysics of language," that is, the grammar of subject and verb. Nietzsche writes:

---

[6] FRIEDRICH NIETZSCHE, ECCE HOMO para. 1, at 295 (Walter Kaufmann ed. & trans., 1989).

[7] *Id.* para. 1, at 297-98.

[8] *Id.* para. 3, at 300.

> Language belongs in its origin to the age of the most rudimentary form of psychology: we find ourselves in the midst of a rude fetishism when we call to mind the basic presuppositions of the metaphysics of language—which is to say, of *reason*. It is *this* which sees everywhere deed and doer; this which believes in will as cause in general; this which believes in the "ego", in the ego as being, in the ego as substance, and which *projects* its belief in the ego-substance on to all things. . . .[9]

This tells us something about the status of the Nietzschean Superman. Knowing that the ego is an illusion, Nietzsche must also know that the creative will of his *Übermensch* is a mere fiction. Indeed, the Superman—the goal, as Zarathustra characterizes him, to which man is only a bridge—is altogether too rational a project in light of the experience of eternal recurrence. The sacrifices and celebrations offered to honor him—the relentless hammering of old ideals, the audacious proclamation of new values, the command to harden oneself so as to face up to the rigorous demands of the post-human—are best understood as public paraphernalia that shelter a more properly *personal* concern with the Moment.

Not that there is an absolute distinction between the exoteric and esoteric dimensions of Nietzsche's knowledge. On the contrary, Nietzsche thrives on dangerously confusing the two, even in his own mind. So Nietzsche does not respond to his experience of the eternal return by allowing his ecstatic vision to illuminate the egoic world, or not exactly. Instead, he relies on Zarathustra's courage and replies: "Was *that* life? Well then! Once more!"[10] Having discovered that life is a dream, Nietzsche elects to go on dreaming. He is a lucid dreamer, dreaming the dream of creative will laying down the law yet knowing all the while that he is nothing more than a moment of relative stability in the flux of sheer becoming. Thus, Nietzsche's two contradictory slogans, carpe diem and *amor fati*. The thought that one is nothing more than a piece of fate is transformed into the belief that to say so is to seize the day. Egoic world-mastery may be illusory, but Nietzsche affirms the value of illusion. He must, because the insight vouchsafed to him is that existence is meaningless. On the one hand, this thought releases him from all responsibility and resentment and prepares the way for joy and affirmation; on the other hand, it plunges him into the abyss of nihilism. Reality is the

[9] FRIEDRICH NIETZSCHE, *'Reason' in Philosophy* para. 5, *in* TWILIGHT OF THE IDOLS 48 (R. J. Hollingdale trans., 1990).

[10] FRIEDRICH NIETZSCHE, *The Vision and the Riddle* para. 1, *in* THUS SPOKE ZARATHUSTRA 178 (R. J. Hollingdale ed., 1969).

eternal return of singular events, and the idea of a subject who adds to that uncontrolled process of becoming by interpreting it is the greatest illusion of all—but that means, not only the most illusory, but also the most beneficial.

But can this really be what Nietzsche, or Zarathustra means by eternal recurrence? Is time simply an illusion? Nietzsche's cleverest readers have not resisted the temptation to answer no, and persuasive evidence can be adduced in support of the denial. Are not the presentations of the doctrine that are given in Nietzsche's own voice thought-experiments, not arguments—parables that invite us to draw the consequences that would follow *if* eternal recurrence were true? Did not Nietzsche have Zarathustra reject his animals' characterizations of eternal recurrence as the mere repetition of identical states of affairs? Does not Zarathustra's recovery from the trauma inflicted upon him by the idea that everything recurs imply that he has discovered a way of understanding recurrence that engenders joy rather than despair? The real teaching, it seems to follow, must be some *reinterpretation* of the idea that is communicated overtly in *The Gay Science* and *Thus Spoke Zarathustra.*

Gilles Deleuze characterizes the real teaching as an understanding of time as "the repetition of difference." His argument is rather elliptical, but its substance is fairly simple. It relies on problems involved in trying, from a first-person perspective, to identify the moments that comprise a temporal sequence. What is it, Deleuze asks, that allows us to identify a moment in time? A moment in time is said to be distinguishable from other moments in that it occurs, say, in the present rather than in the past or future. But it must also be similar to those other moments in that it is, generically, "a moment in time." Saying that, however, seems to imply some kind of atemporal Model Moment to which we can compare real moments so as to establish their identity. It presupposes a criterion that is somehow outside of time, permanently accessible as an unchanging measure, like the quasi-mythical Paris meter discussed by Wittgenstein. How plausible is that? We cannot move through time at will—we cannot leave the present in order to compare it with the past or future, to say nothing of leaving the temporal continuum altogether in order to consult some atemporal criterion that would allow us to verify the continuity of the present moment with those of the past. Thus it seems that there is no ground for saying that the present moment has any relationship at all with the past or future. The present moment, so far as physical time is concerned, was not *caused by* the past, nor is it *causing* the future. That idea of time is merely the perspective of the animal that learned to make promises (as Nietzsche characterizes human beings in *On the Genealogy of Morals*) and that therefore sees its actions in instrumental terms, in which one's future is "produced" by one's actions in the present and in which one's past consists of actions for which one is responsible because they were one's doings. Real time, on the other hand, is sheer event like uniqueness, and apparently inconceivable. In so far as we wish to view time as a series of moments that are identical except for their location in a temporal series, that series is properly understood as the repetition of difference.

With his characteristic love of paradox, Deleuze expresses this idea by saying that temporality of this sort only "begins" with the "third" repetition, i.e., the future:

> [T]he Before and the During are and remain repetitions, but operate only once and for all.... The frontier is no longer between a first time and a repetition that it renders hypothetically possible, but between the conditional repetitions and the third repetition or *repetition within the eternal return* which renders impossible the return of the other two. Only the third Testament turns on itself.
>
> ....
>
> ... What is essential is that we find ... no *prior identity*, no *internal resemblance* ... different relates to different *by means of* difference itself.[11]

A single moment of time cannot be "first," the earliest of a series of repeated moments, apart from a "second" or later moment in contrasting opposition to which the first moment *is* "earlier." The unity of these two moments establishes relations of similarity, analogy, resemblance, and identity, as each of them arises "mutually" and so are measured against one another. The past and present form a stable, balanced, and harmonious pair. The "third" instance, however, undoes all that, for the third is connected to the first only as a link in a chain: there is no direct contact between them, and that is enough to undermine the normative power of resemblance and continuity over the flow of time. That is what Deleuze means by saying that the first two repetitions happen "only once," after which, so to speak, time goes on in a manner entirely disconnected from norms. No moment of time bears any intrinsic resemblance to any other—or to put it differently, eternal recurrence is a vision of reality as sheer chaos,

---

[11] GILLES DELEUZE, DIFFERENCE AND REPETITION 296-99 (Paul Patton trans., 1994). For the sake of clarity, the author has taken the liberty of rearranging the order in which Deleuze's sentences appear.

or again, that at each moment *anything and everything is possible.*

Deleuze's intention in part is to refute those who argue that time is unreal, such as the British idealist J.M.E. McTaggart. In his nomenclature, to say of a moment, *M*, that it is present, will be past, and has been future:

> [M]eans that *M* is present at a moment of present time, past at some moment of future time, and future at some moment of past time. But .... [i]f *M* is present, there is no moment of past time at which it is past. But the moments of future time, in which it is past, are equally moments of past time, in which it cannot be past.[12]

McTaggart observes that "the moments at which *M* has any one of the three [tenses, of past, present, and future] are also moments at which it cannot have that [tense]."[13] Time is something about the way we see things, he concludes, and has no physical reality; time, in effect, is an illusion. It is as if Nietzsche, on Deleuze's reading, accepts McTaggart's premise but denies the conclusion: each moment is utterly unique, but not at all unreal. Since the present is not merely all that is, but *everything*, any present is eternal. The idealist, impressed by his discovery that the present is defined in relation to past and future but that past and future are logical impossibilities, draws the conclusion that the present is unreal. Nietzsche seems more impressed by the irrelevance, to the problem of living one's life, of time in the physical sense. Once the metaphysics of physical time have been abandoned, we are left with the time of our lives, which is the living through of an eternal present—one that becomes deeper and richer as it "goes on," as we reinterpret earlier events in light of later ones, regard the future on the basis of a continually enriching past, and allow everything there is to emerge. Being in time becomes a matter of seeing how things turn out, and evaluating them, not being swept along a putatively physical, "automatic" temporal sequence.[14] To take responsibility for one's past actions, to act now for the sake of future generations—none of this is a fixed law of nature or human nature, but rather a way of being human. It is possible to see oneself as an identity that remains constant, and, equally so, to see oneself as a process that simply takes place. The trick, Nietzsche seems to think, is to regard oneself as both: an amoral process, beyond good and evil, and an identity that persists through the

[12] 2 JOHN MCTAGGART ELLIS MCTAGGART, THE NATURE OF EXISTENCE 21 (C. D. Broad ed., 1968) (1927)

[13] *Id.*

[14] Kierkegaard, Bergson, Dummett, and, of course, Heidegger have offered similar observations.

process and makes choices, decisions, evaluations.

To say that the central aspect of a doctrine is an experience that can be pointed to, that ought to be sheltered, but that cannot and must not be justified, is to suggest a cultic practice, one that is hostile to public scrutiny and its dull and indiscriminate standards. Cult is *cultus*, *colere*—to cultivate, nurture, form, foster, and refine, with more ancient connections to such meanings as inhabit, dwell, sojourn. A cult, we might say, is a way of being, of dwelling or inhabiting or occupying the world, of leading a life, and Nietzsche's Moment is an insight to be cultivated, perhaps indicated, but not demonstrated or argued or enjoined. Academicians commonly regard Nietzsche as a cult figure rather than a serious thinker, but academic philosophy merely sacrifices to different gods, above all the Apollonian forces of the public arena. The latter honor stark oppositions and sharp distinctions, and arguments that shore up the oversimplifications thus derived. Argument, according to Nietzsche, is like war and the danger of war is that it makes us not evil, but unsubtle and indelicate. The cultivation of *gnosis*, on the other hand, requires flights into concealment and resort to masks. The cultivator of insight sometimes exploits the withering attention of the public to weaken doctrines he wishes to attack, but this decision is itself not based on the desire to prevail in argument and does not recognize argument and demonstration as standards according to which the value of an insight is decided.

Nietzsche cultivates above all by means of style. For Nietzsche, contra Plato and a long philosophical and metaphysical tradition, it is not that we become truly human by acquiring truths, but rather that truths become lively when their utterance is inflected by an individuated personality. Philosophy is primarily a matter of tone, attitude, style, and stance, and what matters most in an argument is how it is said. But because Nietzsche emerges from the experience of the eternal return having affirmed egoic illusion rather than dissolved it, the philosophical voice that he constructs is heroic and, it must be said, severe, caustic, and imperative. Even so, because Nietzsche's attitude is of one who seeks to win the game of spiritual power over humanity yet knowing all the while that the outcome will be determined by anything but his ego, his imperious tone is accompanied uneasily by an almost divinely modest self-mockery. Nietzsche's insight that life is meaningless and value is an illusion requires him to pursue the difficult task of forgetting what he has learned without wholly succeeding in doing so. Concretely, this means living out the fantasy of being a poetic lawgiver who would stamp his will on millennia, with occasional comic asides indicating his awareness that he is only dreaming. Nietzsche's philosophy is all-too-modern—an elaborate cult for Everyone and No One designed both to reveal, and protect himself from, the nihilism whose presence he senses at the door of Western civilization.

But there is one more turn to the argument. In Zarathustra's third speech to his followers, he seems to offer the rules or guidelines for a new type of human being, the creator. The creator, we have been told, will establish a new table of laws to hang over a new people, a new system of cruelty to produce a new race of beings. But these laws do not embody values; rather, they adumbrate ways to invent them. And there is no reason at all to suppose that Zarathustra's ways of invention should serve for anyone else. He is interested in himself, not others. Zarathustra (and Nietzsche) *are* antichrists. Whereas Jesus told his followers to deny themselves and take up the cross, Zarathustra and Nietzsche deny what they have been told of morality and law and responsibility for the sake of cultivating the unique moment that each is. It is true that this leads Nietzsche, somewhat regressively, to individuate himself as the one who is powerful enough to affirm even meaningless duration, and, in line with previous lawgivers, to project from that accomplishment a new dispensation for humanity. But this stance implies another: "'This—is now *my* way: where is yours?' Thus I answered those who asked me 'the way.' For *the* way—does not exist!"[15] In the end, as in the beginning, Nietzsche's gnosis yields only the rule that there are no rules, or rather less than that, like Jidda Krishnamurti's conviction that "truth is a pathless land." But Zarathustra should have the last word: "Now I bid you lose me and find yourselves. . . ."[16]

---

[15] FRIEDRICH NIETZSCHE, *Of the Spirit of Gravity* para. 2, *in* THUS SPOKE ZARATHUSTRA 213 (R. J. Hollingdale ed., 1969).

[16] FRIEDRICH NIETZSCHE, *Of the Bestowing Virtue* para. 3, *in* THUS SPOKE ZARATHUSTRA 103 (R. J. Hollingdale ed., 1969).

[8]

FRIEDRICH NIETZSCHE, THE CODE OF MANU, AND THE ART OF LEGISLATION

*Roger Berkowitz**

"Now, the gods who govern life are the meters, for it is thanks to the meters that all living things here below are sustained."

—*Satapatha Brahmana, 8, 2, 2, 8*[1]

"*Wir müssen das Irren lieben und pflegen, es ist der Mutterschooß des Erkennens. Die Kunst als die Pflege des Wahnes—unser Cultus.*"

("We must love and care for error, it is the womb of knowledge. Art as the care of illusion—our cult.")

—*Friedrich Nietzsche*[2]

INTRODUCTION

Political and legal theorists ask the question: What should law be? In so doing, they implicitly or explicitly overlook what law is.

---

* Visiting Lecturer, Amherst College, Departments of Political Science and Law, Jurisprudence, and Social Thought. J.D., 1997, University of California (Berkeley); Ph.D. University of California (Berkeley), Jurisprudence and Social Policy, 2001. I would like to thank Philippe Nonet, Karl Shoemaker, and Jenny Lyn Bader for reading and generously commenting on earlier drafts of this essay.

1 ROBERTO CALASSO, LITERATURE AND THE GODS 148 (Tim Parks trans., 2001).

2 9 FRIEDRICH NIETZSCHE, *Nachgelassene Fragmente 1880-1882*, *in* KRITISCHE STUDIENAUSGABE 504 (Giorgio Colli & Mazzino Montinari eds., 1988) [hereinafter 9 NIETZSCHE, *Nachgelassene 1880-1882*]. All citations from Nietzsche are translated by the author from the *Kritische Studienausgabe*. For some passages in Nietzsche's *Nachlass*, the author has helpfully consulted the unpublished translation of selections from Nietzsche's notebooks, *From Nietzsche's Notebooks: The Notes From "The Will to Power" Restored to Their Integrity and Chronological Order*, by Philippe Nonet (manuscript on file with author). Unless otherwise noted, emphasis in the quotations from Nietzsche's *Nachlass* follows the conventions instituted by the *Kritische Studienausgabe*, the now standard edition of Nietzsche's work. Accordingly, all italicized words are those Nietzsche underlined once. Boldfaced words are those he underlined twice.

This preference for the normative as opposed to the ontological approach to law is rooted in the assumption that law serves social and political ends.

Indeed, in deference to its normative interests, legal scholarship has embraced a diversity of social sciences to assist in the discovery of the best laws. For example, the marriage of law and sociology seeks social norms of fairness according to which particular laws should be understood and interpreted. Similarly, the science of moral philosophy strives to isolate intersubjective moral norms that will guide legislation and legal interpretation. Positivist legal science strives to determine rules of recognition for the identification of valid laws that guaranty the certainty and security promised by the rule of law. Most recently, the sciences of both rational and behavioral economics have emerged as powerful tools, facilitating the discovery of those laws that maximize efficiency.

These various sciences of law embrace different ends governed by their different understandings of justice. However, as important as these differences are, these legal sciences share an equally important and often overlooked assumption about the nature of law. Law, according to normative-positivist-socio-economic legal scholars, is something knowable through scientific inquiry. In other words, the different positivist sciences of law presuppose a common subordination of law to science. As a result, the reduction of law to an object of science threatens to transform law into a means to an end so that law's foundation in justice, as opposed to politics, becomes, at best, questionable, and at worst, impossible.

No thinker has been so struck by the transformation of law from an activity into a knowable object of science as Friedrich Nietzsche. Against the belief that scientific truth leads to justice, Nietzsche affirms the necessity of illusion and error. As Nietzsche writes in the above epigraph, art, as "the care of illusion," must replace truth as the "womb of knowledge." Art, Nietzsche writes, "*is worth more* than "truth."[3] Just as truth is set within the aesthetic realm of creative action, so too must law be, in truth, a work of art.[4] In other words, law is given not through science but in the act of artistic legislation.

To understand what Nietzsche means by the art of legislation,

[3] 13 FRIEDRICH NIETZSCHE, *Nachgelassene Fragmente 1887-1889*, *in* KRITISCHE STUDIENAUSGABE para. 14[21], at 227 (Giorgio Colli & Mazzino Montinari eds., 1988) [hereinafter 13 NIETZSCHE, *Nachgelassene 1887-1889*].

[4] I am indebted to Philippe Nonet who first inspired me to investigate the relation between law and the work of art.

this essay turns to his writings on the Code of Manu. What Nietzsche refers to as the *Gesetzbuch des Manu* first appears within his discussion of "The 'Betterers' of Mankind," in *Twilight of the Idols*.[5] Nietzsche's notebooks from 1888, especially notebooks fourteen and fifteen, are filled with references to Manu, the ancient Hindu God and legislator. These pages show Nietzsche's intense efforts to work through the significance of the Hindu religion as expressed in the Manu Code. And nowhere is Nietzsche's intense attraction to the Manu Code more evident than in his problematic book, *Der Antichrist*, the first and only completed volume of Nietzsche's projected four-volume work, the *Revaluing of All Values*.[6] As Giorgio Colli rightly saw, the Manu Code made an "enormous and exaggerated impression on him."[7]

It has long since been determined that what Nietzsche knew of the Manu Code he got from the translation by Louis Jacolliot.[8] Jacolliot, an amateur Indiophile, claimed to have completed his translation, with the help of a learned Brahmin, from an authentic edition of the Manu Code he discovered in the Tamil region of southern India.[9] Unfortunately, the original text from which Jacolliot worked has never been found.[10]

Jacolliot's translation of the teachings of Manu has been universally discredited.[11] It differs widely from the more scholarly editions, sometimes significantly; as a result, many of Nietzsche's citations from Manu are nowhere to be found in the authoritative texts.[12] In one important instance, Nietzsche's citation of Manu's

---

[5] 6 FRIEDRICH NIETZSCHE, *Götzen-Dämmerung*, *in* KRITISCHE STUDIENAUSGABE 100 (Giorgio Colli & Mazzino Montinari eds., 1988) [hereinafter 6 NIETZSCHE, *Götzen-Dämmerung*].

[6] Nietzsche at times suggested that the Antichrist was itself the complete Revaluing of All Values: "Meine *Umwerthung aller Werthe*, mit dem Haupttitel '**der Antichrist**' ist fertig. In den nächsten zwei Jahren habe ich die Schritte zu thun, um das Werk in 7 Sprachen übersetzen zu lassen; die *erste* Auflage in jeder Sprache c. eine Million Exemplare." Letter from Nietzsche to Paul Deussen, Nov. 26, 1888, *in* 8 FRIEDRICH NIETZSCHE, KRITISCHE SAMMTLICHE BRIEFE 492 (Giorgio Colli & Mazzino Montinari eds., 1986). *But see* Giorgio Colli, *Die Schriften von 1888*, *in* 6 NIETZSCHE, *Götzen-Dämmerung*, *supra* note 5. Such sentiments reflect Nietzsche's already failing mental state in 1888, his increasing "loss of contact with reality," and his abandonment of his philosophical project of the "*Wille zur Macht*" in favor of a more personal and polemical attack on modernity.

[7] 13 NIETZSCHE, *Nachgelassene 1887-1889*, *supra* note 3, at 667 ("[G]roßen, ja übertriebenen Eindruck auf ihn.").

[8] LOUIS JACOLLIOT, LES LÉGISLATEURS RELIGIEUX: MANOU, MOÏSE —MAHOMET (1876).

[9] *See* Annemarie Etter, *Nietzsche und das Gesetzbuch des Manu*, *in* 16 NIETZSCHE-STUDIEN 340, 346 (Ernst Behler et al. eds., 1987).

[10] *Id.*

[11] *See generally Introduction* to THE LAWS OF MANU xvi-xxii (Wendy Doniger & Brian K. Smith trans., 1991). For a more sustained critique, see Etter, *supra* note 9.

[12] *See* Etter, *supra* note 9.

regulations governing the Chandala in *Götzen-Dämmerung* is taken neither from the Manu text, nor from Jacolliot's free translation. Rather, it is appropriated from a rambling twenty-two page footnote in which Jacolliot defends his inconceivable theory that the Manu Code was written in its final formula 13,300 years before the birth of Christ and that all Semitic cultures are traceable back to an emigration of Chandala occurring between 8,000 and 4,000 years before Christ.[13] At the same time, Jacolliot opines that western civilizations, including the peoples of Europe and Egypt, are the result of emigration by the Hindus, and the higher castes, under the influence of the Manu Code. Annemarie Etter, in a thorough analysis of the reliability of Nietzsche's impression of the Manu Code, characterizes Jacolliot's notes as "scientifically worthless curiosities."[14] Her evaluation of Nietzsche's image of the Manu Code is similarly critical.[15]

Despite the unreliability of Nietzsche's source material, however, an understanding of the Manu Code is an essential part of any inquiry into the role of art in Nietzsche's legal as well as his metaphysical thinking. On one level, the Manu Code is an example of Nietzsche's identification of positive law (*Gesetz*) and art. Both *Gesetz* and art are artifices. They are semblances (*Schein*). As such, they are delusions and errors that are the foundations and justifications for all claims to truth. Just as truth is a lie that has come to be believed, so too is law (*Recht*) a posited law (*Gesetz*) that has come to be accepted as just.

On another level, Nietzsche's claim that *Gesetz* founds *Recht* reveals that positive law does not merely reflect a higher, more natural law. Positive law (*Gesetz*) is not simply the expression of a prior idea of law, but names, instead, a revolutionary and decisively modern understanding of law itself. *Gesetz* comes to justify *Recht*, so that what is right and just is indistinguishable from what is legally posited. In other words, *Gesetz* stands above *Recht* as art stands above truth, thereby inverting the traditional hierarchies.

The priority of *Gesetz* and art over *Recht* and truth reveals an important relation between *Gesetz* and art. *Gesetz*, for Nietzsche, is always given in art.

If law is positive law given through a work of art, then law awaits at least two potential fates. One is that law, and with it art, becomes an object of science. Since law is an artifice that must deny its artificiality, it is fated to become law whose absolute

[13] *See id.* at 349.

[14] *Id.* at 351.

[15] *See id.* at 342-44, 352.

separation from morality leaves it in need of justifications—justifications that are increasingly sought in various legal sciences. To the extent that law today is increasingly the province of science (be it social science, psychology, or economics), the scientific fate of law is our own. And the fact that opposing sciences now provide opposing justifications is simply a reflection of modern nihilism—the thoughtless belief in the truth of science in spite of an equally firm conviction that science is an instrument of politics rather than truth.

A second possible fate of positive law, however, is that law might escape its fate and abandon its need for scientific justification. While positive law is in need of rationalization to defend its authority, non-positive law disdains justification. Nietzsche's interest in the possibility of a non-positivist idea of law leads to his hypothesis of the relation between law and art. Insofar as law is known through the artistic creation of a beautiful form that calls the members of a culture to the law, then law, as a creative and life-affirming positive law, operates as a "thou shall't" beyond science, morality, and politics. Nietzsche struggles towards just such a non-moral and non-scientific ideal of positive law—a modern *Sittlichkeit der Sitte* as opposed to a *Moralität der Moral*—throughout his work.

To explore these two potential fates of law—to become science or art—this essay asks four questions. First, how does positive law establish itself in a work of art? Second, what is the proper end of artistic legislation? Third, why is law—and with it art—necessary? Fourth, and finally, how can positive law erect natural law and in so doing redeem life? As a whole, the essay seeks to shed light on Nietzsche's statement, first formulated in *The Birth of Tragedy* and reaffirmed throughout his work, that, "only as an *aesthetic phenomenon* is existence and the world to be eternally *justified*."[16]

I. THE HOLY LIE OF LAW (*GESETZ*): ART

Nietzsche's interest in the Code of Manu is, in part, an example of how law establishes itself through art and artifice. The

[16] 1 FRIEDRICH NIETZSCHE, *Die Geburt der Tragödie*, *in* KRITISCHE STUDIENAUSGABE para. 5, at 47 (Giorgio Colli & Mazzino Montinari eds., 1988) [hereinafter 1 NIETZSCHE, *Die Geburt*]. See also Nietzsche's "Attempt at Self-Criticism" published with the reissue of the *Birth of Tragedy* in 1886 in which he links the artist-metaphysics of the *Birth of Tragedy* to his lifelong pursuit of a pessimism beyond good and evil. *Id.* at 17.

authority of law is derived from what Nietzsche calls a "Holy Lie."[17] The core thought of the Holy Lie is that for law to be spoken in the imperative as a "thou shall't," it is also necessary that the law be taken as true.[18] Paradoxically, for law to speak the imperative of truth, law must lie. Positive law, Nietzsche insists, depends upon a lie, an artifice, so that law, like the world itself, can only be redeemed through a "semblance," (*Schein*).[19] Specifically, positive law must appear as a beautiful semblance, one with the power to awe and to seduce man to its authority. Positive law, as the Holy Lie, is posited in the work of art.

The identity of positive law and art is a consequence of law's need for semblance that strikes the Nietzschean legislator. Even as Nietzsche insists that the good lawgiver is the nobleman who naïvely and confidently issues commands that he expects to be obeyed, he recognizes as well that the imperative tone of a good *Gesetzbuch* is as priestly as it is noble. Only the priest, as the mouthpiece of God, has both the "right to lie" and "the *cunning* of revelation."[20] It is as a knower of hidden and sacred law that the priest-legislator asserts his authority.[21] As the priest says: "The truth is there,"[22] so must the legislator say: "*Das Gesetz* is there." The legislator, as the priest, achieves his goal—power—through a lie—namely the erection of the lie as truth and of the *Gesetz* as the natural and true law of God's will.[23] The legislator, like the priest, must be an artist, skilled in artifice—the art of transforming semblance into truth.

The "art of legislation" is the art of the Holy Lie, the creative act through which the legislator positively erects his will as the truth for a people. To say that priestly legislation is an art is to say that legislation is a means to the creation of truth. The art of *Gesetzgebung*, in other words, is the name for the "*Origin of Morality*,"[24] the creative act through which the legislator posits his will as the truth for a people. The great legislator is a gifted artist. What unites the artist and the legislator is their ability to institute truth and to posit *Recht*.

The Holy Lie allows the Manu Code to speak, as any good

---

[17] 6 FRIEDRICH NIETZSCHE, *Der Antichrist* para. 55, *in* KRITISCHE STUDIENAUSGABE 239 (Giorgio Colli & Mazzino Montinari eds., 1988) [hereinafter 6 NIETZSCHE, *Der Antichrist*].

[18] *Id.*

[19] 1 NIETZSCHE, *Die Geburt*, *supra* note 16, at 17.

[20] *Id.*

[21] *See* 13 NIETZSCHE, *Nachgelassene 1887-1889*, *supra* note 3, at 382.

[22] *See* 6 NIETZSCHE, *Der Antichrist*, *supra* note 17, at 239.

[23] *Id.*

[24] 13 NIETZSCHE, *Nachgelassene 1887-1889*, *supra* note 3, at 382.

code must, in the imperative, because it allows positive law (*Gesetz*) to appear as natural and true law (*Recht*). "A *Gesetzbuch*," Nietzsche writes, "never explains the uses, grounds, the casuistic in the pre-history of a *Gesetz*: to do so, it would lose the imperative tone, the "you shall," the presupposition for being obeyed."[25] On the basis of the Holy Lie, the authority of the Manu Code "is grounded on the thesis: God *gave* it, the forefathers *lived* it."[26] God and the forefathers, "*revelation*" and "*tradition*," are the "double wall" that underlie the legislator's unquestioned authority to set down the law without having to prove or justify it.[27] By creatively securing the truth of the illusion as nature, revelation, and tradition, the legislator-priest succeeds in giving his commands not only the authority of force, but the authority of reason and custom—the ultimate and necessary authority for law.

The Holy Lie is central to Nietzsche's understanding of proper legal authority; the successful artifice of the Holy Lie, however, is not in itself sufficient for Nietzschean legislation. The Christian Code, just as much as the Manu Code, was an artistic achievement of a Holy Lie that granted its Commandments imperative force. Even more successfully than the Manu priests, Christian priests have insinuated Christian morality into the history and fiber of the Western World. And yet it is against the success of Christianity's Holy Lie and as a critique of the Christian artist that Nietzsche imagines his book, *Der Antichrist*, to be a curse upon Christian legislative morality. Great artistry, while necessary, is not a sufficient criterion of a good lawbook.

What elevates the Manu Code, from Nietzsche's perspective, is not the artistic means, but rather, the ends for which the Manu legislators enact the Holy Lie. "In the final account," Nietzsche writes, everything "depends on what end (*Zweck*) is lied for."[28] The overriding question of legislation then becomes: To what end does one prevaricate?

II. The Order of Castes and the Sanction of Nature

Following Nietzsche, we must ask: What ends does the Manu Code serve that necessitate and sanctify its Holy Lie?

Nietzsche asserts three fundamental ends that elevate the Manu Code above other legal and moral codes, particularly the

[25] 6 Nietzsche, *Der Antichrist*, *supra* note 17, at 241.
[26] *Id.* at 242.
[27] *Id.* at 241.
[28] *Id.* at 239.

canons of Christianity. First, Nietzsche's preference for the Manu Code is its valuation of preservation over destruction. "In fact," Nietzsche writes, "it makes a difference . . . whether one [with the lie] preserves or *destroys*."[29] Law, like art, is valuable only insofar as it furthers life. The art of legislation, simply put, must be evaluated under the optic of life.[30]

From the perspective of life, the *Gesetzbuch des Manu* is preservative whereas Christian morality is destructive. Christianity erects its Holy Lie in the name of a "beyond" and thus commits itself to the destruction of this world and the imposition of a slave morality. In order to gain power, the Church had to tear down all of the leading institutions of the Ancient World, including both the Jewish priesthood and the Roman empire. The Code of Manu, on the other hand, sought to preserve, rather then destroy, the hierarchical authority. In part, this is simply a historical matter. The Brahmin priests who received the revealed laws of the Manu *Gesetzbuch* were already esteemed members of India's ruling class. In propagating the Holy Lie, therefore, they sought not to destroy the civilization over which they reigned, but to preserve and sustain its existence. The Holy Lie of the Manu Code, therefore, emerges, not out of a hateful spirit of revenge against the rulers, but out of the Brahmin priests' desire to maintain and augment their own power.

A second advantage of the Manu *Gesetzbuch* is that it seeks to preserve social rank. Christianity, on the other hand, attacks the powerful and noble by "taming" and, ultimately, leveling mankind.[31] While this leveling, with the aim of improving man in the name of some higher ideal, has a rich history it is particularly virulent in Christianity. To make man less prideful, weaker, and more moral, Christianity turns man against himself by preying on his guilt. The guilty man is tamed, but Nietzsche disputes that he is thus "improved."[32] Rather, he is "weakened," "disfigured," and "fundamentally castrated."[33] Improvement is better characterized as a taming of the beast that requires a harming of the beast. Neutered and tamed, Christian man is rendered harmless.

Contrary to the Christian desire to tame man, the Manu Code seeks to "breed" him.[34] It does not take as its enemy the powerful

---

[29] *Id.* at 245.

[30] *See* 1 NIETZSCHE, *Die Geburt*, *supra* note 16, at 14.

[31] 6 NIETZSCHE, *Götzen-Dämmerung*, *supra* note 5, at 99.

[32] *See generally* 6 FRIEDRICH NIETZSCHE, *Die "Verbesserer" der Menschhleit* [*The Improvers of Mankind*] para. 2, *in* 6 NIETZSCHE, *Götzen-Dämmerung*, *supra* note 5 [hereinafter 6 Nietzsche, *Die "Verbesserer"*].

[33] 13 NIETZSCHE, *Nachgelassene 1887-1889*, *supra* note 3, at 445.

[34] *See generally* 6 NIETZSCHE, *Die "Verbesserer"*, *supra* note 32, para. 3, at 100.

"Man-the-beast" that must be tamed, but sets its sights on the impure man, the *Nicht-Zucht-Menschen*, the mish-mash-man, the Chandala.[35] This Chandala must be rendered harmless and bred to his servitude. To this end, the Chandala must be made sick: This is what Nietzsche reads into the sanitary rules of the Manu *Gesetzbuch* that require the Chandala to eat unclean vegetables, that limits their sustenance to garlic and onions, and that stipulates that their water cannot be taken from wells or ponds, but only out of marshes and puddles.[36] Through these and other rules, the Manu wages war not on the few and the powerful, but against the many, die "*grossen Zahl*."[37] Instead of taming the strong, it breeds the weak for their assigned societal roles. The many will be sick; however, the great benefit of the Manu Code is that the few, the powerful, are bred into strength and health.

Third, and most importantly, the superiority of the Manu Code rests upon Nietzsche's assertion that its division of society into four castes, each with its own particular obligations and rights, is a desired end because it reflects the natural order of society. "The *order of castes*," Nietzsche writes, "the highest, the most dominant *Gesetz*, is only the sanction of a *natural-order*, natural-legal-positing of the first rank, over which no willfulness, no 'modern idea' has power."[38] It is nature, he insists, not Manu or the Brahmin legislators, that divides the predominantly intellectual from those who are predominantly physically or temperamentally strong, and both of these from the mediocre, who are extraordinary in neither intellect nor strength.[39] The Indian caste system is an artifice, a Holy Lie—but it is a lie that serves natural ends.

The order of castes rests upon the observation that there are at times either three or four kinds of men in nature.[40] First comes the "highest caste," of whom Nietzsche says: "I name them the fewest."[41] They are the "*geistigsten Menschen*."[42] Only these "most spiritual men" have the privilege (*Vorrecht*, literally, a prior right) to establish beauty and the good upon the Earth. It is from their ranks that the artists and legislators emerge. The second

[35] *Id.*

[36] *Id.* at 101.

[37] *Id.* at 100.

[38] 6 NIETZSCHE, *Der Antichrist*, *supra* note 17, at 242.

[39] "*Die Natur,* nicht *Manu, trennt die vorwiegend Geistigen, die vorwiegend Muskel-und Temperaments-Starken und die weder im Einen, noch im Andern ausgezeichneten Dritten, die Mittelmässigen, von einander ab* . . . ." *Id.* at 242.

[40] *See* 13 NIETZSCHE, *Nachgelassene 1887-1889*, *supra* note 3, at 394.

[41] *Id.* at 395.

[42] 6 NIETZSCHE, *Der Antichrist*, *supra* note 16, at 243.

kind of man is the muscular man—the members of the warrior class. Following Plato, Nietzsche calls these men "the guardians of *Recht*."[43] They are exemplified, above all, by the king, as both warrior and judge—the executive of the most *Geistig*. The third kind of man includes the mediocrities, encompassing not only the businessmen, handworkers, and farmers, but also the scientists, academics, and the largest part of artists, those who busy themselves with a career.[44] Finally, the fourth kind of man—whom Nietzsche at times leaves out of his reckoning—is the one of the lower and submissive kind, recognized to be a servant race.[45]

Together, these three ends—the preservation of power, the breeding of each to his proper social role, and the sanctioning of the order of castes—comprise the core of Nietzsche's defense of the Holy Lie of the Manu *Gesetzbuch*. In short, what Nietzsche values in the Manu Code is the creative and artistic sanction of a natural and life-affirming inequality. Whereas Christianity is dominated by the teaching of the equality of the soul, the equality of man, and the equality of right, the Manu Code creates, teaches, and perpetuates the natural "feeling of distance between man and man," that is the "*presupposition* for every elevation and every growth of culture. . . ."[46] If the doctrine of equality is a weapon "against *ourselves*, against all nobility, gaiety, big-heartedness on the earth, against our happiness on the earth," the feeling of difference first opens the possibility for the affirmation of life.[47]

In *Beyond Good and Evil*, the pathos of distance is not only that which separates noble men from slaves, but also is that internal feeling of "a demand for an ever newer widening of distance within the soul itself, the production of ever higher, rarer, further, more-wide-reaching, more-encompassing conditions, in short, just the elevation of the type 'man,' the advanced 'self-overcoming of man,' to take a moral formula in an over-moral sense."[48] The pathos of distance, as Andreas Urs Sommer has

---

[43] *Id.*

[44] *See id.* at 244.

[45] *See* 13 NIETZSCHE, *Nachgelassene 1887-1889*, *supra* note 3, at 395. That this basic tripartite division of man that Nietzsche adopts is in many ways closer to Plato's division of men between philosophers, warriors, and handworkers in the Republic than to the order of castes in the Manu Code does not detract from Nietzsche's insistence on the all-important naturalness of the division. *See* ANDREAS URS SOMMER, FRIEDRICH NIETZSCHES "DER ANTICHRIST" EIN PHILOSOPHISCH-HISTORISCHER KOMMENTAR 573 (2000).

[46] 6 NIETZSCHE, *Der Antichrist*, *supra* note 16, at 218.

[47] *Id.*

[48] 5 FRIEDRICH NIETZSCHE, *Jenseits von Gut und Böse*, *in* KRITISCHE STUDIENAUSGABE para. 257, at 205 (Giorgio Colli & Mazzino Montinari eds., 1988) [hereinafter 5 NIETZSCHE, *Jenseits*].

suggested, becomes a "fundamental condition for what first makes possible higher forms of individuation, the 'breeding' of a higher man."[49] Differentiation, and with it inequality, are natural drives of man.

What cannot be emphasized enough is that Nietzsche insists that the pathos of difference and the order of castes sanctioned by the Manu Code is a natural division. "To say it again," Nietzsche reiterates, "nothing is arbitrary, nothing is 'made.'"[50] The positing of the order of castes into *Gesetz* only sanctifies the natural division of man into physiological types. In Nietzsche's words: "[T]he *order of castes* is only the sanctioning of a natural difference between more *physiological types* (characters, temperaments, etc.)—it is only the sanction of experience, it does not precede experience, less still does it cancel experience."[51]

Gesetz, as positive law, formulates and sanctions the natural order. It is, as *Schein*, i.e., as the semblance of the rank order of castes, that the legislative order of castes preserves and defends life. Nietzsche writes: "The order of the castes, the *rank-ordering*, only formulates the highest *Gesetz* of life itself, the division of the three types is necessary for the preservation of society, for the possibility of the higher and highest types."[52] The order of castes serves the final goal of life by justifying the natural division of man into the three types. This division of man into castes, satisfying the need for distinction among men, is the highest law of life.

What Nietzsche stresses is not the specifics of any particular division of nature, but rather that nature—and with it life—demands distinctions among men. Life, understood as will to power, is the natural drive for man and all beings to assert themselves in their difference and superiority over others.[53] The pathos of distance is what first allows a ruler to issue his command with the expectation of obedience; it predates even the "*Sittlichkeit der Sitte*" (in English, the customariness of custom, or the ethic of the ethos) as the original source of law and morality.[54] "The

---

[49] SOMMER, *supra* note 45, at 414.

[50] 6 NIETZSCHE, *Der Antichrist*, *supra* note 17, at 243,

[51] "[D]*ie* Ordnung der Kasten *ist nur die Sanktionirung eines Naturabstandes zwischen mehreren* physiologischen Typen *(Charakteren, Temperamenten usw.)—sie ist nur die Sanktion der Erfahrung, sie geht ihr nicht voraus, noch weniger hebt sie dieselbe auf*. . . ." 13 NIETZSCHE, *Nachgelassene 1887-1889*, *supra* note 3, at 395.

[52] 6 NIETZSCHE, *Der Antichrist*, *supra* note 17, at 243.

[53] *See* 5 NIETZSCHE, *Jenseits*, *supra* note 48, para. 13, at 27.

[54] *See* 3 FRIEDRICH NIETZSCHE, *Morgenröthe*, *in* KRITISCHE STUDIENAUSGABE 21-24, 26-28, 29 (Giorgio Colli & Mazzino Montinari eds., 1988). *See also* 5 FRIEDRICH NIETZSCHE, *Zur Genealogie der Morale*, *in* KRITISCHE STUDIENAUSGABE 293-94 (Giorgio Colli & Mazzino Montinari eds., 1988) [hereinafter 5 NIETZSCHE, *Zur Genealogie der Morale*].

pathos of distance," Nietzsche writes, namely, "[T]he feeling of differentiation of rank, lies as the ultimate ground of all morality."[55]

Since inequality and distinction are necessary in nature, the sanctioning and justification of natural distinction and inequality is the presupposition for the possibility of life itself. The Manu *Gesetzbuch*'s succes as an artistic creation, its success in justifying a life-affirming inequality, is precisely what induces Nietzsche to firmly embrace the ancient Brahmin code as a Holy Lie in the name of life.

III. The Need for Art: Nature, Pessimism, and the Problem of Time

Given Nietzsche's apparent naturalism, the question arises: If the division of man into different "breeds" is natural, why is the artistic division of man into an order of castes in the Manu *Gesetzbuch* necessary for the preservation of society? This mirrors the question that bedevils Lockean and Kantian theories of a social contract: If natural law already exists in the state of nature, why is there a need of a contract to move into civil society? Similarly, we may ask of Nietzsche: If the highest law of life develops unformulated and unsanctioned in nature, why is there a need for it to be set out in artistic legislation?

To understand why the positive sanctioning of the highest *Gesetz* of life in the Manu Code is necessary, it is helpful to recall Nietzsche's statement that art "is the great enabler of the possibility of life, the great seducer to life, the great stimulant of life."[56] Art, as does the posited sanction of the order of castes in the Manu legal code, enables life. The absence of art would render life unbearable; hence, for the sake of life, we need art.

What in life is unbearable that necessitates the redemptive power of art, and by extension, a posited legal code? The youthful Nietzsche of the *Birth of Tragedy* discovered the "source of art—and of all *Schein*" to lie in the unbearable Dionysian insight into the necessary suffering and contradiction of the truth of being, "the Silenian wisdom that the best thing for man is not to be born

[55] "*Das Pathos der Distanz, das Gefühl der Rangverschiedenheit liegt im letzten Grunde aller Moral.*" 12 FRIEDRICH NIETZSCHE, *Nachgelassene Fragmente 1885-1887*, *in* KRITISCHE STUDIENAUSGABE (Giorgio Colli & Mazzino Montinari eds., 1988) [hereinafter 12 NIETZSCHE, *Nachgelassene 1885-1887*].

[56] 13 NIETZSCHE, *Nachgelassene 1887-1889*, *supra* note 3, at 521.

and the second best is to die quickly."[57] From his earliest writings, Nietzsche was compelled to the "metaphysical assumption" that "the true being and *Ur-Eine*—as the eternally suffering and full of contradiction—needs the delighting vision, the lustful *Schein*, for its constant redemption."[58] Nietzsche's "particularly dark and unpleasant" pessimism—dictating that "there is only one world, and this is false, cruel, contradictory, seductive, [and] without sense. . ."[59]—is what he later emphasizes as the central insight of the otherwise brash and romantic youthful work. Faced with the unbearable pessimism of the world, "[*w*]*e have need of lies*" and of art "in order to live[.]"[60] The core thought of Nietzsche's metaphysics is that the unbearable "[c]ontradiction, the bliss born of pain,"[61] is the root of man's unquenchable need for art as the justification for life.[62]

In Nietzsche's later writings, the suffering in man's existence is formally attached to his temporality. Man's suffering, in short, proceeds from out of his powerlessness before the onslaught of time. The passage of time shows us repeatedly our inability to control what is past. It is beyond the power of man's will to influence the past: "The will cannot will backwards; that it cannot break time and time's desire, that is the will's most lonely affliction. . . . This, yes this alone, is *revenge* itself: the will's counter-will (*Widerwille*) against time and its 'It was.'"[63] Because every will cannot will backwards, every will suffers from its powerlessness against its past—"thus willing itself and all life were supposed to be punishment!"[64] Time, the uncontrollable flux of becoming, guarantees that we always, as Nietzsche says in the preface to the *Genealogie*, miscount the bells that wake us to ourselves: "We remain necessarily strange to ourselves, we do not understand ourselves, we *must* mistake ourselves . . . ."[65] At all times, such severe suffering threatens to lead to a pessimism of nihilism.

Against the suffering of will and life at the fate of time—a suffering that leads to the nihilistic denial of life—Nietzsche holds out art as the antidote: "Art here counts as the single superior

[57] 1 NIETZSCHE, *Die Geburt*, *supra* note 16, para. 3, at 36.

[58] *Id.* para. 4, at 38.

[59] 13 NIETZSCHE, *Nachgelassene 1887-1889*, *supra* note 3, at 193.

[60] *Id.*

[61] 1 NIETZSCHE, *Die Geburt*, *supra* note 16, para. 4, at 41.

[62] *See id.* para. 5, at 47.

[63] 4 FRIEDRICH NIETZSCHE, *Also Sprach Zarathustra*, *in* KRITISCHE STUDIENAUSGABE 180 (Giorgio Colli & Mazzino Montinari eds., 1988) [hereinafter 4 NIETZSCHE, *Also Sprach*].

[64] *Id.*

[65] 5 NIETZSCHE, *Zur Genealogie der Morale*, *supra* note 54, at 247.

counter-force against all willing for the denial of life."[66] Art, *der Schein* or semblance, is the lie that makes living possible, and art is the antidote to man's powerlessness—to man's feeling of powerlessness against time.

As life without art is unbearable because of the problem of time, so is life without the *Gesetzbuch* similarly unbearable because of the cold hard fact of inequality. Inequality exists in nature. Indeed, inequality is a fundamental law of nature: "The *inequality* of rights (*Recht)* is first the condition that there are rights at all."[67] Each kind of man has a pre-historical and natural way of being that precedes *Gesetz*. The highest men have the privilege (*Vorrecht*) of finding their blessedness and lust in their instinctive self-discipline and asceticism.[68] The warrior kings have the *Vorrecht* to rule, and the mediocre have the great *Vorrecht*—not to be undervalued—of being a cog in the wheel.[69] None of these privileges come easily. It is the creation of the Holy Lie (*Gesetz*) through the *Gesetzbuch* that ennobles, elevates, and justifies the harshness of the labyrinth that is life. Just as art is a stimulus to life, so too is the caste-order legislated by the Manu Code. The ultimate end of the Manu Code must be the willful and artistic creation of a beautiful lie that makes the actuality of existence bearable.

IV. THE FREE FORM OF ART AND GESETZ

The question imposes itself: How can Nietzsche's art of legislation succeed in redeeming life by erecting *Recht*?

Again, guidance is to be sought through the analogy between *Gesetz* and art. Art redeems and justifies truth insofar as it does not simply reflect the suffering and tragedy of the world, but does so in a way that beautifies, ennobles, and thus redeems the world in spite of its temporality and contradictions: "Art is essentially *affirmation, blessing, deification of existence*."[70] In the creation of beauty, art elevates and justifies existence—giving it beautiful form. Artistic creation gives form that may further life, depending on the strength of its creative force and its capacity to seduce.

Artistic creation is the activity of giving form. The essential

[66] 13 NIETZSCHE, *Nachgelassene 1887-1889*, *supra* note 3, at 225.

[67] 6 NIETZSCHE, *Der Antichrist*, *supra* note 17, at 243.

[68] *See id.* ("*Die schwere Aufgabe gilt ihnen als Vorrecht*", i.e., as a privilege and prior-right).

[69] *See id.* at 244.

[70] 13 NIETZSCHE, *Nachgelassene 1887-1889*, *supra* note 3, at 241.

artistic state, what Nietzsche calls rapture, is an explosive state of creative force. The artist seizes this rapture and bestows form upon things, compels them to take from us, violates them, and, ultimately, idealizes them.[71] From the feeling of rapture and abundance, the rapture of sexual excitement and "the rapture of an overflowing, swollen will"[72]—the artist creates both himself and the world. As Eli Eilon has observed: "Abundance is the aesthetic principle of man's self-creation."[73]

Artists form things; they create. For that reason, they "should see nothing as it is, rather fuller, rather simpler, rather stronger: to that end a kind of eternal youth and spring, a kind of habitual rapture must be in their limbs."[74] The idealizing and creative activity of the artist is to give form to the world in himself. As Nietzsche writes:

> The greatness of an artist does not measure itself by the "beautiful feelings" that he arouses: little women may believe that. But according to the degree to which he nears the great style, to which he is capable of the great style. This style has this in common with great passion, that it disdains to please; that it forgets to persuade; that it commands; that it *wills* . . . To become master over the chaos that one is; to compel one's chaos to become form; to become necessity in form: to become logical, simple, unambiguous, mathematic; to become *law* [Gesetz]—: that is here the great ambition.[75]

Art, in other words, is measured by force, the "feeling or fullness of *stowed-up force*,"[76] through which the artist comes to master the chaos that he himself is. The artist, in "compelling one's chaos to become form," wills himself into being and becomes a law for himself—the essential Nietzschean conclusion.

Nietzsche's art of legislation has unmistakable Kantian echoes. The Nietzschean artist claims his freedom to be who he is, to give himself law, and to master and command himself. However, while the Kantian man experiences the feeling of freedom as a universal duty—I ought freely to act such that I am a law unto myself—Nietzsche embraces the freedom of law as a challenge—"an attempt"[77] to make oneself lawful.[78] If Kant's law

[71] 6 NIETZSCHE, *Götzen-Dämmerung*, *supra* note 5, at 116.

[72] *Id.* *See also* 3 FRIEDRICH NIETZSCHE *Die Fröhliche Wissenschaft*, *in* KRITISCHE STUDIENAUSGABE para. 301, at 540 (Giorgio Colli & Mazzino Montinari eds., 1988) ("Wir erst haben die Welt, *die den Menschen Etwas angeht*, geschaffen!").

[73] Eli Eilon, *Nietzsche's Principle of Abundance as Guiding Aesthetic Value*, 30 NIETZSCHE-STUDIEN 219 (2001).

[74] 13 NIETZSCHE, *Nachgelassene 1887-1889*, *supra* note 3, at 295.

[75] *Id.* at 246-47.

[76] 12 NIETZSCHE, *Nachgelassene 1885-1887*, *supra* note 55, at 555.

[77] 4 NIETZSCHE, *Also Sprach*, *supra* note 63, at 265 ("[A]n attempt, oh my brother!

is a freely assumed moral imperative for all rational beings, Nietzsche's is an aesthetic imperative for artistic souls. The freedom of creating, of making art, and of legislating is always first the imperative to create oneself through the art of legislation.

The artist as creator is a legislator who gives himself and the world the law (*Gesetz*). The artist, a "preliminary stage," must go under so that the "world" becomes "a work of art [that] gives birth to itself."[79] In other words, the rapturous creation of the artist works to let the law shine forth in its splendor. As described by Nietzsche in a note entitled "Physiology of Art," art grasps at the typical and reveres the lawful:

> An overpowering of the fullness of the living is in it, measure becomes master, that *repose* of the strong soul lies at its bottom, which moves itself slowly and has a counter-will toward the all-too-living. The general case, the law, is *honored* and *lifted* out; the exception, conversely, is set aside, the nuance wiped away. The firm, powerful, solid, the life that rests broad and reigning and harbors its force—that "*pleases*": i.e. that corresponds with what one holds of oneself.[80]

The artist creates the work of art; more accurately, he lets it be created, so that the law shines forth from within it. Further, the work of art has the potential, in its beauty, to draw others into the original rapture of its creation. It works back upon the artist and his audience as the call to the law. "What alone can restore us?" Nietzsche asks. Only "[t]he *visage of the perfect*."[81] From the longing of strength and overfullness, the artist comes to sacrifice himself to the engendering of that which will call him to himself. The sight of the perfect, that which the artist's work evokes, restores him to himself.[82]

In that art brings man to himself through its beautiful and seductive externalization of the rapturous feeling of form, art is not merely something subject to rules and laws. Rather, as Martin Heidegger has articulated, art, for Nietzsche, is "thought" as law itself.

> Art stands not only under rules, it has not only to follow laws (*Gesetz*), but it is in itself legislation; only as such is art true art. The inexhaustible and to be created is the law (*Gesetz*). What

And no 'contract'!").

[78] 5 NIETZSCHE, *Zur Genealogie der Morale*, *supra* note 54, at 291 ("To breed an animal that *dares to promise*—is that not precisely that paradoxical task itself that nature has set for itself in regard to man?").

[79] 12 NIETZSCHE, *Nachgelassene 1885-1887*, *supra* note 55, at 119.

[80] *Id.* at 290.

[81] 13 NIETZSCHE, *Nachgelassene 1887-1889*, *supra* note 3, at 507.

[82] See the insightful discussion by Babette Babich in NIETZSCHE'S PHILOSOPHY OF SCIENCE 1, 12 (1994).

> the art that dissolves style into mere bubbling of feelings misses is, in its essence, the unrest of finding the law (*Gesetzesfindung*), which only comes to work when the law (*Gesetz*) veils itself in the freedom of form (*Gestalt*), in order that it come into open play.[83]

Only as freedom, at once veiled and made manifest in beautiful form, does law arise as that which raises man over himself and saves him for himself. The creative explosion of the art of legislation is the foundation for the positive establishment of any system of *Recht*. Positive law is, insofar as it is understood as a free and spontaneous work of art, paradoxically resistant to the efforts of the various legal sciences to subordinate law to social or political ends.

CONCLUSION
THE DANGEROUS PARADOX OF THE ART OF LEGISLATION

Art stands to truth as *Gesetz* stands to *Recht*—in a founding relation. This is true, not just for the Manu Code, but for Christianity as well. What distinguishes the Manu Code is simply the *Gesetz* that is given. Whereas Christian morality establishes the law of revenge in its battle against the ravages of time and worldly transience, the Manu Code glorifies the brutality of life itself—its inequalities, its humanity, and its tragedy. In celebrating and elevating *this* life in the art of legislation, the Manu Code—if it is successful—seduces those who are struck by it to life.

Yet, in the end, the question remains, whether art and *Gesetz*, as willful semblances, can indeed justify life. Will not the Holy Lie, once successful, devolve into a calming and intoxicating illusion? How, in other words, does the art of *Gesetzgebung* persist in its creative force?

In a fragment from "Towards a Critique of the Manu *Gesetzbuch*," Nietzsche emphasizes that the entirety of the Manu Code rests on the Holy Lie, namely, that the entire system is inspired by the semblance of the good of man. In actuality, however, the entirety of the Manu Code rests upon the Brahmin Priests. As Nietzsche explains: "We find a kind of man, the *priestly*, that feels itself the norm, the peak, as the highest expression of the type man: they take the concept of 'to better' from out of themselves."[84] These priests believe in their own superiority and "will" it in fact—"the cause of the holy lie is the

---

[83] 1 MARTIN HEIDEGGER, NIETZSCHE 153-54 (1961).

[84] 13 NIETZSCHE, *Nachgelassene 1887-1889*, *supra* note 3, at 439.

will to power."[85]

The Holy Lie and the art of legislation are, in the end, thought from out of the artistic creation that is the will to power. "The lie," Nietzsche writes, "as supplement of power—a new concept of 'truth.'"[86] The Manu Code, Nietzsche's example of a "good" *Gesetzbuch*, is not posited simply as a "thou shall't," but depends essentially on an artistic conception of *Recht*, one that is founded upon *Gesetz*. This positing of *Recht is* necessary, because the urge to posit *Gesetz* as a standard for others demands that the legislator believe, in some way, in its truth and goodness. It is in the *Gesetzgebung*, the giving of the code itself as a work of art, that the Manu Code grants to its world the *Gesetz* that founds its *Recht*.

As a work of art, *Gesetz* founds *Recht*. This is the inversion of the traditional relation between *Recht* and *Gesetz*, an inversion that Nietzsche announces in sections 10 and 11 of the *Genealogie*.[87] "The most decisive act that the supreme" and legislating "power performs . . . is the institution of *Gesetz*, the imperative declaration of what in general counts as *Recht* in its eyes, and what counts as *Unrecht*."[88] And yet, legislation, as the ultimate artistic act that erects an entire system of truth in positive law, is also a consequence of man's desperate will to power—his need to stamp being on becoming. All creative spirits, by whom Nietzsche means "*Genuine philosophers*" who are most essentially "*commanders and legislators*," speak in the imperative:

> [T]hus it *shall* be! They first determine the whither and for what of man . . . . With a creative hand they reach for the future, and all that is and has been becomes a means for them, an instrument, a hammer. Their "knowing" is *creating*, their creating is a legislation, their will to truth is—will to power.[89]

The art of legislation is the becoming creative of the will to power.

In the art of legislation, *Gesetz* is instituted as the ground of *Recht*. Insofar as the institution of *Recht* necessarily claims for itself the status of truth and goodness (for why else would it be instituted?), *Recht* depends upon its justice (*Gerechtigkeit*) that is founded by *Gesetz*. This is why Nietzsche insists that justice has its source in the active will to power that manifests itself in philosophers[90] and master thinkers as the lust for power

[85] *Id.*

[86] *Id.*

[87] For what follows, see the inspired account by Philippe Nonet. Philippe Nonet, *What is Positive Law*, 100 YALE L.J. 667, 669 (1990).

[88] 5 NIETZSCHE, *Zur Genealogie*, *supra* note 54, at 312.

[89] 5 NIETZSCHE, *Jenseits*, *supra* note 48, at 219-20.

[90] *Id.* at 20. *See also* LAURENCE LAMPERT, NIETZSCHE'S TASK 31 (2001).

(*Herrschsucht*).[91] Even the "noble soul," who "accepts the fact of his egoism without any question," names the will that springs from his self-assertion as "justice itself."[92]

The word for justice is *Gerechtigkeit*, and *Gerechtigkeit* is a past participle related to the German concept of *richten*, to set right. As a past participle, *Gerechtigkeit*, like its source *Gesetz*, is static, posited, and historical. *Gerechtigkeit*, or a posited standard of justice, is what happens when the legislative artist stamps being on the becoming of *Sittlichkeit*, the customary, fitting, and ethical world. Thus, *Gesetz* stands to *Recht* as *Gerechtigkeit* stands to *Sittlichkeit*.

As an expression of its lust to rule and in its need for justification, positive law exemplifies the "reduction of nature to morality."[93] And just as morality is a pale reflection of *Sittlichkeit*, so too is *Gesetz*, a "school of the *dumbing-down*"[94] of man culminating in the debasement of man. Thus is the institution of *Recht*, as an expression of will to power, "a partial restriction of the will to life" and of the will to power itself.[95]

The paradox of Nietzsche's account of the Manu Code is that the grand promise of artistic legislation—the successful promulgation of life and will to power through the Holy Lie that sanctions the order of castes—threatens to petrify into a lifeless and will-less morality of justification. The art of legislation carries with it at all times the grave danger, that the institution of a new *Recht* will solidify into a new *Gerechtigkeit*, a morality hostile to life:

> A legal order (*Rechtsordnung*) thought of as sovereign and universal—not as a means in the struggle between power-complexes, but as a means *against* all struggle overall, something like the communist cliché of [Eugen] Dühring's, that every will has to take every will as equal—[such a legal order] would be a principle *hostile to life*, a destroyer and dissolver of man, an assassination on the future of man, a sign of weariness, a slinking path to nothing.[96]

---

[91] 5 NIETZSCHE, *Zur Genealogie*, *supra* note 54, at 310; *see also* 4 NIETZSCHE, *Also Sprach*, *supra* note 63, at 237-38 (*Von den drei Bösen*).

[92] *Id.*

[93] 13 NIETZSCHE, *Nachgelassene 1887-1889*, *supra* note 3, at 385.

[94] *Id.* at 386.

[95] 5 NIETZSCHE, *Zur Genealogie der Morale*, *supra* note 54, at 310.

[96] *Id.* at 313.

[9]

AFRICAN NIETZSCHE: POETRY, PHILOSOPHY AND AFRICAN LEGAL THINKING

*Adam Gearey**

I. A BEGINNING REMARKABLE BEYOND MEASURE

To describe a possible African jurisprudence as "Nietzschean" is not to claim that it is written in homage. It is not an attempt to remain true to a name and a legacy. Even if there are references, and an ongoing dialogue with Nietzsche's text, this is part of a continuing reflection on the conditions of the production of African thought. Our concern in this essay is with a peculiar style of thinking that chooses to relate itself back to Nietzsche as a means of imagining its own constitution: a kind of poetical philosophy, or a jurisprudence of necessary fictions. This is, of course, part of a more generic theme in African and African-American thought; it is not surprising that it should also run through a determination of a jurisprudence adequate to African realities. Thus, the primary concern of this essay is with a new thinking that does not simply assume the correctness of previous worldviews, but announces its autonomy and "right" to create its own versions of the world. It is, of course, presumptuous to talk of an African jurisprudence in an article of this length—to try and embody these claims by reference to the poet/philosopher, Taban lo Liyong. However, it is hoped that this piece will be read in a spirit of experiment; this is but a note to a preface, an outwork, the imagination of a possible path for a journey—no more and no less.

The argument will proceed as follows. After a brief consideration of the constitution of African philosophy as the thought of rupture, we will examine the space that the Nietzschean

* Lecturer in Law, Birkbeck College, University of London, Visiting Professor, Makerere University, Uganda. I would like to thank the Faculty of Law at Makerere, and in particular Professor Joe Olaka Onyango for making me most welcome. Thanks also to Mary Gearey, Bob Woffenden, Antja Eckoldt, and Joan Kelly.

text prepares for its interpreter. In other words, if Nietzsche was working towards a legal philosophy when madness overtook him, could one form of its continuation and embodiment be the work we are about to examine? It would appear that a thinking of law could finally be related to an honesty; a healthy form of thinking. Law must be imagined as a creation. It is not a repository of truth, but rather, the deployment of the strategies that are considered necessary. These themes will be developed by reference to what could be described as lo Liyong's "doctrine of experience." His poetry engages with the notion of an authentic or adequate law for African realities. This is related to his refusal to write the great epic poem of law's reception, but still to imagine Africa as a continent defined by a law. Above all, he proceeds carefully, incrementally, examining the law's penetration of his emotions and his political identity.

II. A Brief Excursus on African Philosophical Thought

Our concern here is with a problematic that envisions the ruins of Europe as the possibility of starting afresh. In broadest outline, we could say that what is at stake is a way of thinking that concerns the relationship of African thought to the European tradition.[1] The ongoing nature of these problems, at a philosophical level, demands the radical criticism and the re-evaluation of the paradigms of colonialist thought. Certainly, there are those African and African-American scholars who would see the notion of African philosophy as offering a profound

[1] Historically, perhaps the most important text here is *African Philosophy: Myth and Reality*. *See* PAULIN J. HOUNTONDJI, AFRICAN PHILOSOPHY: MYTH AND REALITY (Henri Evans trans., 1983). For a useful overview of this position, see V.Y. MUDIMBE, THE INVENTION OF AFRICA: GNOSIS, PHILOSOPHY, AND THE ORDER OF KNOWLEDGE (1988). The philosophical legacy of colonialism has played itself out in the creation of a body of thought that creates Africa and the African as the other that confirms the self-identical nature of the same. *See id.* at 12. It would be possible to trace the mutations of this way of thinking through the philosophy of the Enlightenment, to the great narratives, accounts and reports of the first western "explorers", and to the classificatory schemas of botanists and anthropologists working in the early nineteen hundreds. Running through these various projects is an "epistemological ethnocentricism" that identifies the operation of science with the western subject as an identifier and classifier of an African object. *Id.* at 15. These scientific texts are in bad-faith to the extent that they claim that they discover anything about Africa; they should be read as an imposition of a particular body of thought that is complicit with a broader political project: "a discourse in which an explicit political power presumes the authority of scientific knowledge and vice-versa. Colonialism becomes its project and can be thought of as a duplication and a fulfillment of the power of Western discourses on human varieties." *Id.* at 16. The question remains as to how this system can be thought and criticized.

challenge to the practice and orientation of philosophical thought.[2] This essay makes the argument that a poetic philosophy of the law continues this thematic. In part, this is an elaboration of the debate on the origins and conditions of African thought that is an explicit theme in African philosophy. This could be connected to a related issue. How does one contest a philosophical inheritance? One of the most useful sites for a thinking that contests the European inheritance are those unresolved tensions that have always embarrassed the tradition, while offering a way out for those who have sought to contest the constitution of their inheritance. In speaking of poetry, we are, of course, returning to the most productive of sites, where the literary and philosophical traditions meet and the former is not welcome.

Lo Liyong's work can be read as working this very tension between poetry and philosophy, creating a hybrid discourse—a form of philosophical literature or literary philosophy.[3] For a

---

[2] It is a question of how western philosophical concepts can be deployed. For a development of this argument, see LEWIS R. GORDON, FANON AND THE CRISIS OF EUROPEAN MAN (1995). See also TSENAY SEREQUEBERHAN, THE HERMENEUTICS OF AFRICAN PHILOSOPHY: HORIZON AND DISCOURSE (1994), for a deployment of a radical hermeneutic philosophy. Hermeneutics allows an articulation of lived reality as a foundation for a philosophy; its starting point is the very difficulty of writing in a discourse that was imposed on Africa as a kind of intellectual colonialism. This is, of necessity, an overcoming of certain limitations of European Hermeneutics. Heidegger's philosophy of interpretation and reflection, or the "courage to make the truth of our own presuppositions" is not foreclosed by his own disastrous political choices, nor his own linkage of the truth of philosophy with a German culture. *See id.* at 4. To employ the terms "horizon" and "discourse" within an African philosophy is to draw attention to these concerns. It is a criticism of African philosophy to date, the various claims of the "professional philosophers," and the "ethnophilosophers." *See id.* at 6. This debate is used up; the point is now to understand philosophically a particular political situation, the movement from the colonial to the post or neo colonial; this is the situation that must be grasped as the root concern of African philosophical thought. At stake is the "challenge" of African "self-transformation," or the realization of a promise of independence that has, as yet, proved ambiguous, or, at worst, destructive. *See id.* at 8.

[3] *See also* WOLE SOYINKA, MYTH, LITERATURE AND THE AFRICAN WORLD (1976). Soyinka's use of myth and ritual theatre is another important resource for an orientation of an African legal philosophy through the use of "literary" sources. He is concerned with Yoruba ritual theatre, a discourse that neither fetishises a past, rejects African modes of thought in preference to Western methods of analysis, nor makes the mistakes negritude: creating false dichotomies between African emotion and Western reason. Recovering the sense in which ritual can be analyzed would be to remember that before the dominant "Platonic-Christian" influence on western thought, there was a different orientation: that of the Greek gods, of "Persephone, Dionysos and Demeter." *See id.* at 3. There are parallels between the Greek pantheon and the Yoruba. *See id.* at 14. In building this argument, Soyinka makes reference to Nietzsche. The Yoruba god Obatala can be compared to Nietzsche's Apollo; Ogun is a Dionysian figure. These comparisons, however, would not adequately represent the dynamic of Ogun's mysteries. In place of Apollonian illusion, and an art of representative plastic form, Yoruba ritual, through the work of the actor, speaks for the Gods. Soyinka goes on to show how a myth of justice operates within Yoruba ritual theatre. As far as the western academy is concerned, this

thinking of law, or, rather, the invention of a discourse that is adequate to a description of law in its African situations, it cannot be a question of simply abandoning the forms of thought inherited from the West. It is more an issue of working within and against them.[4]

III. THE EXUBERANT DANCE

This next section is not so much a summary of Nietzsche as a theory that his work prepares itself for a reading that, to remain true to its spirit, must contest it—must depart from the work's original problematic so that a broader project can be endeavored. Perhaps the mark of authenticity is to conceive Nietzsche as an enemy. Although concerns with the strong reading and the enemy recur throughout the Nietzschean oeuvre, the present focus will be on *Ecce Homo*. This work prepares the broader philosophy for its future reading. Tragedy suggests itself as a focus for the strong reading, as this marks the point where Nietzsche himself broke into the tradition with an eccentric argument that served as a foundational claim for a mode of subsequent philosophy. Tragedy is similarly, by an admission in *Ecce Homo*, an idea that holds together the earliest and latest texts. The problematic announced in the *Birth of Tragedy* is recovered in the *Twilight of the Idols*—a book where a provocation for a future jurisprudence announces itself most completely. To pull this argument together: the Nietzschean text anticipates its own reading—its provocation of projects that are to come.

Tragedy has indeed been suggested as a possible thematic for African thought.[5] In sketching a theory for the reception of Nietzsche, though, it is principally necessary to begin by thinking of tragedy as the departure from a single tradition. Tragedy is the summoning of the necessary energy to begin again—to commence the painful activity of a thinking that can understand the conditions of its own production—a work that begins in and against a dominant tradition in the search for its own identity.[6]

---

work suggests a new direction for both law and literature and the study of African Nietzsche.

[4] Literature was always important in the definition (at least by western philosophers) of an African intellectual voice. This, to some extent, harks back to Sartre and negritude. *See* JEAN-PAUL SARTRE, BLACK ORPHEUS (S. W. Allen trans., 1976). *But see* SOYINKA, *supra* note 3 (providing a critique of Sartre).

[5] *See* Lewis Gordon, *Tragic Dimensions of our Neocolonial "Postcolonial" World, in* POSTCOLONIAL AFRICAN PHILOSOPHY 241 (Emmanuel Chukwudi Eze ed., 1997).

[6] Nietzsche's racism is a complex subject, but, for an introduction to the issues, see

Expanding this argument provides further points of reference and contestation for the development of a "Nietzschean" style of thinking. If it is possible to suggest that tragedy makes life bearable as an aesthetic phenomenon, the aesthetic in a broader sense is a discourse about a creative will to interpret the personal and communal circumstances of existence. Given the confines of this essay, no attempt will be made to explicate the substance of this thinking; besides, its importance is probably a question of style, a way of living, a strategy. If, as Nietzsche himself insists, this way of thinking coincides with the end of the *Gay Science* and the composition of *Thus Spoke Zarathustra*, it is also a movement south, towards the Mediterranean, and away from the mud and rain of old Europe. Developing the "exuberant dance song"[7] may mean continuing on this southern trajectory, abandoning Europe all together, and heading towards dryer airs and different rhythms.

A departure is necessary so that one can take a backward glance, and begin to reinvent one's own identity. This is not a return to the old metaphysics of essences, but a celebration of the creative activity that is powerful enough to create new forms. Given the identification of the work and the man in *Ecce Homo*, when Nietzsche writes that his philosophy allows one to "become what one is," the "one" is a complex token. A text, a body of writing, can be related to the biography of the writer, but the writer's struggles are merely one of the possible metaphors of its own production. Tragic thought is an "[a]ffirmation of life even in

---

KEITH ANSELL-PEARSON, AN INTRODUCTION TO NIETZSCHE AS POLITICAL THINKER (1994). Nietzsche's thought was a response to a "sickness:" a cultural crisis that infects the very possibility of thought. Of course, one way Nietzsche has been read has been to focus on the resolution of these problems through the cult of the new aristocracy, a "junkers philosophy," and to link certain texts with the Nazi appropriation of Nietzsche's thought. The racist elements of the text are precisely those moments when the project failed, when the possibilities opened by the project were least glimpsed, and could be interpreted as spirit of gravity weighing down the re-evaluatory project whose target was these very forms of ressentiment. To re-appropriate the wider project of these texts, then, it is necessary to show that the key dynamic is an overcoming of a thinking which tends to racism, or any form of a denial of other forms of life that resist its logic. Racism is a decadence: a form of thought that represents an end point of a tradition, the furthest extension of a particular way of living and thinking. It may be possible to imagine it from a Nietzschean perspective as a denial of life; a form of resentment, a kind of revenge on the sickness of living. This same question reappears at the beginning of *Twilight of the Idols*—there it is interpreted as Socrates' own admission that life is worthless. If this argument is expanded, it suggests that Greek philosophy itself has never been able to affirm life, that it has missed the point—the vision of the affirmation. This is why "we must overcome even the Greeks." FRIEDRICH NIETZSCHE, THE GAY SCIENCE 272 (Walter Kaufmann trans., 1974). This overcoming of the Greeks can be taken up as a reading of the Africans.

[7] FRIEDRICH NIETZSCHE, *The Gay Science* para. 1, *in* ECCE HOMO 68 (R. J. Hollingdale trans., 1979).

its strangest and sternest problems"[8] and authorship is only one of those problems. What is essential is the need to preserve a form of energy as definitional of an intellectual activity that can take joy in its own becoming, even if this becoming is inseparably linked to "destruction."[9] The destruction that allows or enables becoming is a joyous energy. It exhausts the husks of old life and forms of being in an announcement of its own beginning. In summary, the breach in the tradition gives birth to a philosophy that is content to live, affirm its difficult beginning, create a sense of its own destiny and to imagine its own reception: "'We new, nameless, ill-understood' . . . 'we premature-born of a yet undemonstrated future, we need for a new goal also a new means, namely a new health, a stronger, shrewder, tougher, more daring, more cheerful health than any has been hitherto."[10]

Associated with this anticipation is the risk of misinterpretation.[11] Let us now trace the precise contours of this issue. Zarathustra is the strongest and the lightest of readers, the one who has gone the furthest—an extremist. The announcement of Zarathustra is frightening: here is one who "*creates* truth, a *world ruling* spirit, a destiny. . . ,"[12] one with an "eternal right."[13] It would seem that the text courts a kind of misunderstanding; a "crisis" to which it is linked. The question of Nietzsche's responsibility is a fraught one. There clearly is a sense in which the text does prepare for the notion of the strong leader who will declare his own law and sweep away the corruptions of the past—who will settle scores and create the "new health." To grapple with this problematic, it may be necessary to return to the notion of a tragic thinking. If one does not accept tragedy as self-critique then one too easily creates the wicker-man Nietzsche, who can so easily become ash in the fires of careless argument. Tragic thought, as self-criticism—as ceaseless meditation on its own anxious problematic—provokes the need to begin again, to offer a diagnosis of the problem, and affirm that thought can engage with the sickness that produced the ruin of Europe. Even if Nietzsche's work was intertwined with an apologetics for National Socialism,

[8] FRIEDRICH NIETZSCHE, *The Birth of Tragedy* para. 3, *in* ECCE HOMO 50 (R. J. Hollingdale trans., 1979).

[9] *Id.* para. 3, at 51.

[10] FRIEDRICH NIETZSCHE, *Thus Spoke Zarathustra* para. 2, *in* ECCE HOMO 71 (R. J. Hollingdale trans., 1979).

[11] Something Nietzsche acknowledges: "I know my fate. One day there will be associated with my name the recollection of something frightful—of a crisis like no other on earth. . . ." FRIEDRICH NIETZSCHE, *Why I am a Destiny* para. 1, *in* ECCE HOMO 96 (R. J. Hollingdale trans., 1979).

[12] NIETZSCHE, *supra* note 10, para. 6, at 76.

[13] *Id.*

then it can also help to think a critique of the conditions that led to this initial association. This is the task of the strong reader who will carry forward a kind of strategy or a way of thinking to other places and problems.

We will see that lo Liyong is a strong reader of Nietzsche. Before we can make this step, however, it is crucial to outline one final feature of this problematic. As suggested above, tragic thinking heads towards a jurisprudence, a thinking of law. Consider the following: "*What laws betray*—It is a serious mistake to study the penal code of a people as if it gave expression to the national character."[14]

Laws "betray" something and cannot be understood merely as an expression of national character. Therefore, it would be wrong to read them at face value. What is hidden behind the form of the law is a fear of the "foreign, strange, uncanny, outlandish."[15] Law is defined, at its core, by the separation it allows between an "us" and a "them," a foreigner that must be resisted. Law thus betrays a logic of opposition, a force of valuation that precedes any organized notion of a people or an identity. This "something" is not a thing so much as a dynamic, a force. The dictator who claims to speak for the people and the health of society, makes a claim to this creative power. This seems the ballast of the argument that accuses the state of being a "lie" when it claims to represent the people: "It was creators who created peoples and hung a faith and a love over them."[16] The law giver understands the essential operation of the law: the "hanging over" suggests (at least in the English translation) a notion of fate—a destiny that is coherent with a law and a man who can speak for a people: "[w]here a people still exists, there the people do not understand the state and hate it as the evil eye and sin against custom and law."[17] The leader claims to be synonymous with destiny; he speaks with a force that can unite a people; throwing off the yoke imposed on their indigenous customs. With the leader and his law, a people coincide with themselves. In the face of the dictator who speaks for the law, it can never be a question of renouncing judgment. The need is to create new judgments.[18] This is a new language, one beyond good and evil. Enough. It is time interrupt this discourse

[14] FRIEDRICH NIETZSCHE, THE GAY SCIENCE para. 43, at 109 (Walter Kaufmann trans., 1974).

[15] *Id.*

[16] FRIEDRICH NIETZSCHE, *Of the New Idol*, *in* THUS SPOKE ZARATHUSTRA 75 (R. J. Hollingdale trans., 1961).

[17] *Id.* at 76.

[18] *See* FRIEDRICH NIETZSCHE, BEYOND GOOD AND EVIL 17 (R. J. Hollingdale trans., 1990).

of a dead European.

IV. TABAN LO LIYONG: SO MANY DAYBREAKS STILL TO COME

"What is Africa to me so that I search myself so much?"[19]

A poetic philosophy built on a question; perhaps a question without an answer; or a question motivated by insecurity and dread? Lo Liyong's poetry and meditations are relevant to an African legal philosophy because they are marked with a mood of anxiety that is simultaneously a sense of immense possibility and of inestimable loss; of failure and sadness. His poetry is based on a hermeneutic risk, a strategy that he shares with Nietzsche: the risk of identification or the immense intellectual and emotional effort that can allow the poet to identify himself with a continent. For Nietzsche what is at stake is an account of western philosophy that is also an account of civilization; for lo Liyong, along with other African philosophers, this civilization is problematic in a different way. It is, for a start, an imposition—a trauma. From this perspective the claims of western thinkers, even radicals like Nietzsche, appear implicated in the colonial project. However, Nietzsche offers a point of internal critique. Indeed, it is worth asking about the points at which Nietzsche appears in lo Liyong's poetry; a hybrid figure of forking traditions:

> A line of Banquos but there are Kants
> And Schopenauers and Einsteins and Goethes
> And Marxes and Hegels and Heideggers
> And Engelses and Nietzsches and Charlemagnes
> And Goths and Fuzzy Wuzzies:
> All breakers of Roman phalanges and
> British Squares.[20]

In this particular genealogy, the western tradition appears to stretch from those implicated in the murder of emperors and kings to those who have broken rules of thought and redefined the terms of thinking. It is a strange list, but for a poet who constantly returns to lists it offers a way of juxtaposing the incongruous, and of suggesting the contingency of any form of ordering. Why should Engels, Nietzsche and Charlemagne appear together? There may be a suggestion in this linking of names that they are the ones who preserve or carry forward a tradition; either that of

---

[19] TABAN LO LIYONG, MEDITATIONS OF TABAN LO LIYONG 143 (1978).

[20] TABAN LO LIYONG, *The Marriage of Black and White*, *in* FRANTZ FANON'S UNEVEN RIBS 96, 105 (1971).

Marxism, western Christianity or western philosophy. This is linked to the trope of reading a tradition differently—of putting it together in different ways—and taking from it ideas that suit one's own imaginative and emotional situation. The clue to the ordering of this list is contained in the allusion to Kipling's poem in the closing lines.[21] Lo Liyong is celebrating the form breaking energy of the thinkers that he has brought together as those who have aided the dissolution of Empire. However, the allusion is more complex than this. Kipling's poem may be a form of tribute to those who resisted, but even though they could break a British square they could not stop the inclusion of their territory into the British Empire. Likewise, for all the military defeat of the Roman Empire, lo Liyong himself appeals to Latin as a suitable language to mourn his father. We have all been included into Empire, perhaps, even at the moment of its defeat and collapse.

We are all implicated. Nietzsche, however, helps the poet to think his way out of this double bind:

> We want to justify the ways of man to man.
> Too long have we tried to justify the ways of God to man
> Becoming blind in the process and expecting to get a reward
> When Nothing cares whether you wrote of Paradise
> With Satan more favourably cast than nothing.
> God is dead!
> Nietzsche shouted it, I take it up.
> Nietzsche is dead, Taban will die.
> Meanwhile, exercise your muscles
> And mind.[22]

The poet's ironic declaration, which echoes the opening of *Paradise Lost*, inaugurates a poetic thinking that is both skeptical of large claims and works within their universe. The task of the thinker who identifies with Nietzsche is to continue this reassessment—to reinscribe the values of the tradition. These lines accept the notion of the death of God, but also the consequences of the often-ignored second line: "we have killed him"—and the continuing examination of this murder that runs through Nietzsche's work. The mark of any people is their ability to create their god. What must replace God in this thinking is the activity of thought and being, the celebration of the body and its muscles. Is this the meaning of the Earth? Perhaps, at this point, we come upon a poetic ontology related to a theme that resonates in literary, philosophical and legal canons: what is it to be human?

---

[21] *See* RUDYARD KIPLING, *Fuzzy Wuzzy*, *in* WAR STORIES AND POEMS 68 (Andrew Rutherford ed., 1999).

[22] TABAN LO LIYONG, *An Excerpt from an Essay on Univen Ribs*, *in* FRANTZ FANON'S UNEVEN RIBS 41, 48 (1971).

The irony in the lines above defends against the difficulties that result from trying to posit the essence of man—to explain what it means to be all too human—every attempt results in a deferral: "Man, know thyself. Now that makes sense. Except that it is not: MAN KNOW YOURSELF. It is more like man, know mankind. Know the ways of fellow men, as you know or seek to know, the ways of ants."[23]

This is, of course, the Apollonian injunction: "Know thyself," accompanied by the imperative "nothing too much."[24] For Nietzsche, this is the principle of individuation, the beginning of self as that initiated as a path through experience. The implicit critique here is that this mistakes the essential task, and can only become a knowledge of the other rather that the self. This knowledge is no more than that of the masses that teem like ants.

V. A Season in Hell

Lo Liyong's argument may affirm the necessity for self knowledge, but not from the Apollonian perspective. As a true poet, he must affirm the Dionysian. Nietzsche identifies the Dionysian spirit with "barbarians," the Titans, Prometheus and Oedipus. These figures are either pre-Apollonian, marked with a "Titanic love" for mankind, or figures of "extravagant wisdom," like Oedipus, who are "cast into a bewildering vortex of crimes."[25] This thinking suggests that if the principle of individuation is to be affirmed it is achieved as a passage through excess—a form of knowledge of the self derived not so much from reason but emotional engagement:

Born a Villon or a Rimbaud
A new Nietzsche or a de Gaulle
I have found the tree
Where I am at home.[26]

The poet is aware that to travel too far down this path is to arrive at negritude, and Senghor's valorization of African emotion over Hellenic reason. As this verse suggests, however, and as the broader context of lo Liyong's reading of Nietzsche confirms, this is not an opposition of the African and the Hellenic. It is a discovery of a resonance within the Hellenic that vibrates in

[23] LO LIYONG, *supra* note 19, at 33.

[24] FRIEDRICH NIETZSCHE, THE BIRTH OF TRAGEDY para. 5, at 26 (Shaun Williams trans., 1993).

[25] *Id.*

[26] TABAN LO LIYONG, *The Throbbing of a Pregnant Cloud*, *in* FRANTZ FANON'S UNEVEN RIBS 19, 29 (1971).

sympathy with a certain African knowledge of the trip to selfhood. It may be that through this strategy the mistakes of negritude can be avoided, while the vitality of a form of thinking sustained. The strange image of the tree is possibly amongst other things, an allusion to the Beatles' *Strawberry Fields Forever* (given the acknowledgement that this is "pop philosophy," coupled with the recommendations for the use of LSD,[27] this is not so unlikely.[28]) What lo Liyong is trying to find is an emotional soul, a personal soul, which, if it can be discovered, can give the mark of authenticity to the experience of the law. If the writer, as William Carlos Williams thinks necessary,[29] must pass through hell, than she must affirm the price that the Dionysian poet has to pay—loneliness and madness:

Nijinski, he was the greatest dancer;
He danced to the level when he became God,
The full embodiment of the dancer and the dance.
(I create on paper
And regard myself
A God, and believe in myself, the best thing to do,
Especially for those who believe in nothing.)[30]

Given Cees Maris's tracing of Nietzsche's relationship to the dancer, this is a vivid understanding of the cost of creative thought. To depart from what is accepted is to risk misunderstanding and loneliness. To name oneself a god is to experience the loneliness of the deity. But in a universe where becoming is preferred to essence and being, these are stations of the cross that have to be experienced; they are marks of personal authenticity. There is another trope here that will have to be investigated presently, a form of leadership or a lawgiver complex that would run through the identifications of Nietzsche's name with that of De Gaulle and Charlemagne. Another central idea has to be grappled with, first of all. The necessity of the law is that it cannot just be willed for the self. The law is necessarily universal. Even if the poet can discover excess as the pure form of himself, as his own law, then, unless this can feed into the creation of new forms of universal validity, all that remains is a person that has been reduced to its finest element and, as such, must fail in an impure world. The following poem demonstrates why impurity must be praised: it is

[27] The poet writes: "Teach me the LSD trip,/And extend my mind/ Beyond normal confines." TABAN LO LIYONG, *Normalcy, Normalcy, I Detest Thee!*, *in* FRANTZ FANON'S UNEVEN RIBS 34, 34 (1971).

[28] *See id.*

[29] Williams may be another reference point for lo Liyong. *See* WILLIAM CARLOS WILLIAMS, KORA IN HELL; IMPROVISATIONS (1957).

[30] LO LIYONG, *supra* note 22, at 42.

the form of thinking law:

> [I]mpurity fills you up like angles of god
> thou art greater than earth and hell
> for impurity limiteth the child in the cradle
> impurity is boundless like my soul.[31]

If the universal figures purely as that which is fallen and inauthentic, then part of the poetic task is to invent its new form. In part this is the leadership complex that lo Liyong nervously skirts around. The leader, who invents a nation, wills a new form. The question remains as to whether this form can escape from corruption, or even from the identification of self with the law that turns the law giver into a dictator. It might appear that the form of the law must then be devoid of a content, and that this content must be posited in the moment of its giving. Is this the nothing that must be discovered? A kind of negative theology of the law?

> Human nature is such
> That incompletion is all
> That remains with us.[32]

It may be that this is one of the endgames that ontology reaches. The law must be emptied of form to become the law, as it must speak for a subject that is, in turn, radically incomplete. Incompleteness is the mark of a subject that is created through its possibilities, through its imaginings, and a teleological process that moves from thought to action. If individuation takes place, it is through a process that shows that there is no essential content of the human, only that which is created through imaginative work. If this is a knowledge that could be described as a re-inscription of the Apollonian injunction to know the shell, the husk of the self, then the problem of the Dionysian reappears. However, the problem is now not so much of the poet, the lonely creator, but the Dionysian energy of the dictator who writes a law for a people.

It is here that the second great Nietzschean moment in lo Liyong appears: the conjunction of the names of Nietzsche and Hitler. This theme is complicated because it is bound up with a criticism of the form that the law takes, a genealogical account of this form, and the search for a thinking of the new form of the law after the rupture has been acknowledged. This is the basis of a political theology that understands "man as a religion."[33] As much as this is a break with the past, it also repeats a difficult problem. Man can now posit his own truths, and what re-emerges with this is the notion that to kill is "divine." A violence that was performed

[31] TABAN LO LIYONG, *With Purity hath Nothing Been Won*, *in* ANOTHER NIGGER DEAD: POEMS 12, 12 (1972).
[32] LO LIYONG, *supra* note 26, at 22.
[33] LO LIYONG, *supra* note 19, at 104.

in the name of God becomes a violence in the cause of an essential essence of the human. This can be plotted in the epics of the *Bhagavad-Gita* and the *Iliad*; they carry the immemorial truth of a violence that defines the human. One suggestion, muttered in the following lines, is that *Thus Spoke Zarathustra* is also an epic of violence. What is this violence? A kind of repetition? A universal form of the law re-appears and is linked to the notion of the hero. This is a skewing of an original insight: it is correct to the extent that it imagines mans' own power to create and incorrect as to the extent that it posits man as an essence—a "hero" who can separate an "us" and a "them"—and declare the latter to be outside the law and worthy of extermination:

> God was dead, said Nietzsche. God was dead, reborn as Napoleon, but that was impure. Reborn as Hitler, and that did it.
>
> Western philosophy, then, turned its attention into the discussion of Hitler and his emergence, and what life is all about, when all the cosmology after Copernicus was broken. That is all existentialism is all about: commentaries on Hitler and the world he created.[34]

Read at face value, this might appear as no more than the conventional position that Hitler was an embodiment of the superman. Read more closely, this sketch of history is the location of a mode of thought that attempts to seize a new form of the law. Hitler is located in a temporal progression that is the playing out of a logic. Hitler is the final embodiment of a Napoleonic energy. In this cod Hegelianism, lo Liyong both uses and abuses the mechanisms of dialectical thought. It is as if the philosophy of history is both summarized and extended in a sentence. Perhaps this mocking is that of a Dionysian. Hitler is the effect of the Copernican Revolution that creates a universe revolving around the Earth. But we should be careful not to take the language of cause and effect without the necessary salt. One can choose patterns of cause and effect. The choice is instructive of the will of the individual. It begs the question of how an individual wants history to appear. Thus, dictatorship, lo Liyong implies, is one meaning of the Earth—one consequence of the doctrine of the superman—but it is not the necessary end point. The search is for a mode of thinking that can understand the necessary implication of dictatorship and superman:

> Sartre, did you hear that? The point is simple: that highfaluting philosophy of Kant had become insubstantial for life. Hegel mediated. The modern break began with Schopenhauer.

[34] *Id.* at 104-05.

> Nietzsche wanted a philosophy of (or for) our time. In a time when aristocracy (even in knowledge) was going, it did not pay to be dispassionate. Combine the what with rabble rousing, with activism. The sort of thing Karl Marx also came and did. The sort of thing Mohammed had done before.[35]

What is a philosophy of life? Do we have no more than the mistakes of past thinkers? In this genealogy, Nietzsche is a condition for Marx. This is philosophy as passion, not as disinterested enquiry. It would appear that its end results are either philosophies of praxis and mass action, or of religious codes, which, it is suggested, are not that dissimilar. In lo Liyong's version, a poetic philosophy of life, these themes are merged.

VI. THE BOOK OF THE LEGISLATOR (A SHORT HISTORY OF LONELINESS)

Lo Liyong's struggle for selfhood, as a philosophy of life, can be read as a series of meditations on the struggle of Africa towards a viable notion of itself as an ethical and political entity, which is simultaneously a self investigation. If the risks taken by a poetic writing of the law pay off, a personal and emotional history is, at the same time, the history of a people that enters the historical record that becomes the material of objective accounts and national stories. The mark of authenticity, though, is the extent to which this identification is both celebrated and negated. Lo Liyong has to be the Caesar that refuses the laurels, the poet who will not write the national epic as a giving of the law. This is why the great African law givers, when they do emerge as characters in his poetry, are ambiguously presented. Nkrumah may be a writer, but he is a writer who can identify a country with himself—an act of hubris that brings the required nemesis. Nyerere may have donated the jeeps that lo Liyong, as a young politico, rode around in, but there is something insubstantial about the gift and the posture that the young man adopts. The theme of the law, then, is linked to a kind of thinking that is edgy, skeptical and ironic; that tries to mediate the past and the future; the dreadful equation of nation and law.

In entering on this path, this act of literary politics and legal fictions, lo Liyong is aware that he is walking in the footprints of those who have joined the debate about the modernization of Africa that has to respect its traditional forms: "[i]t is a very

[35] *Id.* at 105.

complex matter. You try to modernize Africa. But you have to be more than traditional to be understood. For, you are to understand and master the old language, then create new ideas, symbols, myths, in order to communicate it."[36]

A poet who knows the dangers of poetry speaks these lines. It is also the statement of one who knows that he too will have to use the same language (perhaps, in the end, it comes down to a question of style, of how one chooses to live ones life: a question that would hold together that of poetic form and lived form, and would also indicate the theme of initiation and the problem of experience). The language of modernization, to date, has been contradictory to the extent that it has been filtered through claims about indigenous African cultural values. This has emerged in both progressive forms, if one considers Nyerere's ujamaa, or negative and destructive ones, Mobutu's authenticité, for instance. Lo Liyong's implicit point is that authenticité is not a deviation from the truth of African socialism, but that which allows either to be posited is precisely the problem. The new language, say, of Mobutu's Zaire, is merely a repetition of the old problem of the "African leader"—which is seen as the problem of the failure of an ethic, or an ethic that is replaced by a politics that has made an informed analysis of the problem impossible.

African dictatorship as a throwing off the yoke of the colonist is only partly justified. It is justified to the extent that it is necessary as part of a liberation struggle. But what has become of that struggle; how can it ultimately make sense? The legacy of the struggle may be what lo Liyong refers to as Fanon's uneven ribs. This cryptic expression may refer to the sense in which African intellectuals are born from one of Fanon's ribs, but this inheritance is somehow crooked or misleading. These themes run through the announcement: "The New African Morality Cometh" dedicated, perhaps only half tongue in cheek to the "members of the East African Legislative Assembly."[37] This dedication relates to a pan-Africanist dream, but, for all the irony of the dedication, for all the flippancy of the conclusion ("How about that for a bout of clarity . . . ."[38]), there is an attempt to confront the failure of the law. The thinking here accepts the form of a nation as a sovereign territory created at independence. The problem is how to imagine a "code of ethics"[39] that will create the nation state as an ethical

[36] *Id.* at 62.
[37] *Id.* at 76.
[38] *Id.* at 80.
[39] *Id.* at 77.

entity. Until then, "[w]e can't judge."[40] Perhaps this is the point at which we can interpret the humor, the evasions of this meditation. Humor, irony and jest are supplements that attest to the absence of an ethic. But because there is as yet no code, there is nothing to inform the reconstruction. Institutions and figures can be undermined and subjected to ridicule, but what will replace them cannot be imagined.

The problem is that Freedom did not "arrive"[41] on the leaving of the colonialists. The notion that "man is the nation"[42] can only be a political reality if the state respects the needs of the human subject. This is not utilitarianism; its reference point is primarily theological, to the New Testament, and to the idea of the leader as the servant of the people. Yet, is it not inconsistent to also talk in terms of "indigenous laws" and "our old sense of justice," given that this must appeal to pre-Christian times?[43] In the course of these meditations, this tension can arguably be read more as an example of eternal return, or a hermeneutic strategy that interprets against a horizon of the now. To address the question properly, one has to accept that there was an imposition of a foreign religion, but that there may be a certain coherence between its belief systems and indigenous ones. The question of Christianity thus opens a search for a resource that can allow the articulation of the necessary truth that laws must "exist" in "human hearts" as well as "law books":[44] "Let us create a human conscience in the man in Africa. Let us give him moral codes appropriate to our times of realizing the facts of nationhood and responsibility in a world little controlled by political boundaries."[45] Here, the notion of conscience turns to the need for an inscription on the heart. If the subject breaches the law, then she/he is the first to accuse. The law thus seems to move from that of an imposed institution to identification with the heart, the hidden place that is most human, corresponding with a human "essence" that poetry must define as the projected, ongoing nature of the human.

At the end of *The New African Morality Cometh* there is a date: "*Eleven a.m. Fifteenth of June 1973.*"[46] At one level, this is the inscription of the momentous event, the record of its arrival. Lo Liyong is aware of this. One has to be careful about the

---

[40] *Id.*
[41] *Id.* at 78.
[42] *Id.*
[43] *Id.*
[44] *Id.*
[45] *Id.* at 80.
[46] *Id.*

pretensions of writing—one has to sever the links between the word and the messiah.

To address this theme, we must backtrack. *The New African Morality Cometh* is part of a wider concern in lo Liyong's poetry: a becoming responsible for the fictions of the self. This theme is bound up with a personal odyssey that forces an examination of a macro and a micro politics. The latter is also connected with urgent questions of self-identity. Women appear as the mark and the limit point of a new ethics and law in the same way that the women are so problematic for Zarathustra. To put this slightly differently, to talk of the personal and the intimate is to trace the impact of world history. We need to proceed in such a way that we do not lose the essential connection of these themes. Marriage, or the law of marriage, divides Taban against his father allows him a precarious definition of himself as an individual, but necessitates an examination of exile and colonialism. We will explore the impact of this theme on the personal, before tracing it through a concern with national constitutions.

Marriage is an "obligation[],"[47] a duty, the point at which one learns the meaning of the law. Law works a genealogy. To marry is to continue the line, moreover, to accept one's place in a culture and a family "automatically."[48] However, for Taban this was not to happen in the prescribed way. Taban was educated, which means that he was "handed over to the white man."[49] His father wanted him to obtain a proper education. This is the point of separation—the definition of a different site of belonging—which defined Taban against the "village boys"[50] who spent their time fighting and wooing the village girls. For his father, though, the dislocations wrought by education are not realized. His son's role was still to marry, to "get [him] a daughter-in-law."[51] Reflecting back on this progressive sense of alienation leads to the following double bind. From the perspective of the "negritudists," Taban's father was misled. However, "daddy was right."[52] In other words, the process of education, when seen in the correct way, is "to go, dare, and do. And then to be," a process fought out against one law, and in the process of defining another law of the self and its amorous attachments.[53]

The law is always built on an exchange, an equation: "[f]ather

---

47 *Id.* at 81.
48 *Id.*
49 *Id.*
50 *Id.* at 83.
51 *Id.*
52 *Id.* at 82.
53 *Id.*

was killed because it was thought happiness and pride would now be his. He was rising up in the public estimation through the status his son had created for him."[54] The law of social exchanges continues its logic despite the son playing a different role. Law would carry on functioning if the "woman" had in turn played her part in the script. Instead, in a refusal that is the analogue to Taban's own, she will not "substitut[e]" for the death of his father—she would not "fill that hole" represented by the dead father.[55] To the extent that this is the primal scene of lo Liyong's poetry it is repeated in an attempt to find the law that it figures: What does this refusal mean? It seems to accord with a kind of logic of substitution. Taban's father was an Ethiopian policeman at the time of the Italian invasion.[56] He lost his job, "sacrificed for someone else's responsibilities,"[57]and fled to the north of Uganda. The return of the dummy, the substitute or the scapegoat, is thus the law of the "curse" that is passed down the family line:

> Father . . . [y]ou made me a man without a past, without a present, but a man for the future . . . . You left your ancestors and their graves; you left the landscape where you first heard the crowing of the cock behind. I grew up, hearing a babble of tongues . . . . Oh, Father, do you know what you have done to me? I live for the future, I am dead to the present. . . .[58]

To the extent that the poet sees himself as "created" by his father he is continuing the law of the curse, the bad faith that sees what is inherited as the determinant of the present, the past as the supplement for a present that will not take shape. At the same time, there is a living for the future and for what might come that is associated with an escape from tradition, with the mixture of melancholy and possibility that this occasions. Living through the law of the curse brings with it the tension between tradition and the modern, determining the balance that one will declare as the law of one's own being and belonging. Perhaps this is never completely achieved, but the process initiates itself with the acknowledgement of the self's necessary hybridity: "I will go on living my mixed life: A Ugandan Acholi of Kuku Sudanese ancestry."[59]

How, then, does this law of the balance, or the necessary hybridity of the self, allow lo Liyong to reassess the space or the absence that should be filled by the amorous other? The

[54] *Id.* at 85.
[55] *Id.*
[56] *Id.* at 88.
[57] *Id.* at 89.
[58] *Id.*
[59] *Id.* at 91.

licentiousness of his poetry, that celebrates moments such as: "The little girl asked the boy:/ Let's go and have a fuck?/ The little boy answered the girl:/ Let's go and have a fuck.// They went/ And had a fuck,"[60] could be read as a distraction from the proper task that he has set himself as a poet: What is the meaning of the amorous object? The perfect exchange of this brief poem is not achieved in the longer pieces that concern amorous encounters. *Telephone Conversation Number Two*[61] engages with the code that must be invented to regulate the love relationship; the poem is set in a bar, and concerns an encounter between the poet and "Helen," who comes in "dishevelled" from the street. It becomes obvious that the woman will trade sex for a place to stay. The poet knows that he cannot take her home "[a]s my wife would object"[62] and so telephones his friend. Whilst he is on the phone, the woman falls into conversation with the chef. The suggestion is that he will take her home. How is this situation to be understood ethically? As exemplary of the law that the individual writes for themselves? It is, of course, about substitution: just as his wife can be substituted for Helen, Helen can substitute him for the chef. In the bar is played out the whole trauma of self; the question is how he judges himself as a character. Is there an admission that he would have tricked her ("Since with a cook//You are always sure/ Of a good meal—/Something you may not get/ From students prone to trickery"[63])—and that her absence is somehow the consequence of his dishonesty? The law of substitution concludes the poem. His failure to act honestly, leads to yet another replacement, an "imagination" of sex with her.

If the law of amorous or intimate association suggests that one must behave responsibly, then how might this impact on the poet's thinking of national law? This seems to lie behind lo Liyong's consideration of the American Constitution. The extended meditation of the Constitution is introduced by an engagement with a notion of why people become subjects of the law.[64] The law

---

[60] TABAN LO LIYONG, *Language is a Figure of Speech*, *in* FRANTZ FANON'S UNEVEN RIBS 5, 10 (1971).

[61] TABAN LO LIYONG, *Telephone Conversation Number Two*, *in* FRANTZ FANON'S UNEVEN RIBS 72 (1971).

[62] *Id.* at 75.

[63] *Id.* at 76.

[64] This is from a poem that advertises itself as an "excerpt" or a "prelude" (*An Excerpt from an Essay on Uneven Ribs: a Prelude*)—it is then unfinished, fragmentary-part of a whole that will perhaps never appear (to the extent that the essay on the Uneven Ribs has not appeared, but is perhaps included by such Borgesian exercises as *Batsiary in Sanigraland*—*see* LO LIYONG, *Batsiary in Sanigraland*, *in* ANOTHER NIGGER DEAD: POEMS 63-72 (1972)—and thus exemplary of a form of thought that would rather not settle with conclusions, but which finds itself constantly threatened by ideas whose time

is related to the "leviathan that we created in our childhood,"[65] an image that brings together Hobbes and Freud, within the context of a discussion that affirms that it is artificial human constructions that need to be dissolved, not the natural constitution of human subjects It is at this point that the Constitution is introduced:

For that matter
I admire
The United States Constitution;
The Constitution which declares boldly
That man is created equal
Though a Negro counts as fourfifths
And the natural Indian no man at all
Since we exist in law.[66]

Although the irony of these lines is obvious, it is necessary to find the point of gravity in the poem as a whole. The Constitution can be denounced as a racist document, but, in the context of the poem, and more widely in terms of the *New African Morality*, this is not an argument against all law. Later, the poem regrets "tir[ing]" us with "[a] page stolen from French romanticism."[67] There is no natural streak in the human, whether this is to respect or rebel against authority. The point is not that one can live without the law, or that all authority is corrupt, but that the law tends to harden into a form that denies life—thus one needs to "build afresh, with each season,"[68] and this is linked directly with this ironic reading of the U.S. Constitution. If the poem recommends a Byronic "jest,"[69] it appears to be suggesting that what is required is a way of writing and living, a question of style, that can allow the necessary balance to be achieved; and, perhaps, also to allow what remains worthy in the Constitution to continue.

Conclusion: The Memorial of a Crisis

Nietzsche has played a contentious role in the opening of the discourse of African philosophy. The Nietzsche that appears in these pages is not the racist irrelevance criticized by Cesaire. Although there is a clear sense in which Nietzsche's work is informed by racism, there is a version of Nietzsche that does not

was meant to have come.

[65] LO LIYONG, *supra* note 22, at 44.

[66] *Id.* at 45.

[67] *Id.*

[68] *Id.*

[69] *Id.* at 43.

simply condemn him.[70] Nietzsche is not absolved of racism, but becomes readable as a thinker who opens a style of thinking, that can ultimately be related to the most radical ways of settling accounts with the racist structures of the western tradition.

So, the coming together of Nietzsche's name with the possibility of an African jurisprudence can be seen as the simultaneous disturbance of the tradition and the appearance of a new beginning. In a wider sense this is associated with the theme of the need to re-assess the colonial legacy in African thought. The law is central to this endeavor as it is central to the imposition of European culture in the colonial period. In terms of an African jurisprudence, we are concerned with the abandonment of, or liberation from, this corrupt tradition, and the enabling of a new way of living and thinking that comes from the husk of the old law. Might it also be that, given that it is precisely at this point that Nietzsche's thought is interrupted, it is also one of the most important sites for the engagement with its legacy?

For lo Liyong, Nietzsche's relevance is in addressing the issue of how we are to live; a question that is inseparable from a concern with the codes of living that we invent for ourselves. Perhaps the only way of uncoupling the association of the law with the law giver, and with the tendency towards a tyranny where the one can speak for the many, is for the individual to become a law giver for themselves. The leadership complex can be criticized, or at least as critique can begin, by suggesting that in giving oneself the law, one determines one's responsibility. As *Ecce Homo* repeatedly suggests, this work is primarily a philosophy of the personal, but the personal as that which is always hostage to history and the various forces and institutions that constitute life. Lo Liyong's poetic philosophy of the law is a form of tragic thinking because it can offer a mode of examination of life as lived. Tragic thought provokes the constant question of life's justification, and the responsibility that one is to create for oneself. In the wake of lo Liyong, is there perhaps a provocation to a new jurisprudence?

No more immemorial truths. Now is the time for necessary fictions.

[70] *See* William A. Preston, *Nietzsche on Blacks*, *in* EXISTENCE IN BLACK: AN ANTHOLOGY OF BLACK EXISTENTIAL PHILOSOPHY 165 (Lewis R. Gordon ed., 1997).

[10]

IT'S A POSITIVIST, IT'S A PRAGMATIST, IT'S A *CODIFIER*! REFLECTIONS ON NIETZSCHE AND STENDHAL

*Richard H. Weisberg**

Argument.

The modern movement called "Pragmatism" either is trivially associated with an absurdly wide range of adherents (including the Legal Panel's principal speakers) or is dangerous in its implications for original, unmediated, and creative thinking. Lawyers instead would benefit from the approach of the *codifier*, who seeks to link a private creative vision to a public political program. The models for the *codifier* come from philosophy and literature and help to challenge Richard Rorty's view that the public and private realms are inevitably disjoined.

Richard Rorty writes that "[n]owadays, Allan Bloom and Michael Moore seem to be the only people who still think pragmatism is dangerous to the moral health of our society."[1] Given the source, I would not contest the generalization. Nor would I seek to correct the adjective about pragmatism used more than once by Professors Rorty and Grey: "banal."[2] Indeed, the popularity of pragmatism may reflect its banality. Its amorphous nature has produced strange alliances. For example, the same Stanley Fish who once declared Richard Posner's humanistic forays to be "execrable" now joins Posner's pragmatic program almost without qualification.[3] If Pragmatism's tent is big enough to cover such disparate personalities, its grounding is unlikely to be distinctive or even

* Richard Weisberg is the Walter Florsheimer Chair in Constitutional Law at the Benjamin N. Cardozo School of Law, Yeshiva University. A related paper, called "The Text as Legislator: *Devoir* and the Millenial Stendhal," has recently been published at 95 *South Atlantic Quarterly* 1029 (1996). Professor Weisberg is the general editor of *Cardozo Studies in Law and Literature*, now in its ninth year of publication.

1 Richard Rorty, *The Banality of Pragmatism and the Poetry of Justice*, *in* PRAGMATISM IN LAW AND SOCIETY 89, 90-91 (Michael Brint & William Weaver eds., 1991).

2 *Id.* at 89, 90; Thomas C. Grey, *Holmes and Legal Pragmatism*, 41 STAN. L. REV. 787, 814 (1989).

3 Fish finds little to disagree with in Posner's approach to legal reasoning, which he calls "Almost Pragmatism." Stanley Fish, *Almost Pragmatism: The Jurisprudence of Richard Posner, Richard Rorty and Ronald Dworkin*, *in* PRAGMATISM IN LAW AND SOCIETY, *supra* note 1, at 47, 55. Fish's harsh assessment of Posner's earlier attempts in the humanities related to Richard Posner's *Law and Literature: A Misunderstood Relation*. For Fish's critique, see Karen J. Winkler, *Controversial Judge and Legal Theorist Jumps Into the Debate on Law and Literature*, CHRON. HIGHER EDUC., Dec. 7, 1988, at A10.

identifiable. On the other hand, when we consider that pretenders to pragmatist status have included Holmes, Cardozo, Brandeis, Pound, Llewellyn, Fuller, Frankfurter, Douglas, Brennan, and Powell, we must ask who was or would be rash enough, imprudent enough, to wish to be excluded?

There is no conceivable way that a skeptic of pragmatism like myself could better summarize the pragmatist program for law than do the papers of Professor Grey or Judge Posner. Judge Posner has characteristically raised the adjectival stakes[4] by calling pragmatism "vague"[5] (which is in some ways worse than banal), and calling the very issue he has explored today "spongy."[6] But I *can* add my name to the tiny list of dissenters. I think that pragmatism is, on the terms offered by its proponents, harmful to contemporary legal thought and practice.

The sources for my brief anti-pragmatist argument are a pair of nineteenth-century writers, one of whom has never been described as a pragmatist, and the other of whom would roll over in his grave in hearing himself so labelled. The latter is Friedrich Nietzsche, and the former a novelist whose non-pragmatic art Nietzsche admired greatly: Stendhal.[7] These writers may help us today to distinguish a kind of legal and judicial temperament that is fundamentally different from that of the pragmatist's and, in my view, far more appropriate to the challenges we face as a culture of law in the late twentieth century.

To situate my sense of pragmatism's untimeliness, I shall note that Professor Grey has elsewhere cited William James to the effect that "in this matter of belief we are all extreme conservatives,"[8] so that—now in Grey's own words—"[o]nly when habit and practice

[4] "Perverse," "hectoring," and "peripheral" are some non-pragmatic adjectives Judge Posner has used in writing about my treatment of a topic to which he returns late in his paper for today—judgment under totalitarian regimes. Richard A. Posner, Law and Literature: A Misunderstood Relation 171, 174-75 (1988) [hereinafter Posner, Law and Literature]. There are those who feel he later came to accept my primary position on adjudication in these regimes—and he surely used my primary evidence!—in a later piece. *See* Richard A. Posner, *Courting Evil*, New Republic, June 17, 1991, at 36 (reviewing Ingo Müller's book *Hitler's Justice: The Courts of the Third Reich*).

[5] Richard A. Posner, *Pragmatic Adjudication*, 18 Cardozo L. Rev. 1, 1 (1996).

[6] *Id.*

[7] On Nietzsche's admiration for Stendhal, in the context of his admiration for one of our modern codifiers, Napoleon, see Friedrich Nietzche, Beyond Good and Evil aphorism 254 (Helen Zimmern trans., 1989); *see also* Friedrich Nietzche, The Twilight of the Idols § 45 (R.J. Hollingdale trans., Penguin Books 1968) (1889).

[8] Grey, *supra* note 2, at 799 (citing William James, Pragmatism: A New Name For Some Old Ways of Thinking 224-25 (1907)).

become problematic is there occasion for inquiry."[9] Such a pragmatic method has appeal and looks like the way most people who think or do law and justice proceed. For me, though, such a method has *itself* become intensely "problematic," for, as I shall discuss briefly towards the end of this response, the events of our century have called into radical question the appropriateness of conservative belief structures, or of only incrementalist growth, for law.

To situate my argument further, I will concede the distinction made in Judge Posner's paper today between pragmatism and positivism; Professor Grey has elsewhere cogently separated pragmatism from formalism and other rationalistic systems (including traditional positivism).[10] If pragmatism and any formalism were indeed similar, few antiformalist contemporary legal thinkers would have become its fellow travellers. Instead, as I mentioned earlier, most of them are card carrying members. But I will also return (and also briefly) to the question of positivism.

The pragmatist/formalist opposition conceded, I want instead to articulate a dichotomy between the pragmatist and another jurisprudential type, the one I argue we need today. Since no school has been built—at least recently—around this type of lawyer, I shall give her[11] a name today: I call her *the codifier*. The distinction between the pragmatist and the codifier has the merit of being tangible rather than spongy, and it may also bring with it the possibility of setting apart this panel's two principal speakers. So, whereas there is no reason to question Grey's sincerity in couching his allegiance to pragmatism in the oxymoronic terms of a "conversion" or at least a "partial conversion" to that banal condition, I argue that Posner is an apostate to pragmatism. He is, rather, a *codifier*.

A codifier is that actor who deliberately seeks to embody into law a revolutionary program already situated pre-legislatively on the brink of social acceptance by the actor's—or group of actors'—political, military, and/or verbal achievements. The actor is sometimes utterly, but always mostly, disinterested in the pragmatic likelihood of her program's implementation or acceptability.

---

9 *Id.* at 800.

10 *Id.* at 789-91. Grey allows that the "instrumental aspects" of pragmatism are harder to distinguish from some means-ends qualities of the positivist program. *Id.* at 852-54.

11 In his response to my remarks at the conference, Judge Posner noted that my pronominal choice de-gendered him even as I was paying him the compliment (?) of calling him a "codifier." But the real pronominal choice relating to his work on legal economics is in my *title*, which is partly meant to convey the abysmal and depersonalizing effect upon the law of Posner's brand of economic reasoning.

There is instead a kind of "prophetic" commitment to the program, in the spirit and often in the manner of unpopular idealists whose ambitions went against the grain of the already imbedded popular agenda. Examples of codifiers are Moses, Jeremiah, Socrates, the Icelandic saga writers, the French and American Revolutionary generations, Napoleon, and Nietzsche. All paid a price for their beliefs, but all succeeded in part because pragmatic "incrementalism" played no part in their enterprise or belief system.

The codifier, from the perspective of pragmatist theory, does not exist. She could not, because the positing of any abstract ideal towards which one works independently of the infinite flexibility of a pragmatic collectivity is, of course, anathema to the pragmatist. Since the codifier creates through act and word the ideal that she then wishes to transform into text—*and especially because the codifier is a solo player, inclined to lead and not to follow the masses*—she cannot and would never wish to be a pragmatist.

But she is alluded to as an *absence* by pragmatists, or perhaps as a shadow in the space recently discovered and emphasized by Richard Rorty in his extraordinary book *Contingency, Irony, and Solidarity*.[12] There Rorty identifies what he sees as an unbridgeable gap between the private person striving for individuality and the public person engaged in social improvement. For Rorty, Nietzsche exemplifies—with Baudelaire and Proust—the quest for the self-created life, a life striving for "private perfection."[13] On the other hand, thinkers like Marx, Dewey, Habermas, and Rawls contribute to a "shared, social effort—the effort to make our institutions and practices more just and less cruel."[14] In the space between them, Rorty situates the pragmatic "liberal ironist," a figure resigned to the unalterable difference between the two types, a difference Rorty couches in the strongest terms:

> We shall only think of these two kinds of writers as *opposed* if we think that a more comprehensive philosophical outlook would let us hold self-creation and justice, private perfection and human solidarity, in a single vision.
>
> There is no way in which philosophy, or any other theoretical discipline, will ever let us do that.[15]

The *codifier* disproves of this uncharacteristically universal statement. And she does so as a construct of the two realms used

12 RICHARD RORTY, CONTINGENCY, IRONY, AND SOLIDARITY (1989).

13 *Id.* at xiv.

14 *Id.*

15 *Id.*

by Rorty to *absent* her: philosophy and literature. Now first it must be noticed that Rorty's move to stories may well be the beginning of his own trajectory towards the codifier. Rorty's book directs us to literary sources as guidelines to the sensitivity of the liberal ironist. (Both Posner and Grey have analogously asked the not always receptive world of lawyers to think about poets, novelists, and other storytellers, although a strain in the legal world that might be classified as "pragmatist" tends to resist this literary suggestion—and Posner here conspicuously cites history and philosophy but *not* literature as appropriate reading for appellate judges.) Rorty's move to stories may join with our burgeoning Law and Literature movement to enhance the lawyer's professional options.

Yet, on his own present terms, Rorty disjoins definitively the act of the creative self-fulfilling individual from the act of the communally-minded person. For Rorty, and for most pragmatists, the private and public realms will not be merged. Our pragmatic social actor might be kinder and gentler because he is well read, or he may develop a keen sense of irony that leaves him free to do what he will—but the ironist is never the codifier.[16]

Suppose, as I deeply believe, that the gap between the self-created life and the public world of law *can be breached*! Suppose that a set of readings, which like that proposed by Rorty focuses on Nietzsche, shows us how the most creative private program leads to a socially useful text?

Stendhal and Nietzsche provide us with our anti-pragmatic program. Nietzsche admired Stendhal, as he admired few other nineteenth-century novelists, precisely because of Stendhal's unpragmatic heroes. These characters, like their creator, refused to be constrained by an insipid notion of collective and conformist behavior. But neither does the thrust of their actions derive purely from an unmediated personal vision. Instead, Stendhal is everywhere concerned in his stories with the notion of *devoir*, or duty. His characters' drive to act well is not, on this model of *devoir*, purely *self*-generated. Often contrasted with mere pragmatism or prudence, *devoir* imposes on the protagonist an externally-inspired set of affirmative and negative constraints. Heroic action, both in the private and public spheres, is defined in Stendhal's world as

[16] Note that the well-read Newt Gingrich has been loudly proclaimed a pragmatist in a *New York Times* headline. Jerry Gray, *Gingrich, Long Seen as a Purist, Shows His Worth as a Pragmatist*, N.Y. Times, Oct. 27, 1995, at A1. Gingrich is proving to be a Rortian ironist more than he is a successful codifier, as attest the Republican Party's recent deletion of references to its "contract for America and its more recent flirtation with terminating his role as Speaker."

both self-willed and socially constructed by external models, particularly by the model of Napoleon as at once conqueror and codifier.

Julien Sorel, the youthful hero of *Le Rouge et le Noir*, conceives of himself this way.[17] He imposes on himself a series of outlets for his ambition, but (as René Girard stresses[18]) these outlets reflect a model of heroism derived from an outside source, in Julien's case, Napoleon. Thus, Julien associates heroism on a smaller scale with each act of duty—each *devoir*—that he imposes on himself in the domains of romance, politics, and thought.[19] Although Stendhal treats his protagonists with irony on occasion, there can be little doubt that he, like his Julien, found the *source* of heroic duty in Napoleon. A man of action in his early life, Stendhal proceeded to imitate the Napoleonic model—a striking merger of action and writing. Napoleon's conquests gave birth to his majestic codes of law, sections of which Stendhal used to read nightly to guide him in creating his own masterpieces.[20] Julien's image of Napoleon equally marries heroic action to legislative text. The narrative associates Napoleon with Julien's self-willed accomplishments more than twenty times; equally to my point today, Julien does Napoleon the seemingly unheroic compliment of memorizing the Napoleonic Codes. When Julien is arrested for the attempt on Mme. de Renal's life, which he at first believes to have succeeded, he announces to the examining magistrate, "I caused death with premeditation . . . I bought the pistols from _____ the gunsmith, and had him load them. Article 1342 of the Penal Code is explicit; I deserve death, and I am ready for it."[21] Julien is probably the only

17 STENDHAL, LE ROUGE ET LE NOIR (Paris, Librairie Générale Francaise 1983) (1830). For an English translation, see STENDHAL, THE RED AND THE BLACK (Catherine Slater trans., Oxford Univ. Press 1991) (1830).

18 *See* RENÉ GIRARD, MENSONGE ROMANTIQUE *et* VÉRITÉ ROMANESQUE (1961) (translated as *Deceit, Desire and the Novel*). To simplify for today's purposes: Girard approaches the characters in Stendhal, and other writers, in terms of "triangular desire": the structuring of the character's self-imposed goals through *another*, through a model whom the character emulates. For Julien, the goal of seducing Mme. de Renal or of achieving certain political ends is a triangulated reflection of Napoleon's own achievements.

19 The word *devoir* ("duty") is employed narratively to characterize Julien's various self-imposed public and private challenges. *See, e.g.*, THE RED AND THE BLACK, *supra* note 17, at 57, 86; *id.* at 59 (the *duty* to embrace Mme. de Renal, especially: "*He had done his duty, his heroic duty*"); *id.* at 343 (the *devoir* of growing personally through self-criticism); *id.* at ch. 21 *passim*; *id.* at 411 (the *duty* to fulfill M. de la Mole's restorationist scheme); *id.* at 444 (the *devoir* of cooling Mathilde de la Mole's passion for him).

20 *See, e.g.*, Letter from Stendhal to Balzac (Oct. 28-29, 1840), *in* III STENDHAL CORRESPONDENCE 1835-1842, at 393, 403 (Henri Maritneau ed., 1968) (in which he reveals that he needed a nightly dose of at least three pages of the Code Civil while writing *La Chartreuse de Parme* in order to attain the proper tone in his own novels).

21 THE RED AND THE BLACK, *supra* note 17, at 470.

transgressing hero in literature who knows in advance of his crime (and by heart) the code section under which he will be tried. His continuing reverence for the code and its codifier is obvious in that he seeks immediate punishment under its terms.

Creator and character join in an admiration for Napoleon as both heroic actor and legislator. In a theme picked up more subtly by Melville in the descriptions of Admiral Nelson from *Billy Budd, Sailor*,[22] Stendhal moves us towards the bridging of the gap that only irony seems to bring about in the late twentieth century. For, in an age of *great codifiers*, individuals are able to think unironically about external standards for their actions, not as a limiting factor only (the law says I can't do this or that) but as a positive inducement to action (the law sets standards that encourage me to act a certain way, say as the codifier might have acted).

The creative individual striving for Rorty's "private perfection" is not, on this view, inevitably disjoined from the public world, even the seemingly banal public world of legislation. But to understand the codifier, we will need to see this process described genealogically, at its origin in the acts and in the thoughts of the codifier herself. We will need Nietzsche.

Nietzsche takes the admiration for Napoleon that he shared with Stendhal one step further.[23] Instead of disjoining a public program from the personal, creative will to power (Rorty's reading),[24] Nietzsche consistently binds the public to the private. Rorty in fact allows, correctly, that Nietzsche is a pluralist (or perspectivalist) only in a fraction of what he writes, thus privileging Nietzsche's more typically hierarchical scheme of moral valuation.[25] But Rorty then errs by seeing the will to power as a merely *private* actor.[26] In fact, the Nietzschean will to power becomes publicly expressed *through law*, that very *locus* denied by Rorty's basic claim that these two worlds can never meet.

---

22 *See* Richard H. Weisberg, The Failure of the Word: The Protagonist as Lawyer in Modern Fiction chs. 8, 9 (1984).

23 *See, e.g.*, Friedrich Nietzsche, On the Genealogy of Morals 490 (Walter Kaufmann trans., 1967).

> Like a last signpost to the *other* path, Napoleon appeared, the most isolated and late-born man there has even been, and in him the problem of the *noble ideal as such* made flesh — one might well ponder *what* kind of problem it is: Napoleon, this synthesis of the *inhuman* and *superhuman*.

Id.

24 Rorty, *supra* note 12, at 106.

25 *See generally* Weisberg, *supra* note 22, at 13-23.

26 *See supra* note 12 and accompanying text.

The great legislator is himself (or herself) conceived of as one whose act of social codification begins with a private program of creative self-fulfillment. Nietzsche goes so far as to *describe* the process by which the creative personal striving at its most positive becomes socialized through a legislative text. Let us listen to this central text from *On the Genealogy of Morals*. In the eleventh aphorism of the second essay, Nietzsche first disposes of the link between justice and knee-jerk revenge or *ressentiment*, and then offers us this account of justice on earth:

> To what sphere is the basic management of law, indeed the entire drive towards law, most connected? In the sphere of reactive people? Absolutely not. Much more so in the realm of the active, strong, spontaneous, aggressive. Historically understood, the place of justice on earth is situated as a battle *against* the reactive emotions, a war waged by means of that active and aggressive power that here uses a part of its strength to quiet the ceaseless rumblings of *ressentiment* and to enforce a settlement. The most decisive move, however, made by the higher power against the predomination of grudge and spite, is the establishment of *the law*, the imperial elucidation of what counts in [the codifier's] eyes as permitted, as just, and what counts as forbidden and unjust. . . . From then on, the eye will seek an increasingly *impersonal* evaluation of the deed, even the eye of the victim itself, although this will be the last to do so.[27]

This is a remarkable passage because it at first seems so different from what post-modernists have made of Nietzsche. He is linking to social justice the most controversial and value laden aspect of his personal moral agenda: the ranking of nobility above *ressen-*

---

[27] FRIEDRICH NIETZSCHE, *Zur Genealogie der Moral*, *in* 6 SÄMTLICHE WERKE 306-07 (1964) (my translation). The original language reads as follows:

> [I]n welcher Sphäre ist denn bisher überhaupt die ganze Handhabung des Rechts, auch das eigentliche Bedürfnis nach Recht auf Erden heimisch gewesen? Etwa in der Sphäre der reaktiven Menschen? Ganz und gar nicht: vielmehr in der Aktiven, Starken, Spontanen, Aggressiven. Historisch betrachtet, stellt das Recht auf Erden . . . den Kampf gerade *wider* die reaktiven Gefühle vor, den Krieg mit denselben seitens aktiver und aggressiver Mächte, welche ihre Stärke zum Teil dazu verwendeten, der Ausschweifung des reaktiven Pathos Halt und Maß zu gebieten und einen Vergleich zu erzwingen. . . . Das Entscheidendste aber, was die oberste Gewalt gegen die Übermacht der Gegen- und Nachgefühle tut und durchsetzt—sie tut es immer, sobald sie irgendwie stark genug dazu ist—,ist die Aufrichtung des *Gesetzes*, die imperativische Erklärung darüber, was überhaupt unter ihren Augen als erlaubt, als recht, was als verboten, als unrecht zu gelten habe . . . von nun an wird das Auge für eine immer *unpersönlichere* Abschätzung der Tat eingeübt, sogar das Auge des Geschädigten selbst (obschon dies am allerletzten . . . .).

Id.

timent, of action above reaction, of the heroic Old Testament code above the rococo, privatized spiritualization of the Gospels.[28] The will to power emerges from the realm of self-perfection into the world of socialized humanity. The individual striver—think of Moses, the Revolutionary generation, or some recent feminists—*devotes some of her time to codewriting!* And, from the time of codification on, as the rest of this aphorism tells us, people's actions are gauged cooly and impersonally along the lines of their *duty*, as prescribed by the codifier.

Happy is the generation whose best private actors are regulated by such a code, and whose mass of people share the same reverence for its codifier! But, as Stendhal shows us through Julien's scorn of the prudent French generation around him, people are quickly overcome by *ressentiment*.[29] They lose sight of the greatness of the code, or they live in times where there simply is no great code. Or, worse still, they live in totalitarian times, where the values of *ressentiment*, of limitless violence, have been codified and are followed by millions of people.

I believe that the lesson of the awful codes of twentieth-century Germany and other European states has largely brought on Professor Rorty's liberal ironist, with her programmatic disjunction of the private and the public realms. She reflects the absence of reverence in our times for the constraints of a code. Put more literally, who among us would emulate Stendhal and voluntarily crack the spine of any legal code written under western skies, much less delve into it for creative guidance? The modern rift between letters and law[30] seems most striking in the difference, say, between the Internal Revenue Code and our favorite novel.

But this does not eliminate the *normative* possibility of the arrival of a new codifier. And for those like Judge Posner and myself, who are sensitive to the shadow of European history, ours is a period that might demand, rather than ironize, the linkage of private and public that the codifier forges. Certain periods mandate codification over pragmatics. Ours is such a generation. As Judge Posner observes in this symposium, evoking a debate he had with me about legal rhetoric during the period of Vichy France,[31] ours is a period in which the example of law in Nazi Europe coerces com-

---

28 *See, e.g.*, NIETZSCHE, *supra* note 7, aphorisms 52, 251.

29 See the phenomenological later work of Nietzsche's student, MAX SCHELER, RESSENTIMENT (W.W. Holdheim trans., 1961).

30 *See, e.g.*, ROBERT A. FERGUSON, LAW AND LETTERS IN AMERICAN CULTURE (1984).

31 *Compare* POSNER, LAW AND LITERATURE, *supra* note 4, at 171-75 *with* WEISBERG, *supra* note 22, at 1-9, 181-82 (introduction and appendix on French lawyer, Joseph Haen-

parisons at every moment to some of our own techniques and practices.[32] As I have suggested, particularly when a system so similar to ours in its basic story—the system under which French lawyers were trained—behaves in the pragmatic manner typical of Vichy law—accommodating incrementally to an evil inversion of the traditional egalitarian story—we must reassess the premises of analogous movements seeking prominence in our jurisprudence. If positivism were the villain, the stakes would still be high; but note that Posner here dissociates Nazi judges from positivism—and I believe he is surely correct, if the referent is also Vichy France—and places them implicitly within the dilemma for pragmatism. Recall that Posner the pragmatist earlier defines the pragmatic judge—and in part his own approach—as follows: "[A] pragmatist judge always tries to do the best he can do for the present and the future, unchecked by any felt *duty* to secure consistency in principle with what other officials have done in the past."[33]

Well, if this be pragmatism, and if the pragmatic judge in fact has no Sorel- (or Dworkin-) like *devoir* to any worthy codifier, what keeps us from replicating the model of European law during World War II? What prevents us from going with the flow of the latest accepted and fashionable movement, however grotesquely out of line with our country's previously long held traditions? Neither Posner's answer here nor in his earlier writings is reassuring; today, he advises that Nazi judges might have resisted more if they had been "backward looking" instead of advancing a radical Third Reich program foreign to their traditions. But this suggestion, which is in the service of Posner's "council of wise elders" approach, only helps if the wise elders have unpragmatically assimilated the egalitarian code as a certain guideline for decision-making. This, however, did not happen in Vichy and Posner's earlier consistently pragmatic suggestions about what lawyers should have done in that situation involve such lower-level questions as how does one get published during times of oppression if one does not at least partially accommodate;[34] how does one manage both to write and to hide one's true feelings;[35] how does one "step forward" to resist directly when "heroes are rare."[36]

nig) *and* RICHARD WEISBERG, POETHICS, AND OTHER STRATEGIES OF LAW AND LITERATURE 127-213 (1992).

32 Posner, *Pragmatic Adjudication*, *supra* note 5, at 15.

33 *Id.* at 3–4.

34 POSNER, LAW AND LITERATURE, *supra* note 4, at 173.

35 *Id.*

36 *Id.* at 174.

It is probably not entirely fair to conclude from what I have read so far about pragmatism that it does not help us (at least no more so than other contemporary patterns of legal thought) with the issue that I have identified and Judge Posner has reflected upon. But Posner's definition of what it means to be a judge seems to me so far from the common understanding of pragmatism that it offers a step in the direction of an answer. For it seems to me that Posner, here and perhaps in his practice as a judge, is more the codifier than the pragmatist. He believes that judges, wise or foolish, old or young, should act on a body of "organized knowledge" or a "disciplined, rigorous, and articulate inquiry," rather than an "unstructured intuition"—surely not on the basis of anterior constraint.[37]

Unanchored from precedent, the codifying judge may seek occasion to instantiate his own sense of social utility. A microeconomic generalization, first impressed upon lawyers by Posner's extra-judicial writings,[38] is now raised to the level of appellate rule.[39]

One need not be a judge to be a codifier. One can also be a law professor or a consultant to municipal governments; here I believe that the example of Catherine MacKinnon is helpful. Like Posner, she has moved from a base of powerful theoretical writing[40] to articulate her private academic beliefs into a socially viable code, in her case *literally* a code.[41]

Unlike pragmatism and some other more recent jurisprudential approaches, the move toward codification has the merit of baring the values of the otherwise private thinker or actor to full social scrutiny. Whatever drove Napoleon to conquer Europe, his lasting contribution in the domain of the written code elucidates the social component of his private ambitions. Perceiving Posner or MacKinnon as codifiers, more than as pragmatic or feminist theorizers, engages our social-policy instincts on their most forceful plane. It is in this legislative domain that Napolean himself fell prey to

---

37 Posner, *Pragmatic Adjudication*, *supra* note 5, at __.

38 *See, e.g.*, William M. Landes & Richard A. Posner, The Economic Structure of Tort Law (1987).

39 See, for example, the decision in *Edwards v. Honeywell, Inc.*, 50 F.3d 484 (7th Cir. 1995), on proximate cause, limiting corporate liability even where the plaintiff is foreseeable at the time of the negligent act.

40 *See, e.g.*, Catherine A. MacKinnon, *Pornography, Civil Rights, and Speech*, 20 Harv. C.R.-C.L. L. Rev. 1 (1985).

41 I am referring to her and Andrea Dworkin's Indianapolis anti-pornography statute. *But see* American Booksellers Ass'n, Inc. v. Hudnut, 771 F.2d 323 (7th Cir. 1985), *aff'd*, 475 U.S. 1001 (1986). Some Canadian jurisdictions have adopted her code.

Holmes's antipathy. After all, Napoleon was not to Holmes's liking[42]—maybe that is why Holmes might be happy to be called a pragmatist rather than a codifier, much evidence about his legal method to the contrary notwithstanding.[43]

But it will be up to us, under the codifier model, not merely to criticize or to rationalize the codes of others that we may not like. The challenge for us is to develop and perfect our own private beliefs and, if they are good enough, to make them public. From then on, we will be treated by *skeptical* others as wrongheaded and ephemeral but at least as "entitled to our beliefs" or as "off the wall" but still within the operations of "the system."[44] *Admiring* others will have a chance to say we are correct and inspired. If we attract a sufficiently large group of admirers, we may ironically produce a form of positivism that Nietzsche of all people seems to endorse in the unlikely scenario of the re-appearance of a codifier worthy of the name.

42 A scan of the many mentions of Napoleon by Holmes in his correspondence reveals his distaste for the French hero/codifier. *See, e.g.*, Letter from Justice Holmes to Harold S. Laski (Apr. 30, 1921), *in* I HOLMES-LASKI LETTERS 260-61 (Mark De Wolfe Howe ed., Atheneum 1963) (1953) (wherein he does express an interest in Melville); Letter from Justice Holmes to Harold S. Laski (Sept. 26, 1921), *in id.* at 287-88; Letter from Justice Holmes to Harold J. Laski (Oct. 9, 1921), *in id.* at 291-93 ("Kant after more than a century counted for more than Napoleon").

43 It was his admirer Cardozo who, in *Pokora v. Wabash Railroad Co.*, 292 U.S. 98 (1934), reluctantly had to correct the bald, unpragmatic assertiveness of Holmes's "stop and get out of his vehicle" railway crossing absolute rule in *Baltimore & Ohio Railroad Co. v. Goodman*, 275 U.S. 66 (1927). For that matter, on the level of style, Cardozo certainly painted Holmes in the terms of the codifier, with his epigrammatic, monarchical "type magisterial." *See* BENJAMIN N. CARDOZO, *Law and Literature*, *in* SELECTED WRITINGS OF BENJAMIN NATHAN CARDOZO 339, 347-48 (Margaret E. Hall ed., 1947). For Cardozo, Holmes might have been a kind of Nietzschean "last signpost" to the times of judges who—on their sole authority—could write boldly and without further justification in pragmatics or (even) experience. On this view, Holmes, while not in the Napoleonic mode, was more a codifier than a pragmatist.

44 STANLEY FISH, IS THERE A TEXT IN THIS CLASS? 357 (1980).

[11]

NIETZSCHE IN LAW'S CATHEDRAL: BEYOND REASON AND POSTMODERNISM

John Linarelli[+]

Nietzsche had very little to say about law, and what he did say is fragmentary and sporadic. Nietzsche's philosophy, however, offers a basis for theorizing about law. This article uses Nietzsche's important works to interpret two major movements in legal thought. The first part of the article examines how Nietzsche's philosophy augments our understanding of deontological theories about the law. Nietzsche produced a substantial ethical theory. The second part of the article examines how Nietzsche's philosophy helps us to understand law and economics. Nietzsche had a great deal to say about the intellectual predecessor to law and economics, utilitarianism, and his critique of utilitarianism offers insights into law and economics and its intellectual history. Further, Nietzsche elaborated a philosophy of science that extends to and offers insights about "analytical" social sciences such as economics.

INTRODUCTION

Nietzsche wrote almost nothing explicitly about law. Unlike Kant, Hegel, and others, Nietzsche offered nothing like a philosophy of law.[1] His limited asides setting forth explicit notions about law, if read without further investigation, reflect an austere Austinian positivism, perhaps reflecting the way law was conceptualized in nineteenth-century Europe, when the great codifications of France and Germany were the subject of

---

[+] Associate Professor of Law, University of La Verne College of Law. I am grateful to Tad Beckman for his encouragement and for helping me to see the value of Nietzsche's philosophy. I also wish to thank Jay Mootz and Jane Egly for helpful comments. Finally, Christine Pente, a law student at La Verne, patiently waded through a draft and offered insights. All references to works by Nietzsche are to section numbers in those works, unless otherwise noted.

1. *See, e.g.*, IMMANUEL KANT, THE PHILOSOPHY OF LAW: AN EXPOSITION OF THE FUNDAMENTAL PRINCIPLES OF JURISPRUDENCE AS THE SCIENCE OF RIGHT (W. Hastie trans. 1887); GEORG W. F. HEGEL, PHILOSOPHY OF RIGHT (T.M. Knox trans. 1967). It would be wrong to assume that Kant's later work on philosophy of law was one of his major contributions. For an overview of Kant's contribution to legal philosophy, see EDWIN W. PATTERSON, JURISPRUDENCE: MEN AND IDEAS OF THE LAW 376-403 (1953). Although the title of the Patterson text is dated, the text nevertheless provides a good basic overview.

public intellectual discussion.[2] In *The Gay Science*, Nietzsche conceives law as a force against Dionysian impulses and the true mores of a people.[3] In *On the Genealogy of Morals*, Nietzsche hints at law as being necessary to protect against *ressentiment*.[4] Nietzsche seems to say that law is meant to protect people of nobility from the "herd" or those with "reactive feelings."[5] Walter Kaufmann, the most influential interpreter of Nietzsche's works, interprets Nietzsche to assume that "only the weak need to rely on the rules of others," and "[m]an, being unique by nature, should be able to generate his own standards, if only he were powerful enough."[6] In Nietzsche's writings there is an almost total absence of any significant political philosophy.[7] Nietzsche's philosophy, according to Berkowitz, applies to individuals. It is about the "best life."[8] Nietzsche was a moral philosopher, arguably one of the most significant ever.[9]

Although Nietzsche said almost nothing directly about law, contemporary legal theorists and philosophers have labeled him a pragmatist and a postmodernist.[10] The discussion of Nietzsche in the

---

2. *See, e.g.*, FRIEDRICH NIETZSCHE, ON THE GENEALOGY OF MORALS, First Essay §§ 10-14 (Walter Kaufmann & R. J. Hollingdale trans. 1967) [hereinafter GENEALOGY OF MORALS].

3. FRIEDRICH NIETZSCHE, THE GAY SCIENCE § 43 (Walter Kaufmann trans. 1974) [hereinafter GAY SCIENCE].

4. GENEALOGY OF MORALS, *supra* note 2, Second Essay, § 11.

5. *Id.*

6. WALTER KAUFMANN, NIETZSCHE: PHILOSOPHER, PSYCHOLOGIST, ANTICHRIST 250 (4th ed. 1974).

7. *See* PETER BERKOWITZ, NIETZSCHE: THE ETHICS OF AN IMMORALIST 1-2 (1995); *cf.* FRANCIS FUKUYAMA, THE END OF HISTORY AND THE LAST MAN 300-01 (1992). Walter Kaufmann did much to dispel the notion that Nietzsche's philosophy supported Nazism. *See* KAUFMANN, *supra* note 6, at 284.

8. BERKOWITZ, *supra* note 7, at 4.

9. ALASDAIR MACINTYRE, AFTER VIRTUE 113 (2d ed. 1984). The author wrote:

> For it was Nietzsche's historic achievement to understand more clearly than any other philosopher—certainly more clearly than his counterparts in Anglo-Saxon emotivism and continental existentialism—not only that what purported to be appeals to objectivity were in fact expressions of subjective will, but also the nature of the problems that this posed for moral philosophy. It is true that Nietzsche, as I shall later argue, illegitimately generalized from the condition of moral judgment in his own day to the nature of morality as such: and I have already said justifiably harsh words about Nietzsche's construction of that at once absurd and dangerous fantasy, the *Übermensch*. But it is worth noting how even that construction began from a genuine insight.

Id.

10. *See, e.g.*, JULES L. COLEMAN & JEFFRIE G. MURPHY, THE PHILOSOPHY OF LAW: AN INTRODUCTION TO JURISPRUDENCE 53 (1984) (placing Nietzsche in the discussion of critical legal studies and feminist jurisprudence and concluding that Nietzsche's "perspective on values" is that values are "simply a product of power relations" and that "there is no moral truth or objectivity and thus no point in taking

legal literature is relatively scant, but still significant enough to be too much to survey for this article, given its plan.[11]

As for judicial use of Nietzsche, two curious references appear in the opinions of Supreme Court Justice Antonin Scalia.[12] Scalia has used Nietzsche to criticize the opinions of other Supreme Court Justices who he believes depart from rules relating to *stare decisis*.[13] In *Harper v. Virginia Department of Taxation*, Scalia criticized a dissent Justice Sandra Day O'Connor wrote, in which Justice O'Connor argued against

---

morality very seriously as a fundamental source of social (including legal) evaluation and criticism"); DOUGLAS E. LITOWITZ, POSTMODERN PHILOSOPHY AND LAW 42-64 (1997) (describing Nietzsche as postmodernist).

11. Legal scholarship that deals with Nietzsche for its core discussion is sparse. Another work using Nietzsche's philosophy to critique natural law is *Postmodern Philosophy and Law*, by Douglas E. Litowitz. This Article differs substantially from Litowitz's work. To mention a few differences: I do not classify Nietzsche as a postmodernist, as does Litowitz. This Article focuses more narrowly on two natural law theorists; Litowitz's book is a wider critique. This Article provides a critique of legal consequentialism in Part II, which is absent from the Litowitz text.

In October 2001, the Yeshiva University, Cardozo School of Law held a conference, Nietzsche and Legal Theory, resulting in a substantial addition to legal literature on Nietzsche. The papers are published in Volume 24 of the *Cardozo Law Review*. A sampling of those papers are included here, along with other sources. *See, e.g.*, Jeanne L. Schroeder, *Can Lawyers be Cured? Eternal Recurrence and the Lacanian Death Drive*, 24 CARDOZO L. REV. 925 (2003); Francis J. Mootz III, *Nietzschean Critique and Philosophical Hermeneutics*, 24 CARDOZO L. REV. 967 (2003); Tatiana Flessas, *Cultural Property Defined, and Redefined as Nietzschean Aphorism*, 24 CARDOZO L. REV. 1067 (2003); Roger Berkowitz, *Friedrich Nietzsche, the Code of Manu, and the Art of Legislation*, 24 CARDOZO L. REV. 1131 (2003); Theresa Aiello, *Nietzsche and Salomé Laws of the Father: Sublimation, Narcissism and Idealization*, 24 CARDOZO L. REV. 1183 (2003); Adam Thurschwell, *Specters of Nietzsche: Potential Futures for the Concept of the Political in Agamben and Derrida*, 24 CARDOZO L. REV. 1193 (2003); Kyron Huigens, *Nietzsche and Aretaic Legal Theory*, 24 CARDOZO L. REV. 563 (2003); Wolfert von Rahden, *Individual Law: On Some Aspects of Nietzsche's Juridical and Aesthetic Discourse*, 24 CARDOZO L. REV. 723 (2003); Jonathan Yovel, *Gay Science as Law: An Outline for a Nietzschean Jurisprudence*, 24 CARDOZO L. REV. 635 (2003); Adam Gearey, *We Fearless Ones: Nietzsche and Critical Legal Studies*, 11 L. & CRITIQUE 167 (2000); Richard A. Posner, *Past-Dependency, Pragmatism and Critique of History in Adjudication and Legal Scholarship*, 67 U. CHI. L. REV. 573 (2000); Richard H. Weisberg, *It's a Positivist, It's a Pragmatist, It's a Codifier! Reflections on Nietzsche and Stendhal*, 18 CARDOZO L. REV. 85 (1996); Peter Berkowitz, *On the Laws Governing Free Spirits and Philosophers of the Future: A Response to Nonet's "What is Positive Law?"*, 100 YALE L.J. 701 (1990); Philippe Nonet, *What is Positive Law?*, 100 YALE L.J. 667 (1990); RICHARD H. WEISBERG, THE FAILURE OF THE WORD: THE PROTAGONIST AS LAWYER IN MODERN FICTION 14-25, 32-33 (1984).

12. *See* Harper v. Va. Dep't of Taxation, 509 U.S. 86, 107 (1993) (Scalia, J., concurring); Planned Parenthood v. Casey, 505 U.S. 833, 996 (1992) (Scalia, J.).

13. *Harper*, 509 U.S. at 102-10 (Scalia, J., concurring); *Casey*, 505 U.S. at 995-1001 (Scalia, J.).

a retroactive application of a Supreme Court decision.[14] The majority held that federal retirees living in Virginia could assert, in their state tax refund claims, that a Supreme Court precedent applied retroactively.[15] The Supreme Court had changed the law on state taxation of federal retirement benefits from a rule permitting taxation to one that did not.[16] In criticizing O'Connor for objecting to the retroactivity of precedent, Scalia said:

> That [the] original and enduring American perception of the judicial role sprang not from the philosophy of Nietzsche but from the jurisprudence of Blackstone, which viewed retroactivity as an inherent characteristic of the judicial power, a power "not delegated to pronounce a new law, but to maintain and expound the old one."[17]

In a stinging dissent in *Planned Parenthood v. Casey*, Scalia criticized the majority for *following* the precedent of the famous *Roe v. Wade*, which sets forth the parameters of when abortion is legal.[18] Scalia stated:

> The Imperial Judiciary lives. It is instructive to compare this Nietzschean vision of us unelected, life-tenured judges—leading a Volk who will be "tested by following," and whose very "belief in themselves" is mystically bound up in their "understanding" of a Court that "speak[s] before all others for their constitutional ideals"—with the somewhat more modest role envisioned for these lawyers by the Founders.
>
> "The judiciary . . . has . . . no direction either of the strength or of the wealth of the society, and can take no active resolution whatever. It may truly be said to have neither Force nor Will, but merely judgment . . . ."[19]

Scalia's scant references could be said to misinterpret Nietzsche, although, to be fair, Scalia was writing judicial opinions, not philosophical essays.[20]

---

14. *Harper*, 509 U.S. at 102-10 (Scalia, J., concurring) (criticizing Justice O'Connor's plurality opinion in *Teague v. Lane*, 489 U.S. 288 (1989)).

15. *Id.* at 89-90.

16. *Id.* at 98-99.

17. *Id.* at 107 (quoting 1 WILLIAM BLACKSTONE, COMMENTARIES ON THE LAWS OF ENGLAND 69 (1765)).

18. Planned Parenthood v. Casey, 505 U.S. 833, 995-96 (1992) (Scalia, J., concurring in part and dissenting in part) (criticizing the majority for following *Roe v. Wade*).

19. *Id.* at 996. The latter quotation is from *The Federalist No. 78*, pp. 393-94 (G. Wills ed. 1982). The prior quotations are from the majority opinion.

20. *See* Mootz, *supra* note 11, at 1040. In the context of Supreme Court decisions that have dealt with the legal status of gays and lesbians, Mootz contends that Scalia "offers what might appear at first glance to be a Nietzschean critique, cutting through surface

This Article explores two themes using Nietzsche's philosophy, based roughly on how legal theory divides between consequentialist and deontological approaches.[21] First, the Article examines how Nietzsche's philosophy deals with legal policy issues that are expressed in deontological terms.[22] Here we must deal with the classic notions of fairness, equality, justice and like concepts. Second, the Article explores whether Nietzsche's philosophy has anything to say about the dominant present day mode of legal thinking—law and economics—a variation of utilitarianism.[23] Law and economics is consequentialist to the core. I do not contend that Nietzsche thought of law or anything else in a consequentialist—deontological dichotomy. I use these categories because of their relevance to contemporary legal theory.

The Article shows that Nietzsche's philosophy says a great deal about contemporary legal ideas and also that Nietzsche offered insights about law that were far ahead of their time.[24] The digestion of Nietzsche's ideas by the legal scholars of his day was implausible. Yet his critiques of science and reason had much to say about the scientism in the German legal academy of his time, and about the method of juridical science that pervades some German and continental European thinking about the law.[25] A discussion of Nietzsche's philosophy and German codification, however, is another article, one that centers on the philosophy of legal history. This Article applies Nietzsche's philosophy to contemporary Anglo-American legal thought.

I. NIETZSCHE AND DEONTOLOGICAL LEGAL PRINCIPLES

"No law can be sacred to me but that of my nature."[26]

A.

Whether morality does or should influence the content of legal rules is one of the more significant debates in jurisprudence.[27] Answers such as

---

appearances to the clash of political power that subtends the doctrinal squabbles," but then concludes that Scalia does not offer Nietzschean or hermeneutical insights because he pits power against reason in the form of politics against doctrinal legal analysis. *Id.*

21. For a fuller explanation of consequentialist versus deontological approaches, see LOUIS KAPLOW & STEVEN SHAVELL, FAIRNESS VERSUS WELFARE 38-58 (2002).

22. *See infra* Parts I.A.-D.

23. *See infra* Parts II.A.-F. The view that law and economics is a variation on utilitarianism is contentious and perhaps not well accepted. *See infra* text accompanying notes 158-66.

24. *See infra* Part I.D.

25. *See infra* note 163. *See generally* Part II. This Article does not provide this critique.

26. RALPH WALDO EMERSON, SELF RELIANCE (1841).

"law should reflect the mores of society" are as tautological as they are certain to be uttered routinely in American law school classrooms. Aligned with the problem of the law-morality connection, concepts related to morality, such as fairness, justice, and equality, have an uncertain location in the legal realm.[28] Nietzsche's moral philosophy offers insights on these concepts.[29] To explain how, this article compares Nietzsche's philosophy to the writings of two of the more significant natural law scholars of the late twentieth century, John Finnis and Michael Moore. These two scholars were chosen because they represent two of the more prominent voices in the contemporary natural law tradition.[30]

In his most influential work, *Natural Law and Natural Rights*, Finnis sets forth a theory of natural law.[31] Finnis writes in the Aquinian tradition.[32] He uses the word "law" in the term "natural law" to mean "any criteria of right judgment in matters of practice (conduct, or action), any standards for assessing options for human conduct as good or bad, right or wrong, desirable or undesirable, decent or unworthy."[33] "Natural," according to Finnis, means that the criteria of right judgment in law are "normative prior to any human choices."[34] Such "prior

27. *See generally* BRIAN BIX, JURISPRUDENCE: THEORY AND CONTEXT 31-86 (3d ed. 2004).

28. Economic analysis of law, widely perceived as the dominant school of legal thought, sits squarely in opposition to justice or fairness-based approaches to the law. It bypasses the difficulties in determining what is just or fair in favor of assessing the efficiency properties of legal rules, and applying a dichotomous analysis of efficiency versus distribution as a substitute for analysis of justice or fairness. See *infra* Part II for an examination of economics of law as a species of utilitarianism. Because Nietzsche had much to say about utilitarianism, the critique of law and economics is carved out for special consideration in the next part.

29. *See infra* Part I.D.

30. I am grateful to Jay Mootz for pointing out that Lloyd Weinreb and Lon Fuller offer other versions of natural law that can be more accommodating of Nietzschean philosophy because their versions do not strictly require the discovery of timeless natural law principles through reason. *See* Francis J. Mootz III, *Law in Flux: Philosophical Hermeneutics, Legal Argumentation, and the Natural Law Tradition*, 11 YALE J.L. & HUMAN. 311, 313-14, 338-67 (1999). There are other natural law scholars that I omit from the analysis as well.

31. JOHN FINNIS, NATURAL LAW AND NATURAL RIGHTS 1 (1980).

32. Though many examples could be given, see in particular JOHN FINNIS, AQUINAS: MORAL, POLITICAL, AND LEGAL THEORY vii (1998) (commenting on the "fundamental superiority" of Aquinas to Plato, Aristotle, and others); *see also* Patrick McKinley Brennan, *Arguing for Human Equality*, 18 J. L. & RELIGION 99 (characterizing Finnis as "perhaps the best known expositor of Aquinas's legal ideas today").

33. John Finnis, *Natural Law: The Classical Tradition*, *in* THE OXFORD HANDBOOK OF JURISPRUDENCE AND PHILOSOPHY OF LAW 1 (Jules Coleman & Scott Shapiro eds. 2002) [hereinafter OXFORD HANDBOOK].

34. *Id.*

standards are not the product of either individual or collective choosing or positing, and cannot be repealed, however much they may be violated, defied, or ignored."[35] To acknowledge these standards is to engage in "practical reason," which is the capacity of a person to act in response to reasons for action.[36]

Practical reason is one of the seven basic goods in Finnis's moral theory: life, knowledge, play, aesthetic experience, sociability, practicable reasonableness, and religion.[37] Finnis views these basic goods as "aspect[s] of authentic human flourishing, . . . real (intelligent) reason[s] for action."[38] They exist as undoubted independent principles for their own sake and not as means to other ends.[39] They are based on the "acts of practical understanding in which we grasp the basic values of human existence and thus, too, the basic principles of all practical reasoning,"[40] which seems to be an elaborate way of saying that they are based on human nature. From these basic goods, Finnis articulates nine "basic requirements of practical reasonableness" which are needed to guide humans to "discern moral reason in everyday life."[41] To Finnis, the basic goods and the practicable principles are obvious, self-evident and unquestionable.[42]

What about unreasonableness? To Finnis, unreasonableness is "human, all too human."[43] It is "unnatural."[44] It is "a way of being less than fully what a human person can be."[45] In addition:

> Poor thinking and choosing not only fails to actualize to the full one's capacities to be intelligent and reasonable, but also results

---

35. *Id.* at 1-2.

36. Steven J. Burton, *Law as Practical Reason*, 62 S. CAL. L. REV. 747 (1989).

37. FINNIS, *supra* note 31, at 85-97.

38. *Id.* at 64; *see* Brian H. Bix, *Natural Law: The Modern Tradition*, *in* OXFORD HANDBOOK, *supra* note 33, at 85.

39. FINNIS, *supra* note 31, at 64-65.

40. *Id.* at 59.

41. *Id.* at 100-26.

> These nine principles are: [1] adopting a coherent plan of life; [2] having no arbitrary preferences among values; [3] having no arbitrary preferences among persons; [4] maintaining a detachment from the specific and limited projects one undertakes; [5] not abandoning one's commitments lightly; [6] not wasting one's opportunities by using inefficient methods; [7] not choosing to do something that of itself does nothing but damage or impede the realization of or participation in one or more of the basic goods; [8] fostering the common good of one's community; [and] [9] acting in accordance with one's conscience.

Bix, *supra* note 38, at 86.

42. FINNIS, *supra* note 31, at 59.

43. Finnis, *supra* note 33, at 2.

44. *Id.*

45. *Id.*

> in actions or omissions which fail to respect and promote the humanity, the nature, of everyone they affect. A community in which the standards by which we identify such failure are violated is not flourishing as it might. Its members, whether they are those acting (and forbearing) or those who should have been benefited not harmed, do not fulfill their capacities. However typical of human affairs, such a condition is unnatural so far as it is disrespectful of human persons. It is unnatural *because* unreasonable, and unreasonable *because* neglectful of the good of persons, the good which is the subject-matter of practical reason's standards.[46]

Add to these principles the "master principle of morality," that humans should act, choose, deliberate, and will only those possibilities which are "compatible with integral human fulfillment," which means "the fulfillment of all human beings and their communities, in all the basic human goods."[47] From this master principle several other principles arise, notably that one's motives should be rational and not involve revenge, that one should follow the Golden Rule (do to others as you would have them do to you), and do not do evil to further a good.[48]

Law fits into Finnis's theory as a system of practical reason embedded in a particular social institution.[49] As a system of practical reason, law can be understood only from an internal perspective, "the way of thinking of someone who treats a rule as a *reason* for action."[50] The practical reason approach to law is to be contrasted with the approach of those who examine law from an external perspective, who typically view law "simply as a prediction or basis for prediction."[51] The external or predictive approach is typically associated with such fields as law and economics and law and pragmatism.[52]

Michael Moore is a moral realist.[53] He believes that moral truth is metaphysically real, and moral reality exists independent of our language.[54] The words used in law and in language generally refer to objects that exist, and the existence of the objects is independent of any

---

46. *Id.* (emphasis in original).

47. FINNIS, *supra* note 31, at 28.

48. *Id.* at 29.

49. *Id.* at 3-18; *see also* JOSEPH RAZ, PRACTICAL REASON AND NORMS 10-13 (rev. ed. 1990).

50. FINNIS, *supra* note 31, at 27 (emphasis in original).

51. *Id.*

52. *See* ERNEST J. WEINRIB, THE IDEA OF PRIVATE LAW 3-21 (distinguishing the internal from external perspective).

53. *See, e.g.*, Michael S. Moore, *The Interpretive Turn in Modern Theory: A Turn for the Worse?*, 41 STAN. L. REV. 871 (1989).

54. *Id.* at 872.

social construction or belief systems of the persons who use or hear those words.[55] Rights and duties, good and evil, are moral entities or "moral kinds."[56] A moral kind is a moral theory that applies to a moral word, such as justice or good, which is based not on human conventions but on "the best theory we are able to articulate about what sort of quality . . . [justice or good] really is."[57] Moore is of the view that there are unique and determinate right answers to moral questions.[58] He considers legal reasoning to be a species of moral reasoning.[59] In interpreting cases, statutes, and constitutions, judges and lawyers should look for the real nature of the things to which the words of the law refer.[60] To get to the right answers in morality and law, Moore articulates a nonfoundationalist coherence theory of epistemology for determining a moral proposition, which seems to dilute his moral reality: a moral value has to be coherent with everything else we believe, in order to achieve the status of a moral value.[61]

B.

In classic Nietzsche fashion of avoiding a dichotomous way of conceptualizing the world, Nietzsche's philosophy both condemns and supports natural law. First, this Article sets forth the basic elements of Nietzsche's condemnation. Second, this Article shows how Nietzsche had a vision of the good that was ethically principled, although he used the terms "noble" or "noble morality" rather than "good." Nietzsche's concept of noble morality offers a reference point from which to make ethical judgments about legal rules.

Natural law necessarily must rest on the foundation that there are some *a priori* or metaphysically real principles that are true and axiomatic, that do not require proof or justification, and that do not require any human choices.[62] These principles have value because they are "right" or "moral," and all we need to do is find them.[63] Nietzsche

---

55. *See* Michael S. Moore, *A Natural Law Theory of Interpretation*, 58 S. CAL. L. REV. 277 (1985).

56. Michael Moore, *Moral Reality*, 1982 WISC. L. REV. 1061, 1145 (1982).

57. *Id.*

58. *Id.* at 1149.

59. Bix, *supra* note 38, at 91.

60. *Id.*

61. *See id.* at 90.

62. A casual review of Finnis's foundation text and the works of other natural law scholars provides the insight. *Cf.* LLOYD L. WEINREB, NATURAL LAW AND JUSTICE 97-126 (1987) ("natural law without nature").

63. Finnis contends that self-evident basic goods, such as knowledge, exist. Finnis, *supra* note 33, at 59. Moore contends that a metaphysical reality exists that is real and knowable, independent of our interpretations of it. Moore, *supra* note 56, at 1149.

would find *a priori* or metaphysically real principles problematic. In *The Gay Science*, Nietzsche wrote:

> Whatever has *value* in our world now does not have value in itself, according to its nature–nature is always value-less, but has been *given* value at some time, as a present–and it was *we* who gave and bestowed it. Only we have created the world *that concerns man*![64]

Thus, to Nietzsche, values come into existence because of human choice. Knowledge is the result of numerous errors made throughout human history.[65] Through time, some errors proved useful, others did not.[66] Those who were lucky enough to stumble upon the useful errors survived, and in time their errors became wisdom.[67] Says Nietzsche:

> Such erroneous articles of faith, which were continually inherited, until they became almost part of the basic endowment of the species, include the following: that there are enduring things; that there are equal things; that there are things, substances, bodies; that a thing is what it appears to be; that our will is free; that what is good for me is also good in itself.[68]

Wisdom is not based on *a priori* truth, but rather on accident, the "dice throw," illogic and error.[69] There is no compelling moral state of affairs.[70]

---

64. GAY SCIENCE, *supra* note 3, § 301 (emphasis in original). In his preface to *On the Genealogy of Morals*, Nietzsche explains "his a priori" as "the question of where our good and evil really *originated*." GENEALOGY OF MORALS, *supra* note 2, Nietzsche's Preface, § 3.

65. GAY SCIENCE, *supra* note 3, § 110.

66. *Id.* §§ 110-11.

67. *Id.* § 110.

68. *Id.*

69. *See, e.g.*, FRIEDRICH NIETZSCHE, THUS SPOKE ZARATHUSTRA: A BOOK FOR ALL AND NONE, Third Part, § 4, "Before Sunrise" (Walter Kaufmann trans., 1995) [hereinafter THUS SPOKE ZARATHUSTRA]. Nietzsche wrote:

> O heaven over me, pure and high! That is what your purity is to me now, that there is no eternal spider or spider web of reason; that you are to me a dance floor for divine accidents, that you are to me a divine table for divine dice and dice players.

Id.; see also GILLES DELEUZE, NIETZSCHE AND PHILOSOPHY 25-27 (Hugh Tomlinson trans. 1983).

70. Though there are many sources for this point, Nietzsche's Preface in his *On the Geneology of Morals* supports it nicely. Nietzsche explains that he is looking for the "origin of moral prejudices." GENEOLOGY OF MORALS, *supra* note 2, Nietzsche's Preface, § 2. Later in the Preface, he explains:

> Let us articulate this *new demand*: we need a *critique* of moral values, *the value of the values themselves must first be called into question* . . . . One has taken the *value* of these "values" as given, as factual, as beyond all question; one has hitherto never doubted or hesitated in the slightest degree in supposing "the

Knowledge is not rational, scientific, ahistorical or analytical; rather, knowledge is really interpretation that rises to the level of habit. Humankind began to question error-produced wisdom only later in its existence, and only in relatively recent times did the concept of "truth" emerge, which Nietzsche calls the "weakest form of knowledge."[71] To Nietzsche, "the *strength* of knowledge does not depend on its degree of truth, but on its age, on the degree to which it has been incorporated, on its character as a condition of life."[72]

One Nietzschean problem of truth in natural law is that of false consciousness.[73] In *The Gay Science* Nietzsche questions whether the so-called realists "can forget your descent, your past, your training—all of your humanity and animality" in order to engage in the cold and sober analysis of reality.[74] Realism is impossible because realists are burdened with the primordial baggage that exists in all humans. They do not understand how the world has its origins in the passions of former centuries.[75]

Nietzsche would find Finnis's and Moore's emphasis on reason problematic. Nietzsche would find them all too Socratic.[76] To Nietzsche,

---

> good man" to be of greater value than "the evil man," of greater value in the sense of furthering the advancement and prosperity of man in general. But what if the reverse were true?

Id. § 6. These sorts of statements are not to be misconstrued to suggest that evil villains such as Saddam Hussein are somehow good. Rather, Nietzsche was raising very sophisticated questions to challenge the moral philosophers of his day and of past ages.

71. GAY SCIENCE, *supra* note 3, § 110.

72. *Id.* (emphasis in original).

73. The Cambridge Dictionary of Philosophy defines "false consciousness" as:

> (1) lack of clean awareness of the source and significance of one's beliefs and attitudes concerning society, religion, or values; (2) objectionable forms of ignorance and false belief; (3) dishonest forms of self deception. Marxists (if not Marx) use the expression to explain and condemn illusions generated by unfair economic relationships . . . . Collingwood interprets false consciousness as self-corrupting untruthfulness in disowning one's emotions and ideas.

THE CAMBRIDGE DICTIONARY OF PHILOSOPHY (Robert Audi, ed., 2d ed. 1999).

74. GAY SCIENCE, *supra* note 3, § 57.

75. *Id.*

76. Kaufmann contends that Nietzsche admired Socrates. In his famous book, Kaufmann wrote an entire chapter on "Nietzsche's Attitude toward Socrates." KAUFMANN, *supra* note 6, at 391-411. Even Kaufmann concedes, however, that Nietzsche finds Socrates "deeply problematic." Walter Kaufmann, Translator's Introduction, in FRIEDRICH NIETZSCHE, THE BIRTH OF TRAGEDY 12 (Walter Kaufmann trans., Random House 1967) (1872) [hereinafter BIRTH OF TRAGEDY]. Socrates was problematic for Nietzsche because of Socrates' "faith" in reason. To Nietzsche, Socrates is in part responsible for the death of tragic art. Nietzsche's main concern was with "aesthetic Socratism," the "supreme law" of which is "to be beautiful everything must be intelligible." *Id.*; *see also* ARTHUR C. DANTO, NIETZSCHE AS PHILOSOPHER 57-58 (1965). Nietzsche disfavored Socratic emphasis on reason, at least as a basis for creating and

Finnis's basic goods and requirements of practical reasonableness,[77] and Moore's moral reality, would turn life into something like a play by Euripides.[78] Nietzsche blames Euripides for the destruction of Greek tragedy.[79] To Nietzsche, the problem with Euripides was that he abandoned the focus of Greek tragedy on the heroic in favor of glorifying the affairs of the common man,[80] producing plays that were rational, comprehensible, and realistic in their portrayal of everyday life and its imperfections.[81] Nietzsche saw the death of tragedy in Euripides because of the lack of Dionysian elements in Euripides' plays.[82] Moore and Finnis represent the embodiment of the Apollonian approach, and seek to remove the Dionysian element from the human state of affairs.[83]

Finally, Nietzsche would find problematic the moral principles that Finnis and Moore contend exist.[84] Natural law fits nicely within Nietzsche's conception of "slave morality."[85] Natural law is the belief system of the "last man"—it is "human all too human." To Finnis, to be unreasonable would be "human, all too human."[86] Nietzsche takes the opposite view; to be *reasonable* is human, all too human. The reasonable person is the "last man," someone satisfied with happiness, striving for mediocrity and moderation.[87] Nietzsche no doubt would refer to natural law as "the brain-sick fancies of morbid cobweb spinners."[88] Nietzsche is by natural law standards immoral, but, as we shall see, he is nevertheless ethically principled.

C.

To produce strident criticism of anything requires contrary positions, and Nietzsche clearly had them. Despite his diatribes, his despising of systematic knowledge, and his scathing *ad hominem* attacks, Nietzsche

---

experiencing art. Nietzsche admired Socratic accomplishment of focusing mankind on reason, because the alternatives would lead to a worse state of affairs. *Id.* at 59.

77. *See generally* FINNIS, *supra* note 31.

78. BIRTH OF TRAGEDY, *supra* note 76, § 12; *see also* KAUFMANN, *supra* note 6, at 393.

79. DANTO, *supra* note 76, at 57.

80. BERKOWITZ, *supra* note 7, at 59.

81. *Id.;* DANTO, *supra* note 76, at 58.

82. DANTO, *supra* note 76, at 59.

83. *See generally* FINNIS, *supra* note 31.

84. *See generally id.*

85. One of the most fundamental tenets of Nietzsche's philosophy is the distinction between slave and noble morality. *See infra* text accompanying notes 122-41, 168-72.

86. *See* FINNIS, *supra* note 31.

87. DANTO, *supra* note 76, at 197; BERKOWITZ, *supra* note 7, at 142-43.

88. FRIEDRICH NIETZSCHE, *Reason in Philosophy, in* TWILIGHT OF THE IDOLS § 4 (R.J. Hollingdale trans., Penguin Books 1968).

constructed an ethical philosophy.[89] He had an elaborate vision of the truth and saw man as being able to choose, and choice as necessary for being.[90] Structuralism was not part of his philosophy, nor was instrumentalism. Contrary to postmodern interpretations of his work, Nietzsche was not a nihilist, though he did attack norms and standards by which he saw nineteenth-century Europeans guiding their actions.[91] Nietzsche did not reject value commitments, though his values differ from what he calls the herd or slave morality of Christianity and Enlightenment philosophy.[92] His elaborations on how the concept of "good" began in primordial history reflecting the qualities of elites, then to be rejected in the slave revolt in morality and the rise of *ressentiment*, set forth an ethical agenda.[93] Nietzsche's last man is to be contrasted with his overman, who seeks not to dominate but to go beyond and to become noble.[94] The overman is not interested in hurting others; his nobility is about transcending the human condition rather than concerning himself with the lives of others.[95]

Nietzsche's works set forth an elaborate "noble mode of valuation"[96] and a noble morality that Russell and Kaufman find akin to the virtuous life that Aristotle articulates in the *Nicomachean Ethics*.[97] Nietzsche's core philosophical conceptions are will to power, overcoming and eternal recurrence.[98] These conceptions are ethical principles that mandate value commitments. Heidegger viewed Nietzsche as one of the most important metaphysical thinkers in Western philosophy.[99] He also is one of the most important moral philosophers in Western philosophy.[100] Here, this Article examines the affirmative side of Nietzsche's philosophy.

Will to power is the struggle of humans over time to learn and develop norms of behavior through species preserving error.[101] It is both creative and destructive.[102] It creates because humans use will to power to

---

89. *See generally* GENEAOLOGY OF MORALS, *supra* note 2.

90. *Id.*

91. *Id.*

92. *See* BERKOWITZ, *supra* note 7, at 141-44.

93. *See* GENEALOGY OF MORALS, *supra* note 2, First Essay, § 10.

94. DANTO, *supra* note 76, at 197.

95. *Id.*

96. GENEOLOGY OF MORALS, *supra* note 2, First Essay, § 10.

97. *See infra* text accompanying notes 130-42.

98. Tad Beckman, *Notes for Nietzsche*, *at* http://www.4hmc.edu:8001/humanities/beckman/nietzsche/reading/also.htm (last visited Oct. 2, 2003).

99. 2 MARTIN HEIDEGGER, NIETZSCHE 1 (David Farrell Krell trans., Harper & Row 1984) (1954).

100. *See supra* note 10 and accompanying text.

101. Beckman, *supra* note 98.

102. *Id.*

produce values and to make sense of existence.[103] It destroys because it must overcome old values that no longer serve us.[104] Nietzschean will to power differs fundamentally from natural law philosophy because the world is chaotic and we cannot understand it through reason.[105] There is no right reason or moral reality that we must ultimately discover if we think or try hard enough.[106] Heidegger interprets Nietzsche's will to power as designating the basic character of being; it is the basic question of the being of beings.[107]

Will to power is a mode of valuation, a method, but not value itself.[108] It does not tell us what is right and wrong, ideas that are uncomfortable in Nietzschean philosophy because they presuppose that values can be sufficiently general or "right."[109] To Heidegger, will to power has to be thought of together with Nietzsche's eternal recurrence in order to fully grasp Nietzsche's philosophy.[110] Using Heidegger's conception of Nietzsche's philosophy, we now can see the conceptual glue being set on Nietzsche's ethics.[111] When will to power and eternal recurrence are read together, they give us a way of being or operating as does Finnis's practical reasonableness.[112]

Heidegger contended that the idea of the eternal recurrence was the fundamental thought in Nietzsche's philosophy.[113] Although Nietzsche explained it allegorically in *Thus Spoke Zarathustra*,[114] he described eternal recurrence succinctly in *Ecce Homo* as "the unconditional and infinitely repeated circular course of all things."[115] Though Nietzsche for a time wanted to prove eternal recurrence scientifically, as a physical

103. *Id.*

104. *Id.*

105. *Id.*

106. *Id.* Will to power is the fundamental human ability to struggle through the incomprehensible accident of the world to make life sensible and practical.

107. 1 HEIDEGGER, *supra* note 99, at 18-21.

108. THUS SPOKE ZARATHUSTRA, *supra* note 69, Second Part; Tad Beckman, *Notes on Thus Spoke Zarathustra*, *at* http://www4.hmc.edu:8001/humanities/beckman/nietzsche/reading/Also.html.

109. 1 HEIDEGGER, *supra* note 99.

110. *Id.*

111. *Id.* at 18.

112. *See generally Notes for Nietzsche*, *supra* note 98; FINNIS, *supra* note 31. Both sets of principles have to do with how to live life.

113. 2 HEIDEGGER, *supra* note 99, at 5. Nietzsche called his idea of the eternal recurrence a "doctrine."

114. THUS SPOKE ZARATHUSTRA, *supra* note 69, Third Part, "On the Vision and the Riddle."

115. FRIEDRICH NIETZSCHE, ECCE HOMO, *Essay on Birth of Tragedy*, § 3 (Walter Kaufmann trans. 1966) [hereinafter ECCE HOMO].

law,[116] he ultimately settled for leaving it as an ethical precept, about a way of life.[117] Because what we do eternally returns, every moment counts.[118] Eternal recurrence gives direction to will to power.[119] We now must promote the highest order of values possible, because what we do now will return in the future.[120]

Finally, Nietzsche specified a set of values for humans to seek to achieve through will to power. He does not see the essence of life in self preservation, but in enhancement of life.[121] Nietzsche was not a moral skeptic.[122] Humans must overcome; the goal is becoming overman, not to model one after a saint or God.[123] Noble values are embodied in the idea of a noble morality, which is to be contrasted with slave or herd morality.[124] The noble moral person is one who has a strong character, a "great souled" character in the style of the Athenian citizen.[125] The noble moral person triumphs over *ressentiment*. To avoid *ressentiment* is an ethical precept.[126] To be kind, humble or silent when one is too weak or timid to act, to be humble when one cannot bear unpleasant repercussions, to make virtue of necessity, to want revenge against the teacher, to have reactive feelings, to be resentful, and to seek and give pity, Nietzsche identified these as attributes of slave morality.[127] To quote Nietzsche, through his *Zarathustra*:

> But if you have an enemy, do not requite him evil with good, for that would put him to shame. Rather prove that he did you some good.
>
> And rather be angry than put to shame. And if you are cursed, I do not like it that you want to bless. Rather join a little in the cursing.

116. 2 HEIDEGGER, *supra* note 99, at 106-09.

117. 2 HEIDEGGER, *supra* note 99, at 122-23.

118. Beckman, *supra* note 108.

119. *See* 3 HEIDEGGER, *supra* note 99.

120. Beckman, *supra* note 108.

121. 3 HEIDEGGER, *supra* note 99, at 15.

122. This is perhaps one of the central themes in BERKOWITZ, *supra* note 7.

123. DANTO, *supra* note 76, at 196-97.

124. GENEALOGY OF MORALS, *supra* note 2, § 10.

125. *See infra* text accompanying notes 131-39.

126. *See* 3 HEIDEGGER, *supra* note 99. In essence, it means that one should be strong and magnanimous.

127. KAUFMANN, *supra* note 6, at 371-72.

> And if you have been done a great wrong, then quickly add five little ones: a gruesome sight is a person single-mindedly obsessed by a wrong.
>
> Did you already know this? A wrong shared is half right. And he who is able to bear it should take the wrong upon himself.
>
> A little revenge is more human than no revenge. And if punishment is not also a right and an honor for the transgressor, then I do not like your punishments either.
>
> It is nobler to declare oneself wrong than to insist on being right—especially when one is right. Only one must be rich enough for that.
>
> I do not like your cold justice; and out of the eyes of your judges there always looks the executioner and his cold steel. Tell me, where is that justice which is love with open eyes? Would that you might invent for me the love that bears not only all punishment but also all guilt! Would that you might invent for me the justice that acquits everyone, except him that judges!
>
> Do you still want to hear this too? In him who would be just through and through even lies become kindness to others. But how could I think of being just through and through? How can I give each his own? Let this be sufficient for me: I give each my own.[128]

In *On the Genealogy of Morals*, Nietzsche says:

> While the noble man lives in trust and openness with himself (*gennaios* "of noble descent" underlines the nuance "upright" and probably also "naive"), the man of *ressentiment* is neither upright nor naive nor honest and straightforward with himself. His soul *squints*; his spirit loves hiding places, secret paths and back doors, everything covert entices him as *his* world, *his* world, *his* security, *his* refreshment; he understands how to keep silent, how not to forget, how to wait, how to be provisionally self-deprecating and humble. A race of such men of *ressentiment* is bound to become eventually *cleverer* than any

---

128. THUS SPOKE ZARATHUSTRA, *supra* note 69, First Part, "On the Adder's Bite" 68-69.

> noble race; it will also honor cleverness to a far greater degree: namely, as a condition of existence of the first importance . . . .
>
> To be incapable of taking one's enemies, one's accidents, even one's misdeeds seriously for very long—that is the sign of strong, full natures in whom there is an excess of the power to form, to mold, to recuperate and to forget . . . . Such a man shakes off with a *single* shrug many vermin that eat deep into others; here alone genuine "love of one's enemies" is possible—supposing it to be possible at all on earth. How much reverence has a noble man for his enemies!—and such reverence is a bridge to love.[129]

Such ideas permeate Nietzsche's works; the above extracts capture the essential concepts.

Russell and Kaufmann compare Nietzsche's concept of the noble man to Aristotle's great souled or magnanimous man found in Book IV of Aristotle's *Nicomachean Ethics*.[130] Aristotle refers to "greatness of soul," an upper class Greek virtue that has no direct translation into present day English, but which is close to magnanimity, proper pride or self-respect.[131] The great souled or magnanimous man "thinks that he is worthy of great things, provided that he *is* worthy of them."[132] "The man who is worthy of little consideration and thinks that he is such is temperate [moderate], but not magnanimous, because magnanimity implies greatness . . . ."[133] Aristotle identifies a number of characteristics

129. GENEALOGY OF MORALS, *supra* note 2, First Essay, § 10 (emphasis in original).

130. Kaufmann, *supra* note 6, at 382-83; BERTRAND RUSSELL, A HISTORY OF WESTERN PHILOSOPHY 176 (1945).

131. ARISTOTLE, THE NICOMACHEAN ETHICS 153 (J. A.K. Thomson trans. 1933) (Translator Notes). The word in ancient Greek is *megalopsuchia*. Though Thomson translates this word to mean magnamity, Rackham says that it means "lofty pride and self-esteem rather than magnamity or high-mindedness (in the modern sense of the word)." *Compare id., with* ARISTOTLE, NICHOMACHEAN ETHICS 213 n.b (H. Rackham trans., 1933).

132. ARISTOTLE, NICOMACHEAN ETHICS (Thomson trans.), *supra* note 131, at § 1123a31-b13.

133. *Id.* Aristotle continues:

> The man who thinks that he is worthy of great things although he is not worthy of them is conceited; but not everybody is conceited who has too high an opinion of his own worth. On the other hand the man who has too low an opinion is pusillanimous: and it makes no difference whether his worth is great or moderate or little, if his opinion of it is too low. Indeed the man whose worth is great might be regarded as especially pusillanimous, because what would his behaviour be if his worth were not so great?

Id.

of the great souled or magnanimous man in his Book IV.[134] Of Aristotle's magnanimous man, Russell remarked, "One shudders to think what a vain man would be like."[135] The connection between Aristotle's and Nietzsche's ethics seem clear.[136] Nietzsche, like Aristotle, is not concerned with how to make people "good" or "moral," but rather

---

134. *Id.* §§ 1124a23-b14 to 1125a5-27.

> The magnanimous man does not take petty risks, nor does he court danger, because there are few things that he values highly; but he takes great risks, and when he faces danger he is unsparing of his life, because to him there are some circumstances in which it is not worth living. He is disposed to confer benefits, but is ashamed to accept them, because the one is the act of a superior and the other that of an inferior. When he repays a service he does so with interest, because in this way the original benefactor will become his debtor and beneficiary. People of this kind are thought to remember the benefits that they have conferred, but not those that they have received (because the beneficiary is inferior to the benefactor, and the magnanimous man wants to be superior), and to enjoy being reminded of the former, but not of the latter . . . . Another mark of the magnanimous man is that he never, or only reluctantly, makes a request, whereas he is eager to help others. He is haughty towards those who are influential and successful, but moderate towards those who have an intermediate position in society, because in the former case to be superior is difficult and impressive, but in the latter it is easy; and to create an impression at the expense of the former is not ill-bred, but to do so among the humble is vulgar—like using one's strength against the weak . . . . He is bound to be open in his likes and dislikes (because concealment, i.e. caring less for the truth than for what people think, is a mark of timidity), and to speak and act straightforwardly (his superior attitude makes him outspoken and candid . . .); and he cannot bear to live in dependence upon somebody else, except a friend, because such conduct is servile; which is why all flatterers are of the lowest class, and humble people are flatterers. He is not prone to express admiration, because nothing is great in his eyes. He does not nurse resentment, because it is beneath a magnanimous man to remember things against people, especially wrongs; it is more like him to overlook them. He does not care for personal conversation; he will talk neither about himself nor about anyone else, because he does not care to be complimented himself or to hear others criticized; nor again is he inclined to pay compliments. For this reason he is not abusive either, not even of his enemies, unless he intends to be insulting. In troubles that are unavoidable or of minor importance he is the last person to complain or ask for help, because such an attitude would imply that he took them seriously.

Id.

135. RUSSELL, *supra* note 130.

136. I am not the first, and probably not the last, to see this. *See id.* at 175. In *After Virtue*, MacIntyre argues that the moral philosophies of Nietzsche and Aristotle present "two genuine theoretical alternatives confronting anyone trying to analyze the moral condition of our culture." MacIntyre, *supra* note 9, at 110. MacIntyre contends that to Nietzsche, modern moral utterance is specific to the person, not determined by reason but by will. In the end, MacIntrye rejects Nietzsche. His logic: The Enlightenment philosophers tried to repudiate Aristotle, but they failed. Nietzsche tried to repudiate the Enlightenment philosophers, which needed to be done because the Enlightenment was a failure. So, our only alternatives are Nietzsche or Aristotle, and certainly we cannot accept Nietzsche. *Id.* at 109-20 (chapter entitled "Nietzsche or Aristotle?").

with how one is to be a successful human being.[137] Aristotle's virtuous person was not a Christian saint, nor was Nietzsche's.[138]

Finally, Nietzsche had no concern about the common good. Nietzsche's herd or slave morality is good for the group or collective but not for the individual; noble morality is about how to make the individual better off, regardless of what the community might need from the individual.[139] But is Nietzsche in this respect so different from any other nonconsequentialist philosopher? Aristotle, clearly not utilitarian, examines the virtues of the good person from the standpoint of the person who has, or lacks, the virtue, and is not concerned with the effects of the virtue on other persons. His discussions of generosity or courage in *Nichomachean Ethics*, for example, consider these virtues only from the perspective of the agent possessing these qualities and not from the perspective of how these qualities are necessary to protect society.[140] Aristotle's concept of the common good is fused with his concept of private good: what is a good virtue for the individual is good for the city.[141]

D.

What do Nietzsche's ethics say about law? If natural law is slave or herd morality, and if we accept that natural law is or should inform the content of positive law, then we must conclude that positive law is or should be based on herd morality. Law is meant primarily for society and can harm persons striving for a noble morality. Nietzsche would ask us to develop a new jurisprudence that preserves freedom to overcome, to pursue noble morality.[142] Positive law can be constructed in such a way because Nietzsche viewed norms embodied in morals and law as social constructions.[143] Nietzsche would prefer a legal system that disables and avoids *ressentiment*, that would promote human freedom in a pluralist setting without interpersonal comparisons.[144] Nietzsche's normative vision is that we should fundamentally reevaluate law and other social systems and reorient towards a noble morality.

---

137. *See* ARISTOTLE, *supra* note 131, Translator's Introduction, at 29.

138. RUSSELL, *supra* note 130, at 175.

139. GENEALOGY OF MORALS, *supra* note 2, Second Essay, § 2.

140. *See* ARISTOTLE, NICOMACHEAN ETHICS (Thomson trans.), *supra* note 131, at 31. This is implicit in Aristotle's concept of eudaimonia. *See* J.L. Ackrill, *Aristotle on Eudaimonia, in* ARISTOTLE'S ETHICS: CRITICAL ESSAYS (Nancy Sherman ed., 1999).

141. ARISTOTLE, NICOMACHEAN ETHICS (Thomson trans.), *supra* note 131, § 1094a22-b12; MacIntyre, *supra* note 9, at 150.

142. *See* GENEOLOGY OF MORALS, *supra* note 2, Second Essay, §§ 2, 11.

143. *Id.*

144. *Id.*

Nietzsche's discussion of the notion of equality provides an example of how we can use Nietzsche's legal theory to inquire about law. In several passages, Nietzsche expressed disfavor with the notion of equality.[145] Nietzsche's thoughts on equality are important because the notion of formal equality and how to implement it pervades the ideal visions of Western legal systems. A fundamental aspect of the human condition that law seeks to address is which sorts of inequality deserve legal redress. Hence, constitutional law mandating equal protection and due process, statutes prohibiting discrimination and cases interpreting these statutes, and the recent affirmative action cases are but examples of the ongoing dialogue between law and society on what sorts of inequalities are permissible and which are not.[146]

In *Thus Spoke Zarathustra*, in a section entitled "On the Tarantulas," Nietzsche metaphorically describes "preachers of *equality*" as tarantulas whose "secretly vengeful" ways make "the soul whirl with revenge."[147] Nietzsche's main concern seems to be about dictatorial preferences: "You preachers of equality, the tyrannomania of impotence clamors thus out of you for equality: your most secret ambitions to be tyrants thus shroud themselves in words of virtue."[148] "I do not wish to be mixed up and confused with these preachers of equality. For to *me* justice speaks thus: 'Men are not equal.' Nor shall they become equal! What would my love of the overman be if I spoke otherwise?"[149]

These passages are easily misconstrued to suggest that Nietzsche was anti-liberal or racist.[150] Nietzsche's conception of will to power does not mean that the strong should subjugate the weak or that there are inherent inequalities among peoples. Nietzsche saw values and the characteristics of humans as socially constructed, so it is difficult to read determinism into his philosophy. Rather, Nietzsche's concern with equality is twofold: first, the striving for equality is a search for the unattainable. People are different and can choose. Some will seek a noble life while others will practice *ressentiment* and bad conscience.[151] If

145. *See* BEYOND GOOD AND EVIL §§ 201-03, 212, 238; THUS SPOKE ZARATHUSTRA, *supra* note 69, at 99-100.

146. U.S. CONST. amend. XIV; Grutter v. Bollinger, 539 U.S. 306 (2003); Gratz v. Bollinger, 539 U.S. 244 (2003).

147. THUS SPOKE ZARATHUSTRA, *supra* note 69, Second Part, "On the Tarantulas" at 99 (emphasis in original).

148. *Id.* at 100.

149. *Id.* (emphasis in original).

150. There are other more obvious and regrettable racist and sexist passages in Nietzsche's works. The problem with many Nietzsche interpretations, however, is selective misquoting. Nietzsche advised against this. GENEALOGY OF MORALS, *supra* note 2, Nietzsche's Preface, § 8, n.5.

151. *See id.* § 10 n.2.

people are free they will make choices about which path to take. Second, in response to the democratic consolidation that started to take hold in Europe in the nineteenth century, Nietzsche is essentially asking the question "is that all there is?" To Nietzsche, equality works much like Christianity, to sap the life out of people, to make them comfortable, complacent, and to furnish incentives to compare their lot with others, even if their state of affairs is dismal, rather than to strive for a higher order on their own, without reference to what others have or do not have.[152] In sum, to Nietzsche, equality is overrated.

But Nietzsche's criticism of equality is vague. His objection could be read as against egalitarianism, an idea important in nineteenth-century European socialist thought. It is doubtful that Nietzsche would have much interest in the minimum fairness standard of treating like cases alike, though if he were to have an interest, it is unlikely that he would strenuously object.[153] Treating like cases alike does not impose the requirement that everyone must *be* the same; it only says that everyone must be *treated* the same *if* they are the same.[154] Nietzsche does not "solve" the question how to determine which value should be permitted and which should not. Rather, his answer would be that this is all well and good, but that such interpersonal comparisons are largely beside the

152. Nietzsche expresses such criticisms of Christianity throughout his works. Though clearly not one of his better works, perhaps his culminating work stating his views on Christianity is FRIEDRICH NIETZSCHE, THE ANTI-CHRIST (R.J. Hollingdale trans. 1968). He soon went mad after writing THE ANTI-CHRIST. *Id.* at 7. For a balanced treatment, see BERKOWITZ, *supra* note 7, at 77-83.

153. For a discussion of the standard of treating like cases alike, see David A. Strauss, *Must Like Cases Be Treated Alike?*, University of Chicago Public Law and Legal Theory Working Paper No. 24, (May 8, 2002), *available at* http://papers.ssrn.com/sol3/delivery.cfm/SSRN_ID312180_code020518530.pdf?abstractid=312180; JOHN RAWLS, A THEORY OF JUSTICE 237-78 (1971).

154. Joseph Raz argues that the treating like cases alike principle is tautological and impossible to attain. JOSEPH RAZ, THE AUTHORITY OF LAW: ESSAYS ON LAW AND MORALITY 226-27 (1979). I disagree. Consider the following syllogism, inspired by Joseph Raz:

> Being or not being Chinese is irrelevant to one's eligibility to enroll in college.
> Jane is Chinese.
> Therefore, Jane's race is irrelevant to her eligibility to enroll in college.

JOSEPH RAZ, THE MORALITY OF FREEDOM 217-44 (1986). What is "same" or "alike" is the subject of volumes of law on permissible and impermissible categories of difference. For example, to discriminate against entry to university on the basis of race is impermissible because it treats applicants differently, on the basis of an impermissible category. Race discrimination produces impermissible inequality. It fails to treat like cases alike, because race is not a legitimate difference. But to discriminate against entry to a university on the basis of SAT scores is permissible because it treats applicants differently on the basis of a permissible category: success on a standardized test. Discrimination on the basis of standardized test scores produces equality; it treats like cases alike.

point of a commitment to the noble life. Nietzsche would have no need for fairness or equality other than to facilitate will to power.

Thus, law to Nietzsche should be committed to freedom to engage in will to power. Nietzsche might have the need for law that frees individuals so that they may pursue noble morality. Given the eternal return of the same, we need to "get law right." Nietzsche explains the purpose of law in *On the Genealogy of Morals*:

> Finally, one only has to look at history: in which sphere has the entire administration of law hitherto been at home–also the need for law? In the sphere of reactive men, perhaps? By no means: rather in that of the active, strong, spontaneous, aggressive. From a historical point of view, law represents on earth . . . the struggle *against* the reactive feelings, the war conducted against them on the part of the active aggressive powers who employed some of their strength to impose measure and bounds upon the excesses of the reactive pathos and to compel it to come to terms. Wherever justice is practiced and maintained one sees a stronger power seeking a means of putting an end to the senseless raging of *ressentiment* among the weaker powers that stand under it.[155]

Written before the introduction of the modern welfare state, Nietzsche's words sound illiberal, even repugnant, to contemporary ears. Nietzsche could be interpreted as rejecting what we call today "social justice" because it manifests *ressentiment.*[156] In such an interpretation, Nietzsche forms a classical vision of the rule of law, in the sense that law should promote human freedom, to stop or deter one person or a group of persons from imposing their morality upon others, to prohibit or reduce arbitrary activities that would permit one person from preying on another.

A contrasting interpretation would not place Nietzsche in a political context. Some may be tempted to label Nietzsche "conservative" or "liberal," "right wing" or "left wing." We must avoid trying to pigeonhole Nietzsche into the politics of the present. Nietzsche would have no patience with such political concepts, seeing them as last man thinking, full of bad conscience. Nietzsche's philosophy asks us to transcend politics. To transcend politics we must imagine a world in which social justice is compatible with Nietzsche's noble morality, as a way of improving the human condition.

---

155. GENEALOGY OF MORALS, *supra* note 2, Second Essay, § 11.

156. BERKOWITZ, *supra* note 7, at 86.

II. NIETZSCHE AND LEGAL UTILITARIANISM

Utilitarians "are right so rarely that it is really pitiful."[157]

A.

Nietzsche's assault on the utilitarians, those "English psychologists,"[158] bears particular relevance for critiquing law and economics, currently the dominant research agenda in the legal academy.[159] This part of the article applies Nietzsche's critiques of utilitarianism and science to law and economics. Nietzsche's complaints about utilitarianism shed light on the scope and force of economic analysis of law. Nietzsche's critique of science proves relevant because law and economics apply "analytical" or "rigorous" social science methods of economics to law.[160] Economics follows very much the scientific tradition of Popperian hypothesis testing.[161] It relies on a rigid distinction between normative and positive analysis. It seeks to "explain," "make findings," and "predict" the consequences or effects of legal rules and processes.[162] In law and economics, we have seen some of the most dramatic examples of scientific analysis of law in the post-realist period. Law and economics differs from nineteenth century approaches to legal science, in that law and economics applies economic science to law. As a result, law is not an "autonomous discipline" in this approach, as it was in the other, older and now discredited scientific approach to law.[163] Hence, a substantial

---

157. GAY SCIENCE, *supra* note 3, § 84.

158. GENEOLOGY OF MORALS, *supra* note 2, First Essay, § 1.

159. *See generally* Robert C. Ellickson, *Trends in Legal Scholarship: A Statistical Study*, 29 J. LEGAL STUD. 517 (2000); James E. Krier & Stewart J. Schwab, *The Cathedral at Twenty-Five: Citations and Impressions*, 106 YALE L.J. 2121 (1997); William M. Landes & Richard A. Posner, *Heavily Cited Articles in Law*, 71 CHI. KENT L. REV. 825 (1996).

160. *See* Charles K. Rowley, *Social Sciences and the Law: The Relevance of Economic Theories*, 1 OXFORD J. LEGAL STUD. 391 (1981); ANALYTIC NARRATIVES 10-13 (Robert H. Bates et al. eds., 1998) (explaining differences between analytical tools of economics and narrative tools of history); KENNETH A. SHEPSLE & MARK S. BONCHEK, ANALYZING POLITICS: RATIONALITY, BEHAVIOR AND INSTITUTIONS 5-8 (1997) (analytical methods in politics); MELVIN J. HINICH & MICHAEL C. MUNGER, ANALYTICAL POLITICS 3-9 (1997) (analytical methods in politics); *see generally* JON ELSTER, NUTS AND BOLTS FOR THE SOCIAL SCIENCES (1989); MARTIN HOLLIS, THE PHILOSOPHY OF SOCIAL SCIENCE (1994).

161. *See* Rowley, *supra* note 160.

162. *See supra* note 160.

163. *See* Richard A. Posner, *The Decline of Law as an Autonomous Discipline: 1962-1987*, 100 HARV. L. REV. 761 (1987).

interdisciplinary movement prevails in legal scholarship, and law and economics is an integral part of that movement.[164]

Legal scholars have disagreed on whether law and economics is utilitarian.[165] I do not engage this dispute in any appreciable level of sophistication here, although the similarities and intellectual connections seem substantial. Rather, I contend that what Nietzsche said about utilitarianism and science furthers our understanding of the jurisprudential niche of law and economics, regardless of whether law and economics is utilitarian. This part of the article dissects what Nietzsche said about utilitarianism, to expose the main tenets relevant to economics, and to show that Nietzsche produced a serious critique that must be inquired into and that must not be overshadowed by the sometimes harsh and regrettable attacks that Nietzsche visited upon utilitarians and "Englishmen."[166]

B.

Nietzsche starts *On The Genealogy of Morals* with an attack on utilitarianism.[167] To Nietzsche, what is good (or, in economic terms, "a good") has nothing to do with utility. Nietzsche looks to the origins of the good in noble morality.[168] Noble morality is internal to the individual and has nothing to do with instrumental effects on others. In dealing with his famous distinction between herd or slave morality and noble morality, Nietzsche used the word "utility" to describe the usefulness of herd morality to the preservation of the herd.[169] Egoism is a herd or slave morality concept.[170] People responding to external incentives in order to maximize utility or welfare engage in herd or slave morality.[171] Utilitarianism in this sense is like religion; religious morality also comes from the outside, but it is revealed in sacred texts. Evolution suffers

---

164. *See supra* note 160; *see also* NICHOLAS MERCURO & STEVE G. MEDEMA, ECONOMICS AND THE LAW: FROM POSNER TO POSTMODERNISM (1998).

165. *See* JULES COLEMAN, MARKETS, MORALS AND THE LAW 95-132 (1998); Richard A. Posner, *Utilitarianism, Economics, and Legal Theory*, 8 J. LEGAL STUD. 103 (1979); H.L.A. Hart, *American Jurisprudence Through English Eyes: The Nightmare and the Noble Dream*, 11 GA. L. REV. 969 (1977).

166. For example, in *Beyond Good and Evil*, Nietzsche is *ad hominem* in his criticism. He refers to the "English-mechanistic doltification of the world" and "mediocre minds." FRIEDRICH NIETZSCHE, BEYOND GOOD AND EVIL: PRELUDE TO A PHILOSOPHY OF THE FUTURE §§ 252-253 (Walter Kaufmann trans., 1966) [hereinafter BEYOND GOOD AND EVIL].

167. GENEALOGY OF MORALS, *supra* note 2, Second Essay, §§ 1-3.

168. *See supra* notes 96-98, 130-41 and accompanying text.

169. BEYOND GOOD AND EVIL, *supra* note 166, § 201.

170. *Id.* § 261.

171. GAY SCIENCE, *supra* note 3, § 116.

from the same defects; it denies the possibility of noble morality because character is determined by genes, an external force. Nietzsche conceptualized the powerful ideas of his day something like this:

Slave Systems	Sources of Normativity
Utilitarianism	Pleasure-Pain Principle/Utils
Religion	Revelation and Ressentiment
Evolutionary Biology	Genes (External Factor)

Utilitarianism relies on goods and evils, pains and pleasures, in order to sum up the satisfactions of individuals, or to find the greatest good for the greatest number.[172] In economics, the analogous concepts are "preference" and utility maximization.[173] Nietzsche throws into question the entire utilitarian project. He could not accept utilitarianism because he rejected the idea that good and evil differ, or at least it could be said that he rejected any simple contrasts or opposing formulas for good and evil.[174] In *The Gay Science*, Nietzsche claims that "the strongest and most evil spirits have so far done the most to advance humanity."[175] Nietzsche believed the abolition of suffering to be undesirable, and that "*we* would rather have it higher and worse than ever."[176] To Nietzsche, only the discipline of suffering has brought about improvements in humankind.[177] Nietzsche finds utilitarianism as "altogether an *impossible* literature, unless one knows how to flavor it with some malice."[178]

It would be a serious misinterpretation to read Nietzsche to mean that he wanted people to suffer or to be evil. To Nietzsche, evil is a concept humans define in society and convention, which has a purpose to improve the human condition.[179] Too much order in society "puts the passions to sleep."[180] Evil reawakens "the sense of comparison, of contradiction, of the pleasure in what is new, daring, untried; they compelled men to pit opinion against opinion, model against model."[181]

172. BEYOND GOOD AND EVIL, *supra* note 166, § 260.
173. *See* DAVID M. KREPS, A COURSE IN MICROECONOMIC THEORY 18-37 (1990).
174. *See supra* notes 179-86 and accompanying text.
175. GAY SCIENCE, *supra* note 3, § 4.
176. BEYOND GOOD AND EVIL, *supra* note 166, § 225.
177. *Id.*
178. *Id.* § 228 (emphasis in original).
179. GAY SCIENCE, *supra* note 3, § 4.
180. *Id.*
181. *Id.*

Nietzsche continues, that what is new is always evil because it "wants to conquer and overthrow the old boundary markers and the old pieties."[182] To Nietzsche, "only what is old is good."[183] In this way, Nietzsche critiques the simple good-evil or pain-pleasure dichotomy that utilitarians propose. "[E]vil instincts are expedient, species-preserving, and indispensable to as high a degree as the good ones; their function is merely different."[184] Nietzsche is saying something similar to George Bernard Shaw's "[t]he reasonable man adapts himself to the world: the unreasonable one persists in trying to adapt the world to himself. Therefore all progress depends on the unreasonable man."[185] To Nietzsche, hardship, striving, unreasonableness—these are all attributes that are required for the enhancement of the human condition.[186]

Nietzsche did not value happiness or welfare; these are not the big issues to Nietzsche. Rather, to Nietzsche, focusing on these values stops people from realizing their full potential.[187] Nietzsche criticized utilitarianism as concerned with trivial matters.[188] To Nietzsche, measurements of human welfare that utilitarianism uses fail to address important problems; "there are higher problems than all problems of pleasure, pain, and pity; and every philosophy that stops with them is a naïveté."[189] Pain and pleasure are "mere epiphenomena and wholly secondary."[190] Well-being or welfare-maximization are states that make humankind "ridiculous and contemptible."[191]

C.

Law and economics assumes that people are rational, which means that people act in their own self-interest to maximize their own satisfaction.[192] Behavioral economists and cognitive scientists are producing research that throws the rationality assumption into

182. *Id.*

183. *Id.*

184. *Id.*

185. GEORGE BERNARD SHAW, MAN AND SUPERMAN: A COMEDY AND A PHILOSOPHY 238 (1903).

186. Nietzsche's complaints about equality apply here too. *See supra* notes 146-57 and accompanying text.

187. BEYOND GOOD AND EVIL, *supra* note 6, § 225.

188. *Id.*

189. *Id.*

190. *Id.*

191. *Id.*

192. *See generally* GARY S. BECKER, THE ECONOMIC APPROACH TO HUMAN BEHAVIOR 3-14 (1976).

question.[193] Using the idea of "bounded rationality," economists model the effects of uncertainty and imperfect information on human choice.[194] Some of these economic models accept that people "satisfice," meaning that they "follow[] ordinary habits and rules of thumb so long as they yield satisfactory results, even if an alternate set of procedures would in theory be superior."[195]

The model of bounded rationality and "satisficing" finds some support from Nietzsche; he would accept that knowledge is not rational, scientific, ahistorical or analytical.[196] Likewise, to Nietzsche, logic originates in illogic.[197] "Innumerable beings who made inferences in a way different from ours perished; for all that, their ways might have been truer."[198] Those who were too deliberate and cautious, not finding things to be equal, perished. Those who survived considered two circumstances equal when there is nothing logical in equality because nothing is equal.[199] Nietzsche's basic point is consistent with behavioral economics, in its claim that logic is not solely or even primarily about rational calculation, but about "satisficing" or rule of thumb thinking about the world, in which error educates.[200]

Nietzsche, however, is dissatisfied with error-produced understanding. To Nietzsche, knowledge stems from a clash between the "impulse for truth" and "life-preserving errors."[201] Nietzsche would prefer that people get out of their error-produced ruts; this is where his normative ethics come in, his will to power and eternal recurrence, which calls upon individuals to enhance their condition beyond traditional understanding.[202]

193. Cass R. Sunstein, *Introduction*, *in* BEHAVIORAL LAW AND ECONOMICS 3-7 (Cass R. Sunstein, ed., 2000).

194. FOUNDATIONS OF THE ECONOMIC APPROACH TO LAW 267-69 (Avery Wiener Katz, ed., 1998) [hereinafter FOUNDATIONS].

195. *Id.* at 268.

196. *See* GAY SCIENCE, *supra* note 3, § 110.

197. *Id.* § 111.

198. *Id.* Nietzsche offers as an example that one could be too deliberate in deciding whether a tiger is dangerous as compared to a snake. Those who exercised lower levels of logical power would consider the element of "danger" to be equal here, while the more deliberate would not and would perish. Of course, Nietzsche ignores that it may be "logical" to presume equality of danger in such circumstances; it is logical to focus on relevant facts and ignore the irrelevant ones. *Id.*

199. *Id.*

200. FOUNDATIONS, *supra* note 194, at 268.

201. *See* GAY SCIENCE, *supra* note 3, § 111.

202. *See supra* notes 98-129 and accompanying text.

D.

In *The Gay Science*, Nietzsche examines altruism and lays the foundation for his later work on *ressentiment* and bad conscience.[203] Nietzsche sees a fundamental contradiction in altruism.[204] He attacks the idea that altruism is virtuous.[205] To be altruistic, one's actions must be "selfless," "unegoistic," and detrimental to the person who possesses the virtue in question, but to Nietzsche, altruism has none of these qualities.[206] The contradiction can be viewed from the perspectives of the giver and the recipient. The giver benefits from altruism, as does the recipient, the "neighbor."[207] Nietzsche stated, "[i]f the neighbor himself were 'selfless' in his thinking, he would repudiate this diminution of strength, this mutilation for *his* benefit; he would work against the development of such inclinations, and above all he would manifest his selflessness by *not* calling it *good!*"[208]

Nietzsche's critique of altruism appears, no doubt coincidentally, similar to the contemporary economic analysis of altruism. An economist assumes that people act rationally to maximize their own utility.[209] Altruism can be a Nash equilibrium strategy when the best possible strategy that a player X can take is altruistic, given the strategies that player X expects player Y to take.[210] In other words, people will coordinate around altruism when it makes them better off. Consider a simple family example. A parent is better off making gifts to his child so that the child can attend college, when the parent has a preference that the child attend college. The child is better off too, if her welfare is increased. Evolutionary biologists make similar findings about non-human behavior.[211]

Altruism is an entire research agenda and not susceptible to full analysis here. I have omitted entirely any mention of research on

---

203. *See* GAY SCIENCE, *supra* note 3, § 21.

204. *Id.*

205. *Id.*

206. *Id.*

207. *Id.*

208. *Id.* § 21 (emphasis in original).

209. *See* Gary S. Becker, *Altruism, Egoism and Genetic Fitness: Economics and Sociobiology*, 14 J. ECON. LIT. 817, 818-22 (1976). A substantial amount of economics literature exists on altruism, but Becker's work pioneered the field. Becker developed a model in which he showed that even egoists have an incentive to be altruistic when they benefit from altruism. Although Becker relied on price theory, there is a game theoretical aspect to all of this.

210. For the fundamentals of game theory, see ERIC RASMUSEN, GAMES AND INFORMATION (3d ed. 2001).

211. For a layman's explanation, see RICHARD DAWKINS, THE SELFISH GENE 4-5 (1989).

altruism in other social sciences, such as in psychology and sociology, and I have not engaged the philosophical literature on altruism. The point is that Nietzsche, writing in the nineteenth century, substantially presaged most of the later research in economics that is so very influential in legal scholarship.

E.

The origin of cooperation among humans has been the subject of considerable theorizing by both philosophers and economists.[212] The characteristics of cooperation are important in a legal utilitarian calculus because the law centers on dispute resolving. Understanding the conditions in which people cooperate can tell us something about the origin of legal rules. Nietzsche was not interested in learning the conditions in which people cooperate, but he provides some guidance in his discussion of the origin of society-preserving morals.[213]

At the beginning of the Second Essay in *On the Genealogy of Morals*, Nietzsche poses the question: "To breed an animal *with the right to make promises*—is not this the paradoxical task that nature has set itself in the case of man? Is it not the real problem regarding man?"[214] Nietzsche then goes on to explain that man's conscience originates in cruelty that humans have visited upon one another over the years.[215] Nietzsche explained that his second essay was based only on conjecture.[216] Anecdotal evidence supports Nietzsche's theory on the medieval origin of common law legal rules on the transfer of real property.[217] Though the

---

212. The literature is vast, but for a start, see ROBERT AXELROD, THE EVOLUTION OF COOPERATION (1984); ROBERT AXELROD, THE COMPLEXITY OF COOPERATION: AGENT-BASED MODELS OF COMPETITION AND COLLABORATION (1997); ELINOR OSTROM, GOVERNING THE COMMONS: THE EVOLUTION OF INSTITUTIONS FOR COLLECTIVE ACTION (1990). These sources are rational-choice influenced and influential in the economics literature.

213. *See infra* notes 214-23 and accompanying text

214. GENEALOGY OF MORALS, *supra* note 2, Second Essay, § 1 (emphasis in original).

215. *Id.* § 3. Nietzsche says:

> Man could never do without blood, torture, and sacrifices when he felt the need to create a memory for himself; the most dreadful sacrifices and pledges (sacrifices of the first-born among them), the most repulsive mutilations (castration, for example), the cruelest rites of all the religious cults (and all religions are at the deepest level systems of cruelties)–all this has its origin in the instinct that realized that pain is the most powerful aid to mnemonics.

Id.

216. *Id.* § 6.

217. An important attribute of real property is the ability to transfer it to successive owners. ROBERT COOTER & THOMAS ULEN, LAW AND ECONOMICS 139 (3d ed. 2000). Transfers require the creation of a record of ownership. *Id.* In the Middle Ages, few people could read, and no agencies of government existed as we know them today,

livery of seisin terminology has survived into the twentieth century, records of title held by the appropriate government bodies are the means by which property transfers are recorded, and the original ceremony is long forgotten.[218]

Nietzsche contended that cruelty leads to conscience, which leads to morality.[219] Social fabric and moral and legal obligation come from "blood" of passion and not reason: "It was in *this* sphere then, the sphere of legal obligations, that the moral conceptual world of 'guilt,' 'conscience,' 'duty' 'sacredness of duty' had its origin: its beginnings were, like the beginnings of everything great on earth, soaked in blood thoroughly and for a long time."[220] Nietzsche argues that retribution is the origin of morality:

> To ask it again: to what extent can suffering balance debts or guilt? To the extent that to *make* suffer was in the highest degree pleasurable, to the extent that the injured party exchanged for the loss he had sustained, including the displeasure caused by the loss, an extraordinary counterbalancing pleasure: that of *making* suffer—a genuine *festival*, something which, as aforesaid, was prized the more highly the more violently it contrasted with the rank and social standing of the creditor.[221]

He then clarifies the origins of the moral human in the exchange relationship of debtor-creditor:

> [T]he feeling of guilt, of personal obligation, had its origin . . . in the oldest and most primitive personal relationship, that between buyer and seller, creditor and debtor; it was here that one person first encountered another person, that one person first *measured himself* against another . . . Setting prices, determining values, contriving equivalences, exchanging—these preoccupied the earliest thinking of man to so great an extent

designed to preserve records of title. To record "title" to land, a ceremony known as "livery of seisin" was conducted in which seller handed the buyer a piece of the turf and a twig from the land. *Id.* The folklore on livery of seisin is that the ceremony included the thrashing of a child who had witnessed the passing of the turf and the twig. *Id.* The child was thrashed severely so that he would remember that day forever, thus creating a living record of the transfer. *Id.; see also* Jeffrey Evans Stake, *The Uneasy Case for Adverse Possession*, 89 GEO. L.J. 2419, 2440 (2001). I use the words "folklore" and "anecdotal" because of the debateable historical accuracy of these aspects of the ceremony relating to the child witness. *See* S.E. Thorne, *Livery of Seisin*, 52 LAW QUARTERLY REVIEW 345 (1956) (not mentioning this aspect of ceremony but discussing the need for observance by witnesses).

218. COOTER & ULEN, *supra* note 217.

219. GENEALOGY OF MORALS, *supra* note 2, Second Essay, § 6 (emphasis in original).

220. *Id.* (emphasis in original).

221. *Id.* (emphasis in original).

> that in a certain sense they constitute thinking *as such*: here it was that the oldest kind of astuteness developed; here likewise, we may suppose, did human pride, the feeling of superiority in relation to other animals, have its first beginnings.[222]

Thus, humans are valuating, calculating agents similar in nature to the utility maximizing persons of utilitarianism and law and economics.

Nietzsche's propositions about the origins of morals share similarities with theorizing economists on why and how people cooperate. These economists are looking for the incentives that assumedly rational or boundedly rational humans require in order to engage in contract or society. Nietzsche was not looking for such a theory, so the comparisons are imprecise, but his morality discussion tells us something about what he saw as a relationship among humans, therefore the claims are worthy of comparison.

The economist Oliver Williamson makes an argument similar to Nietzsche's argument. Williamson is not looking for the basis or morality. His limited theory searches for the factors that support cooperation. His theory is that exchange is based on the idea of taking hostages. In his article, *Credible Commitments: Using Hostages to Support Exchange*, Williamson explains that the origins of cooperation are in the bargaining exchange over a hostage.[223]

The hostage relationship sets up a relationship similar to Nietzsche's debtor-creditor relationship. Williamson does not discuss, however, the hostage theory anthropologically, or from a natural history viewpoint.[224] But the connection to Nietzsche's theory seems clear. People engage in debtor-creditor relationships all the time. If one wants to buy a house, one becomes a debtor and gives the creditor bank a hostage—a security interest in one's home. Security interests have their origins in possessory pledges of property in which the creditor holds the property until the debt is paid.

Another fruitful comparison is Nietzsche's origins of morals with the prisoner's dilemma.[225] Here, the infliction of tit-for-tat sanctions in an

---

222. *Id.* § 8 (emphasis in original).

223. *See* Oliver E. Williamson, *Credible Commitments: Using Hostages to Support Exchange*, 83 AM. ECON. REV. 519-20 (1983). Medieval kings guaranteed peace among themselves by exchanging their children. When a king's child was in the court and country of his rival, he was less likely to start a war. A good hostage is one that the hostage-giver values highly and the hostage-taker values little. If the king was to give his rival diamonds, then deterrence is weak because his rival will place a high value on diamonds, will go to war, and will keep the diamonds. COOTER & ULEN, *supra* note 217, at 221.

224. Williamson's approach is consistent with the ahistorical approach of economics as an "analytical" social science.

225. *See generally* ROBERT AXELROD, THE EVOLUTION OF COOPERATION (1984).

infinitely repeating game produces cooperation.[226] Again, the origin of cooperation lies in a negative sanction. Even Nash equilibrium, a strategy in game theory in which a player takes the best move he can, given the move the other player is expected to take, seems to have as its origins in the measuring and evaluating in the "debtor-creditor" relationship that Nietzsche explores.[227]

I have taken some liberties with these theories, and have examined them in ways that economics does not permit. But the basic point here—that "sanctions," "prices," or "payoffs" form a base for Nietzsche's morality as well as for economic analysis—suggest that Nietzsche was not so far away from law and economics approaches as one would typically suspect.

F.

Nietzsche's "pitiful" quote, set forth at the beginning of the second part of the Article, comes from a discussion of poetry in *The Gay Science*.[228] Nietzsche poses the question whether utilitarianism is an adequate or complete theory of human behavior, when it cannot account for something like poetry.[229] Here, Nietzsche says he sides with the utilitarians, in that poetry in ancient times had great utility, to influence the gods.[230] The utility in poetry originated in superstition.[231] Poetry was useful to the ancients.[232] It represents an older form of utilitarianism designed to impress deities.[233] Nietzsche's utilitarian analysis of poetry can hardly be taken literally. Nietzsche was likely offering a critique of utilitarianism: try as it may to be scientific and rational, its origins are primordial, in superstition, in the approach of ancient rhyme whose rhythm is intended to serve as supernatural.[234]

In Book Three of *The Gay Science*, Nietzsche sets forth the core of his epistemological thinking. Although this part of *The Gay Science* says very little about utilitarianism, it offers a powerful examination of the concepts of science and explanation, relevant for reflecting on methodologies used in legal scholarship.[235]

---

226. *Id.* at 27.

227. *See* FRIEDRICH NIETZSCHE, HUMAN ALL TOO HUMAN § 92 (Walter Kaufmann trans., 1966).

228. *See supra* note 157 and accompanying text.

229. GAY SCIENCE, *supra* note 3, § 84

230. *Id.*

231. *Id.*

232. *Id.*

233. *Id.*

234. *Id.*

235. *Id.* §§ 167-220.

Explanation is impossible, according to Nietzsche.[236] Nietzsche contended that we are better at describing states of affairs, but we are no better at explaining them than we were in pre-modern times.[237] Nietzsche was ahead of his time in his critique of scientific explanation. "How should explanations be at all possible when we first turn everything into an *image*, our image!"[238] As for cause and effect, "in truth we are confronted by a continuum out of which we isolate a couple of pieces . . ."[239] Here, Nietzsche presages much of the postmodern attack on the use of scientific method in the social sciences, including the problem of false consciousness, and the weaknesses of empiricism in the social sciences, in which we try to isolate phenomena and control for others in order to develop the idea of statistical inference and probabilistic analysis.

To put Nietzsche in the proper perspective, his criticism of science was not of science *per se*, and particularly not of the natural sciences. Nineteenth-century continental Europeans had a far broader notion of science than do twentieth-century Americans. Nietzsche's critique of science centered on the blind application of the scientific method to social phenomena and art. The Germans, for example, conceptualized law as a science in the nineteenth-century, and the idea that law is a science still clings in the official version of German law, in the German legal academy, in the courts, and among legal practitioners trained in the academy.[240] In the juridical science of continental jurists, determining what is the appropriate legal rule is a scientific enterprise, the product of reason; the contents of legal rules can be determined autonomously as a scientific endeavor.[241] German juridical science (or French for that matter) is not mathematical, but systematic. Economic analysis of law tends towards the mathematical but often is not, and a significant economically influenced legal scholarship exists, which uses economics as a kind of utilitarian moral philosophy to inquire about the effects of law.[242]

Nietzsche was an early critic of such approaches as a kind of scientism. In *The Gay Science*, Nietzsche used the word "faith" to describe scientific

236. *Id.* § 172.

237. *See id.*

238. *Id.* § 112 (emphasis in original).

239. *Id.*

240. *See, e.g.,* John Linarelli, *Anglo-American Jurisprudence and Latin America*, 20 FORDHAM INT'L L.J. 50, 67 (1996).

241. *Id.*

242. *See generally* David A. Hoffman & Michael P. O'Shea, *Can Law and Economics Be Both Practical and Principled?*, 53 ALA. L. REV. 335 (2002).

method.[243] In science, theories are always subject to revision through hypothesis testing and falsification. But such theories, in Nietzsche's philosophy, are subject to prior convictions, things *a priori* and necessary for the scientific method to exist as a discipline. Science does not exist without presuppositions. The particular presupposition required is that truth is needed and more important than everything else.[244] Science rests on a faith in truth.[245] He is critical of faith in "a 'world of truth' that can be mastered completely and forever with the aid of our square little reason."[246] Nietzsche says:

> What? Do we really want to permit existence to be degraded for us like this—reduced to a mere exercise for a calculator and an indoor diversion for mathematicians? Above all, one should not wish to divest existence of its *rich ambiguity*: that is a dictate of good taste, gentlemen, the taste of reverence for everything that lies beyond your horizon.[247]

To Nietzsche, scientific method inquires about only "the most superficial and external aspect of existence—what is most apparent, its skin and sensualization . . . ."[248] Such a scientific interpretation of the world might be "one of the *most stupid* of all possible interpretations of the world," in other words, "the poorest in meaning."[249] Nietzsche's concern was that if we subjected the social world or art to the scientific method, we would have an "essentially mechanical world," which is "an essentially *meaningless* world."[250]

The first essay in *Beyond Good and Evil* is entitled "On the Prejudices of Philosophers."[251] It sets forth several ideas of relevance here. Early in the essay, Nietzsche questions analytical and systematic methods. Nietzsche was passionate in his dislike of German systematic reasoning.[252] These methods reflect what Nietzsche elsewhere calls the bad conscience. On the surface, the scholar's work is articulated and presented as a process of disinterested discovery, "self-development of a cold, pure, divinely unconcerned dialectic."[253] The reality is that it is not analytical. "[I]t is an assumption, a hunch, indeed a kind of

---

243. GAY SCIENCE, *supra* note 3, §§ 344, 373.
244. *Id.*
245. *Id.* § 344.
246. *Id.*
247. *Id.* (emphasis in original).
248. *Id.*
249. *Id.* (emphasis in original).
250. *Id.*
251. BEYOND GOOD AND EVIL, *supra* note 166, §§ 1-23.
252. *Id.* § 11.
253. *Id.* § 5.

'inspiration'—most often a desire of the heart that has been filtered and made abstract—that they defend with reasons they have sought after the fact."[254] Analysis is a way to mask prejudice.[255] Logicians have superstitions, logic is therefore superstitious.[256] Narrative is more important than method; philosophy is the "personal confession of its author and a kind of involuntary or unconscious memoir."[257]

In the essay entitled "Natural History of Morals" in *Beyond Good and Evil*, Nietzsche continues his attack on reason.[258] Reason cannot explain what is good. It is instrumental; reason serves good. Nietzsche criticizes morality as irrational, what Christianity calls faith, Nietzsche deems "herd" instinct.[259] Authority does not concede to reason; it is the other way around.[260]

Nietzsche continues his critique of reason and science in his essay "We Scholars" in *Beyond Good and Evil.*[261] Here he asserts the importance of experience over reason, and emphasizes that philosophy cannot be taught, because one must know it from experience.[262] Nietzsche's metaphor is that philosophy, or, to generalize, learnedness, without experience is like a blind man examining colors.[263] In response to

254. *Id.* § 5; *see* Hal R. Varian, *How to Build an Economic Model in Your Spare Time*, *in* PASSION AND CRAFT: ECONOMISTS AT WORK (Michael Szenberg ed., Univ. of Michigan Press 1997) (copy on file with author). In advising economics graduate students on how to develop an economic model, Varian explains:

> I think that you should look for your ideas outside the academic journals—in newspapers, in magazines, in conversations, and in TV and radio programs. When you read the newspaper, look for the articles about economics . . . and then look at the ones that aren't about economics, because lots of the time they end up being about economics too. Magazines are usually better than newspapers because they go into issues in more depth. On the other hand, a shallower analysis may be more stimulating: there's nothing like a fallacious argument to stimulate research. Conversations, especially with people in business, are often very fruitful. Commerce is conducted in many ways, and most of them have never been subjected to a serious economic analysis. Of course you have to be careful not to *believe* everything you hear—people in business usually know a set of rules that work well for running their own business, but they often have no idea of where these rules come from or why they work, and this is really what economists tend to find interesting. In many cases your ideas can come from your own life and experiences.

Id.

255. *See* BEYOND GOOD AND EVIL, *supra* note 166, § 5, at 12-13.

256. *Id.* § 17, at 24.

257. *Id.* § 6, at 13.

258. *See generally id.* pt. 5.

259. *See supra* notes 169-72 and accompanying text.

260. *See* BEYOND GOOD AND EVIL, *supra* note 166, § 191, at 103-04.

261. *See generally id.* pt. 6.

262. *Id.* §§ 204, 213, at 121, 139.

263. *See id.* § 204, at 121.

utilitarian criticisms of philosophy as dealing with questions that cannot be answered and that were not worth answering, Nietzsche referred to the "color blindness of the utility man who sees nothing in philosophy but a series of *refuted* systems and a prodigal effort that 'does nobody any good.'"[264]

CONCLUSION

Nietzsche remains a mysterious and misunderstood figure in legal philosophy. His intractability to legal theorists is undoubtedly the result of his acerbic prose, his iconoclasm, and his heaping of scorn on Socrates, Christianity, Judaism, Enlightenment, democracy, socialism, women and their emancipation, the notion of human equality fundamental to liberalism, and just about everything else associated with modernity.[265] His ethical principles and his insights on the human condition make him an important philosopher worthy of study by legal theorists. Nietzsche provides an ethical and critical perspective about science and reason that offers a great deal to assist us in understanding how to theorize and engage in interdisciplinary inquiries about law.[266] What Nietzsche said about classical studies is relevant to our thinking about him in the context of legal theory: "I do not know what meaning classical studies could have for our time if they were not untimely—that is to say, acting counter to our time and thereby acting on our time and, let us hope, for the benefit of a time to come."[267]

---

264. *Id.* at 122 (emphasis in original).

265. *See* Berkowitz, *supra* note 7, at 1.

266. *See generally* Friedrich Nietzsche, *On the Uses and Disadvantages of History for Life*, *in* FRIEDRICH NIETZSCHE, UNTIMELY MEDITATIONS (R.J. Hollingdale trans., 1997).

267. *Id.* at 60.

Part III
Legal Critique

[12]

LAW AND MODERNITY

Peter Goodrich

> "Error (belief in the ideal) is not blindness; error is cowardice . . . I do not refute ideals; all I do is draw on my gloves in their presence."[1]

THE discipline of law constitutes one of the most prodigious and formidably utopian of human social endeavours. It aims to rationalise sociality, that is to say that it claims to confine social interaction within the boundaries of reason or, in one relatively mild doctrinal formulation, law is "the enterprise of subjecting human conduct to the governance of rules."[2] In this traditional representation the discipline of law is always, in the last instance, an enterprise in strict reason or logic and human social behaviour is correspondingly, in its most basic principles at least, to be viewed legally as the consequence of reasoned intentions and explicitly formulated goals. In short, lawyers have always been indecently zealous to reduce behaviour to rules and, in constructing the abstract world of the doctrine and science of law, have tended to be forgetful both of the irrationality and chance embedded in social life as well as of the instability and change intrinsic to human purpose and human personality. In so far as present debates in legal studies, in their broader implications, have challenged the doctrinal conception of legal regulation as a rigidly scientific and peculiarly rational enterprise in the exegesis of legal texts, it would seem fitting to discuss, by way of introducing the question of the influence of modernity upon the legal institution, the status of a (critical) legal studies centred upon the hermeneutic and rhetorical features of legal power. We will do so first, by briefly examining the character and role of legal rules, and secondly, by redefining the concept of the legal text in the light of theories of reading the law. The first issue relates most broadly to the problems of the source of law and the definition of the legal text, the second issue relates more closely to the question of the characteristic manner of interpreting legal texts, an issue which is in large measure predetermined by the doctrinal resolution to the first problem, that

---

[1] F. Nietzsche, *Ecce Homo* (1911) p.13.
[2] Lon Fuller, *The Morality of Law* (1975) p.96.

of the authoritative status of the legal text as the expression of the sovereign source of law.

1. Nihilism and Legal Studies

The faith which the legal community places in the doctrinal ideal of the foundational rationality of law and in the correlative concept of the comprehensiveness of legal rules has always been a matter of degree. In terms of legal practice the professional community has a powerful interest in sanctioning and protecting the varied rhetoric and symbols of justice as reason but it would be inaccurate in the extreme to ignore the generally instrumental and pragmatic character of practical legal reason in the self-consciousness of the law. Even at the level of legal doctrine and of education in the law history indicates a degree of caution and clearly evidences that the community of legal science is far from immune to self-doubt and crises of faith in which the foundational value and objectivity of the law has been denied.

Interestingly enough the last major instance of such crisis within the common law world dates back to the end of the nineteenth century and to a movement within legal education which came later to be known as (American) legal realism. In its origins legal realism may plausibly be traced back to the legal expression of a more general social pessimism, insecurity and radical doubt associated with the *fin de siècle* or twilight of the nineteenth century. Aligning themselves most closely with philosophies of pragmatism and scepticism, the legal realists expressed their loss of faith in the legal ideals or idols in terms of the "hard-headed" educational claims that students of law ought to focus less upon the law in books or "paper rules" and more upon official practice, informal processes and the empirical effects of the law more generally as an instrument of discipline and control. The law was defined as what happened to people in legal settings and the study of law was consequently to move from the library to the courts and from abstraction, brooding "omnipresence in the sky", to the concrete practices of everyday legal routines. While the more general and theoretical of the realist proposals were to be superficially accepted by the legal community and tentatively incorporated into the legal curriculum the traditions of textbook and casebook jurisprudence survived the challenge of realism with relative ease and only minor reform.[3]

The intellectual and cultural climate of the late nineteenth century was, in Europe at least, strongly imbued with the atmosphere of radical transition. The industrial revolution had, with unprecedented speed, begun to destroy the traditional agriculturally based communities and customary orders throughout Europe. The emerging modern nation State had not yet begun to

[3] See, M. Tushnet, "Legal Scholarship" (1981) 94 *Yale Law Journal* 1205.

tackle the social ill-effects of the unbridled pursuit of profit and the poverty, dislocation, industrial injury, pollution and ill-health that accompanied rapid and uncontrolled industrialisation. Urbanisation for long remained largely unregulated by either administrative or legal agencies. The widespread cultural sense of dispossession, disinheritance and disorder received striking expression in the political philosophies of the period. The radical, rapid and uncontrolled economic and social change threw up the mildly apocalyptic sense that everything was possible, that the world would soon be either lost or gained, destroyed or saved, that the immediate future would, in the terms of Karl Marx, be one of either barbarism or socialism. The thought of the period correspondingly fluctuated between the polar opposites of radical pessimism and equally radical utopianism, between the revolutionary programmes of anarchism and socialism, and the more inward and individualistic predictions of philosophical pessimism and nihilism.

The cultural alternatives posed in such a fashion towards the end of the nineteenth century expressed strong sentiments of foreboding, of alienation, incomprehension and fear for the future. While these developments clearly had some degree of influence upon legal studies in helping to radicalise and politicise legal education, their effect was immediate, relatively anodyne and short-lived. It is a century later, towards the close of the twentieth century and in the context of a renewed pessimism most obviously associated with the various forms of nuclear power and pollution, with the renewed intensity of the technological revolution and with the perceived failure of reformist and revolutionary movements in the western industrialised economies, that the legal institution is most likely to be affected by a general tide of cultural self-doubt. The cultural context of such contemporary *fin de siècle* ill-ease is to be found in terms of renewed sentiments of pessimism and nihilism, of loss of faith in ideals or absolute values, and in a fear for the future which finds varied expression in the philosophies of modernity and post-modernity and, in more academic terms, in theories of discourse and deconstruction, difference and decay.[4]

Obviously it is not our purpose here to provide any adequate account of the very extensive range of theories of modernity as applicable to literature, art and social science more generally. Our concern is simply to locate the intellectual context and condition within which legal studies have, as yet rather superficially, come to debate the foundational rationality and attendant value of law. Legal studies have been infected by modernity and the legal educational institutions have unwillingly begun to come to terms with the need to debate, if not yet to teach, the rhetorical status of

[4] See, *e.g.* P. Anderson, "Modernity and Revolution" (1984) 144 *New Left Rev.* 96; F. Jameson, "The Politics of Theory" (1984) 33 *New German Critique* 53; J. Lyotard, *The Postmodern Condition* (1984); H. Foster (ed.), *Postmodern Culture* (1985).

law, the political character of legal discourse[5] and even the relation of nihilism (of the refusal to believe in absolute values) to the exegetical exposition of law as a system of rules.[6] In such a context it is clearly relevant to examine briefly the key terms of the debate over modernity before examining their import for legal studies. In broad terms our argument will be to the effect that the various forms and expressions of modernism have been misunderstood by (critical) legal studies and misapplied to the analysis of law. On the one hand, metaphors, images and fashionable expressions of mood and lifestyle have been uncritically transposed onto legal studies and used as therapeutic consolation for a somewhat neurotic dissatisfaction with the state of the legal discipline. The catchphrases of a superficial eclecticism can all too easily stand in the place of historical consciousness and political argumentation. On the other hand, the fundamental conditions, concerns and concepts debated under the rubric of postmodernity deserve careful examination and stand to contribute much to the renewal of legal studies.

At the risk of presenting far too selective an account of the principal themes of postmodernism, the inter-related social experiences of powerlessness, irrationality and loss of faith (nihilism) are the three issues most closely connected to critical debates within legal studies. Each theme has an extensive history as well as specific usages within particular disciplines and the following remarks are intended solely in terms of introductory commentary. The first two themes may be dealt with together: the experience of modernisation and of modernity as fundamentally irrational processes engenders a sense of powerlessness and of incomprehension which, while it dates back as far as the industrial revolution itself, appeals with particular force to the growing apocalyptic sense associated with the close of the century. The sense of irrationality is directed towards the political structures and institutions of modern state bureaucracies which seem largely irrelevant to the lives, needs and desires of modernist existence while at the same time appearing impervious to fundamental change. On the one hand, "to be modern is to experience personal and social life as a maelstrom, to find one's world in perpetual disintegration and renewal, trouble and anguish, ambiguity and contradiction: to be part of a universe in which all that is solid melts into air" and all that is sacred is profaned.[7]

[5] A. Hutchinson and P. Monahan, "Law, Politics and Critical Legal Scholars" (1984) 36 *Stanford Law Review* 199; J. Boyle, "The Politics of Reason" (1985) 4 *University of Pennsylvania Law Rev.* 686.

[6] See, G. Rose, *The Dialectic of Nihilism* (1984); J. Singer, "The Player and the Cards" (1984) 94 *Yale Law Journal* 1; P. Goodrich, "Review" (1985) 12 *Journal of Law and Society* 241.

[7] M. Berman, *All that is Solid Melts into Air* (1982) p.15; see also, F. Jameson, "Postmodernism, Or, The Cultural Logic of Late Capitalism" (1984) 146 *New Left Review* 53; T. Eagleton, "Capitalism, Modernism and Postmodernism" (1985) 152 *New Left Review* 60.

The experience of this atmosphere of disorder is a fluctuating one and incorporates both exhilaration and disturbance, self-enlargement and self-derangement, the expansion of possibilities as well as the destruction of moral boundaries and personal bonds. Irrationality in its modernist cultural guise is never to be thought an unmitigated disadvantage and its essential *insight* is beautifully captured in a recent work on the *Critique of Cynical Reason*: "what appears in reality as an objective state of affairs is . . . what we consider in logic a paradox and in literature a joke. This shapes a new consciousness of 'objectivity'."[8] The sense of powerlessness adverted to in terms of the experience of irrationality is also two-sided, it is both a potential motive for political change and for resistance to power and also, in other contexts, an incapacitating view of the world, a form of resignation to the "power of things" and of cynicism as to the possibility of change. In its most negative sense the experienced condition of powerlessness is well expressed as the cynicism of incorporation and conformity, of loss of hope in the face of perceived necessity—the counter-enlightenment begins at £800 per month. Cynicism here means acquiescence to a power structure experienced both politically and morally as unjustifiable. It is an unhappy consciousness of the absurdity and iniquity of officialdom and bureaucratic structure combined with a certain knowledge that "the objective situation and the instinct for self-preservation speak the same language" and pose the stark alternatives of integration into a social world which one neither created nor desired or self-sacrifice upon the altar of impossible revolutionary Utopias, the various dreams of totality and plenitude.

Underlying the experiences of both irrationality and powerlessness is the much broader and more pervasive experience of nihilism. Nihilism may be provisionally defined as a combination of elements, as a sense of the absurdity of existence and of the unwarranted pretention of social life, as a perception of the nothingness to which all things lead and as the consequent realisation of the contingency of all values and the fragility of all claims to objectivity. Very briefly, the term nihilism in its modern artistic and cultural usages derives from the work of the classicist and philosopher Nietzsche and is to be understood as a specific stage in the history and especially the modernisation of European culture. Although Nietzsche does not provide any comprehensive analytical account of a concept of nihilism, it is reasonably apparent that certain ideas associated with nihilism were of particular significance and may be listed here. First, "What does nihilism mean?—That the highest values are losing their value."[9] Nihilism is thus defined initially in negative terms as the expression of a generalised loss of belief in the extant order and as a breakdown in the credibility of

[8] P. Sloterdijk, "Cynicism—The Twilight of False Consciousness" (1984) 33 *New German Critique* 190.

[9] F. Nietzsche, *The Will to Power* 1 (1909) p.9.

the prevailing religious and political ideologies, the dominant contemporary modes of social organisation and belonging. The loss of purpose associated with nihilism is thus not absolute, it is rather the expression of incomprehension and disbelief in a specific order and specific values. Secondly, following on from the latter comment, nihilism, which Nietzsche explicitly linked to modernity, is based in the rejection of the rationalist tradition of the 19th century and the Christian moral culture to which it belonged. Nihilism is born in the heart of Christian morality. It is the natural law tradition of divine reason as the source of morality and law which nihilists have wished to jettison and eschew. In this sense, it is "the belief in the categories of reason" which is the cause of nihilism and nihilism, as the rejection of Christian doctrines of "unity," "purpose" and "being," is an historical consciousness of the death of a particular mode of organising and belonging to society and the rejection of the values and "truths" upon which that moral culture was based.

Thirdly, nihilism represents an "intermediary condition"[10] and "is an expression of the uselessness only of the *modern* world, not of the world and existence as such."[11] Here we face one of the most paradoxical of the features of nihilism, the possibility of viewing nihilism as a powerful positive force and as an essentially affirmative and active will to create new values, new modes of organisation and of collective belonging. Nihilism is weariness and despair in the face of a transcendental and life destroying moral culture, of a church bound to archaic principles of hierarchy and value, in short a decayed culture. Nihilism is also, however, the hedonistic possibility of displacing that culture and those values and of creating new forms of community and virtue.

Despite the prevalent tendency to caricature nihilism and to present it as an absurd philosophy preaching absurdity and despair we hope to have outlined a fuller meaning of nihilism as an active historical and political consciousness. Nihilism was and is a reading of and response to rationalist Christian ideology which concludes that the orthodox and highly legalistic definitions of truth and of lawful knowledge have outlived their purpose and are indeed absurd when placed in the context of modernity. Nihilism as a philosophy and mode of life denied the claims of religious metaphysics and proposed, in the place of divinely given certainties, a rational dialogue as to the choice of values and as to the terms of collective existence, "happy, unlike the metaphysicians, to possess in oneself not an immortal soul but many *mortal* ones."[12] Nietzsche's injunction was not that we acquiesce in irrationality and purposeless absurdity but that we become aware of and participate in the social conditions of value choice, or in Rose's terms, not that we cease reading our culture but that we read it better, more competently

[10] *Ibid.* at p.15.
[11] *Ibid.* at p.29.
[12] F. Nietzsche, *Human All Too Human* 2 (1911) p.13.

and more thoroughly.[13] In short, the nihilist attack upon the objectivity and unity of a divinely given real world was to clear the way for a movement beyond the old community and values, the tradition and establishment, of the late nineteenth century. Interestingly, however, Nietzsche always claimed to be writing not for his contemporaries but for an audience which would come into being a century later. He saw himself as writing not for the immediate future but for the modernity and community which would develop by the close of the twentieth century. If we turn now to nihilism and legal studies we find, fittingly enough, that Nietzsche's definitions of nihilism, of reason and value in the history of a culture, are peculiarly relevant to contemporary experience, not least by virtue of having been in turn vilified, forgotten and misunderstood.

The concept of nihilism at work within what has come to be termed critical legal studies is on many occasions a peculiarly vacuous and ill-informed one. While the problems raised and debated by the reference to nihilism are important ones for an understanding of law, modernity and the future development of legal studies, the arguments against legal doctrine and the false ideals of textual objectivity and deductive rule application are only likely to be effective if initially proposed in moderate and serious terms before moving to the equally valuable terrains of satire and polemic. To that end we will here follow the account of modernity and nihilism outlined above and will put forward first a brief outline of legal modernity in terms of the experiences of irrationality and powerlessness, and then will comment upon the basic characteristics of legal nihilism understood in its full historical and political context.

First, the related legal experiences of irrationalism and powerlessness, of absurdity and cynicism, as the expressions of a belated legal encounter with modernity. We have already noted in passing the close of the century atmosphere within which legal realism challenged the orthodoxies of legal doctrine at the end of the nineteenth century. Rather than viewing law in terms of the guaranteed objectivity of textually established rules, realism had given expression to a confused sense that the rules of precedent were so vague and so numerous as to make any outcome legally possible. Within a jurisdiction in which reported cases often seemed quantitatively "as grains of sand on the beach", the legal tradition's claim to the objectivity of rules and the rationality of their application sounded hollow to the realistic educators. Legal doctrine and the legal academy survived the challenge of realism and it is in that context, that is in the context of a continuing tradition of legal objectivism, of a doctrinal faith or orthodoxy which continues to

[13] G. Rose, *op. cit.* at p.209. "What did Nietzsche call for? Qua scholar, he asked that the law tables be subjected to philological and historical investigation since he would have us know more and not less about the law."

assert the rationality of law as a "system" of rules, as a "grammar" of norms or even as the "correct" expression of fundamental legal principles and rights, that the various expressions of the critical legal studies movement are to be understood. The sentiment of irrationalism is not new and it is indeed something of a commonplace to hear legal practitioners talk in terms of the ad hoc or fundamentally contingent and pragmatic character of legal decision making. Cynicism, however, as to the actual role of rules in the process of law application, should not be confused with a more fundamental and more serious debate at the level of legal tradition, especially at the level of doctrine and education in the law.[14]

The refusal to continue to believe and promulgate an unreflective ideal of legal rationality has a dual significance. On the one hand it represents an endeavour to open the law to debate. The refusal to acquiesce in the shallow orthodoxy of a determinate system of legal rules is in effect a demand for dialogue within the law and a plea for systematisations of the law that will take into account more than the singular internal logic of legal texts themselves. The other feature to the sense of legal irrationality flows from the first. The demand for dialogue is not radical in itself but it is radical in the context of the prevailing orthodoxy and legal educational practice. It is a paradoxical feature to the development of the legal discipline during the past half century that while it has frequently been acknowledged, even by the highest ranks of the English and American judiciary, that decision making involves discretion, or that experience governs legal development quite as much as logic, these acknowledgements in no whit alter the formalism and objectivism, the authoritarianism and orthodoxy, of legal textual practice. Even within the legal academy the situation is not one of debate but rather of cynicism. While most members of the legal community have certainly experienced the contingency, the elements of irrationality, choice and subjectivity, that enter into the application of law, the overwhelming response has been reactive, fearful and self-protective. Such are the elements of legal cynicism and of a thorough-going legal "resistance to theory" which reduces the real message of the legal curriculum to teaching that "a mixture of low level skills and high grade sophistic techniques of argumentative manipulation is all that there is—all there is and can be—to legal analysis and, by implication, to the many methods by which professional expertise influences the exercise of state power."[15] Cynicism precludes active participation in the development of law being viewed as an intrinsically historical and political form of activity; cynicism refuses to address the question of what, at the level of everyday activity, the law might strive for and the lawyer might strive to do; "the attitude of professionalism thus ends up

[14] R. M. Unger, "The Critical Legal Studies Movement" (1983) 96 *Harvard Law Review* 563.

[15] *Ibid.* at p.669; see also, D. Kairys (ed.), *The Politics of Law* (1983) Chap. 3.

recommending submission to the status quo because it cannot imagine alternatives and does not think it should. This is the real cynicism of the legal profession: that there is not much that anyone can do about the way things are, that we must accept 'reality' as a soldier accepts his orders."[16] In short, the sense of the irrationality of legal development, the experience of a textual tradition which is arbitrary in its authorities and narcissistic in its elaboration of meanings, engenders a sense of powerlessness within the profession and academy alike. The law is perceived to be subject to forces that it cannot control as well as being the object of powers external to it. The only feasible response to the uncontrolled and irrational development of the law is consequently resignation or simple cynicism, the recourse of the profession being to a model of the lawyer as a "technician of practical knowledge" for whom issues of value, belief, aspiration and political hope are essentially only aspects of private life and private desire.

In the context of professional cynicism, legal nihilism arrives as an essentially optimistic force bent upon rejoining the humanity of private aspirations with the language and roles of public life. Nihilism in the context of legal studies simply means loss of faith in the community of legal doctrine and refusal to succumb, acquiesce or otherwise believe in the foundational myths of legal doctrine and legal regulation. Legal nihilism speaks to the possibility of a public language of legal modernity and of open debate as to the values contained in and resulting from the practice of the law. The point is a crucial one in the light of frequent and possibly wilful misinterpretations of the meaning of nihilism within legal studies. The prevalent reaction to the term has indeed been one of exclusion and caricature, of "defining out" those who would admit to even passing acquaintance with the siren of nihilism. Nihilism is here taken to mean no more than purposelessness and despair engendered by the impossibility of arriving at objective, or singular and "correct" interpretations of legal texts. In the following somewhat extravagant defence of the American Constitution, a professor of law at Yale University suggests that "nihilism would drain the great public text of modern America, the Constitution, of all meaning . . . it [nihilism] calls into question the very point of Constitutional adjudication; it threatens our social existence and the nature of public life as we know it in America; and it demeans our lives."[17] Such a statement, of course, says nothing much more than that the old order feels threatened and sees a need to lash out to protect itself. In turning now to the more specific issues of rule, interpretation and value, we will hope briefly to rectify the profound conservatism underlying the rejection of nihilism.

[16] R. Gordon *et al.*, "Nihilism and Academic Freedom" (1985) 35 *Journal of Legal Education* 1; also see, T. Finman, "Critical Legal Studies" (1985) 35 *Journal of Legal Education* 180.

[17] M. Fiss, "Objectivity and Interpretation" (1982) *Stanford Law Review* 739.

2. Legal Values, Legal Interpretations and Legal Texts

If one is incapable of imagining any alternative to the established values and order of social life then loss of faith in those values and that order is bound to appear as a loss of purpose and, more profoundly, as despair. In such circumstances the unwilling nihilist would be left denuded of hope, most likely becoming an agnostic with little else left to do save tend to the garden (Voltaire) or revert to nature (Rousseau). It is precisely such lack of imagination and lack of political will which underpins the refusal seriously to debate the political values, choices and future possibilities contained within legal texts and available to a critical reading of those texts. The legal institution is everywhere concerned to inculcate values, to teach modes of living and belonging, to authorise texts and interpretations as the written embodiment of the reason underlying the law. As a totality of discourses and practices the legal institution continuously strives to present the legal code as the symbolic representation of an ideal sociality, as a way of life and as the fundamental morality of belonging to the social whole.

To challenge the values specifically established in legal texts and legal practices, to question the morality of the written symbols of justice, to refuse passively to accept the legal communities' doctrinal equation of law with reason, these positions are quite the opposite of the insignia of despair, they are the last vestiges of hope, the final flailing of historical consciousness and of political sensibility in the face of a pathological cynicism. The nihilist, to paraphrase Nietzsche, is fearful that "in so far as we believe in law, we condemn existence" and consequently seeks to displace the world of legally established transcendental values with an account of the everyday world of the law, with an account of a very fragile, very finite, very mortal world in which human beings and human institutions are constantly in the process of becoming, for "from this standpoint, the reality of becoming is the only reality that is admitted."[18] To be human, in short, is to become, to become other and to cease.

Legal doctrine, as constituted by and expressed in legal science or the jurisprudence of legal rules, endeavours to avoid the transiency of positive law and the contingency of legal values by establishing and authorising a tradition of written texts. In the face of purely polemical and usually rhetorical claims to the effect that "all interpretations are possible," that legal texts hide a limitless plurality of meanings, the legal institution responds by asserting the written form of law, the conjunction of *logos* and *graphos*, as representing the immortality of the law and the transcendental objectivity of legal meaning. The law comes from books and it is the books of the law that guarantee it permanence, its survival beyond the momentary legal order constituted in each act of law

[18] Nietzsche, (1909) at p.14.

application. The conjunction of writing and law is intrinsic to the foundational value of western legal order: writing places the law beyond the spatial and temporal limitations of oral tradition and unwritten power. The written texts of the law, legal doctrine implies where it does not explicitly so state, provide the legal order with an objectified existence independent of any specific historical institutions sustaining that tradition. In short, it is because it is written, because of the ideational unity which the written law claims to represent, that the textual tradition of the law manages to maintain its status of incontestable professionalism guaranteed by a priesthood of interpreters empowered to gloss but never to create the law.[19]

The concepts of text and of textual meanings as rules presented by legal doctrine are the explicit object of a varied group of critical polemics. While we have thus far outlined motives for ceasing to believe in that doctrine it remains briefly to outline a position which would displace that faith and those idols while posing the question: would it be easy to be a postmodernist in law? The answer presented here by way of provisional definition and conclusion is necessarily partial and non-dogmatic and it should also be clear that the modernity we allude to as the contemporary context of legal studies is stratified and complex in its attack upon the exegetical concept of legal text.

The first point to be made is one of ample common sense. To deny the claims of legal doctrine as to the monumental or documentary status of legal texts is *not* the same thing as denying the existence of the historical community of legal doctrine and the textual teachings and disciplinary rules in which it places its faith. It is simple obfuscation to propose that the claim that texts are inherently ambiguous or polysemic is the equivalent of saying that "anything goes" or that "all meanings are equally possible."[20] The explicit political and interpretative task of the historical legal community as a profession has been precisely that of restricting and constraining the scope of possible interpretations, that of defining the dictionary of legal language and of establishing the paradigm of normal legal knowledge: one cannot drain texts of meaning simply because they were never repositories of settled meaning to begin with.[21] Similarly, what meanings may be established at any given time and in any given context is always a complex negotiation between reader and text, between the hermeneutic or interpretative community and the audience that such a community speaks to: "readers will have a range of plausible meanings set by the conventions of the historically and socially situated communities of interpretation to which they belong."[22]

[19] J. Derrida, "Scribble (writing-power)" (1979) *Yale French Studies* 117.
[20] See, *e.g.* M. Fiss, *op. cit.*, p.763.
[21] S. Fish, "*Fish* v. *Fiss*" (1984) 36 *Stanford Law Review* 1325. See also, W. Mitchell (ed.), *The Politics of Interpretation* (1982).
[22] R. Gordon, *op. cit.*, p.13.

Legal doctrine represents the manner in which lawyers read legal texts and those readings are by and large predictable once the history and contemporary constituents of that interpretative community have been studied. What is at issue, however, in the debate as to law and criticism is not so much the reality of the meanings and values wearily peddled by the legal doctrinal community but rather whether or not it is desirable to allow the profession to continue to transmit those values and doctrines, that ideology and those myths, without being made explicitly accountable for the political choices underlying the development of the law. Although that issue is much broader, it can be usefully posed in relation to legal education and the more general pedagogy of the legal text. The second point we would raise is thus one which may be broadly termed that of deconstructing the written law, that of opening law to the dialogues and disciplines which legal doctrine has traditionally endeavoured to exclude from legal studies.

Initially it is necessary to expand somewhat the concept of legal doctrine to include not simply the concepts and values transmitted within the legal tradition but also to recognise legal doctrine as the instantiation of hierarchy. A body of doctrine is an organised set of "truths" but it is also a mode of transmitting those "truths": "their authority is incorporated into the transmission of the doctrine. To be more accurate, it is inherent in the relationship linking a plurality of receivers with a single sender who stands above them".[23] Doctrine is a way of administering and teaching discourse which consistently presents the doctrinal teaching in the form of a monologue, as the elaboration of a scientifically established and so incontestable authority, as the exegesis of a primary text. Doctrine as teaching demands obedience on the part of its students or pupils and it is consequently less than surprising that the doctrinal community should treat those who do not believe the teachings or who wish to engage in dialogue with the primary texts as schismatics, heretics or other counsellors of despair: the critics of legal doctrine, we are told, have "an ethical duty to depart the law school," in precisely the same fashion that "a professor of divinity for whom atheism is the primary message to profess ought to recognise that he has a conflict of interests."[24]

It is, of course, the function of doctrine to provide an authoritative and closed discourse for its disciples and the doctrinal community guards the boundaries of that discourse by administering the criteria of inclusion and exclusion, of orthodoxy and heterodoxy. The desire to deconstruct the primary texts of legal doctrine, however, also has strong historical support: power creates resistance and, in more specific literary and linguistic terms, texts necessarily

[23] R. Debray, *Critique of Political Reason* (1983) pp.246–247; see also, T. Grey, "The Constitution as Scripture" (1984) 37 *Stanford Law Review* 1.

[24] P. Carrington, "Of Law and the River" (1984) 34 *Journal of Legal Education* 227; also, Correspondence, (1985) 35 *Journal of Legal Education* 10.

engender the "conflict of interpretations." For a postmodernist, or let us say deconstructive, reading of the legal tradition it is not the unified textual teachings of the law that are to be studied and obeyed but rather it is the conditions under which those teachings are possible that should be opened to dialogue. The shift of emphasis is a crucial one: the issue raised by the conflict of interpretations is that of the text as an intersection of competing discourses, the text as a point of fracture in which different systems of signs are transposed, translated and articulated to form the contemporary utterance. The text is here to be understood as productivity, as the active "absorption and transformation of a multiplicity of other texts,"[25] together constituting the space of "intertextuality" in which the text is conceived and read as a tissue built from and leading to other texts and other discourses.

The principle of intertextuality may be loosely summarised in the view that the logic of modernity refuses to recognise any singular or unitary and unifying textuality. The text inevitably refers to and incorporates other texts. More than that, however, the principle of intertextuality opens the way to an analysis of the text as discourse: an analysis of the manner in which the intrinsic dialogue of the text, the polysemy, plurality, polyphony and play of the textual discourse is controlled by the imposition of meaning, by the power of the political and doctrinal communities to define the discourse and to silence dissent. Thus we may have to examine the nature of a deconstructive reading of legal texts by comparing legal intertextuality with what may be termed legal interdiscourse, the latter term referring to the manner in which the legal text may be read as an active gesture, as a speech act or intervention into the texts and discourses of a heteroglot and frequently irrational sociality. First, we would note the sense in which legal method is almost entirely contained within the process of defining and controlling legal intertextuality. From the work of the Glossators to that of contemporary textbook jurisprudence legal method has, for practical purposes, limited itself to the study of the means of textual restriction and recollection (*procedere ad similia*). The legal text and legal judgment are to be presented within the literary canon of jurisprudence as complex (philological) reconstructions of the figures, metaphors and meanings elaborated in earlier texts. Citation and quotation dominate legal writing. Concentration upon the explicit elaboration of intertextual meanings should not, however, detract attention from the indicative silences of the legal text as to its role as discourse, as intervention into the order of discourse and the hierarchy of social meanings.

Whereas legal exegesis searched behind the legal text, as behind a ready-made veil, for a more or less hidden meaning (truth), the deconstructive reading is more open and more hedonistic: the

[25] J. Kristeva, *Semeiotike* (1969); J. Kristeva, *The Revolution of Poetic Language* (1984).

nihilist has no confidence in the text as a transcendental value and meaning; the doctrinal unity of the text, far from hiding the voice or speech of its source, rather veils the historical and political conditions of its existence as meaning. The text is here to be constituted as a generative and creative act of meaning. The signs, symbols and figures of which the text is composed are consequently to be read historically and politically as indicators of semantic choice: the text is semantically structured according to the manner in which it supplements given meanings and discourses,[26] according to the mode in which it administers the insignia of inclusion and exclusion at the linguistic level of assembling the legal surface text. There is, in short, no text, legal or other, which cannot be read as an exercise in organising the signs of belonging. The text is only ever an apparent unity; and to understand that appearance requires a reading of the margins of the text, a reading of its figures of incorporation, of translation and inclusion, but also and more radically a reading of its demarcation of self and other, of the points of diffraction of discourse wherein the discourse of the text becomes incompatible with the discourses external to it.[27]

Finally and by way of conclusion, a third point concerning the interplay of modernity, temporality and the unity of the legal text. As befits a conclusion we must here alter the level and context of discussion. From the doctrine of the unity of the text we need to move to doctrines of the unity of life, from linguistics to metaphysics, and more crudely from questions of how we live to questions of what we live. The natural law tradition is in essence based upon the unity of life as perceived through the eyes of God. In terms of temporality Christian theology has always refused to accept the finality of death, a position whose consequence is that of a linear conception of deferred (incomplete) time: each moment is a step in the direction of a metaphysical plenitude. At the level of biography the temporality of individual life is to be measured against the conditions and unities of an "after-life," while in terms of human history social life moves from ignorance and disbelief towards the inevitable "second coming," the much vaunted and much delayed millennium. In relation both to biography and to history the temporal rationality or indeed unity of human existence is situated at a point external to it, and only beyond living does life have a meaning. The temporality of the individual is fulfilled (unified) in death-live each day as your last; while the temporality of historical sociality is only to be fulfilled once Christ has returned and the human political order has given way to the rule of God on earth.

The Christian conception of time as preparation for judgment and as prelude to a future unity is hardly the temporality of modernity; nor is it easily recognisable as a description of the lived

[26] J. Derrida, *Positions* (1981) pp.37 *et seq.*
[27] M. Foucault, *The Archaeology of Knowledge* (1972).

time of contemporary secular communities. The abstract religious metaphysic, however, still guards and guides the forms and categories of the legal text. In the crudest of terms we need merely observe that the community of legal doctrine still clings to the metaphysical certainties of time, tradition and text: the law remains the same and certain over time, and as a consequence the temporality of human biography can be rendered linear by reference to the unifying rules and goals represented in the legal text. A life lived in the gaze of the law is a life rendered rational over time by the arbitrary metaphysical plenitude of legality. The legal biography, like the Christian biography, is rendered unitary and rational for the purposes of judgment by reference to a point beyond temporality and external to the contingent and merely human biography of becoming. For the law, a biography is a museum cluttered with relics, past deeds, each or any of which deeds may be isolated and excised to be linked in a linear and causal fashion to the contemporary legal subject. For the law there is only one biography, the legal record of a life; and the biography is a unity which transcends both time and context to lead its second life (its after-life) within the abstract contours of the legal text. In the harsh reality of linear time the individual life is always already past: like linear temporality itself, the legal life is built up of moments succeeding one another, each moment being potentially definitive in itself of the individual legal subject to which it is attached. In the rhetoric of modernity, individual and collectivity, subjectivity and history, cannot be so separated. Not only does the individual necessarily possess numerous interrelated and conflicting biographies, but the plural temporality of historical existences means that all actions are to be correlated to the contingent terms of collective life. Rather than creating the singular causal narrative of individual biography by removing the legal subject from both time and history, the logic of modernity points in the direction of individual biography as a constantly changing production within a history which constantly needs to be changed. Legal nihilism as we defined it earlier at least allows for that possibility of change.

P. GOODRICH*

* Lecturer in Law, University of Newcastle. My thanks are due to Iain Stewart and David Walliker for comments on an earlier draft of this article.

[13]

WE FEARLESS ONES: NIETZSCHE AND CRITICAL LEGAL STUDIES *

ADAM GEAREY

ABSTRACT. Abstraction destroys life.

KEY WORDS: Lazarus, rise!

INCIPIT COMEDIA

Nietzsche's thought is for those fearless ones who accept contradiction. This paper will not recommend a project, a set of values or an all-encompassing direction for critical thought that can be summed up in a name. Its ambition is to demonstrate that the law itself generates its own critique and that critical thought has to take this 'foundation' seriously. The perceived failures of Critical Legal Studies will also be addressed as an essential aspect of this promblematic. To argue that Critical Legal Studies remains in the future[1] is to confuse a perceived intellectual failure with a Nietzschean imperative to set to work: "all kinds of individual passions

* For Mary in Africa. Thanks to Costas Douzinas, Tatiana Flessas, and Alexander Carnera Ljungstrom.

[1] There is a great trilogy of articles that offers a diagnostics of the state of critical legal studies, particularly in its British incarnation. If nothing else, one could suggest that critical legal studies is untimely. In 1992, it was announced that "it is in all probability too early to speak of an English critical legal studies." See P. Goodrich, "Critical Legal Studies in England: Prospective Histories", *Oxford Journal of Legal Studies* 12 (1992), 196–236. The future was still a space that critical legal studies could address with an overreaching beyond itself in "Sleeping with the Enemy: On the Politics of Critical Legal Studies in America", in *Law in the Courts of Love* (London: Routledge, 1996), 185–220. See also P. Goodrich, "The Critic's Love of the Law: Intimate Observations on an Insular Jurisdiction", *Law and Critique* 10 (1999), 343–360, 343: "the political project of critical legal studies in England remains overwhelmingly in the future." Perhaps it is in these meditations, in asking these difficult questions, that Goodrich is most possessed by the spirit of Nietzsche. For a consideration of a peculiarly utopian English Nietzsche, see A.R. Orage, *Nietzsche in Outline and Aphorism* (London: T.N. Foulis, 1907). As far as the wider debate in legal theory is concerned, there is perhaps a need to further distinguish between a British and a European critical legal studies. For key texts towards a definition of the latter, see P. Minkkinen, *Thinking Without Desire: A First Philosophy of Law* (London: Hart Press,

have yet to be thought through." Indeed, it is a work that would involve "generations of scholars."[2] Rather than pronouncing the death of Critical Legal Studies one might borrow from Mao's reply when he was asked whether the French Revolution was a success or a failure: it's too soon to say.

Received from the disturbance in the tradition that is named 'Nietzsche' is a courage to continue with a way of thinking. From Nietzsche, one can take the idea that critical thought had its beginnings in values that give birth to their own overcoming. Nietzsche set out to demolish morality in the name of morality. Likewise, the questioning of the law opened a contradiction between the laws of morality and a "thou shalt", or "the last moral law" whose imperative was "to live."[3] These enigmatic statements will be explained presently, for there are a couple of aphorisms that can be used to orientate more generally this way of thinking.

Occurring at the beginning of the fifth book of *Human All Too Human* is a note that tells the reader not to take beginnings too seriously.[4] One should not glorify origins as this has the effect of making the origin a fetish of the "valuable and the essential." If beginnings lose their hold, if thought becomes groundless, then one need not read in terms of opposites, but of "transitions".[5] The key 'contrast' is between the doctrines and what they occult, between what appears most fixed and that which is most fleeting. The drift of the metaphors is towards appreciating the reliance of one term on its silent or shadowy other, or, most importantly, the rootless nature of what appears to be fixed. This kind of thinking is inherently problematic. Just as one of the problems of the criticism of morality is its apparent complicity with the terms of the philosophy that it rejects, critique of law appears unable to escape the terms of the law. Once again, critical thought can learn from the spirit of the underground man. In writing one must face the following contradiction: "faith in morality is withdrawn

1999) and *Polycentricity: The Multiple Scenes of Law*. ed. A Hirvonen (London: Pluto Press, 1998).

[2] Friedrich Nietzsche, *The Gay Science*, trans. Walter Kaufmann (New York: Vintage, 1974), 82. Throughout this piece, the book *The Gay Science* will be distinguished from the broader notion of Nietzsche's work as an exemplification of Gay Science. Gay Science will thus designate a collective sense of the books considered in this essay.

[3] Friedrich Nietzsche, *Daybreak*, trans. Roger Hollingdale Kaufmann (Cambridge: Cambridge University Press, 1982), 4.

[4] Friedrich Nietzsche, *Human All Too Human*, trans. Erich Heller (Cambridge: Cambridge University Press, 1986), 302.

[5] *Supra*, n. 4, 326.

... *Out of morality*."[6] Critical thought is propelled by its contradictions to an appreciation of the necessary, difficult, passionate place of life itself.

Developing this argument has necessitated a division into a number of sections. The first section describes Nietzsche's reception within Anglo-American critical legal thought and argues that this obscures as much as it reveals. A slightly later concern with rhetoric reoriented the understanding of the relationship of critical thought to its object, to itself, and to 'life'; and it is indeed this aspect of the inheritance that is most vital today. It is necessary to elaborate how this style of thought is still relevant, and to show how it can help articulate a reflective, engaged way of thinking. Do not despair. *The Gay Science* can be read as a treatise on law and those who would write against the law.

Working for the Yankee Dollar

Nietzsche's name returned in post-war Anglo-American legal culture at a moment when the post war consensus broke down. Critical Legal Studies, as the inheritor of diverse influences offered a home to this most homeless of philosophers.[7] It is interesting that the defences against Critical Legal Studies were first organised against its perceived nihilism. This was not specifically linked to an interest in Nietzsche, since critical thought turned more properly to his work at a somewhat later date.[8] However, although this response to nihilism is more of a generic phenomenon, its context is still of interest to any discussion of Nietzsche's influence, as its terms influence the way that Nietzsche is viewed by critical scholars.

Although there is a vast literature on nihilism in American scholarship alone, Joseph Singer's work will be taken as an orientating point.[9] At the risk of distorting complex arguments, it might be suggested that nihilism

---

6 *Supra*, n. 3, 4.

7 Describing this as the beginnings of a postmodern jurisprudence would hide as much as it reveals. To make this linkage would return to the well rehearsed themes of the collapse of the great liberatory meta narratives and the associated loss of faith with Marxism and Liberalism. Associated with these concerns is the problem of groundlessness and the questioning of the very constitution of reason itself. These themes, in turn, are part of a wider nexus of problems that can be traced back to the ruptures of modernity and the faultlines that run through legal culture. Contemporary thought is perhaps still experiencing the shock waves of the great crises of the nineteenth century.

8 Work on Nietzsche is perhaps more of a mark of British and European, rather than American, scholarship.

9 J. Singer, "The Player and the Cards: Nihilism and Legal Theory", *The Yale Law Journal* 94 (1984), 1.

took a pragmatic form in the States.[10] Nihilism is conventionally thought to rest on the assertion that as there are no moral truths any action is justified. Singer explicitly rejected this interpretation. To parody nihilism in this way was to detract from its more radical and challenging aspects. Nihilism was presented as having both epistemological and moral aspects;[11] it forces the question of how one is to live the good life in the absence of any rational justification of one's position. For legal theory the problem is most acute. Extending to law the argument that reason is unable to resolve conflicts between values suggests that legal reasoning cannot provide determinate solutions to disputes. The idea that law can provide a guide to action or a restraint to government can no longer be sustained. But where does this leave us? Is the conclusion of this argument merely a surrender to totalitarianism? After nihilism, must one accept that only might makes right?

Once the old philosophies have loosened their hold, thinking about the world in a new way becomes possible. This challenging of reason appears to carry forward a certain Nietzschean spirit. Whether or not this is accurate will be discussed once the outlines of this 'new thinking' have been glimpsed. One need not be trapped in the polarities of reason and emotion, law and politics, objectivity and subjectivity. In the field of legal theory, one need not mourn the death of reason: reason's passing allows a conceptualisation of legal reasoning as a form of conversation[12] in which value claims are made and contested in the absence of right answers. Indeed, the conversation itself presupposes that no discussant has a privileged claim, but that all must be weighed up in coming to a pragmatic conclusion. Legal reasoning is not "the expression of an innate antecedently existing decision procedure of rational consensus that unites all persons involved."[13] Restraint does not come from these shibboleths, but from groundless passions, that are then subjected to the tribunal of debate. Nihilism, then, is both normative and devoid of content: it makes no claim to a universal truth, and by the same token does not allow any one to accuse another of being wrong. Law, in this model, appears to remain more or less in its present form: it is theorised as a set of political compromises open to a debate that must only ever be closed in what are presumably pragmatic interests.

---

[10] For a similar development of this theme, but with reference to Derrida's reception in America, see Christopher Norris, *Deconstruction Theory and Practice* (London: Methuen, 1982), 90–122.

[11] *Supra*, n. 9, 4.

[12] *Ibid.*, at 51.

[13] *Ibid.*, at 51.

As has been suggested in another context, this is a reinvented form of American democracy that "balances every thing very nicely."[14] One could even suggest, in a more radical spirit that the list of edifying "general goals" for law that conclude this article remain blind to the problems that cause them in the first place. It is perhaps necessary to link this with the more pronounced reception of Nietzsche's nihilism to elaborate the scene of Nietzsche's reception, and also to initiate a Nietzschean re-wakening of the joy of Critical Legal Studies.

Beyond American Nihilism

The next wave of critical legal thinking is a modification of Singer's position that leads to a more hard-edged politics.[15] Emblematic of this approach is Peter Goodrich's *Legal Discourse*. His championing of a rhetorical account of law returns to Nietzsche's 'nihilism.' Legal language does not carry any immemorial truth about the world. Law, with its peculiar traditions, customs and organisation, creates a view of the world that is then presented as fixed. Indeed, this endeavour is so successful that law is represented as the very foundations of social life. To think of law in terms of rhetoric would see through this confidence trick. Language does not provide a natural link to the world; it is a code composed of conventions that construct a version of the world, a particular truth.[16] How is this insight a movement on from American nihilism? As has been commented,[17] and as critical scholars have always taken seriously, the re-evaluation of values

[14] J. Culler, *Framing the Sign* (Oxford: Blackwell, 1988). Discussing the deconstructive work of Clare Dalton and Jerry Frug, Culler suggests that American legal deconstruction shows that there is no "outside" to the text of law. It describes "symmetrical or reciprocal structures". This is unusual in that most deconstructive readings tend to isolate structures that are hierarchical. Culler suggests that perhaps these deconstructive readings never escape from the ideology of American law, which "balances everything very nicely." This might suggest that it is American nihilism that prepares the ground for deconstruction; both are of course responses to Nietzsche's work.

[15] The notion of the "waves" of critical legal thought is drawn from Gary Minder's, *Postmodern Legal Movements* (New York: New York University Press, 1995), 116–127. Although Minder defines a second wave of Critical Legal thought as that which engages with deconstruction and other strands of post structuralist thought, he does not discuss British or European scholarship in detail.

[16] These ideas have such currency in debate at present that the point of this discussion is not to offer yet another explication, but to suggest that they define a direction of thought that is still yet to fully realized.

[17] See P. Goodrich, *Reading the Law* (Oxford: Blackwell, 1986), 210–217. This later consideration of nihilism is an elaboration of the earlier engagement in *Legal Discourse*. Nihilism can be thought of as a "powerful positive force . . . an essentially affirmative and

implies not a rejection of values, but the establishment of different values. Goodrich's intriguing references to socialism in *Legal Discourse* come out of this re-evaluation. The Nietzschean project is not linked to Singer's notion of conversation but to a particular political philosophy. Its appearance here is unusual. and it will be suggested that it prompts an interesting distortion both of itself and Nietzsche.

Socialism in *Legal Discourse* is not in any way doctrinaire. It conjoins a notion of re-evaluation to a rhetorical understanding of ideology that provides a broader theory of law. Law cannot be individuated from the social world. What stabilizes any system of values cannot be a foundational logic, but a grounding in a form of life which mandates a particular ideology. Building this line of attack borrows directly from Nietzsche's epigram in *Daybreak*: "surprise at resistance."[18] The critic is surprised that despite seeing through "a thing" and believing that it has no further hold, one remains in its grasp. This enigmatic statement is developed as follows. Producing a rhetorical account of law is necessary, but it is not enough. Law's hold is maintained because it reproduces itself at a doctrinal level through a pedagogy that passes on its institutional forms in a quiescent way. The need is for both a critical theory and a critical practice: "the legal institution still awaits the "twilight of the idols."[19] There is an intriguing mixture of critical registers here. One can hear echoes of the Marxian conjunction of theory and practice; with reference back to a theory of resistances, one can perhaps also appreciate a psychoanalytic register.

There are of course tensions and correspondences between these two positions. One resolution of these difficulties might be a psychoanalysis that retreats from the public arena to the safety of the analyst's couch; at the other extreme is a political engagement that hopes to resolve the problems of theory in the fire of praxis. A more nuanced continuation might develop as follows: if one accepts that law is, at root, a mode of belonging how does one contend with its values and force into becoming new values? To play aphorism off against aphorism, "Where one fails to explain, one learns how to create."[20] How can one locate this creativity? If the word socialism has any measure in *Legal Discourse* it is perhaps linked to this concern. This is not the place to rehearse arguments about the dialectic. It is important to appreciate that Goodrich is arguing for a form of sensuous thinking that can engage with modes of belonging and the tensions that

active will to create new values, new modes of organisation and of collective belonging" (214).

18 P. Goodrich, *Legal Discourse* (London: Macmillan, 1987), 205.

19 *Supra*, n. 18, at 210.

20 *Supra*, n. 3, 28.

arise within them. It places on the agenda a thinking that can examine a personal life and its interaction with institutions. Tracing the possibilities of this kind of thought requires a return to the Nietzschean text; but this is not a quest for origins from which later deviations can be plotted and reformed. The search is for the energy of deviation; the ability to find in the old, the beginnings of the new.

Ashes and Guilt

Any approach to Nietzsche would have to begin with the experience of reading Nietzsche. The Nietzschean text enacts a kind of reflexive reading that performs the very re-evaluation it describes. A starting point is the often repeated caveat that there is an inherent difficulty in presenting any reading of Nietzsche that seeks to isolate and explicate a theme in his work; a difficulty that is exacerbated by any attempt to trace a theme through a number of texts. This scholarly technique may work on texts that are written to be explicated, but for those that shirk this obligation, the problem is how to remain true to the writing's restless spirit. One might initially think that any account of the law as a 'theme' faces the double problem of collating and organizing passages that are spread throughout different volumes, and which obviously occur in a variety of contexts. It would clearly be wrong to impose a false consistency on these passages, and equally unsettling to the reader to fail to offer any organizing form. One way forward is to take seriously the text's own 'advice' for those who are undertaking this strange endeavour. Nietzsche's texts offer themselves to creative appropriations because they seem to mimic this process in their very constitution as texts. The text presents itself as something that constantly returns to itself, and comments upon its own return, its own re-reading of itself. It both anticipates those readings that are to come, and places them in a series of readings that the text has itself initiated. It prevents the text from closing, from revealing a single, stable reading. This potentially infinite process is a figuring of the creative activity that is at the heart of the Gay Science. In any individual text this process can be observed at many levels: the repetition of certain themes, injunctions to the reader and questionings of itself. To aid in the demonstration of this concern, the key metaphor of the wanderer will be focused upon.

The wanderer appears in the last book of *The Gay Science*. In both *Daybreak* and *Human All Too Human* the wanderer has already appeared as a figure of the philosopher. In *The Gay Science*, he appears in dialogue with his shadow. The wanderer is on a journey with no final destination.

His work celebrates change and transience.[21] The wanderer's opinions are passions that come from force of spirit. It is only inertia that rigidifies opinions into conventions. However, if the thinker remained true to invention, the flux of his thought would make him a "thinking snowball." Precisely because one cannot achieve this intensity, because one is a "compound", both heated up and cooled down by the rigours of thought, one must "kneel before justice as the only goddess we recognise over us."[22] Justice recognises that thought is impure. One can only proceed as a "noble traitor", betraying with no sense of guilt.

The wanderer as noble traitor realises the condition of a Gay Science. This could be put less cryptically as follows: the flexible thinker realises the consequences of the conditions of thought. The thinker must also be a creator and make use of a wider disruptive and foundational energy. *The Gay Science* establishes the paradox of thought: the new must be generated within the old, but this new form does not realise the 'essence' of the old form and supersede it. The new repeats the necessary errors that realize themselves as conditions of thought: "What are man's truths ultimately? Merely his irrefutable errors."[23] If there is an eternal recurrence, it is the repetition of this moment of thought's realization of itself as a necessary error that justifies the world. *The Gay Science* does not deal in truths. As a science, it is primarily the art of experimentation. Science, as understood here, is precisely not a form of knowledge, the apotheosis of thought. If it finds patterns and laws in the world, and replaces God with the well ordered regularity of creation, it does no more than perform the original function of religion as it provides an interpretation of the world that seeks to present itself as unquestionable. It has done no more than replace one myth with another, and effectively blind those who mistake its creativity for truth. If it is asserted that it all comes down to a question of style, this is meant in the complex sense that style and content cannot be separated. The thinker, to disturb and interrupt, may juggle the conventional expectations, may assert polemically that what is of final importance is style, but this chicanery reveals the reliance of creativity on both new forms and new contents.

How is this reading relevant to an understanding of the law?

21 *Supra* n. 4, 302.

22 *Ibid.*, at 203.

23 *Supra* n. 2, 19.

Weights and measures

Law can be traced to the discovery of "weights and measures" that is synonymous with the very idea of man. Indeed, Nietzsche derives the word man from *mensch*, the measurer.[24] This cryptic etymology, though, discovers the very source of measure as that which exceeds the possibility of measurement;[25] measure leads to realms "that are quite unmeasurable and unweighable, but originally did not seem to be."[26] Law both gives rise to and exceeds itself. Presently this excess will be related to ethics, but first one has to address some further reflections on the contradictions of law.

For the contemporary reader, it is perhaps necessary to try and deflect some obvious objections to this way of thinking and writing lest it appear anthropologically ill informed, or even uninformed and universalistic. The reflections on customs and law are not presented as historical truth, but as a meditation on certain conditions of the philosophical tradition. Indeed, they "precede history"[27] and escape the written record. But at the same time that these presuppositions escape traditional scholarship, they represent a foundation for what becomes reason: "So far, all that has given colour to existence still lacks a history."[28] This invented history can perhaps be appropriated as imaginative engagements with what reason seems to presuppose.[29]

One can hear in some of Nietzsche's passages echoes of a Kantian contractarianism. Rather than the rule of law as the kingdom of rational ends, the Nietzschean contract preserves a kind of irrational violence that expresses itself, irrationally, in a theory of equilibrium. The rule of law, then, is a means to bring feuding to an end; it is a "compact" between equals that will survive so long as the power between individuals is itself roughly equal. Thus, if one party became more powerful than another, the same result would be achieved: there would be no "squandering of forces" between those of equal strength. The same reasoning can be applied to rights. Rights derive from an "agreement" which can be imagined as made in some time past. Although this pact is not renewed explicitly, it is given the force of tradition and eventually considered to be an "immutable"[30] and "sacred" state of affairs. It is in this "compulsion" of tradition that

24 *Ibid.*, at 310.

25 *Ibid.*, at 311.

26 *Ibid.*, at 311.

27 *Ibid.*, at 17.

28 *Ibid.*, at 81.

29 For an elaboration of this concern, see Jacques Derrida, "The Force of Law: The Mystical Foundations of Authority", *Cardozo Law Review* 11 (1990).

30 *Supra* n. 2, 319.

the "weak" rely upon. These adjectives of strength and weakness must be taken at a metaphoric as well as a literal level. The discussion of law is as much a reflection on the enabling conditions of Nietzsche's own thought; a theme that must perhaps be demonstrated rather than explained.

Law and justice, then, are related to a "principle of equilibrium" that conceals a prior violence. Law is not so much the triumph of reason as violence taking a somewhat different form. What has to be held to one side for a moment is a precise definition of this violence. Firstly, one has to consider the following thought experiment that subverts common expectations. The outlaw and the man of power who undertakes to defend a community from the violence of the outlaw are, in fact, similar figures, although they obtain what they want in different ways: the outlaw through "force", the man of power through "levies" imposed upon the community. In both cases an "equilibrium" is achieved where the weak community is protected against superior forces. If the outlaw was a single individual, the situation could be resolved by a single blow, but, where, as is more likely, there is a clan or a tribe, then a single violent solution is not possible, and an uneasy peace develops. An understanding of the balancing of forces can also found a notion of justice. Indeed, "equilibrium is ... a very important concept for the oldest theory of law and morality; equilibrium is the basis of justice". This would derive all law from the lex talionis. *An eye for an eye* means that equilibrium has been restored. An act of violence that upset the communal order has been balanced by another act of violence that restores it. To give this power to the law means that an individual need not take upon herself the "blind animosity of revenge."[31]

Systems of punishment can be examined in a similar way. Punishment deploys ideas of "disgrace." Where a criminal has obtained advantages through transgressions of the law, punishments which disgrace and "outweigh" those advantages serve to show that the criminal has been placed outside of the community and those "advantages" which are attached to communal life. The criminal is no longer effectively seen to be an "equivalent" member of the community. Exile from the community is the final form of this logic of punishment. In banishment, the criminal is returned to the state of nature: the boundary that defined her as a human is erased.

This analysis does not fetishise an origin. Origins are spoken of in order to show both their effect on the present, and to examine their legacy. To fathom this, to engage with the question of violence, one needs to return to an earlier age and confront the figure of the lawmaker. In comparison with this previous epoch, the contemporary appears most impoverished;

[31] *Ibid.*, at 312.

the hold of morality and custom over the soul and the imagination almost dissipated. Any question of opposing violences has been forgotten. This is why the assessment of morality, and any associated ways of evaluating the world, as no more than obedience to customs appears in itself inadequate to modern minds. But this proposition does carry an insight. If one accounts for morality as the obligation of abiding by tradition, then the "free individual" who "determines" their own values is "immoral" because she lives apart from tradition. In this rude state, "evil signifies the same as 'individual', 'free', 'capricious', 'unusual', 'unforeseen', 'incalculable'."[32] Tradition thus appears as a "higher authority"[33] whose "commands" are "obeyed" because they are the tradition itself speaking: strictly the individual has no place in this order. A later meditation explains how customs as apparently ridiculous as that forbidding the "impaling of coal on a knife" serve to keep in the consciousness of the individual those customs which are essential both to the foundation and the perpetuation of ordered social life.[34] Any question of values that are "useful" to the individual cannot be grasped because custom is the source of social life. However, if one again contemplates the "free individual" one might appreciate that this understanding of custom and tradition is inadequate. Any set of customs may, more precisely, reflect a "set of motives which founded the tradition."[35] The lawgiver has to "elevate" herself above the tradition to mandate new laws and customs, which then harden again into a tradition that cannot be challenged. The significance of Plato as a lawgiver, or at least one dangerous potential of Platonic philosophy is that the doctrine of reason and the laws of conduct that it mandates are threatening to the community. An individual may choose to give herself the law in contradiction to those hallowed by custom and usage. The ambivalence towards Plato is repeated in the attitude to Christianity. Roman hostility to Christianity is directed at a belief in personal salvation that removes the individual from the political community. The violence of the persecution of the early Christians is the physical reflex of a system of ideas and beliefs that felt challenged by a new system that seemed to move beyond it and to mandate new laws.

Violence, then, is as related to symbolic or interpretative phenomena as it is to physical force. Interpretative violence is bound up with the possibility of Nietzsche's own thought. These great and terrible themes can only be touched upon here, but if this concern with the emergence of modes of thought were to be traced, one would first have to account for

---

32 *Supra* n. 3, 10.

33 *Ibid.*, at 9.

34 *Ibid.*, at 16.

35 *Ibid.*, at 10.

another violence: the emergence of Christianity from Judaism. To some extent, this theme has already entered into and influenced critical legal thought. Ressentiment, the reaction of the Christians to the heroic ethic of the Old Testament, becomes a way of thinking the legal mind which cannot imagine a way of life or connect its discourse with the world.[36] This approach can only be partial if it is not associated with a broader theme: Nietzsche's rejection of religion from within religion. Once again, though, an adequate engagement with this issue would necessitate broader discussion of the antagonistic encounter between Christianity and Judaism in the Nietzschean oeuvre. Within the confines of the present article, it can be suggested that running through this concern with the rejection of dominant world views is the discovery of the explosive one, the interrupter, who realises that it is only as an aesthetic phenomenon that the world can be justified. In different ways; Socrates, Moses, Christ, Caesar and Napoleon. Just as poets are responsible for gods, men can generate their own possibilities. Gods represent a particular manifestation of this power, this will or *vis creativa*. To remain in the thrall of a god or gods is to operate with a bad conscience. It is to refuse to take upon oneself the creative power to fashion a world and create a table of values, to "realise [that] the weights of all things must be determined anew."[37] When Nietzsche writes "You shall become the person that vou are"[38] this power to determine. this will to power, is being eulogised.

The You is older than the I

The supreme task is to become the person that you are. This can be linked back to the idea that there is energy always in excess of the form of law, and forward to the idea that the supreme creative act is to will an ethics. In essence, this is the doctrine of Zarathustra. Its complexity can only be hinted at in this piece; its central conceit is the figure of the friend. The notion of friendship both operates with and disrupts the logic of the law. Friendship is everyday; it is constantly before us. To argue that it is the site of supreme creativity is to appropriate a logic of the law. Just as the law aims to keep its own customs and rules in daily consciousness, friendship has to be constantly created. The rules of friendship are authored in creative activity rather than handed down by the lawmaker. Furthermore, the friend provides a challenge, a spur to creativity. Zarathustra comments: "I and Me are always too earnestly in conversation with one another: how

---

[36] See Richard Weisberg, *The Failure of the Word* (New Have: Yale University Press, 1984).

[37] *Supra* n. 4, 218.

[38] *Ibid.*, at 218.

could it be endured if there was not a friend."[39] Although one should be careful in explicating any of the voices that speak in Nietzsche's text, these words might suggest that the 'doctrine' of Zarathustra is not one of solipsism. The friend, it would seem, is the interlocutor, the one to whom one speaks and engages in dialogue. "I and Me" suggest the reflexivity, the necessary sense in which one has to become an object of study for oneself. The "Me" appears here as the object of the "I", but all these relationships are constituted in "conversation" and thus should not be seen as essential. They are rather, positions that can be adopted. The relationship to the friend is a matter of difficulty. When the friend interrupts the conversation with the self, she does so not to support the self's comforting fictions: the true friend has to appear as an enemy. Indeed, the friend must steadfastly resist the friend: although a reflection of the self, his "face a rough and imperfect mirror"[40] he must remain "near to" rather than identical with: this proximity is that of a defining distance.

This ethic of friendship is itself a product of a history of moral sensations. Zarathustra's thinking addresses a particular moment. The problem with ethical expressions to date is the non existence of an adequate moral language. Returning to the central commandment to "Love one's Neighbor", the re-evaluator faces a complex nexus of problems. Not least is a variation of what interrupts the hermit's meditations: "the 'You' is older than the 'I'."[41] The ethical situation is that of the priority of the other. This temporal chronology can also be understood as an existential dilemma. As the hermit has found, the conversation with the other is necessary to the dialogue with the self. The existence of the other is not only inseparable from the appearance of the self, but is somehow prior. "You" is in this sense "consecrated"; it could be said that it is the meaning of the earth. If the doctrine of the superman is to become what one already is, then this return to a primal relation with the enemy/friend is central to becoming. The consecration of the "I" can only take place in an ethical language that can articulate this simultaneous return and advance. It is a language of exhortation: "Do I exhort you to love of your neighbor? I exhort you rather to flight from your neighbor and to the love of the most distant."[42] A distance must separate contemporary ethical terms from what they must become: the neighbor in this sense is the friend that has been and will be: the other as "you".

---

[39] Friedrich Nietzsche, *Thus Spoke Zarathustra*, trans, R.J. Hollingdale (Harmondsworth: Penguin Books, 1986), 82.

[40] *Supra*, n. 39, 81.

[41] *Ibid.*, 86.

[42] *Ibid.*, 87.

For Zarathustra, the distance can be described as love. But this has to be read as an approximation; for virtue has to be "too exalted for the familiarity of names."[43] This can be understood by referring to a notion of law, and even to a Christian sense of love as a law above the law. If love was to become a virtue definable by principles and rules, then it would be no longer true to itself: love has to fail to correspond with any description, because it is the experience of the response that is not governed by any precedent or analogy. Love is "unutterable", a "torment", a "delight" and a "hunger". As an experience, this hunger suggests that it is not self sustaining: it is not a love of the self but what makes the self insubstantial; something that responds passionately to something that is outside of it. When one affirms love, one thus affirms that which goes beyond the self. This law of love is realized in the quotidian: "I do not want it as a law of God, I do not want it as a human statute: let is be no sign-post to super earths and paradises."[44] This forceful expression has to be read very carefully. The statement that it is not to be conceived as either natural or positive law brings to light its peculiarity. It cannot be the law of God, as its metaphysical underpinnings would have to return to a fixed point of validity; it is not a statute, as it is not given by the state. The law has to be mandated by the self as a personal understanding of ethical compulsion. Nor does it appear that this is a conventional rule of morality that seeks to mandate "good" conduct. Its good is only ever "*my*" good. In affirming this good, though, the "my" has to be seen as the self that needs to rely on the other as enemy or as contender. Love is the name for the creation of this law, this ethic, of over-reaching.

Zarathustra does not announce the truth of a god who can stand for and guarantee the meaning of a moral code or a law. In the place of the absent god there can only be self justifying and self validating aesthetic activity. The aesthete as creator bears the burden of the creation of her own code of conduct; "Can you furnish yourself with your own good and evil and hang up your own will above yourself as a law? Can you be the judge and avenger of your law?"[45] A code has to take shape against an existent one. The activity of creation is always an agonistics. The form of the announcement of this agonistic new law has to echo and distort that of the law it attempts to supplement. The four part division recalls, in a distant way, the four Gospels. However, instead of a narrative that moves towards a conclusion that proves the truth of the story it has told, the annunciation of Christ, Zarathustra circles back towards his own beginning. Nietzsche's

[43] *Ibid.*, 63.
[44] *Ibid.*, 63.
[45] *Ibid.*, 89.

text both begins and ends with the address to the great star that welcomes the new day. In keeping with a 'teaching' that has to validate itself or which has to seek validation in its own repetition of the need to create anew, the book has to return the reader to the starting point of her reading and invite another reading. The concluding valediction to "work" is to interpretations of the text that may or may not affirm similar readings; the reader, like Zarathustra, can "only aspire after [his/her] work."[46]

Eternal Recurrence: How to prevent the replacement of life with a dull imitation of itself

If the Nietzschean reading of law suggests that it is open to transformations, one question remains. In whose name, in whose cause is this work to be performed? The answer invokes eternal recurrence.

Answering this question necessitates an examination of the way that Nietzsche deploys the term "life." This in turn begs an engagement with the appearance of this term in the earlier discourse of Critical Legal Studies. To summarise this difficult and radical concern, 'life' was imagined as that which was outside of the distortions of the law.[47] It represented a more authentic engagement with the social world which was not filtered through rules that ultimately related to reified economic relationships. From the perspective of today, such a concern may appear a romantic irrelevance, but 'life' can still perhaps be thought of as an essential provocation to the claims of the law. In some senses any critical thinking must – either explicitly or implicitly – invoke a notion that occupies the same difficult and problematic function.

The problem could present itself as follows. 'Life' can never be thought of as somehow pure, unaltered by the law, a space of uncontaminated communication. Life is as much a space of judgement as the law. Life is always about to manifest its codes of morals and laws. But is there something about the way that life always exceeds its representations in

46 *Ibid.*, 336.

47 See Peter Gabel, "Reification in Legal Reasoning", *Research in Law and Sociology* 3 (1980), 25–51. Life has to be saved from alienation. This theme returns in different forms. Clare Dalton sees the role of deconstruction as a kind of utopian insight. See "An Essay in the Deconstruction of Contract Doctrine", *Yale Law Review* 94 (1985), 997. See also J. Balkin, "Transcendental Deconstruction, Transcendent Justice", *Michigan Law Review* 92 (1994), 1131–1183. One can sense the disruptive influence of 'life' at the heart of Balkin's version of deconstruction. Life is the distinction, the "gap", between the forms of justice and their problematic articulation. Balkin's notion of transcendental justice is understood not as a search for ideals that exist outside of the society that conditions them but by an acknowledgement that to be human is to be marked by a need to evaluate. Deconstruction negotiates the space between experience and value.

codes of morals? In a wider sense, this is the problem of the relationship between life and the structures that represent and speak for those that are meant to be living. Nietzsche's point about ethics, moral codes and life is directly analogous. Life can never simply be lived; it has to be justified, and is justified by those "heroes", those prophets who invent moralities and codes that explain the chaotics of the lived, the "rerum concordia discors".

Life is inarticulate: but it is constantly being pressed into form. Recurrence should be seen as the key formulation of this central problematic: "This life as you now live it and have lived it, you will have to live it once more and innumerable times more; and there will be nothing new in it, but every pain and every joy and every thought and sigh and everything unutterably small or great in you life will return to you, all in the same succession and sequence."[48] Conventionally, this passage has been read as a vision of a life without God, without values; no more than a repetition of the brute force of life. Remember that these are the words of the "demon" which express in a negative sense what the creator must affirm. One must create from the material of one's experience.

Why, though, is this introduced as the greatest weight? Although one could not hope to fathom the depths of the metaphoricity of this term, there is at least one line of associations that can be usefully traced. One metaphor that describes the temporal movement of thought, and hence the necessary interruptions that have been touched upon above, is that of the fall, of the slackening of energy, of corruption and degeneration. At one level this describes the loss of the pagan world, the sharp perspectives and poetical sense of life of the Greeks who realised the need for myth, a need perverted by Christianity and was lost even more in contemporary science. This is the "spirit of gravity", the movement towards rest, the slackening of creative tension and the triumph of form over form creating energy. To realise the greatest weight is to arrest the fall, to bear on one's shoulders the fate of a culture. If this is overblown, arrogant to an impossible degree, it is this superfluity that is precisely a figuring of the creative energy that can contend with gravity, that can counter the certainty of the fall with the lightness of the dance.

Joy is the only energy that can contend with the demon that presents the world as merely succession, repetition of the same, and offer a "tremendous moment"[49] when the demon appears as a god. This transformation is significant because it represents the instant when the creative will transfigures, produces the "luminous though" in which gods act as an embodiment of creative will. To "crave" recurrence is to crave the kind of

[48] *Supra* n. 2, 273.

[49] *Ibid.*, at 273..

thought that has the energy to realise itself, to make itself anew in the face of the world.

The greatest weight is, in one sense, the ability to will one's own life and hence create values. In keeping with the joy of the *Gay Science*, though, this weight must be taken lightly: in must be born in the correct spirit. In other words it is, again, a question of temperament and style. It is the "most dangerous point of view"[50] because it accepts the affirmatory quality of risk taking in the construction of the self as a work of art: "what I do or do not do now is important for everything that is yet to come as is the greatest event of the past." You must consider yourself equal to the greatest events of the past; the artist must write her own "history of the everyday."[51] There is a kind of double perspective to the history of the everyday. To see the everyday as worthy of a history, of memory and recording, is to raise it, and hence become aware of its importance; at the same time, one must not become obsessed with the minutiae of the everyday. The desirable attitude to the quotidian is the lightness of touch that is perhaps best phrased as simply turning away from what one finds distasteful: "looking away should be [the] sole negation."[52] If this carries with it an association of value choice, so much the better, for 'eternal recurrence' is the recurrence of this obligation to joyously affirm.

In the face of time, one has to make a choice; you can be changed or crushed: do you fall into despair, or "have you experienced a tremendous moment"? To adopt the correct attitude to any act, any expression of will, one would have to answer the following question in the affirmative: "Do you desire this once more and innumerable times more?"[53] It might be easy to argue that this position is bankrupt. Simply believing in an act, no matter how perverse or abhorrent, will not provide justification. But, as *The Gay Science* acknowledges, it takes a terrible risk. It throws itself towards those who may misinterpret. But by this same token, it lends itself to those who seek to achieve what they consider a responsible engagement with the world. What returns in Nietzsche is the need for an ethic of solidarity, a recovery of the sense of life as that which is lived between people who seek to discover and create what they consider to be their own truths of the world: co-operation, mutual aid and friendship. Law cannot be insulated from this sense of life, this active creation of 'law-like' value.

---

50 *Ibid.*, at 212.

51 *Ibid.*, at 246.

52 *Ibid.*, at 223.

53 *Ibid.*, at 274.

Many happy returns

A Nietzschean trajectory might represent a development of the 'classic' Critical Legal Studies position. This held to the indeterminacy of principles, and drew various conclusions about the nature of law and the need for a political practice from this position. The so called "question that killed Critical Legal Studies" in its American incarnation, and the problems that bedevilled the 'movement' resulted from the inability to think through the difficulties inherent in the critical position. A Gay Science would carry forward the passion of Critical Legal Studies, but in a different way. It would accept that life in law is defined by principles and rules that determine and restrain interpretative activity and political possibility, but it would see this as the challenge to the joyous interpreter to develop counter strategies within the law. A Gay Science would insist that the only authenticity is that of a mood, of a sensibility that informs the world.

It is not a question of realising policy of objectives, of necessarily changing the world out there, but in believing in and sustaining the utopian charge of writing; of allowing writing to become and remain the place of counter imagination, of mad schemes and impossible manifestos. American Critical Legal Studies was engaging when it had this passion. It killed itself when it started to take itself too seriously, and when it lost its faith in engaged philosophy. Furthermore, to say that a kind of thought has failed is to assert that there are modes of thought that have succeeded. Although this may be a sustainable position within certain philosophies of enquiry, for any kind of thought that understands itself as critical, it is an error precisely because it conflates what is with what could be. Just because a mode of thought is accepted and becomes dominant, does not mean that it has 'succeeded.' If this appears to the jaded reader as repetition, all the better. It is now necessary to affirm the Critical Legal Studies has not 'failed'; the critical tradition continues to reinvent itself.

Perhaps Critical Legal Studies was always the preserve of dreamers; of restless, disaffected youth.

We should never grow so old again.

Department of Law
Birkbeck College
Malet Street
London WC1E 7HX
UK

[14]

Agonal Communities of Taste:
Law and Community in Nietzsche's Philosophy of Transvaluation

H. W. Siemens

I. Introduction: Against the Standard Political Reading

The post-war years have seen the emergence of a broad consensus on Nietzsche as a political thinker. Most commentators are in agreement on his strength as a *critic* of modernity, as they are on his weakness as a *constructive* political thinker. While exposing the failure of our most progressive projects and institutions (liberalism, democracy, enlightenment, etc.) to furnish rational justifications for themselves, Nietzsche is unable to offer us viable alternatives or anything positive to build on, capitulating instead to a blind, irrational voluntarism. Nietzsche's "tyrannophilia" (Staten), his "politics of domination" (Warren), his "religion of power" as "totalitarian rule" (Grau): these are the refrains to which we have become accustomed. In what can be called the standard political reading of Nietzsche's thought,[1] three moments stand out: Nietzsche is first and foremost an *autarkic individualist* (Stern, MacIntyre), philosophically insensitive to the sphere of social relations and deaf to the ethical claims of community. In the wake of a total critique of reason as will to power, Nietzsche (secondly) *abandons the claims of reason* altogether, turning instead to aesthetic and archaic values such as the "Tragic," the "Dionysian" and the "Noble" (Habermas). Since, on his own terms, modernity is too decadent or depleted to sustain such values, he (thirdly) entrusts our salvation to a *mighty act of will* on the part of superhuman redeemers (*e.g.*, the Übermensch, Dionysos) who are yet to come. In MacIntyre's words, "let will replace reason and let us make ourselves autonomous moral subjects by some gigantic and heroic act of the will."[2]

In my contribution, I would like to challenge such readings by exploring the communitarian and pluralistic impulses in Nietzsche's thinking. These impulses will be used to contest the three key claims of the standard political reading: that Nietzsche is (1) an autarkic individualist, who (2) abandons reason in favour (3) of a radical voluntarism. My argument is not that they are unfounded, but rather that they are one-sided and fail to do justice to the perspectival range and tensions in Nietzsche's thought. In neglecting competing pluralistic and communitarian impulses, I believe they underestimate the positive, constructive potential in Nietzsche for political thought.[3] The argument falls into two parts. First, radical individualism (1) is contested through a relational reading of Nietzsche's use of the word "genius" (*Genie, Genius*). Out of this confrontation, the question of community is opened. I then go on to examine community under the sign of taste and agonal conflict. By embedding Nietzsche's individualism and voluntarism (1, 3) in an agonal conception of community that is far from irrational (2) I hope to bring valuable, constructive impulses in Nietzsche's thought to light.

In order to open the question of community, I shall first examine the nature and status of exceptional individuals in Nietzsche's thought under the sign of "genius." Although subject to complex and conflicting tendencies, "genius" is essentially a *relational* concept for Nietzsche: the meaning and value of genius is always determined in relation to a larger context or collective, specifically the open-ended enhancement or perfection of human existence. Nietzsche's relational conception of genius completely transforms the *individualist* and *voluntarist* moments of the standard reading. His demand for self-transformation cannot be read as a solipsistic glorification of power; for it is inseparable from the creation of ethical communities within an ethical project of open-ended human perfectionism.

In Section III, I shall examine Nietzsche's sense of ethical community by asking: What is the character of ethical law in Nietzsche's thought? Here I follow the direction set by Daniel Conway, who has argued that Nietzsche's sense of community is encapsulated in a relation to ethical laws that bind collectively, but only within particular groups. For Conway, however, Nietzschean communities consist only of aesthetic-affective bonds between self-sufficient beings who associate around an *Übermensch*-figure. It is unclear what place ethical laws or rational-cognitive interaction of any kind can have on this account. It seems only to strengthen the *irrationalist* moment of standard readings whereby Nietzsche capitulates to the "other" of reason.

Yet the aesthetic clearly *does* house both ethical and cognitive resources for Nietzsche when, for instance, he speaks of *"die intelligente Sinnlichkeit"* as the mother of all moral phenomena (14[117]/13).[4] For a richer, genuinely pluralistic conception of community in Nietzsche, I shall draw on the concept of taste (*Geschmack*) and the egalitarian model of the *agon* he develops. At its most ambitious, my thesis is that Nietzsche's philosophy of transvaluation, in the service of human perfection, is predicated on the formation of "agonal communities of taste" on the part of his readers; and conversely: the project of transvaluation has not even begun until "we" begin to recognise this. In the present context, I shall restrict the argument to

Nietzsche's direct engagement with the Greek *agon* in 1870s; that it forms the basis for a sense of community informing the whole of Nietzsche's thought, I can only state as a thesis.

II. NIETZSCHE'S RELATIONAL CONCEPT OF GENIUS

Without question, genius is intrinsically valuable for Nietzsche and an object of sustained attention across his writing. His critique of the worship or cult of genius is no less persistent, running from 1870/1 through 1887. It would, however, be wrong to read the latter as a total rejection of *Genie*, either as a phenomenon or as a (normative) concept. Even in MA, where Nietzsche's critique is most virulent, his aim is not to demolish, but to demythologise genius, reducing it to purely human qualities and conditions by analysing the "becoming" or "genesis"[5] of its works. His critical targets are moreover specific: the Wagnerian concept of *Genie*, central to the *Künstlermetaphysik*, which Nietzsche now rejects; and the "superstition" of genius cultivated by Wagner, that is: *Genie* as an ideological construct serving specific cultural-political forces and dubious psychological motives. Not only are there also a good many positive uses of *Genie* (*e.g.* it elevates and liberates its public: MA 168 2.157; 29[19]/8; VM 407 2.533; also MA 157 2.148); the very notion of the "free spirit" or *Freigeist*, which displaces *Genie* as the central figure of Nietzsche's thought, is best understood as a reconceptualisation, not a rejection, of *Genie*. The "genesis [*Entstehung*] of the complete *Freigeist*" is treated as a special case of the genesis of the *Genius*,[6] and several problems faced by the *Freigeist* are worked out on the basis of a new anti-Wagnerian model of genius.[7]

If we then ask what qualities Nietzsche sees and values in the genius, we are faced with a myriad different answers. One can almost say that for every quality ascribed to *Genie*, there is a text where it is denied, or the opposite is affirmed. Thus, the mark of genius is creativity and *Können*, but then it is also receptivity, sensibility or "intellectual sensitivity [*Reizbarkeit*]" (FW 24); the genius is truthful [*wahrhaftig*], but then he is also the "enemy of truth"[8]; he is a suffering and melancholy being, but Nietzsche also writes of cheerfulness (*Heiterkeit*) and the *"genial-frohe Temperament"*[9]; geniuses make the best critics and judges—and the worst; they are the epitome of strength and control, but also "half-crazed ones" at home only in extremes; they are one-sided beings developed "in one direction," but then they are supremely complex, harmonious or contradictory beings. Of these apparently contradictory, opposed qualities, many belong to the different fields or types of genius that populate Nietzsche's text, from the *"moralische," "psychologische"* genius, to the

"Genius des Erkennens," "des Könnens," "der Mittheilung," and the *"Genie im Hass,"* the *"Genie des Herzens,"* the *"Genie zum Krieg."*[10] There are, however, also real discrepancies in Nietzsche's accounts of genius. Some of them represent revisions or corrections of earlier views and beliefs; as a privileged site of self-critique and re-orientation, the concept of genius is particularly susceptible to U-turns of this kind. Other discrepancies represent genuine, unresolved equivocations that point to a deep-rooted problem in Nietzsche's relation to genius. Others still represent equivocations that are eventually resolved by differentiating genius into dichotomous types. The issue of judgement is a good example of this: initially, Nietzsche identifies geniuses or "creators" as "the only heads truly capable of judgement" (*wahrhaft urtheilsfähige Köpfe:* 2[23]/7); after 1875 (the break with Wagner) this gives way to an emphasis on the injustice (*Ungerechtigkeit*) of genius (VM 192, 186 2.463, 461; 3[41]/9); an opposition resolved by differentiating *Genie* into two types (Wagner vs. Goethe), according to their natures ("a wild tree of untamed egoism" vs. a "noble tree": 34[15]/8; *cf.* WS 210 2.644) and their "strength" (*Kraft*: M 542 3.311f.; 11[43]/9; *cf.* 5[180]/8). The break with Wagner does, however, appear to generate a fundamental dichotomy in Nietzsche's thought, or rather: a will to distinguish a strong type that he would affirm from a weak/sick type that he rejects.[11] It is, therefore, of the former, the genius of "strength," that we must ask: What qualities does Nietzsche see and value in genius?

Four intrinsic qualities, above all, are consistently affirmed across Nietzsche's writing:

1. The genius is a creator of new visions, new works, new values (34[8]/7.795; ZB IV 1.722; MA 230; 11[43]/9). That is to say, the genius is and feels *unzeitgemäss* (UB III 3 1.351; GD *Streifzüge* 44 6.145); juridically, he is a criminal, since, in creating new values, or rather a new *standard or law of evaluation*, he breaks (with) received laws and standards (GD *Streifzüge* 45 6.148; 25[259]/11; 9[120]/12.406).
2. As creator, the genius is a squanderer of surplus energy. That is to say, the genius is an *economic type*, one who can afford to hate and to create because he has at his disposition the enormous resources this requires (5[180]/8; MA 231; GD *Streifzüge* 44 6.145; 10[118]/12.524).
3. More than raw physiological energy or strength, genius requires *strength of will* to coordinate, bind and channel its energy in creative acts of legislation (M 548; 10[118]/12). That is to say, the genius is a *voluntarist type:* "To will a lofty goal *and* the means towards it" (VM 378).
4. Finally, it is a matter of *creative fullness* of the will, not just strength (10[118]/12). That is to say, the genius is a *formal type* who embodies and conjugates conflicting impulses (M 263; 25[202]/11). Indeed, genius is a matter of "capaciousness and multiplicity" (*Umfänglichkeit*

> *und Vielfältigkeit*) of "wholenss in diversity" (*Ganzheit im Vielen*, JGB 212): as the richest and most complex form of life (14[133]/13), the genius co-ordinates a maximal range of perspectives, conflicting value-schemes and impulses.

With these qualities Nietzsche describes the *inner constitution* of genius; as intrinsic qualities, they attest to the intrinsic value of individual genius for Nietzsche. Yet they are hard to separate from *extrinsic* qualities. The genius does not just *feel unzeitgemäss*, he *is unzeitgemäss*, "*necessarily* a man of tomorrow and beyond tomorrow [*Übermorgens*]" (JGB 212), who "enters into the most hostile contradiction with the existing forms and orders" (UB III 3 1.351). The appearance of genius may be a "lucky strike" (*Glücksfall der Entwicklung*), a brief spell of beauty *"sui generis"* (14[133]/13), yet his strength and fullness of will do not emerge *ex nihilo:* "No river is great and rich of itself: but rather that it takes up so many tributaries and takes them further, that is what makes it such" (MA 521 2.324). Genius is, in other words, "the end result of the accumulated work of generations [*Geschlechtern*]," a matter of amassed forces presupposing the gathering, accumulation, saving, and preserving of historical and physiological resources (G-D *Streifzüge* 44, 47 6.145, 148).

Now, if we push the questions of value and meaning—why does Nietzsche value genius? what significance does he see in geniuses?—Nietzsche's text directs us from intrinsic towards extrinsic qualities, towards a *relational* conception of genius: it is always in relation to an external, impersonal context, collective, or institution that individual genius derives its meaning and value for Nietzsche. These contexts range from *"das Ureine"* of Nietzsche's *Künstlermetaphysik*, the people (*Volk*), the masses, the state, the institutions of culture and education, prevailing values, the accumulated historical/physiological resources of the present, to the human species and humankind. From a survey of different texts it becomes clear that the relation of individual genius to larger contexts is a recurring preoccupation throughout Nietzsche's work, the site of an unresolved problem or ambivalence in his relation to genius. Considering two such contexts will serve to lay bare this problem; at the same time, it will establish the axiological framework for a communitarian reading of Nietzsche's political thought.

There are countless texts from Nietzsche's youth that affirm the supreme value of the outstanding individual or genius. Against liberal optimism, for instance, he argues: "that the genius is not there for the sake of humankind: while he himself is the peak and final goal of humankind. There is no higher cultural tendency than the preparation and procreation of genius. Even the state is, despite its barbaric origin and domineering gestures, but a means to this goal" (11[1]/7). At issue in this polemical reversal of means and ends is, for one, the value of ordinary human existence. With slogans such as the "dignity of work" and the "dignity of man," liberalism[12] elevates ordinary human existence to the supreme value and goal to be served and protected by our cultural and political institutions. For Nietzsche, this devotion is a pretext for complacency and self-satisfaction, served by a static, hollow "species-concept of the human" (*Gattungsbegriff Mensch:* UZ 145) or "humankind." To dignify the human or humankind with supreme value is simply to ignore the problem; for it is human existence that forces us to question whether existence has any meaning or value. For Schopenhauer as for Nietzsche, ordinary human existence is no different from animal existence in general, consumed in self-preservation—the satisfaction of egocentric needs—and reproduction. But if everything serves the perpetuation of human existence, then what does *it* serve? Nietzsche's answer is unequivocal: "every human being, with all its activities only has dignity [*Würde*] to the extent that it is an instrument [*Werkzeug*]—conscious or unconscious—of the genius; from which the ethical consequence can immediately be drawn that the 'human in itself' [*Mensch an sich*], the absolute human being, possesses neither dignity, nor rights, nor duties; only as a fully determined being in the service of unconscious goals can the human excuse its existence" (10[1]/7). Yet this is deceptively simple, for Nietzsche goes on to refer the 'intrinsic' value of genius, as the goal of humankind, to an extrinsic context: "But this goal points beyond humankind [*die Menschheit*][. . .] What it is that the existence of genius intimates, what kind of sublime goal of existence [*Daseinsziel*] it is, can only be sensed right now with awe" (11[1]/7).

With these words Nietzsche intimates a difficulty that becomes explicit in an unpublished text called *Ursprung und Ziel der Tragödie* (UZ). The difficulty is first broached where Nietzsche focuses his polemic with liberalism and the "dignity of man" on the following question: At what point does individual human existence acquire worth? He answers: "precisely there where the individual goes fully out of itself and need no longer procreate [*zeugen*] and labour in the service of its continued existence [*Weiterleben*]" (UZ 145); that is, in a sense, where it *ceases* to be an individual. The problematic status of the individual becomes virulent when Nietzsche's thought moves on the metaphysical plane. For in this text, geniuses are not just the goal of the human race (UZ 151, 161); they are the "aim and final purpose of nature" itself (UZ 142). And yet, Nietzsche writes:

> In the end they too are no more than instruments of the will and have to suffer the nature of the will in themselves: but *there is something in them* for which the dance of stars and states is staged as a theatre-piece. (UZ 151)

Is it, then, as an end that Nietzsche values genius, or as an instrument for something else? As an individual, or only as one who "goes fully outside of himself" as individual? Commenting on this text, Staten writes: "the individual who is an end in himself, without reference to a higher will, is meaningless; but on the other hand the individual who is merely a tool is *no individual at all*. The genius is at the same time instrument and end, *Werkzeug* and *Zielpunkt*."[13]

No doubt, Nietzsche's equivocation in this text is tied up with a metaphysics reaching its breaking point and the inherent limitations of means-ends thinking. But beneath these exoteric forms is something taking them to breaking point, something they cannot accommodate: the *ethical* impulse motivating Nietzsche's preoccupation with genius, a two-fold commitment that persists after his metaphysical skin has been shed. This can already be seen in Nietzsche's reflections on Schopenhauer as educator, where the same pattern of equivocation we have just seen is repeated, without the metaphysical baggage. Schopenhauer, Nietzsche notes, is "exemplary in his way of coming to himself and thereby [going] beyond himself" (34[8]/7). In UB III 3, we encounter the familiar claim that "the procreation of the genius" is "the goal of all culture" (1.358), only to read a few lines later that Schopenhauer's "genius promised him the highest—that there would be no deeper furrow than that which his ploughshare is digging in the ground of modern humankind [*der neueren Menschheit*]" (*ibid.*). It is, then, both as an end in himself, the goal of culture, and as a tool for a "modern humankind" that Schopenhauer's genius is valued. Let us consider each in turn:

1. It may seem strange for Nietzsche to appeal to humankind in light of his polemic with the humankind hypostasised by liberalism. In fact, the word "modern" or "newer" (*die neuere Menschheit*) divides Nietzsche's ethical concept from a metaphysical one. It indicates what was at stake in Nietzsche's quarrel with liberalism, and what will be at stake in later years in his quarrel with social Darwinism: the intensification (*Steigerung*) of life towards new or "newer" possibilities against the preservation of meaningless existence. The "species-concept of the human" and the "preservation of the species [*Art*]" (14[182]/13) both name a static hypostasis of the human *"an sich,"* a calcination of human possibilities, endowed with dubious worth. The "newer" or "modern humankind" served by Schopenhauer's genius expresses for Nietzsche the only chance of value for human existence in a dynamic, open-ended vision of new possibilities. The antithesis of the "absolute human," it is radically underdetermined, more imagined than conceived. Nonetheless, it constitutes what Conway has called the enduring "ethical core of Nietzsche's political thought," a commitment to human perfection that is as absolute as it is indeterminate; a virtually inarticulable perfectionism fuelled by aversion and antagonism towards our current attainments as humans. If it is from this commitment that Nietzsche values individual genius, it is because he has the creative will ("to will a lofty goal *and* the means for it") (qualities 1 & 3 of genius), the energetic resources and the formal complexity (qualities 2 & 4) to extend the concept "human."

2. But the genius is at the same time "the goal of culture," a *telos* of intrinsic worth. This certainly sounds like an equivocation of means and ends designed to shift the status of "absolute human being" from ordinary to outstanding individuals. Nietzsche's design is not, however, metaphysical; it is *practical*. The elitist, pyramidal models of culture, politics, history (19[10]/7) and education (14[11, 13]/7) in his early writing are all attempts to put his perfectionism into practice. As practical guidelines, they derive from the basic conviction that it is *only in relation to a concrete ethical community* that individual genius stands a chance of extending and perfecting the concept "human."

Underpinning this conviction is Nietzsche's insight into the *social origins of the individual*. It is astounding how so many proponents of the standard political reading have been blinded to Nietzsche's sociological insights by his individualistic gestures and anti-communitarian pathos.[14] Autarkic individualism in any naive sense is ruled out by these considerations that bind Nietzsche's perfectionist interest in individual genius to an interest in its social, political, and moral conditions. This is not to dismiss the claims of autarkic individualism altogether. On the contrary, the perfectionist task of individual genius can only be performed in *a non-coercive community that accommodates the freedom of genius to break with established mores and create a new law or standard of evaluation*. The quasi-Platonic, pyramidal institutions that dominate Nietzsche's early thought are one solution to this problem. They are not, however, the only one. The creative legislation of genius does not *necessitate* a centralised regime of power, and with his growing estrangement from Wagner, the tyrannical model of power becomes increasingly problematic for Nietzsche. In this context he develops an alternative, pluralistic model for genius, a regime of power inspired by the signature institution of archaic Greek culture: the *agon* or contest. The *agon* is best understood as both an *alternative* and *a form of resistance* to tyrannical genius for Nietzsche, in his text as in his own life: "that is the crux of the Hellenic notion of the contest: it abhors the rule of one [*Alleinherrschaft*] and fears its dangers; it desires, as a *protection* against genius—a second genius" (*Homer's Wettkampf*, KSA 1.789), a line that needs to be read together with the remark (of Nietzsche's student, Kelterborn) that Nietzsche honoured Wagner "in the first instance not just as the genial musician and *dramatist*, but above all else as a cultural force, a *fellow fighter next to him* (not above him) in the struggle for a higher German culture.[15]

In the next stage of my argument, the *agon* will be used to reconstruct a resolutely pluralistic account of community as the ideal context for geniuses to perform autonomous acts of creative legislation in the service of human perfectionism. In this way, I hope to challenge the standard view that Nietzsche has nothing constructive to offer political thought. At this stage, the standard political reading already requires substantive revision. Whether we emphasise the centralised, tyrannical regimes in Nietzsche's texts or his anti-tyrannical, pluralistic *agon* of geniuses, one thing is clear: the affirmative conception of genius in Nietzsche's early thought is inseparable from two external contexts): concrete ethical communities on the one hand, and the ethical project of human perfectionism on the other. The relational reading of genius, if correct, completely transforms the *individualist* and *voluntarist* moments of the standard reading. Nietzsche's demand for self-transformation cannot be a blind, solipsistic glorification of power if, as I have argued, it is inseparable from the creation of ethical communities within an ethical project of open-ended human perfectionism.

III. THE CONCEPT OF COMMUNITY IN NIETZSCHE'S EARLY THOUGHT: THE *AGON* AS A COMMUNITY OF TASTE

In examining Nietzsche's sense of ethical community, I shall take as my guiding thread the question: What is the character of ethical law in Nietzsche's thought? Here I follow the direction set by Dan Conway in his book *Nietzsche & the Political* (see note 1). In the context of a perfectionist, relational reading of the *Übermensch*, he argues that exceptional individuals are valued by Nietzsche for enhancing the life of particular ethical communities that spring up around them (24, 30ff., 47ff., 93f.). Nietzsche's sense of community is encapsulated in a relation to ethical laws that bind collectively, but only across a limited group of people—particular communities. This is a valuable suggestion that steers the only viable course between two extremes strongly criticised by Nietzsche: moral universalism (a relation to universal laws) on one side, and libertarian individualism or "misarchism" (hatred of the law: BGE 188; GM II:12) on the other. However, the actual account Conway offers makes for a weak and problematic sense of community. First, it is dominated by the *Übermensch*-figure as centre, at the expense of more egalitarian models that reflect a genuine pluralism in Nietzsche's thought. Secondly, the notion of law, so well formulated by him, is not developed. According to Conway, Nietzschean community is decidedly aesthetic and exclusive in character, but its purported "signature morality" (24) is not clarified. Indeed, the communities he describes are no more than accidental associations between self-sufficient beings with a "similar capacity for affective engagement and expression" (93). Such communities clearly lack any genuine sense of reciprocity and interdependence, and it is unclear what place morality or ethical laws could possibly have in them. More seriously, they seem to exclude rational principles altogether, confirming the standard political reading of Nietzsche as one who capitulates to the other of reason. In short, Conway's insight into the status of law in Nietzsche's thought is short-changed by reducing aesthetic interaction to irrational affective bonds.

But it is precisely in a community of taste (*Geschmack*), for Kant, that reason loses its moorings and the rift with sensibility is crossed or crossed out. Kant's key notions—genius (nature gives the law, originality as a new rule for art); aesthetic ideas (defying articulation and conceptualisation); reflective judgement (non-subsumptive thought); and especially lawfulness without a law (law-like behaviour without coercion, harmonisation both within and between subjects)—all enabled him to exploit the traditional social characteristics of taste in order to shore up the fragmentation of reason. His systematic interest in a strict separation of beauty (aesthetic judgement), truth (cognition), and goodness (morality) as three autonomous discourses did, however, entail a loss, an impoverishment of earlier concepts of taste and the community of taste.[16] A far richer, genuinely pluralistic sense of community can be located in Nietzsche's thought if we attend to the social, ethical and epistemic qualities ascribed to taste in the philosophical tradition up to Kant. By tracing various moments from this tradition to Nietzsche's text, I shall draw out a sense of community with substantive ethical and epistemic dimensions. Nietzsche's "agonal community taste," I believe, makes a strong case against the irrationalist moment of the standard reading, and the dismissal of Nietzsche as a constructive political thinker.

A. Taste (*Geschmack, Gusto*), Wisdom (*Sapientia*), and Community as Conflict

With the help of Gadamer and Schümmer,[17] we can examine the concept of taste in its long history prior to Kant in which it was neither exclusively nor even primarily an aesthetic category. Although used as an aesthetic term for speech and conduct by the likes of Quintilian, Petronius, and Cicero (Schümmer 121f.), it was as an epistemic and moral concept that taste was taken up in the 17th century with such enthusiasm that it became known as *"das Zeitalter der Geschmackskultur"* (Schümmer 124). Tracing the *epistemic* meaning of taste as a particular way of knowing (*Erkenntnisweise*) to Nietzsche's text will serve to dismiss any simple irrationalism from Nietzsche's community of taste. It also provides a first clue to the nature and status of law therein.

Four moments, above all, go to make up the epistemic qualities of taste. In the first instance, taste names an immediate, animal sense bound up with pleasure and pain. But as a pleasurable reception or painful rejection of items that present themselves to our senses, it already implies (1) a *mental capacity to discriminate* (*geistige Unterscheidungsvermögen*). For Gracian it represents a "spiritualisation of our animality" and holds an anomalous place as a middle term linking sensory drives on one side and freedom of the mind on the other: having taste requires a capacity to (2) *distance oneself from mere drives, impulses, preferences* (*Abstand nehmen von blossen Trieben und privaten Vorlieben*), so as to attain the freedom to consciously discriminate, choose and judge. Indeed, taste acts as a *corrective* against private preferences and prejudices in the name of a more general point of view, a collective that it intends and represents. This social reference in taste is evident in the peculiar *normative power* invested in its judgements: the acceptance or rejection expressed with such certainty in a judgement of taste goes hand-in-hand with its (3) *claim to general validity* (*Normkraft, allgemeine Geltungsanspruch*). The normative, law-like power of judgements of taste is, however, peculiar insofar as they are ungrounded: despite their certainty and decisiveness, such judgements are indefensible, undemonstrable (*unbeweisbar*): (4) *universally binding conceptual standards of judgement* (*begrifflich allgemeine Massstäbe*) are neither given nor sought. Hence the old refrain: *"de gustibus non est disputandum"* and Kant's remark that matters of taste allow for conflict (*Streit*), but not for disputation (Gadamer 33).

Taste, then, names a social *episteme* that is normative or law-like, without there being any actual laws or norms that could be used to ground or demonstrate its judgements. The epistemic moment of certainty is articulated, not through recourse to a universal standard of judgement, but through the exclusion of bad taste: "Certainty of taste is certainty in the face of the tasteless. [*Sicherheit des Geschmacks ist also Sicherheit vor dem Geschmacklosen*]" (Gadamer 33). It is this negative, exclusive gesture that we usually encounter in Nietzsche's early use of the term *Geschmack:* in his polemics against David Strauss and other *"Bildungsphilister"* (UB I), against the judges and historians of art (UBII 2 1.264), against the "Old men of the historical sense" (UB II 9 1.322) and others, he is concerned above all to show that those who lay claim to taste are in fact tasteless. There are, however, also some positive uses of the term. One in particular carries strong epistemic traces from the tradition. In his account of pre-Socratic philosophy (*Philosophie im tragischen Zeitalter der Griechen* [= PHG] 1873), Nietzsche remarks:

> The Greek word that designates the "wise one" belongs etymologically to *sapio*, I taste, *sapiens*, he who tastes, *sisyphos*, the man with the keenest taste; a keen savouring and identifying, a significant discriminating [*Unterscheiden*] makes up the peculiar art of the philosopher, in the eyes of the people.[18]

Isidorus' etymology "sapientia a sapore" (Schümmer 124) serves Nietzsche to connect taste with the activity of thought, inscribing the first epistemic moment of *mental discrimination*. The second moment of *distance from mere drives* takes an idiosyncratic form in Nietzsche's text. Drawing on Aristotle, he defines philosophical discrimination as a "selecting and setting apart [*Auswählen und Ausscheiden*] of what is unusual, astonishing, difficult, divine [*des Ungewöhnlichen Erstaunlichen Schwierigen Göttlichen*]", and continues:

> Science [*Wissenschaft*] throws itself without this selectivity, without this refinement of taste, upon everything that can be known in the blind desire to know everything at any cost; philosophical thinking, by contrast, is always on the scent of those things that are most worth knowing [*wissenswürdig*], the great and important insights.[19]

Philosophical legislation entails an evaluation of what is important or worthy of knowledge (*wissenswürdig*). As such, it presupposes a standard of evaluation, a rule through which it forms and grounds its judgements; that, at least, is what one would expect of a philosopher. But nowhere is such a standard or rule given or even sought in Nietzsche's text. In the absence of a universally binding conceptual standard—the fourth epistemic moment of taste—philosophical judgement rehearses the familiar gesture of certainty through exclusion:

> When Thales says: "All is water," humans are stung out of the worm-like probing and crawling around of the separate sciences, he senses [*ahnt*] the last resolution of things and through this sense, overcomes the common [or vulgar: *gemein*] confinement of the lower grades of knowledge.[20]

This is, as Nietzsche's says elsewhere, a case of "*unbeweisbare* (undemonstrable) *Philosophiren*" (PHG 3 1.814), a law-like thinking without any actual law; in short, an episteme of taste.

Clearly, the relation of distance between *Weisheit* and *Wissenschaft* is crucial to understanding Nietzsche's epistemic conception of taste. Here again, several moments from the history of taste play into his text; and they do so in a way that precludes any simple irrationalism. We are reminded, for one, of Leibniz and the opposition between *"Mönchsgelehrsamkeit"* and the *"Geschmack der Wissenschaft"* to be cultivated outside the cloisters in the vulgar tongue (Schümmer 135). More importantly, Nietzsche's text re-activates a medieval use of taste against its later contraction to mere feeling in the 18th century: Master Eckhart's *"gesmecken gotes"* and Lyly's "taste of heauenly things" both name a thoughtful relation to the highest, worthiest objects of thought, contents that cannot be adequately grasped through the power of *ratio* (Schümmer 122–124). From this perspective, Nietzsche's concept of philosophical taste intends an *empowerment* of thought beyond the limitations imposed by *ratio*, not a flight from reason. For Nietzsche, the inadequacy of *ratio* is bound up with the tools and methods of *Wissenschaft*, what he calls the "calculating Understanding" (*rechnende Verstand*) and its "thinking in measures" (*abmessende Denken*, PHG 3 1.814). In wisdom, by contrast, thinking disposes over sensory and anomalous media, such as: *"Phantasie," "geniales Vorgefühl," "blitzartiges Erfassen und Beleuchten," "Ahnung," "philosophische Intuition"* (814, 816). These and similar terms were already associated with taste by 18th century thinkers such as König, concerned to articulate a form of immediate sensory knowledge (*alsfortige sinnliche Erkenntnis:* Schümmer 138f.). In this light, Nietzsche like König takes part in the movement (associated with Baumgarten's *"cognitio sensitiva"*) to re-evaluate the senses and to rethink sensory faculties [*Sinnlichkeit*] as a medium of thought. In Nietzsche's account, the senses do not mislead or obfuscate thought (*"cognitio confusa,"* or Leibniz's *"dumpfe Denken"*), they elevate philosophy into the "more divine companion" (*göttlichere Gefährte*) of the cripple "Understanding" (PHG 3 1.814), reaching in thought what *Wissenschaft* cannot think in its own medium. This is not, however, to dismiss *Wissenschaft* or annul its results. If König insisted that the immediate judgements of taste need not contradict judgements of the Understanding, Nietzsche himself insists that Thales "made use of *Wissenschaft* and the demonstrable [*das Beweisbare*]" (816), before springing beyond them. There is, in short, no question of Wisdom simply *replacing* Wissenschaft. Next to binding (*Bändigen*) and guiding the indiscriminate impulses of *Wissenschaft*, next to using its results, wisdom is to make good the shortcomings of ratio *for the sake of thought*. It names not the "other" of reason, but its *necessary correlative* and *supplement*.[21]

With this relation, Nietzsche's text makes contact with a key figure in the history of taste, Balthasar Gracian. It is Gracian who first identified, as features of taste, the key epistemic powers of Nietzsche's wisdom, the capacities to discriminate and to distance oneself from mere drives. But taste or *"gusto"* names only one pole of Gracian's thought, which turns on the relation between *"gusto"* or *"genio"* (and associated terms like *"cor,"* *"naturaleza"*) one side, and *"razon"* or *"ingenio"* (and associated terms like *"entendimiento,"* *"arte"*) on the other. These two poles are related in ways that resonate with Nietzsche's account of *Weisheit* and *Wissenschaft:* they are opposed yet inseparable, correlates that derive their meaning in relation to each other. "There is," Gracian says, "an education or formation (*cultura*) of taste (*gusto*), as well as the mind (*ingenio*)" (quoted in Schümmer 125). With this formulation, Gracian gives us new coordinates for interpreting Nietzsche's conception of taste as wisdom. For it indicates that Gracian's *gusto* figures not within a strictly epistemic problematic, but rather: within a pedagogic or *Bildungs*-problematic that is oriented towards a new moral ideal, what can be called "an ideal of authentic humanity" (Gadamer 32) or the "art of living" (Schümmer 124). Gracian, then, conceives *gusto* (taste) *as the correlative and supplement of ratio within a Bildungs-programme geared towards a new ideal of humanity (or: the "art of living").*

Gracian's essentially moral concept of taste uncovers a further dimension to Nietzsche's concept of wisdom, locating his epistemic considerations within an underlying (pedagogic-) moral problematic. If it is "in consideration of life, through an ideal life-need [*Lebensbedürfniß*]" that the Greeks bound their "insatiable knowledge-drive [*Wissenstrieb*]"; if it is as "men of culture and with the goals of culture" that they philosophised (PHG 1 1.807), then we can say: Nietzsche conceives *sapientia (taste) as the correlative and supplement of ratio (Wissenschaft) within a Bildungs-programme geared towards a new ideal of humanity (or: life as culture).*

It is, in fact, a new, anti-Humanist ideal of humanity that Nietzsche tries to articulate through his account of the Greek *agon.* As a way into this account, I take again Gracian's account of *gusto.* Gracian's man of taste is conceived as member of a social ideal, what Gadamer calls a *"Bildungsgesellschaft"* (Gadamer 32) that is beyond differences of class. Similarly, when Nietzsche describes his ideal *"Gebildeten"* in 1874, he insists: "He is to be found in all classes [*Ständen*], with all levels of instruction [*Unterrichtetheit*]" (34[26]/7). By cultivating his taste, Gracian's *Gebildete* wins the inner and outer distance that enables him to discriminate, choose, and judge freely and consciously. But the man of taste is a social being, and when Gracian comes to characterise con-genial taste, his account is markedly pluralistic and conflictual; it is, in fact, an agonal community of taste. Amongst the plurality of *gustos*, one *gusto* can completely contradict another, to the point of annulling its judgement; and yet, he insists, each is thoroughly right and complete. Conflict is not a shortcoming in this community, a problem to be resolved through argumentation. On the contrary, *"de gustibus disputare"* would be a problem: to argue about taste, erecting an explicit, collectively binding rule or standard of judgement by which differences could be settled once and for all, would be in effect to dissolve taste. For the variety and conflict (*Gegeneinander*) of *gustos* is, for Gracian, the essence of taste (Schümmer 129).

With this account we have the key principles of the Greek *agon*, as presented in Nietzsche's short essay *Homer's Wettkampf* (= HC, 1872). A strong analogy can be drawn between Gracian's concept of taste and Nietzsche's concept of the *agon* on four points:

1. If the variety and conflict of *gustos* designates the essence of taste, then taste is what it is by virtue of a conflict between different positions or judgements; to have taste *means* to be embroiled in (a potential) conflict of taste with other judgements. Taste cannot therefore be understood from the subject-position, as a particular kind of judgement or attitude that makes the "man of taste." Like the *agon*, it names a *social* phenomenon, a *clash* of judgements, and can only be characterised from an *intersubjective* or *medial* position in the *relations* of conflict; what Nietzsche, in the case of agonal conflict, calls the dynamics of "reciprocal provocation to deeds, as also a reciprocal holding within the bounds of measure" (HC 1.789).
2. The dynamics of conflict in the community of *gustos* are determined, first and foremost, by the absence of any explicit, collectively binding

rules or laws for adjudicating right and wrong: there is no standard of judgement that could serve to resolve and settle the various conflicts that arise. Similarly, Nietzsche's agonal community is characterised by the absence of any codified rules or standards that could be used to adjudicate victory and defeat for all the contests that take place. A contest begins by throwing any prevailing standards in question, and antagonists strive not just to win, but to determine what counts as winning; it is not just victory, but the very standard or rule of victory that is at stake in each contest.[22]

3. To erect an explicit and binding rule by which all conflicts and differences of taste could be resolved once and for all, would be to destroy or dissolve the possibility of taste; taste can only thrive where conflict is radically inconclusive or open-ended. Similarly, to erect a standard of victory that is beyond contention is to destroy or dissolve the *agon*. Like taste, the *agon* names a radically inconclusive form of conflict; it was, Nietzsche recounts, the conclusive victory of Alexander over all other contestants that put an end to the Greek *agon*.[23]
4. Within the conflictual plurality of *gustos*, each position or judgement is right and complete. With this formulation, Gracian touches on a paradox of justice (*Gerechtigkeit*). For how can two contradictory judgements both be right? For both judgements to be "right" some form of adjudication or justice must be in play; the conflict of *gustos* is not simply law-less. Yet it does preclude any actual, explicit code of laws. We can therefore speak with Kant of a *lawfulness without a law* (*Gesetzmässigkeit ohne Gesetz*).[24] The paradox of justice is, moreover, resolutely impartial, giving right to each judgement; it cannot therefore be identified with the subject-position, for judgements of taste secure their certainty by excluding conflicting judgements as wrong (*i.e.*, "bad taste"). The paradox of justice can therefore only be situated in the medial position, at the interspace of conflict, as function of its particular dynamic.

In the *agon*, too, we must speak of lawfulness without a law. A law or standard that could adjudicate victory for all contests, apart from the course taken by each, is lacking; any such law, if established beyond contention, dissolves the *agon*. It is not, however, law-less. In the first place, the *agon* is a social phenomenon, and social life is inseparable from the establishment of law for Nietzsche.[25] It is moreover against the *Vernichtungskampf*, the pervasive and lawless struggle for annihilation, that Nietzsche seeks to delimit the *Wettkampf* or contest. With reference to Heraclitus, Nietzsche identifies the *agon* as the continuous articulation (*Wirken*) of "unified, lawful, rational [*vernünftige*]" concept of justice (*Dike*, VPP p272). This justice is, he insists, immanent: "The contest is what distinguishes the Greeks, and above all the immanent lawfulness in deciding the contest [*immanente Gesetzmässigkeit im Entscheiden des Wettkampfes*]" (*ibid.*). Justice, or the standard of victory, is immanent to the course of each contest. It cannot, however, be identified with any individual contestant, for "every single being [*Einzelne*] fights as if it alone were in the right [*berechtigt sei*]: but an absolutely certain measure of adjudicating judgement [*Mass des richterlichen Urtheils*] decides where victory is leaning" (*ibid.; cf.* PHG 5 1.825). But what *is* this standard (*Mass*) of judgement? How is immanent agonal justice to be understood? One thing, at least is clear: as in the conflict of *gustos*, justice must be located in the medial position, as a function of the agonal play of forces (*Wettspiel der Kräfte*). These dislocations of justice in Nietzsche's thought are bound up with the moral-pedagogic problem animating his early explorations of the Greek *agon:* rethinking humanity against Humanism is inseparable from a rethinking of justice in human terms.

B. Nietzsche's New Ideal of Humanity: The *Agon* Between Our "Human" and "Inhuman" Qualities

In an early draft, Nietzsche opens *Homer's Contest* with the question: "Was ist Humanität?" The text continues:

> When one speaks of *humanity* [*Humanität*], it is on the basis of the idea that it be that which *parts* and distinguishes human beings from nature. But there is in reality no such separation: the "natural" qualities and the so-called "human" [*menschlich*] are inseparably entwined. Human beings in their highest and noblest capacities are wholly nature and bear her uncanny double-character with them. Their frightening capacities, those considered inhuman [*unmenschlich*] are perhaps even the fruitful soil from which alone all humanity [*Humanität*] can grow forth in impulses, deeds and works.[26]

It is clearly for the sake of open-ended human perfection (*their highest and noblest capacities*) that Nietzsche takes issue with Humanism in these lines. His aim is not to annul the concept or the term *"Humanität,"* but to redefine it with reference to perfectionism, to rethink the human in its growth, its "impulses, deeds and works." Nietzsche's confrontation with Humanism in HC involves both a critical-destructive moment and a constructive moment. In its conception of the human being as *"animal rationale,"* Humanism wages what Nietzsche goes on to call a *Vernichtungskampf* (as distinct from the *Wettkampf*) against our natural impulses on behalf of the so-called "human" in us. This involves: *first*, an absolute and false separation of qualities ("human" and "natural") that are in reality "inseparably entwined"; and *second*, the negation or attempted annulment of our "natural" impulses on behalf of our "human" qualities. The Humanist *Vernichtungskampf* against our nature can take various forms. For one, our natural impulses are condemned through moral judgement as something that *"nicht sein soll"* (*"il faut tuer les passions":* GD *Moral als Widernatur* 1 6.82), an attitude that contrasts sharply with the "openness," "passion" (*Offenheit, Leidenschaft:* 3[49]/8), and "freedom of mind" (*Freisinnigkeit*) of agonal Greek culture:

> The wisdom of their institutions lies in the lack of distinction between good and evil, black and white. Nature, as it shows itself, is not denied, but only *ordered*, restricted to determinate cults and days. This is the root of all freedom of mind [*Freisinnigkeit*] in antiquity; a measured release [*mässige Entladung*] was sought for the forces of nature, not their annihilation or negation. [*Vernichtung und Verneinung*]—(5[146]/8.79)

But moral judgements are only part of the *practical* regime fostered by Humanism to educate or form (*bilden*) our nature (conceived as passive substrate), bringing it under the control of reason, identified as the fulfilment of being human. But to subject our "nature" to universal rational principles (*das vernünftig Allgemeine*) is to suppress our particularity in favour of universal, uniform modes of practice. Again, this contrasts sharply with agonal Greek culture that Nietzsche, with Burckhardt, identifies with the "unleashing of the individual" (*Entfesselung des Individuums*, 16[22]/7; *cf.* MA I 237) and a fostering of diversity and plurality unequalled by any culture except perhaps the Renaissance. Despite the intensity of communal life, despite the harsh, repressive laws of the polis, Nietzsche notes: "The individual intensified to the highest power by the polis"; and "Remarkably *many individuals*, ought that not count as a higher morality?" (3[49]/8, 5[70]/8).[27] These remarks reveal Nietzsche's fascination with the remarkable social and ethical dimensions of agonal culture. But first we must consider the second, constructive moment of his polemic against Humanism.

If Humanism is criticised for waging a *Vernichtungskampf* against our "natural" qualities, Nietzsche models his alternative, anti-Humanist conception of humanity on a *Wettkampf* between our human and "inhuman" impulses. It is important to see that the opening paragraph of HC does not contest the difference between our "highest and noblest capacities" as humans and "those considered inhuman"; what Nietzsche contests is their forced, dualistic separation into distinct spheres, in favour of a more complex, but unified conception of humanity and nature, in her "uncanny double-nature." Nietzsche's agonal conception of human nature involves two claims: *first*, that each aspect—human and inhuman—of human nature is what it is only through antagonism towards the other; and *second*, that each is transformed through its antagonistic relation to the other. I shall deal with each claim in turn.

The first names the *inclusive* moment of agonal relations, since it claims that each antagonist requires the other in order to be(come) what it is. This is illustrated by the most celebrated *agon* in Nietzsche's writing: the Apollinian only comes to signify *Maass* or measure in antagonism with *Dionysian Übermaas*; *Dionysian Übermaas* in turn only comes to signify the "truth" in antagonism with Apollinian illusion (GT 4 1.41). Similarly, in HC it is only as a striving against human measure that the heroic pathos of victory comes to signify *Übermaas* and *hubris*; and it is only in striving against heroic *Übermass* that the human signifies *Maass* in the creation of bounded works. Without the resistance of human measure, the heroic dissolves into chaos, the pervasive, lawless *Vernichtungskampf* (*bellum omnia contra omnes*)[28]; in the absence of hubristic impulses, human works calcinate into positive law, rigid conventions, moral ideals or imperatives. This brings us to the second claim.

The series of transformations on both Apollinian and Dionysian sides are charted in GT and need not detain us here. In HC, Nietzsche is at pains throughout to show how excessive natural drives such as hatred, revenge, etc., are transformed from destructive forces into constructive agonal affects such as envy and ambition which stimulate (*Reiz*) cultural production (HC 1.786f. Also: 16[18], [26]/7). Similarly a human work that provokes agonal envy is transformed from being the prevailing standard of taste or convention into stimulant (*Reiz*) to deeds that surpass and limit its authority (HC 1.788).

This entire dynamic of human nature is, however, predicated on an approximate equilibrium of forces (*ungefähre Gleichgewicht der Kräfte:* Gerhardt 115ff., 124). What Nietzsche calls the *Wettspiel der Kräfte* presupposes "that in a natural order of things, there are always *several* geniuses who stimulate each other reciprocally to deeds, as they also hold each other reciprocally within the limits of measure" (HC I.789).[29] But the concept of equilibrium amongst more-or-less equal forces goes well beyond the *agon*; for Nietzsche, as Gerhardt has shown, it is the basis for the establishment of law and justice, indeed for social life *überhaupt*. Thus, Nietzsche's agonal *model of human nature* is tied to the *agon*, as a *model of social interaction*, and its presupposition of approximate equilibrium. Indeed, the interdependence of these two dimensions of the *agon* is one of the central ideas developed in HC: the superlative human achievements made possible by agonal interaction are a function of agonal regimes of human nature; such regimes, in turn, are a function of agonal interrelations among social beings.

C. The *Agon* as a Social Phenomenon

In the social sphere, agonal relations mirror the dynamic pattern in Nietzsche's concept of humanity. Each antagonist only becomes what it is in "impulses, works and deeds" through antagonistic relations with the other; relations through which each is continuously transformed. Thus a Greek poet only composed in order to win, when provoked by envy and ambition to surpass others (MA I 170; HC 1.788); the significance and authority of his achievement shaped, and was itself shaped by, the deeds of others (past, present and future). Such relations of reciprocal provocation and reciprocal limitation encapsulate Nietzsche's fascination with the *agon* as a social phenomenon. First, there is the remarkable wealth of different characters in Greek culture. Rooted in the "unleashing of the individual," it is connected by Nietzsche to envy, jealousy, and competition (3[49], 5[70]/ 8), that is, to the agonal dynamic of reciprocal provocation and empowerment. But that is only one side of the coin. Like Huizinga and Simmel,[30] Nietzsche was struck by the paradox that (institutionalised) conflicts such as the *agon* house unique generative social powers. In his illuminating discussion, Schröter[31] maintains that the *agon* is for Nietzsche the *"Element der Gemeinsamkeit"* and the source of social life. As when Nietzsche writes:

> For the ancients the goal of agonal education was the welfare of the whole, the state society. Every Athenian, for example, was supposed to develop his self in the contest to that degree that would be of greatest advantage to Athens and do it the least harm. [. . .]: it was of the well-being of his maternal city that a youth thought when running or throwing or singing in competition; it was her fame that he wanted to increase through his; [and] the wreaths that the judges of the contest placed in honour upon his head, he dedicated to the gods of his city. Every Greek felt from childhood on the burning wish within himself to be an instrument for the good [salvation] of his city in the contest of the cities: here his egoism [*Selbstsucht*] was enflamed, here it was also checked and bounded [*gezügelt und umschränkt*]. (1.789f.)[32]

At issue, as Schröter notes, is a quarrel with the modern state on the question of primary political goods. With Burckhardt, Nietzsche takes exception to the prioritisation of *security* by the modern state, and in particular: the regulated subordination of all social processes to the supreme goal of securing the reproduction of living conditions.[33] For the young Nietzsche, the state is to act as a "brace [*Klammer*]" or as an "armed comrade and companion" (ZB V 1.709) for a social life oriented towards the ethical "goal" of human perfection, and that means: an unleashing of free, spontaneous and unpredictable individuals that could extend and re-define the concept "human." Hence the value he places on the agonal dynamic of reciprocal provocation. But the regulation of life by the modern state has its rationale in the need to constrain or limit individual excesses so as to secure the "welfare of the whole." Thus, the security-orientation of the state can only be plausibly contested by Nietzsche if he can show that it is not needed to secure the limits of measure. That is precisely what he means when he names the "welfare of the whole" as the "goal of agonal education." In exploring the *agon*, Nietzsche's aim is to show that the very conditions for "unleashing the individual" also generate the measure needed for general well-being; or in Schröter's words, that "the conditions for maintaining the contest generate its constraint [*die Bedingungen der Erhaltung des Wettkampfes seine Bändingung hervorbringen*]" (112). How, then, can the conditions for agonal conflict generate this non-coercive form of constraint?

D. Agonal Measure (*Maass*) and Its Sources in the "Play of Forces"

As a clue to this question, I take Nietzsche's remark:

> *Wonderful* process, how the generalised conflict [*Kampf*] of all Greeks gradually comes to acknowledge one Dike in all areas: where does this come from? The contest unleashes the individual: and at the same time, it restrains [or measures: *bändigt*] the individual according to eternal laws. (16[22]/7)[34]

We want to know the character and sources of these "eternal laws" of measure; that is, the "measure of judgement" (VPP 272) or standard of victory in the *agon*. The *agon* does not presuppose the existence of such standards, as an explicit, governing instance; on the contrary, it was the *agon*, Nietzsche tells us, that led to a gradual recognition of a common sense of justice among Greeks. The key condition or presupposition for the *agon*, we have seen, is the existence of a plurality of more-or-less equal forces. From this angle, the claim that justice developed from the *agon* prepares for the "Principle of Equilibrium" developed in MA, and the derivation of law from the equilibrium of forces (MA I 92, 93; WS 22, 26, 28, 29, 33, 39, 57). The attempt to ground law in power is deemed a serious "category mistake" in the philosophy of law. In Nietzsche, it signifies a reversal of the traditional primacy of law over power, grounded in a refusal to grant law its prior, ideal or transcendental status, as a false, dualistic separation of the one "uncanny" nature (Gerhardt 112). In the context of the *agon*, the derivation of law from power is crystallised in the view that the *law or standard of victory is a product of specific configurations of power, holding between more-or-less equal forces*. As a model of lawfulness it is worked out by Nietzsche against state regulation and Humanist morality, as an alternative to coercive regimes of subjection or self-subjection under pre-established laws.

The agonal configuration of power is encapsulated in the key principle of Hellenic pedagogy: "Every gift must unfold through contestation" (*Jede Begabung muss sich kämpfend entfalten*, HC 1.789). This principle implies *first* a necessary relation of individual qualities to others, and *second*, a necessary relation of individual qualities to the public domain (*Öffentlichkeit*).

What this means is well illustrated by Homer's heroes. The great deeds of the *Iliad* do not emerge from a private, inner process of deliberation, as the result of unified acts of the will. As Bruno Snell and others have shown, Homer's heroes are transparent and highly pervious to their surroundings; more like open fields of forces in which conflicting impulses or qualities, with the help of the gods and mortals, alternate or combine to yield their actions.[35] This, then, is what Nietzsche means by the "visibility of the soul in actions" (*Sichtbarkeit der Seele im Handeln*, 3[49]8), praised as a great ethical quality of the Greeks. What the *Iliad*, at the heart of Greek pedagogy, illustrates is an ethic of openness (*Offenheit*) or freedom of mind (*Freisinnigkeit*), radically opposed to Humanist morality:

> The pleasure of *intoxication*, the pleasure of *guile*, of *revenge*, of envy, of *slander*, of *licentiousness* [*Unzüchtigkeit*]—all this was *acknowledged* by the Greeks as human, and on that basis ordered into the edifice of society and mores. The wisdom of their institutions lies in the lack of distinction between good and evil, black and white. Nature, as it shows itself, is not denied, but only ordered [*eingeordnet*], restricted to determinate cults and days. This is the root of all freedom of mind [*Freisinnigkeit*] in antiquity; a measured release [*mässige Entladung*] was sought for the forces of nature, not their annihilation or negation.—(5[146]/8.78)[36]

If we ask how the Greeks acquired their *Freisinnigkeit*, Nietzsche appeals to their nearness to sensory reality and the "depth of mind [*Tiefsinn*] with which they grasped and glorfied what is nearest [*des Nächsten*]" (5[70]/8). In the present context he speaks of their "sharpness of observation and sense for the actual [*Thatsächliche*]":

> Where do the Greeks draw this freedom from? No doubt already from *Homer*; but whence does he draw it?—The poets are not the wisest and logically most cultivated beings; but they take pleasure in the particulars of reality of every kind and do not want to negate it, but still to measure it [*mässigen*] so that it does not kill everything else around it. (*id.*)[37]

Thus, the ethos of *Offenheit* and *Sinnlichkeit* in Greek pedagogy and its chief source, Homer, returns us to the question of measure (*Maass*). The key to this question lies in the *social ontology* implicit in Homer and Greek pedagogy. The principle that every gift must unfold or flourish through contestation (*"Jede Begabung muss sich kämpfend entfalten":* HC 1.789) is in fact rooted in the social ontology of agonal interaction: *each particular quality, force or genius can only become what it is through antagonistic striving [Gegenstreben] against others*. Earlier, this idea was encountered in Gracian's community of taste, where to have taste means to be embroiled in conflict [*Gegeneinander*] with others (III.A). Further on it was encountered as the *inclusive* moment in Nietzsche's agonal concept of humanity, whereby our human and inhuman qualities need the resistance of the other to be what they are (III.B). As a principle of social ontology, it makes for a strong, resolutely pluralistic concept of community, grounded in the reciprocity and interdependence of antagonism. Such communities contrast sharply with the aesthetic communities described by Conway (III). There can be no question of an accidental association between self-sufficient beings, where each being needs antagonistic relations with others for its self-defining deeds and works. Nor can any single force or genius be so dominant as to exceed contestation by others.

It is to these relations that we must look for the moment of measure. In the *agon*, each force or being encounters the other as both a stimulant to deeds and a source of resistance or limit to deeds. We can therefore say: it is via the antagonists *in the relations of conflict* that limits are encountered. Agonal measure needs to be grasped from the medial position in the play of forces, as an intersubjective achievement, a product of equilibrium between more-or-less equal forces. This contrasts with the inner agony of conscience, and the ascetic regimes of "inward turned aggression" criticised in GM. More important in the context of HC is the contrast with Humanist morality, where measure is determined by a universal-rational law to which the individual must subject himself. Here measure *precedes* action within a coercive regime of regulation. In the *agon*, by contrast, the play of forces precedes measure, which is itself formed in the course of contestation (Schröter 114); measure is, in this sense, situation-bound and *post hoc*, rather than universal and *a priori*. As a consequence, agonal measure is radically contingent and unpredictable; it is dynamically bound to risks that Humanism seeks to preclude through regulation under a pre-established law. The *agon* cannot of itself guarantee the achievement of measure. This, Nietzsche claims, is the originary sense of ostracism: to enforce limits by excluding those forces or geniuses whose absolute supremacy over others dissolves the possibility of measure through contention (HC 1.789). The price of unleashing the individual in the *agon* is a radical insecurity, a *fragility of measure*.

Schröter offers two explanations for the attainment of measure in the *agon*. The first appeals to pleasure:

> In the 'logic' of the contest, the present stimulus to deeds through the will to be better ("*Stimulanzmittel*") also has the consequence of holding 'each other within the bounds of measure' [. . .] 'Agonal thinking,' the pleasure of contestation, is of itself the enemy of any 'monarchic' principle. Although everyone is out to be the best, the pleasure of contestation prohibits a totalising egocentricity. (113)[38]

For Nietzsche, however, the *agon* is driven by pleasures of a destructive kind, such as "the pleasure of *intoxication*, the pleasure of *guile*, of *revenge*, of envy, of *slander*, of *indiscipline* [*Unzüchtigkeit*]" (5[146]/8). Like Burckhardt, Nietzsche maintains that "In his secret wishes, every Greek was a tyrant; and everyone who could be, was in fact a tyrant" (6[7]/8; *cf.* MA I 261). "The hardness, the arrogance [*Übermut*], the tyrannical" in the blood of Greek philosophers (6[7]/8; 23[1]/7) was by no means unique to them. If the *agon* is inimical to any monarchic or tyrannical principle, it is so *in spite of* the pleasure principle. It cannot therefore be Nietzsche's view, when Schröter writes: "At bottom the 'Hellenic will' did not primarily want 'victory' (success) as such, but only the latter for the sake of the contest" (115). For Nietzsche, following Plato's *Gorgias*, writes: "All Greeks (from *Gorgias* in Plato) believed the possession of power as tyrant to be the enviable happiness" (4[301]/9). This same note can in fact be used to formulate a Nietzschean response to Schröter, when Nietzsche writes: "The equality [*Gleichheit*] of citizens is the means for avoiding tyranny, their reciprocal invigilation and constraint" (*Die Gleichheit der Bürger ist das Mittel zur Verhinderung der Tyrannei, ihre gegenseitige Bewachung und Niederhaltung*). In the *agon*, tyranny is curbed by a equality or equilibrium (*Gleichheit, Gleichgewicht*) of tyrannical forces; it is, therefore, from a medial position *in the relations of conflict* that measure must be sought. Schröter's explanation falls short because pleasure, whether tyrannical or counter-tyrannical, is inseparable from the subject-position of the antagonists.

Schröter's second explanation fares better in this respect. His starting point is the ambivalence of agonal culture towards tyrannical impulses and the temptation to hubris and *Übermaass*. The *agon* between inhuman and human impulses, Nietzsche's concept of humanity in HC, is referred by Schröter to an enduring fascination with the world of heroes and heroic excesses at a historical juncture where the Greeks were already aware of the need for measure and constraint (114). The *agon* and with it, agonal measure, are hereby identified with an important moment of human self-awareness, what can be called the transition from the heroic-superhuman to the problematic-human.[39] At issue is the step from the hero's unconditional passion to something more complex, a diremption and conflict of the psyche that is clearly visible in the ambivalent attitude to *envy* amongst agonal Greeks. On one side, envy was praised and valued as the "effect of a beneficent deity," the good Eris who stirs men to new deeds; on the other side it was feared in the fear of divine envy reminding victors of "the transitoriness of every human lot [*das Vergängliche jedes Menschenlooses*]" (HC 1.787). Clearly it is the latter, as an experience of human finitude, that articulates the call for measure and restraint. But it is important to see that fear of divine envy was only one side of an ambivalent attitude, and inseparable from a celebration of human envy. Together they express an experience of the human in *new, untold possibilities*, as well as its limits.

Now it is these two poles of the possible and its limits that are activated and combined in the agonal dynamic of reciprocal provocation and reciprocal limitation within the bounds of measure. There is, in short, a clear link between the dynamic character of the agonal play of forces and the moment of human self-awareness described by Schröter; they are isomorphic. If the experience of human finitude is bound up with the experience of human possibilities, *it is because they are a product of agonal interaction*, not solitary reflection.[40] By embedding agonal measure in this experience of the human, rather than the pleasure of contestation, Schröter's perspective thus moves from the subject-position to a medial position in the *intersubjective* dynamics of agonal conflict. This is a significant improvement on his first explanation of agonal measure. Not only does it allow for the tyrannical impulses emphasised by Nietzsche; it brings us much closer to the unique character of agonal measure that fascinated him, as the product of an equilibrium of tyrannical forces.

IV. Justice and Measure in Nietzsche's *Agon* and Homer's *Iliad*

In my closing remarks, I would like suggest a third perspective on agonal measure. In doing so I shall build on Schröter's insight into the historical juncture of the *agon* and agonal measure. The transition from the heroic-superhuman to the problematic-human, from unconditional *pathos* to the conflictual diremption of the human soul, is usually identified with the age of tragedy. These are, however, the words used by Karl Reinhardt to describe the very first work of Greek literature: Homer's *Iliad*. The *Iliad* is usually read as *the* heroic text of Western civilisation, a poem about Achilles' wrath that embodies the heroic values of honour, courage, loyalty and the immortality of fame. It is also common to see the *Iliad* as a national poem; according to Hegel, it asserts and justifies the world of the Greeks as absolute by pitting them against a foreign nation in a way "that leaves nothing over for those defeated."[41] These views have been discredited due largely to the work the philologists Karl Reinhardt and Wolfgang Schadewaldt.[42] They have argued that, next to the wrath of Achilles, the *Iliad* sings his *death* in a way that portrays his absolute self-assertion as an act of hubris. Indeed for Reinhardt, the entire *Iliad* is a *Todesdichtung*, with its battles for the fallen and its finale in the contrasting fates of two corpses: "In the lamentation over the dead, the human [*das Menschliche*] seems to free itself for the first time, to become the purest of songs" (Reinhardt 16). Schadewaldt, too, speaks of the "conciliatory humanness [*Menschlichkeit*]" (198) at the close of the *Iliad*. It is the reconciliation between Achilles and Priam over Hector's corpse that shows most clearly the distance separating the *Iliad* from the heroic age. The victory of the Greeks is not celebrated here; it *problematised* in a way that curbs their unconditional, unmeasured will-to-victory. Far from justifying the Greek nation as absolute, this scene places limits on the heroic pathos of victory in favour of an agonal acknowledgement of their opponents (Schröter 78). On this reading, then, the *Iliad* marks the transition from the *Vernichtungskampf* to the *Wettkampf*, from the heroic pathos of absolute victory to the transient, questionable victory of agonal humanity. But how is this transition managed? How is the agonal moment of measure inscribed in the *Iliad* such that the pathos of unconditional victory gives way to an acknowledgement of both victors and losers? Pursuing these questions opens an important perspective on agonal measure.

The sense of measure in the *Iliad* cannot be understood from the subject-position in its heroes. Subjects with self-identity and developmental continuity centred in an inner will are absent from Homer's world, as mentioned. Nor can we speak of self-restraint in any sustained sense on the part of individual characters, whose actions bear all the marks of unmeasured, willful heroes. As Reinhardt points out, they are crossed by sharp oppositions and typically illuminated from their sudden turning points: from the cruel to the human (Achilles), from narrow-mindedness to conciliatory openness (Agamemnon [Reinhardt 15, 17]). It would be equally inappropriate to appeal to a transcendent concept of justice as the source of measure. Explicit laws, imperatives or ideals that would govern or even adjudicate human actions are absent from the *Iliad.* As Hegel rightly notes, the poem pre-dates the level of morality, since there is no reflexive self-determination with reference to a universal standard. What, then, takes the place of morality as the source of measure? According to Reinhardt, a "division" or "equilibrium of sympathy" (*Spaltung, Gleichgewicht der Sympathie*) is the "foundation" of the *Iliad*, its "Grundgesetz" applied in different variations throughout (Reinhardt 11, 13). It is, however, a curiously inarticulate law, felt rather than stated: no victor celebrates for long before others, losers, appear to compete for our sympathy; no figures are so bad or worthless as to be utterly god-forsaken; there is, in Nietzsche's words, a lack of distinction between black and white (5[146]/8). The equilibrium of sympathy can be seen in the gods and especially Zeus, whose sympathies become so divided as to approach weakness (Reinhardt 13). As the highest god, he is also the one closest to the human problematic, fighting out the conflicts within himself until he pronounces judgement. The more impartial he is, the more dirempt and tragic he becomes. That the highest god should be the most indecisive: this, for Reinhardt, is Homer's "most sublime thought" (13).

The predicament of Zeus is symbolised by the scales (*Waage*) that he holds, a word that Nietzsche connects etymologically with the word *agon* (16[23]/7). This connection is particularly apposite if, I suggest, Zeus' predicament describes the status of law in the *agon*, as the source of agonal measure. The "equilibrium of sympathy" in Homer's Zeus is the counterpart to the "equilibrium of forces" in Nietzsche's *agon*. Both Homer and Nietzsche allow for tyrannical forces and heroic excesses in their diversity and particularity. Adjudication and measure cannot therefore be identified with, or reduced to, the deeds of individual antagonists. They must, however, be immanent: in the absence of explicit, pre-established universal laws or standards of judgement covering every conflict that arises, adjudication and measure must be responsive to particular conflicts, formed in response to the particular claims or deeds that arise on both sides. They must, in short, be human; or as human as can be without falling prey to particular interests on one side or the other. It is this third position between human particularity and the rigid universality of law that Zeus, as the most "captivated spectator," occupies; a place that best describes the lawfulness without a law that is the source of agonal measure. As a figure of law and justice, Zeus is not as reassuring as we would wish: a reminder of the fragility of measure, not its guarantor. But as a figure of indecision, he does guarantee that the question of justice is opened and re-opened through the *agon* of judgements amongst us mortals.

University of Leiden

1. See Daniel W. Conway, *Nietzsche & the Political* (New York: Routledge, 1997), chap. 7, esp. 119–128. I am indebted to Conway, not just for his brilliant summary of Nietzsche's political legacy, but for his overall treatment of Nietzsche as a political thinker in this book. My essay is an attempt to think with and against him on a number of key issues he raises: first, his central thesis that an open-ended perfectionism constitutes the perduring ethical core of Nietzsche's political thought; second, his relational reading of the *Übermensch* as a concrete empirical type whose value lies in extending the range and horizon of human achievement (20–27); and third, his actual treatment of Nietzsche's sense of community (esp. 30–34, 47–60).

2. Alasdair MacIntyre, *After Virtue* (Notre Dame: Notre Dame University Press, 1984), 114.

3. This view is shared by a number of authors, who form a growing counter-current concerned to retrieve constructive moments from the standard political reading. In addition to Conway, see, *e.g.*, David Owen, *Nietzsche, Politics and Modernity* (London: Sage, 1995), esp. 139–169, Lawrence Hatab, *A Nietzschean Defense of Democracy* (Chicago: Open Court, 1995), and Stanley Cavell, "Aversive Thinking: Emersonian Representations in Heidegger and Nietzsche," in *Conditions Handsome and Unhandsome: The Constitution of Emersonian Perfectionism* (Chicago: University of Chicago Press, 1990), 33–63.

4. References to Nietzsche's works follow the standard German abbreviations as used in the *Kritische Studienausgabe* (=KSA), G. Colli and M. Montinari, eds. (Munich and Berlin: dtv and de Gruyter, 1980), with section / aphorism numbers and/or names, as appropriate. Where necessary volume and page numbers are given from the KSA, unless otherwise stated. References to the *Nachlass*, also from the KSA, follow the notation therein (*e.g.*, 2[13]/7.23 = note 2[13], KSA vol. 7, p. 23). The unpublished text *Ursprung und Ziel der Tragödie* (=UZ) and the lectures *Die vorplatonischen Philosophen* (=VPP) are cited from: *Nietzsche Werke, Kritische Gesamtausgabe*, G. Colli and M. Montinari, eds. (Berlin: de Gruyter, 1967ff.), vol. III-5/2, p.142ff., and vol. II-4 respectively. Emphases are original, unless otherwise indicated. Translations are mine, although I have leaned on Hollingdale, Kaufmann and others. Square brackets are mainly used in quotes for alternative translations, interpolations or comments of mine.

5. For "becoming" (*Werden*) see MA 145 2.141; for "genesis" (*Entstehungsgeschichte*), see: 16[14]/10; MA 231, 252 2.194, 210; 24[2]/8; *cf.* MA 258 212f.

6. MA 231; see MA 230 – 235, 241; 19[66]/8 on the question of the "generation [*Erzeugung*] of the genius" and cultural renewal.

7. See, *e.g.*, the (free spirit's) problem of liberation "vis-à-vis one's provenance" (MA 230; *cf.* GD Streifzüge 45 6.148) and genius as liberation from imprisonment, disorientation, mutilation (MA 231; cf.17[60]/8 on the necessity of hindrances). These themes are encapsulated in the definition of *Genie:* "To will a lofty goal *and* the means towards it" (VM 378, and 5[141]/8 for "gift" (*Begabung*). See also: MA 241; MA 282 on "genius of meditation"; P. Heller, "*Von den ersten und letzten Dingen*" (Berlin: de Gruyter,1972), 428 on "*Zielsetzungen.*"

8. For *Wahrhaftigkeit*, see: UB III 4 1.371f.; 34[36] 7; 7[121]/7.168; JGB 209 ("*Genie zum Kriege*" as "*Skepsis*"); JGB 295 5.238; EH Schicksal 1 6.365 (*anständig*); 15[25]/13.412 ("*instinktive Genie*" and "*Rechtschaffenheit*"). For genius as the "enemy of truth," see: MA 636; 23[156]/8; *cf.* 11[415]/13 ("*Genie der Lüge*"); 30[9]/8 (against "*Erkenntniss*"); FW 361 and JGB 256 on actors as "*unvernünftig,*" "*Feinde der Logik.*"

9. See 25[9]/11.12: "It is self-evident that I know all of that which one calls the sufferings of genius: non-recognition, neglect, superficiality in all its grades, the suspicion, the maliciousness." See also, GT 9 1.68 (Prometheus); relativised to ambition in MA 157 2.147; rejected (of Wag.) WA 7 6.27. See also: 5[76]/8 (Schopenhauer on melancholy); M 50 3.55 (dissatisfaction). But also: 5[77]/8 (contra "*gravitas*"); 5[70]/8 ("*genial-frohe Temperament*") and 7[55]/7, 11[1]/7.356 on Greek cheerfulness and the generation of genius.

10. See, *e.g.*, FW 136; FW 353; MA 157; GD Streifzüge 24; AC 42; JGB 295; JGB 209.

11. Matthias Polyticki, *Umwertung aller Werte? Deutsche Literatur im Urteil Nietzsche's* (Berlin: de Gruyter, 1989, 219f.) speaks of an "immoral genius of strength" (*e.g.* 10[118]/12.523f.), a master of control and discipline (*Bändingung, Zucht*), and the genius "of sickness and weakness" (*e.g.* 14[182]/13.365f.; FW 366 3.615f. on lack of discipline). This clear-cut dichotomy needs to be qualified in my view to: a *wish* or *need* on Nietzsche's part to distinguish the strong from the weak type. For there are competing qualities of his thought that see through simplistic dichotomies of any kind. Thus, the fragility of "strength" and the extraordinary historical power of "weakness" are both emphatic themes in the late 1880s. We also encounter: a rethinking of health and sickness in non-oppositional terms (*e.g.*, 14[65]/13; 14[119]/13.297; 14[182]/13.366); doubts concerning the feasibility of Nietzsche's positive notion of *Genie* (29[16]/8; 4[244]/10); a total identification of genius with sickness (25[35]/11; *cf.* 11[79]/13); and ambivalence on the value of sickness and health (FW 24; MA 214; 14[75]/13).

12. For a good account of the German Liberalism attacked by Nietzsche (as by Grillparzer), see W. Seitter, "Franz Grillparzer und Friedrich Nietzsche; ihre Stellung zueinander," in *Jahrbuch der Grillparzer-Gesellschaft* 3, Bd.8, 1970.

13. H. Staten, *Nietzsche's Voice* (Ithaca: Cornell University Press, 1990), 110.

14. On this point and on the social origins of law in Nietzsche's thought, see V. Gerhardt, "Das 'Prinzip des Gleichgewichts'," in *Nietzsche-Studien* 12 (1983): 111–133, esp. 113 and 129ff. Also on this point and on the social origins of individuality, see M. Warren, *Nietzsche and Political Thought* (Cambridge: MIT Press, 1988), 58–61. Warren misunderstands Simmel as claiming that Nietzsche's individualism was a "social ideal" (59); in fact, this is referred to Liberalism *against* Nietzschean individualism by Simmel, who argues that Nietzsche "vielleicht die Bedeutung unterschätzt hat, die die sozialen Formungen auch für die Herausbildung jener rein individuellen Werte haben" (*Schopenhauer und Nietzsche. Ein Vortragszyklus.* [Munich & Leipzig: von Duncker & Humbolt, 1920], 209–210).

15. "*einen* Mitstreiter neben, *nicht über ihm*": original emphasis. Dated 1875, from the *Nachbericht, Beck'sche Ausgabe der Briefe* (*Friedrich Nietzsche: Werke und Briefe. Historisch-kritische Gesamtausgabe*, Munich: C.H.Beck'sche Verlagsbuchhandlung, 1933–1940), Bd. 4,

351. See also: 32[32]/7: "Die 'falsche Allmacht' entwickelt etwas 'Tyrannisches' in Wagner. Das Gefühl ohne Erben zu sein—deshalb sucht er seiner Reformidee die möglichste Breite zu geben und sich gleichsam durch Adoption fortzupflanzen. Streben nach Legitimität." (*cf.* MA 577). 32[34]/7: "Der Tyrannensinn für das Colossale. Es kommt ihm gar keine Pietät entgegen, der ächte Musiker betrachtet ihn als einen Eindringling, als illegitim." 32[32]/7: "Der Tyrann lässt keine andre Individualität gelten als die seinige und die seiner Vertrauten. Die Gefahr für Wagner ist gross, wenn er Brahms usw. nicht gelten lässt: oder die Juden." Also: 32 [61]/7.

16. See Gadamer, H.-G., *Wahrheit und Methode* (Tübingen: Mohr, 1972), I.1 b) δ Geschmack, 31ff., esp. 37f., 40f.

17. Gadamer, *op. cit.*; Fr. Schümmer, "Die Entwicklung des Geschmacksbegriffs in der Philosophie des 17. und 18. Jahrhunderts," in *Archiv für Begriffsgeschichte*, ed. E. Rothacker, (Bonn: Bouvier, 1955), Bd. I, 120–141.

18. "Das griechische Wort, welches den 'Weisen' bezeichnet, gehört etymologisch zu sapio ich schmecke, sapiens der Schmeckende, sisyphos der Mann des schärfsten Geschmacks; ein scharfes Herausmerken und -erkennen, ein bedeutendes Unterscheiden macht also, nach dem Bewußtsein des Volkes, die eigenthümliche Kunst des Philosophen aus." (PHG 3 1.816)

19. "Die Wissenschaft stürzt sich, ohne solches Auswählen, ohne solchen Feingeschmack, auf alles Wißbare, in der blinden Begierde, alles um jeden Preis erkennen zu wollen; das philosophische Denken dagegen ist immer auf der Fährte der wissenswürdigsten Dinge, der großen und wichtigen Erkenntnisse." (id.)

20. "Wenn Thales sagt 'Alles ist Wasser,' so zuckt der Mensch empor aus dem wurmartigen Betasten und Herumkriechen der einzelnen Wissenschaften, er ahnt die letzte Lösung der Dinge und überwindet, durch diese Ahnung, die gemeine Befangenheit der niederen Erkenntnißgrade." (*id.*)

21. These terms are taken from the end of GT Ch14 where Nietzsche has the dying Socrates wonder: "Perhaps art is even a necessary correlative and supplement of theory [*Correlativum und Supplement der Wissenschaft*]?" (GT 14 1.96). I take this to be a decisive statement of the relation between art (including tragic wisdom) and theory (*qua Wissenschaft*) for Nietzsche. It is also a decisive moment in Nietzsche's early *Umwertung* of art from *ancilla* to philosophy under Plato (GT 14 1.94), into its necessary consequence or telos. This line of thought is then pursued under the sign of wisdom (*Weisheit*) in PHG and contemporaneous notes (see esp. notebook 19, KSA 7 and notebooks 2, 3, 5, 7, 18, 19, KSA 8).

22. See esp. the account of Pericles' wrestling contest in HC 1.788 and MA 170 on "artistic ambition": "The Greek artists, the tragedians for example, poetised in order to win; their entire art cannot be conceived without the contest: the Hesiodic Eris, ambition, gave wings to their genius. Now this ambition demanded above all else that their work should attain the highest excellence *in their own eyes*, that is, as *they* understood this excellence, without concern for the dominant taste and the general opinion concerning excellence in a work of art [. . .] Thus they strive for victory over rivals in their own estimation, before their own seat of judgement, they really want *to be* more excellent; they then demand consensus on this their own estimation from others outside, confirmation of their judgement."

23. HC 1.792. See also 1.788f.on ostracism, and KSA 7: 3[73], 16[16], 16[43], 38[7].

24. Kant, *Kritik der Urteilskraft*, W. Weischedel ed. (Frankfurt: Theorie-Werkausgabe, 1968, Bd. X, 325), §22, *"Allgemeine Bemerkung zum ersten Abschnitte der Analytik."*

25. See Gerhardt (n. 14).

26. "Wenn man von Humanität redet, so liegt die Vorstellung zu Grunde, es möge das sein, was den Menschen von der Natur abscheidet und auszeichnet. Aber eine solche Abscheidung giebt es in Wirklichkeit nicht: die 'natürlichen' Eigenschaften und die eigentlich 'menschlich' genannten sind untrennbar verwachsen. Der Mensch, in seinen höchsten und edelsten Kräften, ist ganz Natur und trägt ihren unheimlichen Doppelcharakter an sich. Seine furchtbaren und als

unmenschlich geltenden Befähigungen sind vielleicht sogar der fruchtbare Boden, aus dem allein alle Humanität, in Regungen Thaten und Werken hervorwachsen kann. (HC 1.783). The *Vorstufe* in manuscript Mp. XII 3 in the Nietzsche Archive begins with the question: *"Was ist Humanität?"*

27. *"Das Individuum zur höchsten Kraft durch die Polis gesteigert,"* and: *"Merkwürdig* viel Individuum, *sollte darin nicht eine höhere Sittlichkeit liegen?"*

28. HC 1.787. *Cf.*: CV 1, esp. 1.772; 10[1]/7.344; 16[15],[18], 26], [28]/7.

29. "daß, in einer natürlichen Ordnung der Dinge, es immer mehrere Genies giebt, die sich gegenseitig zur That reizen, wie sie sich auch gegenseitig in der Grenze des Maaßes halten."

30. J. Huizinga, *Homo Ludens* (Amsterdam: Pantheon Vlg, 1940), chap. 3: *"Spiel und Wetteifer als kulturschaffende Funktion,"* esp. 78, 82f.; Simmel, G., *Conflict and the Web of Group Affiliations*, tr. Kurt Wolff and R. Bendix (New York: Collier-Macmillan, 1964).

31. H. Schröter, *Historische Theorie und Geschichtliches Handeln* (Mittenwald: Mäander, 1982), esp. 106–122, *"Agon und Geschichtlichkeit."*

32. "Für die Alten [. . .] war das Ziel der agonalen Erziehung die Wohlfahrt des Ganzen, der staatlichen Gesellschaft. Jeder Athener z.B. sollte sein Selbst im Wettkampfe soweit entwickeln, als es Athen vom höchsten Nutzen sei und am wenigsten Schaden bringe. [. . .]: an das Wohl seiner Mutterstadt dachte der Jüngling, wenn er um die Wette lief oder warf oder sang; ihren Ruhm wollte er in dem seinigen mehren; seinen Stadtgöttern weihte er die Kränze, die die Kampfrichter ehrend auf sein Haupt setzten. Jeder Grieche empfand in sich von Kindheit an den brennenden Wunsch, im Wettkampf der Städte ein Werkzeug zum Heile seiner Stadt zu sein: darin war seine Selbstsucht entflammt, darin war sie gezügelt und umschränkt."

33. Schröter 115, 112. See also: A. von Martin, *Nietzsche und Burckhardt. Zwei geistige Welten im Dialog* (Basel: E. Reinhardt Vlg., 1945), 113ff.

34. "Wunderbarer *Prozeß, wie der allgemeine Kampf aller Griechen allmählich auf allen Gebieten eine dike anerkennt: wo kommt diese her? Der Wettkampf entfesselt das Individuum: und zugleich bändigt er dasselbe nach ewigen Gesetzen.*"

35. Bruno Snell, *The Discovery of Mind in Greek Philosophy and Literature*, tr. T. Rosenmeyer (New York: Dover, 1982), chap. 1: "Homer's View of Man"; Erich Auerbach, *Mimesis*, tr. W. Trask (Princeton, NJ: Princeton Univ. Press, 1991), chap. 1: "Odysseus' Scar"; Lawrence J. Hatab *Myth and Philosophy: A Contest of Truths* (La Salle: Open Court, 1990).

36. "Die Lust am Rausche, die Lust am Listigen, an der Rache, am Neide, an der Schmähung, an der Unzüchtigkeit—alles das wurde von den Griechen anerkannt, als menschlich, und darauf hin eingeordnet in das Gebäude der Gesellschaft und Sitte. Die Weisheit ihrer Institutionen liegt in dem Mangel einer Scheidung zwischen gut und böse, schwarz und weiss. Die Natur, wie sie sich zeigt, wird nicht weggeleugnet, sondern nur eingeordnet, auf bestimmte Culte und Tage beschränkt. Dies ist die Wurzel aller Freisinnigkeit des Alterthums; man suchte für die Naturkräfte eine mässige Entladung, nicht eine Vernichtung und Verneinung."

37. "Woher haben die Griechen diese Freiheit? Wohl schon von Homer; aber woher hat er's?—Die Dichter sind nicht die weisesten und logisch gebildesten Wesen; aber sie haben die Lust am einzeln Wirklichen jeder Art und wollen es nicht verneinen, aber doch so mässigen, dass es nicht alles todt macht."

38. "In der 'Logik' des Wettkampfes hat der gegenwärtige Anreiz zur Tat durch den Willen, der Bessere zu sein ("Stimulanzmittel"), zugleich die Folge, 'sich gegenseitig in der Grenze des Maasses' zu halten. [. . .] Das 'agonale Denken,' die Lust am Wettkampf, ist aus sich selbst der Feind jedes 'monarchischen' Prinzips. Obwohl es jedem darum geht, der Beste zu sein, unterbindet die Lust am Wettkampf eine totalisierende Egozentrik."

39. Reinhardt, K., 1948 "Das Parisurteil" (1938), in *Von Werken und Formen* (Godesberg, 1948), 36. Quoted in: W. Schadewaldt, *Von Homers Welt und Werk. Aufsätze und Auslegungen zur homerische Frage* (Stuttgart: Koehler Vlg, 1944), 199.

40. According to Schröter, it is the experience of the human in its possibilities and limits

that "grounds their belonging together, the sphere of society" (113). If so, this opens a second angle on the generative social powers of *agon*.

41. G.W.F. Hegel, *Aesthetik*, ed. Fr. Bassenge (Berlin/Weimar, 1965), Bd. II, 423.

42. See esp. Schadewaldt, and Reinhardt, "Tradition und Geist im Homerischen Epos," in *Die Krise des Helden* (Munich: dtv, 1962), 7–18.

[15]

Rationalized Violence and Legal Colonialism: Nietzsche contra *Nietzsche*

Joseph Pugliese

This essay is concerned with examining the practices of western law in the context of Australia's colonial governance of Papua New Guinea. I situate my study of these practices in the context of a narrative by an Australian Patrol Officer who was stationed in Papua New Guinea from the time of World War II to the time of Independence (1975). In writing on colonial issues from the institutional site of the western academy, I am concerned with the politics of positionality and the possibility of re-activating neo-colonial ideologies even as I attempt to articulate a decolonizing practice. I deal with these issues in a detailed manner in a paper which emerged concurrently as I worked on this very project.[1]

In examining the colonial practices of western law in Papua New Guinea, my approach is critically oriented by a desire to discursify these practices, specifically, to articulate the relationship between the discourses of colonialism and the discursive practices of the law. This relationship is structured by constitutive homologies and points of diffraction. In the first instance, or what could more appropriately be termed the inaugural instance of foundation, a discourse achieves the critical parameters governing the bounded operations by which it constitutes its objects of inquiry precisely through the invocation and consequent inscription of a rule of law. This rule of law establishes the conditions of possibility of a discourse: in other words, in demarcating the range and specificity of speaking and writing positions for its subjects, it simultaneously inscribes the limits of its exteriority, beyond which lies cultural mutism or unintelligibility. To exceed or to transgress these limits is to invoke those juridico-political mechanisms which legitimize their operations under the rule of law.

The moment of foundation referred to above should, in fact, be pluralized so as to read: *moments of foundation.* These are the moments in which anterior practices, and their attendant legal systems, are systematically erased in order to nullify the contestatory possibilities of prior claims and alternative systems of law.[2] And it is here that I want to begin to inform this study of colonialism with Nietzschean theories of power and the law. In specifically drawing upon the work of Friedrich Nietzsche in an analysis of systems of colonial domination, I am mindful of the potential contradictions that such an invocation might generate. I am referring here to Nietzsche's advocacy, throughout much of his writings, for a social and political organization based on the rule of a cultural aristocracy, in contradistinction to the "herd," which he sees as constituting the "base" of this socio-political hierarchy. I mark this imperial political structure precisely in order to avoid the sanitization of Nietzsche into a type of postmodernist liberal.[3]

Simultaneously, however, I also want to affirm the extraordinary subtlety and complexity of Nietzsche's writing on questions of power, domination and the law. Inscribed in his corpus are a series of speculative and incisive analyses of such questions, which allow the reader to use Nietzsche *contra* Nietzsche, so to speak. And I have no doubt that this very Zarathustran strategy would be heartily endorsed by one who tauntingly declares: "How does one compromise oneself today? By being consistent. By going in a straight line."[4] My divergencies are sanctioned by the non-linear structure of Nietzsche's speculative philosophy; my mobilizing of Nietzschean theory *contra* the imperial politics of the colonizer is enabled by the trenchant analyses and critiques of systems of racism, domination and exploitation that also constitute Nietzsche's *oeuvre.*

In Nietzschean genealogical terms, the anterior plurality of moments of origin needs to be reduced to an autochthonous singularity in order to maintain the illusion of an originary irreducibility from which the truth of law is said to begin. Nietzsche takes his analysis one step further to demonstrate how this moment of mythical, singular, and autochthonous foundation is inextricably linked to language. In this mythical moment of foundation, argues Nietzsche, "a uniformly valid and binding terminology for things is invented and the legislation of language also enacts the first laws of truth. For now, for the first time, the distinction between truth and lying arises."[5] In the legislation of language is inscribed the rule of law. The rule of law, with its capacity to determine and enforce the difference between criminality and civil behavior, between transgression and obedience, achieves its enunciative function in the legislation of language or, more specifically, *discourse*, understood here in a strictly Foucauldian sense, as a language formation that institutionally authorizes and delimits the possibility for speech and writing.

In my discussion of colonialism and the law, I want to track this process of linguistic legislation, and its complex relationship with regimes of truth and legality. I specifically want to focus on the way in which this process of linguistic legislation is necessarily predicated on violence and the simultaneous erasure of the violent scene that has produced it.

In this study, I focus on the figure of the Patrol Officer because he (and I use the gender-specific term precisely because Patrol Officers were, without exception, male) may be read as a symbolic incarnation of white law. The Patrol Officer served as an instrumentality by which the apparatus of colonial governance extended and consolidated the rule of white law. In focusing on the role of the Patrol Officer, I wish to make visible the discursive practices constituting the colonized space and its subjects. The figure of the Patrol Officer is invariably represented as a type of colonial factotum who performs a seemingly heterogeneous series of roles, including magistrate, "explorer," doctor, census-taker, tax collector, and mediator between indigenous cultures and the colonial regime. In the course of his "field work," the Patrol Officer emerges in colonial narratives as an extraordinarily mobile figure, who traverses vast tracts of terrain in order to extend the rule of colonial law to the furthest reaches of the occupied territory. Viewed in this light, the Patrol Officer can be seen to play a crucial role in the establishment and enforcement of colonial law. As a mobile factotum of colonial rule, the Patrol Officer possesses an extraordinarily infiltrative capacity: his myriad roles, all underpinned and authorized by the power of colonial rule, enable him to infiltrate virtually all levels of indigenous culture. Most importantly, it is the Patrol Officer who enacts and enforces at the local level the supplanting and outlawing of indigenous law by colonial law.

Underpinning these strategies of supplanting and outlawing indigenous law is a series of occulting operations whereby indigenous law, and its attendant cultural practices, is reformulated by the colonizer as mere "custom," "superstition," or "primitive"; it is consequently dismissed as "barbaric" or "anarchic." Indigenous law is thus scripted as essentially a-legal; it is then legislatively deemed to be illegal and thus suppressed. In his discussion of indigenous law in Papua New Guinea, Peter G. Sack, for example, produces a sequence of strategic denigrations: "Primitive [*sic passim*] law is not a battle between right and wrong where one side has to win and the other to lose; primitive law is not an attempt to establish the higher order of justice." Indigenous law is here scripted as necessarily amoral (as it fails to participate in the "battle between right and wrong") and thus a-legal: its failure to stage an adversarial struggle which will differentiate between "right and wrong" vitiates its claims to establishing or ever achieving "the higher order of justice." Indigenous law, Sack continues, "is an endless series of compromises," as though western law were not thoroughly inscribed by a series of compromises. Sack's racist logic culminates in a reasoned demand for exterminatory violence: "Primitive law and the primitive group as a political unit have to be destroyed and a colony has to become a state before a western type of law can begin to rule."[6] In the call for the establishment of the state is encoded the violence of a colonial domination which will gather together and suppress the heterogeneity of indigenous cultures into the simulacrum, to quote the Hegelian statist formula, of "*one* Being, the spirit of *one* people."[7]

The rule of colonial law posits and produces its primitive and barbaric others; it needs to construct these categories even as it claims to transcend them in its universality. Colonial law secures its positional superiority through a systemic denigration and othering of all that fails to be assimilated into the law of the same. In positing itself as the privileged repository of legality as such, it generates the illegality of the other.

Colonial law's self-identity is predicated on an unacknowledged economy of dependence and exchange: its self-identity is founded on acts of expropriation, subordination and assimilation. Yet what is elided in the texts of colonial law is this very system of dependence on the other. In these colonial texts, as I will illustrate below, western law promotes itself as a metadiscursive practice, that is, western law is represented as *meta-legal*: it thereby is seen to have the capacity and right to evaluate and judge all other systems aspiring to the status of law. From this locus of meta-legality western law's claims to universality arise. In its privileged meta-legality, western law reserves the right to adjudicate all other legal (i.e., western), proto-legal and a-legal (i.e., non-western) systems. In dispatching all other non-western systems of law to the realm of proto- or a-legality by decreeing that they are primitive, irrational and/or barbaric, western law generates the space from which it can define itself as the embodiment of reason, impartiality and universality. This seemingly transcendent space is marked, significantly, by the erasure of the very site-specific, socio-culturally bounded factors constituting its conditions of possibility and determining its cultural intelligibility. The colonial imposition of western law, then, is articulated in an aporetic movement: in order to be intelligible and thereby effectively transmuted into practice, colonial law must reproduce the ethnocentric conditions under which it maintains its coherence and *modus operandi*; simultaneously, driven by the logic of a transcultural universality, it claims to transcend the very ethnocentric conditions the colonial regime labors to establish, conditions maintaining their viability only at the cost of constant surveillance and violent enforcement.

The legacy of Australia's colonial rule in Papua, New Guinea, over a period spanning 1906 (when South-Eastern New Guinea, or Papua, was formally "handed over" to Australia by Britain) to 1975 (when Papua New Guinea achieved Independence) is characterized by the systematic manner in which it outlawed and supplanted indigenous law with an alien and Anglocentric model of law. As Edward P. Wolfer's has observed, "the legal system of Papua New Guinea now embodies — by virtue of the adoption of common law — a great deal of English and Australian tradition, but scarcely recognizes the beliefs, customs, and age-old dispute settlement procedures of the country's indigenous inhabitants."[8] In this study of the relationship between colonialism and the law, I focus on the multiple strategies and mechanisms by which colonial rule virtually ensured this type of result.

I now want to turn my attention to the study of a particular text, *The Fate of O'Loughlin* by Dudley McCarthy, which will elaborate and contextualize the theoretical propositions outlined above. *The Fate of O'Loughlin* will constitute my primary textual site for a number of reasons. Firstly, the text, as the blurb on the dust-jacket observes, represents "the perils of opening up the unknown interior of the country [Papua New Guinea], with its mysterious natural forces, savagery and superstition, madness, violence and death."[9] The text, the reader is also told, "spans the period of New Guinea's development from an unknown and primitive land, through the war years to full Independence." Historically, then, the text can be seen to encompass the historical frame within which Australia exercised its colonial rule of law; and, as is lexically evident ("unknown interior," "primitive land," and so on), the text is unambiguously constituted by the discourses of colonialism. My decision to work on this text was also informed by the fact that the author, Dudley McCarthy, was himself a Patrol Officer in Papua New Guinea and therefore part of the apparatus of colonial rule. Furthermore, I was interested in the text's representation of the nexus of gender and colonialism.[10] The text reproduces a type of boys'-own-adventure as it maps the colonial exploits of a Patrol Officer in his travels through the colonized countryside. The colonial regime demanded that the Patrol Officer literally patrol and maintain the borders of the colonial regime and, simultaneously, he was required to extend these borders through "explorative" forays designed to build bases from which to establish the conditions for colonial dependence and domination.

The opening lines of *The Fate of O'Loughlin* enunciate the practical application of the rule of colonial law:

> They hanged the five men that afternoon in a clearing on the bank of the big river.... Then, in that silence, at last he [the District Officer] spoke. "You will take no more heads — or else you will die as these men have died. The day of the bamboo beheading knife is over. You have known of the law for many years, but some of you have been very slow to learn.... See that no new heads are hung in the house tambarans. If they are, the men who took them will be brought to the court and the court will say: 'Take them back to the place where they did these things and hang them by the necks until they are dead, in front of all the people there.'" (p. 2)

Inscribed in these opening lines is the violent scene in which the rule of colonial law represents itself as the rule of reason. As a type of violence authorized by the subjugating rule of western reason, colonial law operates under the logic of a double gesture: in the first instance, it clears the colonized space of any traces of previous systems of law and declares the traces surviving this process of cultural annulment to be nothing more than superstitious and irrational remainders which will be overcome in the indigene's movement toward "modernity," constituted by "reason," "development," and "progress."[11] It is when these remainders of indigenous law, in this case the pay-back system of head-hunting, refuse to be consigned to the scrap-heap of history and are subversively re-activated and re-deployed by the colonized subject that the other side of the same gesture is put into play by the colonizing regime: under the pretext of stopping a barbaric and immoral practice, the colonial authorities perpetrate an act of violence which is sanctioned by a moral lexicon designed to differentiate its act of "civilizing" violence from the "barbaric" violence of the indigene. This moral lexicon functions to rewrite the violence of the colonizer as an act of law and as an exercise of reason. What the public hangings of the indigenes dramatize is nothing if not a mockery and ventriloquy of justice. The imposition of western law on a colonized territory mimics the performance of justice precisely because it establishes its purchase on legality by systemizing a violence that calls itself reason.

Encapsulated in the statement "You will take no more heads — or else you will die as these men have died" is the Nietzschean insight into the immorality of systems of morals which represent themselves as transcendent systems beyond the struggles and political contingencies of violent and unequal relations of power. In Nietzschean terms, the colonizer bestows upon her/his system of violence the legitimating imprimatur of "reason." Effectively mobilized here is what Nietzsche ironically terms "supplemental rationality": that form of the will to power that strategically effaces reason's often insalubrious (because irrational) origins. "All things that live long," writes Nietzsche, "are gradually so saturated with reason that their origin in unreason thereby becomes improbable."[12] The structure of the supplement enables the tactical overcoding or semiotic saturation of the irrational order of violence perpetrated by the rule of the colonizer as the cool exercise of reason. Brought into sharp focus here is the exorbitant question concerning improbable origins; in Derridaen terms, the supplemental structure of reason paradoxically functions to articulate and legitimize "what is indeed 'inconceivable to reason'" — the irrationality of violence.[13]

It is through the act of consecration of the colonial system "as a law, as *dominating*" that the imposed system becomes "venerable, unassailable, holy, true; it is part of its development that its origin should be forgotten — That is a sign that it has become master."[14] It is thus that Nietzsche explains his genealogical thesis that the mythologization of origins follows the mastery of signs: the colonizer's system of law, in effacing its historically constructed nature and representing itself as always already prior and transcendent to other legal systems, places itself beyond the purview of such mundanities as power and contestation. Western colonial law's claim to universality finds its enunciative conditions in this elaborate process of mythification.

In the execution of the Papuans who have perversely continued to perform their own acts of indigenous law, the colonial regime establishes its system of control literally upon the bodies of the indigenous subjects. In the colonial exercise of the law, violence has already profoundly operated upon the bodies of its colonized subjects. In this instance, the bodies of the indigenes are seized, marked as transgressive in the simulacrum of a western court, and subsequently inscribed as exemplars in their moment of death. Within the simulacrum of a western court, constituted by a meager collection of props (the Bible, the colonizer's flag, a typewriter, a desk) symbolizing the new juridical order, the indigene is interpellated by an alien language producing and delimiting the parameters of criminality. For the colonizer, the symbols of the new juridical order cannot be overestimated; as the paternalistic narrator observes, "it's a nice bit of ceremonial.... Impresses the natives." (p. 176) The arcane symbols of colonial law are active in producing the sacral and ceremonial dimension of the law; that dimension, in other words, which is instrumental in mystifying the operations of the law in order to position the colonial subject into a type of enthralled submission.

The execution of the five indigenes is staged within the symbolic configuration of "a clearing on the bank of the big river." Their execution is topographically situated at the point of intersection between the law (and its penal machinery) and the marketplace (metonymically signified by the jetty) with its colonial-mercantile economy of expropriation and exploitation.[15] The hangings in this public space — "hang them [the indigenes] by the necks until they are dead, in front of all the people there" — are instrumental in producing what Nietzsche termed the *theatrics* of public punishment and execution: punishment as a public performance whereby the acts of punishment and torture inflicted upon the body of the criminal serve as symbolic reminders to the spectating public of the power and necessity of the law in maintaining the social order.[16] The hanged bodies of the indigenes signify the material power of the colonizer's law, as it re-articulates its hold corporeally and makes possible the public epiphany of the colonizer's power in the moment of execution.

What is staged in these public hangings, orchestrated and overseen by the Patrol Officer, is what Nietzsche terms "the terrible and strange technique of mnemonics" — whereby the power of the rule of law is corporeally etched on the body of the colonized subject in order to guarantee a mnemonic retention of the colonizer's power to discipline and punish. In *Papuan Epic*, Keith Bushell, "Sometime Native Police Officer and Magistrate in New Guinea," writes of the punishments meted out to a group of transgressive indigenes while he was on patrol:

> These latter would be liberated, but not until they had been given a requisite number of lashes across their naked backs to remind them of the white man Government's visit to their country, and of the futility of their trying to impede his official entry into their mountain villages.
>
> Their "hides" being naturally very thick, the thrashing would not prove anything like so painful as on a more tender white skin, but sufficient to warn the owners not to fight against the police when next they came.[17]

The difference between "hide" and "tender white skin" opens up the racist possibility for a biological difference between the colonizer and the other that sanctions the violence perpetrated against the indigene. This racist difference strategically situates the indigene, as Nietzsche affirms, in one of his most profoundly illiberal moments, in the colonial category of the "primeval man." (*GM*, II, 7) The "requisite number of lashes" will mnemonically inscribe the epidermic text, the "hides," of the indigene with the rule of the colonizer's law. This passage through violence will ensure their elevation to a "higher system of morals" and to the very system of law they are presumed to lack. "With the aid of this sort of memory," Nietzsche sardonically remarks, "people finally come to 'reason!'" (*GM*, II, 3) This nexus of the body and textual incarnation of the law is most graphically dramatized in Franz Kafka's "In the Penal Colony," where the body of the sentenced subject is literally intextuated by the iron spike of the harrow.[18] In the context of the fictitious penal colony, the lived practices of colonialism are enacted: the harrow proceeds, slowly and methodically, to engrave the inscription demanded by the legal sentence on the condemned body of the victim; in the conjunction of the colonized body and the legal machinery of the colonial regime is enunciated the mnemonic guarantee that the violent instrumentality of the colonial rule of law will prevail.

In seizing, controlling and effectively marketing the body of the condemned indigene in the marketplace there is also, for the colonizers, the production of pleasure in the public display of their superior power. By contextualizing the spectacle of public executions in the clearing of the marketplace, this Nietzschean nexus of power, pleasure and punishment can be viewed in economic terms. "[T]o what extent can suffering be a compensation for 'debts'?" asks Nietzsche. "To the degree that *to make* suffer is pleasure in its highest form, and to the degree that the injured party received an extraordinary counter-pleasure in exchange for the injury and distress caused by the injury: to *make* someone suffer, — a true feast." (*GM*, II, 5) Inscribed in this scene, then, is a complex psycho-juridical economy exercising its power on the body of the indigene, simultaneously as it extracts illicit pleasures from it. In the deployment of colonial power, the indigene is disinvested of her/his own body: it becomes objectified under the colonial gaze and commodified in a system of exchange and re-investment that re-intextuates the colonized body as a symbolic corpus. Within the political economy of colonial regimes, the body of the transgressive indigene is charged with a new semiotic, as it is transformed into a general symbol placed in the service of the colonial body politic.

Within this Nietzschean scene, a genealogical reading of the colonial order of law discloses that the processes and practices of colonialism are *not* to be seen, in Nietzsche's words, as a "*progressus* towards a goal, still less is it a logical *progressus*... instead it is a succession of more or less profound ...processes of subjugation." (*GM*, II, 12) In his deployment of the genealogical method, and with characteristic acuity, Nietzsche here routs the teleological pretensions of such institutions as the law by staging a disarticulation between idealized goal and lived effect. In the process, he prefigures the possibility for Foucault to declare that "The system of right, the domain of the law, are permanent agents of these relations of domination, these polymorphous techniques of subjugation."[19]

These processes of subjugation and of corporeal intextuation are not, however, unidirectional. On the contrary, the body of the colonizer is also situated within the intextuating regime of these processes, and it is also thereby symbolically marked; specifically, the body of the Patrol Officer, vested with the official signs of the colonial order, serves to signify the localized embodiment of colonial law. Patrol Officer O'Loughlin, for example, succinctly articulates this to a group of indigenes described as "Stinking bush kanakas, apes out of the trees": "I told you before that there was a new law and that, for you, I am that law." (pp. 41-45) Dramatized here is the dissymmetry of power between the indigene and the colonizer. The Patrol Officer is represented as a figure in sovereign possession of the law: through his injunctions, he perpetuates the illusion of bestowing a system of legality on a people bereft of any sense of legal order. This illusion hinges on establishing a type of *tabula rasa* which effectively obliterates any traces of indigenous law. This illusion, however, is troubled by the contradiction of having to confront and systematically overthrow the very indigenous legal order officially deemed not to exist:

> It had troubled him [Patrol Officer O'Loughlin] often that the law recognized nothing of this kanaka thinking. It was in fact a white man's law and made by white men for white man's society. But it was the law he had to uphold. Within that law he was officially both a policeman and a judge. And now he was asked to connive against that law, which he represented, and with a primitive man to whom it had no meaning — an ignorant savage, black and dirty, little better than an animal, a cannibal, by God, the most disgusting thing there was. (p. 44)

Faced with the contradiction of having to overthrow an indigenous system of law purported to be non-existent,[20] the Patrol Officer finds his solution in the invocation of a lexicon of animality and barbarity that rewrites the indigene as a sub-human subject embedded in the pre-cultural order of "nature." This chaotic order of "nature" effectively constructs the demand for colonial intervention: it is under the rubric of bringing "civilization to the natives" that the practices of colonialism are rationalized. The positioning of indigenous culture within the order of "nature" generates a vast archive of colonial texts that will speak for the indigene without history, without culture, and without law. This archive articulates the collective need for colonial apparatuses to set the indigenous culture onto the path of "modernity." O'Loughlin, for instance, sees Australia's colonial role in Papua New Guinea as primarily driven by the need "to create a modern society where no vestige of it existed before." (p. 151)

Underpinning colonial discourses on modernity is an Hegelianism which finds its most imperial articulation in *The Philosophy of History*.[21] Modernity, as an historical symptom of the West, defines its intelligibility against an horizon of exteriority constituted by the absolute others of the west. This horizon of exteriority is, however, conveniently open to the synoptic vision and the exegetical practices of western colonialism: under the rubric of "exploration," the west will "discover" and "map" the inhabited spaces of non-western cultures; and with the disciplines of anthropology and ethnography, the west will explain to the indigene the workings of her/his own culture: the indigenes' mere "stories" will be transmuted by the western scholar into "knowledge."[22] I am reminded here of Emmanuel Levinas' incisive critique of the Hegelian concept of modernity: "modernity," writes Levinas, "i.e., domination as knowledge of new forms, *other* forms."[23]

These colonial practices are characterized by a type of ongoing internal dialogue, in which the west maintains and secures its self-identity through a seemingly dialogic process professing to define and thematize the other. In effect, this process of defining forgets, to put it in Derridaen terms, the defining of the definition, as that which necessarily relates colonial knowledge of non-western peoples back to the discursively constitutive operations of the west. What remains unacknowledged in this process, then, are the Eurocentric systems of conceptuality by which the west speaks about itself while under the illusion that it is speaking about its others. Instead of an ethical relation of proximity, which refuses an assimilation of the other simultaneously as it recognizes that the irreducible differences of its others are constitutive of its self-identity, the west demands that its others be assembled in readiness to address its imperial summons and serve its colonial needs.

In the context of colonialism, this process of assembling is facilitated by the technology of the book, as that which interpellates, as in a pedagogical roll-call, the colonized subject. Throughout his travels across the Papuan landscape, Patrol Officer O'Loughlin, who has been commissioned to "penetrate the dark reaches" (p. 131) of the country (the relationship between colonialism and this phallic language of penetration will be discussed shortly), carries with him the Village Book. The Village Book is a discursive technology which is instrumental in producing the colonized subject. When asked by the indigene, Somangi, to explain the function of the Village Book, the Patrol Officer replies that the book "tells me among other things that your name is Somangi." (p.116) The Village Book is thus famed to have an incantatory role which reinscribes the past into the actuality of the present: "There is a thing," says the Patrol Officer, "— a book — which the first kiap [government official] who came left here, saying it would speak the names of these people to other kiaps." (p. 17)[24]

The Village Book, however, has an even more momentous role to play in the history of colonialism:

> This is the beginning for the better or worse. For two thousand, three thousand, God knows how many thousand years, the lives of these people have not changed. They have lived and fought and died as they are now, using the same tools, eating the same food, knowing nothing of the world outside these mountains or of the people in it. Unchanging in all those thousands of years. And they would stay that way for thousands of years more, but for me and people like me. But I personally, I O'Loughlin, I myself, I am the first change in all that time. I am the first thing, I am the very first thing, in their recorded history, for in this book and only in this book their record begins. (p. 34)

The Village Book enunciates the erasure, in the very act of colonial inscription, of the subjugated country's history, while simultaneously establishing the enabling condition which inaugurates the colonized country's entry into (western) history. The movement of the colonizer's pen across the white page mimics his/her movements across the a-signifying texture of the *terra nullius* landscape. This a-signifying texture, in its blankness, nullity and unintelligibility, only assumes the dimensions of legibility, order and knowledge under the thematizing gaze of the colonizer, which ensures, as Levinas has remarked, "the gathering of all alterity into presence, and the synchrony of presence"; "intelligibility," adds Levinas, "signifies the reduction of the other [*Autre*] to the Same."[25] This synchrony of presence is, however, already undone by the very differential structure of writing and its relationship to an ungovernable alterity which is simultaneously its condition and antecedent. It is this structure, this relationship, which interrupts the colonizer's dream of inscribing the originary mark enunciating the colonial theology of a beginning without prior origins. In Derridaen terms, this mythical moment of origin is nothing more than the after-effect of a system of language which already signals the interminable structure of originary reproduction.

Informing the Patrol Officer's mythology of origins and the commencement of history is an unacknowledged Hegelianism. The Hegelian philosophy of history, which, as mentioned above, pervades so many colonial texts, turns on a teleological schema in which the attainment of "spirit" (as a form of self-consciousness which can articulate its own ends, interests, and the principles which underlie them) guarantees a nation's entry into (western) history. This Eurocentric schema achieves its own privileged purchase on history precisely by constructing all other non-western nations as entities without "spirit" embedded in a primordial strata of unconsciousness, unreflexiveness and torpid corporeality.[26] These static nations are thus effectively scripted as awaiting the interventions of the European patriarch in order to insert them into the symbolic order of (western) history. As the Patrol Officer's narrative discloses, the time prior to this colonial intervention is one devoid of temporality and change, a catatonic state of timeless fixity which is finally interrupted by the first mark inscribed with the pen/phallus of the colonizer on the virginal text/body/terrain of the colonized nation. In *The Fate of O'Loughlin*, the paternalistic role of the Patrol Officer consists in helping the indigenous culture come to terms with this startling entry into history and the awesome backlog of history that remains to be negotiated: O'Loughlin views himself as "trying to make the whole historical process that's caught up with them a little less painful for them." (p. 148)

Papua New Guinea's "entry into history," in this Hegelian schema, literally takes place in the moment when the League of Nations deems the country to be a Mandated Territory, that is, a country placed under the colonial administration of Australia, whose role will be to guide the dependent nation in its inexorable progress towards modernity: "they all had to go forward together," says the narrator, "or they would go backwards." (p. 334) And, as is dramatized in another kiap narrative, the possibility of going backwards, as an attempt to disengage oneself from this teleologically driven Hegelian logic of modernity and progress, will only result in death: "they [the Papuans] must suffer... in order to understand that we are caught up in history and must go along with it, or drop out and die quietly."[27] Both these seemingly polarized choices are informed by a type of death for the colonized subject. The agonistic process of being subjected to the colonizing practices of western modernity is mitigated by the ruse of being inscribed by a previously denied historicity allowing the colonized subject to live, paradoxically, by becoming interred in the logos of the colonizer. From this position, the colonized subject will reflect back to the narcissistic colonizer poor copies that never quite measure up to the western models: "Excluding the extensive tracts of Western Papua which remain virtually *terra incognita*," writes Captain Frank Hurley in *Pearls and Savages*, "where the native population is slowly coming under the influence of the [Australian] Administration [it] gradually, through a process of passive subjugation, is passing from crude barbarity into a state of *pseudo-civilization*."[28] This process of passive subjugation through which the indigene must pass effectuates the violence of western colonial law in the name of a triumphant because instrumental reason. This instrumental reason demands passivity as it attempts to envelop the alterity of the indigene and to transmute it into a pseudo-image of the colonizer.

As I argue elsewhere, however, the heterotopic space which is opened up by this slippage between bad indigenous copies and their western models generates the possibility for instances of indigenous agency.[29] In such instances, the indigene dissimulates western codes and models and thereby opens up that equivocal interspace occupied by the logic of the pseudo; in this interspace, the imposture of western colonial law is reflected back in the mocking forms of indigenous "pseudo-civilization." These indigenous pseudo-copies escape the calculations and the logic of the colonizer, even as they perform the imposed normative imperatives in order to alleviate the colonizer's rationalized violence. These dissimulative indigenous forms put to play the Nietzschean axiom recognizing "untruth as a condition of life" — as "life-promoting, life-preserving" in the face of pain and suffering.[30]

1 *See* Joseph Pugliese, "Parasiting 'Post'-Colonialism: On the (Im)Possibility of a Disappropriative Practice," *Southern Review*, Special Issue: Framing (Post-Colonial) Cultures (1995).

2 *Compare* Richard Weisberg, "The Law In and As Literature," *The Comparative Perspective on Literature*, Koelb and Noakes, eds. (Ithaca: Cornell University Press, 1988), pp. 221-232.

3 This contemporary sanitization of Nietzsche was critically examined, from a variety of different positions, by David Haber, J. C. Smith, Steven Taubeneck, Richard Weisberg and myself during the discussion devoted to Nietzsche and the Law.

4 Friedrich Nietzsche, *Twilight of the Idols*, R. J. Hollingdale, trans. (London: Penguin, 1990), XI, 18 ("On the Subject of 'Intellectual Conscience'").

5 Friedrich Nietzsche, "On Truth and Lying in an Extra-Moral Sense," *Friedrich Nietzsche on Rhetoric and Language*, Sander L. Gilman, Carole Blair and David J. Parent, eds. and trans. (New York and Oxford: Oxford University Press, 1989), pp. 247-248.

6 Peter G. Sack, *Land Between Two Laws* (Canberra: Australian National University Press, 1973), p. 18.

7 *See* Joseph Pugliese, "Embodied Economies of Colonialism and Desire in Hegel's Empire of Reason," 4 *Social Semiotics* 163 (1994).

8 Edward P. Wolfers, *Race Relations and Colonial Rule in Papua New Guinea* (Sydney: Australia and New Zealand Book Company, 1975), p. 4. *See also* D. R. C. Chalmers and A. H. Paliwala, *An Introduction to the Law in Papua New Guinea* (North Ryde: The Law Book Company, 1984); and B. J. Brown, ed., *Fashion of Law in New Guinea* (Sydney: Butterworths, 1969).

9 Dudley McCarthy, *The Fate of O'Loughlin* (Sydney: McGraw-Hill Book Company, 1979), text on dust-jacket. All further references will be to this edition. I am grateful to Paul Sharrad for bringing this and the Maslyn Williams text to my attention.

10 This is something I examine in detail in "Mandatory Colonialism: The Law and Colonial Regimes," work in progress.

11 For a detailed discussion of the colonial dimensions of this Hegelian series, *see* Pugliese, "Embodied Economies," *supra* note 7.

12 Friedrich Nietzsche, *Daybreak: Thoughts on the Prejudices of Morality*, R. J. Hollingdale, trans. (Cambridge: Cambridge University Press, 1989), I, 1.

13 *See* Jacques Derrida, "The Chain of Supplements," *Of Grammatology*, Gayatri Chakravorty Spivak, trans. (Baltimore: Johns Hopkins University Press, 1976), p. 157.

14 Friedrich Nietzsche, *The Will To Power*, Walter Kaufmann, trans. (New York: Vintage, 1968), III, 514.

15 Indeed, even as I write, the Australian steel and mining giant, BHP, is mobilizing to push through legislation, prepared by BHP lawyers, which would effectively compromise the sovereignty of the Papua New Guinea government and encroach on human rights by making it "a criminal offense, punishable by fines of up to K100,000, with a daily fine of K10,000, to take legal action to seek compensation" for the pollution and environmental devastation caused by its operations at the Ok Tedi mine in Papua New Guinea. Regardless of the fact that Papua New Guinea achieved Independence in 1975, the rule

of colonial law, and its imbrication with expropriative economic regimes, is ongoing. See Cameron Forbes, "Ok Tedi law plan under fire," *The Australian*, 30 August 1995.

16 Friedrich Nietzsche, *On the Genealogy of Morals*, Carol Diethe, trans. (Cambridge: Cambridge University Press, 1994), II, 5 and 6. All further references will be to this edition and will consist of an abbreviation of the title, followed by chapter number and the section number.

17 Keith Bushell, *Papuan Epic* (London: Seeley, Service and Co., 1936), p. 273.

18 Franz Kafka, "In the Penal Colony," *Stories 1904-1924*, J. A. Underwood, trans. (London: Macdonald and Co., 1981), pp. 147-178.

19 Michel Foucault, "Lecture II: 14 January 1976," *Power/Knowledge*, Colin Gordon, Leo Marshall, John Mepham, Kate Soper, trans. (New York: Pantheon, 1980), p. 96.

20 *See* Richard Scaglion, ed., *Customary Law in Papua New Guinea: A Melanesian View* (Papua New Guinea: Law Reform Commission of Papua New Guinea, 1983).

21 For a detailed discussion of the colonial implications of Hegel's The Philosophy of History, *see* Pugliese, "Embodied Economies," *supra* note 7.

22 On the politics of the colonial ethnographer and the "native informant," *see* Gayatri Chakravorty Spivak, "Entering the Third World," *In Other Worlds* (New York and London: Methuen, 1987), pp. 179-268; and Trinh T. Minh-ha, "The Language of Nativism: Anthropology as a Scientific Conversation of Man with Man," *Woman Native Other* (Bloomington: Indiana University Press, 1989), pp. 47-78 and 79-118.

23 Emmanuel Levinas, "The Old and the New," *Time and the Other*, Richard A. Cohen, trans. (Pittsburgh: Duquesne University Press, 1987), p. 128.

24 For a dramatic account of the role of the Village Book and the conflict between kiaps and Papuan villagers, see John Waiko, "The Unexpected Hawk," *Through Melanesian Eyes*, Ganga Powell, ed. (South Melbourne, 1987), 51-66..

25 Levinas, *Time and the Other*, *supra* note 23 at 97-99.

26 Pugliese, "Embodied Economies," *supra* note 7 at 170-176.

27 Maslyn Williams, *The Far Side of the Sky* (Melbourne: F. W. Chesire, 1967), p. 24.

28 Captain Frank Hurley, *Pearls and Savages: Adventures in the Air, on the Land and Sea in New Guinea* (New York and London: Putman, 1925), p. 4. [Emphasis added.]

29 "Mandatory Colonialism," work in progress.

30 Friedrich Nietzsche, *Beyond Good and Evil: Prelude to a Philosophy of the Future*, Walter Kaufmann, trans. (New York: Vintage, 1996), I, 4.

[16]

SPECTERS OF NIETZSCHE: POTENTIAL FUTURES FOR THE CONCEPT OF THE POLITICAL IN AGAMBEN AND DERRIDA

Adam Thurschwell[1]

> *The community I am speaking of is that which will exist virtually from the fact of Nietzsche's existence (which is the demand for such a community) and that each of Nietzsche's readers undoes by shirking—that is, by not solving the posed enigma (by not even reading it).*
>
> —Georges Bataille[2]

I take it that a major premise of this conference is that we legal scholars are today inheritors, in one form or another, of Nietzsche's legacy to thought. However one evaluates or interprets it, that proposition seems indisputable. Whether one

---

[1] "Every written work can be regarded as the prologue (or rather, the broken cast) of a work never penned . . ."—Giorgio Agamben, echoing, as always, Walter Benjamin. GIORGIO AGAMBEN, INFANCY AND HISTORY: THE DESTRUCTION OF EXPERIENCE 3 (Liz Heron trans., Verso 1993) (1978). *See* WALTER BENJAMIN, *One-Way Street*, *in* WALTER BENJAMIN: SELECTED WRITINGS VOLUME 1 1913-1926 (Marcus Bullock & Michael W. Jennings eds., Harvard Univ. Press 1996) (1928) [hereinafter BENJAMIN, SELECTED WRITINGS] ("The work is the death mask of its conception."). For this broken cast, much gratitude to Peter Fitzpatrick, who first started me down this particular path and without whose generous willingness to play interlocutor to my halting preliminary attempts to articulate these ideas this paper would never have come to be. Thanks also to Peter Goodrich for his editorial advice, and unspeakable thanks to Catherine Robertson for her critical interventions and patience. The "work never penned" I dedicate to Drucilla Cornell. This is an abbreviated version of a longer work in progress, which can be found at http://www.law.csuohio.edu/faculty/thurschwell/publications.html. Earlier versions of different sections were presented at the 2001 and 2002 Law, Culture & the Humanities Conferences in Austin, Texas and Philadelphia, Pennsylvania, and the 2001 British Critical Legal Conference in Canterbury, England. Much of the work was supported by a faculty summer grant from the Cleveland-Marshall Fund. Needless to say, all errors are mine alone.

[2] JACQUES DERRIDA, POLITICS OF FRIENDSHIP 47 (George Collins trans., Verso 1997) (1994) (quoting MAURICE BLANCHOT, THE UNAVOWABLE COMMUNITY (Pierre Joris trans., Station Hill Press 1988) (1983)) [hereinafter DERRIDA, POLITICS OF FRIENDSHIP].

deplores or rejects this legacy,[3] embraces it,[4] or—most frequently remains in its grip without any conscious awareness of doing so,[5] we are all, legal scholars along with so many others, haunted by Nietzsche's multiple specters. For, as Jacques Derrida reminds us in the book to which my title alludes, "[o]ne never inherits without coming to terms with [*s'expliquer avec*] some specter," and therefore, he adds, "with more than one specter."[6]

Perhaps, someday, the community to which Bataille alludes in my epigraph will come to include more of us in the American legal academy. Despite his influence on the *zeitgeist*, Nietzsche's legacies to political and legal thought remain all but unexplored in the American legal academy as a basis for comprehending the dilemmas that today confront Anglo-American legal and political philosophy at every turn. Note that I speak here of legacies and not of Nietzsche himself—the challenge that Bataille throws down is to constitute a community of readers, not of followers. To set up Nietzsche's texts as authoritative and immune from interpretation, critique, and, of course, transvaluation would be contrary not only to Bataille's suggestion but Nietzsche's own teachings. It is in that spirit that I focus here not on Nietzsche's texts themselves, but on the Nietzschean specters in the political and jurisprudential writings of two of his contemporary philosophical inheritors, Jacques Derrida and the Italian philosopher Giorgio Agamben. Their two different Nietzschean registers, so close to each other and at the same time so opposed, permits a highly enlightening triangulation of the present situation of Anglo-American legal and political philosophy despite the apparent distance between these traditions and their philosophical vocabularies and topoi. Thus, although my approach here to Agamben and Derrida's work consists primarily of comparative textual analysis, my (perhaps utopian) subtext is the possibility of encouraging such a larger

[3] *See, e.g.*, Paul Schiff Berman, *Telling a Less Suspicious Story: Notes Toward a Non-Skeptical Approach to Legal/Cultural Analysis*, 13 YALE J.L. & HUMAN. 95 (2001); John Finnis, *On the Incoherence of Legal Positivism*, 75 NOTRE DAME L. REV. 1597 (2000).

[4] *See, e.g.*, Richard A. Posner, *Past-Dependency, Pragmatism, and Critique of History in Adjudication and Legal Scholarship*, 67 U. CHI. L. REV. 573 (2000).

[5] *See, e.g.*, Finnis, *supra* note 3, at 1597:

> Today the promoters of this radical kind of "exclusive positivism" are the followers, conscious or unconscious, of Nietzsche or of others who like him reduce ethics and normative political or legal theory to a search for the "genealogy," the historical (perhaps partly or wholly physiological) sources of ethical, political, or legal standards.

See also Philippe Nonet, *What Is Positive Law?*, 100 YALE L.J. 667 (1990).

[6] JACQUES DERRIDA, SPECTERS OF MARX: THE STATE OF THE DEBT, THE WORK OF MOURNING, AND THE NEW INTERNATIONAL 21 (Peggy Kamuf trans., Routledge 1994) (1993) [hereinafter DERRIDA, SPECTERS OF MARX].

constructive engagement.

In the wake of the disillusioning communitarian disasters of fascism and Soviet Communism, the attempt to articulate a post-metaphysical conception of politics and community—a "community of those who have no community," in Georges Bataille's phrase—has been a theme of much post-war Continental political thought. Broadly construed, both Derrida and Agamben's political writings fall within this tradition, which defines the common philosophical field in which other contemporary Continental political thinkers of the left now toil as well.[7] If this political theory has appeared incomprehensible and utopian to most American legal theorists, that is at least in part because of the absence of both the extreme rightist and leftist communitarian traditions that have so tempted and bedeviled European history. As the complementary pathologies of the "middle way" of neo-liberalism have become increasingly apparent, however, on the domestic and international cultural, political and economic fronts, Anglo-American jurisprudes and political philosophers have themselves increasingly looked to various communitarian perspectives for potential cures. Apart from their intrinsic value, it is the manner in which these contemporary Continental thinkers help interrupt the endlessly revolving circle of the liberalism-communitarianism debates that

[7] Derrida has noted his resistance to using the term "community." *See* DERRIDA, POLITICS OF FRIENDSHIP, *supra* note 2, at 304-05: "I was wondering why the word 'community' (avowable or unavowable, inoperative or not)—why I have never been able to write it, on my own initiative and in my name, as it were." *Id.* Derrida here alludes to the work of Maurice Blanchot and Jean Luc Nancy, two others who, like Agamben, have attempted recently to articulate post-metaphysical conceptions of political community. *See* MAURICE BLANCHOT, THE UNAVOWABLE COMMUNITY (Pierre Joris trans., Station Hill Press 1988) (1983); JEAN-LUC NANCY, THE INOPERATIVE COMMUNITY (Peter Connor ed., Peter Connor et al. trans., 1991). *See also* DERRIDA, POLITICS OF FRIENDSHIP, *supra* note 2, at 46-48 (placing these works in the general context of his reading of Nietzsche). Derrida goes on to suggest that his "reticence" with respect to the term "community" is "fundamentally the essential part of the disquiet which inspires this book. . . ." *Id.* at 305. Yet, if *Politics of Friendship* is undoubtedly a relentless interrogation of the "commonality" that would seem to have to underwrite any form of "community," it is also the case that this interrogation itself is carried out in the name of a political ideal that resonates with our own form of political community—the notion of a "*democracy* to come [*une démocratie à venir*]." *Id.* at 104, 306. Although Derrida shares the general historico-philosophical problematic confronting all of these thinkers—Blanchot, Nancy, and Agamben, among others—as I argue below, what crucially distinguishes him from Agamben and Nancy is a certain tilt toward an understanding of the problem of politics in ethical rather than ontological terms. Blanchot's position is another matter. For an argument that he falls on the ethics side of the ethics/ontology divide, see Robert Bernasconi, *On Deconstructing Nostalgia for Community within the West: The Debate between Nancy and Blanchot*, 23 RES. IN PHENOMENOLOGY 3 (1993). As is apparent, I am leaving out of this discussion entirely any reference to European neo-liberalism, which is another political-philosophical reaction to this historical situation.

Anglo-American philosophers ignore at their own expense.

Derrida is the better known of the two within the American legal academy, but Agamben's name-recognition is growing here as his work is translated into English. Like Derrida, Agamben is not primarily a political or legal philosopher (although he does have a degree in law). Agamben only began to write about politics and law after prolonged engagements with phenomenology, the philosophy of language, medieval scholasticism, aesthetics and literature.[8] Both Derrida and Agamben, moreover, are also what might be called "left-Heideggerians" whose recent political-philosophical[9] work has been significantly influenced by Walter Benjamin (albeit much more profoundly in Agamben's case than for Derrida). Their writings intersect at a number of crucial issues and texts, sometimes lightly touching, sometimes crossing at the same point, going, so to speak, in different directions, and thus often resembling each other without, however, there being an actual identity of viewpoint. The differences, although sometimes subtle, are real. Indeed, as I explain below, Agamben has formulated his own thought in part through a critique of Derrida's position. My overarching thesis is that, subtle though these intersections and differences may be, they reveal two incompatible yet inextricable axes of contemporary political thought, blueprints of the competing visions of the political between which, for the foreseeable future, philosophical thinking will have to choose (which is not to foreclose entirely *other* conceptions of politics arriving from the unforeseeable future, the unforeseeable future being in Derrida's account, as we will see, the only future worthy of the name). In this paper I hope to show that these axes can be articulated around two ways of inheriting Nietzsche's legacy—two

---

[8] These engagements, it ought to be said, make for a writing style that is quite spectacular in its encyclopedic erudition and range of reference, as well as in its frequent arc-lamp bursts of insight. *See, e.g.*, GIORGIO AGAMBEN, LANGUAGE AND DEATH: *THE PLACE OF NEGATIVITY* (Karen E. Pinkus & Michael Hardt trans., Univ. of Minn. Press 1991) (1982) [hereinafter AGAMBEN, LANGUAGE AND DEATH]; AGAMBEN, *supra* note 1; GIORGIO AGAMBEN, THE END OF THE POEM: STUDIES IN POETICS (Daniel Heller-Roazen trans., Stanford U. Press 1999) (1996).

[9] "Political philosophy" is a term that I use with some trepidation, conscious that with respect to both writers, as we will see, their "political" philosophy is difficult to separate from their other philosophy, as indeed, at least with respect to Agamben, his politics is difficult to separate from philosophy *tout court*. Derrida, as might be expected, has in particular complicated in advance any attempt to thematize his work in terms of "political philosophy." *See* Jacques Derrida, *Marx & Sons*, *in* GHOSTLY DEMARCATIONS: A SYMPOSIUM ON JACQUES DERRIDA'S *SPECTERS OF MARX* 214-17 (Michael Sprinker ed., 1999) [hereinafter Derrida, *Marx & Sons*]. Despite these warning signs, I am nevertheless (to quote Derrida out of context) "rushing headlong into, the defeat to which, as another French expression has it, my discourse is doomed [*est promis*]." *Id.* at 217 (emphases omitted).

forms of his specter.

Indeed to inherit is also to choose, Derrida tells us, just because inheritances are always multiple and contradictory.[10] It is in that spirit of ineluctable decision that I argue here on behalf of Derrida's reconstruction of the political as a secularized messianic demand for a "democracy to come" over Agamben's version of political messianism, which remains too much in Heidegger's shadow and takes the real possibility of a political-ontological eschatology a bit too seriously for my taste. In what follows I attempt to provide a philosophical basis for that choice.

In particular, I focus on two points of (near) intersection between the two: the highly elaborated notions of "possibility" or "potential" that both Agamben and Derrida locate at the base of their analyses of the political and the ethical, and their competing notions of political messianism. The significance of this difference-within-similarity lies in their fundamentally different approaches to the classical question of the relationship between ethics and politics. To articulate the distinction much too crudely (I will complicate it below), Agamben and Derrida understand the category of ethics in two different and (at least *ab initio*) opposed ways.

Agamben conceives of "possibility" in terms of Heidegger's interpretation of human *Dasein* as "potential" being, in the sense of the being "'whose own Being is at issue in its very Being.'"[11] This is for Agamben (as it is for Heidegger) at the same time a concept of ethics: ethics as "*ēthos*," as "ethical way"[12] in the sense given to that term by Heidegger, i.e., as the thought of the "abode of man" in his (or her) relationship to Being.[13] This ontological conception of ethics in turn determines a politics whose goal is the full "actualization" of humanity's potential, or to be more precise, a complete overcoming of the distinction between "potential" and "actuality" in what Agamben calls a social "form of life" that is lived purely and simply for its own sake.[14]

---

[10] *See* DERRIDA, SPECTERS OF MARX, *supra* note 6, at 16.

[11] GIORGIO AGAMBEN, HOMO SACER: *SOVEREIGN POWER AND BARE LIFE* 153 (Daniel Heller-Roazen trans., Stanford Univ. Press 1998) (1995) [hereinafter AGAMBEN, HOMO SACER]. *See also* GIORGIO AGAMBEN, *The Passion of Facticity*, *in* POTENTIALITIES: COLLECTED ESSAYS IN PHILOSOPHY 200 (Daniel Heller-Roazen ed. & trans., 1999).

[12] AGAMBEN, *supra* note 1, at 9-10.

[13] *See* MARTIN HEIDEGGER, *Letter on Humanism*, *in* BASIC WRITINGS FROM *BEING AND TIME (1927)* TO *THE TASK OF THINKING* (1964) 235 (David Farrell Krell ed., 1977).

[14] AGAMBEN, HOMO SACER, *supra* note 11, at 188. *See also* GIORGIO AGAMBEN, *Form-of-Life*, *in* MEANS WITHOUT END: NOTES ON POLITICS 9 (Sandra Buckley et al. eds., Vincenzo Binetti & Cesare Casarino trans., Univ. of Minn. Press 2000) (1996) [hereinafter AGAMBEN, *Form-of-Life*].

Derrida, by contrast, displaces the concept of "possibility" onto Nietzsche's notion of the "dangerous perhaps," invoked at the beginning of *Beyond Good and Evil.* There Nietzsche appeals to the new philosophers of the "dangerous perhaps" who reject the metaphysical values of truth, the Good, knowledge, and the binary logic of judgment in general.[15] In Derrida's hands, this "dangerous perhaps" becomes not only the condition of the "undecidability" for which he is best-known in the American legal academy, but, far more important, the basis of ethics—or to be more precise, the condition of possibility of the ethical relationship in general. For Derrida, however, "ethics"—in contrast to Agamben (and Heidegger)—denotes first a relationship of responsibility to the Other, an understanding that he inherits from Emmanuel Levinas. This understanding also derives, as we will see, from his deconstructive reading of Nietzsche.

After briefly discussing these different conceptions of ethics, I then examine more closely the relationships of these different ethical conceptions to the competing notions of politics that they support. For both Agamben and Derrida, there is an absolute break or hiatus between the ethical as such and any politics that takes a statist or juridical form. The notion of such a conceptual break or hiatus is hardly unique to them or to the traditions in which they write; indeed, the broken continuity between the ethical and the political is the abyss around which all modern political philosophies, including those of Anglo-American jurisprudence in both its liberal and communitarian forms, continue to revolve.[16] What is unique, however, is the manner in which both Agamben and Derrida explicitly employ the religious vocabulary of messianism in articulating this break and how it may be crossed, overcome, or experienced, and so become a basis for political action. I attempt to specify the implications of Agamben and Derrida's political philosophies by focusing on their two different notions of political messianism. For Agamben, his notion

---

[15] Note that I have substituted the English "perhaps" for "maybe" in Kauffman's translation in the text, *infra*, for the sake of consistency with Derrida's English translations. DERRIDA, POLITICS OF FRIENDSHIP, *supra* note 2, at 28-29. *See* FRIEDRICH NIETZSCHE, *On The Prejudices of Philosophers*, *in* BEYOND GOOD AND EVIL: PRELUDE TO A PHILOSOPHY OF THE FUTURE (Walter Kaufmann trans., Vintage Books 1989) (1966):

> But who has the will to concern himself with such dangerous maybes? For that, one really has to wait for the advent of a new species of philosophers, such as have somehow another and converse taste and propensity from those we have known so far—philosophers of the dangerous "maybe" in every sense.

Id. para. 2, at 10-11.

[16] *See, e.g.*, Adam Thurschwell, *Friendship, Tradition, Democracy: Two Readings of Aristotle*, 5(2) LAW TEXT CULTURE 271, 288 (Penny Pether & Austin Sarat eds., 2001).

of the political calls for a radical overcoming of every form of sovereignty and law—political philosophy as "thinking the end of the State and the end of history together and mobilizing the one against the other," as he puts it.[17] Derrida's notion of messianism, on the other hand, leads to a conception of politics determined by an ethical demand for justice and responsibility to others.

Ultimately, as already indicated, I hope to show that Derrida's conception better serves the needs of our present politico-juridical philosophical situation than does Agamben's fundamentally romantic approach. But I also hope to show in the final section of the paper that this is not a choice that can be made with the certainty or confidence that would allow one to repose in the kind of theoretical "good conscience" that Nietzsche so despised. Relatedly, I conclude with some observations on the necessary role of faith and religion in Derrida's political thought. This will return us one last time to Nietzsche—in particular, to his mocking incredulity at that "stroke of genius called *Christianity*" in *On the Genealogy of Morals*—and to Derrida's own lack of faith in that incredulity.[18]

I.

Derrida's inheritance of Nietzsche's thought is marked by a paradox. Michel Haar has shown the irreducible inconsistency of Derrida's most important insights with many of Nietzsche's substantive views—Nietzsche's vitalism, his naturalism, his privileging of the musicality of the voice over the secondary status of the written, and so on. Yet from his earliest writings Derrida has returned to Nietzsche again and again, as a touchstone of his own thought and more: "a screen, a forerunner and sometimes a mouthpiece," as Haar puts it.[19] That paradoxical relationship to Nietzsche (if paradox is the correct word for it) has continued through Derrida's increasingly Levinas-inflected, political, ethical and jurisprudential writings of the 1990s, in which Nietzschean motifs and engagements play a prominent role—from the "dangerous perhaps" that is the critical leitmotif of *Politics of*

---

[17] AGAMBEN, HOMO SACER, *supra* note 11, at 60.

[18] JACQUES DERRIDA, THE GIFT OF DEATH 112-15 (David Wills trans., Univ. of Chicago Press 1995) (1992) (discussing FRIEDRICH NIETZSCHE, *On the Genealogy of Morals*, *in* ON THE GENEALOGY OF MORALS & ECCE HOMO (Walter Kaufmann ed., Walter Kaufmann & R. J. Hollingdale trans., Vintage Books 1989) (1967)).

[19] Michel Haar, *The Play of Nietzsche in Derrida*, *in* DERRIDA: *A CRITICAL READER* 52, 53 (David Wood ed., Will McNeill trans., 1992).

Friendship, to the concluding appeal to the "'scholar' of the future, the 'intellectual' of tomorrow" in *Specters of Marx*,[20] to the engagement with *On the Genealogy of Morals* at the end of *The Gift of Death*.[21]

In each case, these motifs and engagements are deployed in support of a thematics of politics as the demand for justice and hyperbolic responsibility for the Other, a respect for and responsibility to the specters of the past, a quasi-religious faith beyond subjective knowledge or will, and an emphatic conception of "democracy to come"—in general, a conception of politics as driven by an ethical impulse of messianic intensity. These thematics could hardly be less Nietzschean, at least according to his conventional interpretation. But of course each of Derrida's heterodox interpretations is also thoroughly orthodox—at least by the standard of Nietzsche's own injunctions—insofar as they involve a "transvaluation" of the conventionally Nietzschean values. One could thus say that Derrida radically displaces Nietzsche's project while remaining faithful to his "spirit."[22] Although I will return in some detail to these Nietzschean motifs in the next section, for now, I want to highlight two aspects of Derrida's political thought for purposes of comparison with Agamben's. First, for Derrida, there is a necessary and unbridgeable hiatus between the ethical relationship, conceived, in Levinasian terms, as absolute responsibility for the Other, and any given form of politics. This is so because ethical responsibility (in

---

[20] DERRIDA, SPECTERS OF MARX, *supra* note 6, at 176. Again, the allusion is to the "philosophers of the future" invoked by Nietzsche. *See* NIETZSCHE, *supra* note 15, para. 2, at 10-11; para. 44, at 56.

[21] DERRIDA, GIFT OF DEATH, *supra* note 18, at 112-15 (discussing the works of Friedrich Nietzsche).

[22] As Derrida himself puts it in *Politics of Friendship*, the most overtly "Nietzschean" of his political works: "Of course, we must quickly inform the reader that we will not follow Nietzsche here. Not in any simple manner . . . . He never demanded such a thing anyway without freeing us, in the same move, from his very demand, following the well-known paradoxes of any fidelity." DERRIDA, POLITICS OF FRIENDSHIP, *supra* note 2, at 33. *See also* Jacques Derrida, *On Responsibility*, *in Responsibilities of Deconstruction*, PLI - WARWICK J. OF PHIL. 19, 22 (Jonathon Dronsfield & Nick Midgley eds., 1997) (interview with Jonathon Dronsfield, Nick Midgley, and Adrian Wilding) ("An heir has to affirm, to reaffirm the heritage, and to reaffirm in the Nietzschean sense doesn't simply mean to repeat . . . .") .

Derrida distinguishes "spirit" from the "specter" on the basis of a certain "phenomenalization" that attends the specter but not the spirit as such. *See* DERRIDA, SPECTERS OF MARX, *supra* note 6, at 7, 135. The question of whether such a "phenomenalization" or "ontologization" can be avoided, of whether one can act rigorously and purely in the "spirit" of Nietzsche, or of Marx—or of Derrida, for that matter, even if one *is* Derrida—without falling into such an "ontologization" is a question that I address elsewhere. *See* "Specters and Scholars: Derrida and the Tragedy of Political Thought," *available at* http://www.law.csuohio.edu/faculty/thurschwell/spectres.pdf.

Levinas' formulation, at least) entails a responsibility that is "absolute" and infinite in the sense that it is *singular*, owed absolutely and uniquely to each singular Other in each unique relationship. The concept of the "political," conversely, necessarily entails the consideration of all those multiple "Others" who must be taken account of—whose interests must be balanced, whose preferences or votes must be counted or otherwise aggregated—and thus requires a form of responsibility that must be *calculable*, rather than infinite or absolute. What this means is that, on one hand, there is an absolute gulf between ethical responsibility and political responsibility, insofar as "I cannot respond to the call, the request, the obligation, or even the love of another without sacrificing the other other, the other others." On the other hand, these "other others" cannot be distinguished from the singular Other of the ethical relationship since "[e]very other (one) is every (bit) other [*tout autre est tout autre*], every one else is completely and wholly other" as well, and the same singular and infinite responsibility owed to the "original" Other is owed to each singular "other other" as well.[23]

From the outset, then, ethical responsibility renders political responsibility—and the "calculation" that it entails—both impossible and necessary. What issues from this paradox, according to Derrida, is an absolute ethical demand that we nevertheless attempt to perform the required political calculations—"incalculable justice [that is, the infinite responsibility of the ethical relationship] *requires* us to calculate."[24] All the while, we must recognize that the results of these calculations will not themselves be "just" precisely to the extent that they are the result of a calculation, an accounting, a balancing or accommodation of interests, rather than the discharge of a singular and infinite responsibility. Justice never is or can be "present" in any given political program or platform, whether realized in practice or represented as an ideal. It remains suspended in the "to come" of a future that never arrives, and therefore can never become the subject of knowledge or representation, because no calculation can do justice to the infinite responsibility that genuine justice demands.[25]

---

[23] DERRIDA, GIFT OF DEATH, *supra* note 18, at 68 (emphasis omitted). Indeed, as many have noted, the "other others" are implicated in Levinas' ethical relationship from the outset. *See, e.g.*, Robert Bernasconi, *The Third Party. Levinas on the Intersection of the Ethical and the Political*, 30 J. BRIT. SOC'Y PHENOMENOLOGY 76-87 (1999).

[24] Jacques Derrida, *Force of Law: The "Mystical Foundation of Authority"*, *in* DECONSTRUCTION AND THE POSSIBILITY OF JUSTICE 28 (Drucilla Cornell et al. eds., 1992) [hereinafter Derrida, *Force of Law*].

[25] *Id.* at 27.

Thus, as Derrida puts it, "[e]thics enjoins a politics and a law . . . . [b]ut the political or juridical *content* that is thus assigned remains undetermined, still to be determined beyond knowledge, beyond all presentation, all concepts . . . ."[26] No determinate content issues from the ethical demand because ethics, in Derrida's (and Levinas's) sense, is non-normative. To derive a legal or political rule of decision from one's ethical responsibility would be, paradoxically, to displace that responsibility onto a "calculation," and thus would itself be unethical precisely to the extent that it relieves one of further responsibility for the decision in any given case. Ethics therefore demands a legal/political decision that can only rest on something like a "mystical foundation,"[27] since such a decision cannot be founded on any determinable rules, reasons or values without abandoning its claim to ethical status. Accordingly, the legal/political decision can only be "determined beyond knowledge, beyond all presentation, all concepts"[28]—which is to say, determined on the basis of something that resembles pure faith.

And in fact, from *Force of Law* through his most recent political and ethical writings, the categories of political thought have been linked to religious categories as well (or, to be more precise, in Derrida's words, to the categories of that philosophical thought "that 'repeats' the possibility of religion without religion").[29] Most apropos for my purposes here, Derrida describes the political decision in terms of a certain "political messianism." This terminology is not gratuitous rhetoric but the logical outcome of his schema: "the messianic" would appear to be an appropriate term of art insofar as politics has the task of crossing the uncrossable divide between the singular and infinite ethical responsibility to the Other and concrete political accountability to "all the other others" on the basis of quasi-religious faith rather than conceptual or calculative reason. But it must be kept in mind that this is a "messianism" conceived in the Levinasian ethical terms discussed above and not a religious doctrine that predicts the coming of a Messiah—it is a "messianic

[26] JACQUES DERRIDA, ADIEU TO EMMANUEL LEVINAS 115 (Pascale-Anne Brault & Michael Naas trans., Stanford Univ. Press 1999) (1997) (footnote omitted) [hereinafter DERRIDA, ADIEU TO EMMANUEL LEVINAS].

[27] *Cf.* Derrida, *Force of Law*, *supra* note 24.

[28] DERRIDA, ADIEU TO EMMANUEL LEVINAS, *supra* note 26, at 115.

[29] DERRIDA, GIFT OF DEATH, *supra* note 18, at 49. For a discussion of the meaning of this phrase in the context of Levinas's thought, see Thurschwell, *supra* note 16, at 319 n.24. For a discussion of the significance of the formula "X without X" in Derrida's thought more generally, see DERRIDA, POLITICS OF FRIENDSHIP, *supra* note 2, at 42.

without messianism."[30]

Within the sphere of political justice, that "messianic without messianism" issues in an ideal that Derrida calls "*une démocratie á venir*"—a democracy-to-come.[31] In *Politics of Friendship* Derrida develops this notion initially from a reading of Nietzsche's thought in *Beyond Good and Evil* of those "free spirits" and "philosophers of the future" who are (or will be) "friends of solitude . . . friends of an entirely different kind, inaccessible friends, friends who are alone because they are incomparable and without common measure, reciprocity or equality . . . [and] [w]ithout a familial bond."[32] By reconceiving political "friendship" in terms of "solitude," Derrida is trying to save the thought of the political-as-ethical in general, and the "dominant concept" of democracy in particular—based as it is on the calculative counting of equally-weighted votes or preferences—by imagining a union of the calculative model with the intensity and responsibility to singularity represented by Levinas's ethics.[33] Thus, his political thought is driven by a thought of ethical singularity and responsibility that would simultaneously bind the political community while purging it of any trace of the identity politics that have deformed every concept of the political up to now (including the identity politics of "State and nation" as well as those of ethnicity, culture and race that have received the most attention in the American legal academy). That the realization of such a community *in actuality* is foreclosed in advance by the aporetic relationship between the ethical and the political discussed above—the unbridgeable hiatus between singular and infinite ethical responsibility on one hand and the calculation required by finite politics on the other—merely displaces it into the future and confirms the inherent *ávenir* of political justice.

Second, in Derrida's later political work, the notion of the "specter" (or "ghost") has become a, if not the, privileged signifier of this perverse temporality of political justice. It is a figure that encompasses many of his earlier themes and obsessions (the "work of mourning," "survival that is reducible neither to living nor dying," the "economy of debt and gift," and "iterability," among

[30] DERRIDA, SPECTERS OF MARX, *supra* note 6, at 73. *See id.* at 89 (defining his notion of "*messianic* affirmation" as "a certain experience of the promise that one can try to liberate from any dogmatics and even from any metaphysico-religious determination, from any *messianism*").

[31] *See* DERRIDA, POLITICS OF FRIENDSHIP, *supra* note 2, at 306.

[32] *Id.* at 35. *See* NIETZSCHE, *supra* note 15, at para. 44, at 56 (addressing himself to those "born, sworn, jealous friends of *solitude*, of our own most profound, most midnightly, most middaily solitude").

[33] *See* DERRIDA, POLITICS OF FRIENDSHIP, *supra* note 2, at 106.

others)—indeed, he says that "the logic of spectrality [is] inseparable from the idea of the idea (of the idealization of ideality as effect of iterability), inseparable from the very motif (let us not say the 'idea') of deconstruction."[34] Moreover, because the specter represents a certain undecidability between the living and the dead, the present and the absent, and the imagined and the actual,[35] it also figures that "out-of-jointness" that characterizes Derrida's view of temporality and historicity (a figure embodied, in *Specters of Marx*, by Derrida's philosophical readings of the scenes in *Hamlet* in which the ghost of Hamlet's father appears). Specters signify both an event of the past and of the future[36] and indeed represent the inextricable confusion of the temporal dimensions of past event and future-to-come[37]—without, however, having any determinable "living presence" in the present moment of perception. Indeed, insofar as the specter/revenant "begins by coming back," it exists, it "is," as nothing other than the promise of its own future return. The law of spectrality thus "dislodges any present out of its contemporaneity with itself," and thereby determines "historicity as future-to-come."[38] In sum, the "specter" is among the most encompassing and potent of the many terms—"iterability," "*différance*," and so on—that Derrida has used as the operative figures of deconstruction.

Turning now to Agamben, in a manner in some ways complementary to Derrida's fidelity to the "spirit" of Nietzsche's philosophy, in respect of its *substance* Agamben's political philosophy is even closer to Nietzsche than is Derrida's. I am thinking of Agamben's valorization, in *Homo Sacer* and other works, of a new politics of life as such[39] and the articulation of the question of politics as a question of "power"—a philosophical framework that for Agamben limits the fundamental question of politics to: "Is today a *life of power* available?"[40] "Power" here

---

[34] DERRIDA, SPECTERS OF MARX, *supra* note 6, at 178 n.3.

[35] *See id.* at 11 (the specter belies "the sharp distinction between the real and the unreal, the actual and the inactual, the living and the non-living, being and non-being ('to be or not to be,' in the conventional reading), in the opposition between what is present and what is not, for example in the form of objectivity").

[36] *See id.* at 10 ("it figures *both* a dead man who comes back and a ghost whose expected return repeats itself, again and again").

[37] *See id.* at 11 ("a specter is always a *revenant*" [a synonym for 'specter' in both French and English] and thus "it *begins by coming back*").

[38] *Id.* at 73.

[39] *See* AGAMBEN, HOMO SACER, *supra* note 11, at 188 ("This biopolitical body that is bare life must itself . . . be transformed into the site for the constitution and installation of a form of life that is wholly exhausted in bare life and a *bios* that is only its own *zoē*.").

[40] *See* AGAMBEN, *Form-of-Life*, *supra* note 14, at 8-9 ("The question about the possibility of a nonstatist politics necessarily takes this form: Is today something like a form-of-life, a life for which living itself would be at stake in its own living, possible? Is

translates the Italian *potenza*, power not in the statist sense but in the more general sense of vital force or strength, capacity, or (to use the term that Agamben privileges) "potential."[41] But of course that sense of "power" is perfectly consistent with Agamben's other Nietzschean overtones.

In essence, Agamben's political-philosophical project combines a messianic-political eschatology—"thinking the end of the State and the end of history together and mobilizing the one against the other," as he puts it[42]—with an ontology of human life-as-potential derived primarily from Heidegger, but whose Nietzschean provenance is also unmistakable. Against received notions of legality, sovereignty and the statist politics that accompanies them, which he understands exclusively in terms of the power of death over what he calls "bare life," Agamben opposes a life that is "absolutely immanent,"[43] a "social praxis that, in the end, becomes transparent to itself,"[44] "a wholly profane mystery in which human beings, liberating themselves from all sacredness, communicate to each other their lack of secrets as their most proper gesture."[45]

If these phrases are initially obscure (as they were for me, at least), especially as articulations of a specifically *political* ideal, they perhaps nevertheless evoke an intuitive sense of what Agamben is attempting here. A political "life for which living itself would be at stake in its own living"[46] is a political life in which *nothing else is "at stake" in its own living*—a "coming community" (the title of the book that sets forth and defends Agamben's affirmative political vision in the most detail)[47] that will no longer depend for its meaning on carrying forward the burdens handed down by a mythic past (for example, fidelity to the blood and soil of one's ancestors); or on living up to a supra-individual identity based on national, ethnic, racial or any other categorical characteristic (like Derrida's, Agamben's vision is the antipodes of

today a *life of power* available?").

41 *Id.* at 143 n.1 (Translators' Notes to *Form-of-Life*).

42 AGAMBEN, HOMO SACER, *supra* note 11, at 60.

43 GIORGIO AGAMBEN, *Absolute Immanence*, *in* POTENTIALITIES: COLLECTED ESSAYS IN PHILOSOPHY 220 (Daniel Heller-Roazen ed. & trans., 1999).

44 GIORGIO AGAMBEN, **Se: Hegel's Absolute and Heidegger's* Ereignis, *in* POTENTIALITIES: COLLECTED ESSAYS IN PHILOSOPHY 137 (Daniel Heller-Roazen ed. & trans., 1999) [hereinafter AGAMBEN, *Se].

45 GIORGIO AGAMBEN, *Kommerell, or On Gesture*, *in* POTENTIALITIES: COLLECTED ESSAYS IN PHILOSOPHY 85 (Daniel Heller-Roazen ed. & trans., 1999) [hereinafter AGAMBEN, *Kommerell*].

46 AGAMBEN, *Form-of-Life*, *supra* note 14, at 9.

47 GIORGIO AGAMBEN, THE COMING COMMUNITY (Michael Hardt trans., Univ. of Minnesota Press 1993) (1990) [hereinafter AGAMBEN, COMING COMMUNITY].

any "identity politics"); or on awaiting or bringing about a promised future, whether salvation in its Christian form or a realization of a regime of "human rights" rooted in some understanding of our "common humanity." Rather, it would be a community in which "humans co-belong without any representable condition of belonging," whose sole and paradoxical condition of membership is each singular member's desire "to appropriate belonging itself, its own being-in-language, and thus reject[] all identity and every condition of belonging."[48] Only such a community of naked "belonging" would be freed of every mythic, religious or otherwise metaphysical predicate and presupposition, and in this sense would be an "absolutely immanent" and "wholly profane" community, "liberat[ed] . . . from all sacredness."

The Coming Community and much of Agamben's other recent work is devoted to explaining how such a community, stripped of every commonality traditionally thought to bind communities together, can remain a "community" in any meaningful sense. It thus lies in the same broad tradition of left-Continental thought as Derrida's political writings on the "democracy to come." Like Derrida, moreover, Agamben is driven to employ the vocabulary of messianism in order to resolve an absolute break between the ethical ideal of community that motivates his work and his concept of the political. Furthermore, Agamben, in a manner at least superficially similar to Derrida's notion of the specter as "revenant," privileges a certain notion of "return"—exemplified in his work by Nietzsche's "eternal return"—as the point of departure for his account of the relation of politics to historicity. And finally, as we will see in the next section, like Derrida, he places a notion of "possibility" at the center of his political thought.

Nevertheless, a number of characteristics distinguish his positions from Derrida's: a political messianism that seems to endorse rather than eschew eschatology and utopianism; a politics of temporal "return" that would *kill off*, rather than attend to, the specter; and above all, an account of ethics and the political that is fundamentally oriented toward ontology and the determinations of Being, rather than toward the singular and infinite responsibility for the Other that characterizes ethics in the Levinasian sense. It is this latter divide which fundamentally separates Derrida from Agamben (and others)[49] on the thought of the political, and that I

[48] *Id.* at 86, 87.

[49] For example, despite his other differences from Agamben, Jean Luc Nancy seems to me also to fall squarely within the "ontological" camp. *See, e.g.*, JEAN-LUC NANCY, BEING SINGULAR PLURAL (Robert D. Richardson & Ann E. O'Byrne trans., Stanford

attempt hereafter first to explicate and then to complicate. Thus, it is the early Heidegger's ontological interpretation of *Dasein's* "*authentic* Being-one's-Self" as "authentic potentiality-for-Being" that primarily determines the form taken by Agamben's ethical/political philosophy, if not its specific content.[50] For Agamben, being human is simply and purely potential-being: "*It is the simple fact of one's own existence as possibility or potentiality*;" accordingly, he says, "this is why the only ethical experience (which, as such, cannot be a task or a subjective decision) is the experience of being (one's own) potentiality, of being (one's own) possibility."[51]

The "ethical" here signifies something entirely different than what it signifies in Derrida's Levinasian discourse of responsibility to and for the Other. In fact, Agamben is explicitly critical of any understanding of ethics as responsibility, which he says represents a confusion between the legal and "genuinely ethical" spheres. Mentioning Levinas by name, he says that "[t]he gesture of assuming responsibility is . . . genuinely juridical and not ethical."[52] Instead, for Agamben, "ethics is the sphere that recognizes neither guilt nor responsibility; it is, as Spinoza knew, the doctrine of the happy life"[53]—which is to say, as the reference to Spinoza suggests, a life of pure immanence freed of any transcendent principle of judgment.

More particularly, Agamben's ethics begins from the thesis that "the good" is not an entity like other entities, that it does not "take place" like such entities, but is itself "the taking-place of the entities, their innermost exteriority."[54] For Agamben, the good is nothing more nor less than the entity's "being-thus," its being what it is and "not otherwise."[55] This "being-thus" (or "being-such") is not itself an entity, nor does it "found" nor "direct" nor "nullify" the existent—it is neither ground nor principle nor *aufhebung*. Instead, Agamben says, the "being-thus" of the existent "is only its being exposed, its nimbus, its limit"—which is to say in another

---

Univ. Press 2000) (1996).

[50] MARTIN HEIDEGGER, BEING AND TIME 313 (John Macquarrie & Edward Robinson trans., Harper & Row 1962) (7th ed. 1953). *See also* AGAMBEN, HOMO SACER, *supra* note 11, at 188 ("Here attention will also have to be given to the analogies between politics and the epochal situation of metaphysics. Today *bios* lies in *zoē* exactly as essence, in the Heideggerian definition of Dasein, lies (*liegt*) in existence.").

[51] AGAMBEN, COMING COMMUNITY, *supra* note 47, at 43-44.

[52] GIORGIO AGAMBEN, REMNANTS OF AUSCHWITZ: *THE WITNESS AND THE ARCHIVE* (HOMO SACER III) 22 (Daniel Heller-Roazen trans., 1999) [hereinafter AGAMBEN, REMNANTS OF AUSCHWITZ].

[53] *Id.* at 24.

[54] AGAMBEN, COMING COMMUNITY, *supra* note 47, at 15.

[55] *Id.* at 93.

way, its being-such-as-it-is-and-not-otherwise, not-something-else.[56] Agamben calls this condition of being-such "the Irreparable": "The Irreparable is that things are just as they are, in this or that mode, consigned without remedy to their way of being .... How you are, how the world is—this is the Irreparable."[57]

The Irreparable is thus the pure immanence of the world, what Agamben also calls its "irreparably profane character." Yet, he says, the world's very "profanation and thingness" is at the same time its salvation: "The world—insofar as it is absolutely, irreparably profane—is God."[58] Thus, following Heidegger and Nietzsche, Agamben is a thinker of radical finitude, of the possibility of meaning (including ethical and political meaning) in a world from which every unearned—which is also to say, metaphysical—presupposition of transcendence has been extirpated. If ethical or political meaning is nevertheless to be found, it therefore must be found in immanence itself. "Redemption is not an event in which what was profane becomes sacred and what was lost is found again," he says; rather, "[r]edemption is ... the irreparable loss of the lost, the definitive profanity of the profane."[59] But, Agamben claims, that "definitive profanity of the profane" only effects its "passage outside the world" in the medium of language. Only in language do entities manifest themselves *as such*; only in its being-called "tree" (and being-called all of its other predicates) *is* a tree—that is, a particular, singular tree—*as* itself, that is, as this tree and not otherwise. Thus only in its relationship to language is *this* tree *this* tree, yet, at the same time, by virtue of this relationship to language which is necessarily a relationship to generality ("a tree" refers to every tree, not just *this* tree), *this* tree is linked in the mode of "belonging" to language to every other singular entity.[60]

---

[56] *Id.* at 100.

[57] *Id.* at 90.

[58] *Id.*

[59] *Id.* at 102. Here, Agamben is tracking and interpreting, *sub silentio* (as he so often does with Benjamin's thought), Benjamin's theses on the oblique but intimate connection of the order of the profane and the order of Messianic redemption. *Compare* WALTER BENJAMIN, *Theologico-Political Fragment*, *in* REFLECTIONS: ESSAYS, APHORISMS, AUTOBIOGRAPHICAL WRITINGS 312 (Peter Demetz ed., Edmund Jephcott trans., 1978) ("From the standpoint of history [the Messianic Kingdom of God] is not the goal, but the end .... The profane, therefore, although not itself a category of [the Messianic] Kingdom, is a decisive category of its quietest approach.") *and Goethe's Elective Affinities*, *in* BENJAMIN, SELECTED WRITINGS, *supra* note 1, at 356 ("Only for the sake of the hopeless ones have we been given hope.") *with* AGAMBEN, COMING COMMUNITY, *supra* note 47, at 102 ("We can have hope only in what is without remedy [i.e., "irreparable"].").

[60] AGAMBEN, COMING COMMUNITY, *supra* note 47, at 9. As Agamben puts it, "[l]inguistic being (being-called) is a set (the tree) that is at the same time a singularity (*the* tree, *a* tree, *this* tree) ...." *Id.* He illustrates this general point by reference to the

By extension to the world as a whole, only in its relationship to language is the immanence of the world transcended as its particular mode of being, its "being thus."

Agamben's "coming community" is not "coming" in the sense of Derrida's *démocratie á venir*, then, not even as the "here and now" of a messianic promise, but is in a real sense available as such *today*—indeed, in sharp contrast to Derrida's account, it is only available *as* a certain form of immediate linguistic and ontological transparency inherent in the notion of the "being such" of entities as their "being called" in language. The members of the coming community are—in Agamben's words—"whatever singularities," and he goes on to explain that "[t]he Whatever in question here relates to singularity not in its indifference with respect to a common property (to a concept, for example: being red, being French, being Muslim), but only in its being *such as it is*."[61] Only by first "being such as" it is—that is, by taking place in language—does the whatever singularity become an entity subject to predication ("being red," "being French," "being Muslim"), but its "whatever being" is not its belonging to those particular classes but its "belonging" to classes (language) in general by virtue of that taking place in language.[62] But this means that *every* being, insofar as every being is "such as it is," "belongs" potentially with every other being, and the "coming community" is nothing other than this ever-present possibility of anonymous and universal belonging—of belonging-to-a-community "before it is a community *of*... (this or that, men, God's creatures, etc.)," as Thomas Carl Wall puts it.[63] In short, the coming community is a community of singular beings that "are expropriated of all identity,

---

phenomenon of the example:

> [The example] is one singularity among others, which, however, stands for each of them and serves for all. On one hand, every example is treated in effect as a real particular case; but on the other, it remains understood that it cannot serve in its particularity. Neither particular nor universal, the example is a singular object that presents itself as such, that *shows* its singularity.

Id. at 10. But this "showing" can take place only in language, in being-called. *Id.* ("Exemplary is what is not defined by any property, except by being-called. Not being-red, but being-*called*-red; not being-Jakob, but being-*called*-Jakob defines the example."). The exemplarity of the example, in other words, resides neither in the generality of its class membership ("being-red") nor in the ineffability of its particularity, which cannot show itself in language, but in the singularity of its status as something (some thing, some particular thing) that is *called* "red." But the linguistic being of the example instantly can be extended to every thing insofar as everything is some "thing" (X) that is called "X."

[61] *Id.* at 1.

[62] *Id.* at 97.

[63] THOMAS CARL WALL, RADICAL PASSIVITY: LEVINAS, BLANCHOT, AND AGAMBEN 121 (1999).

so as to appropriate belonging itself."[64]

Agamben's conception of ethical community seeks to fuse the notion of human *Dasein* as pure potential with the notion of an absolutely immanent and profane life—a life in which entities simply *are* "as such"—in the medium of the entity's pure relationship with language, its "being called" in the taking-place of language itself. Human-being-as-potential is in fact nothing but a complete openness or receptivity to that linguistic relation to the world as such, its being-thus. For Agamben, the "coming community"—the community of a redeemed humanity—would be the community whose only bond is a shared openness to the world manifested through its pure linguistic being, its pure being-called.

Agamben sums up this utopian conception of community in the notion of an *experimentum linguae*—"an experience which is undergone only within language . . . in which what is experienced is language itself." The "only content," he says, of this *experimentum* "is that *there is language*"—a result that cannot be represented by the fact that there is "*a* language, . . . a state or a patrimony of names and rules which each people transmit from generation to generation." That is, the object of the *experimentum* is not any particular language, "that there is English, or Italian, or French, etc.," but that there is *language as such*. The radical openness to the world required by human-being-as-its-own-potentiality can only be represented, or rather experienced, as this experience of this bare fact of language itself that is the final and presuppositionless presupposition of the "being-*thus*" of beings—"the unpresupposable non-latency in which men have always dwelt, and which, in speaking, they move and breathe." This fact of language is a "non-latency" because it is actualized in every speech act, since every act of speech, in disclosing the world, simultaneously and necessarily manifests "that there is language."

Yet, Agamben observes, "[f]or all the forty millennia of *Homo sapiens*, man has not yet ventured to assume this non-latency, to have the experience of his speaking being." What then, Agamben asks, *would* be the "correct expression for the existence of language" that man has avoided for forty millennia? To this he replies, "[t]he only possible answer to this question is: human life, as *ethos*, as ethical way. The search for a *polis* and *oikìa* befitting this void and unpresupposable community is the *infantile* task of future generations."[65]

In this condensed passage one can already see the outlines of the messianic political program that I will interrogate in the

---

[64] AGAMBEN, COMING COMMUNITY, *supra* note 47, at 11.

[65] AGAMBEN, *supra* note 1, at 9-10.

remainder of this essay. The task of creating a *polis* allotted to "future generations" is "infantile" in the specific sense that Agamben gives to that term in his writings. To be "infantile" is to inhabit one's potentiality-for-Being without reserve, to "reject[] any specific destiny and any determined environment" and thus be "ecstatically overwhelmed, cast out of [oneself], not like other living beings into a specific adventure or environment, but for the first time into a *world*."[66] Even more to the point, it is to be cast out into *no particular* language or tradition, insofar as the "world" into which one is cast is the world of "whatever being"—the world in which all that is shared is the predicate-less linguistic being shared by every entity as such, in its taking-place in language. Only on that day when these future generations find this common yet "unpresupposable" relationship to language—and this has not happened for forty millennia, a long time to wait for the Messiah—"when time has come to fullness . . . will men be able finally to construct a history and language which are universal and no longer deferrable, and stop their wandering through traditions," and thus finally achieve a *polis* that is a genuinely universal community—that is, based on no particular linguistic, national or ethnic tradition—of whatever singularities.[67] And, Agamben concludes, "[t]his authentic recalling of humanity to the infantile soma is called thought—that is, politics."[68]

To restate this: authentic politics, for Agamben, is a "recalling"—or "return"—to a life of absolutely immanent potential effected in "thought." Or as Agamben also puts it, "philosophy" is the proper name of politics.[69] Along with its eschatological and immediate character, the two motifs of politics-as-thought and politics-as-return define the parameters of Agamben's political messianism. Before turning to Agamben's account of state sovereignty in the next section, I will address the significance of "return" in his philosophy, since it is a node around which many of his key concepts ("immanence," "messianism," "life," for example) turn, as well as his most important point of contact with Nietzsche's philosophy.

---

66 GIORGIO AGAMBEN, *The Idea of Infancy*, *in* IDEA OF PROSE 96 (Michael Sullivan & Sam Whitsitt trans., State Univ. of New York Press 1995) (1985) [hereinafter AGAMBEN, *Idea of Infancy*]. *See generally* AGAMBEN, *supra* note 1.

67 AGAMBEN, *Idea of Infancy*, *supra* note 66, at 98.

68 *Id.*

69 "For politics is the sphere of the full, absolute gesturality of human beings, and it has no name other than its Greek pseudonym, which is barely uttered here: philosophy." AGAMBEN, *Kommerell*, *supra* note 45, at 85. Agamben expresses this notion repeatedly in a number of ways throughout his writings. *See, e.g.*, AGAMBEN, HOMO SACER, *supra* note 11, at 47; AGAMBEN, *Form-of-Life*, *supra* note 14, at 11.

In *Language and Death: The Place of Negativity*, Agamben analyzes the entire Western philosophical tradition as a response to the condition first described in Heraclitus's fragment, *ethos anthropo daimon*, which Agamben interprets as "'*Ethos*, the habitual dwelling place of man, [is that] which lacerates and divides.'"[70] "Habit," the mode in which one is most at home, "the dwelling in which one always already exists," Agamben suggests, is (in the Western understanding, at least) a "place of scission," and therefore "one can never really be [there] *from the beginning*, but can only return [there] *at the end*."[71] It is this originary or pre-originary scission that determines the place and task of philosophy in the Western tradition. Philosophy is the thought that, beginning "at home" in unselfconscious habitual being, is driven out of itself by this scission to a position of self-reflection (the "wonder" or "marvel" with which the ancient Greeks first identified the philosophical attitude) in order to return to itself, thereby completing and fulfilling itself.[72] According to this tradition (the supreme exemplars of which, for Agamben, are Hegel and Heidegger), the task of philosophy is, upon its return, to be "at home in the marvel and in the division," that is, to make the negativity of its origin its own.[73]

It is from this perspective that the outlines of Agamben's critique of Derrida comes into view. Referring to Derrida obliquely in another work, Agamben notes that

> [i]t is hardly an accident, therefore, that an authoritative current of contemporary French thought posits language in the beginning and yet conceives of this dwelling in the *arkhē* according to the negative structure of writing and the *gramma*.... In other words: language, which is in the beginning, is the nullification and deferral of itself, and the signifier is nothing other than the irreducible cipher of this ungroundedness.[74]

---

[70] GIORGIO AGAMBEN, LANGUAGE AND DEATH, *supra* note 8, at 93. A more traditional translation of this fragment is "a person's character is his fate (divinity)." Heraclitus, FRAGMENTS Fragment 119, at 69 (T.M. Robinson trans., 1987).

[71] AGAMBEN, LANGUAGE AND DEATH, *supra* note 8, at 93.

[72] *Id.*

[73] *Id.* at 94. Agamben extended this analysis of Hegel and Heidegger in the essay *Se: *Hegel's Absolute and Heidegger's* Ereignis, which takes it in the direction of his later political thinking. *See* AGAMBEN, *Se, *supra* note 44, at 116, 135-37 (discussing sacrifice and *homo sacer*).

[74] GIORGIO AGAMBEN, *The Idea of Language*, *in* POTENTIALITIES: COLLECTED ESSAYS IN PHILOSOPHY 200 (Daniel Heller-Roazen ed. & trans., 1999). Agamben regularly mentions Derrida by name in other versions of the same objection. For some of these other versions, the latter two citations directly pertaining to the implications of this debate for the status of law, see AGAMBEN, LANGUAGE AND DEATH, *supra* note 8, at 38-40; GIORGIO AGAMBEN, Pardes: *The Writing of Potentiality*, *in* POTENTIALITIES:

Agamben's accusation against Derrida is thus an echo of Derrida's own accusation against Heidegger—that he has unknowingly remained within the metaphysical tradition that he thought to have identified and escaped by trying in a new way to "make negativity its own."[75] For Agamben, however, that tradition is not defined by the value placed on "presence," as it is for Derrida, but on a form of "absence." To the extent that the philosophical tradition (whether it has recognized this fact or not) has rested on a negative structure of writing and the *gramma*, Derrida's "grammatology" cannot overcome it but only bring this tradition to fruition.

It is the traditional philosophical interpretation of "return" as re-appropriation of the negative that Agamben seeks to contest. What Hegel and Heidegger were really after—or should have been after, had they been entirely true to their deepest philosophical intention, Agamben suggests—is not an appropriation of the negativity of the originary scission, but a return to the "before," so to speak, of that originary scission: a return that "returns to that which never was and to that which it never left."[76] Such a return returns to "that which never was" in the sense that thinking and being, in their traditional sense, themselves *begin* in, and as, that originary scission—in the binarism of essence and existence, subject and object, profane and divine, and so on,[77] so that a "return" to that which lies before, beneath or beyond those dualities can only be a return to "that which never was." At the same time, no metaphorics of "before, beneath or beyond" will ever capture the meaning of what it is that is returned-to, either, because what is returned to is at the same time "that which it never left"—that which thought and language (that is to say, philosophy) necessarily presuppose in every cognitive-linguistic act, the "thing itself" of language and the being-thus of the entity. Agamben gives the name "habit" to the "thing itself" of human life that philosophy has never managed to leave behind.[78]

COLLECTED ESSAYS IN PHILOSOPHY 209-19 (Daniel Heller-Roazen ed. & trans., 1999); GIORGIO AGAMBEN, *The Messiah and the Sovereign: The Problem of Law in Walter Benjamin*, *in* POTENTIALITIES: COLLECTED ESSAYS IN PHILOSOPHY 170-71 (Daniel Heller-Roazen ed. & trans., 1999) [hereinafter AGAMBEN, *The Messiah*]; AGAMBEN, HOMO SACER, *supra* note 11, at 54, 57.

[75] *See* AGAMBEN, LANGUAGE AND DEATH, *supra* note 8, at 39 (Derrida "*believed he had opened a way to surpassing metaphysics, while in truth he merely brought the fundamental problem of metaphysics to light*").

[76] *Id.* at 97.

[77] Agamben himself lists "living and language, nature and culture, ethics and logic." *Id.* at 96.

[78] *Id.* at 97. It goes by other names in his work as well—"manner" (AGAMBEN, COMING COMMUNITY, *supra* note 47, at 27), "the full, absolute gesturality of human

It is against the background of this notion of "return" that one must understand Agamben's claim that, in the redeemed world, "'[e]verything will be as it is now, just a little different.'"[79] "Everything will be as it is now" in that the Messiah does nothing other than effect a return to our habitual dwelling place. Nevertheless, it will also be "just a little different" in that that dwelling place, that home where we have never actually lived while never having left, assumes a "glow" or "halo" that our mundane, pre-messianic habitual life lacked. Agamben describes this "halo" as "a zone in which possibility and reality, potentiality and actuality, become indistinguishable."[80] By this he means that the redeemed entity's pure, irreparable being-thus, its being-such-as-it-is-and-none-other, can neither be necessary nor contingent. It cannot be necessary because necessity implies some supplemental principle in addition to its own being that maintains it in its being-thus, and such supplementarity is precisely what is foreclosed by the entity's pure, presuppositionless being-itself-and-none-other.[81] On the other hand, insofar as it is irreparable, "consigned without remedy to [its] way of being,"[82] neither is the entity's being simply contingent (at least to the extent that "contingency" is interpreted to mean that the being, in itself, could be, at that very moment of its being, otherwise). Rather, pure being-thus—that is, the entity's redeemed, post-messianic being—would be a modality of being that shares the characteristics of both necessity and contingency (and, relatedly, actuality and potentiality as well) without being reducible to either of them. "Being-thus is not contingent; it is necessarily contingent. Nor is it necessary; it is contingently necessary."[83] Redeemed humanity's "infantile soma" would be precisely this coincidence of an unpresupposed being-what-it-is-and-none-other (its "contingent necessity") with a pure potentiality-for-being that opens each singular human being to the ineradicable possibility of being other than he or she is (its "necessary contingency"). The "coming community" is thus the community of beings who are singularly

---

beings" (AGAMBEN, *Kommerell*, *supra* note 45, at 85), and "the social praxis itself that, in the end, becomes transparent to itself" (AGAMBEN, *Se, *supra* note 44, at 137), among many others.

[79] AGAMBEN, COMING COMMUNITY, *supra* note 47, at 53 (quoting Walter Benjamin).

[80] *Id.* at 55, 56.

[81] To formalize this: "It is necessary that X exist" necessarily implies, whether explicitly stated or not, some explanatory supplement in the form of "because [proposition A]," where [proposition A] is the explanation of *why* it is necessary that X exist. By contrast, the proposition "X exists" carries no such necessary implication and logically can stand on its own.

[82] AGAMBEN, COMING COMMUNITY, *supra* note 47, at 90.

[83] *Id.* at 105.

themselves while sharing this absolute opening to each other in the form of the potentiality of each to be the other.

The philosophical figure to which Agamben most often turns in attempting to articulate this constellation of necessity, contingency, radical immanence and human transcendence is Nietzsche's notion of the "eternal return." While his evaluation of Nietzsche's success has varied over the years,[84] what has remained constant is his understanding of Nietzsche's underlying philosophical intention. For Nietzsche, the doctrine of the eternal return is designed to overcome the will to power's inability to master the past, the "'[i]t was'" that names the "'will's gnashing of teeth and most secret melancholy,'" the fact that "'[t]he will cannot will backwards.'"[85] Agamben shares Nietzsche's understanding up to a point; like Nietzsche, he views liberation from the past—humanity's "wandering through traditions"[86]—as the goal of both philosophy and politics. But as Agamben also notes, it is not simply the past that brings the will up against its limit, but the present moment as well. The "'principle of conditioned necessity,'" he points out, dictates that no matter how equipoised a being is in its potential between being and non-being, no matter how clearly, that is, that it is contingent in the sense that it *could have been different*, "nevertheless, in the instant in which it actually is, it cannot be otherwise."[87] In the tradition of Western thought against which both Nietzsche and Agamben are reacting, contingency can only take the form of a *could have been*; in the present moment of being itself it disappears in the face of the necessity of what *is*.

Nietzsche's solution is to embrace the eternal return (and its related doctrine of the *amor fati*, loving one's fate), and thus transform every "'thus it was'" (and, by extension, every "thus it is" as well) into a "'thus I willed it'"—"'this alone is liberation,'" he says—and so return to it the character of contingency.[88]

---

[84] *Compare* Giorgio Agamben, *The Eternal Return and the Paradox of Passion*, 6 STAN. ITALIAN REV. 9, 14 (1986) [hereinafter Agamben, *Eternal Return*] *with* GIORGIO AGAMBEN, IDEA OF PROSE 56 (Michael Sullivan & Sam Whitsitt trans., State Univ. of New York Press 1995) (1985) *and* GIORGIO AGAMBEN, *Bartleby, or On Contingency*, *in* POTENTIALITIES: COLLECTED ESSAYS IN PHILOSOPHY 200 (Daniel Heller-Roazen ed. & trans., 1999) [hereinafter AGAMBEN, *Bartleby*].

[85] AGAMBEN, *Bartleby*, *supra* note 84, at 267 (footnote omitted).

[86] AGAMBEN, *Idea of Infancy*, *supra* note 66, at 98.

[87] GIORGIO AGAMBEN, *Philosophy and Linguistics*, *in* POTENTIALITIES: COLLECTED ESSAYS IN PHILOSOPHY 75-76 (Daniel Heller-Roazen ed. & trans., 1999).

[88] AGAMBEN, *Bartleby*, *supra* note 84, at 267 (footnote omitted). *See* FRIEDRICH NIETZSCHE, *Thus Spoke Zarathustra: Third Part*, *in* THE PORTABLE NIETZSCHE 103, 278 (Walter Kaufmann trans., 1968) ("Verily, it is a blessing and not a blasphemy when I teach: 'Over all things stand the heaven Accident, the heaven Innocence, the heaven Chance, the heaven Prankishness.'").

Agamben, however, because he rejects Nietzsche's metaphysics of the will, ultimately rejects this solution to the problem that Nietzsche has otherwise so accurately identified. Rather, for Agamben, as we have seen, the key to "liberation" is not human will but human *potential*. "Contingency" is thus not a modality of the world conceived as subject to transformation by the will, but the perfect human receptivity to that world, the infantile potentiality-to-be-otherwise that can only be realized in the immediate relationship to language.

By bending the will in the direction of the necessity of what has been and what is, Nietzsche, for Agamben, fell into an unpardonable philosophical, ethical and, ultimately, political error: uttering a "'yes'" to "that worst moment when truth seems to close itself off forever in a world of things."[89] Agamben's notion of "return," by contrast, returns to "that which *never was*" even while remaining at home with "that which it never left," and thus intends to bend necessity in the direction of contingency and potentiality even while endowing contingency and potentiality with the mantle of necessity worn by existence itself in the moment of its actuality. The question can still be asked, however, whether his *political* thought has entirely managed to avoid Nietzsche's error. That is, one can ask whether his work is an adequate basis for thinking a response to the fundamental political-philosophical dilemma of our time, the severing of any form of ethical transcendence from the immanence of political life—or, in the vocabulary of jurisprudence, the inability to articulate an emphatic conception of justice in any terms beyond those of positive law. It is to that question that I now turn in the following sections.

II.

In the concluding section of *The Coming Community*—titled "Tiananmen"—Agamben posits the "coming politics" that corresponds to the "coming community" as an absolute antagonism between the community and the state.[90] The state,

[89] GIORGIO AGAMBEN, *The Idea of Truth*, *in* IDEA OF PROSE 56 (Michael Sullivan & Sam Whitsitt trans., State Univ. of New York Press 1995) (1985) [hereinafter AGAMBEN, *Idea of Truth*] (noting that the eternal return, "[t]his monstrous compromise between destiny and memory, whereby that which can only be object of memory (the return of the same) is each time seized on as destiny, is the discontorted image of the truth with which our times are unable to come to terms").

[90] *See* AGAMBEN, COMING COMMUNITY, *supra* note 47, at 85 ("The novelty of the coming politics is that it will no longer be a struggle for the conquest or control of the State, but a struggle between the State and the non-State (humanity), an insurmountable

Agamben says, can negotiate any community's claim to an identity, no matter how antithetical that identity or its aims may appear to the state's own ends, but what it cannot negotiate—and therefore cannot tolerate—is that "singularities form a community without affirming an identity, that humans co-belong without any representable condition of belonging." Thus, he concludes, "[w]hatever singularity . . . is the principal enemy of the State."[91]

In a condensed paragraph, Agamben indicates the source of this antagonism in a discussion that trades on the ideal of an absolutely immanent "life for which living itself would be at stake in its own living"[92] that we have explicated at length above. He says that "[a] being radically devoid of any representable identity would be absolutely irrelevant to the State," and thus, he suggests, the state must endow such a "life" with a representable identity in order to make it "relevant"—that is, to include it within the field of its sovereign power, which is to say, within the law. In the Western tradition, he goes on to say, the "representable identity" assigned to life as such has assumed both a quasi-theological sanctity—"the hypocritical dogma of the sacredness of human life"—and a strictly legal form—"the vacuous declarations of human rights." The hypocrisy and vacuity stem from the reality that these specious identifications are intended to obfuscate: "*Sacred* here can only mean what the term meant in Roman law: *Sacer* was the one who had been excluded from the human world and who, even though she or he could not be sacrificed, could be killed without committing homicide."[93]

In *Homo Sacer: Sovereign Power and Bare Life*, this cryptic reference to Roman law blossoms into the figure of *homo sacer*, the emblem of Agamben's entire philosophical account of law and the state form. Even while sacralizing and celebrating human life in (impotent, un-enforced) declarations of human rights, the state *qua* sovereign treats this life as what Agamben calls "bare life," biological life that is separated from its humanity as such so as to become the raw material of its governmental processes. "*It can even be said that the production of a biopolitical body is the original activity of sovereign power*," as Agamben puts it in a formula

disjunction between whatever singularity and the State organization.") (emphasis omitted).

[91] *Id.* at 87. This is how Agamben reads the crushing of the peaceful Tiananmen Square demonstrations of May 1989, the demands of which, he says, were too diffuse to endow the demonstrators with any particular political identity or to have posed any actual danger to the State.

[92] AGAMBEN, *Form-of-Life*, *supra* note 14, at 9.

[93] AGAMBEN, COMING COMMUNITY, *supra* note 47, at 86-87.

whose importance he emphasizes by italicizing.[94] Sovereignty and law are nothing other, in essence, than the separation of the person into a politically spiritualized entity—the "citizen" to whom formal rights and legal recognition attach—and the person's living substance ("bare life"), which, like the eponymous *homo sacer*, is consigned in its entirety to a meaningless mortality: *Homo sacer* is the person who may be killed by anyone without legal consequence, while such death is at the same time deprived of any higher significance insofar as it may not be offered as a sacrifice, that is, consecrated to the divine.[95] The political state is nothing other than the mechanism for this separation of the form of humanity from bare life.[96] And the political task of the "coming community" is accordingly to negate the state form *tout court*, and this dualism along with it, in the name of the integral unity of that "life for which living itself would be at stake in its own living."[97]

The consequences of this analysis for contemporary politics are dramatic, insofar as it is the state form *as such*, and not just particular forms of the state, that are implicated in this political task. Thus, while denying that he is simplistically identifying modern democracies with fascism and Stalinism, Agamben is nevertheless driven to note an "inner solidarity" among them in the form of the "biopolitics" that, however different its particular

---

[94] AGAMBEN, HOMO SACER, *supra* note 11, at 6. Agamben here refers to Foucault's understanding of politics in terms of "biopolitics." *Id.* at 3 (emphasis omitted).

[95] *See id.* at 8-10.

[96] Agamben traces this distinction back to the Greeks and their distinction between *bios*—"the form or way of living proper to an individual or a group"—and *zoē*—"the simple fact of living common to all living beings (animals, men, or gods)." *Id.* at 1. It is no coincidence, Agamben argues, that classical thought excluded "simple natural life" as such (*zoē*) from the *polis*, confining it in the form of reproduction to the home (*oikos*). *Id.* at 1-2. Notably absent from Agamben's philosophy is any consideration of the significance of gender or the sexual difference. The consignment of "bare life" to the household that he notes in this passage would be one point from which such a consideration could have departed.

[97] AGAMBEN, *Form-of-Life*, *supra* note 14, at 9. The echoes of Marx's analysis of the abstraction of law and human rights in capitalist democracies are apparent. *See* Karl Marx, *On the Jewish Question*, *in* THE MARX-ENGELS READER 24-51 (Robert C. Tucker ed., Norton 1972) (1963). Agamben in fact conceives of his political project, at least in part, as a radicalization and extension of the Marxist analysis. *See* AGAMBEN, *Form-of-Life*, *supra* note 14, at 6-7. In many ways, he retains the formal outline of a classical Marxist theoretical structure, from its secularized messianicity and end-of-history thesis to its positing of dialectical forces immanent to society itself driving it toward a (potentially) final crisis. *See* AGAMBEN, COMING COMMUNITY, *supra* note 47, at 63-65. But Agamben displaces this historical dialectic from labor as the medium of social relations (Marx) to communication, both in the concrete form of a thoroughly media-tized "society of the spectacle" and ultimately language itself as the immediate form of mediacy in general. *See id.* at 65; GIORGIO AGAMBEN, *Language and History: Linguistic and Historical Categories in Benjamin's Thought*, *in* POTENTIALITIES: COLLECTED ESSAYS IN PHILOSOPHY 61 (Daniel Heller-Roazen ed. & trans., 1999).

forms, ultimately joins "the society of mass hedonism and consumerism" to "modern totalitarianism."[98] In a real sense, then, Agamben is not only seeking to articulate a political ideal of community beyond the carnage of twentieth century Europe, but also to understand how that carnage "could have happened here" in the first place, in the midst of the enlightened West. "[O]ne ends up identifying with an enemy whose structure one does not understand," Agamben warns, and his political philosophy is a response to that challenge.[99]

What both totalitarianism and democracy share is the state form itself, the "logic of sovereignty" that Agamben identifies in its essence with Carl Schmitt's famous definition of the sovereign: "Sovereign is he who decides on the exception,"[100] where the exception is that state of emergency in which the sovereign assumes its absolute power to ignore its own legal limitations and norms—where the law itself definitively steps outside the law. For both Schmitt and Agamben, the decision on the exception is the condition of possibility of the rule of law in general. It is the flip-side of that "factual regularity" which is the necessary presupposition of the effectiveness of any particular rule of law, since it "belongs . . . to the rule's immanent validity."[101] Thus, "[t]he exception does not only confirm the rule; the rule as such lives off the exception alone," insofar as the possibility of the exception—that is, the possibility that the sovereign will decide that the situation is "irregular" and therefore that the law will no longer apply—cannot be separated from the opposite decision, which is the condition of possibility of the rule of law itself—that is, that the situation *is* regular (or "normal," as Schmitt also puts it) and thus that the rule of law will continue in force.

Although remaining firmly with the Schmittian problematic, Agamben's political theory broadens and deepens it in three fundamental respects. First, he elaborates the logic of the exception in terms of the specific form of relationship that he calls the "ban" or "abandonment."[102] By "abandonment" Agamben means that paradoxical relation in which something is included in a class solely by virtue of its exclusion. The exceptional situation is held in the law's ban precisely in this sense, insofar as it is in fact a category of law—the legal name for the situation in which the law

---

[98] AGAMBEN, HOMO SACER, *supra* note 11, at 10, 11.

[99] *Id.* at 12.

[100] CARL SCHMITT, POLITICAL THEOLOGY: FOUR CHAPTERS ON THE CONCEPT OF SOVEREIGNTY 5 (George Schwab trans., MIT Press 1985) (1934) (footnote omitted).

[101] *The Logic of Sovereignty*, *in* AGAMBEN, HOMO SACER, *supra* note 11, at 16 (citation omitted).

[102] *Id.* at 28 (crediting Jean-Luc Nancy for the term).

no longer applies, created solely by virtue of the decision of the sovereign legal authority—yet at the same time remains "outside the law," excluded from the law by the very decision that maintains it as a legal category. Understood as ban, the sovereign exception thus represents a "zone of indistinction" or undecidability in the borders that define the limits of a class—"the radical crisis of every possibility of clearly distinguishing between membership and inclusion, between what is outside and what is inside, between exception and rule."[103]

But, second, Agamben goes on to suggest that the key to understanding the sovereignty of the sovereign decision is not its formal structure as ban in the abstract, but what in particular is included by its exclusion from law in both the extreme case and most general sense—human life. As Agamben puts it, the sovereign decision is not best understood as "the expression of the will of a subject hierarchically superior to all others," but rather as "the inscription within the body of the *nomos* of the exteriority that animates it and gives it meaning."[104] What "animates it and gives it meaning" is not the abstraction of the legal decision itself—a decision on "the licit and illicit"—but rather life itself, "the originary inclusion of the living in the sphere of law . . . which the law needs."[105] Law needs life not only because it is a meaningless abstraction without some living connection to the life of human beings, but, more specifically, because "[t]here is no rule that is applicable to chaos."[106] "Life" signifies simultaneously and indeterminately both that "chaos" which is necessarily excluded from every proper legal decision, and that which, at the same time, is incorporated within law in every legal decision in the form of the presupposition of the underlying "regular situation" that is sufficiently ordered for a rule of law to apply meaningfully to it. "There is a limit-figure of life, a threshold in which life is both inside and outside the juridical order, and this threshold is the place of sovereignty."[107] In sum, "[Schmitt's] statement 'The rule lives off the exception alone' must therefore be taken to the letter . . . . [The law] nourishes itself on this exception and is a dead letter without it."[108]

The archaic Roman figure of *homo sacer*, who is included as a legal person in both profane and divine law only by virtue of his

---

[103] *Id.* at 25.
[104] *Id.* at 25-26.
[105] *Id.*
[106] *Id.* at 16 (quoting Schmitt).
[107] *Id.* at 27.
[108] *Id.*

exclusion from both spheres (he may be killed by anyone without secular legal consequence but not sacrificed), is the symbol of this victimization of life by the law. And indeed, Agamben's central historical thesis is that we live today in an age in which law has abstracted and generalized itself across the entire field of life, beyond any determinate content or norms, to the point that it is "in force without significance"[109]—a legal order in which the Schmittian "exception" has become the rule. This generalized rule of the exception is at the same time the generalized rule of the sovereign power of death over "bare," biological life, which is itself merely a cipher for that sovereign power. The extreme figure of this rule of the exception—one that in its very extremity emblematizes all of its lesser manifestations in a political and social life lived increasingly in the shadow of the virtually unreviewable discretion of impersonal bureaucracies—is the Nazi extermination camp. The camp, says Agamben, in which life was indeed excepted *in toto* from the legitimacy of any recognizable rule of law and placed instead under the sign of arbitrary death, yet at the same time was absolutely routinized, regularized and even mechanized in its rule-like character, is "the hidden matrix and *nomos* of the political space in which we are still living."[110] We are all *homines sacri* now, and in this latest (and apparently last) historical unfolding of the essence of sovereignty our supreme political task has become to throw off the yoke of the law in its entirety—to drive a stake through the heart of the legal *revenant* so that it returns no more.[111]

Agamben thus assigns an historical dialectic to the progressive envelopment of law by its exception, a progression whose end-state we are now experiencing. The sovereign exception is also, however, as we have seen, the purely logical structure of the rule of law in general. This logical structure, moreover, is identical to

---

[109] *Id.* at 53.

[110] *Id.* at 166. *See* GIORGIO AGAMBEN, *What Is a Camp?*, *in* MEANS WITHOUT END: NOTES ON POLITICS 37 (Sandra Buckley et al. eds., Vincenzo Binetti & Cesare Casarino trans., Univ. of Minn. Press 2000) (1996).

[111] *See* AGAMBEN, HOMO SACER, *supra* note 11, at 111. Although derived from Carl Schmitt, Agamben's opposition of life to law could be brought into direct relationship with key elements of Nietzsche's account of law and life as well. Nietzsche also would limit law—which potentially represents a "principle hostile to life"—so as to keep it subordinate to life as a "means" and not an end in itself, lest it become a "secret path to nothingness" (a warning to which one should compare Agamben's claim that law's "*Being in force without significance*" is equivalent to the "Nothing of Revelation" revealed as the truth of law in Kafka's *Trial* (the phrase is Gerschom Scholem's, *see id.* at 50-51; I return to this passage below). *See* FRIEDRICH NIETZSCHE, *On the Geneology of Morals*, Second Essay para. 11, *in* ON THE GENEALOGY OF MORALS & ECCE HOMO 76 (Walter Kaufmann ed., Walter Kaufmann & R. J. Hollingdale trans., Vintage Books 1989) (1967) [hereinafter NIETZSCHE, *On the Genealogy of Morals*].

one that we have already touched on above—the relationship of being to language. At the outset of *Homo Sacer*, alluding to Aristotle's essential linkage of human beings' having language and living in cities, Agamben declares: "The question 'In what way does the living being have language?' corresponds exactly to the question 'In what way does bare life dwell in the *polis*?'"[112] This is so, Agamben explains, because both the force of law and linguistic signification depend for their effectiveness on the same structure, the structure of "abandonment" and "exception."[113]

In other words, Agamben's politics is absolutely continuous with his metaphysics of language.[114] Thus, when he says that "[t]here is politics because man is the living being who, in language, separates and opposes himself to his own bare life and, at the same time, maintains himself in relation to that bare life in an inclusive exclusion,"[115] the political solution that he has in mind to healing that schism is as much an exercise in fundamental ontology as it is in politics in the usual sense. In particular, that politico-metaphysical solution is the "return" to a life of "habit" that was discussed at the end of the last section. In sum, politics is ontology and ontology, politics.

Derrida's critique of political sovereignty, by contrast, takes a very different but, as we will see shortly, no less Nietzschean route. In *Specters of Marx* he begins to articulate his own critique and vision of a politics "beyond the sovereignty of States" (he calls it "the New International")[116] around the "logic of the specter" that he develops in that book. His description of the New International, in its spectrality, resembles in certain significant respects Agamben's "coming community," which is another community "without common belonging to a class":

> [The New International] is an untimely link, without status, without title, and without name, barely public even if it is not clandestine, without contract, 'out of joint,' without

---

[112] AGAMBEN, HOMO SACER, *supra* note 11, at 8.

[113] *Id.* at 21:

> [J]ust as language presupposes the nonlinguistic as that with which it must maintain itself in a virtual relation (in the form of a *langue* or, more precisely, a grammatical game, that is, in the form of a discourse whose actual denotation is maintained in infinite suspension) so that it may later denote it in actual speech, so the law presupposes the nonjuridical (for example, mere violence in the form of the state of nature) as that with which it maintains itself in a potential relation in the state of exception.

Id. at 20-21.

[114] *See, e.g.*, AGAMBEN, HOMO SACER, *supra* note 11, at 8 ("[p]olitics . . . appears as the truly fundamental structure of Western metaphysics"; "the 'politicization' of bare life [is] the metaphysical task *par excellence*").

[115] *Id.*

[116] DERRIDA, SPECTERS OF MARX, *supra* note 6, at 84.

> coordination, without party, without country, without national community (International before, across, and beyond any national determination), without co-citizenship, without common belonging to a class.[117]

Despite that shared appearance, I want to note preliminarily two crucial differences.

First, while Agamben's coming community is a community whose links are based ultimately on fundamental ontology, the shared "belonging to belonging" of every entity insofar as it participates in the taking place of being in language, Derrida's New International is a community of ethical commitment in the sense of responsibility for the suffering of the Other. "It is," he says, "a link of affinity, suffering, and hope," one based on the shared recognition and ethical response to the fact that "never have violence, inequality, exclusion, famine, and thus economic oppression affected as many human beings in the history of the earth and of humanity."[118]

Second, unlike Agamben, Derrida's discourse does not conclude in an end to the State *tout court*, nor is simplistically anti-statist in any other way. Derrida says this explicitly, in a carefully phrased passage:

> Despite appearances, what we are saying here is not simply anti-statist: in given and limited conditions, the super-State, which might be an international institution, may always be able to limit the appropriations and the violence of certain private socio-economic forces. But without necessarily subscribing to the whole Marxist discourse . . . and, on the other hand, *without suspecting the juridical idea in itself*, one may still find inspiration in the Marxist "spirit" to criticize the presumed autonomy of the juridical and to denounce endlessly the *de facto* take-over of international authorities by powerful Nation-States, by concentrations of techno-scientific capital, symbolic capital, and financial capital, of State capital and private capital.[119]

"Without suspecting the juridical idea in itself"—in this language one sees the critical practical distinction between Agamben and Derrida's philosophies of law and sovereignty. For Derrida, law is both inevitable and necessary in the ethical sense, because justice without the calculations, guidance and limitations of law would be, as he puts it in *Force of Law*, too close to "the worst," in that "it [could] always be reappropriated by the most

[117] *Id.* at 85.
[118] *Id.*
[119] *Id.* at 84-85 (first emphasis added).

perverse calculation."[120] For Agamben, on the other hand, law and sovereignty *are* the "worst," in that they are the pure form of the ontological schism between beings and their being-in-language that humanity's politico-ontological task is to appropriate and abolish.

If this passage makes Derrida sound like more of a reformer than a revolutionary, one should keep in mind that he has rejected the reform/revolution distinction as an unhelpful abstraction from the concrete demands of particular political situations.[121] That said, there is no doubt that, in stark contrast to Agamben's politico-ontological eschatology, and despite the vocabulary of "messianicity" (to which I return shortly), Derrida's is a politics of ethical responsiveness that rejects neither the State nor the law in their entirety, but seeks to intervene in both according to the needs of the moment, whether those needs are for revolution or for reform. In the remainder of this section I attempt both to articulate more clearly the nature of this pragmatic difference between the two, and also to suggest that, as a philosophical matter, Derrida's ethical messianism provides a more coherent basis for a concept of the political than does Agamben's linguistic-ontological variety.

Towards those ends, let me begin with the overarching framework of Agamben's political theory in *Homo Sacer*, Carl Schmitt's definition of the sovereign as the one who "decides on the exception," which Derrida also treats at length in *Politics of Friendship*—not, however, as his framework but as his chief object of critique.

First, Agamben's exclusion of the ethical relation in Levinas's sense from the realm of the political is already determined by his privileging of this moment in Schmitt's thought as his own starting point for his political reflections. This becomes clear when it is recognized that for Schmitt, the relation of sovereign to decision and exception was not the fundamental political distinction, but derivative of another: he announces in the first sentence of *The Concept of the Political* that "[t]he concept of the state presupposes the concept of the political,"[122] and goes on, famously, to define the political in terms of the distinction between "friend" and "enemy." Schmitt himself is explicit that sovereignty is an incident of a prior constitution of the friend/enemy grouping—"[i]f such an entity [i.e., one constituted on the basis of the

[120] Derrida, *Force of Law*, *supra* note 24, at 28.

[121] *See* Derrida, *Marx & Sons*, *supra* note 9, at 242.

[122] CARL SCHMITT, THE CONCEPT OF THE POLITICAL 19 (George Schwab trans., 1976).

friend/enemy distinction] exists at all, it is always the decisive entity, and it is sovereign in the sense that the decision about the critical situation, even if it is the exception, must always necessarily reside there."[123] The relation between sovereign and subject, as a vertical relation between constituted political power and human being, is and can be nothing other than a relationship of power. Not so, however, with respect to the relationship of friend to enemy, which is necessarily a horizontal relationship between human beings, and therefore already an ethical relationship. Thus, by taking the sovereign exception as fundamental, Agamben elides the ethical configuration that underlies it in Schmitt's own philosophy.[124]

Indeed, the situation is actually more complicated than this summary suggests. Schmitt himself rejected the characterization of the friend-enemy distinction as an ethical configuration; he insisted on the theoretical purity of his concept of the political with respect to other fields, including especially morality and ethics, and relatedly insisted that "enemy" is a term of public, impersonal (i.e., political in the statist sense) hostility, and not a matter of personal enmity (or, therefore, of ethical concern). What makes Schmitt's arguments problematic, however, is a certain circularity that inheres in the grounding of sovereignty on the friend-enemy distinction, because the friend-enemy distinction is itself necessarily, first of all, a friend-enemy decision—a decision on who is the enemy. *The Concept of the Political* makes clear that that decision is itself a decision on the exception, indeed the decision on the exception *par excellence* insofar as it simultaneously determines the identity of the sovereign itself. This circularity thus threatens the fixity of the identity of the friend *qua* friend and enemy *qua* enemy, and the priority of the friend/enemy grouping over the sovereign decision, in a manner that undermines the entire Schmittian edifice.

Derrida shows in *Politics of Friendship* that the strategy that Schmitt employs to stabilize this potential fault line is the notion of "real possibility," the "presence" of a "real possibility" of war that

---

[123] *Id.* at 38. On this point, see Ernst-Wolfgang Böckenförde, *The Concept of the Political: A Key to Understanding Carl Schmitt's Constitutional Theory*, *in* LAW AS POLITICS: CARL SCHMITT'S CRITIQUE OF LIBERALISM 41-42 (David Dyzenhaus ed., 1998).

[124] It should be noted that Agamben recognizes that he is rejecting Schmitt's own understanding of the priority of politics to the state. He says in *Homo Sacer* that "[t]he fundamental categorial pair of Western politics is not that of friend/enemy but that of bare life/political existence, *zoē/bios*, exclusion/inclusion." AGAMBEN, HOMO SACER, *supra* note 11, at 8, 110 ("This relation is more original than the Schmittian opposition between friend and enemy, fellow citizen and foreigner."). He does not follow up on the significance of this difference, however.

involves the killing of other human beings (indeed the concept of "real possibility" is the *leitmotif* of the three chapters devoted to Schmitt):

> The friend, enemy, and combat concepts receive their real meaning precisely because they refer to the real possibility of physical killing. War follows from enmity. War is the existential negation of the enemy. It is the most extreme consequence of enmity. It does not have to be common, normal, something ideal, or desirable. But it must nevertheless remain a real possibility for as long as the concept of the enemy remains valid.[125]

As Derrida suggests, by formulating war and the physical killing of others as neither actual nor potential in the classical Aristotelian sense of the distinction between potential and act, but instead already or always "present as a real possibility," Schmitt can stabilize his discourse by allowing the "real possibility" notion to oscillate between its two poles. Insofar as the possibility of war and killing—in which the friend and enemy groupings are manifest—is "present" and "real," the required decision over who is the enemy has already been made, and the problem of circularity is resolved. But insofar as the possibility of war and killing is merely a "possibility," Schmitt's formulation retains the form of a transcendental condition of possibility, not a reality or actuality of individual, personal hostility—personal "enmity" in its most extreme form, deliberate "physical killing"—that would compromise the conceptual purity of "the political" with ethical or personalistic overtones.[126]

And yet again, the situation is still more complicated, because the notion of "real possibility" is not *just* a rhetorical ruse. Whatever its rhetorical effectivity, the need to decide cannot ultimately be avoided; one (but who? Derrida asks) must still decide whether that "real possibility" is "present" or not. Derrida quotes Schmitt: "What always matters is the possibility of this decisive eventuality taking place[], the actual war[], and the decision whether this eventuality is or is not the given case."[127] Thus the circularity cannot be avoided, and both "the [sovereign] decision" and "this eventuality"—the fact or non-fact of the presence of war or its "real possibility"—are cut free from any grounds or mooring, swinging free in a pure state of possibility with nothing to determine or decide between its occurrence and its

[125] SCHMITT, *supra* note 122, at 33 (translation slightly modified to correspond with *Politics of Friendship*).

[126] DERRIDA, POLITICS OF FRIENDSHIP, *supra* note 2, at 124, 125.

[127] *Id.* at 127 (citation omitted).

non-occurrence. In this sense, Derrida concludes, "the [sovereign] exception is the rule," but the "rule of what takes place, the law of the event, the real possibility of its real possibility." And the event itself is impossible without "the 'perhaps,' . . . that which may not happen, that which happens only in so far as it might just as well not happen, this undecidable eventuality *qua* real possibility, that informs decisions and forms truth."[128] In sum, it is the "real possibility" of this "undecidable eventuality," "that which happens only insofar as it might not happen," that is the (undecidable) source of the sovereign decision on the exception. And just to that extent, it rends that decision in advance just as much is it guarantees it, by rendering the friend-enemy distinction indeterminate even while presupposing it.

Derrida notes that this "law of the event," the "perhaps" as the "real possibility of its real possibility," is at the same time "the very law of spectrality" that "haunts" Schmitt's discourse.[129] An aside in *Politics of Friendship*, this "law of spectrality" is the primary focus of *Specters of Marx*, where Derrida elaborates it as "the question of the event as question of the ghost."[130] I will return to the role of "spectrality," but for now I want to focus more closely on Derrida's notion of the "perhaps," which is its close correlate.

Beyond the specific context of the critique of Schmitt's decisionism, the notion of the "perhaps" is the dominant motif of *Politics of Friendship* as a whole. Derrida's original discussion of it, the one that orients his reading of Schmitt's notion of "real possibility" and indeed the entire book, begins with a reading of that "dangerous perhaps"[131] that Nietzsche invokes at the beginning of *Beyond Good and Evil* when he appeals to those new "philosophers of the dangerous 'perhaps'"[132] who reject the metaphysical values of truth, the Good, knowledge, and the binary logic of judgment in general. In a compact manner, the scene of this invocation—and Derrida is here interested even more in the *performance*, *event* and *form* of this call to the future than he is in its content (although in his reading, these cannot ultimately be separated)—comprises all of the key thematics of the book and of Derrida's political philosophy more generally: the relation to the Other as an event of the future; the future itself as the coming of an event that must not exclude its own impossibility from its

128 *Id.* at 128.
129 *Id.* at 129.
130 DERRIDA, SPECTERS OF MARX, *supra* note 6, at 10.
131 DERRIDA, POLITICS OF FRIENDSHIP, *supra* note 2, at 28-29.
132 NIETZSCHE, *supra* note 15, at 10-11.

possibility in order to remain "future" in the emphatic sense of *à venir*; and thus the ethical relationship itself as an event fundamentally *à venir*, so as to maintain the relationship to the Other beyond any knowable calculation, program, or process.[133] In addressing himself to the philosophers of the future, in inviting them, explicitly and implicitly to come, to join *us*—"we free spirits," Nietzsche says—and thus in that very moment of calling to a future and future of friendship that Nietzsche cannot "know," cannot have any certainty of—and therefore must qualify with a "perhaps"—in that very moment and by virtue of that call's very enunciation, he constitutes the community of "free spirits" (that "we") in the first instance. Or to be precise, he performatively constitutes two communities of "friends": the community of "we free spirits" in the present moment, who call out to the coming philosophers, and the virtual community that exists between those who call and those who are called, the philosophers of the future together with "we" of the present.[134]

Derrida coins the word "teleiopoetic" to describe Nietzsche's sentences, which bring about in the here-and-now of the enunciation addressed to an absolute future *à venir* the very possibility of the community that—by definition of the fact that the address is in fact to the *à venir*—at the same time remains structurally "to come."[135] Derrida emphasizes that a call to others who remain "to come"—beyond knowledge, familiarity, affection, and so on—that constitutes in this very call the caller as a member of these others' community *avant la lettre*, has a messianic structure. If we cannot share a community with the Messiah him/herself, Derrida suggests, we can nevertheless, in the teleiopoetic address, participate in a community of messianic "precursors," who herald his/her arrival.[136] And, Derrida says, a

---

[133] *See* DERRIDA, POLITICS OF FRIENDSHIP, *supra* note 2, at 29:

> Now, the thought of the "perhaps" perhaps engages the only possible thought of the event—of friendship to come and friendship for the future. For to love friendship, it is not enough to know how to bear the other in mourning; one must love the future. And there is no more just category for the future than that of the "perhaps." Such a thought conjoins friendship, the future, and the *perhaps* to open on to the coming of what comes .... For a possible that would only be possible (non-impossible), a possible surely and certainly possible, accessible in advance, would be a poor possible, a futureless possible, a possible already *set aside*, so to speak, life-assured. This would be a programme or a causality, a development, a process without an event.

Id.

[134] NIETZSCHE, *supra* note 15, para. 44, at 56 ("that is the type of man we are, we free spirits! And perhaps *you* have something of this, too, you that are coming? you *new* philosophers?").

[135] DERRIDA, POLITICS OF FRIENDSHIP, *supra* note 2, at 37.

[136] *Id.*

doubled responsibility corresponds to this doubled community of those to come ("they," the philosophers of the future, the Others) and those of today ("we," the same):

> I must answer *at the same time* before the philosophers of the future to come (before *them*), before the specter of those who are not yet here, and before the philosophers of the future that we (*we*) already are, we who are already capable of thinking the future or the coming of the philosophers of the future.[137]

As we will see, it is not just these unique sentences of Nietzsche's that are teleiopoetic, and thus messianic, but, according to Derrida, *every* enunciation, every speech act, has a similarly messianic-teleiopoetic structure. For now, however, the critical point is that that structure remains at all times under the sign of the "perhaps." Messianic though it be, nothing can guarantee that the Messiah will in fact come—indeed, any such guarantee (in the form of evidence, rational argument, signs and portents, or so forth) would be sufficient proof by itself that the person coming could *not* be the Messiah, since the Messiah by definition comes when he/she comes, and not according to anyone's plans, programs, calculations, or expectations. Thus the most one can say of Derrida's own "coming community"—which is both "coming" in the strongest sense of the messianic *à venir*, never actually to arrive in the present, and yet at the same time effective *here and now*, insofar as the teleiopoetic speech act constitutes the possibility of the "precursor" community of those who look and call to the future for the Messiah's arrival in the here-and-now—is "perhaps." Perhaps the Messiah will come, perhaps the precursor community of those who call for the Messiah's arrival—which, let us not forget, is also "messianic" in that it is the community of those who demand that justice be realized—is here with us today, but, at the same time, perhaps not. One can call for the Messiah, one can look to and join with others whom one believes share one's sense of justice and ethical responsibility, but no knowledge will ever allow one to rest in the good conscience or assurance that either of these communities exist in fact. Because of the "perhaps," the double responsibility can never be allayed.

If we now return to Agamben, we find formulations that are at first glance strikingly similar to Derrida's deconstruction of the relation of the sovereign exception to its "real possibility" in the form of war and physical killing. Indeed, the heart of *Homo Sacer* is Agamben's claim that in "describing the most authentic nature

---

[137] *Id.*

of potentiality, Aristotle actually bequeathed the paradigm of sovereignty to Western philosophy." More specifically, Agamben explains:

> [T]he sovereign ban, which applies to the exception in no longer applying, corresponds to the structure of potentiality, which maintains itself in relation to actuality precisely through its ability not to be. Potentiality (in its double appearance as potentiality to and as potentiality not to) is that through which Being founds itself *sovereignly*, which is to say, without anything preceding or determining it . . . other than its own ability not to be. And an act is sovereign when it realizes itself by simply taking away its own potentiality not to be, letting itself be, giving itself to itself.[138]

Thus, as he also puts it, "potentiality and actuality are simply the two faces of the sovereign self-grounding of Being," and, from the other side, "the sovereign is precisely [the] zone of indistinction" at the limit where "pure potentiality and pure actuality are indistinguishable."[139]

Phrased in this way, the ontological structure of sovereignty and its (non-)relation to bare life in the form of the ban determines a specific, if highly abstract, political program.

> [O]ne must think the existence of potentiality without any relation to Being in the form of actuality—not even in the extreme form of the ban and the potentiality not to be, and of actuality as the fulfillment and manifestation of potentiality—and think the existence of potentiality even without any relation to being in the form of the gift of self and of letting be. This, however, implies nothing less than thinking ontology and politics beyond every figure of relation, beyond even the limit relation that is the sovereign ban.[140]

By now these types of formulas should be familiar, even if they are given a slightly different twist in the context of the critique of sovereignty. Because the essence of political sovereignty is nothing other than Being's own ontological sovereignty, one cannot be overcome without overcoming the other. And, as in *The Coming Community*, the result of that (messianic, eschatological) overcoming will be a revision of the ontological categories of potentiality and actuality—specifically, a merging of the two in the "absolutely immanent" life to which we have referred above. "Immanence" in the present context refers to that complete "absence of relation" that Agamben here insists is a condition of a redeemed politics. A redeemed political life

---

[138] AGAMBEN, HOMO SACER, *supra* note 11, at 46.

[139] *Id.* at 47.

[140] *Id.*

would be "relationless" in the sense of "without presupposition," neither an "actuality" whose essence or potential lies elsewhere, nor even a "potential" in the classical Arisotelian sense which would be marked by the unrealized possibility of its actuality. It would thus be, in the words of *The Coming Community*, "a zone in which possibility and reality, potentiality and actuality, become indistinguishable."[141]

Among the notable features of this formulation is how closely it mirrors Agamben's description of that which is to be overcome in the messianic moment, the ontological structure of sovereignty as ban. Agamben says that "the sovereign is precisely [the] zone of indistinction" at the limit where "pure potentiality and pure actuality are indistinguishable."[142] This is virtually the same description that Agamben provides in *The Coming Community* of the redeemed world. This convergence is best understood along two lines. First, it represents a certain classical model of revolution as "overturning": Bare life, which under state sovereignty was *subject to* the sovereign ban in the form of its radical exclusion, becomes, in the redeemed world, the *subject of* that same structure of exception, with its "zone of indistinction," and so on. Or rather, I believe Agamben would say, *almost* the same structure—"just a little different."[143] The "tiny displacement" in the model of sovereignty effected in the redeemed world comprises precisely that "beyond relation" that Agamben says is the touchstone of genuine redemption. The sovereign ban, no matter how negative its form (inclusion solely by virtue of exclusion) and how much a limit case it represents, itself remains a "form of relation" between the mutually presupposed elements of sovereign power and bare life. Redeemed, immanent life, however, regardless how much it otherwise resembles the sovereign ban, presupposes nothing, and instead "appears as an indissoluble cohesion in which it is impossible to isolate something like a bare life."[144]

---

141 AGAMBEN, COMING COMMUNITY, *supra* note 47, at 56.

142 AGAMBEN, HOMO SACER, *supra* note 11, at 47.

143 AGAMBEN, COMING COMMUNITY, *supra* note 47, at 53 (quoting Walter Benjamin).

144 AGAMBEN, HOMO SACER, *supra* note 11, at 153. The formal outlines of this political program—overturning of a binary hierarchy (sovereignty/bare life), followed (structurally) by a displacement that retains the old name of the formerly subordinated element ("life"), but moves it "backward" to designate a structural presupposition of the system (the fact that "there is language," etc.) even more fundamental than the formerly dominant element—ought to be recognizable to anyone familiar with the old formalistic descriptions of deconstruction (including Derrida's own descriptions) in identical terms. *See generally* JACQUES DERRIDA, POSITIONS 41-42 (U. of Chicago Press 1981) (1972) (interviews in which Derrida discusses deconstruction in terms of overturning, displacement, and "*relever*").

Second, once again, the means of that political redemption is thought—"thinking ontology and politics beyond every figure of relation," as he puts it. Thought is not simply the *means* of redemption for Agamben, however; it is also its model. Thought is certainly the medium in which the dualisms imposed by sovereign power—above all the dualism of "power" (*potenza*, potential) and bare life—are overcome.[145] But "thought," for Agamben, also signifies the exemplary figure of the confluence of potentiality and actuality, necessity and contingency, that his political program dictates as its goal. In *Homo Sacer*, he alludes to this only in passing,[146] but that terse acknowledgment is expanded elsewhere in a manner that defines the ontological essence of his politics.

On one hand, he argues (following Aristotle), "thought" is a pure passivity, a pure faculty in the form of a receptivity to stimuli, argument, and so on—thought as "pure knowability and receptivity (*pura receptibilitas*)" or *nous*.[147] Thought is thus a potential-to-think that may realize itself in any *particular* thought whatsoever without itself being any such particular, realized "thought." In that sense, thought must be as much a potentiality-not-to-think as it is a potentiality-to-think, because otherwise, thought-as-potential would not be something separate from its actualized, particular thoughts (just as, in the language quoted above, Agamben describes the sovereign act as taking place "when it realizes itself by simply taking away its own potentiality not to be").[148] But at the same time, thought cannot remain potential—to be "thought," it has to *think something*, that is, spontaneously actualize itself in particular acts of thought (thought as *noesis*). The figure of "thought thinking itself" thus becomes the solution to the problem that Agamben sets himself in his political

---

[145] *See, e.g.*, AGAMBEN, *Form-of-Life*, *supra* note 14, at 9.

[146] *See* AGAMBEN, HOMO SACER, *supra* note 11, at 47 (noting, after identifying the sovereign as that "zone of indistinction" in which "pure potentiality and pure actuality are indistinguishable," that "[i]n Aristotle's *Metaphysics*, this corresponds to the figure of the 'thinking of thinking,' that is, to a thinking that in actuality thinks its own potentiality to think").

[147] AGAMBEN, *Bartleby*, *supra* note 84, at 251. In this passage, Agamben is closely tracking Aristotle's argument in Book Λ• of *Metaphysics* that the "most excellent of things" is the "thinking on thinking," that is, thought thinking itself. *See* THE BASIC WORKS OF ARISTOTLE 884-85 (Richard McKeon ed., 1941).

[148] AGAMBEN, HOMO SACER, *supra* note 11, at 46. This is a particular instance, albeit a privileged one, of Agamben's more general insight that the key to understanding the ontological category of "potentiality" as such is to recognize that all "potentiality-to-be" is just as necessarily "potential-not-to-be;" otherwise, potentiality would have no ontological status distinct from its actualized instances. *See, e.g.*, AGAMBEN, *Bartleby*, *supra* note 84, at 250. Although this argument is a central motif—indeed, possibly the central motif—of Agamben's philosophical work over the past twenty years, I touch on it here only insofar as is necessary to explicate the manner in which it determines his political philosophy.

philosophy, that is, the location of a "zone in which possibility and reality, potentiality and actuality, become indistinguishable."[149] A thought that thinks itself actualizes (in a particular act of thought) that very "potentiality-not-to-be" that is characteristic of thought-as-potentiality, and thus brings together "possibility and reality, potentiality and actuality."

Everything thus turns on the status of this synthesis of thought-as-passive-potential and thought-as-actualized-spontaneity. Too much emphasis on spontaneity, activity, and actuality, and this figure begins to resemble Nietzsche's metaphysics of the will-to-power that ends in a "'yes' uttered in that worst moment when truth seems to close itself off forever in a world of things,"[150] an assent to the sheer positivity of what exists (including the sheer positivity of "positive law").[151] Too much emphasis on potentiality and passivity, however, and the reverse is the case—thought begins to hide *from* that "world of things" that it must necessarily engage if it is to be effective, certainly if it is to be *politically* effective in any meaningful sense. In any event, what raises one's suspicions about this figure, at least if one comes to it from the perspective of a philosophy of ethical alterity like Levinas's, is not so much the notion of a synthesis of potentiality and activity as such but, in this particular instance, its essentially idealist provenance—the fact that it is derived from a self-reflexive act of thought, "thought thinking itself," that seems of necessity to exclude everything outside itself. Let us recall in this regard that, with respect to thinking, even Nietzsche perceived the priority of a kind of passivity and exteriority ("a thought comes when 'it' wishes, and not when 'I' wish"), as did the later Heidegger when he reformulated his fundamental understanding of thought in terms of a "listening" rather than a "questioning."[152] The question I would raise here is whether Agamben's ontological model of politics is capable of fully accounting for that moment of passivity and exteriority, or whether these Nietzschean and late-Heideggerian (and Levinasian and Derridian, too, of course) insights into passivity and the priority of the Other rather instead return to haunt that ontology.

---

149 AGAMBEN, COMING COMMUNITY, *supra* note 47, at 56.

150 AGAMBEN, *Idea of Truth*, *supra* note 89, at 56.

151 *See generally* Nonet, *supra* note 5.

152 NIETZSCHE, *supra* note 15, para. 17, at 24; MARTIN HEIDEGGER, *The Nature of Language*, *in* ON THE WAY TO LANGUAGE 71 (Peter D. Hertz trans., 1971) (suggesting that the most proper stance of thinking is not active questioning but a passive "listening to the grant, the promise of what is to be put in question").

III.

Let us now step back from the details of Agamben's proposal for overcoming the ontological structure of sovereignty and asks how it differs from Derrida's account of how the "perhaps"—the "real possibility of the real possibility" of the event as such—undermines the structure of the sovereign decision. My concern here is not simply with the philosophical distinctions but with the practical implications of these distinctions. For all their abstraction and erudition, neither Agamben and Derrida forget that politics is first of all a matter of practical action in the here and now, even if (at least in Agamben's case) one has to identify a distinctly utopian and idealist bent to that practical impulse. In that spirit, it seems to me that the key difference is this: In Derrida's account, the undermining of the sovereign decision effected by the "perhaps"—which, we should note, is different than an "overcoming" insofar as the "perhaps" is what supports *as well as* undermines the structure of the sovereign decision—has already "taken place," in fact has always already taken place. Schmitt's stabilization of the sovereign decision in the "real possibility" of war *has already* deconstructed itself, has already left open a point of attack that is practical as well as theoretical, insofar as there always remains room to argue about, even after the sovereign decision on the friend and enemy purports to have been made, just who is *really* the friend and who the enemy. "This *already of the perhaps* acts," Derrida says; "[i]t acts within itself—in immanent fashion;" and thus "[w]e have already undergone the effects of its action."[153] Where Agamben's analysis issues in a call for a future task aimed at a future result (the task of the coming philosophy, as Agamben frequently repeats, a task that has not been undertaken "[f]or all the forty millennia of *Homo sapiens*"[154])—a massive task, indeed a messianic task in the eschatological sense—Derrida's issues in an identification of an *existing* crack or rupture in the edifice in question (here, the Schmittian doctrine of the sovereign decision), a flaw that represents, one might say, not a messianic future task so much as an opportunity for thought and for politics in the here-and-now (an opportunity that Derrida acts on in *Politics of Friendship* by demonstrating how Schmitt's categories of "friend" and "enemy" turn in on themselves).

---

[153] DERRIDA, POLITICS OF FRIENDSHIP, *supra* note 2, at 42.

[154] AGAMBEN, *supra* note 1, at 9.

A number of questions could be put to Agamben under the general heading of this "always already." Here I will address only one of them—the question of messianism—because of its centrality to both Derrida and Agamben's political thought, and because it crystallizes the specific difference between Agamben's thought of "potential" on one hand, and Derrida's thought of the "perhaps" and the "spectral" on the other.

For Agamben, the status of the Messiah is "the point of greatest proximity between religion and philosophy"—in particular, the Messiah is "the figure through which religion [and philosophy] confront[] the problem of the Law, decisively reckoning with it."[155] The Messiah is called at that moment when the sovereign exception generalizes itself across the entire field of law. In this critical moment, normative law, the law of the "normal situation," devolves into a permanent, non-normative state of exception in which the sovereign exerts absolute unbridled discretionary power over every aspect of life in which legality (the rule of law as the "law of rules") once held sway. (One example of this situation is marshal law; another, Agamben's favored illustration, is the "law" of the concentration camp.) Agamben calls this situation of the totalized sovereign exception the "pure form of law," in which the law is "'in force without significance.'"[156] That is, in the exceptional moment the law remains in force *qua* "force," a power of enforcement, but has been emptied of any content whatsoever in the form of rules, guidance or norms. It thus appears as a force that is both arbitrary and deadly, a pure power of death over life.

Let us recall again that this point simultaneously has the character of an historical moment—Agamben continually returns to the idea that the law's "being in force without significance" is the characteristic dilemma of our age, our epoch, the epoch of the camp, and so on—and at the same time is the very "logic of sovereignty" in general: "the exception is the originary form of the law."[157] In this latter sense, the pure "being in force without significance" is also the quasi-transcendental condition of possibility of law and sovereignty in general, and is implicated in every legal act, whether part of the "normal" situation of the rule of law or the exceptional state of emergency in which the rule of law is suspended.[158] The pure form of law thus plays a structural,

---

[155] AGAMBEN, *The Messiah*, *supra* note 74, at 163 (emphasis omitted).

[156] AGAMBEN, HOMO SACER, *supra* note 11, at 51.

[157] *Id.* at 26.

[158] This is less dramatic a claim than it may sound. The exception is the "originary form" even of law in the non-exceptional, "normal" situation simply because legal rules

"spectral" role in Agamben's discourse that is homologous to the role played by the "real possibility" of war in Schmitt's discourse that is identified by Derrida. Because it is "present" in every legal act as its condition of possibility, it is simultaneously possible and real, law's logic and its history, the potentiality that drives the historical *telos* of law toward its end-state of "being in force without significance" and the actuality of that state in every present moment of the legal tradition. As such, moreover, it represents that "zone of indistinction" that signifies the pure form of sovereignty itself, which, while itself standing beyond these oppositions, acts by separating bare life from the immanent "life for which nothing is at stake but its own living," the sacred from the profane, potentiality from actuality, humanity's traditions and historicity from its being-in-language, and so on. But it is also, as we have seen, at the same time the form of sovereignty's opposite—the messianic "zone in which possibility and reality, potentiality and actuality, become indistinguishable."[159]

Agamben's "logic of sovereignty," in short, is haunted in all its moments by Derrida's "logic of spectrality," hovering ambiguously not only between logic and history but also between the violent disjointure (or scission, as we called it above) that is the law of law on one hand and, on the other, the messianic "return to that which never was and that which it never left" that is Agamben's ideal of political justice. The difference between the two philosophers lies in the question of whether one term of the spectral binary can or should overcome the other—whether, in short, the spectrality that haunts and produces these various disjunctions itself can or should be overcome. By interpreting the "logic of sovereignty" in terms of a historico-messianic destiny—a destiny that assigns to us the ultimate political task of a messianic return to the "before" of the various scissions that that logic calls into being—Agamben determines a teleology (law's historical evolution into the stage of "being in force without significance") and an eschatology (the final overcoming of law by justice in that end-stage). We would thus indeed seem to have encountered here, beyond the ontology with which Agamben himself identifies his theory of the political, what Derrida calls a "hauntology," a "logic of haunting [that] would not be merely larger and more

are not self-executing—some interpreter is required to interpret them in the particular case. It is this moment of authoritative application of the generality of the rule to the particularity of the facts which can never *itself* be constrained in advance by any rule or law, that constitutes, even in the "normal" situation, law's "pure form"—its "being in force without significance."

[159] AGAMBEN, COMING COMMUNITY, *supra* note 47, at 56.

powerful than an ontology or a thinking of Being," but would also "harbor within itself... like circumscribed places or particular effects, eschatology and teleology themselves."[160] But, let us also be clear, in its intention at least, Agamben's teleo-eschatology would itself exceed the bounds of any such "hauntology," insofar as it *also* sets for itself as its ultimate end, beyond the particularities of the "end of the state" or the "end of history," the goal of the final destruction of the "logic of spectrality" as well.

Indeed, Agamben says as much in almost as many words in a short article that represents (as far as I am aware) his most sustained engagement with Nietzsche's idea of the eternal return and its relation to potentiality. Without going into the intricacies of his argument (which, characteristically, passes through early Christian theology),[161] in this article Agamben articulates the

---

[160] DERRIDA, SPECTERS OF MARX, *supra* note 6, at 10. In the original French, "hauntology [*hantologie*]" is a characteristically Derridian play on words. The French word for "ontology" (*ontologie*) is pronounced the same as *hantologie* even though it is written differently (e.g., like *différence* and *différance*).

[161] *See* Agamben, *Eternal Return*, *supra* note 84, at 9. In the article, Agamben reconstructs Nietzsche's position via an explanation of an equivalent problem in early Christian theology. In Christian theology, the doctrine of a final resurrection that would give the dead final rest in eternal life posed an epistemological problem about the form of that final resurrection: the question of who, or what, exactly, would be resurrected, "the problem of the risen body's substance and form." *Id.* at 11. Would the resurrected dead appear in their final bodily incarnation, aged, mutilated (if they died in an accident, for example) and so on, or would they appear as youthful? And, if the latter were to hold true, at what age? As Agamben notes, however "absurd" these questions may appear to us now, they were highly significant to the central theological concept of resurrection, and raised an epistemological problem that, despite its theological form, has continuing relevance: "how to recognize the individuality and identity of the person resurrected." *Id.* Agamben cites, approvingly, the solution to this problem achieved by the third century philosopher Origen, a solution "in which the theme of salvation is linked to that of the image, and both are linked to the theme of the eternal return":

> Faced with the implicit paradoxes of a strictly material conception of the resurrection (the resurrection of the corpse or, at least, of a certain quantity of matter), Origen affirms that what resurrects is not the matter of the body but its *eidos*, its image, which remains unchanged throughout all its material transformations. On the other hand, precisely because Origen still considered the *eidos* a material principle, albeit a spiritual and, literally, subtle matter, it was possible for the resurrected to fall again and to occupy a coarser body until the moment of *apocatastasis*, or final resurrection, in which the subtle matter of the *eidos* would be totally consumed. Yet even at this point the process could start over, in which case the image was virtually ineradicable.

Id. at 11-12.

Despite this last equivocation on the ultimate status of the *eidos*/ghost, Agamben ultimately opts for an interpretation of the eternal return in which it is in fact "totally consumed": "As an image of nothing, the *like* disappears in its own enduring, and is destroyed through its own salvation." *Id.* at 11, 12, 17. Here the "like" is an "image of nothing," Agamben explains, because in Nietzsche's doctrine of the eternal return, the "like" (*Gleich*) that returns is an "*Abbild*, an image which precedes both what it is the image of, and what it is impressed upon: a like, a likeness which anticipates both terms being compared, being likened." The "return" of (and to) such a pre-originary "like" in "eternal return of the same" as a redemption or salvation that, familiarly enough by now, is the "final identity" of passivity/receptivity (which he here identifies with Aristotle's *potentia passiva*) and activity/spontaneity (*potentia activa*). At the same time, however, he describes the eternal return in terms of an "image" that "is destroyed though its own salvation." That "image" is at once the Platonic *eidos* or Form that allows for all knowledge, but also, literally, a "ghost": Agamben traces the etymology of the German "*Gleich*" (as in Nietzsche's phrase "*ewige Wiederkehr des Gleichen*," the "eternal return of the same") to the word "*Leich*"—corpse—and thence to the image of the dead person that is its "ghost," that is, that "threatening and uncomfortable presence, which is none other than the image of the deceased, his likeness that returns obsessively." The doctrine of the eternal return, then, would be the attempt to think a de-Christianized "final resurrection" of the past (emblematized here by the dead) that would once and for all put to rest its obsessive and disconcerting return in ghostly form, a "final resurrection, in which the subtle matter of the *eidos* would be totally consumed."[162] Thus, to crystallize their specific difference in a phrase, for Derrida, the spectrality of the ghost is the very condition of possibility of politics, while for Agamben the goal of politics is the killing off—the final destruction—of the ghost and its "threatening and uncomfortable presence."

Against that larger background, Agamben's account of the politico-legal role of the Messiah comes into clearer focus. According to Agamben, the Messiah arrives on the scene in the historico-logical moment in which law assumes its destiny as pure form, pure "being in force" without further signification. What is the Messiah's role at this point? Agamben says that the Messiah effects an almost invisible yet critical displacement of this already ethereal structure, a "tiny displacement" dramatized in correspondence between Walter Benjamin and Gershom Scholem on the meaning of a scene in Kafka's *Trial.* Scholem had claimed that Kafka's *Trial* stood for a stage of law in which, although emptied of its meaningful content, still remained in force "without significance" as the "Nothing of Revelation." Against which interpretation, Agamben claims, Benjamin proposed an even more radical nihilism, a "messianic nihilism that nullifies even the

---

the "eternal return" is thus indeed, to use Agamben's expression from *Language and Death*, a "return to that which never was and that which it never left." And, as we have just seen, in the political salvation that this "return" also represents for Agamben, the specter—"*eidos*," "image," "ghost"—is finally also put to rest.

[162] *Id.* at 12.

Nothing and lets no form of law remain in force beyond its own content."[163] In the terms that we have been using, the Messiah is the slayer of the specter.

In this drama of opposing nihilisms, deconstruction, according to Agamben, represents the endorsement of Scholem's position. He compares deconstruction elsewhere to "a petrified or paralyzed messianism, that, like all messianism, nullifies the law, but then maintains it as the Nothing of Revelation in a perpetual and interminable state of exception, the 'state of exception' in which we live.'"[164] Agamben evidently means by this the following: Deconstruction destroys the authority of tradition, but then, instead of going deeper and thinking the overcoming of historicity, or that which causes the transmission of tradition without itself being transmitted (humanity's being-in-language, that "non-latency" that humanity must "assume . . . to have the experience of his speaking being," and so on), deconstruction leaves the *form* of tradition in place, now empty of its authoritative content, but otherwise continuing in force as all we have, since deconstruction denies the possibility of decisively going beyond tradition as such—the genuinely messianic step that Agamben wants to take.[165] The difference would thus be between a messianic moment emptied of all content—"without significance"—that remains operative in every "historical" moment of a tradition (Derrida), and a messianic moment that brings that history and tradition to an end (Agamben). Lurking behind this accusation is the critique of deconstruction discussed above, that is, that it remains within the tradition that it seeks to deconstruct by virtue of its maintaining the presuppositional form of language, thought and being instead of overcoming it. Deconstruction, according to Agamben's reading, maintains that presuppositional form while emptying it of all content, revealing the originary form of metaphysics not to be substance, but simply the negativity of presupposition itself (thematized in deconstruction by Derrida's notions of always pre-originary arche-writing, "trace," and so on).

Is Agamben's accusation that deconstruction is a false Messiah justified? Certainly, at least at first blush, his description of deconstruction's formal characteristics seems apt, not only in the apparent negativity of its presuppositional thematics but specifically with regard to the Derridian account of law as well: the messianic—but contentless—injunction that ethics directs to law and politics in Derrida's account indeed resembles, in certain

---

163 AGAMBEN, HOMO SACER, *supra* note 11, at 53.

164 AGAMBEN, *The Messiah*, *supra* note 74, at 171.

165 AGAMBEN, *supra* note 1, at 9.

respects, a law that is "in force without significance." Nevertheless, before attempting a definitive answer to that question—which will disclose what is fundamentally at stake in Derrida's reading of Nietzsche's "dangerous perhaps" as well as in Agamben's dispute with Derrida—let us return one more time to the relationship between messianism and language, this time, however, in Derrida's rather than Agamben's account.

How then does Derrida's articulation of the "messianic moment" of language differ from Agamben's? Derrida has himself spoken to the relationship between language and the messianic in an oral presentation from another context that provides a first pass at an answer:

> [The messianic in deconstruction] is not a question of messianism that one could easily translate in Judaeo-Christian or Islamic terms, but rather of a messianic structure that belongs to all language. There is no language without the performative dimension of the promise, the minute I open my mouth I am in the promise. Even if I say that "I don't believe in truth" or whatever, the minute I open my mouth there is a "believe me" at work. Even when I lie, and perhaps especially when I lie, there is a "believe me" in play. And this 'I promise you that I am speaking the truth' is a messianic apriori, a promise which, even if it is not kept, even if one knows that it cannot be kept, takes place and *qua* promise is messianic. And from this point of view, I do not see how one can pose the question of ethics if one renounces the motifs of emancipation and the messianic.
>
> . . .
>
> I would not call this attitude utopian. The messianic experience of which I spoke takes place here and now; that is, the fact of promising and speaking is an event that takes place here and now and is not utopian. This happens in the singular event of engagement, and when I speak of democracy to come (*la démocratie à venir*) this does not mean that tomorrow democracy will be realized, and it does not refer to a future democracy, rather it means that there is an engagement with regard to democracy which consists in recognizing the irreducibility of the promise when, in the messianic moment, 'it can come' . . . . There is the future . . . . There is something to come . . . . That can happen . . . that can happen, and I promise in opening the future or in leaving the future open. This is not utopian, it is what takes place here and now, in a here and now that I regularly try to dissociate from the present. . . . I try to dissociate the theme of singularity happening here and now from the theme of presence and, for me, there can be a here and

now without presence.[166]

In this passage we again see the characteristics of Derrida's political messianism: messianism as a question of the promise, the very "futurality" or opening of the future, the event, the non-utopian occurrence of the messianic event in the "here and now," and so on. But I want to focus on another aspect, one brought into relief by Agamben's very different conception: Here the messianic promise is instituted in the moment *of enunciation*—in the "the minute I open my mouth" to speak "here and now," regardless of the particular words I use. The messianic is not, in other words, the human confrontation with *the fact of language in general*—the fact that language exists as such—as it is for Agamben, but the promise and the appeal ("believe me!") embodied in each "singular event of engagement" with a concrete Other, in every individual act or performance of language.

Agamben's philosophy, political and otherwise, is devoted to discovering the philosopher's stone of language, its "thing itself," the naked fact of its existence, as the messianic key that will bring language, and therefore the linguistic being of humanity, back to itself in its own possibility. But for Derrida, that messianic possibility inheres not in the fulfillment of this massive historico-philosophical task, but already exists "here and now," and thus is already "real," it is a "real possibility"—in the singular acts of speech that each incorporate this promise and appeal to the Other who is being addressed by that enunciative act. It is this structure—a messianism that arises out of the concrete and singular "engagement" with the singular Other *today*, "here and now," in fact at every moment, and for that reason is not a "utopian" messianism but a quotidian messianism, an eminently practical messianism—that explains why Derrida says that "the question of ethics" is not even *askable*, it "cannot be posed," without adopting this "point of view." My thesis would be that it is because he focuses on the ontological question—the question of "language as such," "that language exists," that we always find ourselves already thrown or fallen into language in the act of speech, and so on—that the "ethical question" in the Levinasian sense is not and indeed "cannot be posed" by Agamben as a question that also concerns the political and political action.

We are now in a position to determine more precisely the relationship of Agamben's conception of potentiality to Derrida's notion of the "perhaps." I have been arguing that for Agamben, the authentic thought of "potentiality" lies ahead of us as a

---

[166] Jacques Derrida, *Remarks on Deconstruction and Pragmatism*, *in* DECONSTRUCTION AND PRAGMATISM 82-83 (Chantal Mouffe ed., 1996).

messianic task, the task of the "coming philosophy." This is not to say that we do not already have a conception of "potentiality"—we do have one, a brilliant one, Aristotle's—but this conception of potentiality itself remains fundamentally unthought, in the ontological sense, and the task of politics, its only chance for a future beyond the permanent "state of exception" in which we find ourselves, is to carry out that ontological project. In other words, the task of both politics and philosophy is to realize the "potentiality of potentiality," to bring into a kind of actuality (the qualifier is necessary because precisely what this will achieve is the overcoming of the potential/actuality distinction) of what now only exists as potentiality—which is to say, to make possibility itself real, to bring into the "here and now"—*for the very first time in history*—a "real possibility."

The Derridian "perhaps," I have already suggested, plays a different role. In particular, I tried to suggest, through the example of Derrida's deconstruction of Schmitt, that the "perhaps" is what guarantees the "always already" of an opportunity of action for thought and politics. We can now sharpen up that suggestion and link it finally to the question of ethics that remains my main interest here, as well as clarifying the ultimate stakes of Agamben's critique of Derrida. In the preceding passage, Derrida says that "[t]here is no language without the performative dimension of the promise." That performative dimension manifests itself, Derrida goes on to explain, in a "singular event of engagement," an event of engagement that represents, first of all, the engagement with the Other, since a speech act is always addressed *to* someone or something (even if that someone or something is sometimes abstract or indeterminate, or addressed to oneself as other). It is that performative promise presupposed in every speech act that is constitutive of the "ethicality" of the ethical relationship in general—the absolute alterity of the Other as indistinguishable from the unpredictable event of a "coming," an *à venir* that is itself the fundamental dimension of the future, but also the condition of the authentic thought of the political as well (*la dèmocratie à venir*, etc.).

But this performative promise is not *simply* a pragmatic reality of the communicative use of language in the singularity of particular encounters with particular others. In Derrida's thought—I am tempted to say, at its furthest reaches and in its deepest grounds—this absolutely presupposed performative engagement takes the form of an affirmation, acquiescence, or assent—a "yes"—to language itself, an "arche-originary *yes*" that is the invisible presupposition and condition of possibility of every speech act. This "arche-originary *yes*," he says, "engages a kind of arche-engagement, a kind of alliance or consent or promise lost in the acquiescence to the utterance which it always accompanies." It is thus "presupposed as the condition of possibility for all other performatives," and as such, "opens the eventness of every event, [but] is not itself an event."[167] To grasp the significance of this notion, let us follow Derrida's original derivation and explication of this "yes," which occurs in a long footnote in a book devoted to Heidegger, but which, it seems to me, applies with equal persuasive force to Agamben's own "[interrogation] of the essence of language."[168]

"What is the essence of language?"[169] Derrida proposes that if one begins with this question—as does Heidegger in his later work, as does, in a different way, Agamben in his own political-ontological analysis of the linguistic being of entities—then one is immediately confronted with a paradox:

> [A]t the moment at which we pose the ultimate question, i.e., when we interrogate . . . the possibility of any question, i.e., language, we must be *already* in the element of language. Language must already be speaking for us—it must, so to speak, be already spoken and addressed to us . . . . Language is *already* there, in advance . . . at the moment at which any question can arise about it.

And thus any *use* of language—even the use of language to question the very possibility of language—has already, in a sense, assented to or acquiesced in language, said "yes" to it, simply by virtue of the fact that every linguistic act is always already in the medium of language, no matter what its form or content. Because language thus remains "in advance" of every utterance, Derrida says that it is "before any contract, a sort of promise of originary alliance," an *a priori* "pledge" that is the condition of possibility of every discourse, no matter how negative, skeptical, or questioning its explicit content.[170]

But, Derrida emphasizes, this "arche-originary *yes*" is not itself a speech act or an event, even if it is the condition of possibility of every speech act and event. Or rather, it is what might be called an arche-event—rather like the contentless ethical

[167] Jacques Derrida, *A Number of Yes*, 2 QUI PARLE 120, 129 (Brain Holmes trans., 1988) [hereinafter Derrida, *A Number of Yes*].

[168] JACQUES DERRIDA, OF SPIRIT: HEIDEGGER AND THE QUESTION 129 n.5 (Geoffrey Bennington & Rachel Bowlby trans., Univ. of Chicago Press 1989) (1987) [DERRIDA, OF SPIRIT].

[169] *Id.*

[170] *Id.*

injunction to which it gives rise, it is the event of pure memory and pure anticipation themselves, without any determined content: "an event of which the memory [*mémoire*] comes before any particular recollection [*souvenir*]."[171] Thus, "it is never *present* as such,"[172] because it has no "being" as such; the *yes* is, as Derrida emphasizes, the unavoidable presupposition of all language only in the form of "an absolute performative," that is, a pure *act* that has no content or result beyond the pure action of its acquiescence.[173] For this reason, the "arche-originary *yes*" appears nowhere in the speech act itself; it accompanies every speech act, but always "silently." Thus, very much like the self-withdrawal of Being in the later Heidegger, "[t]hat which translates this non-presence into a present *yes*, in the act of an utterance or in any act, dissimulates the arche-originary *yes* in the very motion which reveals it." Accordingly, because it itself lacks "being"—the ontological status of an entity—the arche-originary *yes* also cannot be the object of knowledge or of historical occurrence: Derrida says that it is "[torn] from the grasp of all knowledge, and in particular from all history."[174]

If we pause at this point to consider the characteristics of this arche-originary *yes*, we will find that it seems to bear a strong resemblance to that "thing itself" of language which is the touchstone of Agamben's politics and ontology. Derrida's *yes*, although it stands beyond language and history, is presupposed in every linguistic act by language itself and by every event. At the same, in its very taking place, the *yes* removes itself from any thematization in the linguistic act and thus remains beyond the sphere of knowledge. These are the very characteristics of the "thing itself" of language that Agamben identifies: that presupposition which makes language "sayable" in the first instance yet which remains unsaid in the speech act itself.[175] Even more fundamentally, Derrida's *yes* would seem to capture the essence of Agamben's political goal of a "zone in which possibility and reality, potentiality and actuality, become indistinguishable."[176] The *yes* is the condition of possibility of speech and events in

[171] *Id.* at 130.

[172] Derrida, *A Number of Yes*, *supra* note 167, at 130.

[173] *Id.* at 129.

[174] *Id.* at 130.

[175] *See* GIORGIO AGAMBEN, *The Thing Itself*, *in* POTENTIALITIES: COLLECTED ESSAYS IN PHILOSOPHY 35 (Daniel Heller-Roazen ed. & trans., 1999) ("The thing itself is not a thing; it is the very sayability, the very openness at issue in language, which, in language, we always presuppose and forget, perhaps because it is at bottom its own oblivion and abandonment.").

[176] AGAMBEN, COMING COMMUNITY, *supra* note 47, at 56.

general that is indistinguishable from their pure taking-place, and thus both their "potentiality" and the pure form of their "actuality," their "possibility" and their "reality." By the same token, the *yes* is the union of pure activity—an "absolute performative," pure taking-place itself—and pure passivity, an act that acts by doing nothing beyond acquiescing, affirming, assenting, in short, a pure *response* without further content and in particular without judgment (which is why Derrida characterizes it as an "arche-originary" *yes* that precedes the distinction between affirmation and negation, "yes" and "no").

It may appear, at this point, that we have encountered a final point of intersection between Agamben and Derrida's thought, a "presuppositionless presupposition" that they themselves share. In that case, of course, one would be constrained to conclude that Agamben is simply mistaken about Derrida when he attributes to the structure of his thought the form of bottomless negativity, presupposition without end. The "arche-originary *yes*" indeed appears to represent precisely the end of that negativity, a non-negative ground of language and of being in general that is structurally homologous to Agamben's "thing itself" of language. For at least two reasons, however, matters are not that simple, and Agamben's characterization of Derrida's thought remains accurate, at least up to a point.

The first reason is that the *yes* itself is not "simple."[177] Insofar as it is a *yes*—an acquiescence, an engagement, a response—it is always already internally divided into more than one, the recall of a past affirmation and the promise of a future affirmation. "Let us suppose a first *yes*," Derrida says, "the arche-originary *yes* which engages, promises and acquiesces before all else."

> On one hand it is originarily, in its very structure, a response. It is *firstly second*, coming after a demand, a question or another *yes*. On the other hand, as an engagement or a promise, it must *at least* bind itself beforehand to a confirmation in a next *yes*. *Yes* to the next, or to the other *yes*, already there but nonetheless yet to come. . . . Promise of memory and memory of promise. This "second" *yes* is a *priori* enveloped in the "first." The "first" would not take place without the project, the bet or the promise, the mission or the emission, the send-off of the second which is already there in it. This last, this first, doubles itself in advance: *yes*, *yes*, previously assigned to its repetition.[178]

[177] Derrida, *A Number of Yes*, *supra* note 167, at 130 (emphasis omitted) ("[T]he *yes* never lets itself be reduced to any ultimate simplicity.").

[178] *Id.* at 130-31.

According to its logical structure, a *yes*—even, or especially, a pure *yes*, an "arche-originary *yes*"—is always already both a response to something that precedes it (which, whether "a demand, a question or another *yes*" is itself always already engaged by its own arche-originary *yes*) and a promise or pledge of another *yes* to follow. Thus Agamben is quite right to describe Derrida's thought in terms of its bringing the pure, presuppositional structure of language to light: the arche-originary *yes* or "pledge [*gage*] which precedes any other engagement in language or action"[179] itself, always already, both presupposes and is presupposed by other *yeses*. By the same token, however, Agamben would appear to be utterly wrong insofar as he characterizes this presuppositional structure in terms of Derrida's endorsement of "negativity" or a "negative ontological foundation" (as he has been doing at least since *Language and Death: The Place of Negativity* was published in 1982),[180] since this presuppositional structure is rather the consequence of a pure *affirmation* that precedes all language and action.

Agamben might nevertheless be able to respond that the name one attaches to this structure ("affirmative" or "negative") is unimportant, and that, functionally, Derrida's arche-originary *yes*—which, after all, precedes the distinction between "affirmation" and "negation"—is "negative" in the only sense that matters for Agamben's purposes, which is that it consigns the final foundation of language, meaning and action (language's "thing itself") to the abyss of infinite deferral. And this response might be well-taken, were there nothing more to the arche-originary *yes* than a formal structure of infinite presupposition. Derrida's *yes* is not, in fact, primarily formal, however, but rather the signifier (or, to be more accurate, a quasi-transcendental signifier)[181] of the

---

179 DERRIDA, OF SPIRIT, *supra* note 168, at 130.

180 AGAMBEN, LANGUAGE AND DEATH, *supra* note 8:

> From this point of view it is possible to measure the acuteness of Derrida's critique of the metaphysical tradition and also the distance that remains to be covered.... To identify the horizon of metaphysics simply in that supremacy of the *phone* and then to believe in one's power to overcome this horizon through the *gramma*, is to conceive of metaphysics without its coexistent negativity. Metaphysics is always already grammatology and this is *fundamentology* in the sense that the *gramma* (or the Voice) functions as the negative ontological foundation.

Id. at 39.

181 Derrida, along with others, has used the term "quasi-transcendental" to describe the various terms ("trace," "*différance*," "iterability," "spectrality," etc.) that he has privileged over the years. What the "arche-originary *yes*" shares with these terms—the characteristic that constitutes the "quasi" of their quasi-transcendental status—is the manner in which it simultaneously serves as a condition of possibility, master descriptor, or similar transcendental term for some domain of thought or action and remains inseparable from,

infinite responsibility to absolute alterity that constitutes the core of his political philosophy. Every act of language, Derrida says, in a formula that could have been lifted directly from Levinas, "answers in advance, and whatever it does, to this pledge and of this pledge. It is engaged by it in a responsibility it has not chosen and which assigns it even its liberty."[182]

Beyond the presuppositional structure that it retains, this responsibility in which the *yes* always already engages every utterance and act is the other characteristic that distinguishes Derrida's arche-originary *yes* from the ontological orientation of Agamben's "being in language" or "thing itself" of language. The ethics of responsibility is not an ethical imperative imposed on language, action or existence from the outside—for example, from the sphere of law, as Agamben suggests[183]—but is rather the originary (or rather arche-originary) structure of each of these domains. The *yes* that accompanies every utterance and event is, in itself and by virtue of the very structure of affirmation as assent or acquiescence, a response to another, and thus, always already and necessarily a response to what might be called an "arche-responsibility" that precedes it. The presuppositional structure of the *yes* is therefore not primarily formal or even ontological, concerned with the mode of its being, but rather *ethical* in the Levinasian sense. In Derrida's interpretation, then, the "arche-responsibility" revealed by the *yes* of language thus turns Heidegger's formula on its head. It is not ethics that is a regional domain of fundamental ontology, but the reverse: Rather than saying that the thought of ethics as "the abode of man . . . is not ethics in the first instance, because it is ontology," one should rather say that the thought of language as "the house of Being" is

or tainted by, that same domain. Thus, in the case of the *yes* or "pledge" ("*gage*," in French), Derrida says that "the fact that it precedes language does not mean that it is foreign to it. The *gage* engages in language—and so always in *a* language." DERRIDA, OF SPIRIT, *supra* note 168, at 130. This "tainting" of the transcendental by the field that it ostensibly transcends and determines has enormous consequences for the form that Derrida's philosophy—*qua* philosophy—takes in all of his work, and, in particular, is one reason for the "presuppositional" form that it retains, to Agamben's dismay. In this regard, one should compare Derrida's insistence that the *yes* (or *gage*) "engages in language . . . always in *a* language" with Agamben's comments, discussed *supra*, regarding the "radical vision of Community" represented by the experience of the fact "that *there is language*"—an experience which, he emphasizes (in diametrical opposition to Derrida's own statement), *cannot* be represented by the fact that there is "*a* language, . . . a state or a patrimony of names and rules which each people transmit from generation to generation." AGAMBEN, *supra* note 1, at 9.

[182] DERRIDA, OF SPIRIT, *supra* note 168, at 130. The specific context is a discussion of the status of "the question" in Heidegger's thought but the statements concerning the "yes" and the "pledge" have general applicability.

[183] *See* AGAMBEN, REMNANTS OF AUSCHWITZ, *supra* note 52, at 22.

not ontology in the first instance, because it is ethics.[184]

It is in this sense that Derrida says that language is always already "engaged by [the *yes*] in a responsibility that it has not chosen." But, in the same sentence, he goes on to say this structure of responsibility also "assigns it even its liberty." What can this mean? How can "liberty" be "assigned," especially by a responsibility that has not itself been freely chosen?[185]

The arche-originary *yes* is a "[p]romise of memory, memory of promise" insofar as, as we have seen, it necessarily both recalls an earlier affirmation to which it is a response and promises another affirmation to come. But, Derrida says, paradoxically "memory itself must forget in order to fulfill what is, since the *yes*, its mission."

> Promised simultaneously with the "first," the "second" *yes* must come as an absolute renewal, again absolutely, once again absolutely inaugural and "free," failing which it could only be a natural, psychological or logical consequence. It must act as if the "first" were forgotten, far enough past to require a new, initial *yes*.[186]

The second *yes*, although already promised by the first, must be no less inaugural and spontaneous because otherwise it would not be a *yes* at all, whatever form it might take. It would instead merely be a causal or logical consequence, and would therefore, in itself, signify nothing beyond the first *yes*—in that sense, it would not be a (separate, distinct) affirmation, assent or acquiescence at all. Or, to put it in the terms of Derrida's more distinctly ethical-political-juridical writings, it would represent a "calculation" rather than a "decision," the mechanical following of the law laid down by the "first" *yes* rather than the unsubsumable singularity of a just decision. In sum, the responsibility always already assumed by the presupposed *yes* of language dictates that this *yes* itself be absolutely free and freely given, undetermined and unconditioned by anything outside itself. That responsibility "assigns it even its liberty."

---

184 MARTIN HEIDEGGER, *Letter on Humanism*, *in* BASIC WRITINGS FROM *BEING AND TIME* (1927) TO *THE TASK OF THINKING* (1964) 243 (David Farrell Krell ed., 1977).

185 Without having the space to elaborate, I will note that in the following argument yet another specter of Nietzsche looms up in the background, one that Derrida again makes very much his own (and that might not be recognizable from the perspective of a more conventional reading)—the Nietzsche of the opening passages of the Second Essay of *On the Genealogy of Morals*, in which he weaves together the themes of forgetfulness and memory, responsibility and freedom, the leveled calculability and uniformity of the mass of humanity and the free will of the sovereign individual, around the figure of man as the "animal *with the right to make promises*." NIETZSCHE, *On the Genealogy of Morals*, *supra* note 111, Second Essay para. 1, at 57.

186 Derrida, *A Number of Yes*, *supra* note 167, at 131.

Pausing again to take stock, it may appear that we have strayed rather far from our starting point—the structure and role of the never-fulfilled, always deferred messianic promise in Derrida's political philosophy and the place of the "perhaps" and the "specter" in that structure. Where, in this complex structure of affirmation and presupposition, memory and promise, responsibility and freedom, do these other specters of Nietzsche manifest themselves?

If my reconstruction is at all accurate, then it *is* a structure of sorts, even a "theory" of the political grounded in the messianic/affirmative structure of language, which Derrida is asserting as "the truth" and is therefore also urging upon us, at least implicitly, as a new understanding and new form of politics to adopt as our own. If so, would this not be another version of the eschatology that Derrida purports to reject—a proposed "answer" for all those unresolved conundrums of politics that would allow for a clean break with the past? Or is it possible that that undecidability and pure contingency—"that which may not happen, that which happens only in so far as it might just as well not happen, this undecidable eventuality *qua* real possibility, that informs decisions and forms truth"[187]—is located somewhere "within" this theory? On the other hand, wouldn't such a theory—precisely insofar as it is a "theory"—necessarily exclude, or, what amounts to the same thing, sublate or capitalize on that undecidability or contingency in the process of generating its conclusions, consequences, or prescriptions? Would it not, to put it another way, reintroduce a surreptitious privileging of the "calculative" (the reasoned, the consistent, the argumentative, the predictable, the legal, the law-like, the mechanical, repetition, iteration—fatality, in a word) over the unsubsumable singularity of the ethical and the just at the level of his own thought? Would it not, in sum, abdicate that very spontaneous responsibility that is the critical element not only of ethics and justice, but of the *yes* of language itself? Has Derrida forgotten to "forget"?[188]

Perhaps not. In *Politics of Friendship*, Derrida himself describes this possibility as the chief "temptation" of his book, posing the question in this way: "if politics were at last grounded in this friendship, this one and no other, the politics of *this* hyperbole [that is, the friendship grounded on the arche-originary, hyperbolic responsiveness, responsibility and assent that accompanies every address to another in language, regardless of how otherwise hostile

[187] DERRIDA, POLITICS OF FRIENDSHIP, *supra* note 2, at 128.

[188] Derrida, *A Number of Yes*, *supra* note 167, at 131 (the "second *yes's*" "memory itself must forget in order to fulfill what is, since the [first] *yes*, its mission").

that utterance might be], would this not be to break with the entire history of the political, this old, tiring and tired, exhausted history?" But he goes on to declare the following:

> [It is a temptation that] this same book owes itself to resist. . . . Not to resist so as to deny, exclude or oppose, but precisely to keep the temptation in sight of its chance: not to be taken for an assurance or a programme. Again the question of the *perhaps*, the paradoxical conditions for an event or a decision.[189]

Derrida is saying here that the *perhaps*—sheer contingency itself, that which lies at the opposite pole from any "assurance or programme"—is the very "chance" of that "temptation" to convert the inherent structure of speech and language represented by the arche-originary *yes* into a theory, and thus that the very condition of possibility of that temptation is the resistance that one brings to bear against it.[190] And thus it is entirely consistent and even logical (in the pretzel-like logic that applies here) that Derrida should on one hand say that the "perhaps" comes "before"—in the non-temporal sense of a presupposition—the arche-original *yes* and its engagement with the other in order "to make [it] possible,"[191] and yet on the other, that "it [could] never be a matter of *grounding* anything, above all of grounding a politics, on the virtue of a 'perhaps.'"[192]

If the *perhaps* is thus indeed a "paradoxical condition of possibility" of the temptation to theorize, it is a perfectly comprehensible one from the ethical (in the Levinasian sense) perspective taken by Derrida's political thought. To repeat what was said above, there is no ethical encounter in the genuine sense outside of the "perhaps," that is, outside the pure, unpredictable, unanticipatably contingent event of its occurrence. Short of that pure contingency, the encounter cannot be "ethical" because the encounter is not with an absolutely Other. To the extent that the encounter *can* be predicted, calculated, or, more generally, *known*—become the object of knowledge in any form—one has also to that extent not opened oneself to alterity as such but only to one's own horizon of expectation, knowledge, and so on.

---

189 DERRIDA, POLITICS OF FRIENDSHIP, *supra* note 2, at 218.

190 Put in these terms, it is difficult not to think of Paul de Man's dictum that theory is nothing but the resistance to theory. PAUL DE MAN, *The Resistance to Theory*, *in* THE RESISTANCE TO THEORY 19 (1986). This is a connection that, whatever its significance, I cannot pursue here.

191 DERRIDA, POLITICS OF FRIENDSHIP, *supra* note 2, at 38 ("Now this *perhaps* not only comes 'before' the question (investigation, research, knowledge, theory, philosophy); it would come, in order to make it possible, 'before' the originary acquiescence which engages the question in advance with [*auprès de*] the other.").

192 *Id.* at 218.

Nevertheless, the "perhaps" is plainly the antithesis of the "knowledge" represented by theory, and it is difficult to understand how it could constitute its "condition of possibility" rather than its abyss. Note, however, that Derrida does not say that the "perhaps" is the condition of possibility of theory, but of the "temptation" to theorize, which is a different matter entirely. When one employs language in order to be understood—which is the minimum threshold description of any utterance that can be categorized as "theoretical"—one does so against the background possibility, whether conscious or unconscious, that this utterance will instead be misunderstood, and this possibility of misunderstanding—of being taken out of its intentional context and "read" in another, where its meaning will be different—is inseparable from the possibility of understanding. This is, in essence, Derrida's insight in his early work on speech act theory and the notion of "iterability" that haunts that theory from the outset.[193] But in *Politics of Friendship* and his other later, ethical-political work, he seems to go further and suggest that this same structure of iterability, or "haunting," is the condition of possibility of the *impulse*, *desire* or *motive* ("temptation") of both the speech act and the event (and the "political event" in particular): "for me *to hope to be understood* beyond all dialectics of misunderstanding, etc., the possibility of failure must, in addition, not be simply an accidental edge of the condition, but its haunting."[194]

When one addresses another in order to be understood, one simultaneously (regardless of one's intentions, conscious or unconscious) responds with an acquiescing *yes* to a prior call of language (whether that call takes the form of a prior utterance of the other addressed or of the always-prior existence of language itself), and promises another *yes* to come. But one cannot *know* in the moment of that arche-originary *yes*—its messianic here-and-now—whether that earlier call was addressed to you (or indeed was "addressed" at all—it may have been an accident of nature (wind whispering in the trees, etc.) that by pure chance appeared to have a signifying intention); nor can one know whether the originary promise of the "first" *yes* will in fact be fulfilled and issue

193 *See* JACQUES DERRIDA, *Signature Event Context*, *in* MARGINS OF PHILOSOPHY (Alan Bass trans., Univ. of Chicago Press 1982) (1972).

194 DERRIDA, POLITICS OF FRIENDSHIP, *supra* note 2, at 218-19 (emphasis added). *See also* DERRIDA, SPECTERS OF MARX, *supra* note 6, at 73 ("This indifference to the content [of the ethical injunction that enjoins political calculation] here is not an indifference, it is not an *attitude* of indifference, on the contrary. Marking any opening to the event and to the future as such, it therefore conditions the interest in and not the indifference to anything whatsoever, to all content in general. Without it, there would be neither intention, nor need, nor desire, and so on.").

in the form of the "second," promised *yes* (nothing can guarantee that any promise will in fact be carried out). More important—and this seems to me to be Derrida's subtlest, and most political, point about the political consequences of the *yes*—one has to not-know in order to *want* to speak or otherwise use language at all, because to the extent that one *does* know—to the extent that one has the assurance that one is acquiescing in another's call and making an affirmation whose echoing confirmation in the form of another *yes* is guaranteed—then one has no need to speak, because one is "communicating" only with oneself.[195] The absolute Other (including the "absolute Other" that even those most familiar to us always remain in crucial part) is the only one with whom one can have any reason or inclination or—strictly speaking—possibility to *communicate*; but the Other, as such, is not "knowable," is not reducible to an object of knowledge.

Three consequences flow from this. First, we can now see how the "perhaps" is indeed "before" the arche-originary *yes* as its "paradoxical condition of possibility"—there could be no *yes*, no pure response or promise, without the inner possibility of its "haunting" by misunderstanding or failure. Accordingly, the messianic promise to which the *yes* gives rise in every speech act and event is inherently undecidable; like the ethical injunction, it promises without content because it *cannot know* the form that the politics it enjoins will or even ought to take. It is tempting to say that this in no way diminishes its ethical and political force; indeed, as the preceding discussion hoped to show, that absence of knowledge is not only a necessary condition but the highest desideratum of any legitimate form of politics. Having thus been tempted, it is a separate question, however, whether one ought to give in to this temptation or to resist it—to resist it in order to give it its very "chance," as Derrida says of the temptation to theorize discussed above. For the following reasons, I hesitate simply to conclude with the proposition that the undecidability of the "perhaps" provides the key to that linkage of the ethical and the political that has been my (and, I believe, Derrida and Agamben's)

---

[195] *See, e.g.*, DERRIDA, POLITICS OF FRIENDSHIP, *supra* note 2, at 219:

> At this point, practical performativity is irreducible to any theorem; this is why we have stressed the performative force which had to prevail in both versions of a sentence which in any case, in addressing another, could not count on any assurance, any purely theoretical criterion of intelligibility or accord; it *could not* count on such assurance, but above all *it had to* and *desired not to want* to count on such an assurance, which would destroy in advance the possibility of addressing the other as such.

Id.; *see also id.* at 220 (noting that ethical desire "must indeed desire that which goes to make the essence of desire: this non-assurance and this risk of misunderstanding").

topic all along, however tempted I am to do so.

Derrida describes the "perhaps"—the "possibility of failure," of misunderstanding, etc.—as "haunting" the structure of the arche-originary *yes* of language. In that sense, one could say that the "perhaps" is the specter of the *yes*, its condition of possibility that is properly indistinguishable from each of the *yes's* own moments (insofar as both memory and promise incorporate in their very concepts the possibility of going astray, failing, etc.). By the same token, however, one could as easily say that the *yes* is the specter of the "perhaps," the incarnated apparition of the pure insubstantial "real possibility" of possibility. The possibility of this reversal, Derrida suggests, is a function of "haunting" or spectrality itself, which "must leave an imprint right on the body it seems to threaten, *to the point of merging indissociably with it, as inseparable from it as its essence or essential attributes*."[196] The spectrality of the ghost thus adds another layer of undecidability to that already supplied by the "perhaps," an undecidability that is considerably more threatening than the benign condition of possibility of the ethical relationship represented by that first undecidability. The undecidability of the specter suggests the possibility not just of not knowing, but of not knowing that one is not knowing, and therefore of mistaking one thing for another—a possibility that is indelible since, Derrida says, the specter cannot be distinguished from the "essence" of that which it haunts. The effects of this spectral undecidability might still be contained if they could be limited to indistinguishable exchanges and misrecognitions among the elements of Derrida's system—the specter, the "perhaps," and the *yes* (although even so limited it would still wreak havoc on the logic of that system itself, since Derrida states unequivocally, for example, that the "perhaps" comes "before" the *yes*—a proposition whose meaning and consequences could no longer be ascertained with any assurance).

But these effects cannot be so limited, and the radical and indeed menacing uncertainty disseminates itself throughout language, rendering any theoretical claim—including a theoretical claim about the priority of ethics to theory—at least suspect. For example, as pointed out above, Derrida compares the *yes* to an "absolute" or pure performative. But the *yes* is never in fact or in practice pure, because it is never found in isolation but only accompanying individual speech acts. And thus we can only refer to it at all *in a (particular) language*—for example, by employing the English word "yes"—with all of the historical baggage, the

[196] *Id.* at 219 (emphasis added).

sometimes violent exclusions, biases or prejudices, that go into the history of every national idiom. The logic of spectrality guarantees that we will never be certain, at the moment that we make a statement about the "*yes*"—no matter how cabined around with additional qualifying or explanatory language—that the *yes* we are expressing is the quasi-transcendental, arche-originary *yes* that "precedes any other engagement in language or action," or rather simply a word "in *a* language," and thus historically conditioned and limited in ways that remain invisible to the idiom itself.[197] It is this doubled, and menacing, spectral undecidability that suggests a certain prudence before dèclaring any final solutions to the problems of politics in the form of the "dangerous perhaps."

Second, it follows from the structure of this spectral undecidability that any politics that acknowledges the primacy of the "perhaps" runs the risk of incorporating the spectral double of ethical responsibility for which the "perhaps" is the condition of possibility. "Theoretically, it can always flip into its opposite," Derrida says. It thus follows that this risk cannot be avoided, and that "[w]ithout the possibility of radical evil, of perjury, and of absolute crime, there is no responsibility, no freedom, no decision."[198] Just as the promissory structure of the "first" and "second" *yeses* (which the logic of spectrality also underwrites) always threatens to lose its affirmative character by turning into a meaningless mechanical repetition, the logic of spectrality dictates that one can never be certain that any apparently ethical impulse is not the product of an obsessive and meaningless "*revenance*"—a Freudian "death instinct or a drive to destruction"[199]—nor can one ever be sure, in Carl Schmitt's political framework, that one's "friend" is not instead, or rather at the same time, one's "enemy."[200] Nevertheless, however potentially disastrous its consequences for ethics and politics, the logic of spectrality remains *at the same time* the only condition of possibility of responsibility, of ethics, and of the future of the political good in the form of "*la démocratie à venir*." For Derrida as much as for

---

[197] DERRIDA, OF SPIRIT, *supra* note 169, at 130:

> [B]efore the word, there is this sometimes wordless word which we name the "yes." A sort of pre-originary pledge [*gage*] which precedes any other engagement in language or action. But the fact that it precedes language does not mean that it is foreign to it. The *gage* engages in language—and so always in *a* language.

Id.

[198] DERRIDA, POLITICS OF FRIENDSHIP, *supra* note 2, at 219. Indeed, Derrida says explicitly that "this possibility, as such, if there is one, must be neither living nor dead," which is to say that it must be spectral. *Id.*

[199] *Id.* at 218.

[200] *Id.* at 217.

Nietzsche, in a register that is at once similar and entirely different, there is indeed never a moment to rest secure in one's "good conscience."

Finally (third consequence), what this doubled and threatening undecidability means is that the problem of politics is intimately bound up with the problem of faith, or rather with that philosophical thought "that 'repeats' the possibility of religion without religion," as Derrida puts it.[201] Insofar as the "perhaps" defeats the possibility of knowledge in the form of a guaranteed response or event, and, beyond that, insofar as the logic of spectrality defeats every attempt to know whether (and what) we know or do not know at any given moment, what links us to the pre-originary ethical engagement of the *yes* (and thus by extension with every ethical engagement) is faith, "a faith which defeats any narrative."[202] This faith "defeats any narrative" both because it is a pure faith—supported by *nothing* beyond a pure act of credence—and because, paradoxically, it is at the same time necessary and unavoidable, a faith that is presupposed (like the *yes* itself) by every speech act and event and therefore cannot be "explained away," demystified, debunked or circumvented by any rationalist discourse.

The emphasis on the philosophical dignity of faith, religion and belief—particularly manifest throughout Derrida's work since the late 1980s—that has accompanied his renewed interest in ethics and politics, may seem particularly perverse from a conventional Nietzschean perspective. But here, too, Derrida turns the tables on Nietzsche's skepticism about the role of religion and belief by remaining true to Nietzsche's own skeptical spirit (or, I should say, one way of interpreting or inheriting that spirit). In *On the Genealogy of Morals*, Nietzsche's skepticism about religious faith receives perhaps its purest expression in his demystifying critique of Christianity as the credulous belief that the supreme "creditor" (God) would sacrifice himself for the sake of his debtors out of "love" alone.[203] Yet, in *The Gift of Death*, Derrida shows that even Nietzsche, in the course of this critique, cannot avoid the spectral logic of the *yes*, which inhabits his own incredulous questions ("can you believe it?") and which he

201 DERRIDA, GIFT OF DEATH, *supra* note 18, at 49.

202 DERRIDA, OF SPIRIT, *supra* note 168, at 130.

203 DERRIDA, GIFT OF DEATH, *supra* note 18, at 114 (quoting FRIEDRICH NIETZSCHE, *On the Genealogy of Morals*, Second Essay para. 21, *in* ON THE GENEALOGY OF MORALS & ECCE HOMO 92 (Walter Kaufmann ed., Walter Kaufmann & R. J. Hollingdale trans., 1989) (God as "the creditor (*der Gläubiger*) playing scapegoat for his debtor (*seinen Schuldner*), from *love* (can you believe it? [*sollte man's glauben?*]) from love of his debtor!").

necessarily presupposes in the form of his own arche-original belief in the belief of the Other to whom his question is addressed.[204]

But, as Derrida also makes clear, that unavoidable, structural "belief" that inhabits even Nietzsche's skepticism itself remains undecidably suspended between and among the creed of the religious believer, the (calculable) credit owed to the creditor, and the sheer credulousness of the fool. There is no avoiding the spectrality of the perhaps, nor should we want or expect any way of avoiding it, to the extent that we want our religion, our ethics and our politics to be worthy of those names. Here, then, is the most profound link between Derrida's interest in religion on one hand and the ethico-political on the other, the link that has determined the largely religious vocabulary that, as we have seen, has come to dominate his political thought ("messianicity," "testimony," "faith," etc.).

Having returned at last to our starting point in the notion of political messianism that Agamben and Derrida (almost) share—or rather, having returned to a point before that starting point, in the spectral logic of the "perhaps" that organizes that messianism in Derrida's thought—we can perhaps bring together the various threads of similarity and difference that I have tried to collect here. Derrida's messianism differs from Agamben's in that it eschews utopianism and eschatology of both the religious and secularized varieties in favor of a pragmatic messianism of the "here and now." The "perhaps" does not lie before us a messianic task of apocalyptic proportions, nor is it the culmination of an *experimentum linguae* that takes its orientation from the idealist model of "thought thinking itself." Rather, the "perhaps"—in the form of the *yes* of language that it makes possible without ever guaranteeing—is what lies always "before" us, "prior" to us, promising both that an affirmative politics of-and-in the here and now is also possible and that it is, or can be, or indeed always

[204] *The Gift of Death* ends with the following passage:

> How can one *believe* this history of *credence* or *credit?* That is what Nietzsche asks, *in fine*, what he asks himself or has asked by another, by the specter of his discourse. Is this a false or counterfeit question, a rhetorical question as one says in English? For what makes a rhetorical question possible can sometimes disturb the structure of it.
>
> As often happens, the call of or for the question, and the request that echoes through it, takes us further than the response. The question, the request, and the appeal *must* indeed have begun, since the eve of their awakening, by receiving accreditation from the other: by being believed. Nietzsche must indeed believe he knows what believing means, unless he means that it is all make-believe [*à moins qu'il n'entende le faire accroire*].

DERRIDA, *supra* note 18, at 115.

already will have been, ethical insofar as the Other will be/is/was (the temporality of verb tenses break down here) always already engaged. It is this affirmative prior engagement with the Other—"prior," that is, in the non-temporal sense of what opens the temporality of the future as the coming of the Other in the first place—that is lacking in Agamben's account of the political.

More fundamentally still, Agamben's entire political-ontological edifice in all of its many aspects and under all of its names—the "coming community" of "whatever singularities" that share only their common "belonging to language" in the form of their "being-called" in language, contingent necessity and necessary contingency, and so on—itself presupposes Derrida's *yes*. Humanity's long-awaited entry into the "fact of language" as such, the full compassing of the simple fact that "there is language" that for Agamben is the touchstone of humanity's political (as well as ontological) salvation, depends—as Agamben also makes clear—on language's "taking place," for example in the entity's "being-called" in language. But language only "takes place" in discourse, and discourse presupposes an Other (sometimes one's self as that Other, sometimes God, but always some form of interlocutor, no matter how narcissistic or abstract). The arche-original *yes* is the logical form of that presupposition, and the "arche-responsibility" that accompanies the *yes* in the form of an absolute and unwilled openness to alterity is its consequence.[205]

It seems to me that Agamben's attempt to uncover the originary presuppositionless presupposition of language is therefore doomed in itself and, *a fortiori*, as a basis for politics. Language presupposes the Other and is accordingly

---

[205] Among the figures that Agamben has returned to consistently as a primary exemplar of what he means by absolute "contingency" and the very "formula of potentiality" is Bartleby the Scrivener's repeated phrase, "I would prefer not to." AGAMBEN, *Bartleby*, *supra* note 84, at 255. It may only be a coincidence then, but if so it is a telling one, that in describing the unavoidable primacy of the *yes* (the *Zusage*, in Heidegger's formulation), Derrida resorts in an interview to citing Bartleby as an example of the absolute reach of this primacy:

> Even this "I would prefer not to," which doesn't measure anything, which is not a refusal, or an acceptance, in which he was simply saying he would prefer not to—neither negation nor affirmation—even in this case the simple fact that he answers "I would prefer not to," even if he said nothing by this sentence, if he accepted nothing or denied nothing, this is a *Zusage*: he finally says "Yes" to the other, "I speak to you, even if I don't say 'Yes,' even if I don't say 'No,' even if I don't say 'Perhaps,' I uttered something, I answered, by not answering I answered something." This answer is a *Zusage*. . . .

Jacques Derrida, *On Responsibility*, *in Responsibilities of Deconstruction*, PLI – WARWICK J. OF PHIL. 19, 35 (Jonathon Dronsfield & Nick Midgley eds., 1997) (interview with Jonathon Dronsfield, Nick Midgley & Adrian Wilding).

presuppositional in its essence. Only by hypostasizing it in the ontological form of "language as such" can Agamben conjure the image of a primordial relationship to language that does not pass through discourse and thus the relationship to the Other. But that suppressed relationship to alterity—the *yes* said with every utterance—nevertheless continues to haunt Agamben's ontological account of language as its (spectral) condition of possibility. In that sense, at least, it would appear that Derrida's "hauntological politics" is indeed "larger and more powerful" than Agamben's politico-ontology, and "would harbor within itself, but like circumscribed places or particular effects, [Agamben's] eschatology and teleology themselves."[206]

If this conclusion sounds like an endorsement of Derrida's concept of the political over Agamben's, that is no doubt how I intend it to be read. But, by that very token, as we have already discussed above, one ought to at least pause to reflect again that this type of decisive theoretical judgment is in one sense deeply (and theoretically) inconsistent with the theory that it is seeking to affirm. Agamben's is an ethics of *ēthos*—authentic and originary human dwelling, the return to the "habitual," what is most one's own—but Derrida's is an ethics of the coming of the "stranger" who (in Levinas's words) "disturbs the being at home with oneself [*le chez soi*]," and thus also any sense of self-satisfaction or repose.[207] Accordingly, while the fundamental mood (or, to use the more philosophically charged Heideggerian term, *Stimmung*) of Agamben's political philosophy is "ease,"[208] the *Stimmung* of Derrida's philosophy might be called "unease," the constant recognition of the radical uncertainty and risk that one's judgments, theoretical and otherwise, might be profoundly *unethical* rather than ethical and responsible. One can therefore at least wonder about the apparent performative contradiction implicit in any truth claim or judgment made under the rubric of a theoretical position so radically opposed to any form of "good conscience" in Nietzsche's sense, including the claim that Derrida's Levinasian account of ethics and politics has theoretical (and ethical) priority over Agamben's Heideggerian-ontological interpretation.

And in fact, in another place, I have tried to demonstrate that such a judgment is perhaps more difficult than I have made it appear—that Agamben's discourse is haunted by a "specter of

---

206 DERRIDA, SPECTERS OF MARX, *supra* note 6, at 10.

207 EMMANUEL LEVINAS, TOTALITY AND INFINITY: AN ESSAY ON EXTERIORITY 39 (Alphonso Lingis trans., Duquesne Univ. Press 1969) (1961).

208 AGAMBEN, COMING COMMUNITY, *supra* note 47, at 25 (chapter titled "Ease").

Levinas" that becomes indistinguishable from the essence of his own position, and that Derrida's political discourse is no less haunted by an "ontologization of the ethical" that it cannot avoid.[209] Had I the time and space, I would have concluded with that discussion here. There is no—or rather ought not to be any—end to theoretical discussions, but other considerations, including above all that recognition of our finitude that is the hallmark of both Agamben and Derrida's ethics, impose the responsibility to decide nevertheless. And so, in no good conscience, allow me to conclude with that caveat and promise of more to be said.

---

[209] *See* Adam Thurschwell, Specters of Nietzsche: Potential Futures for the Concept of the Political in Agamben and Derrida (long version), at 124-50, *available at* http://www.law.csuohio.edu/faculty/thurschwell/nietzsche.pdf.

Part IV
Timely Reflections on the Scholarly Enterprise

[17]

WE SCHOLARS

Friedrich Nietzsche

204

At the risk that moralizing will here, too, turn out to be what it has always been-namely, according to Balzac, an intrepid *montrer ses plaies*—I venture to speak out against an unseemly and harmful shift in the respective ranks of science and philosophy, which is now threatening to become established, quite unnoticed and as if it were accompanied by a perfectly good conscience. I am of the opinion that only *experience*-experience always seems to mean bad experience?—can entitle us to participate in the discussion of such higher questions of rank, lest we talk like blind men about colors—*against* science the way women and artists do ("Oh, this dreadful science!" sigh their instinct and embarrassment; "it always gets to the *bottom* of things!").

The scholar's declaration of independence, his emancipation from philosophy, is one of the more refined effects of the democratic order—and disorder: the self-glorification and self-exaltation of scholars now stand in full bloom, in their finest spring, everywhere—which is not meant to imply that in this case self-praise smells pleasant. "Freedom from all masters!" that is what the instinct of the rabble wants in this case, too; and after science has most happily rid itself of theology whose "handmaid" it was too long, it now aims with an excess of high spirits and a lack of understanding to lay down laws for philosophy and to play the "master" herself—what am I saying? the *philosopher*.

My memory—the memory of scientific man, if you'll forgive me—is bulging with naïvetés of overbearing that I have heard about philosophy and the philosophers from the lips of young natural scientists and old physicians (not to speak of the most learned and conceited of all scholars, the philologists and schoolmen, who are both by profession). Sometimes it was the specialist and nook dweller who instinctively resisted any kind of synthetic enterprise and talent; sometimes the

1. FRIEDRICH NIETZSCHE, BEYOND GOOD AND EVIL: PRELUDE TO A PHILOSOPHY OF THE FUTURE (Walter Kaufmann trans.) (Vantage Books: New York, 1966), excerpting pages 118-23, 134-40 without the Editor's commentary.

industrious worker who had got a whiff of *otium* and the noble riches in the psychic economy of the philosopher which had made him feel defensive and small. Sometimes it was that color blindness of the utility man who sees nothing in philosophy but a series of *refuted* systems and a prodigal effort that "does nobody any good." Sometimes the fear of masked mysticism and a correction of the limits of knowledge leaped forward; sometimes lack of respect for individual philosophers that had involuntarily generalized itself into lack of respect for philosophy.

Most frequently, finally, I found among young scholars that what lay behind the arrogant contempt for philosophy was the bad aftereffect of—a philosopher to whom they now denied allegiance on the whole without, however, having broken the spell of his cutting evaluation of other philosophers—with the result of an over-all irritation with all philosophy. (Schopenhauer's aftereffect on our most modern Germany, for example, seems to me to be of this kind: with his unintelligent wrath against Hegel he has succeeded in wrenching the whole last generation of Germans out of the context of German culture—a culture that was, considering everything, an elevation and divinatory subtlety of the *historical sense*. But precisely at this point Schopenhauer was poor, unreceptive, and un-German to the point of genius.)

Altogether, taking a large view, it may have been above all what was human, all too human, in short, the wretchedness of the most recent philosophy itself that most thoroughly damaged respect for philosophy and opened the gates to the instinct of the rabble. Let us confess how utterly our modern world lacks the whole type of a Heraclitus, Plato, Empedocles, and whatever other names these royal and magnificent hermits of the spirit had; and how it is with considerable justification that, confronted with such representatives of philosophy as are today, thanks to fashion, as much on top as they are really at the bottom—in Germany, for example, the two lions of Berlin, the anarchist Eugen Dühring and the amalgamist Eduard von Hartmann—a solid man of science *may* feel that he is of a better type and descent. It is especially the sight of those hodgepodge philosophers who call themselves "philosophers of reality" or "positivists" that is capable of injecting a dangerous mistrust into the soul of an ambitious young scholar: these are at best scholars and specialists themselves—that is palpable—they are all losers who have been *brought back* under the hegemony of science, after having desired *more* of themselves at some time without having had the right to this "more" and its responsibilities—and who now represent, in word and deed, honorably, resentfully, and vengefully, the *unbelief* in the masterly task and masterfulness of philosophy.

Finally: how could it really be otherwise? Science is flourishing today and her good conscience is written all over her face, while the level to which all modern philosophy has gradually sunk, this rest of philosophy today, invites mistrust and displeasure, if not mockery and pity. Philosophy reduced to "theory of knowledge," in fact no more than a timid epochism and doctrine of abstinence—a philosophy that never gets beyond the threshold and takes pains to *deny* itself the right to enter—that is philosophy in its last throes, an end, an agony, something inspiring pity. How could such a philosophy—*dominate!*

* * * *

210

Suppose then that some trait in the image of the philosophers of the future poses the riddle whether they would not perhaps have to be skeptics in the sense suggested last, this would still designate only one feature and *not* them as a whole. With just as much right one could call them critics: and certainly they will be men of experiments. With the name in which I dared to baptize them I have already stressed expressly their attempts and delight in attempts: was this done because as critics in body and soul they like to employ experiments in a new, perhaps wider, perhaps more dangerous sense? Does their passion for knowledge force them to go further with audacious and painful experiments than the softhearted and effeminate taste of a democratic century could approve?

No doubt, these coming philosophers will be least able to dispense with those serious and by no means unproblematic qualities which distinguish the critic from the skeptic; I mean the certainty of value standards, the deliberate employment of a unity of method, a shrewd courage, the ability to stand alone and give an account of themselves. Indeed, they admit to a pleasure in saying No and in taking things apart, and to a certain levelheaded cruelty that knows how to handle a knife surely and subtly, even when the heart bleeds. They will be *harder* (and perhaps not always only against themselves) than humane people might wish; they will not dally with "Truth" to be "pleased" or "elevated" or "inspired" by her. On the contrary, they will have little faith that *truth* of all things should be accompanied by such amusements for our feelings.

They will smile, these severe spirits, if somebody should say in front of them: "This thought elevates me; how could it fail to be true?" Or: "This work delights me; how could it fail to be beautiful?" Or: "This artist makes me greater; how could he fail to be great?" Perhaps they do not merely have a smile but feel a genuine nausea over everything that is enthusiastic, idealistic, feminine, hermaphroditic in this vein. And whoever knew how to follow them into the most secret chambers of their hearts would scarcely find any intention there to reconcile "Christian feelings" with "classical taste" and possibly even with "modern parliamentarism" (though such conciliatory attempts are said to occur even among philosophers in our very unsure and consequently very conciliatory century).

Critical discipline and every habit that is conducive to cleanliness and severity in matters of the spirit will be demanded by these philosophers not only of themselves: they could display them as their kind of jewels—nevertheless they still do not want to be called critics on that account. They consider it no small disgrace for philosophy when people decree, as is popular nowadays: "Philosophy itself is criticism and critical science—and nothing whatever besides." This evaluation of philosophy may elicit applause from all the positivists of France and Germany (and it might even have pleased the heart and taste of *Kant*—one should remember the titles of his major works); our new philosophers will say nevertheless: critics are instruments of the philosopher and for that very reason, being instruments, a long ways from being philosophers themselves. Even the great Chinese of Königsberg was merely a great critic.—

211

I insist that people should finally stop confounding philosophical laborers, and scientific men generally, with philosophers; precisely at this point we should be strict about giving "each his due," and not far too much to those and far too little to these.

It may be necessary for the education of a genuine philosopher that he himself has also once stood on all these steps on which his servants, the scientific laborers of philosophy, remain standing—*have to* remain standing. Perhaps he himself must have been critic and skeptic and dogmatist and historian and also poet and collector and traveler and solver of riddles and moralist and seer and "free spirit" and almost everything in order to pass through the whole range of human values and value feelings and to be *able* to see with many different eyes and consciences, from a height and into every distance, from the depths into every height, from a nook into every expanse. But all these are merely preconditions of his task: this task itself demands something different—it demands that he *create values*.

Those philosophical laborers after the noble model of Kant and Hegel have to determine and press into formulas, whether in the realm of *logic* or *political* (moral) thought or *art*, some great data of valuations—that is, former *positings* of values, creations of value which have become dominant and are for a time called "truths." It is for these investigators to make everything that has happened and been esteemed so far easy to look over, easy to think over, intelligible and manageable, to abbreviate everything long, even "time," and to *overcome* the entire past—an enormous and wonderful task in whose service every subtle pride, every tough will can certainly find satisfaction. *Genuine philosophers, however, are commanders and legislators:* they say, "*thus* it *shall* be!" They first determine the Whither and For What of man, and in so doing have at their disposal the preliminary labor of all philosophical laborers, all who have overcome the past. With a creative hand they reach for the future, and all that is and has been becomes a means for them, an instrument, a hammer. Their "knowing" is *creating*, their creating is a legislation, their will to truth is—*will to power*.

Are there such philosophers today? Have there been such philosophers yet? *Must* there not be such philosophers?—

212

More and more it seems to me that the philosopher, being *of necessity* a man of tomorrow and the day after tomorrow, has always found himself, and *had* to find himself, in contradiction to his today: his enemy was ever the ideal of today. So far all these extraordinary furtherers of man whom one calls philosophers, though they themselves have rarely felt like friends of wisdom but rather like disagreeable fools and dangerous question marks, have found their task, their hard, unwanted, inescapable task, but eventually also the greatness of their task, in being the bad conscience of their time.

By applying the knife vivisectionally to the chest of the very *virtues of their time*, they betrayed what was their own secret: to know a *new* greatness of man, of a new untrodden way to his enhancement. Every time they exposed how much hypocrisy, comfortableness, letting oneself go and letting oneself drop, how many lies lay hidden under the best honored type of their contemporary morality, how much virtue was *outlived*. Every time they said: "We must get there, that way, where *you* today are least at home."

Facing a world of "modern ideas" that would banish everybody into a corner and "specialty," a philosopher—if today there could be philosophers—would be compelled to find the greatness of man, the concept of "greatness," precisely in his range and multiplicity, in his wholeness in manifoldness. He would even determine value and rank in accordance with how much and how many things one could bear and take upon himself, how *far* one could extend his responsibility.

Today the taste of the time and the virtue of the time weakens and thins down the will; nothing is as timely as weakness of the will. In the philosopher's ideal, therefore, precisely strength of the will, hardness, and the capacity for long-range decisions must belong to the concept of "greatness"—with as much justification as the opposite doctrine and the ideal of a dumb, renunciatory, humble, selfless humanity was suitable for an opposite age, one that suffered, like the sixteenth century, from its accumulated energy of will and from the most savage floods and tidal waves of selfishness.

In the age of Socrates, among men of fatigued instincts, among the conservatives of ancient Athens who let themselves go—"toward happiness," as they said; toward pleasure, as they acted—and who all the while still mouthed the ancient pompous words to which their lives no longer gave them any right, *irony* may have been required for greatness of soul, that Socratic sarcastic assurance of the old physician and plebeian who cut ruthlessly into his own flesh, as he did into the flesh and heart of the "noble," with a look that said clearly enough: "Don't dissemble in front of me! Here—we are equal."

Today, conversely, when only the herd animal receives and dispenses honors in Europe, when "equality of rights" could all too easily be changed into equality in violating rights—I mean, into a common war on all that is rare, strange, privileged, the higher man, the higher soul, the higher duty, the higher responsibility, and the abundance of creative power and masterfulness—today the concept of greatness entails being noble, wanting to be by oneself, being able to be different, standing alone and having to live independently. And the philosopher will betray something of his own ideal when he posits: "He shall be greatest who can be loneliest, the most concealed, the most deviant, the human being beyond good and evil, the master of his virtues, he that is overrich in will. Precisely this shall be called *greatness*: being capable of being as manifold as whole, as ample as full." And to ask it once more; today—is greatness *possible*?

213

What a philosopher is, that is hard to learn because it cannot be taught: one must "know" it, from experience—or one should have the pride *not* to know it. But nowadays all the world talks of things of which it *cannot* have any experience, and this is most true, and in the worst way, concerning philosophers and philosophical states: exceedingly few know them, may know them, and all popular opinions about them are false.

That genuinely philosophical combination, for example, of a bold and exuberant spirituality that runs *presto* and a dialectical severity and necessity that takes no false step is unknown to most thinkers and scholars from their own experience, and therefore would seem incredible to them if somebody should speak of it in their presence. They picture every necessity as a kind of need, as a painstaking having-to-follow and being-compelled. And thinking itself they consider something slow and hesitant, almost as toil, and often enough as "worthy of the *sweat* of the noble"—but not in the least as something light, divine, closely related to dancing and high spirits. "Thinking" and taking a matter "seriously," considering it "grave"—for them all this belongs together: that is the only way they have "experienced" it.

Artists seem to have more sensitive noses in these matters, knowing only too well that precisely when they no longer do anything "voluntarily" but do everything of necessity, their feeling of freedom, subtlety, full power, of creative placing, disposing, and forming reaches its peak—in short, that necessity and "freedom of the will" then become one in them.

Ultimately, there is an order of rank among states of the soul, and the order of rank of problems accords with this. The highest problems repulse everyone mercilessly who dares approach them without being predestined for their solution by the height and power of his spirituality. What does it avail when nimble smarties or clumsy solid mechanics and empiricists push near them, as is common today, trying with their plebeian ambition to enter the "court of courts." Upon such carpets coarse feet may never step: the primeval law of things takes care of that; the doors remain closed to such obtrusiveness, even if they crash and crush their heads against them.

For every high world one must be born; or to speak more clearly, one must be *cultivated* for it: a right to philosophy—taking that word in its great sense—one has only by virtue of one's origins; one's ancestors, one's "blood" decide here, too. Many generations must have labored to prepare the origin of the philosopher; every one of his virtues must have been acquired, nurtured, inherited, and digested singly, and not only the bold, light, delicate gait and course of his thoughts but above all the readiness for great responsibilities, the loftiness of glances that dominate and look down, feeling separated from the crowd and its duties and virtues, the affable protection and defense of whatever is misunderstood and slandered, whether it be god or devil, the pleasure and exercise of the great justice, the art of command, the width of the will, the slow eye that rarely admires, rarely looks up, rarely loves—

Name Index